Musical
Notes

MUSICAL NOTES

A PRACTICAL GUIDE TO
STAFFING AND STAGING STANDARDS
OF THE
AMERICAN MUSICAL THEATRE

Carol Lucha-Burns

GREENWOOD PRESS
New York • Westport, Connecticut • London

Library of Congress Cataloging-in-Publication Data

Lucha-Burns, Carol.
Musical notes.

Bibliography: p.
Includes index.
1. Musical revue, comedy, etc.—United States—
Production and direction.   2. Musical revues, comedies,
etc.—Stage guides.   I. Title.
MT955.L8   1986   782.81'07'1   85–10017
ISBN 0–313–24648–3 (lib. bdg. : alk. paper)

Library of Congress Catalog Card Number: 85–10017
ISBN: 0–313–24648–3

First published in 1986

Greenwood Press, Inc.
88 Post Road West
Westport, Connecticut 06881

Printed in the United States of America

The paper used in this book complies with the
Permanent Paper Standard issued by the National
Information Standards Organization (Z39.48–1984).

10 9 8 7 6 5 4 3 2 1

To my parents, my teachers, my students, and
the memory of Jean Mattox, colleague and friend

Contents

Preface

My interest in show business began in the early 1950s and was nurtured by my parents, a teacher of musical comedy, countless Broadway shows and the times. My father, a club manager who as a child had spent his after-school hours in the balconies of vaudeville and burlesque houses, sparked my interest by his many stories of the performances of such stars as Jimmy Durante, Eddie Cantor, Fanny Brice, Gypsy Rose Lee, Sally Rand, Ethel Merman, Bert Lahr and Ed Wynn. My mother, a former Latin teacher with a love for the songs of Rodgers and Hammerstein, Jerome Kern, George and Ira Gershwin, Cole Porter and Victor Herbert, introduced me to the musical side of the genre, and Bob Scarpato, a teacher at Syracuse University, who in 1958 had one of the first musical comedy classes at a major University, developed my knowledge of history, performing and directing.

1964 found me in New York studying at the American Musical and Dramatic Academy (AMDA) under Lehman Engel, Philip Burton, Sandford Meisner, Sande Campbell, Karen Gustafson and Joyce Worsely. It was a time to be in New York for during that very rich era, now known as the "Golden Age Of Musical Theatre," one could walk down Broadway and see *Funny Girl, Hello, Dolly!, Fiddler on the Roof, The Roar of the Greasepaint—The Smell of the Crowd, Sweet Charity, Mame, How to Succeed in Business Without Really Trying, Oliver!, A Funny Thing Happened on the Way to the Forum, She Loves Me*, and a City Center production of *My Fair Lady* at affordable prices. My classmates and I saw more than ten performances of *Hello, Dolly!* from the last row in the balcony at $3.50 a ticket and AMDA students got free tickets to *Anyone Can Whistle, High*

Spirits, Do I Hear a Waltz?, Foxy (Bert Lahr's ill-fated hit), and *Flora, The Red Menace* (Liza Minnelli's first Tony Award performance). We were a generation raised on a combination of musical theatre and Elvis Presley.

In 1977, after seven years of teaching musical theatre at the University of New Hampshire, I discovered the majority of students in my classes had not heard of Jerome Kern, George Gershwin, *Show Boat* or *West Side Story*. This was rock music's new generation. Hence the beginning of *Musical Notes*. In its original form the book was designed to introduce students to musicals which had scripts, scores and records in our library. Since that time the book has been expanded, the library collection has grown, and many of our graduates have moved to Broadway.

The revised version has been changed to include reference data, more detailed synopses, production advice and song charts to assist those seeking numbers to perform, either in a class or revue situation.

The problem of choosing a musical when there are so few published scripts available is formidable. It often means reading catalogues, sending for perusal materials and having an entire committee read the material before making a choice. For many groups it is just too time-consuming a process. As a result amateur groups often compete with one another by producing the more famous shows, usually ones that have been adapted to screen or video. This competition is usually due to a lack of knowledge of the broad spectrum musical theatre has to offer. It is hoped that these synopses and production notes will give directors and producing organizations enough background and encouragement to produce lesser known shows that are worthy of becoming standards.

The term *standards* usually signifies works that have become part of a cultural tradition; however, for the purpose of this book, the term has been broadened to include shows that should be seen more often at schools, regional and community theatres around the globe.

Acknowledgments ─────────────

This is to acknowledge the following people who helped in the preparation of the manuscript. Many are former students; most are connected with the University of New Hampshire or are experts in the field.

Chris Leavy for vocal and instrumentation expertise; Rena Hart, Bob Douglas, Bob Reed, and the Reference and Reserve Staff at the UNH Library; Gene Lauze, Martha Levesque, Lauren Rydgreen, Darlene DesFosses, Merrill Clark, Trish Malone, Barbara Whitney, Kim Stuart, and John M. Burns, for word processing assistance, Margaret Lucha, Ginger Christie, Gene Dingenary, Ken Mandelbaum, Peter Landroche, Erik Haagensen, John Lenehan, Nancy Irving, the University of New Hampshire Central Research Fund, Juanita Lewis and the staff of Greenwood Press.

Organization of the Book ─────────

The entries are arrranged alphabetically. Those in the main body of the text provide in-depth synopses of shows that require detailing for the reader to understand scope and performance details. A supplementary section, entitled *Concept, Rock, Nostalgia and Others*, contains entries providing abbreviated overviews instead of more detailed synopses. Many of these shows do not require a detailed synopsis for the potential producing organization to consider a production. Others are not often done because of limited commercial appeal, production or casting difficulties; however, a more adventurous group may want to be introduced to the potential of such shows. Those listed are presently available (as of March 1986) for nonprofessional performances.

The book concludes with a chronology of the plays in the work, a bibliography listing works of related interest, and information on sources for obtaining scripts, scores, etc.

Each entry begins with the name of the show, authors, composers, lyricists, and the title of the source the show is based on. This introductory data is followed by information on the *Original Production*. This includes the name of the theatre, date of opening, number of performances, director, choreographer, musical director, arranger, principals and their vocal type. Immediately following is a section entitled *Chorus and Smaller Roles*. This is usually not according to the original production but a recommended minimum. Many of the pre–1970s musicals had separate singing and dancing choruses which brought the total cast size to approximately fifty. It was decided that a suggested minimum would be more advantageous because it is always possible to expand but often difficult for someone unfamiliar with the show to minimize.

The production information is followed by an in-depth synopsis of each show with musical numbers in parentheses for quick reference. This section attempts to give the reader a feeling of the show by detailing the story, capturing the essence of the characters, and giving specific scenic locations.

The *Notes on the Production* section includes Tony Awards, a brief comment which may be used in a program insert, ideas on technical and costume requirements, possible pitfalls and budget suggestions.

Songs of Special Interest details certain songs suitable for classroom study and revues. This information also appears in the ready reference song charts at the end of the book.

Instrumentation gives the full orchestration provided by the various rental organizations. It is possible to trim the size, but this is best left to each musical director.

The entry concludes with data on published materials and the names of the various licensing agencies. The agencies' full names and addresses are given in the appendix on sources. Many scripts are not published, but are available in manuscript form from the rental agencies. These are listed with an NP. The music and records of most shows have been published, and their publishing houses are listed. *Score* means the full score was printed in its complete form while *Selections* refers to the collection of the more popular songs from the shows. This collection is usually geared for the home piano player, not written in the original key. If *Score*, *Selections* or *Record* is not included it means the material is not yet commercially available.

A Guide to Abbreviations and Special Terms

The following terms and abbreviations, used throughout the book, will prove helpful to the reader.

Chorus—This term refers to musical numbers which are most often performed by a group in some sort of physical unison. In the song charts in the back of the book the chorus numbers are specifically geared to the beginning choreographer and success in a classroom or revue situation. There are many chorus numbers that require a seasoned choreographer, excellent dancers and gruelling rehearsals. For that reason they do not appear except in the synopsis.

Concept Musical—This term generally refers to a show that originated from a concept, is fairly free flowing, and has characters that do not need to interrelate. *A Chorus Line*, *Working* and *Runaways* are examples of these. The primary interest of both these shows is the treatment of the topic and how the individual character feels about himself.

Duet—This term applies to a song sung by two people.

In One—This term refers to a scene or musical number that is played in front of a drop to facilitate a set change. Many numbers begin in full set and end in front of a closed curtain or drop. This usually implies there are not set props available, thus most In One numbers are performed standing up. "Elegance," in *Hello, Dolly!*, is an example of this type of song.

Linear . . .—Linear, most often used to define duets, refers to a song where two people sing together but from different areas of the stage. They usually do not physically relate to each other. However, the lyrics may refer to and involve the other person. Linear duets are usually not appropriate for dramatic scene to duet class work for there is no interrelationship.

L to . . . —This phrase refers to lines which directly precede a song. This information is included because of the difficulty in bridging the gap between spoken dialogue and song. Lines may mean a monologue prior to a solo song or a few lines at the end of a scene that flow into the song.

Octet—An octet is a song sung by eight people; it is only mentioned if the number specifically requires that exact amount for vocal reasons.

Quartet—This term describes a song sung by four people.

Quintet—A quintet is a song sung by five people.

Sc to . . . —This phrase applies to scenes that precede musical numbers. These are most often small scenes with two or three characters with action directly leading to the song and its development. All the characters need not have lines in the scene, and all need not sing in the song. There are many scenes to solos which require the other person to be onstage prior to the song and often throughout the song without taking a vocal part in the song.

Solo—A solo is a song sung by one person, sometimes to another who does not sing. In cases where the response of the nonsinger is important to the singer it is advised that the two rehearse together. It is suggested that "reaction" numbers be part of all students' training. "Miracle of Miracles" and "Far from the Home I Love," from *Fiddler on the Roof*, are two examples of how the nonsinger helps the singer. In the first, Tzeitel's reactions to Motel's enthusiasm lead him to greater heights, and in the second, Tevye's response to Hodel and her subsequent reactions make the drama heartbreaking.

Stage Directions—Stage directions, as we know them, go back to Shakespearean times when performers played on a raked stage, and the poorer members of the audience most often stood on the ground. In order to allow these standees to see the action at the rear of the stage the stage was raked with the highest end farthest from the audience. When an actor walked away he was walking upstage. Thus the term *upstage* refers to action farthest from the audience and downstage refers to that which is closest. All stage directions are given from the actor's viewpoint, which means that *stage right* and *stage left* refer to the actor's right and left.

Trio—This term refers to a song sung by three people.

Triple Threat—This relatively new term refers to performers who act, sing and dance. Prior to the seventies performers usually excelled in either singing, dancing or acting and were termed singers who danced, dancers who sang, actors who sang or actors who danced. The rising cost of Broadway musicals necessitated that chorus size be trimmed, thus the disappearance of separate singing and dancing choruses. *A Chorus Line* is a show that requires a company of triple-threat performers.

VTI—This abbreviation stands for vocal type interchangeable. This primarily refers to those who only sing in trios, quartets, or as a member of the chorus. The character is not altered by a change in vocal type.

VTNE—This abbreviation stands for vocal type not essential; it is usually applied to a nonsinging role.

Musical
Notes

IN-DEPTH SYNOPSES

A

ALLEGRO

Book and Lyrics: Oscar Hammerstein II
Music: Richard Rodgers

ORIGINAL PRODUCTION

Majestic Theatre, October 10, 1947 (315 perf.)
Director and Choreographer: Agnes de Mille
Orchestra Direction: Salvatore Dell'Isola
Orchestration: Robert Russell Bennett
Principals: Joseph Taylor, Jr.—John Battles—Tenor; Marjorie Taylor—Annamary Dickey—soprano; Dr. Taylor—William Ching—baritone; Jenny—Roberta Jonay—mezzo; Emily—Lisa Kirk—alto; Beulah—Gloria Wills—soprano; Grandma—Muriel O'Malley—alto; Charlie—John Conte—baritone; Millie—Julie Humphrey—soprano
Chorus and Smaller Roles: Minimum 6M/6F, if the production is done in a theatricalized choral manner, the principals may join the chorus when they are not specifically featured in a scene.

SYNOPSIS

The show opens in a midwestern town in the year 1905, with the townspeople lauding Marjorie Taylor, the proud mother of a baby boy (Joseph Taylor Jr.—Mixed Chorus). Grandma Taylor envisions the future the baby will have (I Know It Can Happen Again—Sc to F Solo).

The chorus quickly forwards the action by performing the thoughts of Joe Jr. as he grows from infancy and experiences the death of his grandmother, his first kiss and his graduation from high school (One Foot, Other Foot—Poor Joe—Mixed Chorus).

Before Joe leaves for college, his parents sit on the front porch and ponder what his future will be. Joe Jr., near an open window, hears every word of the conversation and interjects his feelings to the audience. Joe Sr. hopes his son will pick the right girl, one similar to his own wife, but Joe feels no girl can compare to his high school sweetheart and childhood friend, Jenny. Joe's father, the warmhearted town doctor, hopes his son will follow in his footsteps and dreams that Joe will help him build a town hospital. Joe Sr. confides to Marjorie that the right wife is important to a man's career, and he is grateful that he picked her. They are a contented couple and comment on the fact (A Fellow Needs a Girl—Sc to M/F Duet).

The time is 1921; the action is transported to a college dance where the students are portrayed as they would like to appear: graceful and elegantly dressed. This is in direct opposition to the awkwardness they actually possess.

Joe, who is studying to be a doctor, enjoys college but discovers it is quite a bit different from his hometown (It's a Darn Nice Campus—M Solo). He meets Charlie, a happy-go-lucky fellow student, football star who is more interested in women than in medicine. He is an opportunistic yet likeable young man who uses Joe to help him pass his courses. Meanwhile, Jenny, who is still back home, has Joe worried because the letters she has been writing haven't been wholly enthusiastic about waiting for him to graduate. Immediate marriage is on her mind.

In a collage of Joe's thoughts and letters, enhanced by choral commentary (You Are Never Away—Mixed Chorus), we learn that Jenny has gone to Europe and is infatuated with another man. Joe, hurt by her infidelity, agrees to a double date picnic with Charlie. On the date, Charlie and his girl leave Joe and Beulah, a swinger of the "new generation," together on a blanket. Her seduction attempts fail when Joe falls asleep (So Far—Sc to F Solo).

Joe returns home to see Jenny, who tells him she is going to wait for him. We soon learn, however, that Jenny has no intention of being the wife of a poor local doctor. When she tells Joe's mother she would prefer that Joe work for her father's lumber and coal company or be a city doctor, Mrs. Taylor attempts to convince her that Joe will be happiest carrying on his father's practice. Jenny, realizing that she must get Joe away from the influence of his mother, declares open war and angrily leaves. Marjorie, who was never very strong, dies of a heart attack. Her death silences the only verbal opposition to the match. Joe and Jenny decide to marry (What a Lovely Day for a Wedding—To Have and to Hold—Wish Thee Well—Mixed Chorus).

Act II opens eight years later in the backyard of the Taylor house. Jenny is hanging up the wash as her father, who has lost his fortune, business, and home in the recent stock market crash, enters. Jenny, angered that she is forced to live in a below-average home, spitefully lets her father know she feels he is a failure.

After her father leaves, Jenny regrets her sharpness but the confrontation has made her more determined than ever to quickly better her circumstances. She invites some neighborhood women over and they commiserate over the luxuries none of them are able to afford (Money Isn't Everything—Sc to F Quintet).

When Joe is offered a partnership with Charlie's uncle, Bigby Danby, a well-known city doctor, Jenny finagles him into taking the position. He enters a superficial world, demonstrated by a typical cocktail party (Yatata, Yatata, Yatata—Mixed Chorus). Joe's nurse, Emily, who recognizes Joe's talents, is infuriated by his overly ambitious wife. She sees that Joe is quickly losing his potential and self-esteem because his major concerns are turning to more social involvement with the leaders of the community. Emily steps into the street during a downpour and vainly attempts to hail a cab. She is obviously attracted to Joe yet angrily comments on his naivete (The Gentlemen Is a Dope—L to F Solo).

Joe, along with Charlie, who also works for Bigby, realizes that Bigby only involves himself with the rich hospital benefactors. They scornfully confer with Emily about the present situation (Allegro—Sc to 2M/1F Trio to Mixed Chorus).

Mrs. Lansdale, a wealthy patient whose husband is the major trustee of the hospital, enters to give Joe a detective's report linking Jenny with Mrs. Lansdale's husband. Joe examines the situation and realizes, in an introspective monologue, that his life is empty. As he is reminded by the chorus that he is always welcome home (Come Home—Mixed Chorus), Bigby Danby and Lansdale enter to offer him the position of physician-in-chief. They leave to announce the news to the board of trustees. Emily and Charlie, left alone in the office, worry that Joe will accept; they both feel he has the ability to be an excellent doctor and should be more than a medical politician.

At the new private pavilion of the hospital, Lansdale begins his speech as the chorus intersperses comments (Yatata, Yatata, Yatata [Reprise]—Mixed Chorus). Joe surprises everyone by declining the offer and announcing that he is going home to help his father build a hospital. The play ends as he leaves for home with Emily and Charlie.

NOTES ON THE PRODUCTION

The play deviates in style from the collaborators' first two popular works, *Oklahoma!* and *Carousel*. Its presentation in a choral/acting manner is the reason Agnes de Mille was hired as both choreographer and director of this difficult theatre piece. The interesting style and use of a Greek chorus made the show innovative, but critics and audiences expected something more along the lines of the collaborators' prior hits.

In 1970, *Equity Library Theatre*, an Equity showcase theatre based in New York, produced the show and demonstrated its worth as a revival piece. There are good singing opportunities for choral/acting work as the entire company may appear as various characters in the scenes and dances when needed. The production would be an excellent choice for a school or university and could be interestingly mounted by the combined talents of the music department's choir and the drama department's actor/singers. A refreshing change from the usual choral offerings, it is a light technical production that may be performed on a small stage with limited wing and fly space. Relatively inexpensive to produce, it can be effectively costumed and designed with stylized pieces.

SONGS OF SPECIAL INTEREST

"A Fellow Needs a Girl," baritone/soprano. Romantic, older couple, charm duet.

"The Gentleman Is a Dope," alto solo. Up tempo, vocally interesting, actually a love song that begins in anger, has charm and ends poignantly.

"Money Isn't Everything," F quintet. Good number for developing character as the girls have individual sections of the verse. Up tempo. Comments on what the rich have that they do not.

Instrumentation: 4 reeds, 2 horns, 2 trumpets, 2 trombones, tuba, percussion, 4 violins, viola, cello, bass, piano/conductor
Script: Knopf, *Six Plays by Rodgers and Hammerstein*.
Score: Williamson
Record: RCA
Rights: R & H

ANNIE

Book: Thomas Meehan (Based on the comic strip *Little Orphan Annie* by Harold Gray)
Music: Charles Strouse
Lyrics: Martin Charnin

ORIGINAL PRODUCTION

Alvin Theatre, April 21, 1977 (2,377 perf.)
Director: Martin Charnin
Musical Director: Peter Howard
Musical Numbers Staged by: Peter Gennaro
Principals: Annie—Andrea McArdle—child mezzo; Daddy Warbucks—Reid Shelton—baritone; Miss Hannigan—Dorothy Loudon—gravelly mezzo; Grace Farrell—Sandy Faison—soprano; Rooster—Robert Fitch—tenor; Lily—Barbara Erwin—squeally soprano
Chorus and Smaller Roles: 7M/4F minimum, 6 young girls ages five to eleven who sing and dance well.

SYNOPSIS

The play opens in a dimly lit orphanage in Manhattan's lower East Side; the time is 1933 and America is in the middle of its worst depression. Six orphans have just been awakened by the nightmares of Molly, the youngest. Annie, an eleven-year-old who has been at the orphanage since two months of age, comforts Molly and shares her feelings about her own parents, who she knows will come back. The other orphans wistfully listen and join in at the end of the song (Maybe—F Solo and Female Chorus). When Miss Hannigan, the mean, liquor-imbibing manager of the orphanage, discovers Annie and the girls awake, she proceeds to put them to work scrubbing the bedroom floor. The girls perform the showstopping number complete with buckets and brushes (It's a Hard Knock Life—F Chorus).

Annie, yearning to find her parents, escapes from the orphanage in the bottom of a laundry basket and wanders the streets of New York looking for a place to call home. She befriends a stray dog, names him Sandy and assures him that things will be all right (Tomorrow—F Solo). Annie discovers a Hooverville under the 57th Street bridge and finds food and friendship with the residents who sarcastically praise President Hoover (We'd Like to Thank You, Herbert Hoover—Mixed Chorus).

At the orphanage, Miss Hannigan, infuriated by Annie's escape and the practical jokes of the orphanage, comments on her hatred of children (Little Girls—L to F Solo). She turns on a radio soap opera but is interrupted by a policeman who enters with Annie. Upon the officer's departure Miss Hannigan starts thrashing Annie about but is interrupted by Grace Farrell, secretary to billionaire Oliver Warbucks. Grace is charmed by Annie and invites her to spend the next two weeks in the Warbucks mansion on Fifth Avenue.

Annie is overwhelmed by the mansion, and especially impressed by the servants (I Think I'm Gonna Like It Here—F Solo to Mixed Chorus). Daddy Warbucks arrives and is upset to discover that Grace has brought him a girl orphan instead of the boy he requested. Annie, however, charms him into accepting her and he invites Annie and Grace to the Roxy Movie Theatre. The three walk the forty-five blocks to the theatre listening to Warbucks tell them how much he loves New York City (NYC—1M/2F Trio with Mixed Chorus at End). They arrive at the theatre and are ready to enter when Warbucks notices Annie's weariness; as he picks her up she falls asleep in his arms.

One week later Grace arrives at the orphanage to tell an infuriated Miss Hannigan that Warbucks intends to adopt Annie. As Grace exits she runs into Hannigan's gangster brother, Rooster, and his bleached blonde girlfriend, Lily. He has just gotten out of prison and has come to Hannigan for money. The devious trio yearn for an easier, richer life (Easy Street—Sc to 1M/2F Trio).

At the mansion Warbucks, while attempting to tell Annie he wants to adopt her, discovers she desires to find her real parents, who left her on the doorstep of the orphanage with half a locket and a letter promising to return. Determined to make her happy, he promises to find them. The servants and Grace assure her that everything will be all right (You Won't Be an Orphan for Long—Mixed Chorus).

Act II opens at a radio station, where Warbucks has offered a $50,000 reward to anyone who can prove they are Annie's parents. The show signs off with Bert Healy and the Boylan Sisters singing the show's theme song (You're Never Fully Dressed Without a Smile—M Solo with 3F Trio).

At the orphanage the orphans listen to the radio and imitate the show's theme song (You're Never Fully Dressed without a Smile [Reprise]—F Chorus). Miss Hannigan sends them to bed as Rooster and Lily arrive disguised as Annie's parents and convince Hannigan to help them fool Warbucks. Hannigan agrees in return for half of the reward money.

In Washington, Annie and Warbucks meet with President Roosevelt and his Cabinet, who are depressed over the nation's economic state. Annie encourages them to look to the future (Tomorrow [Reprise]—Mixed Chorus). The festivities are soon stopped when Warbucks receives a telegram saying that hundreds of people, all claiming to be Annie's parents, are jamming the streets outside the mansion. Warbucks and Annie return home to discover that all claims of parentage are false. Warbucks attempts to bolster Annie's spirits by telling her he wants to adopt her (Something Was Missing—M Solo). She agrees that the search was futile and happily consents to his proposed adoption (I Don't Need Anything but You—Sc To M/F Duet). The servants enter to prepare for the adoption party and enthusiastically sing a tribute to the little girl that brightens their lives (Annie—Mixed Chorus). The high point of the number occurs when an enormous Christmas tree surrounded by multitudes of presents is wheeled out.

The party is interrupted by Rooster and Lily, who arrive disguised as Annie's parents, showing as proof a birth certificate and the missing half of Annie's childhood locket. Annie is disappointed, and Warbucks and Grace are suspicious of these two odd characters who leave Annie to say her farewells. Warbucks turns to President Roosevelt and the FBI, who discover that Annie's real parents have been dead for many years and the couple claiming to be her parents are false. Annie is free to be adopted by Warbucks.

Miss Hannigan and the orphans arrive for the Warbucks' Christmas party followed by Rooster and Lily, who claim Annie. The three are arrested by the Secret Service and Warbucks promises the orphans a better life. The entire company excitedly looks to the future (A New Deal for Christmas—Mixed Chorus). The number peaks when Sandy arrives in a huge wrapped gift-box . . . the perfect end to a Merry Christmas and the beginning of a wonderful life (A New Deal for Christmas—Mixed Chorus).

NOTES ON THE PRODUCTION

Annie won seven of a possible nine Tony Awards (Dorothy Loudon and Andrea McArdle were nominated for the same award, which Miss Loudon received): Best Choreography, Actress, Score, Book, Costumes, Set, and Musical. The production was a lively and exciting one for children, one of the few semilavish family shows since the 1965 Tony Award winner *Fiddler on the Roof*.

It takes some extremely talented children and good character actors to plausibly portray the principals and the smaller vignette roles, namely Roosevelt's Cabinet. There is also a need for a dog with enough training not to upstage the entire production.

The sets are fairly lavish and difficult to trim, although set pieces may be used if the budget is limited. The Christmas tree is extremely important to the overall show as it helps peak the musical number and is essential in the finale. The costumes are period thirties with servants' and a policeman's uniform. Nothing is terribly difficult.

At the present time the royalty is quite high, a strong consideration when choosing this show. It is also frequently performed, and too many productions of *Annie* in nearby communities will definitely hurt ticket sales.

SONGS OF SPECIAL INTEREST

"Easy Street," 2F/1M trio. Up tempo, movement-oriented. Emphasis is on broad characterizations and character interaction and reaction.

"I Don't Need Anything but You," baritone/child mezzo duet, charming number, good for relationship and soft shoe as it is done on the vaudeville style.

"Little Girls," mezzo comedic character solo. Emphasis is on solid characterization through strong acting. Good exercise for an actress who has trouble taking on strong characters.

"We'd Like to Thank You, Herbert Hoover," a delightful, up tempo chorus number which allows much room for individual characterization and simplistic staging arising from lyrics and situation.

Instrumentation: 5 reeds, 2 trumpets, 2 trombones, tuba, violin, cello, bass, guitar/banjo, percussion I & II, piano/conductor
Script: NP
Score: Big Three
Record: Columbia
Rights: MTI

ANNIE GET YOUR GUN

Book: Herbert and Dorothy Fields
Music and Lyrics: Irving Berlin

ORIGINAL PRODUCTION

Imperial Theatre, May 16, 1946 (1,147 perf.)
Director: Joshua Logan
Choreographer: Helen Tamiris

Musical Director: Jay Blackton
Orchestration: Philip J. Lang, Robert Russell Bennett, Ted Royal
Principals: Annie—Ethel Merman—alto belt; Dolly Tate—Lea Penman—alto;
Buffalo Bill—William O'Neal—baritone; Frank Butler—Ray Middleton—baritone; Charlie Davenport—Marty May—tenor; Pawnee Bill—George Lipton—baritone
Chorus and Smaller Roles: 4 children 3F/1M, 9M/9F minimum, various shapes
and sizes to portray Indians, society and townsfolk.

SYNOPSIS

Outside the Wilson House hotel on the outskirts of Cincinnati, Ohio, Charlie
Davenport, manager of Buffalo Bill's Wild West Show, enters with his sister,
Dolly Tate, to drum up business for the show. They dramatically enact the heroic
escapades of their boss as a crowd of onlookers becomes involved (Colonel
Buffalo Bill—M/F Duet to Mixed Chorus).

Foster Wilson, the hotel proprietor, enters. Furious that Charlie has advertised
a shooting contest between the town's best sharpshooter and Frank Butler, the
show's star, on the hotel grounds, he orders them off the premises. Charlie sends
Dolly into the hotel to charm Wilson, a bachelor. Frank Butler, left alone with
the young girls of the town, warns them about his reputation (I'm a Bad, Bad
Man—M Solo to F Chorus).

Dolly enters after failing to change Wilson's mind and sits down to rest near
a hedge. A shot rings out, knocking a decorative bird off Dolly's hat. She looks
around fearfully as Annie Oakley, a tomboyish, rather grubby girl in well-worn
clothes, enters. Wilson arrives to see Annie pointing a gun at Dolly, who hastily
exits. Annie attempts to sell some game birds to Wilson, who is impressed by
her shooting. When he orders twenty-four, Annie has to call her three sisters
and brother Jake to count the birds. Since they can only count to twenty, Annie
promises to deliver that number. Wilson questions her about the family's lack
of reading and writing, but she replies that folks back home didn't need book
learning (Doin' What Comes Natur'lly—Sc to F Solo to Children's quartet).

Wilson offers her five dollars to enter the shooting match against Frank Butler,
whom he refers to as a swollen-headed stiff. Annie agrees and confidently begins
cleaning her gun but is interrupted by the handsome Butler, who is appalled by
the antiquity of her rifle and the bluntness of her manner. She, on the other
hand, is overwhelmed by his outstanding good looks and listens closely as he
tells her of his ideal woman (The Girl That I Marry—Sc to M Solo). He tips
his hat and exits.

Annie, realizing she has to be more than a good shot to trap someone like
Frank into marriage, ponders her situation (You Can't Get a Man with a Gun—
L to F Solo). She marches off as Buffalo Bill arrives to referee the contest.
When Wilson introduces Annie, everyone is shocked that he has entered a girl
against Frank Butler, but they are outwardly impressed when she wins.

Despite Frank's unenthusiastic response to the idea, Buffalo Bill encourages

Charlie to offer her a job with the show. Frank, assured that Annie will only assist him in the act and not do any fancy shooting that might endanger his status as number one, agrees. The three men tell her of the perils and thrills of show business (There's No Business Like Show Business—Sc to 3M/1F Quartet).

The show moves by train, and the scene shifts to the Pullman parlor of a train at night. The car is full of Indians with wash and living items scattered about. Dolly enters, furious that Annie has given the Indians permission to use her car, but Charlie comes to Annie's defense and Annie settles down with Little Jake to study her spelling. The two are interrupted by Frank, with whom Annie is hopelessly in love. He is also becoming fond of her and asks if she has ever been in love with anyone. Each is afraid of the other's reaction so they talk of the things they've heard about love (They Say It's Wonderful—Sc to M/F Duet). By the end of the number Frank realizes he loves her; they embrace.

Charlie and Buffalo Bill, in hopes of getting business away from competitor Pawnee Bill, asks Annie to perform a motorcycle riding and shooting trick in Minneapolis. Convinced that Frank will be proud of her, she agrees.

Her brother and sisters are enjoying the excitement of show business so much that it is difficult to get them to sleep. They beg Annie for a lullaby and she agrees as the trainman, waiter and porter join in (Moonshine Lullaby—F Solo to M Trio).

Frank, feeling threatened when he sees a large poster of Annie outside the performance arena, warns Charlie that he will quit the show if the posters stay up. Charlie and Buffalo Bill, knowing the show is in financial difficulty, have no choice but to have Annie perform her trick shooting. Charlie begins the pitch to draw an audience as the company joins in (Wild West Pitch Dance—Mixed Dance Chorus). Charlie's spiel is cut short by the entrance of Pawnee Bill and Sitting Bull, who have come to see Annie perform. Charlie and Buffalo Bill attempt to interest the oil-rich Sitting Bull in making an investment, but the chief refuses to invest in "show business."

Frank attempts to propose to Annie, but she insists that he wait until after her performance; he agrees and tells his friends he is going to be married (My Defenses Are Down—M Solo to M Chorus).

The stage goes dark and the lights suddenly rise on Annie, who is lying on a motorcycle, steering with her feet and shooting at lighted candles attached to a wheel on the main tent pole. The crowd goes wild, but Frank refuses to follow such a tremendous spectacle. Annie enters, anxious to discover Frank's reaction but is unable to talk to him because Sitting Bull, who labels her the best marksman he has ever seen, announces his wish to adopt her as his daughter.

The ceremony begins (Wild Horse Ceremonial Dance—M Dancers), and Annie becomes Sitting Bull's daughter (I'm an Indian Too—F Solo to Mixed Dance Chorus). At the end of the ritual Annie is exhausted and surprised to receive a letter from Frank; in the excitement she didn't realize how upset he was. She enlists the aid of Papa Bull, who reads that Frank has left with Dolly to do his old act at Pawnee Bill's show. Annie is crushed and sadly reprises (You Can't Get a Man with a Gun—F Solo) as the curtain falls.

Act II opens with the troupe camped atop the deck of a cattleboat in New York harbor; they have just returned from a successful tour of Europe and are penniless because European royalty doesn't pay for command performances— they only award medals. Charlie tells Annie that they are broke and the U.S. Government has placed Papa Bull on a small weekly allowance. Their depression is interrupted when someone from Pawnee Bill's outfit arrives to invite them to a reception in New York. Papa Bull suggests that the two shows merge and Annie, anxious for a chance to reunite with Frank, agrees. She quietly sits alone and remembers (I Got Lost in His Arms—F Solo with Offstage Mixed Chorus).

At the ballroom of the Hotel Brevoort in New York, Pawnee Bill, Frank and Dolly tell Mr. and Mrs. Adams, two wealthy society patrons, about the perils of show business (There's No Business Like Show Business [Reprise]—2M/1F Trio). The subsequent meeting between the two owners is a disaster, for they discover neither has any money. Papa Bull saves the day when he realizes that Annie's medals are worth $100,000, enough to finance the merger. Charlie warns Annie that she is giving up her only tangible wealth, but she retorts that she has enough in life (I Got the Sun in the Morning—F Solo to Mixed Chorus). Frank joins in and the two are reunited.

Frank proposes and begins to describe the wedding he wants, but Annie envisions a very large wedding, in direct opposition to his need for a simple one (An Old-Fashioned Wedding—Sc to M/F Duet). The two argue and decide to have one big shooting match to determine who is the best sharp shooter in the world.

On the loading platform for the ferry to Governor's Island, Dolly attempts to sabotage Annie's guns but is stopped by Papa Bull and her brother Charlie. Charlie is furious, but Papa Bull knows that if Annie wins the match she will lose Frank, so he and Charlie sabotage the guns.

At Governor's Island the shooting match is about to begin, but Annie and Frank delay things by arguing about their talents (Anything You Can Do—Sc to M/F Duet). The competition begins with Annie missing two simple shots. Frank offers her one of his guns and she gets a hit. Papa Bull, worried that she may win with Frank's gun, takes her aside to explain she must lose the competition in order to marry Frank. She purposely misses the next shot and the two agree to be lifetime partners as the two shows merge (Finale—Mixed Chorus).

NOTES ON THE PRODUCTION

Ethel Merman starred in a variety of musical comedy roles including *Girl Crazy*, *Anything Goes*, *DuBarry Was a Lady*, *Call Me Madam*, *Happy Hunting*, *Red, Hot and Blue*, *Gypsy* and *Hello, Dolly!*. More roles were written for her than for any other musical star. In fact, she changed the emphasis of musical theatre from the typical ingenue soprano heroine to the more interesting older, three-dimensional leading lady.

The score is considered to be Irving Berlin's most memorable one; it is interesting to note that producers Rodgers and Hammerstein II originally hired Jerome Kern, whose untimely death forced them to find another writer. Berlin's wonderfully melodic score and charming lyrics, combined with a well-written musical libretto, helped chalk up a long run.

When the show was revived in 1966 for a limited engagement at Lincoln Center, Berlin wrote a new song for Miss Merman, "Old-Fashioned Wedding." The script was changed to trim Dolly's and Charlie's roles as the secondary love interest by cutting their song "Who Do You Love I Hope" and redefining them as brother and sister. The acting version available for production is based on the revival, but the older scores have the cut-out song and some companies have chosen to negate the brother and sister relationship by including the original song.

The show is an extremely popular one and may be produced in all sizes and types of theaters without losing any of the production quality. The major problem is determining the best way to handle the trick-shooting sequence on the motorcycle. Smaller community groups and those performing in the round have often had the sequence "performed" offstage and utilized an onstage audience's reactions to establish the mood.

It is possible to perform the show on a unit set with prop pieces to establish more specific locations. The homespun charm of the story and songs is what makes the show enjoyable and enables it to be performed with a limited set and costume budget.

The production calls for an Annie with tremendous vocal and physical stamina—she rarely leaves the stage for a breather. Do not attempt this musical, which was written for a star, without two talented female performers, one to perform the role and one to be an understudy or alternate.

SONGS OF SPECIAL INTEREST

"Buffalo Bill," good small chorus number that calls for minimal staging, features 1M/1F; emphasis is on enthusiasm and energy with vocal and physical build.

"I'm an Indian Too," comic song with good potential as an alto audition number since it shows off energy, comedy, movement and pitch.

"Moonshine Lullaby," nice alto ballad, charm song.

"There's No Business Like Show Business," showstopping quartet, presentational staging, basic movement patterns and simplicity.

"They Say It's Wonderful," good romantic duet for an alto/baritone.

"You Can't Get a Man with a Gun," alto comic problem song which forces actress to relate to audience, good for developing believability and eye contact.

Instrumentation: 4 violins, viola, cello, bass, 4 reeds, 3 trumpets, 3 trombones, percussion, harp, guitar, piano/conductor
Script: Irving Berlin

Score: Irving Berlin
Record: RCA/Capitol
Rights: R & H

ANYONE CAN WHISTLE

Book: Arthur Laurents
Music and Lyrics: Stephen Sondheim

ORIGINAL PRODUCTION

Majestic Theatre, April 4, 1964 (9 perf.)
Director: Arthur Laurents
Dances and Musical Numbers: Herbert Ross
Musical Director and Vocal Arrangements: Herbert Greene
Orchestration: Don Walker
Principals: Cora Hoover—Angela Lansbury—alto; Comptroller Schub—Gabriel
Dell—baritone; Chief Magruder—James Frawley—VTI; Treasurer Cooley—Ar-
nold Soboloff—VTI; Doctor Detmold—Don Doherty—VTNE; J. Bowden Hap-
good—Harry Guardino—baritone; Nurse Fay Apple—Lee Remick—mezzo; Mrs.
Schroeder—Peg Murray—soprano
Chorus: 10M/10F, 1F child.

SYNOPSIS

The curtain rises on the main square of a bankrupt town, with a crooked,
dilapidated City Hall on one side and the crooked, desolate Hotel Superbe on
the other. The citizens are dressed in rags and glare sullenly at the audience.
The only thriving business in town is *The Cookie Jar*, a sanitarium for the
"socially pressured" who dared to be individuals in the outside world. The
patients, in direct contrast to the townsfolk, are well dressed and happy (I'm
Like the Bluebird—Mixed Chorus).

The angry citizens of the town picket outside City Hall, to protest the cor-
ruptness of Chief of Police Magruder, Treasurer Cooley, Comptroller Schub,
and Mayor Cora Hoover Hooper, who arrives laden with diamonds and carried
by four handsome young men. Undaunted by the angry townsfolk who hurl rocks
at her, she comments on the dismal state of affairs (Me and My Town—F Solo
and M Quartet). Cora, knowing it will take a miracle to save the town, goes
along with the unethical plan of her lecherous right-hand man, Schub; womanizer
Magruder; and ex-preacher Cooley.

An unusual rock formation rolls on and the three officials carry out their
miracle, which involves Baby Joan Schroeder, an extremely odd-looking seven-
year-old who thirstily licks the rock, which instantly spews forth a waterfall
fountain. The waterfall is proclaimed a miracle, and Baby Joan a saint. The

excited townspeople and pilgrims laud the event (Miracle Song—Mixed Chorus) as the flowers brighten and the buildings straighten.

The rock revolves, showing Magruder at a water pump and Schub working on some electrical wires. Cooley is thrilled at the success of the waterfall and begins thinking of ways to make more money from their miracle. Cora discovers her three officers in the cave and congratulates them on their brilliant scheme, which will financially benefit the town, for pilgrims are arriving daily.

Nurse Fay Apple, from the sanitarium, brings her cookie charges to take the cure, but Treasurer Cooley refuses to sell them any admission tickets, for he knows the failure of the water to cure the cookies will bring exposure of the fraud. While they are arguing, the cookies blend in with the pilgrims and Cooley is unable to convince Fay to separate them. She escapes from the town, chased by the town officials, and sings of a hero she knows will come to save her (There Won't Be Trumpets—Sc to F Solo).

A flash of lightning is seen, and a clap of thunder is heard as a trumpet blasts to announce J. Hapgood's arrival. Mistaken for a famous psychiatrist, he is enlisted to separate the cookies from the pilgrims. He proceeds to confuse everyone by his analytical method of dividing the people into group A or group One, neither of which has any significance to the discovery of the cookies (Simple— Sc to M Solo and Mixed Chorus). Hapgood terrorizes the town officials by questioning them about the sense of paying government taxes to make bombs which will eventually kill everyone, including themselves. The onstage chorus chant and circle around Cora as they ask for answers to life's questions. Hapgood pronounces everyone in the audience mad, and the act closes with the characters onstage laughing at the audience. ''Who is crazy?''

In Act II groups A and One parade through town with placards praising Hapgood and proclaiming their sanity (A-One March—Mixed Chorus). Fay returns to town, sexily disguised as a French lady from Lourdes sent to test the miracle. Schub invites himself to her apartment but she refuses the invitation, saying she must see if the miracle is legitimate. Schub hastily exits, leaving Fay to smile at Hapgood, who appears on the hotel balcony. Fay waves to him, and the entire set and Hapgood move toward her. The two converse in French as English subtitles are flashed on the set. Fay entices him to leave the balcony as she seductively and comically dances (Come Play Wiz Me—Sc to M/F Duet).

At the end of the song, Hapgood leads Fay onto the balcony and into his room. The balcony revolves to reveal a small room with a Murphy bed. Hapgood orders another bed sent up, and an enormous, tacky one rolls on. Fay, without removing her disguise or her accent, reveals to Hapgood her true identity and her belief that the fountain is a fraud. She tells him she has stolen the records of all the patients, but Hapgood is too involved in removing her clothes to be too interested. When he removes her wig the illusion is shattered as she becomes controlled Nurse Fay Apple, who can't get drunk, laugh, be held or kissed without the aid of her wig. Hapgood accuses her of wanting the waters to be real because she needs the miracle for herself, a fact she readily admits. She sings about her inability to whistle and hopes he can help her shed her inhibitions (Anyone Can Whistle—L to F Solo).

Outside, groups A and One, parading for Hapgood, cause Cora to worry about the town's rejection of her and their sudden adoration of Hapgood (A Parade in Town—F Solo with Mixed Chorus Interspersed).

Meanwhile, Hapgood urges Fay to destroy the records of her cookies and thereby free them, which in turn will free her. Her refusal causes him to angrily comment on the problems caused by the outside world (Everybody Says Don't—Sc to M Solo). He tells her he's not a doctor but a new patient, committed because he protested at the UN by playing his trumpet. He has five degrees and was adviser to the President until he quit because he was too idealistic. Touched by his story, Fay rips up his hospital record and begins destroying the records of all her charges. As she tears the records, the room disappears and the cookies begin dancing. The wild, infectious ballet of the freed cookies crescendos as Fay joins in (Cookie Ballet—Mixed Dance Chorus). The stage empties as Hapgood appears on his balcony and Fay slowly walks toward him with her arms outstretched.

In Act III Cora and her three officals meet in Cora's solarium. They decide to discredit Hapgood by turning off the miracle, certain that the townspeople will blame Hapgood. She congratulates them on their clever scheme (I've Got You to Lean On—1F/4M Quintet which ends as a Tap Dance with Cora and Her Four Boys).

In the town square the defunct rock is in full view and an angry crowd calls for Hapgood, demanding that he identify the cookies because they are certain that his refusal to comply has stopped the miracle. As the crowd gets angrier he and Fay hide in the cave and thus learn that the miracle was a fraud. Cora and her three cohorts discover them and announce that they are going to take anyone they can find to fill the sanitarium by sundown. The four exit to begin rounding people up.

Fay wants to stop Cora and her gang by exposing the pump and the fountain as a fraud, but Hapgood tells her the people need to believe in a miracle. Even if they are shown it is a fake, they will still believe. She is furious at his withdrawal and slaps him for failing her. She runs away from him but stops to angrily sing (See What It Gets You—Sc to F Solo).

Meanwhile, Cora begins to randomly choose townspeople to fill her quota (Cookie Waltz), but Fay frees everyone as fast as they are captured. After a frenzied ballet chase, Fay's true identity as Nurse Apple is revealed by Dr. Detmold, the sanitarium psychiatrist, who orders her to expose the cookies to save the innocent. The nurse has no way out and thus obeys her orders. The cookies happily march off with Dr. Detmold.

Hapgood and Fay are left alone onstage. She was unable to turn him in because she feels he and others like him could possibly change the world. He asks her to come with him, but she can't break that far away from herself. He thanks her for their secret moments together and she returns the thanks (With So Little to Be Sure Of—Sc to M/F Duet). At the end of the song they exit in opposite directions.

Cora arrives onstage to see everyone, including Magruder and Cooley, running to a miracle statue in the next town. She is left standing with Schub, who suggests they make a profit by turning the whole town into a cookie jar. Cora readily agrees, realizing that she and Schub are meant for each other (I've Got You to Lean On [Reprise]—Sc to M/F Duet). The two dance crazily off into City Hall.

The arrival of a cold, orderly female psychiatrist forces Fay to see her former self. Unable to find Hapgood, she desperately whistles for him—he appears and carries her off as the "miracle waters" pour on them.

NOTES ON THE PRODUCTION

Anyone Can Whistle was an innovative musical not destined for a long Broadway run. The show is best described by the term "alienation/theatre of the absurd," a form that commercial audiences of the sixties could not accept. Its small cast makes it ideal for adventurous community theatres; the musical is memorable and the characters well drawn.

Technically it isn't too complex and may be inexpensively mounted. Some production companies with limited offstage space and funds have kept the town square and its buildings onstage throughout the production, rolled on the bed and the rock and relocated Cora's message area to the town square. There are few props necessary to the play; the waterfall is the only technical aspect which is a bit complex, but a good electrician and utilization of waterproof paint should alleviate any problems.

The costumes are modern and may be "pulled" from the everyday wardrobe. Cora's costumes are more elaborate than others but are still of modern vintage. The four "chorus" boys, who dance well, should probably be costumed alike, but this may be left to the discretion of the designer.

The song "There Won't Be Trumpets," although in the published version of the script and score, was eventually cut from the original production. The song may be heard on the album *Marry Me a Little* (RCA).

SONGS OF SPECIAL INTEREST

"Anyone Can Whistle," mezzo ballad. The number appears simplistic yet needs strong acting talents to keep the emphasis on the lyric meaning.

"Come Play Wiz Me," fun duet, effective for loosening up an inhibited mezzo actress. Movement is helpful.

"Everybody Says Don't," scene to baritone solo. Angry, dramatic, with emphasis on the emotions.

"There Won't Be Trumpets," tormented, anguish, strong mezzo number.

"Me and My Town," up tempo, movement-oriented, alto character song.

"See What It Gets You," Angry and dramatic, up tempo with limited movement. Mezzo.

"With So Little to Be Sure Of," poignant romantic farewell love duet. Mezzo/baritone.

Instrumentation: 5 reeds, 2 horns, 3 trumpets, 2 trombones, 5 cellos, bass, accordion, piano/conductor (also celeste)
Script: Random, Leon Amiel
Score: Chappell
Record: Columbia
Rights: MTI

ANYTHING GOES

Original Book: P. G. Wodehouse and Guy Bolton
Revised Book: Howard Lindsay and Russel Crouse
Music and Lyrics: Cole Porter

ORIGINAL PRODUCTION

Alvin Theatre, November 21, 1934 (420 perf.)
Director: Howard Lindsay
Choreographer: Robert Alton
Musical Director: Earl Busby
Orchestration: Robert Russell Bennett and Hans Spialek
Principals: Reno Sweeney—Ethel Merman—alto; Billy Crocker—William Gaxton—baritone; Moon Face Martin—Victor Moore—baritone; Hope Harcourt—Bettina Hall—soprano; Bonnie Latour—Vera Dunn—squeally soprano; Sir Evelyn—Leslie Barrie—baritone
Chorus and Smaller Roles: Various ages and types, the young female chorus members must tap-dance, minimum 12M/12F.

SYNOPSIS

Aboard the luxury liner SS *American*, headed for London, a reporter and press photographer dash about getting information on the passengers. The audience is introduced to the travelers: Mr. Elisha J. Whitney, a pompous Wall Street executive; Sir Evelyn Oakleigh, a staid British aristocrat; Hope Harcourt, his fiancée, and her mother, Mrs. Harcourt; Bishop Henry T. Dobson of the Chinese Anglican Church; and the boisterous Reno Sweeney and her "angels," an evangelist turned nightclub singer.

Billy Crocker, a long-time friend of Reno and the ex-general manager for Mr. Whitney, enters. Reno promptly asks him to be the master of ceremonies of her act and go to London with her, but Billy insists that Reno is the one with talent

(You're the Top—L to M/F Duet) and declines the offer, knowing that Mr. Whitney will hire him back.

When Billy realizes that his former girlfriend, Hope Harcourt, is sailing, he decides to stow away in an attempt to convince her to give up Sir Evelyn and marry him.

Moon Face Martin, Public Enemy Number 13, disguised as a preacher, arrives, followed by the FBI who know of Moon's disguise. They mistakenly apprehend Bishop Dobson and proceed to remove him from the ship as it is about to set sail (Bon Voyage—Mixed Chorus).

Billy meets Moon and his high-spirited, flirtatious girlfriend Bonnie. The two suggest that Billy disguise himself as Snake-Eyes Johnson, Moon's partner who has missed the ship, and give him the gangster's ticket.

Later that evening, Billy finds Hope and her fiancé, Sir Evelyn, on the ship's deck, but Evelyn becomes seasick and leaves them alone. Billy reminds her of the special time they shared together as they both comment on the romantic nature of the evening (It's Delovely—Sc to M/F Duet).

The next morning, Billy tells Moon that his boss, Mr. Whitney, is in the cabin next door and if Whitney discovers Billy he will be fired again. Moon decides to steal Whitney's eyeglasses so that he can't see Billy, but Billy has bigger problems. It seems the FBI have discovered their mistake and alerted the ship's crew to be on the lookout for Snake-Eyes Johnson. Moon, Billy and Bonnie decide it would be best if Billy changed his disguise to that of a member of the crew.

Bonnie, mistaken for one of Reno's angels, decides to show that she's just as talented as the rest (Heaven Hop—F Solo with F Tapping Chorus).

On deck, Sir Evelyn discovers that Hope and Billy were out until seven in the morning; his lack of concern bothers Hope. Billy appears, dressed as a sailor, to remind Hope that he still loves her and wants to marry her.

Billy, hoping that Mrs. Harcourt will stop Hope's wedding, decides to discredit Sir Evelyn and enlists the aid of Moon in persuading Reno to trap Sir Evelyn into a compromising situation (Friendship—Sc to 2M/1F Trio).

In Evelyn's stateroom, when Evelyn mistakes Reno's sexual advances as American slang, she is charmed by his innocent manner and intrigued by his wealth. Alone on deck, in a dreamy daze, Reno sings about the Englishman that's on her mind (I Get a Kick out of You—F Solo).

Meanwhile, on the afterdeck, Billy, now disguised as a woman, is seated next to Hope and Evelyn but quickly exits when Mrs. Harcourt discovers his identity. He returns dressed as a chef, later as a purser and finally as a Count. When his false beard falls off he is mistaken for Snake-Eyes Johnson, and only the excited behavior of the passengers, who feel they have a celebrity on board, keeps him from the brig. Reno leads the company in the Act I Finale (Anything Goes—F Solo to Mixed Chorus).

In Act II the passengers praise Billy (Public Enemy Number One—Mixed

Chorus) and Bonnie leads the company in a rousing number that symbolizes her philosophy (Let's Step Out—F Solo).

Billy meets Hope, who is upset by his behavior, but he assures her he will try to put an end to his popularity. Reno and Evelyn enter, obviously enamored with each other, and a miffed Hope exits. Evelyn and Reno are left alone to share their mutual admiration (Let's Misbehave—Sc to M/F Duet).

At a revival "religious service" Billy confesses to the passengers that he is not Snake-Eyes Johnson, but a simple stockbroker down on his luck. The angry Captain orders Billy and Moon into the brig as Reno continues the revival (Blow Gabriel—F Solo to Mixed Chorus).

Five days later, the ship reaches England, with Billy and Moon still in the brig. Billy can't keep his mind off Hope, who is in another part of the ship thinking about him (All through the Night—M/F Solos). Realizing that Billy is depressed by the sudden turn of events, Moon tries to cheer him up (Be Like a Bluebird—Sc to M Solo). Bonnie appears upside down at the cell's porthole (she's being held by her ankles by a sailor friend) to see if she can help. Billy sends for Hope who arrives with the news that Mrs. Harcourt has insisted that Hope and Evelyn be married immediately by the Captain. Hope sadly leaves after admitting her love for Billy.

Meanwhile, on deck, Reno and her angels are getting bored with shipboard life and yearn to return to New York (Take Me Back to Manhattan—F Solo with F Chorus). Evelyn tells Reno he must maintain his honor and marry Hope despite his preference for Reno.

Billy and Moon, determined to stop the wedding, escape the brig disguised as Chinese immigrants. They convince Reno to join them, and the three arrive at the ceremony and convince everyone that Sir Evelyn deflowered Plum Blossom (Reno) and dishonored their family name. Evelyn and Hope, who recognize Billy and Reno, go along with the action and agree that the only way to right the wrong is to have Evelyn marry Plum Blossom, and Plum Blossom's brother (Billy) marry Hope. The couples are quickly wed (Finale—Mixed Chorus).

NOTES ON THE PRODUCTION

The show established Ethel Merman's career and provided audiences with another Cole Porter score. The production was revived in 1962 with the addition of the following six Cole Porter tunes: "It's Delovely" (*Red Hot and Blue*), "Heaven Hop" (*Paris*), "Friendship" (*Du Barry Was a Lady*), "Let's Step Out" (*Fifty Million Frenchmen*), "Let's Misbehave" (*Paris*) and "Take Me Back to Manhattan" (*The New Yorkers*). The preceding synopsis adheres to the 1962 revised script, which is the version available for production.

The show is extremely popular and often performed by community theatres and high schools alike. There are a number of scenes, but most may take place on the deck of the ship with the ship's smokestacks forming a background. The brig is usually a small cell-type arrangement placed in front of the ship structure.

The cabin scenes may also use this arrangement, which simplifies the technical and budgetary requirements.

The costumes are styled in the 1930s. Most of the female chorus have two costumes for the show and the principals have at least two, depending on the look the designer chooses. The majority of the male chorus is composed of the ship's crew and may utilize one costume throughout; the male passengers should have several outfits.

SONGS OF SPECIAL INTEREST

"Be Like the Bluebird," baritone solo. Emphasis on comic characterization and absurd, angular movements.

"It's Delovely," romantic, period style, à la Astaire and Rogers, helps make this a memorable number for a soprano and baritone.

"I Get a Kick Out of You," alto solo. Very workable in a nightclub situation.

"You're the Top," M/F baritone, alto duet. Emphasis on reacting to praise and instant response. Simple dance movement.

Many of the numbers from the revised version would be successful in a club, revue, or class situation and are worth a closer examination.

Script: NP
Score: Harms, also see *Cole Porter Songbook*
Record: Smithsonian, Epic
Rights: TW

APPLAUSE

Book: Betty Comden and Adolph Green (Based on the film *All about Eve* and the original short story by Mary Orr)
Music: Charles Strouse
Lyrics: Lee Adams

ORIGINAL PRODUCTION

Palace Theatre, March 30, 1970 (896 perf.)
Director and Choreographer: Ron Field
Musical Director: Donald Pippin
Orchestration: Philip J. Lang
Principals: Margo Channing—Lauren Bacall—alto; Eve Harrington—Penny Fuller—mezzo; Buzz Richards—Brandon Maggart—tenor; Bill Samson—Len Cariou—baritone; Duane Fox—Lee Roy Reams—baritone; Karen Richards—Ann Williams—alto; Howard Benedict—Robert Mandan—VTNE; Bonnie—Bonnie Franklin—mezzo
Chorus and Smaller Roles: Mixed chorus of dancers and singers—minimum

number advisable, if performers are triple threat, is 8M/8F. If two separate choruses are used, a configuration of 12 dancers and 8 singers (equally divided M/F) with additional actors for smaller roles is suggested.

SYNOPSIS

The play opens at a Tony Awards ceremony where Margo Channing, a successful, middle-aged star, has just presented the Best Actress Award to Eve Harrington, Margo's former protégé. We soon find out, however, that Margo's feelings towards Eve are anything but admirable.

Flashback. It is now a year and half earlier, and we are in Margo's busy dressing room where she has just opened in another stellar production. The dressing room is filled with fans, friends, and first nighters (Back Stage Babble— Mixed Chorus). Finally Margo's dressing room clears, leaving only Margo with her friends: Bill Sampson, her slightly younger, thirty-nine–year–old director/ lover; Duane, her hairdresser/confidant; Buzz Richards, the author of the show, and his wife Karen.

Karen enthusiastically introduces Margo to Eve Harrington, a seemingly meek young fan who has spent all her money to see Miss Channing perform. Margo is preoccupied with Bill, who will soon be leaving to direct a film in Rome. The two are temporarily left alone, and she attempts to convince him not to leave. He patiently tells her how nice it will be when he returns (Think How It's Gonna Be—Sc to M Solo).

Margo, who can't face the opening night party without Bill, decides to have her own party with Duane and Eve at a Greenwich Village discotheque. Margo has a rousing time with "the boys," who are frequent customers (But Alive— F Solo to M Chorus).

Later that evening, in Margo's apartment, Margo, Duane, and Eve learn that the reviewers declare the show a hit. It is the end of a perfect evening for Eve, who expressively thanks Margo for including her (The Best Night of My Life— Sc to F Solo). Margo enjoys the flattery and invites Eve to stay in her apartment as a companion. Happening to see a late-night television movie of herself at age nineteen, she comments to Eve on the changes she has undergone (Who's That Girl?—Sc to F Solo).

Four months have passed, and Eve, much to Duane's dismay, has become girl Friday to Margo and friend to the play's production staff. Margo trusts Eve who is using their friendship as a way to establish her own career. The younger woman ingratiates herself with Producer Howard Benedict, who invites her to Joe Allen's, an after-theatre spot, and asks her to understudy Margo. The two are entertained by Bonnie, a Broadway dancer, and her fellow "gypsies" who sing about the theatre (Applause—F Solo to Chorus).

Later that evening, in her apartment, Margo urges Bill, via long distance, to come home because she misses him desperately (Hurry Back—F Solo). He promises to get there as quickly as possible.

Two weeks later, Bill arrives at one of Margo's parties and exchanges flirtatious quips with Eve, a scene Margo happens to witness. Threatened by Eve's youth, she becomes extremely vicious, and the guests sense the chill in the air (Fasten Your Seatbelts—Mixed Chorus).

Several days after the party, Eve reads for the part of Margo's understudy and impresses everyone with her talent. Margo bitterly welcomes Eve to the difficult world of show business (Welcome to the Theatre—Sc to F Solo). Eve quietly leaves during the number; she has achieved the first step in her rise to stardom. When Margo jealously accuses Bill of helping Eve get the understudy role, he is no longer able to cope with her constant insecurity and walks out, leaving her alone as the curtain falls.

Act II, set a few weeks later, begins with Margo enjoying a quiet afternoon at Buzz and Karen's Connecticut home. She plans on returning to the city for the evening performance but Karen, who is furious at Margo's behavior toward Eve, drains the gas tank. They are stranded and Eve performs the starring role. Buzz, Karen and Margo think over their respective situations (Inner Thoughts— Sc to 2F/1M Linear Trio). Margo is upset because it is the first performance she has ever missed, and Karen feels guilty about betraying Margo. Buzz tries to clear the air while strumming the banjo (Good Friends—Sc to 2F/1M Trio).

In New York, Eve has received rave reviews for her performance. When Bill comes into her dressing room, Eve tells him how much help he was and makes strong, flirtatious advances, which he refuses. Feeling rejected, Eve accepts an invitation from an elated Howard, who asks her to join him at Joe Allen's, where she purposely snubs Bonnie and the other gypsies who comment on her overnight sensation (She's No Longer a Gypsy—Mixed Chorus).

During the filming of a coffee commercial in her living room, Margo falters from the pressure of Eve's reviews, but Bill assures her that Eve can't begin to approach her talent (One of a Kind—Sc to M/F Duet).

Eve has secretly taken up with Buzz, whom she is trying to manipulate into writing her a new show. She is on top of the world, but she can't forget her hatred of her father, who once called her a whore. As she stands backstage, she remembers (One Hallowe'en—Sc to F Solo). Howard, who wants Eve for himself, enters to insist that she drop Buzz. She has no alternative if she wants to continue her career, for Howard is a very powerful man. She has been trapped by someone more clever and vicious.

Two weeks later in Margo's dressing room, Karen and Margo are reconciled when Karen seeks Margo's advice about Buzz, who has written his new play for Eve. Margo, knowing that Eve will get the starring role, finally realizes there is more to life than the theatre. She excitedly informs Bill that he means more to her than starring roles (Something Greater—Sc To F Solo M/F Duet). (Finale—Mixed Chorus).

NOTES ON THE PRODUCTION

This show marked Lauren Bacall's musical debut, for which she won the Tony Award for Best Actress (1970). Other awards were Best Musical, Book, Direction, and Choreography.

The show is presented in the style of the late sixties and should remain relatively close to that period if the 1940s-style "Who's That Girl?" number is to remain plausible. Possibly it could be updated to 1975 if Margo's age is in her fifties and Eve's in early thirties. Neither period is difficult to costume. It is important that the "Gypsies" be colorfully adorned since their numbers call for flamboyance to help ensure that they will be showstoppers.

Although the original production had nine different sets comprised of wagons, a curtain and flying scenery, it is possible to simplify this by deleting Margo's bedroom and playing the scene in the already used living room; using one restaurant set instead of a restaurant and a disco; and using the backstage area instead of the dressing rooms. A company may want to consider keeping the backstage area onstage throughout the play as a general backdrop. The audience can accept seeing the backstage with its flats and walls as a background for minimal set pieces used to establish definite locations.

The music is memorable, and the lesser characters and chorus smaller parts are interesting for young actors to portray. The role of Margo is extremely demanding as she must move fairly well and be able to portray a vital though aging star.

SONGS OF SPECIAL INTEREST

"Applause," a tribute to theatre, is often used for the closing or encore of a revue. The song is usually performed by a chorus of dancers; however, movement may be kept extremely simple as it is the energy that really sells the song.

"But Alive," alto. Good for a club act, up tempo, may be done as a solo in a revue situation or as a solo with chorus.

"One Hallowe'en," dramatic number for a mezzo. A good acting exercise as there are several mood shifts and transitions.

"Who's That Girl?," alto comment on the movies of the forties, calls for specific knowledge of forties dances and social history. Good for movement, loosening up a stiff performer, eye contact and warmth.

Instrumentation: 2 violins, viola, cello, bass, 5 reeds, 3 trumpets, 2 trombones, 1 bass trombone, 2 percussion, guitar/banjo/mandolin, harp, organ, piano/conductor
Script: Random, *Great Musicals of the American Theatre Volume II*
Score: Edwin H. Morris
Record: ABC
Rights: TW

THE APPLE TREE

Book: Sheldon Harnick and Jerry Bock; additional book material by Jerome Coopersmith (Based on stories by Mark Twain, Frank R. Stockton, and Jules Feiffer)
Music: Jerry Bock
Lyrics: Sheldon Harnick

ORIGINAL PRODUCTION

Shubert Theatre, October 18, 1966 (463 perf.)
Director: Mike Nichols
Choreographer: Lee Theodore; Additional Musical Staging: Herbert Ross
Musical Director: Elliot Lawrence
Orchestration: Eddie Sauter
Principals: Adam/Cpt. Sanjar/Flip—Alan Alda—baritone; Eve/Princess/Ella—
Barbara Harris—mezzo; Snake/Balladeer/Narrator—Larry Blyden—baritone
Chorus and Smaller Roles: SM/SF needed for the middle and last pieces.

SYNOPSIS

The Diary of Adam and Eve. Time: June 1st. Place: Eden.

The lights rise on Adam, slowly waking to the sound of a voice which commands him to name the creatures on Earth and warns him not to eat the fruit of a certain apple tree. Adam begins his task rather haphazardly but soon decides he had better keep an accurate record of the momentous occasion, so he begins to take notes on all he sees. As he attempts to categorize the creatures he realizes, quite happily, that he is the sole man. His elation is short-lived as he clutches his rib in pain and a sleeping Eve rolls onstage. He looks curiously at the creature but chooses to name her later.

Eve awakens, overwhelmed to find herself in a very nice, new world. She begins taking notes, knowing that this knowledge will someday be important to historians (Here in Eden—L to F Solo). At the end of the song Eve spies Adam, who wanders on carrying a fish. She screams at him to drop the pickerel; he quickly climbs a nearby apple tree and yells at her to get out. The argument ends when Adam drops the fish. Eve exits, having won their first battle.

Adam isn't pleased by Eve's presence, but she is attracted to him and examines her emotions (Feelings—Sc to F Solo). During the song's interval Eve begins creating fire, which initially intrigues but quickly disenchants Adam, who burns his fingers on the hot coals. Eve continues thinking up ways to interest him.

Adam is attracted to Eve and attempts to analyze his mixed emotions. It starts to rain and Adam refuses Eve shelter in his hut. When she begins to cry, he is amazed for he has never seen a person "rain." He kindheartedly manages to squeeze Eve into his new home, but once inside she begins badgering him about redecorating. He is simultaneously infuriated and fascinated by this interesting creature (Eve—Sc to M Solo).

Eve puts Adam to work fixing up their living quarters and the area around the hut. She good-naturedly listens to his first joke—about a chicken crossing a road—and sends him to cut the grass.

Meanwhile, Eve, infatuated with her reflection in the nearby pond, sings to her new friend that is like a sister (Friends—F Solo).

When a snake she has befriended impresses her with a scientific explanation of the reflection process, she defers to his knowledge and eats the forbidden fruit (The Apple Tree—Sc to M Solo).

Adam, innocently bathing and enjoying the beauty of the world (Beautiful, Beautiful World—M Solo), becomes aware that the animals are fighting and realizes death has come to the garden. He accuses Eve of eating the apple and bringing disaster upon them, but she convinces him his bad jokes are at the root of the problem and he will gain knowledge if he eats the apple. Adam takes the fatal bite and he and Eve are forced to leave the garden and seek refuge elsewhere.

In order to survive, Adam often travels great distances to forage for food. After one such trip he discovers Eve with a new creature that looks like a small human but acts like a fish and a bear. He tries to determine exactly what this new object is (It's a Fish—L to M Solo).

Eve cautiously comes from the hut, hoping she is alone with this new creature, and quietly sings a lullaby (Go to Sleep, Whatever You Are—F Solo). She exits and Adam reenters, holding his recently bitten hand, to comment on the growth of the strange animal (Fish II—M Solo).

Time passes; the boys have been named and are fully grown. Adam is worried about Cain's disagreeable nature, but having Eve to confide in makes up for his lack of trust in his son. He realizes he would be very lonely without her.

Adam and Eve are much older, Cain and Abel are both dead and they feel very much alone. Eve brings up the subject of death, admitting she could not physically survive without him, but he changes the topic by telling her a favorite joke. After he exits Eve considers life without Adam and ponders her reasons for loving him (What Makes Me Love Him?—L to F Solo). She slowly enters the house.

Eve has died. A saddened Adam enters—he realizes he never really lost Eden until he lost Eve. He crosses to the flower garden and begins to tend the flowers as the curtain falls.

The Lady or the Tiger. Time: Olden days. Place: An imaginary kingdom.

The actor who previously portrayed the snake enters as a guitar-playing and singing balladeer to tell a story about jealousy in love (I'll Tell You a Truth—M Solo). As he finishes, the lights brighten and the company enters carrying King Arik and his daughter, Barbara (Make Way—Mixed Chorus). The balladeer tells of King Arik's peculiar system of justice, which requires an accused prisoner, to choose between two doors. Behind one door is a ferocious tiger—behind the other a beautiful woman.

The balladeer introduces Captain Sanjar, who has just returned from battle victorious and exhausted. Barbara eagerly ministers to him for they are actually secret lovers who have no hope of marriage because of the difference in their stations (Forbidden Love—Sc to M/F Duet). They plan to run away to a place Sanjar has heard of (In Gaul—Sc to M/F Duet) but honor stops them. After all, Barbara is a princess and Sanjar has his career to think of. They decide to continue their secret relationship and madly embrace, but they are discovered by an angered King Arik, who orders Sanjar to stand trial.

Barbara bribes the reluctant tiger keeper, played by the balladeer, to tell her which door conceals the lady (Forbidden Fruit—M/F Duet) and excitedly promises to save Sanjar. She imagines his feelings when she tells him the answer (I've Got What You Want—F Solo).

When the princess discovers that her lovely maidservant Madjira is to be the lady behind the door, she contemplates what she should tell her lover. It seems that the girl must marry the prisoner if he chooses the right door, and Barbara knows that Sanjar is attracted to Nadjira (Tiger, Tiger—F Solo).

The ritual is about to start (Make Way [Reprise]—Mixed Chorus) when the troubador stops the action to analyze the outcome (Which Door?—Mixed Chorus); the audience is left to draw its own conclusions.

Passionella. Time: The sixties to the present. Place: NYC.

The lights rise on a New York rooftop where Ella, a chimney sweep who yearns to be a beautiful movie star, is working. The narrator describes Ella's dream in tones not unlike the "Queen for a Day" television show. Ella animatedly sings (Movie Star—F Solo).

The narrator outlines Ella's life of work and television dreaming. One day her boss tells her she is no longer needed since chimney sweeping has become automated. Ella, unable to find work elsewhere, sadly returns home to watch television. As she watches, her neighborhood godmother appears and promises to grant her wish. A series of flashes turns Ella into a gorgeous Marilyn Monroe–style movie star. Ella is ecstatic (Gorgeous—F Solo) until her godmother warns her she will only be gorgeous between the seven o'clock news and the late show.

Ella rushes off to El Morocco via subway and everywhere she goes people wonder about her (Who Is She?—Mixed Chorus). She confidently tells everyone that she is Passionella. A producer signs her to a lifetime contract, she rises to stardom and is adored by everybody. Secretly she yearns for true love (I Know; Wealth—Mixed Chorus to F Solo).

At the opening of a Sunset Strip psychedelic drugstore she meets Flip, her Prince Charming, who is the idol of millions for he is dirty and "real." When he scoffs at her beauty and expensive clothes (You Are Not Real—Sc to M Solo With Mixed Chorus), she desperately attempts to change his mind and makes a film about chimney sweeps which gains her the Academy Award. After she gives her Oscar thank-you speech, Flip asks her to marry him. The happy couple retires to her home where they eagerly embrace while watching Garbo in *Camille* on late-night television. At the end of the movie, a voice announces that programming is completed—it is 4:00 A.M. and the movie is over. Both freeze in fear. Blackout. There is a huge flash and the lights rise on Passionella, who is once again a lowly chimney sweep. She looks around to see a mousy businessman staring at her. They are stunned but happy to discover they have something in common. (George—L to M/F Duet).

NOTES ON THE PRODUCTION

Barbara Harris won the 1967 Tony Award as Best Actress in a musical, winning over Lotte Lenya in *Cabaret* and Mary Martin in *I Do! I Do!* The show is a charming small-cast musical where each act can be performed by different actors or the entire show by the same ensemble of actors.

It is inexpensive to produce as each act is self-contained and in a different production style. *The Lady or the Tiger* sequence is traditionally performed in a large-scale style. The *Adam and Eve* sequence needs a simplified garden with small set pieces to represent the hut and the tree. The tree is usually practical because Adam climbs it, but in some productions he hides behind it, which saves on building costs and structural techniques. The final piece is done in a story theatre style which calls for very little in the way of set and props as much is covered through narration.

The directors and designers need to find sets and styles that will truly represent each playlet while cohesively tying the three productions together. It is important that the audience have the feeling they have spent an "evening in the theatre."

The *Adam and Eve* sequence may be used in one-act play contests, for assembly presentations, or for entertainment at a meeting. It is the most charming of the three selections, appeals to grades five and up, and only requires three actors and minimal set pieces. Be sure to specify the desire to perform only one act when applying for royalties.

SONGS OF SPECIAL INTEREST

"Eve," introspective, charm song, good to develop male sensitivity, doesn't require a strong voice; baritone.

"Forbidden Fruit," strong character baritone, comic in tone, good for getting a stiff actor to move as the movement is eccentric in style.

"Here in Eden," number requires mezzo actress to visualize the various images she sees and make them real to an audience, calls for variety in expression, challenges the performer to search for differences in vocal delivery.

"It's a Fish," comic, baritone story song, sometimes used in audition to show ability to handle comedy, good to work on in a class situation because the song is interspersed with monologues and gives the actor experience in handling lines to song.

"I've Got What You Want" and "Tiger, Tiger" are both good for development of hard characters. Both numbers require strong and sensual movement, mezzo.

"Movie Star" into "Gorgeous." The combination shows mezzo versatility and characterization change. Could be adapted for an audition situation if time were permitted.

"What Makes Me Love Him?," simple mezzo ballad, old age delivery, charm song.

Instrumentation: 4 reeds, 3 trumpets, 3 trombones, horn, 2 percussion, guitar, harp, violin, viola, cello, bass, piano/conductor
Script: Random
Score: Hansen
Record: Columbia
Rights: MTI

B

BABES IN ARMS

Book: Original Book: Lorenz Hart and Richard Rodgers. Revised Book: George Oppenheimer
Music: Richard Rodgers
Lyrics: Lorenz Hart

ORIGINAL PRODUCTION

Shubert Theatre, April 14, 1937 (289 perf.)
Director: Robert Sinclair
Choreographer: George Balanchine
Music Director: Gene Salzer
Orchestration: Hans Spialek
Principals: The acting manuscript was rewritten in 1959 and all the characters except Val and Gus were renamed. In order to avoid confusion, a description of the character is used instead of the cast member in the original production. See notes section for further details. F—Terry—comedic, lovestruck—alto; M—Gus—clumsy apprentice—tenor; M—Valentine—composer, romantic—high baritone; F—Susie—enthusiastic, attractive—mezzo; M—Seymour Fleming—theatre owner—VTNE; F—Bunny—Eve Arden type—alto/mezzo; M—Lee Calhoun—southern playwright—VTNE; F—Jennifer Owen—stage mother—VTNE;

M—Steve Edwards—Broadway producer—VTNE; F/M—Press Agent—Narrator—VTNE

Chorus and Smaller Roles: 4F/3M but may be expanded.

SYNOPSIS

The play opens on the exterior of the Surf and Sand Playhouse where a press agent congenially welcomes everyone and gives some background on Seymour Fleming's failing Cape Cod Theatre. He introduces the apprentices, in their mid to upper teens, who perform and demonstrate varying degrees of talent.

Gus, a comically awkward young man, accuses Terry, his coquettish girlfriend, of ignoring him. She agrees with his perception and plans on continuing her behavior. Valentine White, a young composer, lyricist and author who is trying to get Fleming to produce his revue, enters, followed by Susie, a bright, enthusiastic girl who idolizes him. The apprentices gather round to hear Val's latest song (Babes in Arms—M Solo to Mixed Chorus).

Fleming, the tyrannical theatre owner, enters and accuses everyone of working on their revue instead of his shows. The theatre's impoverished co-owner, Bunny, interrupts to tell him Phyllis Owen is on the phone to discuss her famous daughter Jennifer's costume. Fleming leaves after telling Bunny she must pay him the money she owes or forfeit her half of the theatre.

Susie tries to bolster everyone's spirits by convincing Val and the apprentices to continue their work on the show and give Bunny the profits to save her theatre. Bunny is overcome and Susie tactfully changes the subject to their forthcoming production "The Deep North," written, directed and acted by Lee Calhoun. The lunch bell rings and the apprentices rush off, leaving Susie to ask Val how he feels about her. She is angered by his response and tells him to stop thinking of her as a younger sister (All at Once—Sc to M/F Duet).

In the theatre, several days later, Gus, the bumbling apprentice, is on a ladder adjusting lights when the arrogant, pint-sized Lee Calhoun enters and begins throwing his weight around. When Gus confronts him about his behavior, Calhoun takes away the ladder and leaves Gus hanging from a light bar. Terry rescues him, and Gus gives her a kiss which she initially resists (I Wish I Were in Love Again—Sc to M/F Duet).

Outside the Playhouse Val is seated at a small piano composing when starlet Jennifer Owen enters and congratulates him on his song. He asks if she has a special man in her life; she flirtatiously responds that she has a fiancé who is in New York and she feels very close to Val (Where or When—Sc to M/F Duet).

Susie enters with Mrs. Owen. Both are upset to see Val and Jennifer in a romantic mood. Val hastily exits as Susie snubs him. The apprentices exit from the Playhouse where Calhoun has insisted on silence, and Bunny asks Val what part he wants her to play in his revue. When he questions her about her vocal type, she responds that she is a western singer from New York (Way Out West on West End Avenue—F Solo).

Later that evening, at an old barn, the apprentices are rehearsing. Jennifer, who has escaped the watchful eye of her mother, enters and tells Val she will try to get Steve Edwards, her fiancé, who is a producer, to see his show. He kisses her as Susie enters to warn them her mother is coming. Jennifer rushes off as Val thanks Susie. He starts to give her a platonic kiss but runs off in confusion, leaving Susie to comment (My Funny Valentine—Sc to F Solo).

Back at the theatre, the dress rehearsal has ended in a shambles. Everyone is on edge when Fleming and Mrs. Owen decide to delay the opening until the week scheduled for the apprentice revue. The kids and Bunny are dejected and consider quitting until Susie bolsters their spirits and urges them to fight (Babes in Arms [Reprise]—Mixed Chorus).

Act II opens on the exterior of the theatre. The apprentices are frozen in dejected poses as the press agent enters to bring the audience up-to-date on the progress of Calhoun's show, which is a flop. He exits. Susie arrives to energize the apprentices (Imagine—F Solo to Mixed Chorus Dance). When Jennifer enters to apologize to Val for not saving his revue, the apprentices hide her from Calhoun and lock him in the cellar. Val, left alone with Jennifer, convinces her to feign sickness and force Fleming to cancel the show and allow the revue to go on (You're Nearer—Sc to M/F Duet).

Bunny and the apprentices enter after Jennifer leaves; Val tells them the good news but is interrupted by Mrs. Owen, who demands to know Jennifer's whereabouts. When everyone sends her in a different direction, she insultingly tells Bunny she should be more ladylike and exits in a huff. Bunny quickly laughs and tells Susie, Val and Gus that she is a different type of woman (The Lady Is a Tramp—F Solo).

Terry comes running on to tell everyone that Calhoun has escaped from the cellar and knows of Steve and Jennifer's plans. The apprentices are dejected, but Susie insists that she can get producer Steve Edwards to watch the revue in the barn after the evening performance.

At the hotel, Susie enters through the bedroom window and warmly greets her brother, Steve. It seems that she hasn't told anyone about their relationship. Terry, Gus and Val discover her in Steve's bedroom, and Susie feigns romantic involvement, hoping that Val will be jealous.

Backstage, while Terry counts the audience, Gus and Susie enter in a panic for they can't find Val. When he enters in a drunken stupor, Susie tells him that Steve is her brother. The show begins and the apprentices sabotage "The Deep North" by turning lights off and on and ringing phones in the wrong places. The frustrated Calhoun tells the audience he can take no more and is returning to the South forever.

On a country road leading to the barn the apprentices are singing as Bunny and Susie are trying to sober Val.

At the barn the press agent comments that the hopes of the apprentices were almost fulfilled and announces the revue. Bunny enters dragging a rocking chair and is surrounded by Terry and Gus dressed as children who beg a story. She tells them about a boy named Johnny (Johnny One-Note—L to F Solo). The song ends and Val rushes onstage with Susie and a check from Steve Edwards, who has commissioned the revue for Broadway. The excited apprentices launch into the finale.

NOTES ON THE PRODUCTION

The original production, with a much different book, featured young and relative unknowns Ray Heatherton, Alfred Drake, Dan Dailey, Mitzi Green, Robert Rounseville and Wynn Murray. The songs, excellent in 1937, are still performed and have become "notable standards." "You're Nearer," originally from *Too Many Girls*, was added to the revised acting version.

The book is quite thin and must be played with believable, charming innocence in order to be enjoyable. It has been reset in the 1950s and works as a show because the music and lyrics are so enjoyable, familiar and memorable. There is something pleasant about seeing songs one has grown up with being performed in a theatrical setting.

The show may be performed using one set for the stage of the theatre and placing all the theatre scenes there. A separate set is needed for the hotel bedroom. The costumes are simple and easily pulled from wardrobes or attics. It is inexpensive to produce and, in the hands of a good director and cast, worthy of a summer theatre or school production.

SONGS OF SPECIAL INTEREST

"I Wish I Were in Love Again," alto/tenor duet for young comics, good exercise for beginning choreographer as the number almost directs itself yet allows for individual creativity.

"Johnny One-Note," story song, possible for children's theatre audition when combined with monologue.

"The Lady Is a Tramp," standard club song, good for revue. Excellent lyrics, emphasizes attitude.

"My Funny Valentine," charm song, good for club.

"Way Out West," F alto solo, presentational, clever lyrics.

Instrumentation: 4 reeds, 3 trumpets, trombone, percussion, 4 violins, viola, cello, bass, piano/conductor
Script: NP
Score: Chappell
Record: Columbia
Rights: R & H

BABY

Book: Sybille Pearson (Based on a story developed with Susan Yankowitz)
Music: David Shire
Lyrics: Richard Maltby, Jr.

ORIGINAL PRODUCTION

Ethel Barrymore Theatre, December 4, 1983 (241 perf.)
Director: Richard Maltby, Jr.
Musical Staging: Wayne Cliento
Music Direction: Peter Howard
Orchestration: Jonathan Tunick
Principals: Lizzie—Liz Callaway—mezzo; Danny—Todd Graff—tenor; Arlene—Beth Fowler—mezzo; Alan—James Congdon—baritone; Pam—Catherine Cox—mezzo/soprano; Nick—Martin Vidnovic—high baritone
Chorus and Smaller Roles: 5F/2M minimum.

SYNOPSIS

A movie scrim drops in and a film of various images begins as a voice narrates the monthly trip of the egg. As the narration continues the music peaks, and the film dissolves to a bedroom in a college town which the twenty-year-old Danny and Lizzie enter. Danny kneels by the bed composing on an electric piano and complains that all the good music has been written. Lizzie stops him from playing and asks him to feel the magic of the moment when two lives begin to merge (We Start Today—Sc to M/F Duet). As she sings, the film bleeds through the scrim, showing continued development of the egg.

The film dissolves to show Alan and Arlene, a couple in their forties, returning from their twentieth anniversary celebration. They comment on how empty the house seems since the last of their three children has gone to school but look forward to their new beginning as a couple with freedom to live their own lives (We Start Today—Sc to M/F Duet).

The film bleeds through to show the further development of the egg and dissolves to the same bed in the room of gym coaches Nick and Pam, a couple in their thirties who desperately want a baby (We Start Today—Sc to M/F Duet). The other two couples join in and the number becomes a sextet as all go on with their daily lives. The scrim passes in front of them, and the film represents an embryo one month later. The film dissolves and the lights rise on passersby and the couples on a spring day in April.

The three women line up outside the doctor's office to discover they are pregnant. Each reacts quite differently to the news. They turn to their respective husbands, who greet them with varied reactions, and the number ends (We Start Today—Sc to Mixed Chorus).

In Danny and Lizzie's apartment, Danny attempts to convince Lizzie that marriage will not ruin their relationship, but she is adamantly opposed. They imagine what the baby will be like (What Could Be Better?—Sc to M/F Duet).

In Arlene and Alan's bedroom the two are exercising and wonder when the event occurred (The Plaza Song—Sc to M/F Linear Duet). He hopes it is twins and feels rejuvenated; she is overwhelmed.

The scene shifts to Nick and Pam's where Nick urges Pam to set aside her feelings of unfemininity and only have positive thoughts around the baby (Baby, Baby, Baby—Sc to M/F Duet to Mixed Chorus). The other two couples join in.

The scrim comes on showing the embryo at five weeks. The three women, now at the doctor's office, introduce themselves and discover they all want the same thing, despite their differences in age and perspective (I Want It All—Sc to F Trio).

Nick, Danny's track coach, advises him on the complexities of women (At Night She Comes Home to Me—Sc to M Solo to M Linear Duet). Danny completes the song in a different area of the stage. Pam enters to tell Nick she isn't pregnant; there was a mistake in the records. He comforts her as the scene shifts to Danny and Lizzie, where Danny informs Lizzie he is taking a high-paying job with a punk rock group. He is insistent of being financially as well as emotionally responsible for the baby (What Could Be Better? [Reprise]—Sc to M/F Duet).

The film shows the embryo with its hand moving, age eight weeks, and the scene shifts to the doctor's office where Nick and Pam discover that their inability to produce a child isn't due to Pam. The doctor suggests adoption but gives them specific rules to follow if they are insistent on having their own offspring.

At the faculty-student baseball game Danny arrives in his new punk rock costume, excited that he is going to be a responsible father. Joined by two other faculty men with definite opinions on fatherhood, Alan, Danny and Nick, who is still determined to father his own child, examine the emotional feelings of being a father (Fatherhood Blues—Sc to M Quintet).

The subsequent scenes show the agony Arlene is feeling about a baby inter-rupting her chance to be alone with her husband; Pam and Nick living their sex life by the rule book; and Danny and Lizzie preparing for their summer separation. Pam, knowing Nick is upset by his failure to create a child, desperately tries to keep humor in their relationship (Romance—L to F Solo. M Necessary for Staging).

The film flashes on showing the embryo at eleven weeks. The lights rise on Lizzie and Danny at the bus station. Danny gives Lizzie a ring and tells her that he is marrying her whether she marries him or not. To honor the occasion he sings the song he has just finished (I Chose Right—Sc to M Solo).

Lizzie, now obviously pregnant, returns to the apartment. Feeling the baby kick, she realizes the importance of the cycle of life (The Story Goes On—F Solo). As she sings she reaches out and the scrim image shows a baby's hand reaching out. The stage goes black.

In Act II Lizzie, on her way to mail a letter to Danny, is greeted by various women who insist on asking about the baby and relating terrifying experiences (The Ladies Singing Their Song—F Chorus).

Arlene leaves the doctor's office after experiencing the sixth-month sonogram, sits on the park bench and sings a lullaby. She is amazed at the scientific advancement during the past twenty years (Baby, Baby, Baby [Reprise]—F Solo).

Pam, tired of the nightly ritual the doctor has prescribed and upset that the romance has gone from their lives, laments (Romance [Reprise]—Sc to F Solo). Nick agrees with her and the two decide to let nature take its course.

Arlene, over a dinner that Alan has solicitously prepared, tells him that they are first and foremost parents and she will always wonder if they could have been more. Alan realizes she is right and admits to himself that children are less threatening than a relationship with an adult (Easier to Love—M Solo).

The scrim shows the baby, nearly full size, as Danny returns to Lizzie, who is now anxious to marry (Two People in Love—Sc to F/M Duet).

Nick, painfully aware of how much Pam wants a child and anxious about their future together, asks her how she will feel if they never conceive. She reassures him (With You—Sc to F/M Duet).

Alan and Arlene confess to each other their belief that the children may have been what kept their marriage together. As they consider how different their lives might have been, they discover that they really are in love (And What if We Had Loved Like That—Sc to M/F Duet).

The couples consider their relationships. Arlene and Alan are committed to being more than just parents, Pam and Nick vow to keep trying, and Lizzie and Danny realize how better prepared they are to handle the responsibility of parenthood. Lizzie goes into labor and the baby is born (The Birth—Mixed Chorus).

Alan and Arlene, Nick and Pam go to the hospital to see the new baby (Finale—Mixed Chorus).

NOTES ON THE PRODUCTION

Baby, originally designed with the use of a film to show time lapses, was effectively presented without the film on the 1984 summer stock circuit. The story line, which is of import to a variety of ages, is universal in its appeal as it centers on the development of three specific relationships. The music is modern in tone, yet the lyrics and situation add enough drama to bridge any age gap.

It is an inexpensive vehicle well suited for stock, colleges, and community theatres. There are more females required in the company than males and everyone, including the chorus, has good singing and acting roles.

The costumes are modern, and the set (if the film is cut) is quite simple. Both the Broadway and stock productions used one bed which was relocated to a different position on stage for each couple's bedroom. The only other specific scenes are the doctor's office, the baseball field, the bus station and the park. Simple set pieces will suffice.

SONGS OF SPECIAL INTEREST

"I Want It All," mezzo trio, up tempo, character reaction and character oriented.

"The Ladies Singing Their Song," F quintet, good for character study and showcase or revue situation.

"What Could Be Better?," tenor/mezzo, reaction-oriented duet. Young couple.

Instrumentation:2 reeds, 3 trumpets, 2 trombones, horn, drum, bass, synthesizer, piano/conductor
Script: NP
Selections: Valando
Record: Polydor
Rights: MTI

BALLROOM

Book: Jerome Kass (Adapted from *The Queen of the Stardust Ballroom*, TV Special)
Music: Billy Goldenberg
Lyrics: Alan and Marilyn Bergman

ORIGINAL PRODUCTION

Majestic Theatre, December 14, 1978 (116 perf.)
Director and Choreographer: Michael Bennett
Co-Choreographer: Bob Avian
Musical Director: Don Jennings
Principals: Bea Asher—Dorothy Loudon—alto; Alfred Rossi—Vincent Gardenia—baritone; Helen/Sally—Jane Heit—VTNE; Jack—John Hallow—VTNE; Marlene—Lynn Roberts—alto; Nathan Bricker—Bernie Knee—baritone; Angie—Patricia Drylie—VTI; Pauline Krim—Janet Stewart White—VTI
Chorus and Smaller Roles: Minimum 11M/10F.

SYNOPSIS

In widow Bea Asher's secondhand shop, her friend Angie urges Bea to get out and enjoy her life, which has been empty since her husband passed away one year ago. Angie vividly describes the Stardust Ballroom and Bea hesitantly decides to give it a try.

Outside the dance hall several couples greet each other warmly before entering. Bea arrives and tries to bolster her confidence by remembering Angie's description (A Terrific Band and a Real Nice Crowd—F Solo).

Inside is a mirrored room and a large orchestra with band singers, Marlene and Nathan. The regular customers are enjoying the dance music (A Song for Dancing—M/F Duet With Dancers for Visual).

Angie introduces the reticent Bea to many of the regulars before she and "Lightfoot," her steady partner, step onto the floor to demonstrate their lindy skills (One By One—Mixed Dancers and Band Singers).

The music changes (The Dance Montage—Mixed Dancers Featured). Bea meets Al Rossi, a quiet middle aged man, who leads her through several dances, ending with a fox-trot (Dreams—Band Singer Solo). When Rossi offers to take her home, she refuses, but ponders the evening (Somebody Did All Right for Herself—F Solo).

In Bea's living room her sister-in-law Helen is anxiously waiting for Bea. Helen is certain Bea has been murdered and is shocked to discover Bea has been at a dancehall. Helen reassures Bea's daughter by phone that everything is all right and Jack, Helen's husband, arrives in his pajamas; he has been driving around the neighborhood searching for Bea. After everyone leaves, the phone rings; it is Al, who tells Bea he hopes she will be back at the Stardust the next evening. Bea makes no promises but is pleased to be wanted (A Terrific Band and a Real Nice Crowd [Reprise]—F Solo).

A month later, at the ballroom, Al and Bea enter the tango contest and thoroughly enjoy themselves (Goodnight Is Not Goodbye, I've Been Waiting All My Life—Mixed Dancers and Band Singers). She invites Al to her house for a cup of coffee, and he tries to tell her how he feels about her. Bea is not ready to deepen the relationship, but for the first time in a year she feels a part of someone's life.

At the junk shop, Bea's daughter, Diane, reproaches Bea, who has reneged on a babysitting commitment so that she can go out on a date with Al. Bea realizes she must live her own life, for she is still young enough to enjoy what life has to offer. She makes a major decision that leaves the family upset.

Later that night, Bea makes a spectacular entrance in a purple disco dress. She has added a reddish tint to her previously graying hair and emerges as a new woman. Everyone admires the new look, especially Al, and Bea feels like a movie star. Al confides his feelings for her as his favorite dancing partner (I Love to Dance—Sc to M/F Duet) Al confesses to Bea that he is married, something that she instinctively knew but preferred not to think about.

The set changes to Bea's living room, where Al is well on his way to winning a Scrabble game. The two discuss how comfortable they feel with one another and then decide to practice their "hustle" steps. They are not aware that Helen has used her own key to come in and is observing them. A startled Bea at last notices Helen's disapproving stare and quickly introduces her to Al. Somewhat uncomfortable, Al bows out. Helen interrogates Bea about her relationship with Al and leaves in disgust when Bea reveals that Al is a married man.

At the ballroom hustle lesson (More of the Same—Mixed Dancers, Band Singers), Bea is nominated for Queen of the Stardust Ballroom. It is an exciting moment, but Al is unable to share it because of his home situation. She realizes how vulnerable she is and rushes home, where her sister-in-law, son and daughter confront her about her affair. Her children are more able to accept their mother's new life than Bea's sister-in-law. Bea is left to contemplate her relationship (Fifty Percent—F Solo) and decides 50 percent is better than nothing at all.

Bea returns to the ballroom (The Stardust Waltz—Dancers), where she is crowned Queen, and thanks everyone for her new life (I Wish You a Waltz— L to F Solo). The dancing continues (Finale—Mixed Dancers).

NOTES ON THE PRODUCTION

Michael Bennett and Bob Avian won the Tony Award for Best Choreography. *Sweeney Todd* won most of the other 1979 Tony Awards. The production requires a solid female lead and a chorus of excellent ballroom dancers. It is a good vehicle for community theatres that have access to experienced "partner" dancers and a choreographer well trained in a variety of dance styles.

The costumes may probably be obtained from cast members, but each of the female dancers should have at least two different dresses. The settings are not complex and consist of the dance hall, Bea's shop and apartment.

The subject matter may not be accepted by all audiences, for it centers around a widow who has an affair with a married man. It can be given a sensitive treatment and is thought-provoking and timely but can only be effective if given a quality production.

SONGS OF SPECIAL INTEREST

"Fifty Percent," dramatic alto solo, where character defends her beliefs.

"Somebody Did All Right for Herself," alto. A good song to complete a two-song character study in a class situation.

"A Terrific Band and a Real Nice Crowd," questioning, decision making, alto solo.

Instrumentation: 4 reeds, 3 trumpets, 1 horn, 3 trombones, 2 percussion, 3 violins, 2 cellos, bass, harp, guitar, piano/conductor
Script: SF
Selections: Schirmer
Record: CBS
Rights: SF

BARNUM

Book: Mark Bramble
Music: Cy Coleman
Lyrics: Michael Stewart

ORIGINAL PRODUCTION

St. James Theatre, April 30, 1980 (854 perf.)
Directed and Staged by: Joe Layton
Musical Director: Peter Howard
Orchestration: Hershy Kay
Principals: P. T. Barnum—Jim Dale—high baritone; Chairy Barnum—Glenn Close—mezzo; Ringmaster/Goldsmith/Bailey—William C. Witter—baritone;

Joice Heth—Terri White—alto; Tom Thumb—Leonard John Crowfoot—tenor;
Jenny Lind—Marianne Tatum—soprano
Chorus and Smaller Roles: Minimum 7M/5F.

SYNOPSIS

As the audience awaits the opening of the theatre, a barker performs magic tricks and sets the scene. His sales pitch is followed by a young woman, Amy Beecher, who guides tours through the exhibition of wonders in the inner lobby. The exhibition is in actuality a re-creation of many of the wonders of Barnum's famous museum. The audience proceeds to a slide show history of Barnum's life and finally into the theatre, which is decorated to give the illusion of a circus tent.

In the center ring, a man in shirtsleeves enters; it is Barnum. He introduces himself and the sights that will follow as the company enters. A woman from a box seat in the audience rises to leave and Barnum excitedly asks her where she is going. It is his wife, who stands for truth and despises the humbug that Barnum loves. Barnum leaps from a trampoline into the box to kiss her as the ringmaster announces the struggle that will take place in the center ring between P. T. Barnum and his wife, Chairy. Barnum slides down a rope to return to the stage and sings an energetic number which reflects his philosophy (There Is a Sucker Born Ev'ry Minute—L to M Solo).

Barnum's first attraction is the oldest woman in the world, the 160-year-old Joice Heath, whom he passes off as George Washington's nurse. She begins singing at the piano and ends leading the tambourinists and Barnum in a tribute to old age (Thank God I'm Old—F Solo).

Barnum's first humbug, a patriotic one, is such a success that he begins signing up other attractions in hopes of making a fortune. He takes his wife Chairy to lunch at the Women's Emporium, where they argue about their different philosophies; Barnum needs excitement, energy and bright colors, while Chairy is practical and wants her life in calmer, more muted tones. Barnum illustrates his needs by changing a decanter of water to purple, a gray napkin to crimson, and the cyclorama to vibrant red (The Colors of My Life—Sc to M Solo). He rushes off to meet his future partner in his museum scheme and leaves Chairy alone to contemplate their differences (The Colors of My Life—F Solo).

The ringmaster appears on a "walking ladder," falls off and introduces the clowns and bricklayers who are to build Barnum's American museum. Everyone chaotically attempts to build the brick building which will house Barnum's latest attractions—the endeavor is a failure which ends as the building topples.

Barnum is defeated until Chairy arrives and tells him she will supervise his workers to *slowly* build (One Brick at a Time—Sc to F Solo to Mixed Chorus). The number ends with the museum completed and the patrons holding up their one dollar admission fees. Barnum describes the sights that are to be found inside (Museum Song—M Solo).

Fourteen years later, in the backyard of their Bridgeport home, Barnum gives

Chairy a pearl necklace to celebrate their anniversary. She is suspicious because their anniversary is not for six months. He confesses that he needs help in his newest venture, the signing of a young Swedish singer. Chairy wants nothing to do with his deals and returns his gift, yet they are still in love despite their age-old differences (I Like Your Style—Sc to M/F Duet). Chairy agrees to go to New York to help sign the star, but the announcement from Amos Scudder, Barnum's partner, that the museum has burned to the ground forces Barnum to change his plans. He undauntedly decides to put his museum on wheels and tour the East coast featuring the twenty-five–inch midget General Tom Thumb.

The ringmaster announces the smallest man in the world as Tom Thumb enters, looking quite impressive in a general's uniform. He is played by an average-sized actor but appears with two stilt-walking performers and oversize props which create the illusion of smallness (Bigger Isn't Better—M Solo). During the song the ringmaster announces Tom Thumb's command performance for the queen and Barnum's acquisition of Jumbo, the world's largest elephant.

Leaving Chairy at a railroad station in Boston, Barnum rushes off to sign Jenny Lind, the Swedish Nightingale, to an American tour. She closes her first hit concert with a special song (Love Makes Such Fools of Us All—F Solo). Barnum proves the truth of the sentiment when he agrees to escort Jenny to a reception. Barnum says goodnight to Chairy and absolves his guilt by reiterating his philosophy of grasping at life (Out There—M Solo). He walks a tightrope to Jenny Lind and the two ascend on a trapeze as the act ends.

As Act II opens, the company enters from the aisles (Come Follow the Band—Mixed Chorus). It is six months later and Barnum, tired of the life he leads with Jenny, decides to return to Chairy a little less colorful. A blues singer paints a picture of the new man (Black and White—F Solo to Mixed Chorus). In the middle of an election for mayor of Bridgeport, which Barnum is losing, Chairy agrees to let him put the color back in his life, and he wins the election.

Chairy dies after Barnum agrees to fulfill her wish that he run for the Senate; however, he isn't nominated by his party because they feel he lacks dignity. He decides to go on a lecture tour and tell everyone about humbug (The Prince of Humbug—L to M Solo), but Bailey enters to offer him a partnership in his circus (Join the Circus—Sc to M Solo to Mixed Chorus).

Barnum agrees to the merger and dubs the show the greatest one on earth. The circus performers join the reprise as Barnum regretfully steps forward to comment that although times have changed and his kind of humbug is gone, he will always remember the days when there was "a sucker born ev'ry minute."

NOTES ON THE PRODUCTION

Barnum won several of the 1980 Tony Awards—Best Actor, Costumes, Scenic Design.

The Broadway production took place in a circus ring complete with trapeze, tightrope, trampoline and other circus paraphernalia. The show's scenes flowed easily into each other by use of simple set pieces to denote new locations. It is possible to expand the circus theme by further simplifying the set pieces and using the tent set to greater advantage. The various settings may be established by simple signs or stylized props. The entire mood of the production is one of fun and circus; the audience can thus readily accept the convention of a unit set with minor changes to establish location.

The majority of the performers were versed in various circus skills such as juggling, acrobatics, baton twirling, and tumbling; star Jim Dale actually walked a tightrope. Most community theatres don't have the fly space to rig an operating trapeze let alone cast performers trained in walking the high wire. Much of the more complex circus routines can be cut or varied without detriment to the story or characters.

The play takes place between 1835 and 1880, and the female noncircus costumes must reflect the time change. The earlier costumes should consist of hoop skirts and crinolines, which require yards of fabric and lots of rehearsal use. It may be advisable to rent Chairy's and Jenny's costumes as they are the most opulent and time-consuming to make.

It is important to cast a Barnum who has the energy and vitality to carry this production, a man who moves well and has the ability to give a charismatic performance. It may be necessary to work with several actors in the audition situation to ensure that the right one is being cast, for without a strong Phineas the show runs the risk of being extremely slow paced. It may be advisable to cast an understudy or alternate with equally strong talents in case of physical mishap.

Tom Thumb should be played by an average-sized adult. In the original production he was surrounded by large props and two men with stilted pants who towered above him. The props are a nice addition but not absolutely necessary, and they can prove to be a backstage storage problem. It is advisable to employ the stilt-walking men to flank Tom Thumb as they establish the illusion that he is twenty-five inches tall.

Barnum is an enjoyable family entertainment and can be as simple or complex as the theatre is able to produce. Each company should make the decision concerning the preshow slide exhibition, informative lecture and circus acts.

SONGS OF SPECIAL INTEREST

''Come Follow the Band,'' good number for opening a revue, energetic chorus-style.

''Thank God I'm Old,'' alto, bouncy, energetic, and presentational, good for audience eye contact.

''There Is a Sucker Born Ev'ry Minute,'' high energy baritone number which requires lots of broad and dynamic movement, good for building gesture strength.

Instrumentation: Violin, cello, bass, 5 reeds, 3 trumpets, 3 trombones, tuba, 3 percussion, guitar/banjo, 2 pianos, piano/conductor
Script: Doubleday

Selections: Notable
Record: Columbia
Rights: TW

BELLS ARE RINGING

Book and Lyrics: Betty Comden and Adolph Green
Music: Jule Styne

ORIGINAL PRODUCTION

Shubert Theatre, November 29, 1956 (924 perf.)
Director: Jerome Robbins
Dances and Musical Numbers Staged by: Jerome Robbins and Bob Fosse
Musical Director: Milton Rosenstock
Orchestration: Robert Russell Bennett
Principals: Sue Summers—Jean Stapleton—mezzo; Inspector Barnes—Dort Clark—VTNE; Sandor—Eddie Lawrence—baritone; Ella Peterson—Judy Holliday—character alto; Jeff Moss—Sydney Chaplin—tenor; Carl—Peter Gennaro—tenor (must dance); Dr. Kitchell—Bernie West—VTNE; Blake Barton—Frank Aletter—VTNE; Gwynne Smith—Pat Wilkes—VTNE; Francis—Jack Weston—VTNE
Chorus and Smaller Roles: 8M/8F minimum. If the minimum number is utilized, all should be good dancers and singers.

SYNOPSIS

The lights rise on eight depressed girls; an advertisement announcer explains that they are sad because they missed that all-important call from the man of their dreams. The announcer's solutions to all their problems is the never-failing Susanswerphone answering service. The girls perk up and extol the benefits of the service (Bells Are Ringing—F Chorus).

The main curtain rises to disclose the Susanswerphone office. Sue Summers, the owner of the company, her cousin Ella Peterson, and operator Gwynne Smith are working. The day progresses; Sue leaves, warning Ella not to get too involved with the clients. Unlike her cousin, Ella believes in taking a personal interest in the customers and portrays different characters when she talks to them. She is in love with client/writer Jeff Moss and sings about the problems of their relationship. They have never met, yet he refers to her as Mom because she uses the voice of a sixty-three–year–old woman (It's a Perfect Relationship—Sc to F Solo).

Two men enter the answering service and introduce themselves to Ella as magazine reporters, Barnes and Francis. They are really Inspector Barnes, an overly anxious, bumbling detective, and his partner Francis, who suspect the answering service is a cover-up for a prostitution ring.

Sue returns to the office and introduces Sandor Prentz, a shady character who has proposed marriage to her. Barnes and Francis warn everyone that one wrong move will quickly shut the company down.

The scene shifts to Jeff Moss's apartment, where he tells a group of his friends that he is excited to be writing without his partner of many years (On My Own— M Solo). In actuality, Jeff is unsure of his ability to write alone, and is stalling on a new script he must have at his producer's office by noon the next day. He phones Ella, "Mom," and she gives him the push he needs to make himself believe in his ability. Unfortunately, he doesn't have enough self-confidence and angrily pushes the blank pages aside.

In a dirty alley, Sandor, who is actually a bookie, is seen teaching a group of disreputable characters his latest code for placing bets via the answering service (It's a Simple Little System—M Solo and Chorus).

At the Susanswerphone office Ella is trying to reach Jeff with his wake-up call while Sandor teaches Sue his system for taking record orders and calling them into the shipping company. Sue, totally ignorant of his criminal nature, believes that Sandor is an extremely brilliant man.

When Ella gets a message from Jeff's producer that he will be fired unless he finishes the first two acts of his play, she decides to go to his apartment to convince him to work on the play. Realizing that she is being followed by Inspector Barnes, she attempts to confuse him (Is It a Crime?—Sc to F Solo). After she thinks she has eluded the inspector, she enters Jeff's apartment, where he is still sleeping.

Ella fascinates Jeff, for she claims to be a psychic named Melisande. She finally convinces him to write an outline and accompanies him to his producer, who likes it.

During the subway ride home, Ella gives Jeff and the other passengers a lesson in friendliness (Hello, Hello There—Mixed Chorus). He is overjoyed at meeting this unusual, honest girl and soliloquizes (I Met a Girl—M Solo).

Meanwhile, Ella has decided to spread her sunshine on some of her other customers: the singing dentist, Dr. Kitchell, and actor Blake Barton. As she does this, Francis and Barnes are right behind her, snapping pictures and trying to build a case against the answering service. They now suspect Sue is running a drug ring.

At Jeff's apartment "Melisande" arrives and claims to be Jeff's secretary. She tells Olga, a girlfriend of Jeff's, that Jeff must begin work. A surprised Olga exits. Melisande starts working as his secretary. As he dictates a memo telling of his love for her (Long Before I Knew You—Sc to M/F Duet) they embrace. The act ends as Detective Francis snaps a picture of the entwined couple.

In Act II, at the answering service, before a date with Jeff Ella gets dancing lessons from Carl, a delivery boy (Mu Cha Cha—Sc to M/F Duet).

Ella meets an excited Jeff in the park, but loses her confidence when she learns that they must attend a scheduled party with Jeff's theatre friends. Feeling terrified, Ella begs him to forget about the party and just take her dancing. To reassure the terrified girl he begins dancing with her in the park (Just in Time— Sc to M/F Duet). A crowd gathers as the two improvise a vaudeville routine.

At the theatre party, where Ella is obviously out of place, a kindly butler advises her to drop a name and assures her that she'll fit right in. She attempts to follow his advice but is a dismal failure (Drop That Name—Mixed Chorus).

Jeff and Ella return to the terrace, where Ella attempts to explain who she really is. His refusal to believe her makes her think he isn't in love with Ella Peterson, but the nonexistent girl she has made up. Left alone by Jeff, who is saying good-bye to everyone, she ponders her situation (The Party's Over—F Solo). Ella writes him a note and disappears.

At a cafe, Sandor, the bookie, discovers that Ella has incorrectly placed an order and he must pay the mob in two hours or suffer the consequences. He decides to marry Sue for her $6,500 savings and the two sing of their future life together (Salzburg—Sc to M/F Duet).

Jeff, upset that Ella has left, goes to a nearby nightclub where a floor show is in progress (The Midas Touch—Mixed Chorus). At the bar Jeff discovers that Dr. Kitchell, one of Susanswerphone's clients, has written songs for the club, and Blake Barton, an actor customer of Susanswerphone's, has been signed to Jeff's new play. He finally realizes that Mom and Melisande are one and the same and runs to the answering service to find her.

At the answering service, Ella is packing her suitcase, preparing to return to her job as a model (I'm Going Back—Sc to F Solo), for she knows she cannot stay and hear Jeff's voice every day. Meanwhile, Sandor, with Ella's help, is captured by Inspectors Barnes and Francis, who ask Sue to accompany them to headquarters to testify against him.

Ella promises to cover the switchboard until Sue returns but learns that Jeff is on his way; she picks up a mop and attempts to disguise herself as an old woman. Jeff see through the disguise and explains to Ella/Melisande/Mom that he loves her no matter who she is. Sue, Gwynne, and Barnes enter, followed by the other subscribers, who thank her for changing their lives (Finale).

NOTES ON THE PRODUCTION

Because the show was written for the talents of Judy Holliday, who became a star in *Born Yesterday*, amateur groups should avoid a production of this musical unless they have a fantastic leading lady with a strong voice and excellent comedic talents.

In 1957, Judy Holliday won the Tony for the Best Actress in a musical. Most of the other Tonys were awarded to *My Fair Lady*.

The show is enjoyable and not produced often enough. The songs are clever, tuneful, and memorable. The characters are broadly characterized and the script quite humorous.

The play may be set in the present, which makes the costuming quite simple since the costumes can be pulled from the modern wardrobe. The set for the answering service calls for one switchboard, which may be angled so that the audience doesn't see that the entire board isn't real. A clever set designer can combine the terrace and the main room of the party and utilize the party set for the nightclub. If the subway car is a problem, the scene could be transferred to an elevator for the desired effect of unfriendly New Yorkers in a closed area.

SONGS OF SPECIAL INTEREST

"I'm Going Back," ragtime, gutsy, club style, brassy alto. Possible audition number as it shows vocal ability, personality and movement.

"Is It a Crime?," comic scene to alto solo. Solid lyrics for effective comedy as parts contain a story narrative.

"It's a Perfect Relationship," comic, alto, character-oriented, problem number.

"Just in Time," vaudeville, soft shoe, movie musical style, with dialogue interspersed, good for class study. Alto/tenor.

"Mu Cha Cha," energetic dance number for tenor, high baritone/alto.

"The Party's Over," poignant ballad for an alto, and movement.

Instrumentation: 4 violins, viola, cello, 5 reeds, guitar, 3 trumpets, 2 trombones, 2 horns, harp, percussion, piano/celeste/conductor
Script: Random House and Theatre Arts (Magazine) 4/59
Score: Schirmer
Record: Columbia
Rights: TW

THE BEST LITTLE WHOREHOUSE IN TEXAS

Book: Larry L. King and Peter Masterson
Music and Lyrics: Carol Hall

ORIGINAL PRODUCTION

46th Street Theatre, June 29, 1979 (1,584 perf.)
Director: Peter Masterson and Tommy Tune
Musical Numbers Staged by: Tommy Tune
Musical Director and Vocal Arranger: Robert Billig
Principals: Sheriff Ed Earl—Henderson Forsythe—high baritone; Doatsey Mae—Susan Mansur—alto mezzo; Mona—Carlin Glynn—alto; Amber—Pamela Blair—VTI; Jewel—Delores Hall—VTI; Shy—Joan Ellis—VTI; Melvin P. Thorpe—Clint Allmon—baritone; Scruggs and Governor—Jay Garner—tenor; Senator—J. Frank Lucas—VTI
Chorus and Smaller Roles: 10M/8F who play a variety of roles.

SYNOPSIS

The production opens with a five-piece orchestra prologue. The orchestra leader/narrator sets the scene of this 1930 Texas whorehouse with its skeletal upstairs rooms and a stairway leading to a large open parlor downstairs.

It seems the house has been in existence since 1890 but didn't become upgraded until the depression when Willa Jean became the madam and accepted vegetables and chickens as payment, thus the nickname "Chicken Ranch." As the song continues, the bandleader brings the audience up to the present while the girls and customers highlight his narrative (Twenty Fans—M Solo to Mixed Chorus).

Willa Jean dies and leaves the Ranch to Mona, the best of the girls, who tells two newcomers, one a hardened city whore and the other an inexperienced, gawky farm girl, the rules of the Chicken Ranch. She enlists the aid of her "girls," who reel off the rules of the place (A Lil' Ole' Bitty Pissant Country Place—L to F Solo and F Chorus). Mona decides to hire the newcomers on a trial basis and renames the hardened girl Angel and the other girl Shy. She attempts to bolster Shy's confidence and urges her to leave the past behind and look toward the future (Girl, You're a Woman—Sc to F Solo To F Trio). During the song, Shy is transformed form an awkward hayseed to a sexily clad, though still awkward, more attractive girl of the night. She greets her first customer, an awkward young farm boy.

The scene quickly shifts to a television studio where the Dogettes, four men wearing Texas hats, sing the show's theme song (Watchdog Theme—M Quartet). They represent Melvin P. "Watchdog" Thorpe, a moralistic news reporter who is appalled by the Chicken Ranch (Texas Has a Whorehouse in It—Mixed Chorus). He vows to close down the Chicken Ranch as the Dogettes and chorus perform a flashlight dance that resembles a revival meeting.

Back at the ranch, Mona overhears Angel secretly talking on the upstairs phone to her mother and young son and offers to let her go home for Christmas. Downstairs, Jewel, the maid, tells the girls she is spending the next twenty-four hours with her husband and promises it will be something special. She steps to the bandstand and sings (Twenty-Four Hours of Lovin'—F Solo and F Chorus) while the girls dance together. Ed Earl Dodd, Mona's lover and town sheriff, arrives to warn Mona of Melvin Thorpe's intentions, but Mona is certain the furor will quickly end.

It is Thanksgiving Day. In the Texas Twinkle Cafe, a local hang out for the town's leading citizens, Doatsey Mae, the wise-cracking waitress, serves Edsel Mackey, the editor of the paper, and the town politicians, who discuss Ed Earl's treatment of Watchdog. As the men freeze, Doatsey Mae dreams of changing places with Mona (Doatsey Mae—L to F Solo).

It is half-time at the Thanksgiving Day football game where the Angelettes are performing a close-order tap routine with look-alike dolls. In this clever choreographic sequence, the lifesize dolls held between each two girls cause the troupe to appear much larger (Angelette March—F Dance Number).

After the game, the team is seated in the locker room dressing for their winning evening at the whorehouse, a traditional reward provided by a distinguished Senator alumnus (The Aggie Song—M Chorus).

At the Chicken Ranch, the boys and the Senator are being entertained by the ladies while Mona and the sheriff reminisce about Mona's first day in town. The act ends in a frantic chase when Melvin P. Thorpe and his cohorts sneak into the Ranch to take pictures of the "happy couples." Ed Earl runs them off as the stage clears and the bandleader promises to continue after intermission.

Act II opens with a repeat of the raid on the whorehouse. The Senator quickly dresses and blames the Communists, claiming he was doped. The reporters, led by Melvin P. Thorpe, confront the recently arrived Governor, who gives his political viewpoint on solving the sticky situation (The Sidestep—M Solo to Mixed Chorus). He agrees to close the whorehouse.

At the Chicken Ranch Mona sends the girls upstairs to pack and tells Jewel she has learned not to expect much from life (No Lies—Sc to F Duet to F Chorus).

In Ed Earl's office, a phone call from the Governor forces him to close the Ranch. He contemplates his true feelings for Mona (Good Old Girl—L to M Solo) and phones to give her the official news.

The girls, in their respective rooms, sing of what they might do with their futures (Hard Candy Christmas—Sc to F Chorus).

The sheriff arrives to ease Mona's departure. She realizes he can never be involved in a more permanent and romantic relationship so they bid each other farewell. She introspectively studies her life (The Bus from Amarillo—Sc to F Solo). As she sings the final verse, the girls slowly move behind her while the Governor's aide presents a plaque for service to Melvin P. Thorpe.

NOTES ON THE PRODUCTION

Tony Awards went to Henderson Forsythe and Carlin Glynn for featured performances. *Sweeney Todd* took most of the major musical awards for 1979. It appears that Mona's song "Bus from Amarillo" in the Boston tryout occurred at the end of Act I, during her reminiscent scene with Ed Earl, but the French version has the song at the end of Act II. Directors may want to consider repositioning the full song at the end of Act I and use the Act II slot for a reprise. It is a solid dramatic number that becomes less important at the end of the show when the audience wants things resolved.

Smaller theatres have successfully utilized a unit set to represent the chicken ranch, and brought on chairs for the cafe and a desk and phone for Ed Earl's office. The main setting is usually sparsely furnished and the upstairs rooms have roll-down blinds that may be raised or lowered according to the scenic needs.

The girls need two or three costumes for the ranch sequences, and if they play the Angelettes and various townsfolk, they will need more. The male chorus needs western-style outfits, and the Aggie boys could use some football equipment for the locker area but may be dressed as if ready for the party rather than in football uniforms.

It is possible to lighten the sexual implications of the script by physically playing down certain sections and not emphasizing sexuality in the choreography. The fact remains, however, that the story is set in a whorehouse. Even though Mona tries to add class to the place by cleaning up the language and manners of the girls, the innuendos remain. It is doubtful that the show will be performed by companies that are worried about their loss of income due to the subject matter.

The characters afford good acting studies because the backgrounds of the female principals give actresses a firm foundation from which to develop a well-rounded characterization. The story, based loosely on fact, is cleverly told and the music popular among those who like a country-western sound. The show has been well received in larger communities and summer theatres where there is a wide audience to draw from. It is popular among college students, and the music and large female cast would make it a good choice for theatre departments with an abundance of females.

SONGS OF SPECIAL INTEREST

"The Bus from Amarillo," poignant, older woman's examination of life, alto.

"Doatsy Mae," character-oriented, semidramatic, good for mezzo with a limited range.

"Hard Candy Christmas," female, character-oriented chorus number, good for beginning director to attempt in a class situation. Emphasis on characterizations in chorus.

"The Sidestep," may be performed as a male baritone character song in a class situation; humorous, good for freeing up a stiff performer as movement may be comedic.

Instrumentation: Reed, trumpet and trombone are optional and not necessary; violin/viola, guitar, rhythm and steel, bass, drums, piano/conductor
Script: SF
Selections: MCA
Records: MCA
Rights: SF

THE BOY FRIEND

Book, Music and Lyrics: Sandy Wilson

ORIGINAL PRODUCTION

Royale Theatre, September 30, 1954 (485 perf.)
Director: Vida Hope
Choreographer: John Heawood
Musical Director: Anton Coppola
Orchestration: Ted Royal and Charles Cooke
Principals: Polly Browne—Julie Andrews—soprano; Bobby—Bob Scheerer—baritone; Tony—John Hewer—tenor; Hortense—Paulette Girard—mezzo; Percival Browne—Eric Berry—high baritone; Maisie—Ann Wakefield—mezzo/alto; Mme. Dubonnet—Ruth Altman—mezzo; Lord Brockhurst—Geoffrey Hibbert—baritone; Dulcie—Dilys Lay—alto
Chorus and Smaller Roles: 3F/3M.

SYNOPSIS

In the drawing room of the Villa Caprice Finishing School, located near Nice, Hortense, the chic maid, admonishes her charges about their behavior. The girls insist they always act properly (We're Perfect Young Ladies—F Solo to Small F Chorus). Dulcie, Maisie, Fay and Nancy, four students at the school, are extremely excited about the forthcoming carnival ball and girlishly comment on their dresses and their dates. When Polly Browne, one of their more quiet friends, approaches the girls with a letter from her boy friend, they beg her for the details (The Boy Friend—F Solo to Small F Chorus to Small M Chorus).

Mme. Dubonnet, the very attractive owner of the school, sends the girls to their classroom but takes Polly aside. She discovers that Polly has made up an imaginary boy friend because her millionaire father thinks men are only after her wealth. Mme. Dubonnet promises to talk to Polly's father, who is arriving this very morning. Polly gratefully rushes off to class.

Maisie, the flirtatious soubrette of the group, enters to retrieve her "dorothy bag," but Bobby Van Heusen, a good-looking, wealthy, young American world traveller, interrupts her search. Maisie is quite chagrined that he is on the premises but secretly pleased when he asks her to dance all evening (Won't You Charleston with Me?—Sc to M/F Duet).

Percival Browne, Polly's father, is shocked to discover that Mme. Dubonnet is his wartime flame "Kiki." She asks if he remembers one of their more romantic moments, but he denies everything. When she re-creates the moment he reluctantly joins in (Fancy Forgetting—Sc to M/F Duet). She is about to kiss him but is interrupted by offstage giggles. The two exit to tour the school.

The girls enter with Polly, who begs off trying on her ball costume and claims she is waiting for her father and her boy friend. Alone in the drawing room she is surprised by Tony who delivers her costume. He eagerly asks her to the ball, apologizes for appearing forward, and bursts into song (I Could Be Happy With You—Sc to M/F Duet). They agree to meet later that afternoon on the beach.

He hurriedly exits, leaving a happy Polly (The Boy Friend [Reprise]—Mixed Chorus).

In Act II the boys and girls are frolicking on the beach (Sur la Plage—Mixed Chorus) as Lord Brockhurst, a wealthy Englishman with an eye for the female figure, enters. He is quickly followed by his domineering wife, who is distraught with grief over the sudden disappearance of their son, Tony.

Polly tells Tony she is Mme. Dubonnet's secretary and quite content with the simple things in life. He is enthused by her response and the two mime their ideal life (A Room in Bloomsbury—Sc to M/F Duet). Hortense arrives, dressed in her Sunday best, and threatens to tell Mme. Dubonnet, but Polly takes Hortense aside and swears her to secrecy.

The boys and girls corner Hortense and try to trick her into telling about Polly's beau, but she refuses and gaily responds (It's Nicer in Nice—F Solo to Mixed Chorus). As the number ends Hortense spies Mme. Dubonnet and hastily exits.

Mme Dubonnet, in a 1920s bathing costume, attempts to involve Percy in the pleasures of Nice, but when he realizes there are other men attracted to her, namely Lord Brockhurst, he attempts to leave. Mme. Dubonnet accuses him of being a "damp" blanket (You-Don't-Want-to-Play-with-Me Blues—Sc to M/F Duet with F Chorus).

Maisie, trying to make Bobby jealous, shows her true spirit by flirting with all the boys on the beach (Safety in Numbers—F Solo and Small M Chorus).

Polly and Tony return as Lord and Lady Brockhurst recognize their missing son. A gendarme is called and Tony hastily exits. Polly assumes he is a thief and sobbingly tells the company she won't be going to the carnival ball (I Could Be Happy with You—F Solo to Mixed Chorus).

Act III opens at the Cafe Pataplon, where the boys and girls have gathered for the carnival ball. During the course of the evening Maisie, Dulcie, Fay, and Nancy are proposed to, respectively, by Bobby, Alphonse, Marcel, and Pierre. While the girls delay their decision making, they decide to pass the time dancing (The Riviera—Mixed Chorus).

Tony meets Hortense, who accuses him of ruining Polly's evening. He persuades her to bring Polly to the ball and promises to make amends. Hortense agrees.

In a corner of the room Dulcie angrily slaps Pierre's face and Lord Brockhurst suggests that she should experiment with older men (It's Never Too Late to Fall in Love—Sc to M/F Duet).

Polly, in a pierrette costume, arrives at the ball alone and terribly hurt by Tony's betrayal, but Mme. Dubonnet tells her an old French legend and assures her that Pierrot will arrive (Poor Little Pierrette—Sc to F Solo). Tony does arrive to tell her that he is not a thief, but the son of Lord and Lady Brockhurst and he wishes to marry her. She consents and tells him that she is the daughter of millionaire Percival Browne. The play ends happily with all the couples, including Mme. Dubonnet and Percy, agreeing to marry (Finale—Mixed Chorus).

NOTES ON THE PRODUCTION

The play is a spoof on the plots and songs of the 1920s musicals, fun to perform for principals and chorus alike. It is a small-cast show, but in larger schools with a great many female students in the drama club, a larger female chorus may be used.

It can be successfully produced by junior high school students and is enjoyable for audiences of all ages. The script calls for three sets, one for the finishing school, one for the beach area, and one for the cafe. Some productions have used the same set for Acts I and III by changing the properties and adding Japanese lanterns.

The entire cast needs approximately three costumes each, one for each act. Act I requires typical 1920s street clothes; Act II, vintage-style bathing suits; and Act III, carnival costumes. It is possible to have the boys in the same costumes in both Act I and II and use the girls to create the visual interest.

SONGS OF SPECIAL INTEREST

"The Boy Friend," F chorus, good revue number which calls for period-style movement and attitudes.

"It's Never Too Late," older male baritone and young alto, character-oriented, humorous.

"Perfect Young Ladies," period F chorus, requires definitive characters.

"A Room in Bloomsbury," tenor/soprano charm song, calls for some mime and soft shoe.

"Won't You Charleston with Me?," period movement-oriented mezzo/baritone duet. Nice scene before to develop character and game playing.

Instrumentation: 3 reeds, 2 trumpets, trombone, percussion, 2 violins, bass, banjo or guitar, piano/conductor
Script: Chappell (London), E. P. Dutton
Score: Chappell
Record: RCA
Rights: MTI

BRIGADOON

Book and Lyrics: Alan Jay Lerner
Music: Frederick Loewe

ORIGINAL PRODUCTION

Ziegfeld Theatre, March 13, 1947 (581 perf.)
Director: Robert Lewis
Choreographer: Agnes de Mille

Musical Director: Franz Allers
Orchestration: Ted Royal
Principals: Tommy Albright—David Brooks—high baritone; Fiona MacLaren—
Marion Bell—high soprano; Meg Brockie—Pamela Britton—alto; Mr. Lundie—
William Hansen—VTNE; Charlie Dalrymple—Lee Sullivan—tenor; Jeff Doug-
lass—George Keane—VTNE; Harry Beaton—James Mitchell—VTNE; Jean
MacLauren—Virginia Bosler—VTNE
Chorus and Smaller Roles: 14M/12F, usually a separate dance chorus 8M/8F.

SYNOPSIS

The curtain rises at the end of the overture and a haunting chorus (Once in
the Highlands—Mixed Chorus) is heard offstage, which fades out as the action
begins.

It is five o'clock on a misty morning somewhere in the Scottish Highlands;
the time is the present day. Two American tourists, Tommy Albright, an attractive, sensitive man in his thirties, and Jeff Douglass, his happy-go-lucky
friend, are lost in the middle of nowhere. The two hear the sound of singing
(Brigadoon—Mixed Chorus) and spy a distant village that isn't on the map. The
two set out for the little town.

The scene switches to the town of Brigadoon where the villagers, dressed in
eighteenth-century Scottish garb, are involved in the town fair. Vendors' calls,
inviting people to the weekly fair (Vendors' Calls—Mixed Chorus), are heard
as the curtain opens on the town's central square (Down On MacConnachy
Square—Mixed Chorus).

Lovely Fiona MacLaren and her shy sister Jean enter with their father to
prepare for Jean's forthcoming wedding to the handsome, well-educated Charlie
Dalrymple. Harry Beaton, Jean's former suitor, greets the girls despairingly. He
is angered that Charlie has graduated from the university and won Jean—two
things he can never achieve.

Fiona leaves to buy milk from the highly spirited, flirtatious Meg Brockie,
who asks when Fiona is going to consider her own marriage. Fiona brightly
responds to Meg and four nearby girls that she is waiting for the right man
(Waitin' for My Dearie—Sc to F Solo to Small F Chorus).

As the song ends the Americans Tommy and Jeff enter, awed by the townspeople who study them curiously. Fiona apologizes by explaining that visitors
don't often come to Brigadoon. The conversation is interrupted by the arrival
of Charlie, who greets everyone warmly and offers a toast to Mr. Forsythe for
postponing the miracle. Tommy begins to question Charlie's statement, but Fiona
promises to tell him later.

Charlie, deeply in love with Jean, tells everyone his feelings (I'll Go Home
with Bonnie Jean—Sc to M Solo to Mixed Chorus to Small Dance Chorus).
Tommy, impressed by Charlie's enthusiasm regarding marriage, tells Fiona he
isn't excited about his own forthcoming marriage. He asks to spend the day with
her gathering heather for the wedding bouquets (The Heather on the Hill—Sc

to M/F Duet). The two exit as the scene shifts to an open shed on the edge of a field on Meg's father's land. The furniture consists of a rocking chair and divan.

Meg hopes to entice Jeff into romance, but he feigns sleep. Unaware that he isn't listening, she proceeds to tell him of her love life and its many problems (The Love of My Life—Sc to F Solo).

The scene shifts to the MacLarens' sparsely furnished living room and a group of girls who are excitedly packing for Jean (Jeannie's Packing Up—F Chorus). Charlie arrives to see Jean but is stopped by her father, who sends him out to sign the family Bible. A disgruntled Harry Beaton delivers a package for Jean's father and tells MacLaren he hates everyone because he is trapped in Brigadoon forever. Charlie calls to Jean, who begs him to leave so she can come down. He stands outside her door and sings (Come to Me, Bend to Me—M Solo to F Ballet). He leaves as Fiona enters to help Jean pack. Tommy tells Jeff, who has managed to escape from Meg, about his day (Almost Like Being in Love—M/F Duet); he is joined by Fiona and the two romantically finish the song. Tommy casually opens the family Bible, which lists Fiona's birthdate as 1722 and Jean's wedding day as 1746. He demands an explanation from Fiona, who insists that he ask the schoolmaster, Mr. Lundie.

The three find the schoolmaster on a bench outside his home and he tells the story of the minister, Mr. Forsythe, who asked God to make Brigadoon and its citizens vanish for 100-year periods. One day out of every 100 years they awaken and lead normal lives, but at the end of the day they sleep for another 100 years. If any of the citizens leaves Brigadoon the spell is broken forever. The ringing chimes herald the arrival of the clans at the church (Entrance of the Clans—Mixed Chorus March).

The wedding ceremony is followed by the wedding dance. As the dance ends Harry Beaton starts a fight and tells the group he is leaving Brigadoon. He runs off, followed by a crowd of frightened citizens.

Act II opens at the forest's edge with the men chasing Harry (The Chase—M Chorus), who is accidentally killed. MacLaren and the town leaders decide it's best not to ruin the wedding by telling of Harry's death, and everyone exits for the celebration but Fiona and Tommy. The two express their love (There but for You Go I—Sc to M Solo).

A short time later the festivities are in full swing and Meg Brockie compares it with her parents' wedding (My Mother's Wedding Day—F Solo to Mixed Chorus). As the song ends, Charlie and Jean exit and the townsfolk, all a little tipsy, continue to dance. Their happiness is interrupted by a mournful bagpipe lament as Harry's funeral begins (The Funeral Procession—F Dance). Tommy spies Jeff and tells him he plans on staying, but Jeff warns that he could be caught in a dream where nothing is real. Tommy reconsiders and tells Fiona she will always be a part of him no matter what happens (From This Day On—Sc to M/F Duet). As the lovers part, Tommy and Jeff watch the town disappear in the highland mist.

Four months later, in a bar in New York City, Jeff is swilling whiskey when Tommy, whom he hasn't seen for a month, enters to tell him he can't forget Fiona. Tommy's fiancée Jane arrives to discuss his absence. As they talk he is reminded of Fiona. The lights dim on the bar and Fiona is seen in the distance (Come to Me, Bend to Me, Heather on the Hill, I'll Go Home With Bonnie Jean, Down in MacConnachy Square [Reprise]—Various Characters). Tommy announces that he is returning to Scotland and invites Jeff to accompany him.

As they approach the moor the chorus is heard in the distance (Brigadoon—Mixed Chorus), and Mr. Lundie appears to take Tommy to Fiona. The music swells and the curtain falls.

NOTES ON THE PRODUCTION

The year 1947 marked the debut of the Tony Awards. There were few categories and no differentiation between plays and musicals. Agnes de Mille received the award for Choreography.

The production is written to utilize drops as scenic backgrounds. For theatres with no space to fly drops it is possible to use two drops, one for the moors, the other, which rolls down in front, for the town. The rest of the scenes—the shed, Jean's home, the church area and Mr. Lundie's cottage—may be set in front of the town drop. At intermission the show can be rerigged to enable a woods drop to be used at the rear wall of the stage. This forest drop can remain until the New York sequence, which may be performed In One. The moor drop may then be rolled down for the final scene.

The costumes are mostly Scottish clan. While there should be two costumes per chorus member to make the march of the clans a high point, it is not absolutely essential if budget is a problem.

SONGS OF SPECIAL INTEREST

"Almost Like Being in Love," romantic soprano/baritone duet, up tempo, relationship-oriented.

"Heather on the Hill," romantic baritone/soprano duet, up tempo, movement.

"I'll Go Home with Bonnie Jean," possible audition for lyric tenor, up tempo yet romantic.

"The Love of My Life," story song, alto, comic, lyric emphasis.

"My Mother's Wedding Day," comic alto, up tempo, good diction and memorization exercise, class study.

"Waitin' for My Dearie," possible audition ballad, romantic yet determined soprano, good pace.

Instrumentation: 2 violins, viola, cello, bass, 5 reeds, horn, 3 trumpets, trombone, percussion, piano/celeste, piano/conductor's score
Script: Chappell (London); Coward, McCann; Ten Great Musicals of the American Theatre, Theatre Arts (Magazine) 8/52

Score: Sam Fox
Record: RCA
Rights: TW

BYE BYE BIRDIE

Book: Michael Stewart
Music: Charles Strouse
Lyrics: Lee Adams

ORIGINAL PRODUCTION

Martin Beck Theatre, April 14, 1960 (607 perf.)
Director and Choreographer: Gower Champion
Musical Director: Elliot Lawrence
Orchestration: Robert Ginzler
Principals: Albert Peterson—Dick Van Dyke—baritone; Conrad Birdie—Dick
Gautier—tenor; Rosie—Chita Rivera—alto; Mae Peterson—Kay Medford—
VTNE; Kim MacAfee—Susan Watson—soprano; Mr. MacAfee—Paul Lynde—
tenor; Mrs. MacAfee—Marijane Maricle—mezzo; Randolph MacAfee—Johnny
Borden—boy soprano
Chorus and Smaller Roles: 11 teen F/7 teen M; 7 adult M/6 adult F minimum
with lots of doubling.

SYNOPSIS

The overture is accompanied by a film sequence of rock star Conrad Birdie
and a small chorus of teen girls who sing from the orchestra pit (We Love You,
Conrad—F Chorus).

The play opens in the office of Almaelou Music where Albert Peterson, thirty-
three–year–old songwriter and founder of the record company, is nervously
talking on the phone about Conrad's draft call. Albert, who makes most of his
income as Conrad's writer/manager, is worried about the future.

Rosie, Albert's secretary, enters to announce her resignation. She wants to
be more than just a secretary, but Albert isn't ready for marriage, due to the
influence of his overly domineering mother, Mae. Rosie urges him to join a
respectable profession and get out of the music business (An English Teacher—
L to F Solo).

Albert, realizing his career as Birdie's songwriter/manager is nearly over,
makes a deal with Rosie: if she helps him with one last publicity gimmick to
push Albert's latest song, he'll make enough money to cover the rest of Birdie's
contract, quit the music business, marry her, and teach English. Rosie readily
agrees and springs into action. She randomly picks a teenage fan to be the
recipient of Birdie's "last kiss" based on a song that Albert will write. Albert

agrees that the idea is a great one, and the call is placed to teenage fan Kim MacAfee.

In Sweet Apple, Ohio, all the phones are busy due to the recent pinning of Kim to Hugo Peabody (Telephone Hour—Mixed Teen Chorus).

Kim considers herself a mature woman although her mode of dress belies the fact as she dons jeans, a baggy sweater, socks and a baseball cap (How Lovely To Be A Woman—F Solo). Her newfound maturity quickly dissipates when she learns she has been chosen to receive Conrad's last kiss.

At Pennsylvania Station in New York, Albert rehearses a group of young fans (We Love You, Conrad—F Chorus). He discovers a sad-faced girl sulking over Conrad's departure and cheers her (Put on A Happy Face—M Solo) only to turn and find another sad girl. He clowns about and dances with them both. After several pratfalls he manages to leave both girls in good spirits.

Rosie enters to urge Albert to get on board the train before anyone can interview Conrad, but Albert insists on waiting for his mother. Mae greets him warmly and tells Rosie how horrible she looks. The reporters arrive, but Rosie and Albert manage to sidetrack their questions and enlist the aid of the teen fans (A Healthy, Normal, American Boy—Sc to Mixed Chorus). They exit to the train as the station sign changes to Sweet Apple, Ohio.

At Sweet Apple the teenagers greet Conrad with cheers and music. Hugo, Kim's boyfriend, takes her aside to urge her not to kiss Conrad, but she and her two girlfriends tell Hugo he is Kim's special boy (One Boy—F Solo to F Trio).

On the courthouse steps the mayor and his wife are preparing to give Birdie the key to the city when Conrad bursts into song (Honestly Sincere—M Solo). The girls and women, including the mayor's rather staid wife, go absolutely wild. At the end of the number the stage is littered with the bodies of Conrad's fans, male and female, who have fainted from all the excitement.

At the MacAffe house, where Rosie, Conrad and Albert are living, Mr. MacAfee, infuriated by the upheaval Conrad is causing, threatens to evict them. Albert, sensing promotional disaster, promises him a guest appearance on the "Ed Sullivan Show." MacAfee, overcome with excitement, gathers the family around him (Hymn for a Sunday Evening—Sc to 2F/1M/1 Ch Quartet) for a tribute to the favorite Sunday night show of the 1950s.

Backstage at the movie theatre which will house the television special, Rosie, infuriated by Albert's inability to face up to his mother, fantasizes various ways to kill him (How to Kill a Man Ballet—F Dance Solo).

At the television taping, Conrad sings Albert's song (One Last Kiss—M Solo) while everyone tries to get on television. As Conrad prepares to end the song with a kiss, Hugo jealously strikes him and the evening ends in chaos.

Act II opens in Kim's bedroom. Rosie and Kim share the same angered mood and wonder what they ever saw in their men (What Did I Ever See in Him?— L to F Solo to F Duet).

When Rosie decides to make up for the eight years she wasted on Albert by painting the town red, Kim vows to join her and runs away from home. Meanwhile, Conrad, fed up with the midwestern celibate image he is forced to maintain, escapes Albert's watchful eye and sets off for a night of fun with the teens (A Lot of Livin' to Do—M Solo to Mixed Chorus).

Mr. MacAfee, discovering that Kim has run off, confides to his wife his confusion about modern teenagers (Kids—Sc to M/F Duet).

Albert, in a one-sided phone conversation, tries to convince Rosie, who is at Maude's Roadside Retreat, that he loves her. His sentiments are echoed by a male quartet who pass by the phone booth (Baby, Talk to Me—M Solo and M Quartet). Rosie, believing Albert will never actually escape his mother's domination, decides to play the role of a wild Spanish girl for a Shriners' party at Maude's (Shriners' Ballet—F Dance Solo with M Movement-Oriented Chorus).

Albert, followed by the Sweet Apple parents, reaches Maude's, where Hugo and Rosie tell them the kids are with Conrad at the Ice House, a notoriously wild hangout.

The scene switches to a darkened barnlike building where Conrad is putting the make on Kim. Realizing she is underage he begins to leave but is mobbed by teen fans and their parents. Conrad is dragged off to jail.

Albert tells Rosie to make the wedding arrangements while he goes to the courthouse to save Conrad. As Albert leaves, his mother enters to tell Rosie she is not pleased he is marrying someone Spanish. Rosie, unabashed by Mae's attitude, plays Spanish to the hilt (Spanish Rose—F Solo).

At the train station, Albert shoves Mae and Conrad, now disguised as an old woman, onto a waiting train. Albert proclaims his love for Rosie by telling her he is applying for a job teaching English in Pumpkin Falls, Iowa, and has sent Mae in the other direction (Rosie—Sc to M Solo to M/F Duet).

NOTES ON THE PRODUCTION

The show marked Gower Champion's first directing job on a "book" musical. Those who saw the show still remember the magnificent "Shriners' Ballet" danced by Chita Rivera, the cleverly simplistic staging of "Telephone Hour" and the hilarious "How to Kill a Man" where Chita Rivera acts out various methods of killing Albert.

1961 Tonys: Best Musical, Best Book, Best Direction, Best Choreography, and Best Actor.

The production calls for a creative and highly organized director. Because it is a satire of the teenagers of the fifties and their relationship with their parents, the actors must have the ability to play comedy and sing with confidence. Rosie and Albert must dance: Rosie should be versed in jazz and Albert in tap and soft shoe. It is also important that Albert be able to do pratfalls and be extremely limber.

The costumes should represent the style of the late fifties and early sixties. Modern styles that do not reflect the period should not be used because the story line, references and situations are not totally applicable to today's teens.

Since the play was written during the period of large multiset shows, the original production had fourteen different locations, many of which were full stage sets. The most essential sets are the MacAfee home, Maude's interior, and the Almaelou office. The train locations can utilize signs and overhanging cutouts in front of a drop to represent a station; the courthouse steps, while nice because they give levels for the choreography, may be represented by a platform for Conrad and the dignitaries; the stage of the theatre and backstage office scenes may be combined and performed on the stage; Kim's bedroom may be included in the home set. Even with this oversimplification the show is technically quite complex, and money should be budgeted accordingly. Most of the costumes may be pulled from people's attics or easily adapted. However, the money saved on costumes is going to have to be expended on sets as too much chintzing will definitely hinder the overall look of the production.

SONGS OF SPECIAL INTEREST

"How Lovely to Be a Woman," mezzo, light comic number which requires youthful sincerity and the visual gag of dressing like a boy.

"Kids," comic duet, strong characterization and emphasis on lyrics needed.

"One Last Kiss," period rock n' roll performed à la Elvis Presley.

"Put on a Happy Face," solo nightclub style number, or done as charm solo with girl needed for dance section.

"Spanish Rose," movement-oriented, up tempo, good for building strength and precision in performance.

Instrumentation: 3 violins, cello, bass, 4 woodwinds, 3 trumpets, 2 trombones, guitar, percussion, piano/conductor
Script: DBS, Chappell (London)*
Score: Edwin Morris
Record: Columbia
Rights: TW
*The British script (Chappell) changed Conrad into a British quartet called Conrad and the Birdies.

C

CABARET

Book: Joe Masteroff (Based on John Van Druten's play *I Am a Camera* and stories by Christopher Isherwood)
Music: John Kander
Lyrics: Fred Ebb

ORIGINAL PRODUCTION

Broadhurst Theatre, November 20, 1966 (1,166 perf.)
Director: Harold Prince
Dances and Cabaret Numbers: Ron Field
Musical Director: Harold Hastings
Orchestration: Don Walker
Principals: Emcee—Joel Grey—tenor; Herr Schultz—Jack Gilford—baritone; Clifford Bradshaw—Bert Convy—tenor; Sally Bowles—Jill Haworth—alto/mezzo; Fraulein Schneider—Lotte Lenya—alto; Ernst Ludwig—Edward Winter—VTNE; Fraulein Kost—Peg Murray—VTNE; Max—John Herbert—VTNE
Chorus and Smaller Roles 8M/8F minimum plus a four-piece onstage all-girl orchestra—one male in chorus must be a very high tenor.

SYNOPSIS

In prewar Berlin, at the Kit Kat Klub Cabaret, the Master of Ceremonies welcomes everyone to an evening of varied entertainment (Wilkommen—M Solo to Mixed Chorus).

The scene switches to the compartment of a European railway car where Cliff Bradshaw, an American novelist and language tutor, is greeted by Ernst Ludwig, a jovial German in his thirties who gives Cliff the name of a boardinghouse for cheap lodging and the location of the biggest night spot in Berlin, the Kit Kat Klub. The train arrives and the two shake hands as the train moves off and the emcee continues his song.

Cliff goes to the boardinghouse, which is run by Fraulein Schneider, a practical woman in her sixties. They agree on a price, one lower than Fraulein Schneider had asked for, but she explains that a little money is better than no money (So What?—Sc to F Solo). Fellow boarders Fraulein Kost, a large woman in her mid-thirties who entertains a variety of sailors in her room, and Herr Schultz, a warm, cheerful Jewish fruit proprietor who is Fraulein Schneider's beau, are introduced.

Cliff, alone in his room, can't concentrate on his writing and goes to the Kit Kat Klub to celebrate the incoming year. He arrives in time to see Sally Bowles, an English girl in her mid-twenties, and the Cabaret Girls perform (Don't Tell Mama—F Solo to F Chorus). The club is a phone club, and as the New Year rings in, Sally phones Cliff and becomes quickly intrigued by this young American writer who speaks her language. The phones become very busy (Telephone Song—F Chorus).

The next day, Cliff is in his room completing an English lesson with Ernst when Sally appears at the door and convinces Cliff to let her move in. It seems she has left the owner of the club, her former lover, who was extremely jealous of her occasional flirtations. She obtains Fraulein Schneider's blessing by offering to pay more for the room and tells Cliff he needs her as a lover/roommate to inspire him (Perfectly Marvelous—Sc to F/M Duet). He agrees to the arrangement.

The scene switches to the Cabaret where the Emcee is singing of the advantages of having more than one girlfriend (Two Ladies—M/2F Trio).

The lights rise on Fraulein Schneider's living room as Fraulein Kost enters with a sailor and proceeds to the door of her room. Fraulein Schneider warns her to be discreet. Herr Schultz greets Fraulein Schneider with a gift of fruit in a brown paper bag. As the two romantically examine the pineapple, it is obvious they are fond of one another (It Couldn't Please Me More—Sc to M/F Duet).

At the Kit Kat Klub, the waiters sing of the future of Germany (Tomorrow Belongs to Me—M Solo to M Chorus).

In his room, Cliff tells Sally he is living in an unreal situation but is loving every minute of it (Why Should I Wake Up?—Sc to M Solo). Realizing Cliff loves her, she tells him she is carrying his child, news which is extremely maturing and motivating. He decides to be realistic and find steady employment, then Ernst offers him seventy-five marks to carry a briefcase of money from Paris to Berlin.

At the Klub, the Emcee continues to entertain with the help of the girls (The Money Song—M Solo and F Chorus).

When Fraulein Kost, who resents Fraulein Schneider's moralistic airs, discovers Herr Schultz leaving Fraulein Schneider's room, Herr Schultz virtuously tells her they are to be married. Herr Schultz and Fraulein Schneider are overwhelmed by his suggestion and decide to seriously consider it. She goes to her room to think the matter through as he stays in the living room (Married—Sc to M/F Linear Duet).

Herr Schultz throws an engagement party in his fruit store and entertains with a Yiddish story (Meeskite—L to M Solo). The party is full of Nazi sympathizers, Ernst being one of them, and they begin singing a party song (Tomorrow Belongs to Me [Reprise]—Mixed Chorus, which builds to a terrifying, foreshadowing, anti-Jewish frenzy, but only Fraulein Schneider and Cliff seem to realize the implications.

Act II opens in the club, where the tone of the music is more military oriented and the audience is aware that the Nazis are achieving power (Tomorrow Belongs to Me—F Dance).

Fraulein Schneider visits Herr Schultz in his store to tell him she fears marriage to a Jew and must survive in her own way. He vainly attempts to change her mind, but a brick crashes through the store window and seals her decision.

The Emcee enters the club with a gorilla and urges the audience to view the gorilla with open eyes (If You Could See Her—M Solo). This song is a direct parallel to the intermarriage situation of Fraulein Schneider and Herr Schultz.

Fraulein Schneider returns Sally and Cliff's wedding gift and tells them the engagement is off because she knows what will happen if she marries a Jew. She asks what they would do in her situation, reminding them that she is older and has settled into her own way of life (What Would You Do—L to F Solo).

After she leaves, Cliff, worried by the political situation in Germany, orders Sally to pack for America and safety. She is upset by his suggestion for she instinctively realizes she can never be a headliner anywhere but the Kit Kat Klub, where she was mistress to one of the owners. Terrified of having to face the truth, she decides to have an abortion and return to the club.

Cliff enters the club to try to force Sally to realize the truth about herself, but she rushes off to perform as Cliff is accosted by Ernst, who has him beaten by two Nazi thugs for his refusal to carry any more money for the party. During the beating Sally begins performing a song that reflects her attitude towards life and Germany's refusal to admit the dangers of the Nazis (Cabaret—F Solo).

Herr Schultz comes to Cliff's room to say good-bye, for he is moving out of the rooming house in deference to Fraulein Schneider. Cliff invites him to leave Germany for America but he responds that he is a German and everything will eventually pass. Sally tries vainly to explain to Cliff her reasons for staying but he leaves her a railway ticket to Paris and exits knowing she will die in Germany.

The lights rise on a railroad car where Cliff is writing about Sally and Germany. The Emcee enters at the wings. The cabaret appears decorated with swastikas and filled with Nazi party members; the various characters are seen recounting their philosophies. The Emcee steps forward to bid the audience farewell.

NOTES ON THE PRODUCTION

1967 Tony Awards: Best Musical, Music and Lyrics, Direction, Choreography, Featured Actor (Joel Grey), Set and Costume Design.

The show, a dramatized version of the evolution and decadence of Nazi Germany, is reminiscent of the Kurt Weill/Bertolt Brecht shows that actually arose from the era. The musical operates on two levels—one the musical story line and the other the club numbers. Because alternate scenes take place in the cabaret, the designer needs to arrange for quick set changes. The audience must realize that the cabaret sequences are commenting on the prior scenes. The other two sets essential to the production are the fruit store, which may be a partial set, and the boardinghouse rooms. The railway car may be set to the side in front of the cabaret. The costumes are period 1930s with the chorus girls having several that are theatrical in style. The rest of the company needs some costumes suitable for New Year's Eve and some military.

Much of the character development of Herr Schultz and Fraulein Schneider comes from their songs, which were cut from the film version due to Director Bob Fosse's decision to use music only in the nighclub numbers. Those familiar only with the movie version should survey the script and score before deciding to produce the show.

The script is an ingenious one, for it captures the temper and mood of Germany during the Nazi takeover. As each scene which involves the major characters ends, the scene switches to the cabaret, where the song and dance action is a commentary on the prior scene. The show becomes horrifying to an audience that knows where the madness will lead. It is a thought-provoking script that requires a sensitive yet strong director to capture its frightening realism.

A word of warning to actresses who try to imitate Liza Minnelli's Academy Award–winning performance: it must be remembered that Sally Bowles is an English girl performing in Germany. The script mentions she is performing in the club because she is the mistress of one of the owners. This is a fact which Sally may not admit to herself but must be seen by the audience. If she were a star performer, she could perform anywhere and this free-thinking, fun-loving girl would readily go to any new opportunity in America. She probably isn't a bad club performer, but she certainly isn't the star the film version portrayed.

SONGS OF SPECIAL INTEREST

"Cabaret," club style, alto, show business, up tempo song, movement-oriented.

"It Couldn't Please Me More," baritone/alto, older characters' charm song. Good for developing characterization skills and relationship.

"What Would You Do?," alto, dramatic, musically soaring.

"Why Should I Wake Up?," tenor, lovely melody, possible audition ballad.

Instrumentation: 2 violins, viola, cello, bass, 4 reeds, horn, 2 trumpets, 2 trombones, percussion, accordion, celeste, guitar and banjo, and piano/conductor. Stage band: tenor sax, trombone, piano, and trap drum set

Script: Random House, Great Musicals of the American Theatre Volume II
Score: Valando
Record: Columbia
Rights: TW

CALL ME MADAM

Book: Howard Lindsay and Russel Crouse
Music and Lyrics: Irving Berlin

ORIGINAL PRODUCTION

Imperial Theatre, October 12, 1950 (644 perf.)
Director: George Abbott
Choreographer: Jerome Robbins
Musical Director: Jay Blackton
Principals: Sally Adams—Ethel Merman—alto; Cosmo Constantine—Paul Lukas—baritone; Ken Gibson—Russell Nype—tenor; Pemberton Maxwell—Alan Hewitt—VTNE; Sebastian Sebastian—Henry Lascoe—VTNE; Princess—Galena Talva—soprano; Congressman Wilkins—Pat Harrington—tenor
Chorus and Smaller Roles: 12M/12F, half of whom must be able to dance.

SYNOPSIS

Sally Adams, a popular and wealthy Washington socialite noted for her parties, has been named ambassador to the Grand Duchy of Lichtenberg. After she is sworn in she asks Secretary of State Dean Acheson where Lichtenberg is. The lights black out and rise In One on guests carrying invitations to Sally's farewell party (Mrs. Sally Adams—Mixed Chorus).

The curtains open on a fabulous Washington party where Ken Gibson, a Harvard-educated international relations graduate, is introduced to various Republican congressmen by his wealthy father. It seems Ken has been assigned to Sally's embassy and plans to help Lichtenberg achieve self-sufficiency. Sally enters and demonstrates her obvious ignorance of Lichtenberg by laughingly explaining that she received her post because she is a marvelous party giver (Hostess with the Mostes'—Sc to F Solo). She demonstrates her abilities as a party giver by ending various political arguments between the Republicans and Democrats (Washington Square Dance—F Solo to Mixed Chorus).

The scene shifts to the town square of Lichtenberg where Cosmo Constantine, present finance minister, introduces himself and explains the problems of the smaller European countries who need to modernize without losing their old-world qualities (Lichtenberg—M Solo to Mixed Chorus).

In the office of the embassy, the anxious, highly efficient Chargé d'Affaires, Pemberton Maxwell, nervously introduces Sally to Tantinnin, the Lichtenberg

Secretary of State who asks for a U.S. loan. Sally refuses and he exits. Moments later the newly appointed Secretary of State Cosmo Constantine arrives to receive Sally's credentials. Overwhelmed by his debonair manner, she asks how much money he needs (Can You Use Any Money Today—Sc to F Solo).

Cosmo calls her a true American but refuses her generosity by explaining that there are things more valuable than money (Marrying for Love—Sc to M Solo and F Solo). After he leaves she looks after him and echoes his sentiment.

The fair, which originally was cancelled due to lack of funds, is in full swing, thanks to Sally's generous private donation. The villagers are in their native costumes (The Ocarina—Mixed Chorus), and Sally is enjoying the occasion with Cosmo. Sally, who thinks Princess Maria would be a suitable companion to her aide Kenneth, defies protocol and invites Maria to sneak through the secret passage from the palace to the embassy.

Sally discreetly exits to another part of the fair, leaving Kenneth alone with Maria. When he questions Maria about Lichtenberg, he is appalled by her lack of knowledge and brashly accuses her of not keeping up with the times. She becomes defensive and angry at his brash manner and turns to go, but he urges her to spend the day with him (It's a Lovely Day Today—Sc to M/F Duet).

In a corridor in the palace, Maria greets Cosmo, who has been elected Prime Minister by the Cabinet. She surprises him by discussing Kenneth's ideas for reform. As Cosmo exits to present his credentials to the King and Queen, a nervous Sally arrives, coached by Maxwell, who urges her to be proper. As she practices curtseying she falls on her face and the lights black out.

In Sally's sitting room, Cosmo enters on "official" business to inform her of the Grand Duke's and Duchess's displeasure at her behavior. He exits but immediately returns on "unofficial" business to explain that the rulers are upset because Maria has been alone with Kenneth in the embassy. He urges Sally to be more careful, for he wants to stay in Lichtenberg. She tells him her only interest is in keeping him happy (The Best Thing for You Would Be Me—Sc to F Solo). A phone call from President Truman granting Lichtenberg the loan pleases Sally, who informs Cosmo. He is upset that she could deceive him by asking for a U.S. loan. He thought she understood his desire to make the country self-sufficient. Sally is helpless; it seems that Sebastian, the former Prime Minister, duped her into thinking Cosmo would want aid *after* he became Prime Minister. Cosmo leaves in anger as Kenneth arrives with a note from Maria refusing to see him again.

In Act II Sally throws an embassy party to introduce some visiting U.S. congressmen to the country, to patch things up between Maria and Kenneth, and to straighten out her relationship with Cosmo (Something to Dance About—F Solo to Mixed Chorus). Kenneth, left alone with Maria, tells her he loves her (Once upon a Time, Today—M Solo).

The congressional loan approval committee arrives to meet the Prime Minister and Cabinet. They are so impressed with Cosmo, who tells them the country needs to help itself, that they double the loan amount. Cosmo resigns, thereby forcing a general election, something the country hasn't had in twenty years.

As the set changes the two Democratic congressmen, Brockbank and Gallagher, ask the Republican Wilkins who his party is running for President (They Like Ike—Sc to M Trio).

In the embassy sitting room, Kenneth attempts to concentrate on business but keeps thinking of Maria. Sally tells him he's in love (You're Just in Love—M/F Counterpoint Duet). Ken opens a letter from his father giving him 90 percent backing for a Lichtenberg hydroelectric plant on the condition that 10 percent be raised locally. Sally, now living in Lichtenberg, promises a personal loan to get things rolling.

Sally is recalled for becoming involved in the elections of a foreign country and says a sad good-bye to Cosmo. She is interrupted by the royal family, who want to thank her for all she has done for the country. Kenneth announces he is staying to help develop the country and Maria, in keeping with royal tradition, asks him to marry her (It's a Lovely Day Today [Reprise]—M/F Duet).

The scene shifts to Washington and another of Sally's galas (Mrs. Sally Adams [Reprise]—Mixed Chorus). Cosmo arrives; he has been reelected Prime Minister and named Ambassador from Lichtenberg. Sally greets him warmly (Finale—Mixed Chorus).

NOTES ON THE PRODUCTION

This is an engaging show that isn't done often enough. The script is witty, the music catchy and enjoyable, the story humorous and the leading role an excellent vehicle for a strong female star.

The show needs to be set in the fifties since it has a lot of political humor that belongs in that time frame. If it is updated the clever male trio "They Like Ike" makes no sense.

The original show utilized several drops for In One scenes. It is possible to cut the number of sets and drops by placing the swearing-in ceremony and the palace corridor in a neutral area, possibly a grouping of panels. Sally's living room in Washington, the reception room in the embassy, and Sally's sitting room may utilize the same background with some different props. The Lichtenberg exterior sequences and the embassy ball may be moved to the reception room rather than the garden. If Sally's sitting room and the reception room are the same, there should be a more intimate downstage right seating arrangement for the smaller scenes. This new scenic configuration would mean one large set for Sally's parties, a neutral panelled location, and a public square.

The costumes are period fifties and native folk with some formal clothes for everyone. The three male congressmen should be able to vocally harmonize and move well to make the "Ike" number a showstopper.

The show works best for an older audience and is excellent dinner theatre fare. Unfortunately, there are more featured male roles than female; however, if one wants to forego the accuracy of a predominantly male congress, it is possible to use females in some of the feature congressman roles.

SONGS OF SPECIAL INTEREST

"Hostess with the Mostes'," F alto subjective, nice rhythm, written for female star, good for learning to take stage and playing an audience.

"It's a Lovely Day Today," charm, up tempo duet, good for movement, fun number, good for revue, soprano/tenor.

"Marrying for Love," F alto possible audition ballad.

Instrumentation: 5 reeds, horn, 3 trumpets, 2 trombones, percussion, guitar, 4 violins, viola, cello, bass, piano/conductor
Script: Chappell (London)
Score: Irving Berlin
Record: Decca
Rights: MTI

CAMELOT

Book and Lyrics: Alan Jay Lerner (Based on *The Once and Future King*, by T. H. White)
Music: Frederick Loewe

ORIGINAL PRODUCTION

Majestic Theatre, December 3, 1960 (873 perf.)
Director: Moss Hart
Choreographer: Hanya Holm
Musical Director: Franz Allers
Orchestration: Robert Russell Bennett and Philip L. Lang
Principals: Merlyn—David Hurst—VTNE; Arthur—Richard Burton—baritone; Guinevere—Julie Andrews—soprano; Sir Dinadan—John Cullum—VTI; Sir Lionel—Bruce Yarnell—VTI; Nimue—Marjorie Smith—soprano; Lancelot—Robert Goulet—tenor; Mordred—Roddy McDowall—baritone; Pellinore—Robert Coote—VTI; Morgan Le Fey—M'el Dowd—mezzo; Sir Sagramore—James Gannon—VTI
Chorus and Smaller Roles: 12F/12M.

SYNOPSIS

The beginning of the play reveals Arthur, the twenty-year-old boyish king of Camelot, hiding in a tree on top of a hill trying to catch a glimpse of his future bride. Merlyn, his wizard friend and teacher, tells him Guinevere is beautiful and his behavior disgraceful. Arthur comments on his subjects' perception of royalty (I Wonder What the King Is Doing Tonight?—L to M Solo).

Arthur returns to his tree as Guinevere comes racing in. She is trying to get a moment alone to pray to St. Genevieve for deliverance from King Arthur (The

Simple Joys of Maidenhood—L to F Solo). Arthur frightens her when he falls from the tree, but they talk easily and enjoy each other. Not knowing he is King Arthur, she tells him she plans to run away and asks him to be her protector. He tries to persuade her that Camelot is really unique (Camelot—L to M Solo). When the royal procession arrives, Guinevere discovers she has been talking to her future husband, but he tells her the story of how he became king and convinces her to stay.

Merlyn knows what the future holds for the newlyweds, but before he can warn Arthur about Lancelot's involvement with Guinevere, a nymph, Nimue, takes all his powers and seals him in a cave forever (Follow Me—F Solo).

Five years later. Arthur and Guinevere are in the study talking about Arthur's achievements, his most famous being a new code of chivalry that centers around "the round table." A young, handsome French knight, Lancelot, is seen in the countryside nearby. He has heard of the knights and vows to join them (C'est Moi—L to M Solo). Arthur meets this idealistic young knight and takes him to see Guinevere, who is partying in the park with the court (The Lusty Month of May—F Solo to Mixed Chorus).

Pellinore, an old man with rusty armor and a dog, stops by the castle and is surprised to learn that the boy he once met in Camelot is now King Arthur. He is invited to spend the night at the castle so he can see the king in the morning.

Lancelot is introduced to Guinevere, who takes an instant dislike to his egotistical manners. In an effort to show him up, she sides with Sir Sagramore, Sir Dinadan, and Sir Lionel in a plan to ensure that he is defeated in the jousting competition (Then You May Take Me to the Fair—Sc to 1F/3M quartet).

Pellinore stays on at the castle and agrees with Guinevere that Lancelot is not likeable, but Arthur is perplexed by her attitude and attempts to puzzle it out. He secretly fears there is something underneath the surface (How to Handle a Woman—L to M Solo).

At the fair, Lancelot overcomes the knights (The Jousts—Mixed Chorus), but it is not until he saves Sir Lionel from death that Guinevere realizes she loves him and prays he will leave Camelot before she becomes involved (Before I Gaze at You Again—F Solo). Arthur knows they are destined for each other and realizes the pain he will undergo as a result. At a ceremony that evening King Arthur knights Lancelot.

Act II is set several years later. Lancelot, on the terrace of the castle, tells Guinevere of his love (If Ever I Would Leave You—Sc to M Solo). The scene continues as Arthur and Pellinore are interrupted by a rude young man, who identifies himself as Mordred, Arthur's illegitimate son. Arthur puts him in the knights' training program, not knowing that Mordred is there to destroy the Round Table. Mordred slyly comments on the sin in the world (Seven Deadly Virtues—M Solo).

A month later, Arthur yearns to banish Mordred, who has caused discontentment among the knights, but he knows that there is nothing he can do. He and Guinevere talk about what it would be like if they weren't King and Queen (What Do the Simple Folk Do?—Sc to M/F Duet).

Mordred finds his aunt, a witch named Morgan Le Fey, and enters her invisible forest to persuade her to play a trick on Arthur. For a basket of candy, Morgan agrees to detain King Arthur while he is in the forest hunting. If she keeps him there overnight, Mordred is convinced he can incriminate Lancelot and Guinevere (The Persuasion—Sc to M/F Duet). While Arthur and Pellinore are hunting Morgan puts an invisible wall around Arthur, who tells Pellinore to run to the castle and warn Lancelot and Guinevere to be careful.

Back at the castle, Lancelot enters Guinevere's room as the knights watch. They discuss their love (I Loved You Once in Silence—Sc to F Solo) but are interrupted by Mordred and the knights, who enter and accuse them of treason (Fie on Goodness—M Chorus). Lancelot escapes but Guinevere is condemned to be burned at the stake. Lancelot returns to save her as the chorus tells of the end of Arthur's dream of the Round Table (Guinevere—Mixed Chorus).

War breaks out, and the new code of chivalry is dead. Lancelot and Guinevere meet Arthur on the battlefield. Arthur learns Guinevere has joined a nunnery to atone for her sins. She looks to him for forgiveness, which he gives. The two leave Arthur, who meets a young lad named Tom, who has come to be a knight. Arthur realizes his dream can still come true and sends the boy home to tell everyone about the Round Table (Camelot—Sc to M Solo).

NOTES ON THE PRODUCTION

Tony Award for the Best Actor (Richard Burton), Musical Direction, for sets, and for costume design.

Camelot might have fared better if it had preceded *My Fair Lady*, for the critics compared it to the previous Lerner/Loewe hit and found it far short of expectations. After the death of President Kennedy, *Camelot* became synonymous with the Kennedy dream. The show ran for two years and was revived in 1980 with Richard Burton, and subsequently Richard Harris, re-creating the role of King Arthur. The Richard Harris version was televised and can occasionally be seen on cable television.

The sets may be trimmed from the opulence of the original. It is suggested that a multilevelled-unit set be utilized throughout with smaller scenes being played in specific locations and the entire set used for larger numbers. The props and costumes are expensive to re-create as there is a lot of armor that must be accurate to the period. The women's gowns require quite a bit of material, and most amateur groups are unable to pull many costumes of this period from their often limited wardrobes.

SONGS OF SPECIAL INTEREST

"I Wonder What the King Is Doing Tonight," "Where Are the Simple Joys of Maidenhood?" and "Camelot" combine as a scene character study for a baritone/soprano in a class situation.

"Seven Deadly Virtues," movement, character-oriented, baritone, emphasis on evil.

"What Do the Simple Folk Do?," dramatically difficult baritone/soprano duet, emphasis on transitions and mood changes, good for class study.

Instrumentation: 2 violins, viola, cello, bass, 5 reeds, 2 horns, 3 trumpets, 2 trombones, percussion, guitar/lute/mandolin, harp, piano/conductor. Also available: 12-piece condensed orchestration
Script: Random House, Dell, Great Musicals of the American Theatre, Volume II
Score: Chappell
Record: Columbia
Rights: TW

CANDIDE (revival)

Book: Hugh Wheeler (Based on the book by Voltaire)
Music: Leonard Bernstein
Lyrics: Richard Wilbur; additional lyrics by: Stephen Sondheim and John Latouche.

REVIVAL PRODUCTION

Broadway Theatre, March 5, 1974 (740 perf.)
Director: Harold Prince
Choreographer: Patricia Birch
Musical Directors: John Mauceri and Paul Gemignani
Orchestration: Hershy Kay
Principals: Candide—Mark Baker—tenor; Paquette—Deborah St. Darr—mezzo; Cunegonde—Maureen Brennan—high, strong soprano; Maximilian—Sam Freed—baritone; Old Lady—June Gable—alto; Dr. Voltaire/Dr. Pangloss/Governor/Host/Sage—Lewis J. Stadler—tenor
Chorus and Smaller Roles: 8M/8F minimum.

SYNOPSIS

This synopsis is based on the script used for the 1974 revival. The show is performed without an intermission.

The audience enters a carnival-oriented theatre lobby where hot dogs, peanuts, and drinks are readily available for patrons to take to their seats. The interior of the theatre allows for the audience and orchestra to be seated around the stage area; the atmosphere is unusual and festive. The overture begins and the lights rise on Voltaire, an old man in a nightshirt and nightcap sleeping in bed. He sleeps throughout the overture. At the end of the overture a servant rushes on with some hot chocolate and exits as Voltaire begins reading his manuscript.

The four teenagers his manuscript centers around are introduced; Candide, the bastard cousin who is well treated; Paquette, the sexy sewing maid who happily grants favors to her master; Cunegonde, the Baron's virgin daughter; and her brother Maximilian, an extremely self-centered, egotistical young man who is constantly admiring himself in a mirror (Life Is Happiness Indeed—Sc to 2M/1F Solo To 2M/2F Quartet).

The focus shifts to Voltaire, now acting the part of the admired teacher Dr. Pangloss, who is joined by his four pupils, in a parade to the schoolroom (Parade—Instrumental).

The castle schoolroom resembles an eighteenth-century American one, complete with desks, a blackboard, and a picture of the Baron that looks like George Washington. The four teenagers seat themselves as Dr. Pangloss begins the lesson (The Best of All Possible Worlds—Sc to 3M/2F Quintet).

At the end of the class, Paquette is privately tutored by Dr. Pangloss, who teaches her sex and physics. The two are observed by Cunegonde, who asks Dr. Pangloss to enlighten her on advanced physics. Using Paquette to help him demonstrate, he explains the specifics of gravity between the male and female bodies.

A delighted Cunegonde leaves the two and searches out Candide in the Baron's orchard, where she proceeds to enlighten him. The two kiss wildly and envision their married life together (Oh Happy We—Sc to M/F Duet). During the song they begin undressing each other. They are interrupted by the Baron, Baroness, Maximilian, Pangloss, and Paquette. When the two lovers entreat the Baron to let them marry, he banishes Candide. The young lad wonders about his lonely future (It Must Be So—M Solo). Two men grab the innocent boy and carry him off in a sack to join the Bulgarian Army.

Back at the Baron's chapel, the Baron and his family are praying for deliverance as the sounds of the battle between the Bulgarians and Westphalians are heard in the distance. The Bulgarians enter and spear all but Cunegonde, whom they carry off to sell her favors at twenty ducats per customer. The chorus mournfully comments (O Miserere—Mixed Chorus).

Voltaire, in another area of the stage, describes the fate of Candide and Cunegonde as their scenes are enacted. Candide escapes when his two abductors are killed, and Cunegonde is left for dead after having been ravished. The two, in separate areas of the stage, lament their fate (Oh Happy We [Reprise]—M/F Linear Duet).

Voltaire continues to outline their adventures. Candide is now an actor portraying female roles quite badly, and Cunegonde is moved from brothel to brothel until she becomes the mistress of a wealthy Portuguese Jew in Lisbon. The scene moves to her bedchamber in Lisbon where she receives a diamond Star of David from the Jew and a diamond cross from the grand inquisitor. Cunegonde, left alone, ponders her life as she examines her jewels (Glitter and Be Gay—F Solo).

Candide is seen in a part of Lisbon that has been destroyed by an earthquake.

As he surveys the disaster he discovers Dr. Pangloss sporting a metal nose as a result of syphilis he contracted from Paquette. The two are arrested for heresy and dragged before the citizens in the central square, who excitedly witness the floggings, hangings and burnings of the inquisition (Auto Da Fe—Mixed Chorus). Cunegonde enters with an old woman and settles down to watch the proceedings. Pangloss is taken off to be hanged as Cunegonde recognizes her old teacher and Candide, who is flogged and left unconscious. He is taken off by Cunegonde's servant and healed but doubts the value of life (This World—M Solo) as the old woman leads him to Cunegonde. The two are happily reunited (You Were Dead You Know—M/F Duet) but are soon interrupted by the arrival of the Jew, who is accidentally killed by Candide, and the subsequent arrival of the Grand Inquisitor, whom Candide purposely kills. The old lady urges them to flee and attempts to gain money for the trip by seducing three Spaniards (I Am Easily Assimilated—F Solo to M Trio) who spurn her efforts. As Cunegonde, Candide, and the old lady await their fate, a businessman offers Candide a job as captain of a ship bound for the new world; the three ponder their future as a Latin rhumba rhythm underscores the scene change.

Voltaire describes Cartogena Columbia while a local whore transforms him into the lecherous provincial Governor. Two young female slaves are whipped onto the slaves' block and instantly recognize each other as Maximilian, who has disguised himself as a girl to avoid the army, and Paquette. The Governor rejects Paquette and chooses Maximilian and begins expressing his emotions (My Love—Sc to 2M Duet). Maximilian attempts to avoid him, but the Governor misinterprets the avoidance as shyness and takes Maximilian to be married in a mock ceremony. After the fake ceremony the Governor fondles Maximilian, realizes that something is wrong, rips open Maximilian's blouse and finds coconuts on a hairy chest. Maximilian pleads for his life.

Four sailors enter to convert the theatre into a ship carrying Candide, Cunegonde, and the old woman. The old lady tells her two companions about her lost buttock which was cut off by a pirate—her extremely descriptive character monologue tells of her capture and ravishment by various villainous groups. The story is interrupted by pirates who carry the women off and leave Candide unconscious.

The scene switches to a cathedral which Candide enters. He is approached by two priests who he discovers are Paquette and Maximilian (Alleluia—Mixed Chorus). When Candide tells Maximilian that Cunegonde lives and he plans on marrying her, the enraged Maximilian attempts to kill him, for Candide is, after all, still a bastard. Candide accidentally hits Maximilian with a statue, assumes he is dead and leaves with Paquette.

Voltaire appears and continues the narrative as a "jungle" of green paper streamers drops in. Candide and Paquette stumble upon Eldorado, a fabled land where life is wonderful; the inhabitants gentle and intelligent; even the animals, represented by two pink sheep, are happy creatures (Sheep's Song—F Duet). Unable to stand the placid life, Paquette and Candide steal two of the sheep and load them with jewels and gold. They return to Columbia where they find the old lady, who tells them Cunegonde is in Constantinople. The Governor arrives, impounds the sheep, takes Paquette to his room and gives Candide to some whores.

Later the Governor and some townspeople bid farewell to Candide, the old lady and Paquette (Bon Voyage—Mixed Chorus) and send them off in an unseaworthy skiff which sinks.

The three land on a desert island, followed by the two sheep still laden with the jewels and gold. They joyously sing (The Best of All Possible Worlds [Reprise]—2F/1M Trio) before setting off for Constantinople.

In Constantinople they find Cunegonde disguised as a belly dancer (You Were Dead You Know [Reprise]—M/F Duet). Candide buys her and a disguised Maximilian. The five set off to find the wisest man in the world, who is none other than their old teacher Pangloss. They journey off to create a true garden of Eden (Make Our Garden Grow—Mixed Chorus).

NOTES ON THE PRODUCTION

Candide, with book by Lillian Hellman, was originally produced on December 1, 1956, for a run of 73 performances. It was later revived in 1974 with a new book, added lyrics and a fresh production concept. The revival was noted for its sheer fun and lively adaptation. The vibrancy of the production and the youthful energy of the performers, combined with a more intimate production, helped make it a theatrical event.

The 1974 version won Tony Awards for Best Book and Direction.

The script is almost a story theatre piece and requires little in the way of a specific permanent set. If desired, set pieces may be brought in by members of the ensemble.

There are quite a few costumes per character, and every effort should be made to define the period, country and style through the costumes. If there is little or no set it is essential that the costumes establish location.

The show is a festive one, and the revised Wheeler script and Prince production are worth emulating. Mr. Prince has an excellent preface in the score which should be absorbed by any director planning to do this production. In its present form the show may not be advisable for some theatre groups as the subject matter involves homosexuality, decadent priests and sexual ravishment and may not be accepted by some members of the audience or by members of the producing organizations.

SONGS OF SPECIAL INTEREST

"Glitter and Be Gay," requires high soprano, ending good for audition, comedic.

"I Am Easily Assimilated," alto, comic, character-oriented.

"Life Is Happiness Indeed," up tempo, good for class study of how to handle music to dialogue to music.

"You Were Dead You Know," tenor/soprano spoof on the operetta style, comic song that requires good direction.

Instrumentation: violin, cello, bass, 2 trumpets, trombone, 2 piano/celestes, electric piano, 3 reeds, percussion
Script: Schirmer as part of score, Macmillan
Score: Schirmer
Record: Columbia
Rights: MTI

CARMEN JONES

Book and Lyrics: Oscar Hammerstein II (Based on Henri Meilhac and Ludovic Halévy's opera libretto, which was adapted from Prosper Mérimée's novel *Carmen*)
Music: Georges Bizet

ORIGINAL PRODUCTION

Broadway Theatre, December 2, 1943 (502 perf.)
Directors: Hassard Short and Charles Friedman
Choreographer: Eugene Loring
Musical Director: Joseph Littau
Orchestration: Robert Russell Bennett
Principals: Carmen Jones—Muriel Smith—soprano; Joe—Luther Saxon—tenor; Cindy Lou—Carlotta Franzell—soprano; Husky Miller—Glenn Bryant—baritone; Frankie—June Hawkins—VTI; Drummer—Cosy Cole—VTI
Chorus and Smaller Roles: 12F/12M minimum. The music would be richer with more in the company, 8 children.

SYNOPSIS

The curtain opens to show the exterior of a parachute factory on the edge of a river near a Southern town; the time is 1943 and an army camp is beyond. The stevedores are carrying cases from the factory onto the loading platform to await shipment, the MP's are on guard and other workers are readying a parachute for folding. The soldiers and workers improvise a work song to keep the pace and encourage the war effort (Prelude—M Chorus).

Cindy Lou, an attractive girl from out of town, attempts to gain entrance to the factory but is stopped by the MP's. Morrell, who considers himself a ladies' man, crosses to greet her, only to discover that she is looking for a corporal named Joe and has no interest in flirting with anyone else. Morrell and the men playfully attempt to entice her, but she laughingly tells them she only likes one man (Opening—M Solo, F Solo to M Chorus).

She exits as the change of the guard begins and a line of street urchins enter, imitating the more formal guard-changing ceremony. The children comically perform the guard change, complete with baseball bats and broomsticks, while the sopranos sing with childlike intonations (Lift 'Em up and Put 'Em Down—Ch and F Chorus). After they complete maneuvers the urchins exit.

Joe enters with the new guard and the foreman informs him Cindy Lou is looking for him. Sergeant Brown, one of the new guards, strikes up a conversation with Joe; Brown is quite swaggering and proud for he is from New York and a real ladies' man. The men inform him that Joe is quite popular among the factory girls, especially Carmen Jones, but Joe shuns all of them in favor of his girl back home. The lunch whistle sounds and the men tell of their hunger for a girl, not food (Honey Gal o'Mine—M Chorus).

Female laughter is heard from the direction of the parachute factory. Lieutenant Eddie Perkins, a flier who used to work at the factory, enters, followed by the factory girls, who are dressed in flat-heeled shoes and dresses. They wish him good luck and hope that if he ever has to bail out he will use one of their parachutes (Good Luck, Mr. Flyin' Man—F Chorus).

Carmen, an extremely sexy, over-dressed girl wearing high heels and a rose in her hair, enters. The crowd is obviously awed except for Sally and Joe. Carmen tells everyone that love is where you find it; it comes and goes (Dat's Love—F Solo to Mixed Chorus). She is the type of woman who wants what she can't have and once she wins she quickly loses interest. At the end of the song she throws a rose at Joe's heart. Everyone exits, leaving Joe alone to ponder this unusual woman.

As Joe slowly picks up the rose Carmen has left, Cindy Lou enters and confesses she has come because his mother has had some superstitious omens—buzzard feathers and a bad tea leaf reading. They are upset by the omens but attempt to put their fear aside by expressing their love (You Talk Jus' Like My Maw—Sc to M/F Duet). At the end of the number the two are in each other's arms. Joe decides to read the letter his mother has sent but Cindy, knowing the letter is a request for Joe to marry her as soon as possible, leaves him alone. He agrees with his mother and is grateful the letter has come before he has succumbed to Carmen's wiles.

Joe prepares to discard Carmen's flower when a terrible row is heard from the factory and Joe rushes to the entrance, which is now filled with the factory girls who are escaping a fight between Carmen and Sally. The girls describe the fight, which verbally continues as Sally and Carmen are dragged on (Murder, Murder—F Chorus). Sergeant Brown threatens to throw Carmen in jail for her actions, but she taunts him, claiming he has no authority over her for he only has military jurisdiction and she is a civilian. He retaliates by ordering Joe to take her to the guardhouse. She runs away from Joe and kisses him when he finally catches her. The crowd comments (Finale of Scene 1—Mixed Chorus).

The chorus, in the orchestra pit, happily sings (Carmen Jones Is Goin' to Jail—Mixed Chorus). On a shrub-lined road, Joe is seen leading Carmen to jail, followed by eight taunting children who reprise the adult song. Joe chases them off and they vow revenge. When Carmen persuades Joe to take her dancing at Billy Pastor's (Dere's a Cafe on de Corner—F/M Duet), he lets her go after she promises to meet him at the cafe. She runs off. Sergeant Brown enters with Cindy Lou to be told by the street urchins that Joe has let Carmen go. Brown is furious, has Joe put in the guardhouse, and goes to meet Carmen at the cafe.

Three weeks later at Billy Pastor's a happy crowd is enjoying the music; Frankie, who is dancing with Rum, a prizefighter's manager from Chicago, expresses her feelings for the music in song (Beat out Dat Rhythm on a Drum— F Solo to Mixed Chorus). There is great excitement among the crowd as the famous Husky Miller, a 6'6" majestic prizefighter, enters. Husky buys drinks for the house and tells the admiring crowd about prizefighting (Stan' up an' Fight—M Solo to Mixed Chorus).

Carmen enters during Husky's song, and his attraction to her forces him to embellish the number. She gives him one bored glance and walks away. Husky tells Rum and his assistant, Dink, that he wants to see Carmen waiting for him when they get off the train in Chicago. If they can't coerce her into going to Chicago they can consider themselves fired.

At Frankie and Myrt's table the two girls confide to Carmen that Rum and Dink want them to go to Chicago and they would like Carmen to join them. Carmen dreams of traveling, and Rum and Dink heighten her interest with a description of the speeding train (Whizzin' Away Along De Track—3F/2M Quintet). Carmen almost gives in but confesses that she is in love with Joe and can't leave while he is in jail. Rum describes the easy life in Chicago and further entices her by telling her how easy it would be for her to work in a nightclub. Carmen promises to reconsider.

Joe arrives, after having finished his three weeks in jail, excited to find Carmen has waited for him. When he shows her the rose she gave him three weeks before (Dis Flower—M Solo), she realizes he is in her power. Carmen invites him to Chicago (If You Would Only Come Away—F/M Duet), but he wants to better himself through flying school. Sergeant Brown overhears this last comment, begins needling Joe and a fight occurs. Brown is knocked out and Joe, thinking he will spend years in prison if he stays, agrees to leave with Carmen. Carmen tells the crowd that Joe is going to flight school, and the company lines up to wish him farewell (Act I Finale—Mixed Chorus).

Act II opens at the classy Meadowlawn Country Club in Chicago where Frankie, Rum and Myrt are obviously out of their element. Carmen arrives, grateful to be away from Joe and ready to meet Husky. Myrt entertains the women by reading cards and telling fortunes (De Cards Don' Lie—F Chorus). Carmen cuts a nine of spades which terrifies her, for it is an omen of death (Dat Ol Boy—F Solo).

Husky and his opponent from Brazil arrive; both are strikingly dressed in evening clothes. The crowd is excited and greets Poncho (Poncho De Panther from Brazil—M/F Chorus). Husky is introduced to Cindy Lou, who has come searching for Joe. When Husky asks her what is so special about Joe, she easily responds (My Joe—F Solo). Husky goes to get Carmen.

Left alone, Cindy Lou surprises Joe, who arrives at the club for Carmen. She desperately urges him to come home, but he refuses and attacks Husky, who has entered the garden with Carmen. Rum and Dink break up the fight and convince Husky to return to the club. Rum, Carmen, Cindy, Frankie and Myrt urge Joe to go home with Cindy to be with his dying mother. He agrees but promises Carmen he will return, for she is his forever (Finale of Scene 1—4F/2M Sextet). Carmen shrugs indifferently and walks into the clubhouse where Husky is waiting.

It is one week later, outside a baseball park on the night of the championship fight; the fans are excited (Git Yer Program for de Big Fight—Mixed Chorus). The crowd is anxiously awaiting Husky (Dat's Our Man—Mixed Chorus) and goes wild with excitement when he enters with Carmen. The police guard escorts him inside, leaving Carmen with Frankie and Myrt, who warn her that Joe is waiting for her. Although they urge her to run, she feels the future is fated and turns to face him.

Joe slowly approaches Carmen to tell her his mother died before he got home. She comforts him but tells him if he is going to kill her to get it over with. He asks if they can begin again (Beginning of Finale—Sc to M/F Duet), but she replies that she needs new fire and their flame is gone. In a grippingly difficult and dramatic twelve-minute musical scene, the two rehash their relationship, with each crying out for something different. As the chorus reprises (Dat's Our Man [Reprise]—Mixed Chorus), Carmen starts to go in to her soon-to-be victorious lover, Husky. Joe is overcome with jealousy and kills her. Behind this downstage death tableau the lights rise, revealing a victorious Husky and a cheering crowd. The lights dim as Joe, on his knees, announces that his death will bring him to his Carmen.

NOTES ON THE PRODUCTION

In Oscar Hammerstein II's introduction to the play he gives a background of his early impression of opera and further theorizes that the reason the form is so successful in Europe is mainly that it is sung in the native language of the presenting country. He feels that opera which has been translated into English has generally failed because the translations have been more scholarly than theatrical. It was for this reason that this creative man wrote *Carmen Jones*.

Hammerstein based his musical play on the Bizet opera *Carmen*. He felt his treatment would enable audiences to understand the story line, the characters and the dialogue and they would be moved to emotional heights by the musical line which underscores the piece throughout. Oscar Hammerstein II wrote the play for Black actors because he felt the American Black had the freedom and abandon necessary to capture the gypsy spirit of Bizet's opera.

Vocally the work is extremely difficult and requires operatic voices. Billy Rose, the producer of the original production, considered the roles too vocally taxing to sing twice a day and double cast the principals.

The show was extremely successful, opulently mounted, visually exciting and musically true to the original. It is the only adaptation of an opera which truly appealed to Broadway audiences and one that is worthy of more public performances.

An interesting note from Abe Laufe's *Broadway's Greatest Musicals*, which should encourage community theatres, is that none of the principals in the original production were professional; all were making their Broadway debut. Certainly a company that has the vocal ability to handle *Porgy and Bess* should consider adding *Carmen Jones* to its repertoire.

The costuming adds color and variety to the show, and all efforts should be made to have a visually exciting grouping of costumes. It is probably more important in this show to spend a larger portion of the budget on the costumes than on the scenery.

There are essentially three sets, the exterior of the parachute factory, the interior of the cafe, and the exterior of the country club. The exterior of the baseball park traditionally is a painted scrim, but this can be trimmed in size and placed to one side of the stage. It is visually better to have the ending scene performed with a scrim, even a small one.

SONGS OF SPECIAL INTEREST

"Finale," scene to tenor/soprano dramatic duet. Extremely difficult and worthy of study.

Instrumentation: 4 reeds, horn, trumpet, 2 trombones, percussion, 4 violins, viola, cello/bass, harp, piano, piano 4/conductor
Script: Knopf
Score: Williamson
Record: Decca
Rights: R & H

CARNIVAL

Book: Michael Stewart (Based on the film *Lili*, by Helen Deutsch; adapted from a story by Paul Gallico)
Music and Lyrics: Bob Merrill

ORIGINAL PRODUCTION

Imperial Theatre, April 13, 1961 (719 perf.)
Director/Choreographer: Gower Champion
Musical Director: Saul Schechtman

Orchestration: Philip J. Lang
Principals: Lili—Anna Maria Alberghetti—soprano; Marco—James Mitchell—
baritone; Paul—Jerry Orbach—high baritone; Rosalie—Kaye Ballard—alto; Jacquot—Pierre Olaf—baritone; Schlegel—Henry Lascoe—baritone
Chorus and Smaller Roles: 6M/6F minimum, circus skills necessary.

SYNOPSIS

The play begins on an empty meadow sometime before sunrise. Jacquot enters
playing a concertina, sits and begins to sing. The other carnival performers and
roustabouts enter to raise their tent for the eventual performance. Schlegel, the
owner, calls for the parade which announces the arrival of the Cirque de Paris.
The performers and their specialties are introduced (Direct from Vienna—Mixed
Chorus) as the parade starts for town.

Lili, a waiflike, recently orphaned teenager, arrives seeking work from her
father's friend, who runs the souvenir concession. Grobert, the abrupt new
souvenir operator, gruffly informs her the man is dead. Lili offers to sell souvenirs
for him (Very Nice Man—Sc to F Solo), and he lustily invites her into his wagon
to discuss the matter.

Marco, the self-centered magician, hears crashing noises from Grobert's and
is intrigued by Lili, who scampers out of the wagon. He charms her with some
magic and showmanship, but Grobert angrily orders her to leave the carnival
and she wanders off.

The lights rise on the puppet booth where Carrot Top, an endearing redheaded
puppet, is singing (Fairyland—M Solo) to Schlegel, who is in a fury about the
incompetence of the act. He yells for the puppeteers, Jacquot and Paul, and
warns them to get a new act or be fired. Paul, the head puppeteer, a former
dancer who was crippled in the war, angrily begins to pack up. Jacquot, his
good-natured caring assistant, begs him to reconsider, but Paul responds that
his present life is meaningless (I've Got to Find a Reason—Sc to M Solo). When
Lili enters looking for Marco, Paul furiously tells her to go home and leave men
like Marco alone. She retorts that he performs magic and Jacquot kindly agrees
with her but also urges her to go home. She tells him how far she has traveled
and how much her town meant (Mira—Sc to F Solo).

The carnival parade returns and Marco invites Lili to have lunch in his wagon.
As he sings of how gallant he is, the roustabouts mock him but the infatuated
Lili doesn't notice (Sword, Rose, and Cape—M Solo to M Trio).

Rosalie, Marco's girlfriend, starts to go to Marco's wagon but Schlegel,
anxious to avoid problems with his star, offers her a drink. Rosalie tells Schlegel
she has a proposal of marriage from a Swiss doctor and is considering accepting.
She sarcastically tells of Marco's nauseating habit of humming at his sexual
successes and revels in the fact that it's her turn (Humming—Sc to F/M Duet).
At the end of the song, Marco enters to ask Schlegel to give Lili a job, and
Rosalie decides to tell the Zurich doctor yes. Schlegel, surprised that Lili is the
girl Marco wants him to hire, agrees to test her for six months at no salary. Lili

excitedly imagines she is in love (Yes, My Heart—F Solo to Mixed Chorus). As she sings, various roustabouts and performers enter and begin decorating the carnival for the evening's performance. Everyone becomes involved in her mood and song.

The company exits as the focus shifts to Jacquot, who tells Paul he is staying with the carnival. Paul angrily urges Jacquot to see the people and show for the mediocre place it is, but Jacquot tells him the ugliness is within Paul himself and exits. Paul looks sadly at Carrot Top, his favorite redheaded, little boy puppet and bitterly wonders if he should be more like the puppet (Everybody Likes You—M Solo).

The lights fade on Paul and rise later that night on the carnival show. Various acts perform and Marco headlines with his magic act assisted by Rosalie (Magic Magic—M/2F Trio). Lili's constant comments to the audience on the magnificence of the act upset Marco, who has her fired. The carnival ballet closes the scene and the carnival for the night.

Lili crosses an empty stage, puts down her suitcase and begins to climb a tall ladder, but the voice of Carrot Top slowly guides her from her contemplated suicide. She meets the rest of the puppets, Horrible Henry, a walrus; Renardo, a clever fox; and the elegant Marguerite. After Renardo insults Horrible Henry, Carrot Top urges Lili to sing Henry a cheerful song, which she does (Golden Delicious—Sc to F/2 Puppets Trio). She then lyricizes the carnival theme (Love Makes the World Go Round—F Solo). The puppets query her about her feelings and Carrot Top's voice gradually becomes that of Paul, who begs her to care about him. The puppets join her in the song, which stops when Lili sees Marco. Carrot Top, in Paul's voice, orders Jacquot to hire Lili for their act and get her away from Marco. As Jacquot leads her off, Paul slowly comes from behind the booth and removes Carrot Top.

Act II opens as the roustabouts, band and performers prepare for the puppet show. The fanfare is played and Marguerite pops up with Renardo and Henry. Lili joins them (Yum Ticky-Ticky Tum—F and Puppets Trio). Schlegel watches the crowd growing at the puppet booth and decides to move the puppet theatre to a more central location.

The lights flash on to the puppet booth, which is larger and freshly painted. The puppets are better costumed (The Rich—F and Puppets Trio). The show continues (Beautiful Candy—F and Puppet Quartet to Mixed Chorus).

When Schlegel announces they will move to the main tent, the three are excited, but Lili breaks the mood when she remembers she is to watch Marco's act. Left alone, Paul agonizes (Her Face—M Solo). During the song, he realizes he has fallen in love. Paul calls to Jacquot to freshen up the puppets and give Lili a new song. Jacquot excitedly imagines their act will be so successful it will play Paris (Cirque de Paris Ballet—M Solo to Mixed Chorus). He is joined by the carnival people.

The next morning, the sudden arrival of Dr. Glass, Rosalie's veterinarian boyfriend who carries some of his patients with him, causes her to have second thoughts. Marco, certain she is leaving, asks Lili to join him in the act, at which point Paul enters and orders her to rehearse. Angered by her attitude of fear, he grabs her tear-stained face and kisses her. Lili denounces him (I Hate Him—Sc to F/M Duet).

The carnival people perform (Cirque de Paris—Mixed Chorus). Rosalie enters to tell Marco she is staying with him and is ready for their sword act. It seems Papa Glass, the owner of a large chain of hotels, pleased that Rosalie is not marrying his son, has booked their act. She gets into the sword box and the two sing as Marco stabs swords into the box and she reacts as if hit (Always, Always You—Sc to M/F Duet).

Rosalie tells Lili that Marco no longer needs her and Jacquot urges her to go home to Mira, for Paul has torn down the puppet booth. When Marco enters to tell Lili he plans on seeing her again, Paul drives him off and angrily calls Lili cheap. She screams that she hates him and he slaps her across the face. She runs off and Paul laments (She's My Love—M Solo). He slowly exits.

Lili informs Marco she has grown up and learned some truth about the world so she won't be seeing him anymore. He kisses her fondly and exits. As she walks by the broken puppet tent Carrot Top and the puppets ask her to stay. As she embraces them she realizes that the puppets are indeed Paul. She lifts the curtain and demands an explanation. He admits to the puppets being aspects of his personality and angrily asks if he must make another puppet in the form of a cripple. Irritated that he has opened up, he angrily orders her out and hurls Carrot Top to the ground. She looks at him. Admitting that he needs her, he reaches out his hand and she runs into his arms. They exit arm in arm.

NOTES ON THE PRODUCTION

A Tony Award went to Anna Maria Alberghetti, who tied with Diahann Carroll of *No Strings* for Best Actress.

This small-cast musical is suitable for family audiences and one of the more inexpensive musicals to produce. It is dramatic, comedic and charming and has something that will appeal to all audiences. The music is melodic and highlights the story quite well.

The costumes are carnival/circus in style. The show is best if placed sometime before World War II when the world was a bit more innocent. The performers only need one costume although Rosalie and Lili should probably have several to help character believability.

Set requirements call for a puppet booth, a wagon for Marco, and a souvenir stand. Usually the puppet booth is the rear of the souvenir stand. Marco's wagon balances the stage and may be left on or moved off as desired. The carnival tent is set up in the beginning of the show by the actors and may be as simple as banners or as elaborate as a full tent. The action is choreographed and lends atmosphere to the opening.

The dramatic numbers are excellent for classroom study. There aren't many musical theatre dramatic songs for a soprano and this show has some fine ones.

SONGS OF SPECIAL INTEREST

"Everybody Likes You," sung to a puppet. Shows the development of the character. Baritone. Good in class situation for characterization study.

"Her Face," solid dramatic baritone solo, good for class situation. Should be performed with the scene for full value.

"Humming," comedic song for character alto.

"I Hate Him," strong soprano dramatic song, best when coupled with the scene before.

"Mira," charm song, soprano/mezzo range, simplistic excitement. Good for two-song character study when coupled with "I Hate Him."

"She's My Love," realization song for male lead, good drama. Baritone.

Instrumentation: 3 violins, cello, bass and tuba, 5 reeds, horn, 2 trumpets, 2 trombones, 2 percussion, harp, guitar, accordion, piano/celeste (piano/conductor). Also available with reduced combo
Script: DBS
Selections: UA
Record: MGM
Rights: TW

CAROUSEL

Book and Lyrics: Oscar Hammerstein II (Based on the play *Lilliom*, by Ferenc Molnár)
Music: Richard Rodgers

ORIGINAL PRODUCTION

Majestic Theatre, April 19, 1945 (890 perf.)
Director: Rouben Mamoulian
Choreographer: Agnes de Mille
Musical Director: Miles White
Orchestration: Don Walker
Principals: Billy Bigelow—John Raitt—tenor; Nettie—Christine Johnson—soprano; Julie Jordan—Jan Clayton—soprano; Louise—Bambi Linn—VTNE—must dance; Carrie Pipperidge—Jean Darling—mezzo; Jigger Craigin—Murvyn Vye—baritone; Enoch Snow—Eric Mattson—high tenor; Mrs. Mullin—Jean Casto—VTNE
Chorus and Smaller Roles: 12F/14M minimum, several children as walk-ons.

SYNOPSIS

The time is 1873–1888 in a New England coastal town. The traditional musical theatre overture is replaced by a dance number which pantomimes the chorus enjoying the sights at a New England amusement park, and the meeting of Julie Jordan and Billy Bigelow. Julie, a quiet, innocent mill worker, is infatuated by the flamboyant Billy, who operates the carousel (Carousel Waltz—Orchestra).

A little distance from the carousel, Julie and her friend Carrie, who have been chased out of the park by Mrs. Mullin, the jealous carousel owner, pause to rest. Mrs. Mullin enters but is stopped by Billy, who demands to know what all the fuss is about. When he learns Mrs. Mullin's anger was caused because he put his arm around Julie, he becomes irritated and defies Mrs. Mullin, who fires him. He tells the girls he will be back and returns to the carousel to pick up his things.

While he is gone, Carrie asks Julie how she feels about Billy and accuses her of being infatuated with this worldly individual (You're a Queer One, Julie Jordan—Sc to F Duet). Carrie proceeds to tell about her fisherman boyfriend (Mr. Snow—Sc to F Solo).

Billy returns with a suitcase and coat, amazed that the girls are waiting. Julie sends Carrie home while Billy questions her reason for staying. They are interrupted by a policeman and Mr. Bascombe, the mill owner who offers to take Julie to the mill boardinghouse and explain her lateness. When Julie doesn't move, the policeman and Bascombe are distressed by her frivolity. After the two leave, Billy becomes more enamored and discovers she has no boyfriends and no plans for marriage. He boldly asks what she would say if he asked her to marry him, and she responds that she would marry him if she loved him. The two imagine how they would act if they were in love (If I Loved You—Sc to M/F Duet). Billy kisses her tenderly.

At Nettie Fowler's Spa, a group of hungry men carrying baskets of clams enter, anxious for the clambake to begin. Carrie tells the men to be ashamed of their loud behavior as the women shout encouragement (Give It to 'Em Good Carrie—F Solo to Mixed Chorus). Nettie passes out hot doughnuts and coffee while wisely commenting that everyone is impatient for the first clambake of the year because it marks the beginning of summer (June Is Bustin' Out All Over—F Solo to Mixed Chorus). Carrie, who hasn't seen Julie since she married Billy and moved in with Nettie, greets her friend with the exciting news that she is going to marry Mr. Snow. She tells Julie and the girls about her plans. As they playact the ceremony Enoch Snow arrives (Mister Snow [Reprise]—Sc to F Chorus and M Solo).

Julie is introduced to Enoch, a preening, straight-laced man with a peculiar laugh, and is pleased to see Carrie starting out her married life with such a homebody. When Billy enters to tell her he isn't going to the clambake, she breaks down and exits into the house.

Carrie and Mr. Snow, left alone, wonder about the future (When the Children

Are Asleep—Sc to M/F Duet). After their dreaming, the men, all seamen, enter and describe their life as whalers (Blow High, Blow Low—M Chorus). They are joined by Billy and Jigger, who later attempts to convince Billy to steal the mill payroll. Their plans are interrupted by Mrs. Mullin, who offers Billy a job on the carousel if he will leave Julie. An anxious Julie comes to the porch and privately takes Billy aside to tell him she is going to have a baby. Overwhelmed by the news, he softens his usually harsh behavior by helping her into the house and returns to tell Mrs. Mullin he is going to be a father. Julie's announcement forces him to consider his sudden responsibility (Soliloquy—L to M Solo). He imagines first his relationship with his son and the outcome if the baby is a girl. Realizing he must have money to protect a daughter from people like himself, he rashly decides to join Jigger in the robbery.

In Act II, on an island later that night, couples are resting and talking about the clambake (This Was a Real Nice Clambake—Mixed Chorus). Nettie sends Enoch to hide the treasure for the traditional male treasure hunt and Jigger takes Enoch's absence as the opportunity to flirt with Carrie. Enoch returns and accuses Carrie of being a loose woman. He sadly turns away to dream of what might have been (Geraniums in the Winder—L to M Solo). As Carrie sobs, Jigger comforts her while telling the arriving chorus that any girl in love with a virtuous man is destined for unhappiness (There's Nothin' So Bad for a Woman—M Solo to Mixed Chorus).

Billy quietly tells Jigger it is time to sneak back to the mainland to steal the payroll. The women, left alone, express various opinions on married life, and Julie tells Carrie her viewpoint (What's the Use of Wond'rin—Sc to F Solo).

On a mainland wharf Billy and Jigger's plan to rob Bascombe is thwarted when Bascombe pulls a gun and yells for the police and ship's crew. Jigger escapes but Billy is trapped. Knowing he could not stand to spend the rest of his life in jail, he stabs himself and cries out Julie's name. Julie and Nettie enter. As Billy calls Julie for one last good-bye, he dies in her arms. Julie quietly says good-bye and tells Billy she loves him. When she brokenheartedly asks Nettie what to do, Nettie tells her she will never be alone (You'll Never Walk Alone—Sc to F Duet).

As Julie and Nettie kneel in prayer, two heavenly friends enter and order Billy to come with them. Billy arrogantly demands to be judged by the Lord himself (The Highest Judge of All—L to M Solo). The two exit with Billy.

In heaven Billy meets the Starkeeper, who informs him that he hasn't done enough good deeds in his life but may return to Earth to help his fifteen-year-old daughter. The stage becomes extremely bright, and Louise is spotted running on the beach with two young ragamuffins. Enoch enters followed by Carrie and their six snobby children. After a variety of short dance scenes which depict various groups of teenagers rejecting and taunting Louise, Billy starts off with the heavenly friend to descend to Earth.

Outside Julie's cottage, Junior Snow is appalled to discover that Louise is going to run away with a man in a theatrical troupe. When he tells her he wants to marry her if his father will agree to let him marry beneath his station, Louise sends him away. Billy appears and talks to her about her father, but she tries to run into the house. He grabs her and attempts to give her a star he has brought with him, but the terrified girl pulls away and he slaps her. She screams for Julie. Billy disappears from their view but watches as Louise describes her meeting with the stranger. Julie sends her into the house, crosses to the star and holds it before exiting. Billy realizes he must do something to help Louise so he decides to attend the graduation.

Later that day, outside the schoolhouse, the students are receiving their diplomas. The principal announces the keynote speaker, the town doctor who looks quite similar to the Starkeeper. The doctor proceeds to tell the graduates the world is theirs. As he continues the group sings (You'll Never Walk Alone [Reprise]—Mixed Chorus), and Billy urges Louise to listen to the words of the song. She moves closer to the group and a classmate embraces her. Billy's last words on earth are to tell Julie he loves her. She smiles, feeling his presence, and Louise gains strength to face her future (Finale—Mixed Chorus).

NOTES ON THE PRODUCTION

The artistic and producing staff names were familiar to those who had seen *Oklahoma*! It is a brilliant work, with a dramatic book, memorable music and excellent characters. The show is worthy of a quality production and requires talented singers and actors in the leading roles. A careful analysis by the director, using the advice of Harold Clurman in his book *On Directing*, can only enhance the acting motivation. Many of the scenes, the "bench scene" in particular, where Billy and Julie talk of love, are subtly contrived yet add much to the character relationships. Billy's dramatic "Soliloquy" is one of the most character-developed songs ever written for the American musical stage. If the song/scenes are not fully acted and directed, much of the dramatic value of the script and the motivation of the characters is lost. This show, considered by some to be Rodgers and Hammerstein II's greatest achievement, needs three-dimensional characters to achieve its artistic potential. Anything less is not worthy of production.

The sets are not terribly complicated, if a practical carousel is not used. The costumes, period 1873–1888, may be the same throughout the show. The strong consideration here is the acting. The choreography may be complex or simple, but there should be at least one good male and female dancer in the company. The opening number is a classic musical theatre piece which establishes the main characters and situation and requires a lot of rehearsal.

SONGS OF SPECIAL INTEREST

"Geraniums in the Winder," tenor charm character song.

"If I Loved You," character development scene/song with lots of specifics to act. Good tenor/soprano duet for class example.

"What's the Use of Wond'rin'," semidramatic, resigned, female solo, good for class or small revue.

"When the Children Are Asleep," tenor/mezzo, charm duet, good for intimate revue.

"You're a Queer One, Julie Jordan" into "When I Marry Mr. Snow," excellent song to scene character study for mezzo/soprano. "Mr. Snow" is also an excellent story song with lots of images for acting.

"You'll Never Walk Alone," often used at graduations and in choral work. Dramatic, tearful scene into song. Good acting exercise in handling drama, 2 sopranos.

Instrumentation: 3 violins, viola, cello, bass, 4 reeds, 3 horns, 2 trumpets, 2 trombones, tuba, harp, percussion, piano/conductor; 2 piano score also available
Script: Knopf; Six Plays by Rodgers and Hammerstein
Selections: Williamson
Record: Decca
Rights: R & H

CHARLIE AND ALGERNON

Book and Lyrics: David Rogers (Based on the novel *Flowers for Algernon*, by Daniel Keyes)
Music: Charles Strouse

ORIGINAL PRODUCTION

Helen Hayes Theatre, September 14, 1980 (17 perf.)
Director: Louis Scheeder
Musical Director/Conductor: Liza Redfield
Choreographer: Virginia Freeman
Orchestration: Philip J. Lang
Principals: Charlie—P. J. Benjamin—tenor; Alice Kinnian—Sandy Faison—soprano; Dr. Strauss—Edward Earle—VTI; Dr. Nemur—Robert Sevra—VTI; Mrs. Donner—Nancy Franklin—mezzo; Little Charlie—Matthew Duda—VTNE; Lita—Loida Santos—mezzo; Frank—Patrick Jude—baritone; Charlie's Mother—Julienne Marie—alto/mezzo; Charlie's Father—Michael Vita—high baritone
Chorus and Smaller Roles: None.

SYNOPSIS

During the overture the lights rise on a New York playground where Charlie Gordon, a gentle thirty-year-old with the mind of an eight-year-old, is waiting for Alice Kinnian, his attractive thirty-year-old teacher. As the music continues Alice warmly greets him with a handshake. They cross the stage and voices of children are heard (I Got a Friend—Mixed Chorus). During the song, small mimed moments are presented to demonstrate Charlie's mental abilities and his reliance on Alice. She tells him to wait, crosses the stage and reads Dr. Strauss's letter. As she reads the letter the taped voice of Dr. Strauss of the Beekman University Clinic is heard. It seems that Charlie is being considered for an intelligence operation, the first ever performed on a human. Alice relates to the audience how she first met Charlie (Charlie Gordon—F Solo).

Charlie and Alice arrive at the office where Dr. Strauss, age fifty, and his associate Dr. Nemur, age thirty, explain their project to replace damaged brain tissue with a synthetic replica. They have successfully experimented on Algernon, a mouse, and are anxious to try out their technique on the perfect human candidate. Charlie endears himself to them (I Got a Friend—M Solo).

Alice leaves Nemur, Strauss and Charlie to begin the testing. One test consists of a maze which Charlie must race against Algernon. He loses and is emotionally upset because he wants to be like normal people so he will not be lonely. Alice, sensitive to his emotions, agrees to the operation.

The scene changes to a hospital room where Charlie is recuperating from the operation. Strauss hands him a diary to record his thoughts, but Charlie is depressed because he doesn't have instant intelligence. The doctors and Alice explain it will take time (Some Bright Morning—Sc to 3 M/F Quartet). During the number Charlie's mind develops and the days pass. He is making progress but wants to return to work at the bakery. As he expresses this desire the scene shifts to the bakery.

Mrs. Donner, the sixty-year-old bakery owner, excited to see Charlie, calls his co-workers, Frank and Lita (Jelly Doughnuts and Chocolate Cake—Sc to 2M/2F Quartet), who are astounded by his ability to work the mixing machine.

Charlie returns to the clinic to tell Nemur and Strauss, who are so amazed at his progress they race him against Algernon in the maze. He beats the mouse and gives Algernon a piece of Mrs. Donner's cake as a booby prize. He excitedly runs about singing (Hey, Look at Me—Sc to M Solo). As he exits with Algernon the song is completed by Alice, who is told of Charlie's development by Strauss.

The set becomes a classroom where Alice questions Charlie on various novels he has read, *War and Peace*, which he finished in one day, and *Dr. Jekyll and Mr. Hyde* (Reading—M Solo with Scenes Interspersed). Impressed with his growth, she tells him he has to learn to make his own decisions. He immediately asks her for a date but she refuses. An embarrassed Charlie runs off, leaving Alice to question their relationship (I Want No Surprises—Sc to F Solo).

The scene moves to a bar where Charlie has gone to celebrate with Frank and Lita (Midnight Riding—Sc to M/F Duet). The two teach Charlie how to dance, but he realizes he has sexual feelings and becomes embarrassed. Frank laughs behind Charlie's back but Charlie, who is still naive in the ways of the world, isn't aware of it.

The set clears but the incident with Frank forces him to recall specific moments from his past. "Little Charlie" comes in the room and tells his mother he played hide and seek with the kids, but they all ran off. His mother tries to comfort him (Dream Safe with Me—Sc to F Solo). Charlie watches and smiles at the memory of human contact. Dr. Strauss enters to compliment him on remembering his childhood. The scene continues as Charlie's father, a beaten-looking man in his thirties, enters and refuses to take Charlie to another specialist. His parents argue about his future; Charlie is upset and becomes violently ill. The scene fades and Charlie painfully tells Strauss that his memory is coming back in disjointed pieces. He sees his parents yell at him about touching girls, then he hears them talking about sending him away. His mother wants him out right away, for she is afraid of what his presence is doing to his sister. She finally forces the father to agree to let him go (Not Another Day Like This—Sc to M/F Duet).

Charlie is emotionally in pain, but the doctor interrupts his thoughts to tell him Mrs. Donner has come to call. She adds to his grief by telling him she doesn't want him to work for her anymore because he is a new person and doesn't fit in with the people at the bakery. The old Charlie was someone she could care for and she loved him, but the new Charlie no longer needs her (Somebody New—Sc to F Solo). It has been three months since the operation and although he has gained superior intelligence he still has no friends. He vows to make his own life and strongly soliloquizes (I'm Somebody New—M Solo).

In Act II Charlie has enrolled at the university and has become a linguist. His voice is heard on tape describing his mental growth. The lights rise on the street where Alice and Charlie are coming home from a movie. He tries to tell Alice how he feels about her but confesses that although he knows eight languages and has memorized the classics he can't express his emotional feelings (I Can't Tell You—Sc to M Solo). When he realizes she is frightened that his mind will outgrow hers, he kisses her and tells her he loves her. Admitting she loves him as well, she asks him to stay (Now—Sc to M/F Duet).

Alice and Charlie begin living together, which upsets Nemur, who demands that Charlie come to the office. It seems he wants Charlie and Algernon as examples at an examination for the grant renewal. Charlie agrees but sarcastically comments to Algernon and proceeds to remove the mouse from his cage. The two perform a vaudeville act during the number (Charlie and Algernon—Sc to M Solo).

In the conference room, Charlie tries to make the visitors realize that his emotions are very important and he is still human. When the doctor puts Algernon to the maze test, the mouse becomes confused and bites Nemur. This action leads the scientists to fear that the mouse has achieved its highest level of intelligence and may be regressing. Charlie, fearing he will also regress, realizes there are no options; if he is going to regress it will happen (The Maze—Sc to M Solo). Nemur, hoping that Charlie's superior intelligence will aid the project, invites him to join the research team.

Alice finds Charlie on the playground, reflecting on the fact that he has found a flaw in the surgery hypothesis. Knowing he will soon be losing his intelligence, he tells her they should break up, but she refuses and wants to stay with him as long as possible. He makes her promise she will go when he tells her, and she agrees to make the most of the time they have left (Whatever Time There Is—Sc to M/F Duet).

The scientists discover Charlie's theory is right; he is regressing. Strauss says they must try again, but Nemur is worried about the emotional impact on Charlie. The two, one leaning toward the humanist, the other strictly a scientist, examine the situation (Everything Was Perfect—Sc to M Duet).

Charlie enters carrying the dead Algernon in a box. He is visibly upset for he knows there is no reversal. While accusing Strauss of treating him as a laboratory experiment and not as a person, he begins to return to the "old" Charlie; his speech visibly slows and his vocal pattern becomes more hesitant. He snaps back to the present and vows to finish his research to help others. Charlie tries to concentrate, but all the people from his past encircle him and he screams out against them (Charlie—Sc to M Solo). He works to fight his past, finishes the report, and slowly walks to the playground.

Alice finds Charlie, who asks her to move out. She agrees, knowing his deterioration will be painful for both of them. They reaffirm their love (I Really Loved You—Sc to M/F Duet) and she walks out of his life.

It is September 21, six months after the operation. Charlie sits on the bench listening to a cassette of his voice outlining his future at the Warren Home. The voice slowly speaks of practicing his reading so he can be better than he was before the operation and urges Alice not to feel sorry for him because he had a lot of experiences he never would have had without the operation. He closes by asking her to put some flowers on Algernon's grave.

NOTES ON THE PRODUCTION

This sensitive treatment of the classic book is an extremely moving theatrical experience in the hands of a talented company and director. It is not expensive to produce if the sets and props are kept to a minimum. In fact, the show works better if the sets do not overpower the actors. It is a perfect community and regional theatre show, for it can only benefit from a smaller production geared for avid theatre patrons.

The show did not last long on Broadway, but this in no way reflects the quality of the piece. Broadway audiences traditionally support lighter fare with more emphasis on spectacle. This is a strong, emotional theatrical experience worthy of smaller productions.

The major problem that confronts anyone considering the production is the portrayal of Algernon. The acting version of the script contains a detailed explanation of training and working with a pet mouse; however, many people are unnerved by the thought of an uncaged mouse onstage and companies may want to consider a shadow puppet or medium-sized marionette to depict Algernon. Most professional puppeteers are able to successfully create and operate a puppet in a manner conducive to enhancing the mood of the play. It is not difficult for an audience to accept the convention of the puppet/mouse, and it makes the show much easier to produce.

SONGS OF SPECIAL INTEREST

"Charlie," dramatic solo, ending vocally demanding, possible for audition, tenor.

"Charlie and Algernon," good for class-style tenor vaudeville number, comic monologue in the interlude.

"Hey, Look at Me!" Audition potential for tenor, up tempo, exciting.

"I Really Loved You," romantic, tenor/soprano duet. It would be effective in a class situation to perform the number as it occurs in the show, when Charlie is still of superior intelligence, and then as his IQ returns to sixty-eight.

"The Maze," semidramatic, situation-oriented male solo, good for class work, excellent for transition work. Tenor.

"Whatever Time There Is," M/F duet, poignant, semidramatic. Soprano/tenor.

Instrumentation: 2 reeds, trumpet, horn, cello, harp, bass, percussion, piano/conductor
Script: DPS
Record: Under London title *Flowers for Algernon*, Original Cast Records.
Selections: NP
Rights: DPC

CHICAGO

Book: Fred Ebb and Bob Fosse (Based on the play *Chicago*, by Maurine Dallas Watkins)
Music: John Kander
Lyrics: Fred Ebb

ORIGINAL PRODUCTION

46th Street Theatre, June 3, 1975 (947 perf.)
Director and Choreographer: Bob Fosse
Musical Director: Stanley Lebowsky
Orchestration: Ralph Burns
Principals: Velma Kelly—Chita Rivera—alto; Amos Hart—Barney Martin—baritone; Roxie Hart—Gwen Verdon—mezzo/alto; Billy Flynn—Jerry Orbach—baritone; Matron—Mary McCarty—low alto; Mary Sunshine—M. O'Haughy—contra tenor
Chorus and Smaller Roles: 6M/6F

SYNOPSIS

Velma Kelly sets the mood of the Chicago gangland era (All That Jazz—F Solo to Chorus) where anything is acceptable, even murder. This opening leads into the story of two murderesses, Velma and Roxie Hart. Roxie, who has just made sensational news for killing her salesman lover, hopes her nebulous husband, Amos, will take the blame for her crime. She sings of her feelings for him in a Helen Morgan–style song (Funny Honey—F Solo). When Amos realizes that Roxie was having an affair with their furniture salesman, he refuses to take the rap and Roxie goes to jail. In the jail six other murderesses, among them Velma, sing of their crimes. Each girl carries her jail cell door, which she hands to another girl during her solo section. On the choral parts the girls form interesting choreographic configurations with their cell doors (Cell Block Tango—F Chorus).

The prison matron introduces herself Sophie Tucker–style, and explains the prison bribery system (When You're Good to Mama—L to F Solo). She advises Roxie to get lawyer Billy Flynn to take her case.

Billy, primarily interested in love and money (All I Care About—M Solo and F Chorus), agrees to take the case for $5,000 and calls in reporter Mary Sunshine for an interview. Mary Sunshine, who always finds good in everyone, is a natural to help Roxie (A Little Bit of Good—M Contra Tenor Solo).

Billy, deciding Roxie's case needs publicity, plans an interview with the press but decides Roxie's language is too abusive and crude for public sympathy. He sets her on his knee like a ventriloquist's dummy, and she mouths the words to the story he invents (We Both Reached for the Gun—M Solo and Mixed Chorus).

Roxie is such a big sensation with the public that she dreams of having her own vaudeville act (Roxie—L to F Solo). Velma, whose notoriety has taken second place to Roxie's, desperately tries to convince Roxie to do a sister act so she can capitalize on Roxie's fame. She describes the act (I Can't Do It Alone—F Solo), but Roxie prefers to perform solo.

Roxie's notoriety is short-lived when a pineapple heiress shoots her husband, and Roxie and Velma realize they can only rely on themselves (My Own Best Friend—Sc to F Duet; Period). Roxie, refusing to surrender her popularity, feigns pregnancy and regains fame among the press.

The second act becomes extremely vaudeville-oriented with short dialogue sequences before musical numbers.

Velma, astounded by Roxie's clever ploy, wonders why she didn't think of pregnancy herself (I Know a Girl—F Solo).

Roxie is a big hit with the press, who leave to write up her story. She removes her hospital garb and performs à la Eddie Cantor (Me and My Baby—F Solo). Amos, imagining he is the father of the baby, hopes that perhaps someone will at last notice him, and performs a Bert Williams–style number complete with a sad clown outfit and oversized shoes (Mister Cellophane—L to M Solo; Period). At the end of the number the spotlight doesn't even follow him off.

In a desperate attempt to regenerate Billy's interest in her case, Velma describes the perfect defense (When Velma Takes the Stand—F Solo and Mixed Chorus). Billy takes all her ideas and promptly uses them to defend Roxie. He prepares for the courtroom (Razzle Dazzle—M Solo and Mixed Chorus).

In the jail, Velma and the matron are listening to a radio broadcast describing the trial when Velma realizes that Roxie has stolen her defense ideas. The two women comment on the basic dishonesty in the world (Class—Sc to F Duet).

Roxie is acquitted, but receives little publicity. Realizing she won't be a big vaudeville headliner, she is dismayed (Nowadays—F Solo) but joins forces with Velma. The MC announces a duo vaudeville act and Velma and Roxie perform (Nowadays, RSVP, Keep It Hot—2F Duet).

NOTES ON THE PRODUCTION

The production is vaudeville-oriented and must be directed/choreographed by someone with an understanding of the people represented and the style of the era. The two main female roles require tremendous triple-threat performers with a lot of energy, charisma and physical stamina.

The show flows very quickly with locations loosely established by a simple set piece here and there. Because it is established as being "theatrical" in tone, the locations are oftentimes on a bare stage with the performers in tight lighting or spots.

Technically the emphasis must be on quality lighting and the bulk of technical monies should be spent in renting more instruments. The show is dance-oriented and should be well side lit to show off the movement to best advantage.

There are a few mildly risqué sections which can be cleaned up, but it is a better vehicle for adult performers than for younger ones.

SONGS OF SPECIAL INTEREST

"All That Jazz," club style, movement and sensuality emphasized, alto/mezzo.

"Cell Block Tango," excellent female chorus number with specific characters and monologues, great for showcase. Unfortunately, the music isn't in the vocal selections.

"Class," comic though slightly crude female duet, emphasis on character and situation, works in class situation, 2 altos.

"Mister Cellophane," low-key, poignant, heavily stylized, good for class, baritone.

"Razzle Dazzle," club potential, baritone.

"Roxie," excellent choice, when combined with monologue that precedes, for inhibited actress who needs to develop presentational style mezzo/alto.

"When You're Good to Mama," brassy solo for big-voiced character alto, audition potential.

Instrumentation: 3 reeds, 2 trumpets, 2 trombones, tuba/bass, percussion, violin, banjo, 2 keyboards
Script: SF
Selections: Chappell
Record: Arista
Rights: SF

COMPANY

Book: George Furth
Music and Lyrics: Stephen Sondheim

ORIGINAL PRODUCTION

Alvin Theatre, April 26, 1970 (690 perf.)
Director: Harold Prince
Choreographer: Michael Bennett
Musical Director: Harold Hastings
Orchestration: Jonathan Tunick
Principals: Robert—Dean Jones (replaced by Larry Kert one month later)—tenor; Joanne—Elaine Stritch—alto; David—George Coe—baritone; Kathy—Donna McKechnie—mezzo; April—Susan Browning—soprano; Sarah—Barbara Barrie—alto; Amy—Beth Howland—mezzo; Jenny—Teri Ralston—soprano; Harry—Charles Kimbrough—baritone; Larry—Charles Braswell—baritone; Marta—Pamela Myers—mezzo; Susan—Merle Louise—soprano; Peter—John Cunningham—baritone; Paul—Steve Elmore—tenor
Chorus: Possibly 4F who represent the vocal minority and sing from the pit.

SYNOPSIS

The set is a unit one where various locations are delineated by use of props. The play opens as Robert, a bachelor whose closest friends are married, is given a surprise party on his thirty-fifth birthday by these friends who feel he should find a wife (Company—Mixed Chorus).

Robert visits Sarah and Harry, a couple in daily competition with each other. Sarah, a student of karate, succeeds in throwing husband Harry, while Joanne, a brassy, blunt but always humorous neighbor, in another area of the stage comments on the scene (The Little Things You Do Together—F Solo to Mixed Chorus). Robert asks Harry if he ever regrets getting married, to which he responds that he is both sorry and grateful (Sorry-Grateful—M Solo and M Linear Chorus).

Robert then goes to Susan and Peter's apartment, where he discovers that the charming, feminine, Southern Susan and her Ivy League husband are divorcing. Robert, visibly shaken by the news, moves on to Jenny and David's.

He finds the stoned couple experiencing pot for the first time. It affects them quite differently: Jenny is babbling a mile a minute while David is nearly comatose. During the course of the conversation, Robert tells them he is ready to marry. In another area of the stage, April, Kathy and Marta, three of Robert's girlfriends, disbelievingly comment (You Could Drive a Person Crazy—F Trio).

The husbands, in their apartments, tell Robert of the various girls they've found for him (Have I Got a Girl for You—M Quartet), but he is looking for a girl with the same qualities of his friends, Sarah, Amy, Joanne and Jenny. He is convinced that he will find her (Someone Is Waiting—M Solo).

Marta, seated on a park bench, comments on life in New York (Another Hundred People—F Solo). Between verses the action focuses on Robert, who in the course of the song talks to his three girlfriends. April feels that she's boring and has nothing to say: Kathy leaves to marry a man she doesn't love because she is tired of playing at life; and Marta tells Robert he is uptight and not a part of the real New York.

In Amy's apartment, the flighty, nervous girl begs her fiancé Paul to call off the wedding. As she pleads, a girl in a white choir robe describes the event (Getting Married Today—F Solo with M/F Solos Interspersed).

The act ends in Robert's apartment with all the guests gathered as in the opening scene.

Act II begins one year later with Robert at his birthday party. Robert tells everyone he doesn't need birthday presents, for he has friends who are more important (Side by Side—What Would We Do Without You?—Mixed Chorus).

The couples leave and April enters in her stewardess uniform. She is apprehensive since it is her first visit to Robert's apartment. As they begin to neck, the wives worry about Robert's being alone (Poor Baby—Mixed Chorus). While Robert and April make love, their inner thoughts are expressed by Kathy's solo dance, which expresses their changing moods (Tick Tock Ballet—F Dance). Early the next morning, as April prepares to leave for her stewardess job, Robert unwittingly asks her to stay (Barcelona—Sc to M/F Duet). She initially refuses, but finally agrees.

In a short scene, Robert brings Marta to visit Peter and Susan, who are happily living together, despite their divorce.

At a private club, Joanne drunkenly comments to Robert and husband Larry about the women patrons who spend their days dining out (The Ladies Who Lunch—L to F Solo). Later, a very drunk Joanne accuses Robert of being weak and not committed to life. When Larry leaves to pay the tab, Joanne offers to take care of Robert. Her proposition forces Robert to realize that his friends have been taking care of him too long and he decides to find someone he can take care of (Being Alive—M Solo).

Once again, Robert's friends are gathered to give him a surprise birthday party, but he doesn't arrive. When they realize that he is not coming, they quietly extinguish the candles and leave him to lead his own life.

NOTES ON THE PRODUCTION

Tony Awards: 1971 Best Musical, Music and Lyrics, Book and Direction.

Those looking for good audition monologues may want to examine April's speech in Act I, as it shows character and is comedic.

A synopsis of *Company* doesn't do justice to the excellence of the script for the plot seems rather disjointed. The play traces the life of a New York bachelor who realizes his friends are jaded and not happy in their relationships.

The show may be inexpensively played on a small unit set with simple props to establish specific location where necessary, for example, a bed, to delineate Robert's bedroom. It is also possible to use one costume per actor and enhance Amy's wedding scene with a veil rather than a full costume. The cast is very balanced, which makes the show a good choice for community groups that want to give opportunities to a variety of their better female performers. Special attention should be given to casting April and Marta, who have precise, rapid diction numbers. One cast member must dance well. The only major company dance number, "Side by Side," requires basic soft-shoe.

SONGS OF SPECIAL INTEREST

"Being Alive," semidramatic, shows off tenor voice, possible last sixteen-bar audition. Good for club.

"Getting Married Today," good for class and precise diction, showcase material, soprano, mezzo, tenor, trio.

"The Ladies Who Lunch," character-oriented song for low alto, hard-nosed.

"You Could Drive a Person Crazy," F mezzo à la Andrews Sisters. Actresses must have individual characters and attitudes to make it work.

Instrumentation: 5 reeds, 3 trumpets, 2 horns, 2 trombones, 3 violins, 2 cellos, 4 female pit singers, electric keyboard/piano conductor, 2 guitars, bass, 2 percussion. Abbreviated instrumentation available
Script: Random, Ten Great Musicals of the American Theatre
Score: Valando
Record: Columbia
Rights: MTI

D

DAMES AT SEA

Book and Lyrics: George Haimsohn and Robin Miller
Music: Jim Wise

ORIGINAL PRODUCTION

Bouwerie Lane, December 20, 1968—moved to Theatre DeLys April 22, 1969 (575 perf.)
Director and Choreographer: Neal Kenyon
Musical Director: Richard J. Leonard
Principals: Mona Kent—Tamara Long—alto; Joan—Sally Stark—mezzo; Hennesey and Captain—Steve Elmore—baritone; Dick—David Christmas—tenor; Lucky—Joseph R. Sicari—baritone; Ruby—Bernadette Peters—mezzo/soprano
Chorus and Smaller Roles: None.

SYNOPSIS

The show opens onstage at a 42nd Street theatre in the early thirties, where Mona Kent, a temperamental Broadway star, is rehearsing her tap solo (Wall Street—F Solo). At the end of the solo part of the number, Mona takes her bow and Joan enters for the chorus part. But before Joan gets very far, Mona refuses to go on. Hennesey, the director, rushes onstage to calm his star as Joan stands by the proscenium and reacts à la Joan Blondell. Mona orders him to have her name in lights as big as those on the Wrigley billboard, but Hennesey begs her to ease up for his nerves are shot. She exits to her dressing room as Joan sarcastically calls her "the Lady Macbeth of 42nd Street."

Ruby, a stagestruck girl from Centerville, Utah, enters the theatre to apply for a job in the chorus, but Hennesey urges her to return home. Joan convinces Hennesey to give Ruby an audition, which he quickly does. Ruby rips off her raincoat to show her tap costume and begins tapping away. Hennesey hires her and exits. Joan offers her a room and goes off to get the starving girl a candy bar. As Joan leaves, Dick, a handsome sailor/songwriter, reminiscent of Dick Powell, arrives with Ruby's forgotten suitcase whose only contents are a pair of tap shoes. It is love at first sight (It's You—M/F Period Duet). They discover they both grew up in Centerville, Utah, she yearning to be a tap dancer and he a famous songwriter. At present, he is a sailor, but he promises to return to New York when his tour is up and take New York by storm.

Joan reenters with Ruby's candy bar, is introduced to Dick and takes Ruby off for a costume fitting as Dick pulls a small piano onstage from the wings and begins composing (Broadway Baby—M Solo). As he completes his composition Mona enters, and expresses interest in his songs and insists that he play one for her. She strikes a dramatic pose on top of the piano and proceeds to sing Dick's torch song as the company humorously acts out the lyrics behind a shadow curtain (That Mister Man of Mine—F Solo). At the end of the song she drags Dick off to her dressing room.

Moments later, Lucky, a sailor friend of Dick's, enters the theatre, spies Joan, a former girlfriend, and begs her to remember their past "good times." She refuses any further involvement without marriage (Choo Choo Honeymoon—Sc to M/F Duet). Joan introduces Ruby to Lucky as Mona enters with Dick and insists that Dick have lunch at her penthouse. Ruby is heartbroken and wants to return to Utah, but Joan takes her aside, bolsters her spirits, orders her to practice and leaves for a date with Lucky.

Dick returns from Mona's car to apologize for breaking his date with Ruby and begs her to understand that Mona could help his career. She beams in understanding and sits down to write President Roosevelt a letter about Dick and the U.S. Navy (Sailor of My Dreams—Sc to F Solo).

Joan, Ruby and Hennesey are rehearsing when Mona rushes on with Dick to insist that one of Dick's specialty songs be added to her show. The company performs the number (Singapore Sue—Mixed Chorus: Period) in the Cagney-Keeler style as Dick outlines how he envisions it being performed. An enormous Oriental idol appears as Chinese lanterns drop into place. Lucky becomes the hero of the show who falls in love with Sue, a Chinese bar girl who is eventually strangled by the idol.

Backstage, Ruby excitedly praises Dick as a loud noise of a building being demolished is heard. Hennesey gathers the company together to tell them the theatre is being torn down for a roller rink, which means the show won't go on. The chorus kids, led by Joan, attempt to cheer their director (Good Times Are Here—L to F Solo to Mixed Chorus). Dick suggests they perform the show on the battleship, but Lucky is convinced the Captain would refuse. Mona discovers she once dated their Captain and assures everyone things will be just fine. As the actors clear the stage, the bricks begin falling.

Act II opens with the Captain watching as Dick and Lucky swab the deck of their ship. During the song, the three girls appear in portholes and join in (Dames at Sea—M Duet to F Trio). The Captain, returning to reality, tells the boys there are no women allowed at sea. Mona grandly enters and informs the Captain that they are opening the show on his ship. He refuses but she calls him Kewpie Doll, and he remembers she was his Consuelo when they met and loved in Pensacola, Florida (The Beguine—Sc to F/M Period Duet). The Captain agrees to let the show be performed on the ship and exits to get the suddenly seasick Mona a bicarbonate of soda. Dick enters and Mona tells him she wants Hennesey to replace the old songs with new ones written by Dick. She quickly and passionately kisses the overwhelmed boy as Ruby enters, sees them and runs off. The Captain is jealous but Mona calms him and they exit.

Ruby, convinced that Dick cares for Mona, is heartbroken. She tearfully begins singing as the company enters in yellow slickers carrying plastic umbrellas covered with silver raindrops; as they move around her they open and close the umbrellas, which gives a rain and pattern effect (Raining in My Heart—F Solo to Mixed Chorus). At the end of the song Dick tells Ruby she is his girl (There's Something about You—Sc to M/F Duet).

The audience begins arriving and Mona, upset to discover that Ruby is in the show, orders her off the ship. Joan defiantly announces that the chorus kids, orchestra and everyone will walk out if Mona doesn't back off. Joan and Lucky, who are fed up with Mona's attitude, decide to make her seasick during one of the show's numbers by moving the spotlight back and forth, simulating the ship's movement (The Echo Waltz—Mixed Chorus). Mona rushes offstage to be violently ill as a distraught Hennesey agrees to let Ruby star in the finale and the girl becomes an overnight sensation (The Star Tar—F Solo to Mixed Chorus). As the number is being performed by the full company, two upstage panels turn to reveal mirrors which make the chorus appear more numerous.

Mona enters, sporting a diamond and quite recovered. The couples unite and the production ends with the girls in wedding dresses. As the ship's cannons roar, the entire stage is immersed in bubbles backed by a rainbow (Let's Have a Simple Wedding—Mixed Chorus).

NOTES ON THE PRODUCTION

A spoof on the Dick Powell, Joan Blondell, Ruby Keeler, James Cagney movie musicals of the thirties, with a special emphasis on *42nd Street*, the show contains many excellent period-style numbers that may be more accessible than their original counterparts. It should not be attempted without a choreographer and cast that tap-dance.

There are two sets; Act I occurs on an empty stage with a brick wall in the back and Act II on board ship. There are technical effects in both acts which are outlined in detail in the synopsis; they are not overly complex but are essential to give the show the "Busby Berkley" quality it demands.

Hennesey and the Captain may be played by one or two actors. The costume needs are minimal. The girls have rehearsal clothes, street dresses, stylized sailor uniforms, Chinese outfits, echo waltz dirndles, wedding overlays and raincoats. The men are in sailor uniforms, except for Hennesey, who is dressed in rehearsal clothes. All have raincoats. Lucky needs a Chinese outfit.

The props are easily obtained but will need to be "dazzled up" to give them a show biz look, i.e., buckets covered with aluminum foil, glitzy cigarette holders.

The smoke special effects may be achieved by fire extinguishers, flash powder or paper, and the bubbles by a child's bubble gun.

The show is a well-written spoof with catchy songs. It demonstrates the talents of the performers, is excellent dinner theatre fare and the first act works well as an entry in a one-act play competition. Schools that need to give more students an opportunity to gain performance experience have increased the size of the chorus in the following numbers: "Good Times Are Here to Stay," "Dames at Sea," "Raining in My Heart," "The Echo Waltz," and "Star Tar."

SONGS OF SPECIAL INTEREST

"Choo Choo Honeymoon," baritone/mezzo period duet, similar in style to "Shuffle off to Buffalo," tap duet.

"It's You," period tenor/mezzo duet performed in the Astaire/Rogers tradition, some dance.

"Good Times Are Here to Stay," small chorus, up tempo, energetic, requires interaction, good thirties-style song for class or revue.

"Singapore Sue," 3M/3F, comic, story song, strong style required, good for showcase.

"Wall Street," period alto tap solo.

Instrumentation: 2 pianos/percussion
Script: SF
Selections: Hastings
Record: Columbia
Rights: SF

DAMN YANKEES

Book: George Abbott and Douglass Wallop (based on *The Year the Yankees Lost the Pennant*, by Douglass Wallop)
Music and Lyrics: Richard Adler and Jerry Ross

ORIGINAL PRODUCTION

46th Street Theatre, May 5, 1955 (1,019 perf.)
Director: George Abbott
Choreographer: Bob Fosse
Musical Director: Harold Hastings
Orchestration: Don Walker
Principals: Lola—Gwen Verdon—mezzo; Joe Hardy—Stephen Douglass—tenor;
Mr. Applegate—Ray Walston—baritone; Van Buren—Russ Brown—baritone;
Gloria—Rae Allen—alto; Joe Boyd—Robert Shafer—baritone; Meg—Shannon
Bolen—mezzo; Sister—Jean Stapleton—soprano; Sohovik—Eddie Phillips—VTI;
Doris—Elizabeth Howell—VTI; Rocky—Jimmy Komack—VTI; Vernon—Albert Linville—VTI; Smokey—Nathaniel Frey—tenor
Chorus and Smaller Roles: 8M/8F minimum, who sing and dance.

SYNOPSIS

The play opens on the front porch and living room of a suburban home near Washington, D.C., where Joe Boyd, a middle-aged baseball fan, is so engrossed in a TV baseball game that his wife, Meg, is unable to converse with him. She and a chorus of wives comment on this seasonal problem (Six Months Out of Every Year—Mixed Chorus).

When Joe's favorite team, the Washington Senators, loses, Joe offers to give his soul to the Devil if he can be a hitter for the team. The Devil, appropriately named Applegate, arrives complete with red socks and tie, and agrees to get Joe on the Senators' team by making him twenty years younger and putting him in top physical condition. Joe writes a farewell note to his wife (Goodbye, Old Girl—M Solo), and leaves the house as a twenty-year-old baseball player named Joe Hardy.

In a corridor under the stands of the Washington Baseball Park, players Smokey, Rocky and Vernon are being told by their coach, Van Buren, to keep up their spirits and they'll beat the Yankees (Heart—M Quartet). Gloria, a reporter, arrives to interview the team as Applegate and Joe enter and introduce themselves to Van Buren. Van Buren agrees to give Joe a tryout and everyone heads for the field. A sound of a ball hitting a bat is heard and the lights rise on the dugout where the team is watching the offstage tryout. He surprises the team with his expertise in hitting and fielding. Van Buren offers him a contract. Gloria attempts to find out Joe's history, but his evasive and hesitating answers only make her more curious. She looks for an angle to describe this new baseball wonder and comes up with the name Shoeless Joe when she learns the shoes he had brought were too small. Gloria decides to write up an article that will make Joe famous (Shoeless Joe From Hannibal, Mo—F Solo and M Chorus).

By a billboard near the park, Sister and Doris, two of Meg's friends, wait with three teenagers to get autographs from the players.

In team owner Welch's oak-paneled office back room, Applegate, knowing he does not have full control over Joe's soul until September 24, decides to distract Joe with a beautiful redhead from Chicago named Lola. Joe isn't interested for he wants his wife (A Man Doesn't Know—Sc to M Solo). The reporters, led by Gloria, arrive and question Joe about the chances of the Senators' winning the pennant. Joe and Welch state they'll have the pennant sewed up by the 24th.

Lola waits on a bench near the billboard for Applegate, who outlines her job. She says it is no problem to seduce Joe for she is an expert (A Little Brains, a Little Talent—Sc to F Solo). Joe goes to his old house to convince Meg to rent him a room. He explains he will be away a lot, and they discuss what it's like to miss someone (A Man Doesn't Know [Reprise]—Sc to M/F Duet). Joe meets Meg's friends, Sister and Doris, ardent baseball fans who are excited to think Joe will be living in the neighborhood.

In the ballpark corridor, the players are commenting on the game while Gloria and Applegate discuss the fact that Joe is finally appearing on TV.

In the locker room, Van Buren tells the team to get some rest before their next game, and everyone gradually drifts off, leaving Joe with Applegate, who introduces him to Lola and leaves. Lola sexily vamps him (Whatever Lola Wants—Sc to F Solo). She drapes herself alluringly across his lap, but Joe puts her aside, apologizes and goes home to Meg. Applegate enters to chide her and she promises to try a new tactic. Several of Meg's friends rehearse a song to honor Joe (Heart [reprise]—3F/1M).

The curtain opens on a hotel ballroom, partially decorated to celebrate the success of the season. Joe enters and spies Lola, who explains she is now an official fan and sincerely starts to make friends with Joe. When Applegate arrives, she goes off to perform (Who Got the Pain?—M/F Duet). At the end of song Lola sees Applegate, who tells her he has spread a rumor that Joe is Shifty McCoy, the missing ballplayer known to have taken a bribe in the Mexican League. Joe is to be questioned by the baseball commissioner the following morning. Joe, upset that he might not be able to play in the pennant-deciding game, proclaims his innocence as the curtain falls.

Act II opens in the locker room; the team is worried about Joe but Rocky tells them to concentrate on the rules and think about the game (The Game—Sc to Small M Chorus).

On a bench in the park, Joe tells Meg everything will be over soon, but Meg tells him she believes in him the way she believes her husband will return (Near to You—Sc to M/F Duet). Applegate, who sees them, is depressed that he may lose Joe's soul and upset that Lola hasn't been of much help. He longs for the successes he had in the past and moves downstage as the curtains close behind him (Those Were the Good Old Days—L to M Solo; Vaudeville Style).

In the commissioner's office things look grim for Joe. He tries to leave before midnight to exercise his escape clause, but time runs out and he thinks he has lost his soul to Applegate.

Later that night, Lola meets Joe on a park bench to tell him that she has drugged Applegate so he won't awaken until after the game, which means that he can't stop Joe from winning. They both know the consequences of fighting Applegate, but decide to spend their last night together. They leave the park, enter a nightclub and begin enjoying life (Two Lost Souls—M/F Duet to Mixed Chorus Dance).

Applegate arrives at the game witth Lola, whom he has turned into an old hag. He angrily changes Joe into his former self, but Joe, as a middle-aged man, manages to catch the final out and the Senators win the American League Championship. Joe returns home to Meg, who eagerly greets him, promising to ask no questions (A Woman Doesn't Know—F Solo).

NOTES ON THE PRODUCTION

The show made Gwen Verdon a star and won the following Tony Awards: Best Musical 1956, Actress, Supporting Actor—Russ Brown, Actor—Ray Walston, Music, Book, Choreography, and Conductor/Musical Director.

This was Adler and Ross's second and last collaboration, for Jerry Ross died on November 11, 1955.

Much of the success of *Damn Yankees* relies on its two stars Lola and Applegate, who have to be charming and talented singer/actors. Gwen Verdon is a remarkable actress who has an appealing and distinctive style; she can portray sex and charm with humor and delight. This style is appreciated by men and women alike and it is important to cast a Lola with this charming yet vulnerable quality. The actress playing Lola must also dance well.

The show was written before the Washington Senators became the Minnesota Twins (1961). The director must decide whether to update the costumes and script or keep it as originally intended. Many of the costumes are baseball uniforms, and none are complex. The props are usual and not overly difficult to obtain. The show was written during the period of the In One scene/song, where there were one or more downstage curtains dropped to allow for set changes behind the curtain. The action was forwarded by either short songs or scenes performed in front of the drop. When the set change was over, the drop rose and a larger set was in view. *Damn Yankees* has many In One scenes which alternate among two billboards, a corridor under the stands, and the major set pieces; Joe's home, Welch's office, the locker room, Applegate's apartment, the commissioner's office, and a nightclub, all of which may be wagons or drops.

For theatres with limited fly space, the sets will need to be greatly adjusted from the original. It is possible to perform the show on a unit set with levels, small set pieces and props to delineate the different areas. The success of the show isn't as dependent on the physical look as other period shows are.

SONGS OF SPECIAL INTEREST

"A Little Brains, a Little Talent," character-oriented, kittenish sexy, good for overcoming movement problems, mezzo.

"The Game," good for showcase, good comic timing and strong characterizations required. Male chorus.

"Heart," comic characterizations required for this male quartet, showstopper, requires harmony, good for revue.

"Those Were the Good Old Days," vaudeville-oriented song and dance style, baritone.

Instrumentation: 5 reeds, 3 trumpets, 3 trombones, horn, percussion, guitar, 4 violins, viola, cello, bass, piano/conductor
Script: Random, Theatre Arts (Magazine) 11/56
Score: Frank
Record: RCA
Rights: MTI

A DAY IN HOLLYWOOD/A NIGHT IN THE UKRAINE: A MUSICAL DOUBLE FEATURE

Books and Lyrics: Dick Vosburgh; additional lyrics by Jerry Herman
Music: Frank Lazarus, additional music by Jerry Herman

ORIGINAL PRODUCTION

Golden Theatre, May 1, 1980-Moved to Royale June 17, 1980 (588 perf.)
Director and Choreographer: Tommy Tune
Co-Choreographer: Thommie Walsh
Musical Direction and Arrangements: Wally Harper
Principals for *A Night in the Ukraine*: Mrs. Pavlenko—Peggy Hewett—soprano; Carlo—Frank Lazarus—baritone; Gino—Priscilla Lopez—mezzo; Serge B. Samovar—David Garrison—high baritone; Nina—Kate Draper—mezzo; Constantine—Stephen James—tenor; Masha—Niki Harris—dancer; Sascha—Albert Stephenson—dancer
All of the above are in the revue *A Day in Hollywood*.
Chorus and Smaller Roles: None.

SYNOPSIS

A Day in Hollywood. At the rise of the curtain, six ushers in Period 1930s uniforms enter through the doors and invite the audience to escape life in Grauman's Movie Theatre (Just Go to the Movies—Mixed Chorus). They describe the stars of the day.

An usher steps forward to give a brief history of Sid Grauman's famous celebrity sidewalk. The overhead platform is revealed where the performers enact the historical event and the forthcoming song. Various film personalities' legs and feet are demonstrated by Niki and Albert: Dick Powell and Ruby Keeler, Charlie Chaplin, Sonja Henie on ice skates, Tom Mix, Judy Garland, Dracula,

Dorothy Lamour, Al Jolson, Mickey and Minnie Mouse. Priscilla and David perform below (Famous Feet—M/F Duet with Dancers).

Peggy enters in her usher costume, wearing a period wig or hat reminiscent of a Jeanette MacDonald character. She carries a life-size cardboard cutout of Nelson Eddy in his Mountie uniform and tells the audience how much she despises her supposedly romantic film partner (Nelson—F Solo).

At the end of the number, Stephen comments on the Hollywood hopefuls, young girls who come from all over America. Priscilla enters to tell the story of a small-town usher who went to Hollywood, made a film which flopped and became an usher in the film capitol (The Best in the World—F Solo).

The company enacts the stories behind the method various composing teams used to write their hit songs. Stephen tells the audience that the theme song for Grauman's Chinese Theatre was a Richard Whiting standard, "Hooray for Hollywood." The company pays tribute to Richard Whiting (It All Comes Out of the Piano—M Solo). The number segues to highlighted Whiting songs with the company singing and playing various instruments (Richard Whiting Medley— Mixed Chorus).

Frank, at the piano, describes a favorite movie setting of the thirties, the cruise ship. He reminisces as "Thanks for the Memories" is played and sung by the onstage "Bob Hope and Shirley Ross" and the overhead stage shows a dancing Astaire and Rogers.

Frank leaves the piano to join the other five ushers who are wearing tap shoes. He describes the censorship rules that set the guidelines for the 1930 moviemakers (Doin' the Production Code—Mixed Chorus).

They invite the audience for a preview of their next attraction starring the Marx Brothers (*A Night in the Ukraine*—Mixed Chorus).

A Night in the Ukraine.   The curtain rises on the morning room of a Russian villa sometime before the Revolution. There is a grand piano stage left, a chaise longue stage right, an easel, two chairs and a desk.

As the lights rise, Masha, the maid, and Sascha, a manservant, are busily working when Carlo enters carrying a large painting of Mrs. Pavlenko, a widow who is going to her first party since the death of her husband eighteen months before.

Mrs. Pavlenko enters to tell everyone she isn't going to the party as she is still too grief-stricken over the loss of her husband. Gino, looking like Harpo Marx, rushes on honking a horn and begins to chase Masha. After exchanging visual comedy routines with Carlo, he succeeds in terrifying Mrs. Pavlenko, who exits for her nerve tonic. Carlo begins playing the piano as Gino waters a fake hand which comes to life and proceeds to tickle him.

Serge B. Samovar, a lawyer, enters; he walks, acts and talks like Groucho Marx. He and Carlo go through typical comedic routines, complete with typical one-line comedy gags, as they introduce themselves (Samovar, the Lawyer— Sc to M Solo).

Samovar has come to see Mrs. Pavlenko to get the money her dead husband owed for legal services. Carlo replies that his job is to keep people from her, but Samovar confuses him, in typical Marx Brothers style, and they both exit as Mrs. Pavlenko enters with her daughter, Nina. The two are talking about Nina's prospective husband, Baron Trofimov, whom she doesn't love. Mrs. Pavlenko scoffs at the word *love* and leaves a disheartened Nina alone to dream of true romance (Just Like That—F Solo). Carlo rushes in to accompany her on the piano.

As the number ends Constantine, the coachman, enters with some legal papers. He bumps into Nina; they turn and realize they are in love. He tells her he is a coachman who dreams of being a playwright, but rejection by the Moscow Art Theatre has forced him to give up. She encourages him and they openly admire each other (Just Like That [Reprise]—Sc to M/F Duet). Constantine asks her to elope and they dreamily exit.

Mrs. Pavlenko hears strains of the Ukraine theme, which reminds her of her dead husband, but her sad mood is interrupted by Samovar who, cigar in hand, climbs on top of the piano meowing like a cat. After several insulting remarks, which Mrs. Pavlenko doesn't notice, Samovar asks her for the money Nicholas owed. She refuses to pay him until her steward returns from town. He doubts she has the money and insults her; she huffily exits as Carlo enters for some slapstick comedy with Samovar, who later exits.

Gino enters whistling for attention; and after several minutes of miming, he finally gets the message to Carlo that Samovar is to be thrown out.

Constantine reenters with Nina, who goes to get her suitcase. Carlo and Gino are amazed that he is marrying Nina. He is so pleased by the confidence she has given him to rewrite his play that he begins reading to them from the script. Nina enters and thinks the lines he is speaking relate to her. Thinking he is only after her money, she throws him out and bursts into song (Again—F Solo). Constantine reenters but Nina slaps him and rushes off, and he continues the song.

Gino enters riding a broken-down bicycle, which he falls from. After several comic turns with the bike where he offers it a carrot, listens to its heart and plays a tune on the spokes (Gino's Harp Solo—Music Only), he leaves.

A distraught Constantine tells Samovar he is going back to Moscow immediately and leaving Samovar behind. Samovar, failing to stop him, spies the play and begins reading but is interrupted by Nina, who realizes Constantine was only reading dialogue which she thought was about their relationship. When she discovers Constantine is leaving, she bursts into tears and rushes from the room.

Carlo and Gino attempt to throw Samovar out, but he outwits them by asking Gino to enact what will happen to Samovar; the scene becomes quite bizarre and physical. Mrs. Pavlenko arrives to discover everyone hurling flowers at her portrait. She sends Carlo for help as Samovar challenges her to a duel which she readily accepts (A Duel! A Duel!—M/F Duet with 2M Needed for Staging). She exits for the pistols.

When Carlo tells the impoverished Samovar of Mrs. Pavlenko's wealth, he decides to marry her for her money and begins wooing her (Natasha—M Solo with F and M Needed for Staging). She agrees to his proposal and falls into his arms. Constantine and Nina are reunited, and Sascha and Masha enter for the finale (A Night in the Ukraine—Mixed Chorus).

NOTES ON THE PRODUCTION

Tony Awards: Choreography and Featured Actress (Priscilla Lopez).

This four male, four female revue and Marx Brothers spoof is excellent summer theatre fare for a multitalented company. The original music, coupled with the nostalgic tunes, makes for a rewarding musical experience. The Marx Brothers sequence is enjoyable, even for non–Marx Brothers fans. In fact, it may be more enjoyable for non–Marx Brothers fans, for it highlights some of their famous routines in capsule form.

The revue section of the two one-acts was performed in front of six revolving doors which represent the lobby doors of Grauman's Chinese Theatre in Hollywood. The doors could totally swing from red to black, and each door contained a circular window, at face height, which opened and closed. This simple set allowed for various visual effects. A platform above the doors, usually covered by a traveler, was effectively used for the overhead "Famous Feet" number. The remaining setting consisted of two benches, a grand piano, and an art deco style bar; all represented the lobby.

The costumes are not complicated, although there are a number of legged specialty ones needed for the "Famous Feet" sequence. The set used in the Broadway production is thoroughly detailed in the acting version of the script and should be utilized.

The show calls for talented singers who tap-dance, an excellent choreographer and a director with a flair for comedy. Although most of Tommy Tune's clever staging is outlined in the acting libretto, the dance numbers must be precise and clean in order to believably imitate the stars they are to portray.

It is possible to perform *A Night in the Ukraine* as a one-act musical and it is a good choice for a one-act play competition. However, practically every comic line is enhanced by a sight gag prop, and all of Gino's bits rely on the visual gag. The props are relatively common but are time-consuming to obtain and the actors will need them in beginning rehearsals because they greatly affect the comic timing.

SONGS OF SPECIAL INTEREST

"The Best in the World," story song, mezzo, good acting exercise.
"Just Go to the Movies," good for opening a revue about films, mixed chorus.
"Nelson," comic number for a soprano.

Instrumentation: 2 pianos, 1 piano onstage. Sound tape available from publisher
Script: SF
Selections: Jewel
Record: ORG
Rights: SF

DO I HEAR A WALTZ?

Book: Arthur Laurents (Based on Arthur Laurents's *The Time of the Cuckoo*)
Music: Richard Rodgers
Lyrics: Stephen Sondheim

ORIGINAL PRODUCTION

46th Street Theatre, March 18, 1965 (220 perf.)
Director: John Dexter
Choreographer: Herbert Ross
Musical Director: Frederick Dvonch
Orchestration: Ralph Burns
Principals: Leona Samish—Elizabeth Allen—mezzo; Signora Fioria—Carol Bruce—alto; Eddie Yaeger—Stuart Damon—baritone; Jennifer Yaeger—Julienne Marie—mezzo; Renato Di Rossi—Sergio Franchi—tenor; Giovanna—Fleury D'Antonakis—mezzo; Mr. McIlhenny—Jack Manning—baritone; Mrs. McIlhenny—Madeline Sherwood—mezzo
Chorus: 2M, 2M children minimum.

SYNOPSIS

The play opens in Venice where Leona Samish, an attractive romantic, marvels at the sights. With a suitcase in each hand, she sings about the miracle of a city floating on water, the enchanting gondolas and pigeons fluttering about the square. A young boy, Mauro, offers to take her to Signora Fioria's and carry her suitcases. Leona is so busy looking at everything she naively plunges into the canal but nothing can dampen her excitement (Someone Woke Up—F Solo).

She arrives at the Pensione Fioria to discover that the guests are Americans. The forty-year-old owner, Signora Fioria, explains how pleased she is at their arrival (This Week Americans—Sc to F Solo). After brief introductions, the guests tell how they came to Italy and reveal the inconveniences of flying (What Do We Do? We Fly—3F/2M Quintet). Leona is left alone to muse over her loneliness, which is amplified by the romantic atmosphere of Venice.

On a morning shopping trip, Leona meets Renato Di Rossi, a forty-year-old owner of a curio shop. When she expresses interest in an antique goblet, Renato enthusiastically expresses admiration (Someone Like You—Sc to M Solo). He gives her a lesson in antique shopping (Bargaining—Sc to M Solo) and manages to obtain her Venice address.

That night, Leona ventures into the Piazza San Marco, where she orders drinks for two at a cafe. She knows no one will join her but doesn't want anyone to think she is alone (Here We Are Again—F Solo). Di Rossi approaches her, sees the two drinks and graciously retreats.

Di Rossi arrives at the Pensione and charms Leona by giving her two precious antique Italian goblets. Mr. and Mrs. McIlhenny arrive and show Leona six of the same goblets, and Leona is outraged that Di Rossi tried to deceive her. After the McIlhennys leave, Di Rossi insists that the goblets he gave her were originals, the others copies. He asks her out and she considers the prospect (Thinking—Sc to M/F Duet). The two agree to meet later.

Eddie Yaeger, a married playboy guest at the Pensione, flirts with Fioria, who is very interested in some late-night romance. Giovanna, Fioria, Eddie and the McIlhennys prepare for the evening (Here We Are Again [Reprise]—Mixed Chorus).

As Leona relaxes at the Pensione garden awaiting Di Rossi's entrance, Vito, a young boy, arrives with the message that Di Rossi will be late. Leona finds out that Vito is really Di Rossi's son and is appalled to think she is dating a married man. Jennifer, after fighting with Eddie, invites Leona to a movie and the two exit. Eddie and Fioria, under the guise of a language lesson to Giovanna, arrange for an assignation in a gondola (No Understand—Sc to 2F/M Trio). Di Rossi arrives and forces Leona, who has returned in time to see Eddie and Fioria's meeting, to make the most of their mutual attraction (Take the Moment—Sc to M Solo). She carefully listens and accepts his offer for an evening on the piazza.

In Act II after a night alone at the movies, Eddie's wife Jennifer, used to his infidelity, hopes that he will return to her (Moon in My Window—F Trio). Fioria and Leona echo the same song from their windows.

Eddie and Jennifer decide to leave Italy in order to save their failing marriage (We're Gonna Be All Right—Sc to M/F Duet).

Di Rossi arrives to bring Leona a garnet necklace, which she can't refuse because she suddenly hears a waltz and knows she is no longer afraid of involvement (Do I Hear a Waltz?—F Solo). She tells Di Rossi she must soon return to America, but he begs her to remain in Venice (Stay—Sc to M Solo).

Before she leaves, Leona decides to throw a party for everyone at the Pensione. They all remark on Leona and Di Rossi's happiness, not aware that he is a married man (Perfectly Lovely Couple—Mixed Chorus).

Leona is angered to discover that Di Rossi didn't pay for the necklace. When a man arrives at the party to collect, she gives Di Rossi the money but vents her anger on all those at the party. She realizes too late that most of her distrust of Di Rossi stemmed from distrust of herself. She thanks him for everything he has done for her (Thank You So Much—Sc to M/F Duet) and returns to America ready to begin again with someone new.

NOTES ON THE PRODUCTION

Some interesting facts about the show can be found in the book *Sondheim and Co*. The songs are good to study in a class situation, and the show might be best presented in capsulized form as part of a dinner theatre offering. It will appeal to audiences who are curious about a Richard Rodgers/Stephen Sondheim collaboration but otherwise will probably not be a large box office draw.

Companies wishing to produce the essence of the show without the expense of re-creating Venice or using a large Broadway-style ensemble may want to stage the production on a very small stage. Making his a more intimate musical without the use of a full chorus would help center on the psychological ramifications of the characters.

SONGS OF SPECIAL INTEREST

"Bargaining," tenor solo, potential for audition if shortened. It allows for varied characterizations.

"Someone Woke Up," mezzo, up tempo solo, possible for audition, some movement, shows warmth and abandon.

"What Do We Do? We Fly," comic, mixed chorus, clever lyrics, good for beginning choreographer.

Instrumentation: 4 reeds, 2 trumpets, 3 trombones, percussion, harp/celeste, guitar/mandolin, 4 violins, 2 violas, 2 cellos, bass, piano/conductor
Script: Random
Score: Williamson
Record: Columbia
Rights: R & H

DO RE MI

Book: Garson Kanin
Music: Jule Styne
Lyrics: Betty Comden and Adolph Green

ORIGINAL PRODUCTION

St. James Theatre, December 26, 1960 (400 perf.)
Director: Garson Kanin
Choreographer: Marc Breaux and Deedee Wood
Musical Director: Lehman Engel
Principals: Kay Cram—Nancy Walker—alto; Hubie Cram—Phil Silvers—baritone; Fatso O'Rear—George Mathews—VTI; Skin Demopoulos—George Givot—VTI; Brains Berman—David Burns—VTI; Thelma Berman—Marilyn

Child—VTNE; Tilda Mullin—Nancy Dussault—soprano; John H. Wheeler—
John Reardon—tenor
Chorus and Smaller Roles: 12F/12M, some doubling required.

SYNOPSIS

Kay Cram, a patient woman in her late forties, waits in a seedy nightclub for
her husband, Hubie (Waiting, Waiting—F Solo), a middle-aged wheeler-dealer.
He arrives in time to witness "The Swingers," a female singing group, pay a
tribute to the head of the juke box industry—John Henry Wheeler (All You Need
Is a Quarter—F Trio to F Chorus). During the song, Hubie moves his chair in
front of Wheeler to get away from the confusion of sitting near the kitchen. Two
waiters pick up Hubie and his chair and carry him out. Kay follows.

Later that night in the Crams' bedroom, when Hubie tells Kay he has to find
a new scheme which will make him rich and important, she implores him to be
satisfied with a job in her father's laundry (Take a Job—Sc To M/F Duet). She
wishes him Happy Anniversary and urges him to be happy, but he remembers
his former hoodlum friends Fatso O'Rear, Skin Demopoulos and Brains Berman
and decides to con them into a partnership. He rushes out the door leaving Kay.

In Fatso's Ice Cream Parlor in Union City, New Jersey, the teenagers are
dancing to the juke box (All You Need Is a Quarter—F Dance). Fatso starts to
lock up, but Hubie enters extolling the honesty of a juke box venture (It's
Legitimate—Sc to M Duet). Fatso agrees and the music continues as Brains and
Thelma Berman are seen in front of a chicken house. Fatso and Hubie mime
their scheme to Brains, who joins them and waves farewell to Thelma. The three
move to a box at the Hialeah race track where they enlist Skin in their business
(It's Legitimate—Sc to M Quartet). The number ends as they move to their new
business on Broadway, Music Enterprise Associates, Inc. (MEA).

When John Henry Wheeler, the juke box magnate, hears of the new company
Hubie has formed, he tells a reporter he is unworried by this new competition
because he knows the formula for records that sell (I Know about Love—M
Solo).

In a Greenwich Village Zen Pancake Parlor, Hubie, Fatso, Skin and Brains
try to put some muscle on proprietor James Russell Lowell III, a Japanese devotee
who promptly karates Brains. Everyone is overwhelmed including waitress Tilda
Mullin.

In the MEA offices, Brains tells a ferrety-looking individual, Wolfie, that he
wants out, but Hubie tells his partners the new record promotion plan isn't
working because they have no talent to perform new songs. He is unable to find
a singer he can afford until he remembers the waitress he heard singing at the
pancake house. After auditioning several untalented performers, a plump Marsha
Denkler, a hillbilly singer named Irving Feinberg, and a German girl playing
the concertina, he searches for Tilda (Audition—F/M Solo Sections).

Hubie auditions Tilda at the pancake house and convinces her that she can be
a sensation (Cry Like the Wind—F Solo/Ambition—Sc to M/F Duet). When

she discovers that people get paid for singing and realizes she could financially help the children back home, she agrees. His hunch pays off because Tilda Mullin, waitress turned singer, is a tremendous success, as evidenced by an announcer reeling off her top forty standing and a reporter commenting.

In an empty recording studio, Kay greets Hubie by telling him she is busy buying things he can't hock when this deal falls through. The musicians and partners enter for the recording session, followed by Wheeler and the Swingers. Tilda enters and sees Wheeler at the same time he notices her. There is a chord as fireworks pop. They are immediately infatuated (Fireworks—M/F Duet). Fatso tells Wheeler to get out of their recording studio and he leaves with the Swingers. Hubie busies himself with the orchestra and demonstrates how to play the various instruments. Everyone watches in amazement.

At the Imperial Room, Tilda is the headliner with a girl backup chorus (What's New at the Zoo—F Chorus). Hubie's gangster-type partners, who discover Wheeler dancing with Tilda (Asking for You—M Solo), are all for roughing him up, but Hubie convinces them to let him take care of the matter. He crosses the room to Wheeler's table, where he proceeds to tell Wheeler about all the old movies on TV featuring Hollywood tough guys. He hopes that Fatso, Skin and Brains think he is forcefully telling Wheeler off (The Late, Late Show—L to M Solo with Imitations of Cagney, Bogart, etc.). Hubie's plan fails when his partners, unable to restrain themselves, get into a brawl and are thrown out of the club. Kay watches Hubie carried off as the curtain falls on Act I.

Act II opens in the Crams' bedroom. Hubie is reading a newspaper article about Kay's former boyfriend, who is now a successful lawyer. Kay tries to bolster his spirits and assure him that she wouldn't want to be married to anyone else (Adventure—Sc to M/F Duet).

In Wheeler's office, Wheeler asks Tilda to marry him (Make Someone Happy—Sc to M/F Duet) and she happily agrees.

The scene moves to the upgraded office of MEA. The partners are upset that Tilda has married Wheeler. Fatso calls in a large psychopathic thug, and Kay worries that things are going too far.

At a Senate investigation committee hearing, the crowd wonders who is "Mr. Big" of the juke box racket (VIP—Mixed Chorus). Fatso, Brains and Skin subsequently take the stand and finger Hubie (VIP—Three M Solos).

The Senate investigation ends Hubie's involvement in the entertainment business. He realizes how empty and phony his life has been and soliloquizes about his failure (All of My Life—M Solo). In the court chambers, where Hubie sits alone contemplating his future, Kay arrives to convince him it isn't too late to start over. Finale.

NOTES ON THE PRODUCTION

The book, occasionally thin, is a good vehicle for two performers who have the qualities of Phil Silvers and Nancy Walker. Some of their duets are excellent studies in character comic timing and Hubie's "Late, Late Show" is a brilliant audition piece for a performer who can handle impressions of old film "tough guys." There are a number of good roles for the gangsters. The part of Tilda, in the hands of a good actress singer, is a talent showcase. The script, with prudent editing of the extraneous material, could be a highlight of any company's season. Some of the scenes, products of the times they were written for, are unnecessarily "big."

The costumes, many of which are for the club chorus girls, are basically contemporary and not complicated to obtain. The sets may be trimmed and combined; for example, the opening nightclub and the Imperial Room, where Tilda eventually performs, could be the same. The ice cream parlor, chicken ranch, and box at Hialeah aren't absolutely necessary as the scenes are very rapid and have an In One quality. The scenes may be played in front of a curtain with simple props to denote location. The proposal scene in Wheeler's office may be located elsewhere to save building a set that is only used for one short scene.

The chorus, considered in terms of the unedited script, is rather large. It is possible to trim it in half if the larger scenes are minimized and the size of the stage is smaller.

SONGS OF SPECIAL INTEREST

"All You Need Is a Quarter," F trio, comedic spoof on singing group of late fifties, good for movement.

"All of My Life," baritone, dramatic solo for a character actor, excellent for dramatic intensity.

"Ambition," up tempo, energetic, baritone con man and soprano, exciting, good for showcase.

"Adventure," comic alto/baritone duet with comedienne featured. Nice actable specifics that show off comic flair. Needs abandon.

"I Know about Love," tenor solo, audition potential, shows range and male strength.

"The Late, Late Show," excellent for an audition. Baritone. Shows characterization skills, comedic flair and acting ability.

"Take a Job," comic counterpoint duet for baritone and alto character actors.

Instrumentation: 3 violins, cello, bass, 5 reeds, horn, 3 trumpets, 3 trombones, 2 percussion, piano/conductor
Script: NP
Score: Chappell
Record: RCA
Rights: TW

E

EVITA

Music: Andrew Lloyd Weber
Lyrics: Tim Rice

ORIGINAL PRODUCTION

Broadway Theatre, September 25, 1979 (1,568 perf.)
Director: Harold Prince
Choreographer: Larry Fuller
Musical Director: Rene Wiegert
Orchestration: Hershy Kay and Andrew Lloyd Weber
Principals: Eva—Patty LuPone—mezzo with low range; Che—Mandy Patinkin—tenor; Peron—Bob Gunton—baritone; Peron's Mistress—Jane Ohringer—soprano; Eva (matinees)—Terri Klausner—mezzo; Magaldi—Mark Syers—tenor
Chorus and Smaller Roles: 12M/12F, all with good voices. Six children's voices.

SYNOPSIS

The play opens in a Buenos Aires film theatre on July 26, 1952, where a movie is being shown; the screen blurs to show images of tragic faces as an announcement is made that Eva Peron has died. Her funeral, equal to that of any Pope, begins as the chorus moves around the coffin (Requiem for Evita—Mixed Chorus). A young revolutionary student, named Che, comments on the insaneness in Argentina over this woman, Eva Peron (Oh What a Circus—M Solo). The crowd continues lauding her as a young girl moves forward and sings the words of the dead Evita (Don't Cry for Me Argentina—F Solo). During the entire funeral sequence, the movie screen depicts the tragic faces of members of the company in mourning.

The screen flies out and is replaced by black strips of cloth. Acting as narrator, Che comments on her life.

The scene flashes back to 1934 and a nightclub in Evita's village, where Magaldi, a man of mediocre talent, is performing (On This Night of a Thousand Stars—M Solo). After a brief affair, Evita asks Magaldi to take her to Buenos Aires, but he is hesitant (Eva Beware of the City—M/F Duet and Mixed Chorus). She relentlessly convinces him to take her to the city (Buenos Aires—F Solo and Dancers). Upon arriving in Buenos Aires she promptly dumps him, for she has set her sights on men who will further her dreams of an acting career. The screen shows Buenos Aires scenes, and Che comments on various lovers that Evita uses as she moves up the social ladder (Goodnight and Thank You—M/ F Duet and M Chorus).

The year is 1943, and five military leaders are seated in a rocking chorus. As they stand to pray, one rocker is removed, leaving one general without a chair and forcing him to leave. The song quickly denotes the "rocky" condition of the Argentinean government in the early forties (The Art of the Possible—M Chorus with F Solo). During the generals' song, Eva, who is now a broadcast news reporter, comments on an earthquake tragedy in Argentina.

At a concert for earthquake victims (Charity Concert—Mixed Chorus), Eva, fascinated by the people's reaction to Peron, steps away from her escort and stands in Peron's shadow for a brief moment. As the two come together, she tells him that she would be good for him (I'd Be Surprisingly Good for You— M/F Duet).

She enters Peron's apartment, where his sixteen-year-old mistress is waiting, packs the girl's things, gives her a fur coat and evicts the girl from the room and Peron's life. The mistress, alone in the hall, contemplates her situation (Another Suitcase in Another Hall—F Solo).

The upper class of Argentina and the military despise Eva's influence over Peron and openly criticize her behavior amongst themselves (Peron's Latest Flame—Mixed Chorus).

Eva is determined that Peron will be President and she plots his campaign, which relies on the workers' support and the help of the secret police (A New Argentina—M/F Duet to Mixed Chorus). The scene moves from their bedroom to the streets where the workers, with union signs, take up the cry. The number builds as men enter with torches, and the act ends on a hopeful note.

Act II opens, it is June 4, 1946. Peron is proclaimed President (On the Balcony of the Casa Rosada—M Duet/Chorus) and Eva receives greater accolades from the crowd than Peron does. She tells the crowd of her need for their love and implores them to stand by her (Don't Cry for Me Argentina—F Solo). The reception is overwhelming.

In Eva's dressing room, Che comments on the contradictions that are Eva Peron (High Flying Adored—M/F Duet). She ponders the distance she will fall if Peron loses power but begins to adorn herself with jewels and elegant designer clothes, for she is on a pinnacle and must enjoy it while she is there (Rainbow High—F Solo and Chorus).

Eva and Peron tour Europe, beginning in fascist Spain, where they are given a warm welcome (Rainbow Tour—2M/1F Trio and Mixed Chorus), and ending in France and Italy with cool receptions. She angrily returns to Argentina determined to concentrate all her efforts on domestic affairs.

The society set of Argentina continues to criticize her behavior (The Actress Hasn't Learned the Lines You'd Like to Hear—M/F Duet and Mixed Chorus).

Eva sets up a foundation, and Che comments on how the money enlisted for the poor fattens the Perons' Swiss bank accounts (And the Money Kept Rolling In (and Out)—M Solo and Mixed Chorus). The people, however, consider her a saint (Santa Evita—Mixed Chorus).

Che confronts Eva, questioning her motives (Waltz for Eva and Che—M/F Duet). She realizes she is becoming ill and begs for 100 more years. The country is bankrupt, the newspapers have been censored, and the generals are angry about Eva's meddling. Peron attempts to defend her (She Is a Diamond—M Solo and M Chorus).

Peron goes to her bedroom to inform Evita that the generals and the Argentinian aristocrats are anxious to be rid of her. She responds by telling him that she must be Vice President (Dice Are Rolling—M/F Duet), but the army and her encroaching illness are too strong for her. She goes to a radio broadcast, physically supported by two men, to announce to the citizens that she must renounce all honors and titles. She momentarily gains her strength and stands free of the two men (Eva's Final Broadcast—M/F Duet).

Eva's life passes before her (Montage—Mixed Chorus)—the end is near. She is taken to the hospital where she ponders her life and hopes that her actions will be understood by the people of Argentina (Lament—M/F Duet). The moment she dies, the embalmers move around to preserve her image for posterity.

NOTES ON THE PRODUCTION

The musical won most of the possible 1980 Tony Awards: Best Musical, Actress, Featured Actor (Mandy Patinkin), Score, Book, Light design, and Direction.

The New York production opened to mixed reviews but the success of the show was nearly guaranteed by its hit record album and the added hype of the sold-out London production.

The show is an interesting study of an individual who rose to international acclaim. It requires three strong singer/actors in the roles of Eva, Peron, and Che. The vocal demands on Eva are tremendous and it would be best to double cast this role, especially if a company plans two shows in one day. The voices need to be heavily miked to balance the rock quality of the music. Money must be set aside for individual mikes for the principals and general mikes for the stage.

Technically, the show may be stark or overblown; it is easily played on a bare stage with minimal set pieces to establish the location, or it may be on a unit stage with levels which represent various areas. It helps to have an elevated platform for the political speeches so the chorus can be at a lower level without blocking the stars.

The chorus portrays common citizens, aristocrats and a variety of military types and will need two to three costumes depending on their roles.

Props are used to establish location and should represent the social status of their owners, especially if the stage doesn't lend itself to establishing specific location. The props aren't terribly difficult to obtain.

SONGS OF SPECIAL INTEREST

"Waltz for Che and Eva," tenor/mezzo confrontation, good for character study.

"I'd Be Surprisingly Good for You," baritone/mezzo. Interaction and reaction are the strong points.

"Another Suitcase in Another Hall," emphasis on mood and character, no movement needed, mezzo to soprano range.

"A New Argentina," establishes character, relationship and reaction also important, builds to an exciting chorus. Showcase.

Instrumentation: 5 reeds, 2 horns, 2 trumpets, trombone, 2 violins, cello, bass, 2 guitars (electric and acoustical), harp, 2 percussion, 2 keyboard (Yamaha, synthesizer, Propatt), piano/conductor
Script: Avon
Selections: Leeds
Record: MCA
Rights: MTI

F

FADE OUT-FADE IN

Book and Lyrics: Betty Comden and Adolph Green
Music: Jule Styne

ORIGINAL PRODUCTION

Mark Hellinger Theatre, May 26, 1964 (271 perf.)
Director: George Abbott
Choreographer: Ernest Flatt
Musical Director: Colin Romoff
Orchestration: Ralph Burns and Ray Ellis
Principals: Pops—Frank Twiddell—VTNE; Roscoe—Bob Neukum—VTNE; Byron Prong—Jack Cassidy—tenor; Hope Springfield—Carol Burnett—alto; Gloria Currie—Tina Louise—mezzo; Myra—Virginia Payne—VTNE; Ralph Governor—Mitchell Jason—tenor; Rudolf Governor—Dick Patterson—baritone; Lou Williams—Tiger Haynes—baritone; Lionel Z. Governor—Lou Jacobi—baritone
Chorus and Smaller Roles: 12M/8F.

SYNOPSIS

The play is set in the 1930s during the heart of the depression when Hollywood represented escapism, fun and frivolity.

Eager fans stand around the famous F.F.F. film studio gate in Hollywood waiting for the various stars. When Nelson Eddy and Jeanette MacDonald arrive in period costumes, they are surrounded by autograph seekers. Billy Vespers, a studio casting director, tells Pops, the gateman, that Hope Springfield is coming from New York for a screen test. She arrives, a surprise to everyone, for she is the antithesis of a Hollywood starlet; however, since she was picked by the owner of the studio, L. Z. Governor, the studio personnel greet her warmly. She climbs on a ladder for a publicity shot and expresses her joy at being in Hollywood (It's Good to Be Back Home—F Solo).

In the executive dining room, the six nephews of L. Z. Governor admit their fear of L.Z.'s changeable temper (Fear—M Solo to M Chorus). When Vespers enters with Hope, the nephews are astounded, but Ralph sends for Byron Prong, who tells the nephews he refuses to play opposite the over-anxious girl. Ralph orders him to play along or the studio won't pay his gambling debts. Byron agrees to be in Hope's film (Fear [Reprise]—Sc to M Solo to M Chorus).

Rudolf enters the wardrobe department to introduce Hope to Myra, the sixty-year-old wardrobe mistress, and is surprised to see Hope in a seminude outfit laden with pearls that clang when she walks. Rudolf gives her his jacket, but she brazenly tells him about her wild life (Call Me Savage—Sc to F/M Duet). As she cavorts about imitating every movie sex goddess, Rudolf contradicts her but enjoys her sincerity.

Ralph tells Hope her new movie script is ready for shooting, hands her a script and exits. Hope puts on a dressing gown and comments on her sudden rise from film usher to stardom (The Usher from the Mezzanine—L to F Solo).

On the set Byron Prong sings as the dancers rehearse (My Heart Is Like a Violin—M Solo). Hope outlines her ideas to the script writer, who gratefully copies down her words. The shooting begins and includes several comic sections with Lou Williams, a Black actor who plays a Step-N-Fetchit ex-boxer, and Hope, who portrays a violinist.

The scene switches to psychiatrist Dr. Traurig's Vienna office where L.Z. is undergoing analysis. They discover he is unable to say the number four because he has a deep fear of his fourth nephew, Ralph, and Ralph's quest for power.

On the set Byron and Hope perform a black-and-white costumed musical number complete with girls costumed as violins (I'm with You—M/F Duet). The film is completed and everyone exits but Rudolf, who wishes Hope would notice him (Notice Me—M Solo).

Meeting Ralph in the executive dining room the next day, Byron claims that his good looks are what will sell the picture. He takes a mirror from his robe and sings himself a love song (My Fortune Is My Face—Sc to M Solo).

L.Z. arrives for the viewing of Hope's picture, calls her at the bungalow and tells her he is changing her name to Lila Tremain. As the film progresses L.Z. discovers that his inability to say the number four had caused him to choose Hope, who was fifth in the ushers' line. He fires Ralph, makes Rudolf head of production and sends him to fire Hope and get the real girl, number four, from New York.

Hope, in her studio bungalow, thinks about the new name the studio has given her and tries to take on the qualities of a Lila Tremain (A Girl to Remember—F Solo). As the song ends, Rudolf enters and sadly watches her miming an Oscar acceptance. The curtain falls.

As Act II opens, Gloria Currie, the dump, sexy blonde who was L.Z.'s real choice for Lila Tremain, enters the wardrobe room to rehearse. Her acting is worse than her line readings but L.Z. covers for her. When Byron is introduced there is an obvious attraction but L.Z., not suspecting the explosive potential of their relationship, is confident they will work well together (Close Harmony—Sc to 2M/F Trio).

Hope, who has been forced to earn her living costumed as Shirley Temple and advertising for a children's school, meets Lou Williams, who is advertising for Madame Barrymore's dance school. The two comment on their present status while spoofing a Shirley Temple/Bojangles number (You Mustn't Be Discouraged—Sc to F/M Duet). As the number ends, Rudolf finds Hope and tells her he loves her and wants to help her.

Dr. Traurig has been flown from Vienna to L.Z.'s office to continue psychoanalysis. L.Z. confesses his past in operatic style (The Dangerous Age—Sc to M Solo). Traurig demands that L.Z. describe his nightmares about Hope Springfield. As he speaks, the dream is enacted with L.Z. pursuing Gloria but being stopped by Hope. The nightmare ends as he approaches a bed which contains Dr. Traurig, who calls L.Z. a dirty old man. The dream ends with L.Z. screaming as the lights fade.

On the set, the final scene for the remake of Hope's film is being shot with Gloria and Byron (The Fiddler and the Fighter—Mixed Chorus). Rudolf refuses to finish the picture and urges his uncle to release Hope's picture instead. Hope, disguised as Charlie Chaplin, warns Rudolf it is the end of his career but he isn't worried (Fade In-Fade Out—F/M Duet).

L.Z., who overhears Gloria describing him to Byron as a stupid, dirty old man, fires both of them and agrees to use Hope's film that Ralph shot.

Five years later, in front of Grauman's Chinese Theatre, Hope imprints her toothy smile in the cement as her new husband, Rudolf Governor, watches.

NOTES ON THE PRODUCTION

The musical, though not well-known, can be artistically successful. It requires a director and choreographer who are able to re-create many of the famous thirties film sequences. There is a Busby Berkley sequence which is hilarious if properly mounted.

Some of the sets may be combined. The executive dining room may be moved onto the film set. Dr. Traurig's and L.Z.'s office may have the same background or utilize the same wagon but vary the decorations and props. The wardrobe department may be a small area established by a costume rack on the edge of the film set. The facade of Grauman's is important, as is the studio gate area, but both may begin as In One numbers. If absolutely necessary, the bungalow scene may also be moved to the movie set and be played under tight lighting to keep the intimate tone.

There are quite a few costumes for the various film sequences. Many can be pulled, but the specialty numbers (e.g., girls as violins) require chorus-type "similar" costumes.

When a company is considering this show, it is essential that it have available a strong female character actress and a solid tenor actor for Hope and Byron. The show is a star vehicle and shouldn't be attempted without two excellent performers for these roles.

SONGS OF SPECIAL INTEREST

"The Usher from the Mezzanine," alto, excitement song, short, good to loosen up beginning performer, presentational.

"You Mustn't Be Discouraged," alto/baritone tap number, styled in Shirley Temple mood, good for period and interrelationship.

"The Dangerous Age," older character song, possible for audition if edited, baritone.

Instrumentation: 3 violins, cello, bass, 5 reeds, horn, 2 trumpets, 3 trombones, percussion, harp, piano/celeste/conductor
Script: Random
Selections: Chappell
Record: ABC-Paramount
Rights: TW

FANNY

Book: S. N. Behrman and Joshua Logan (Based on the trilogy of Marcel Pagnol)
Music and Lyrics: Harold Rome

ORIGINAL PRODUCTION

Majestic Theatre, November 4, 1954 (888 perf.)
Director: Joshua Logan
Choreographer: Helen Tameris
Musical Director: Lehman Engel
Orchestrations: Philip J. Lang
Principals: Fanny—Florence Henderson—soprano; Panisse—Walter Slezak—tenor; Admiral—Gerald Price—baritone; Marius—William Tabbert—tenor; Cesar—Ezio Pinza—baritone/bass; Honorine—Edna Preston—VTNE
Chorus and Smaller Roles: 4M/4F minimum.

SYNOPSIS

The curtain opens on the waterfront at Marseilles where the Admiral, a strange character whose main occupation is to provide women for the sailors (Octopus Song—M Solo), promises Marius, a young man who yearns to travel, a job on a square-rigger sailing vessel. Marius confides that he forgets his girlfriend Fanny and his obligation to manage his father's bar when he sees a beautiful sailing ship (Restless Heart—L to M Solo). Honorine, Fanny's mother, enters to sell her oysters as Fanny watches Marius go off.

Honorine urges Fanny to marry for Honorine wants to retire and let Fanny take care of her. Panisse, a fifty-four–year–old wealthy widower, tells a group on the waterfront he is going to find a new wife (Never Too Late for Love—M Solo and Mixed Chorus/Cold Cream Jar—M Solo). He privately proposes to Fanny, who is appalled by the offer. Marius jealously sends him away and Fanny wonders if Marius knows she loves him (Does He Know?—F Solo).

Marius's father, Cesar, knows Fanny loves Marius and desperately wants his son to marry her and settle down. He tries to teach him how to woo her (Why Be Afraid to Dance?—M Solo and Mixed Chorus). Honorine enters in her best clothes to greet Panisse, who she believes is going to propose marriage to her. When Panisse arrives to tell her he hopes to marry Fanny, Honorine is certain he is too old for a young girl. They are interrupted by Cesar, who is running off for an assignation. Honorine and Panisse joke with him (Never Too Late for Love—F Solo to M Duet).

Cesar returns home and tells Marius that coming home is the nicest thing about going away (Welcome Home—L to M Solo). Marius, unable to tell his fatther he has signed on a ship that sails in the morning, attempts to ease the pain he knows will come (I Like You—Sc to M Duet). After Cesar leaves for bed, Fanny arrives, determined to take advantage of a moment alone with Marius (I Have to Tell You—F Solo). Marius tells her he loves her (Fanny—L to M Solo), and takes her to his room.

Two months later, in Cesar's bar, several of the customers urge him to stop being angry at Marius for leaving. He refuses, but excitedly listens as Fanny reads him a letter from Marius. Cesar discovers that Fanny told Marius she was going to marry Panisse because she didn't want Marius to stay in Marseilles simply because she and Marius had slept together.

Fanny discovers she is pregnant by Marius and tells Honorine, who urges her to seek help from Panisse. Fanny goes to Panisse's sail shop, where he eagerly consents to the marriage if the chld can be raised as his own (Panisse and Son— L to M Solo). Cesar, furious that Panisse would marry someone so young, threatens to kill him but quickly changes his mind when he is named godfather.

At the wedding celebration Fanny grows faint and dreams that she is marrying Marius, but the scene quickly becomes realistic and Fanny finds herself dancing with Panisse (Wedding Dance—Mixed Chorus).

The act ends as Honorine rushes out to tell everyone that Fanny has a baby boy. Panisse and Cesar attach the letters *& Son* to the end of Panisse's shop sign.

In Act II everyone is at Panisse's celebrating the baby boy's first birthday (Birthday Song—Mixed Chorus). Panisse toasts Fanny (To My Wife—L to M Solo).

Marius, ashore on leave, visits Fanny and begs her forgiveness for leaving her with a child. She tells him that she forgave him long ago and asks him about his life. He tells her his adventures were wonderful but she was always in his heart (The Thought of You—Sc to M Solo). As he kisses her, Cesar interrupts and orders Marius to leave Fanny, who is now married to Panisse. Panisse enters, panicked that Marius will interfere with his happiness, and tells Marius he can have Fanny, but never the child. Cesar explains that Panisse is actually the boy's father because it was his love that nurtured the baby (Love is a Very Light Thing—L to M Solo). Fanny refuses to leave because of Panisse's kindness and her love for her son (Other Hands, Other Hearts—Sc to F Solo).

Time passes through a series of vignettes showing Panisse, Cesar and Honorine. Years later, Cesario, age twelve, tells Fanny, Cesar and Panisse he wants to go to sea. Fanny tries to explain their reluctance to let him go since he is only twelve years old (Be Kind to Your Parents—F Solo).

Cesario, determined to escape the confines of Marseilles, leaves his birthday party to meet Marius, who works in a garage down on the waterfront. He begs Marius to take him to America and threatens to stow away if Marius won't.

Panisse, bedridden since Cesario left, argues with Cesar about the will to live. He angrily rises from the bed as Marius enters to return Cesario. The grateful Panisse collapses. He later realizes he is dying and asks Cesar to draft a letter to Marius asking him to live in his home, marry Fanny and raise his child. Cesar does his bidding (Welcome Home—M Solo), and Panisse dies a happpy man, knowing he has done the right thing.

NOTES ON THE PRODUCTION

Ezio Pinza, well known for his singing in *South Pacific*, proved that his acting talents equaled his great voice. Much of the charm, warmth and humor in the story lies in the relationship of Panisse and Cesar. Walter Slezak won a Tony Award for his performance.

The Broadway production, a large-scale one, lost much of the charm inherent in the stories. It might be advantageous to trim many of the larger chorus numbers and scenes in order to regain the warmth that is in the script. Too much of the story is interrupted by extraneous material. Most of the scenes can take place on the waterfront set, or Panisse's home scenes can be played in a garden area in front of the shop and Cesar's cafe can be outside—which means the entire show may be performed on one set.

Readapting the script allows it to be placed on a more compact stage with a smaller company. There are sexual innuendos that surround the Admiral that high school productions have managed to "clean."

The music is pleasant, the characters well drawn and the moments range from dramatic to comedic. It is a good choice if the theatrical pacing can be kept.

SONGS OF SPECIAL INTEREST

"Fanny," lovely tenor solo, shows off the voice, good for audition.

"Panisse and Son," tenor, older character actor solo. Lots of actable specifics, story song.

Instrumentation: 4 violins, viola, mandolin, cello, bass, 5 reeds, 2 horns, 3 trumpets, 2 trombones, harp, percussion, concertina, piano/celeste/conductor
Script: Random House
Score: Chappell
Record: RCA
Rights: TW

THE FANTASTICKS

Book and Lyrics: Tom Jones (Based on Edmund Rostand's play *Les Romanesques*)
Music: Harvey Schmidt

ORIGINAL PRODUCTION

The Sullivan Street Playhouse, May 3, 1960 (still running)
Director: Word Baker
Musical Director and Arrangements: Julian Stein
Principals: The Mute—Richard Stauffer—VTNE; Matt—Kenneth Nelson—tenor; El Gallo—Jerry Orbach—high baritone; Hucklebee—William Larsen—baritone; Luisa—Rita Gardner—soprano; Bellamy—Hugh Thomas—baritone; Henry—Thomas Bruce; Mortimer—George Curley—VTI; The Handyman—Jay Hampton—VTI
Chorus and Smaller Roles: None.

SYNOPSIS

As the audience enters the theatre, the stage is in full view and contains a platform with a tattered drape across the front. The overture begins and the company sets out a prop box, removes the curtain and prepares to perform.

The narrator, El Gallo, sets the mood of the play (Try to Remember—M Solo) and introduces the main characters: a boy, Matt; a young girl, Louisa; and their fathers, Hucklebee and Bellamy. During this, the mute, in the tradition of Oriental theatre, handles the props and scenery. El Gallo focuses on the impressionable girl, who tells the audience how wonderful her life is and expresses her youthful dreams (Much More—L to F Solo).

El Gallo introduces the impressionable twenty-year-old Matt. As he points to the wall their fathers built to keep them apart, the mute holds up a stick between Luisa and Matt.

Matt, eager to talk to Luisa, climbs the wall and sings to her (Metaphor—M/

F Duet). As they secretly kiss, Matt's father, Hucklebee, enters, tells about himself, orders his son from the wall and escorts him inside. Bellamy, Luisa's father, enters, introduces himself and sends Luisa inside. When he is sure she has gone, he yodels for his friend Hucklebee, who yelps back. They climb the wall to congratulate themselves on tricking the children into loving each other because their parents are "enemies" (Never Say No—Sc to M Duet). They decide to end the imaginary feud and hire El Gallo, a professional abductor, to stage a ravishment. El Gallo enters to negotiate the cost and describes the various options (It Depends on What You Pay—Sc to 3M Trio). He sends the fathers off and hires two actors to assist in the abduction. The older actor, Henry, a rather faded, Shakespearean, dust-worn type, attempts to remember the famous roles he once played but jumbles everything together.

El Gallo describes the season and place, as Matt and Luisa, seeking shelter from an impending storm, play out a more romantic setting (Soon It's Gonna Rain—Sc to M/F Duet).

The actors and El Gallo arrive in the woods to stage the extravaganza (*The Rape Ballet*) and Matt saves Luisa from El Gallo, as planned. The families are united and it "appears" to be a bright, happy life for all (Happy Ending—3M/1F Quartet). The family freezes as El Gallo wonders how long they can hold the mood and calls for intermission.

El Gallo and the mute return and Act II begins. The music underscoring the mood is sour as the families begin to argue first in solo and then in chorus (This Plum Is Too Ripe—3M/1F Quartet). When the fathers angrily tell the children that the abduction was staged, the children are hurt and insulted. The fathers begin to fight but El Gallo stops them. Matt grabs a sword from the mute and prepares to attack Luisa's bandit but is easily disarmed by El Gallo. Luisa chides Matt, they argue and she slaps him. Matt leaves to see the world despite the narrator's warning of what lies ahead (I Can See It—M Duet). Mortimer and Henry enter from the prop box to portray Socrates and Romanoff, two odious types who offer to show Matt the world.

The fathers, on their respective properties, watching the mute rebuild the wall, gradually begin to talk to each other. They comment on the fun they used to have, their mutual love of gardening and the reliability of vegetables when compared to children (Plant a Radish—Sc to M Duet).

Luisa begs El Gallo, whom she fondly calls her bandit, to take her out into the world. He makes her wear a smiling mask so the world will always seem happy. She sees Matt undergoing great horrors, but she can only laugh because her face is frozen by the mask (Round and Round—M/F Duet to Chorus). El Gallo takes her necklace, but Matt begs El Gallo not to hurt her by leaving. The bandit strikes him down. A brokenhearted Luisa, realizing El Gallo has left, bursts into tears. As Matt comforts her the two realize that while the world has changed, their love for each other has remained strong (They Were You—Sc to M/F Duet). (Finale—Mixed Chorus).

NOTES ON THE PRODUCTION

The show opened to mixed reviews, but the producers were able to build an audience and make it the longest running show in New York history. The long run is made possible by the fact that the theatre only seats 150. The small cast, set and orchestra requirements, which make it ideal for dinner theatres, schools and summer stock, may have contributed to its popularity. The play is familiar to most theatre-goers and is often revived as a first show of a summer stock season. It is inexpensive to produce, as it has one set and only requires one costume per character with various extra pieces for the two ''actors,'' has family appeal and is a charming evening's entertainment. The first act is often entered in play festivals since it is fairly complete in itself.

SONGS OF SPECIAL INTEREST

''Much More,'' good for movement, character-oriented, pleasant, possible audition for soprano.

''Plant a Radish,'' vaudeville-style baritone duet for two character men, good for revue, showstopper.

''Soon It's Gonna Rain,'' romantic charm duet with lots of actable images, tenor/soprano.

''Try to Remember,'' club-style solo, any voice.

Instrumentation: piano, harp, bass, drum, conductor
Script: Avon, DBS
Score: Chappell
Record: MGM
Rights: MTI

FIDDLER ON THE ROOF

Book: Joseph Stein (Based on stories by Sholom Aleichem)
Music: Jerry Bock
Lyrics: Sheldon Harnick

ORIGINAL PRODUCTION

Imperial Theatre, September 22, 1964 (3,242 perf.)
Director and Choreographer: Jerome Robbins
Musical Director: Milton Greene
Orchestrations: Don Walker
Principals: Tevye—Zero Mostel—baritone; Golde—Maria Karnilova—alto; Tzeitel—Joanna Merlin—mezzo; Hodel—Julia Migenes—soprano; Chava—

Tanya Everett—mezzo; Yente—Beatrice Arthur—alto; Motel—Austin Pendleton—high baritone; Perchik—Bert Convy—tenor; Lazar Wolf—Michael Granger—tenor Chorus and Smaller Roles: 10F/10M, 2 young girls, must have one tenor who can hold G above middle C.

SYNOPSIS

The curtain rises on the exterior of Tevye's house in 1905. A fiddler sits on the roof playing, as Tevye, a poor Jewish milkman with five daughters and a habit of talking to God, introduces the villagers of Anatevka, a little town in turn-of-the-century Czarist Russia (Tradition—Mixed Chorus).

In the kitchen of Tevye's house, Golde sends her daughters Tzeitel, Chava, Hodel, Shprintze and Bielke outside to complete their chores while she talks with Yente, the old, absent-minded matchmaker. When Yente tells Golde she can arrange a match for Tzeitel with Lazar Wolfe, a wealthy, middle-aged butcher, she is overjoyed but worried that Tevye won't be happy with an uneducated son-in-law. Yente urges Golde to send Tevye to talk to Lazar and rises to leave.

The girls enter to discover what Yente wanted, but Golde refuses to tell them. She exits as Hodel romantically wonders if Yente has found a husband for her older sister. Both Hodel and Chava, Tevye's daughters who are next in line for marriage, are excited to find out whom Yente has found, but Tzeitel warns them that arranged marriages are not the ideal way to find a husband (Matchmaker, Matchmaker—Sc to F Trio).

Outside, Tevye enters pulling his cart. It seems his horse lost a shoe and Tevye has to hurry and deliver the milk orders before sunset. He wonders why he wasn't chosen to be wealthy and thinks of how his life would be different (If I Were a Rich Man—L to M Solo).

The villagers arrive looking for their dairy orders and begin discussing the political implications created by the Czar's recent eviction of the Jews from Rajanka. Perchik, a young student activist from a Kiev university, enters. Tevye, drawn to the idealistic intellectual, offers him room and board if he will educate Tevye's daughters. Perchik agrees and the two enter the house.

In the kitchen, now prepared for the Sabbath meal, Tevye introduces Perchik to his daughters and Motel, the young tailor who has come to visit Tzeitel. Golde sends everyone out to wash up and sets the table for the guests. She urges Tevye to see Lazar Wolfe about an urgent matter. Tevye assumes the butcher wants to buy his new milk cow and agrees.

Tzeitel, returning with Motel, urges him to ask Tevye if they can be married but Motel is too afraid. Everyone gathers around the table as Golde lights the candles (Sabbath Prayer—Mixed Chorus).

At an inn, the next night, an anxious Lazar Wolfe waits for Tevye to arrive. He talks with several of the other Jewish men, but their conversation ends when Fyedka, a young, handsome Russian, enters with several of his Gentile friends. Tevye arrives, greets Lazar and begins discussing the reason they are meeting.

Lazar assumes that Tevye knows he wants to marry Tzeitel but Tevye, left in the dark by Golde, thinks Lazar wants to buy his milk cow. After a humorous dialogue the two discover their mistake and Tevye agrees to the marriage. They drunkenly toast the match and join some townsmen in a Russian dance (To Life—Sc to M Duet to M Chorus).

On the way home, Tevye meets the constable, who warns him of an unofficial demonstration that is to be staged in Anatevka. After he leaves, Tevye asks God why the Jews must be persecuted. The fiddler enters, circles Tevye and the two dance off.

Outside the house, the next day, Hodel is watching Perchik teach her younger sisters, Shprintze and Bielke, when Golde calls them to help her with Tevye's chores. Left alone with Perchik, Hodel is cynical about Perchik's radical new ideas that break tradition, but is soon taken in by his charm.

Tevye slowly enters, obviously sporting a hangover, and sends Hodel to get Tzeitel. Golde enters in time to hear Tevye tell the stunned Tzeitel she is to marry Lazar. Golde rushes out to tell Yente the happy news. A heartbroken Tzeitel begs Tevye to cancel the agreement. As he agrees, a distraught Motel arrives to beg Tevye for permission to marry Tzeitel and confesses they have given each other their pledge to marry. Tevye, realizing his daughter loves Motel, considers the request (Tevye's Monologue—M Solo) and agrees. He exits to think of a way to break the news to Golde. Motel excitedly expresses his feelings as Tzeitel watches (Miracle of Miracles—Sc to M Solo).

That night, in Tevye and Golde's bedroom, which is completely dark, Golde is awakened by Tevye's frenzied screams and assumes he is having a nightmare. She turns on the lamp, which only lights the bed, and insists on a description of his dream. As he details the dream, the chorus enacts the song (The Tailor Motel Kamzoil—Sc to M/F Duet to Mixed Chorus). When the story is finished Golde is convinced that Tzeitel should marry Motel.

On the village street and the interior of Motel's tailor shop, villagers are spreading the news that Tzeitel is going to marry Motel. Chava, alone in Motel's shop, is confronted by some young Russians who pretend to congratulate her. Fyedka forces them to leave her alone and attempts to interest her in himself. He is impressed by the fact that she is an avid reader and offers to loan her a book. She is hesitant but takes the book, which means she will see him later.

In the yard of Tevye's house the wedding is beginning. At the wedding Golde and Tevye reminisce about how fast children become adults (Sunrise, Sunset— M/F Duet to Mixed Chorus). When Lazar Wolfe, upset that Tevye has broken his promise, vents his anger, the guests begin to argue. They are stopped by Perchik, who shocks everyone by announcing that love is more important than a matchmaker. He begins dancing with Hodel. Tevye, to save face, dances with Golde and eventually everyone joins in the merriment (Wedding Dance—Dance). The constable and a group of Russians enter to enact their "demonstration" and the act ends on an ominous note.

In Act II, two months later, Perchik tells Hodel he must journey to Kiev to join the fight against the Czar. In a dramatically moving scene he asks her to marry him and expresses his happiness when she agrees (Now I Have Everything—Sc to M Solo to M/F Duet). Tevye enters, dumbfounded by Perchik's announcement that he and Hodel are going to get married. After much contemplation (Tevye's Rebuttal—M Solo), he gives the young couple his blessing.

He begins to wonder if Golde, his wife of twenty-five years, loves him and calls her out of the house to discuss the matter. After telling her he has given Perchik and Hodel permission to marry, he questions Golde (Do You Love Me?—Sc to M/F Duet).

Gossip is being spread by Yente. She has seen Chava and Fyedka together and has also opened a letter to Hodel from Perchik saying he has been sent to Siberia (I Just Heard—Mixed Chorus).

At a lonely train stop, Hodel tries to explain to her father why she must go to Siberia to join Perchik (Far from the Home I Love—Sc to M/F Duet). She promises a traditional marriage and Tevye sadly says goodbye.

Back in Anatevka, the villagers gather in Motel's shop to see the new arrivals, a used sewing machine and a baby, while outside Chava begs Tevye for permission to marry Fyedka. He refuses, telling her it is wrong to marry outside the faith.

The next day, Golde rushes to the road to tell Tevye, who is pulling his cart, that Chava and Fyedka have been married by the village priest. Tevye tells Golde to go home and to forget Chava and poignantly sings of his favorite daughter (Chavelah—Sc to M Solo).

In a new edict from the Czar, the Jews are ordered to leave their town in three days. As they pack, they comment on the meaning of leaving (Anatevka—Mixed Chorus).

In a touching scene, Chava and Fyedka come to say good-bye and tell Tevye they are moving to Poland. Tevye acknowledges her presence and Golde urges her to write to them in New York. The family slowly exits while Tevye, pulling his wagon, is followed by the fiddler.

NOTES ON THE PRODUCTION

Fiddler on the Roof is the third longest running musical in Broadway's history. It was surpassed by *Grease* in 1980 and in 1983 by *A Chorus Line*. The show won nine Tony Awards: Best Musical, Actor, Featured Actress, Music and Lyrics, Book, Director, Choreography, Costumes, and Producer (Hal Prince).

Possibly one of the most finely crafted of the book musicals, the play has been performed professionally in small towns and large cities around the globe and translated into practically every conceivable foreign language. Its universal theme makes it applicable to every ethnic group, and its well-drawn characters, rich music and quality lyrics make it a script worthy of production.

The scenic requirements and costume demands are not particularly heavy, for the emphasis is on the characters and story line more than the production. Much of the show takes place in or around Tevye's home with scenes in the tavern,

Motel's shop, and at a train stop. The costumes are primarily turn-of-the-century peasant clothes with the exception of the wedding party costumes and the constable's uniform.

Anyone who is considering a production of *Fiddler*, should read *The Making of a Musical*, which outlines the original production and has many directorial and character notations.

SONGS OF SPECIAL INTEREST

"Do You Love Me?" comic yet poignant character song for baritone/alto. Good for class study or revue.

"Far from the Home I Love," dramatic soprano ballad with tremendous emotional impact for the actress. Potential audition choice.

"If I Were a Rich Man," strong images to act, lots of specifics, mood changes, potential for audition or class character study. Baritone.

"Now I Have Everything" through "Tevye's Rebuttal" is also an excellent scene to song to scene character study. Good for class situation.

"The Tailor Motel Kamzoil," comedic, character-oriented chorus number. Good for beginning directors as the number allows for simple movements and is full of specifics that are easily enacted.

"Tevye's Monologue" including the scene into "Miracle of Miracles," a class study for dramatic scene to comic song. The unit is excellent for transitions and as an acting exercise. "Miracle of Miracles" is also a good audition song as it shows specifics, movement and characterization ability.

Instrumentation: 5 reeds, 3 trumpets, trombone, horn, accordion, guitar, percussion, 3 violins, viola, cello, bass, piano/conductor
Script: Brown, Pocket, Ten Great Musicals of the American Theatre
Score: Times Square
Record: RCA
Rights: MTI

FINIAN'S RAINBOW

Book: E. Y. Harburg and Fred Saidy
Music: Burton Lane
Lyrics: E. Y. Harburg

ORIGINAL PRODUCTION

46th Street Theatre, January 10, 1947 (725 perf.)
Director: Bretaigne Windust
Choreographer: Michael Kidd
Musical Director: Milton Rosenstock

Orchestration: Robert Russell Bennett
Principals: Sharon—Ella Logan—soprano; Og—David Wayne—baritone; Finian—Albert Sharpe—baritone; Susan Mahoney—Anita Alvarez—VTNE; Woody—Donald Richards—tenor; Senator Rawkins—Robert Pitkin—tenor
Chorus and Smaller Roles: 12M/12F. The chorus numbers need a full-volumed sound. Mixed Black and White, 2 children.

SYNOPSIS

Around the well, the Missitucky meeting place, a crowd of Blacks and Whites gather around Sunny, a Black sharecropperr who plays the harmonica. When the sheriff arrives to sell Woody Mahoney's land for back taxes to Buzz Collins, Susan, sister of Woody Mahoney, who "speaks" by dancing, urges the sheriff to wait until Woody arrives. The sharecroppers sing in order to bide time (This Time of the Year—Mixed Chorus) and spontaneously carry the sheriff and Buzz off.

Finian McLonergan enters with his daughter, Sharon, and a carpetbag full of leprechaun gold. When she hears a skylark sing, Sharon is reminded of their home in Ireland (How Are Things in Glocca Morra?—F Solo and Chorus). She begs to return, but her father wants to plant his gold in the ground near Fort Knox and wait for it to multiply. When they hear the sharecroppers returning, they hide in a tree to protect the gold.

Woody prepares to pay the taxes but discovers that the added interest leaves him without the full amount. Sharon is so taken with his plight that she throws down enough gold to pay off the sheriff. After Buzz and the sheriff exit, Finian comes down from the tree to tell Woody he needs some of Woody's land to bury his carpetbag. Woody agrees and asks Sharon about herself: she responds with a Glocca Morra legend (Look to the Rainbow—Sc to F Solo to Chorus).

In the light of the moon, Finian buries his carpetbag then relaxes with his whiskey jug. He is suddenly confronted by Og, a leprechaun who has followed Finian to America to recover the stolen gold. It seems that Finian's theft is causing the leprechauns in Ireland to become mortal. Og has already become 50 percent mortal and is beginning to have human emotions.

Woody, who has fallen in love, confides his dreams to Sharon as the two watch the moon (Old Devil Moon—Sc to M Solo).

At Senator Billboard Rawkins's estate, Buzz explains that he was unable to obtain Woody's land. This news infuriates Rawkins, who is further upset when he learns that two federal men have discovered a heavy concentration of gold buried on Woody's property.

At the wall, where Sharon is pulling up water for the wash, Og arises and proclaims his love (Something Sort of Grandish—Sc to M/F Duet). Og is so upset by these uncontrollable human emotions that he jumps back down the well.

Woody plans on leaving for New York, but Finian and the sharecroppers trick him into staying and marrying Sharon. Susan, Woody's sister who doesn't speak, is so happy for her brother that she dances. Her moves are interpreted by Woody and the chorus (If This Isn't Love—Mixed Chorus). After everyone leaves, Og begs Finian to return the crock of gold, but Finian refuses and threatens to have Og deported for entering the country without a passport. Two children meet the saddened Og and promise to help him find the gold if he will give them a wish. He agrees (Something Sort of Grandish [Reprise]—Sc to M Solo).

At the meeting place, the sharecroppers, busy sorting tobacco leaves, dream of faraway places (Necessity—Mixed Chorus). Senator Rawkins, determined to get Woody's land, arrives and orders him evicted for allowing Negroes on the property. Sharon is so mad that she wishes the Senator were Black—a wish that comes true because she is standing over the buried gold. The Senator, an extremely bigoted man, rushes into hiding.

When the Shears and Roebust Company hear of Finian's wealth, they extend him unlimited credit, and Woody urges the sharecroppers to buy tractors and really raise acres of tobacco (That Great Come and Get It Day—Mixed Chorus).

In Act II the people, carried away with their new credit, purchase all sorts of unnecessary items; Sharon comments on this age-old problem (When the Idle Poor Become the Idle Rich—F Solo and Mixed Chorus). Og, while searching for the gold, finds the missing senator, now Black, hiding in the woods. He rightfully decides the senator's attitude needs changing and casts a spell which causes Rawkins to begin singing old spirituals. Three Black gospel singers passing by interest him in joining their group (The Begat—Sc to M Quartet).

The sheriff, who has been unable to find Rawkins, arrests Sharon for witchcraft. Everyone is in an uproar.

Later that day, Og, who has become 90 percent mortal, falls in love with Susan, whom he sees sitting by the well. He can't understand how he can love both Susan and Sharon (When I'm Not Near the Girl I Love—Sc to M Solo). When Og wishes Susan could talk, she surprises him by telling him she loves him. It seems Og made his wish while standing over the crock of gold. He decides to use his third and final wish to free Sharon by making the senator White. The play ends happily with Og betrothed to Susan, Sharon and Woody happily married, the senator gaining compassion for his fellowman, and Finian leaving for new vistas (Finale—Mixed Chorus).

NOTES ON THE PRODUCTION

The first Antoinette (Tony) Perry Awards were given in 1947 to honor Broadway's best artists. David Wayne received the Featured Actor Award, and Michael Kidd, choreographer, tied with Agnes de Mille (*Brigadoon*).

The show may be performed with two sets, the well area and the senator's plantation house. Both may utilize the same background drop. The costumes are country style, skirts and blouses for the women and overalls or jeans for the male chorus. It is possible to use the same costumes throughout. Susan's costume should be very movement-oriented. Companies have the freedom to set the show, costume wise, from the mid-forties through the early sixties—before the majority of people became aware of the civil rights movement.

The songs are excellent and enhance the script, which appeals to a wide variety of audiences. Although a lighthearted fantasy, it makes a strong comment on many social problems. Not as familiar as many other early hits, it is worthy of more productions and may be labeled among the more inexpensive shows to mount.

The treatment of the Blacks by the senator and his associate is typical of the times and should be given the humorous treatment it deserves. Modern audiences, who may have felt uncomfortable with the subject in the sixties and seventies, should be able to laugh at the absurdity of the situation. The labelling of Blacks as Negroes should be kept to give an authenticity to the period.

SONGS OF SPECIAL INTEREST

"How Are Things in Glocca Mora?" nice ballad style, romantic, nostalgic, mezzo range. Good for audition.

"Old Devil Moon," charming, romantic duet, lovely melody, imaginative lyrics, good up tempo for leads. Revue potential. Soprano/Tenor.

"Something Sort of Grandish," charming, up tempo, good for character study for Og; quick movements for Og make this a good number to lighten up a usually heavy performer. Baritone/mezzo.

"When I'm Not Near the Girl I Love," comic baritone solo, character-oriented, good for movement and working on developing abandon.

Instrumentation: 2 violins, viola, cello, bass, 5 reeds, 2 trumpets, 2 trombones, 2 horns, percussion, harp, piano/celeste, guitar/banjo, piano/conductor
Script: Random, Berkley, Theatre Arts (Magazine)
Score: 1149 Chappell
Record: Columbia
Rights: TW

FIORELLO!

Book: Jerome Weidman and George Abbott
Music: Jerry Bock
Lyrics: Sheldon Harnick

ORIGINAL PRODUCTION

Broadhurst Theatre, November 23, 1959 (796 perf.)
Director: George Abbott
Choreographer: Peter Gennaro
Musical Director: Harold Hastings

Orchestration: Irwin Kostal
Principals: Fiorello—Tom Bosley—tenor; Neil—Bob Holiday—tenor; Morris—
Nathaniel Frey—baritone; Marie—Patricia Wilson—mezzo; Ben—Howard Da
Silva—baritone; Thea—Ellen Hanley—high soprano; Dora—Pat Stanley—alto;
Floyd—Mark Dawson—VTNE; Mitzi—Eileen Rodgers—alto
Chorus and Smaller Roles: 12M/12F.

SYNOPSIS

Time: 1915. The law office of Fiorello La Guardia.
Several of New York's poor wait to see La Guardia while Neil, the energetic
young clerk, is busy at the switchboard and Morris, the serious, reserved office
manager, converses on the phone. The two have different viewpoints about
working for a man who believes in helping the unfortunates of New York (On
the Side of the Angels—Sc to 2M Duet and Chorus).
Dora, a friend of Fiorello's secretary, Marie, enters to beg for legal aid. She
is followed by Fiorello, who tells Marie he plans on running for Congress against
the Tammany Hall Democrats, an especially ambitious task since no Republican
has ever won in the 14th District. He asks Marie to introduce him to Republican
district leader Ben Marino and promises to help Dora.
In Marino's office, some political hacks sit around playing poker while Ben
tries to concentrate on choosing a candidate (Politics and Poker—L to M Chorus).
At this point Fiorello walks in with Marie and confidently expresses his wish to
be nominated. Ben agrees to back him, as the rest of the political hacks continue
playing cards.
Fiorella rushes off to the exterior of the shirtwaist factory to help Dora. It
seems the women workers at the factory where Dora works need Fiorello to
defend their right to picket. He boosts their morale and instructs them in the art
of protesting (Unfair—M Solo with F Chorus).
When Fiorello meets Thea, a beautiful Italian girl who is the leader of the
strikers, he is charmed by her spirit and forgets a prior engagement for dinner
with Marie. Marie, disappointed at his lack of thoughtfulness, tells Morris she
wishes there were laws against inconsiderate men (Marie's Law—Sc to F/M
Duet).
Fiorello campaigns on street corners throughout the district. With the help of
Ben, Neil, Morris and Thea, he is able to address the various ethnic groups (The
Name's La Guardia—M Solo and Mixed Chorus).
It is election eve. Ben and his political hacks, staggering from intoxication
and disbelief at Fiorello's success, worry that Fiorello may become too inde-
pendent (The Bum Won—M Chorus).
On the roof of Dora's apartment building, Dora confides that she is in love
with Floyd, the rude policeman who tried to stop the shirtwaist strike by arresting
Thea (I Love a Cop—Sc to F Solo).
In Washington, La Guardia is causing a commotion by his support of the draft

act. Against Ben's and Marie's wishes Fiorello goes ahead with his support of the draft and even enlists himself.

After Fiorello's going away party, Fiorello asks Thea to marry him. She is at first hesitant, but agrees after Fiorello promises to win Trieste from the Germans (Till Tomorrow—F Solo to Mixed Chorus).

News reports of Fiorello's heroic deeds show his achievements as a soldier (slide or film presentation). At the end of the war he returns to New York where he is greeted by the voters (Home Again—Mixed Chorus).

Act II opens at the La Guardia home. Thea, now Fiorello's wife, speaks with Ben on the telephone about the La Guardia campaign for mayor against the corrupt Jimmy Walker. Dora tells Thea of Floyd's promotion and inquires about Thea's weakening health. After Dora and Fiorello leave, Thea wonders when she first fell in love with her ambitious husband (When Did I Fall in Love?—Sc to F Solo).

Floyd and Dora have married and Floyd is high in the ranks of the politically corrupt Walker government. He invites the politicians and some shady mob characters to his new penthouse to show off his newly acquired clout. The guests are entertained by Mitzi and some chorus cuties, who perform a tribute to the mayor (Gentleman Jimmy—Sc to F Solo and F Chorus/Tap Dance).

In Fiorello's office, Ben and Fiorello come to blows as Ben tries to advise Fiorello on his political tactfulness. At the same time Dora informs Marie of a plot to kill La Guardia. Fiorello tries to stop this act by having Morris and Neil watch out for trouble but they are distracted when they find out Thea has died.

Morris, Neil and Marie wait in Fiorello's office to tell him of Thea's death. La Guardia's bereavement coupled with the loss of the election has him emotionally beaten. He feels the city has turned its back on him, yet vows to fight the Walker corruption in the courts.

In the Republican meetinghouse, where Ben Marino and his hacks are playing poker and reading the daily news accounts of the trial, they sarcastically comment (Little Tin Box—M Chorus). Marie enters to convince Ben to back Fiorello in the next campaign.

Morris questions Marie about her personal plans, which involve living a life of her own and finding an eligible husband (The Very Next Man—Sc to F Solo). Ben arrives at the office to ask Fiorello to run for mayor and Marie forces him to accept. Realizing that he needs and loves Marie, Fiorello proposes marriage. She agrees (Finale—Mixed Chorus)

NOTES ON THE PRODUCTION

Fiorello! was the fourth musical to win a Pulitzer prize for drama. The others were: *Of Thee I Sing*, 1932; *Oklahoma!* (special award), 1944; *South Pacific*, 1950. The show tied with *The Sound of Music* for the following 1960 Tonys: Musical, Book, Producer, and Composer. The individual awards went to Tom Bosley, Featured Actor, and George Abbott for direction.

Fiorello! is a well-written libretto about an interesting and unusual man, a perfect role model for high school students and an excellent choice for this age group. Unfortunately, some companies feel the subject matter has limited appeal outside the New York area and are hesitant to risk a production. The show, although based on the life of La Guardia, has a universal theme with marvelous music and lyrics written by the team that wrote *Fiddler on the Roof*. *Fiddler*, the story of Russian Jewish peasants, is popular around the globe because of its universal theme. The same should hold true for *Fiorello!* The excellent book, soaring music and adroit lyrics of this prize winner are certainly worthy of more productions in the country of its origin.

The sets are usually drops and wagons. The World War I La Guardia film sequence may be adapted to a slide show with pictures of the company's Fiorello placed over the faces of real World War I heroes and reproduced in slide format.

The costumes span from pre–World War I to 1925 and each chorus member has at least two if not three changes.

SONGS OF SPECIAL INTEREST

Final Scene beginning with "The Very Next Man," class study and as part of a character study for mezzo/soprano.

"I Love a Cop," for alto with limited range, story song. Comedic, problem song.

"Marie's Law," spunky soprano/mezzo. Good for character study.

"Unfair," F chorus with baritone solo, requires slight movement, good for helping shyer performers achieve volume and anger. Class study.

"When Did I Fall in Love?" extremely high soprano, Possible audition.

Instrumentation: 3 violins, cello, bass, 5 reeds, 3 trumpets, 3 trombones, guitar/banjo, percussion, piano/conductor
Script: Random Great Musicals of the American Theatre, Volume Two.
Selections: Valando
Record: Capitol
Rights: TW

FLOWER DRUM SONG

Book: Oscar Hammerstein II and Joseph Fields (Based on the novel by C. Y. Lee)
Music: Richard Rodgers
Lyrics: Oscar Hammerstein II

ORIGINAL PRODUCTION

St. James Theatre, December 1, 1958 (600 perf.)
Director: Gene Kelly
Choreographer: Carol Haney

Musical Director: Salvatore Dell'Isola
Orchestration: Robert Russell Bennett
Principals: Mei Li—Miyoshi Umeki—mezzo; Madam Liang—Juanita Hall—
alto; Linda Low—Pat Suzuki—alto; Wang Chi Yang—Keye Luke—baritone;
Sammy Fong—Larry Blyden—baritone; Wang Ta—Ed Kenney—tenor; Helen
Chao—Arabella Hong—soprano; Frankie Wing—Jack Soo—baritone; Madam
Fong—Eileen Nakamura—VTNE; Dr. Lu Fong—Chao Li—VTNE; Dr. Li—
Conrad Yama—VTNE
Chorus and Smaller Roles: 8W/6M minimum. If minimum is used, all must be
able to play teens as well as adults. 2F/2M children (optional).

SYNOPSIS

The curtain rises on an average living room in modern-day San Francisco
Chinatown. In it is Madam Liang, a middle-aged, Americanized Chinese woman
who lives with her overly traditional sixty-year-old Chinese brother, Wang Chi
Yang, and his two sons. Ta, the eldest son, tells his aunt of his interest in a
young girl he plans on plying with romantic Chinese poetry. The two musicalize
the poem (You Are Beautiful—Sc to M/F Duet).

Ta's father, determined that Ta should marry a girl from the old country,
decides to allow Sammy Fong's picture bride, Mei Li and her father Dr. Li to
stay in his home. Mei Li sings the charming flower drum song (A Hundred
Million Miracles—Sc to F Solo with Small Mixed Chorus) and is embraced by
Madam Liang.

On a hill overlooking San Francisco Bay, Linda Low, a pretty, westernized
Chinese girl and nightclub singer, tells Ta of her aim to be a success as a woman.
She hints that she is cold, and when he naively misses her cue and runs off to
get her a sweater, she sings about the joys of being female (I Enjoy Being a
Girl—F Solo). Ta returns and asks her to marry him. Knowing he has money,
she readily accepts.

At the Wang house, everyone is busy preparing for Ta's graduation from
college and Madam Liang's from citizenship school. Mei Li is introduced to Ta
and is immediately entranced (I Am Going to Like It Here—F Solo).

In Ta's simply furnished bedroom Mei Li, curious about western ways, shyly
asks Ta how he would ask a girl to marry him; he responds (Like a God—Sc
to M Solo).

At the citizenship graduation party, in Wang's garden, Madam Liang announces her pride in being both American and Chinese (Chop Suey—Sc to F
Solo to Mixed Chorus). The party ends in disaster when Linda Low arrives,
announcing that her brother, Frankie, consents to her marriage to Ta. Wang is
shocked because Ta knows nothing of women, especially fortune hunters, and
Linda Low appears to be fast. Sammy Fong, who loves Linda and has been
dating her for five years, tells Mei Li she has to get busy or she will have to
marry him, according to his mother's previously arranged marriage agreement
(Don't Marry Me—Sc to M/F Duet).

Various party-goers congratulate Linda and inquire where she will live after she is married. She quickly responds that she must be where the action is (Grant Avenue—Sc to F Solo to Mixed Chorus).

In Linda's dressing room at the Celestial Bar, Linda prepares for her final show, which Sammy has insisted on. Helen Chao, her dresser, envies Linda her forthcoming marriage to Ta for she has admired him herself (Love Look Away—F Solo).

The specialty act is going on at the club (Fan Tan Fanny—F Solo with F Dancers) as the Wang family arrives. It seems Sammy wants to make sure Linda does not marry Ta. As Frankie, Linda's "pretend" brother, emcees, a variety of scantily clad girls, including Linda as the star attraction, enter (Gliding Through My Memoree—M Solo with F Showgirls). The family, greatly upset, leaves a dazed Ta alone in the club.

Act II opens at Helen's apartment; Ta, in a drunken stupor, dreams. Various girls dance through his mind (Dream Ballet). In the morning, Mei Li arrives to have Mr. Wang's suit mended and notices Ta's suit jacket; she quietly leaves. Ta thanks Helen for her assistance and says he will call her. After he leaves, she knows they will never date again and sadly laments (Love Look Away [Reprise]—F Solo).

In Wang's living room, Wang and Madam Liang comment on the strangeness of the younger generation (The Other Generation—Sc to M/F Duet). Ta enters to beg forgiveness and is pleased that Mei Li is his father's choice of a bride for him. When she tells him she cannot marry him because she knows he was in Helen's room, he feels he has lost someone very special. Dr. Li and Mei Li prepare to leave Wang's house.

At Sammy Fong's, where Linda has come to pack her things, Sammy asks her to marry him. The two romanticize about their future life (Sunday—Sc to M/F Duet).

In a large ballroom, the family association insists that Sammy honor his contract with Mei Li. The young people despair because Sammy wants to marry Linda, and Mei Li doesn't know what she wants.

Mei Li promises Ta, at Sammy's apartment, that she will try to think of some way to stop the marriage, and her answer comes from a late-night television show about a Mexican wetback. At Mei Li's and Sammy's wedding Mei Li announces to Madam Fong she is a wetback for she has entered the country illegally. Madam Fong refuses to let her son marry an alien and gladly accepts Linda Low into her family. The play ends with Ta and Mei Li, and Sammy and Linda united.

NOTES ON THE PRODUCTION

An enjoyable show with memorable music by Richard Rodgers and lyrics by Hammerstein II. Juanita Hall, of *South Pacific* fame, again delighted Rodgers and Hammerstein followers. Although most of the season's Tony Awards went to *Redhead*, the musical direction received an award.

This "generation gap" musical is enjoyable to audiences of all ages and may easily be performed by high schools and communities alike. High schools may want to simplify and tone down the nightclub sequence, but this change requires very little on the part of the director.

There are very good roles for males and females; the songs are familiar and the show quite saleable. The roles of Linda and Helen require strong singing voices, but the rest of the songs are mainly character-oriented and may vary from role to role. The original production had separate singing and dancing choruses, but this isn't absolutely necessary, especially if the dance sequences are trimmed.

The sets may be simplified by playing more scenes in the Wang living room and not utilizing the Wang bedroom or garden. The family association may also meet at the Wangs' and the final scene could possibly be in the living room. A backdrop of San Francisco Bay is recommended for Act I scene 2 and as a general background for the living room. It may also be utilized, with the addition of signs and storefront cutouts, as the Grant Avenue background.

It is important that the show be quickly paced. Quick scene changes and script tightening will help this show, which should sell well and is a worthy production.

SONGS OF SPECIAL INTEREST

"Like a God," possible audition, shows off the voice, good ballad, tenor.

"Love Look Away," semidramatic, requires strong soprano voice, good for audition or class study.

"The Other Generation," comic duet, older M/F, relationship and reactions important. Possible for revue and class study. Alto/baritone.

Instrumentation: 6 reeds, 2 horns, 3 trumpets, 2 trombones, 4 violins, viola, cello, tuba, percussion, bass, harp, guitar/banjo/mandolin, piano/conductor
Script: Chappell (London), Farrar, Straus
Score: Williamson
Record: Columbia
Rights: R & H

FOLLIES

Book: James Goldman
Music and Lyrics: Stephen Sondheim

ORIGINAL PRODUCTION

Winter Garden Theatre, April 4, 1971 (522 perf.)
Directors: Harold Prince and Michael Bennett
Choreographer: Michael Bennett

Musical Director: Harold Hastings
Orchestration: Jonathan Tunick
Principals: Sally—Dorothy Collins—mezzo; Roscoe—Michael Bartlett—tenor; Phyllis—Alexis Smith—alto; Hattie—Ethel Shutta—alto; Benjamin Stone—John McMartin—baritone; Buddy—Gene Nelson—tenor; Heidi—Justine Johnston—soprano; Solange La Fitte—Fifi D'Orsay—alto; Carlotta—Yvonne DeCarlo—alto; Young Phyllis—Virginia Sandifer—soprano; Young Ben—Kurt Peterson—tenor; Young Buddy—Harvey Evans—tenor; Young Sally—Marti Rolph—soprano; Emily Whitman—Marcie Stringer—mezzo; Theodore Whitman—Charles Welch—baritone
Chorus and Smaller Roles: 12F/8M, various ages.

SYNOPSIS

The play takes place on the soon-to-be-demolished stage of the Weismann Theatre where a reunion is being held to honor the beautiful Weismann chorus girls that once performed there. The lights rise on the once replendent theatre that now contains little but planks and scaffolding. A pale young showgirl is seen, the ghost of a former performer; as she slowly moves another showgirl appears. The ghostlike girls are only seen by the audience and are never noticed by the onstage performers. A majordomo breaks the mood of the past when he enters, followed by waiters and waitresses who pass through the showgirls.

Sally Durant Plummer, a small, blonde, energetic, forty-nine–year–old former Weismann girl, enters, and her youthful counterpart moves towards her. Phyllis Rogers Stone, an extremely sophisticated and attractive woman also in her late forties, arrives with her handsome and successful husband Ben. Young Phyllis moves to her as a Young Ben moves to Ben. Phyllis comments to Ben about their past, but he feigns disinterest; there is an underlying tension in their relationship.

More guests arrive; among them is Buddy Plummer, Sally's husband, who is looking for Sally. Mr. Weismann enters, and greets his guests as Roscoe, an elderly tenor, introduces the showgirls from 1918 to 1941 (Beautiful Girls—M Solo to Mixed Chorus).

As the party continues, the audience meets former Weismann performers Max and Stella Deems, now store owners in Miami; Solange La Fitte, who has a men's perfume named after her; Hattie Walker, who has lost five younger husbands; Vincent and Vanessa, former dancers who now own an Arthur Murray franchise; Heidi Schiller, who once had Franz Lehar write a waltz in her honor; and Carlotta Campion, a film star who has embraced all life has to offer and benefitted from every experience.

Throughout the various introductions the story of Ben, Phyllis, Buddy and Sally dramatically unfolds in a series of present-day scenes which are intertwined with scenes from the past played by their younger counterparts. It seems that Phyllis and Sally were once roommates, and Ben and Buddy best friends.

Suddenly, Sally sees Ben, her former lover. She greets him self-consciously

(Don't Look at Me—Sc to F Solo to M/F Duet). Carlotta reenters to comment that she is tired of listening to everyone's stories and just wants someone to listen to her. The scene quickly cuts, film style, to Ben, Sally, Phyllis and Buddy, who are reminiscing about the old days of their courtship and the theatre. They are joined by their young counterparts (Waiting for the Girls Upstairs—Sc to 4M/4F Octet). The song ends with the four visibly shaken by the realization of what they have become. They angrily finish the song as the stage goes to blackout.

The lights rise on Willy Wheeler, a portly man in his sixties, who performs a cartwheel for a photographer. Emily and Theodore Whitman, two ex-vaudeville performers in their seventies, perform an old routine (Listen to the Rain on the Roof—M/F Duet). They are followed by Solange La Fitte, still fashionable at sixty-six (Ah, Paris!—F Solo), and Hattie Walker, a tough seventy-year-old who performs her showstopping number (Broadway Baby—F Solo); the performance ends with the three songs being sung simultaneously.

Sally is awed by Ben's life, which she assumes is a glamorous one, yet Ben wonders if he made the right choices and considers how things might have been (The Road You Didn't Take—L to M Solo with 2M Scene Interspersed). Phyllis and Buddy comment and move off as Vincent and Vanessa tango (Bolero d'A-mour—Dance). Sally tells Ben how her days have been spent since she left the Follies and attempts to convince him and herself that Buddy keeps her life from being mundane (In Buddy's Eyes—Sc to F Solo). In the middle of the song Young Sally and Ben are seen. Young Sally is in love with Young Ben and terribly hurt, for he is marrying Young Phyllis but still wants Young Sally's sexual favors. Sally shakes loose from the memory and tragically continues singing about Buddy. As the song ends she and Ben embrace and begin to dance but are interrupted by Phyllis, who takes Sally aside for a rather biting encounter. The two are interrupted when the ex-chorines line up to perform an old number (Who's That Woman?—F Solo and F Chorus), mirrored by their former selves.

After the number the depth of the two couples' unhappiness is uncovered. Sally has never been in love with Buddy, who adores her, while Phyllis and Ben are angry at their lives and their relationship, which has become numb and unemotional.

Carlotta breaks the scene by telling of her dramatic solo number that was cut from the Follies because the audience found it humorous. Somehow the number works when she sings it at age fifty (I'm Still Here—L to F Solo).

Ben confides to Sally that his life is empty. She yearns to be held by him, but Young Sally slips between them and the three move together (Too Many Mornings—Sc to M/F Duet). Ben, caught up in the memory, kisses Sally but is startled by the reality of the moment and the parallel between the present and the past. He tells Sally it was over long ago and exits, as Sally dreams of a marriage that can never be.

Buddy angrily sings about the girl he should have married, the one who would have loved him and made him a somebody (The Right Girl—M Solo). After a frantic dance he soliloquizes his thoughts about Sally. Sally overhears but tells him Ben has asked her to marry him. Buddy knows she is either crazy or drunk but doesn't care because he has helped her through the alcohol rehabilitation clinics and mental hospitals and can't take anymore.

Meanwhile, Ben drunkenly propositions Carlotta, who refuses his advances and tells him she is involved with a twenty-six–year–old. The scene is broken when Heidi Schiller, a Viennese lady in her eighties sings with her counterpart, Young Heidi (One More Kiss—F Duet).

Ben tells Phyllis he wants a divorce because he must find something to care for. Phyllis, hurt and angered because she loves Ben and has given him her whole life, contemplates his request (Could I Leave You?—Sc to F Solo).

The two couples and the young counterparts argue furiously and insanely about how foolish they were when they were young. Suddenly, at the peak of madness and confusion, the couples are surrounded by the ensemble dressed as Dresden dolls and cavaliers, singing of love (Loveland—Mixed Chorus).

Young Phyllis and Young Ben come to life and sing to each other the hopes for their future (You're Gonna Love Tomorrow—M/F Duet). They are followed by Young Buddy and Young Sally, who express similar hopes (Love Will See Us Through—M/F Duet). This section ends with the young couples vocally joined in counterpart.

As the number ends, a show curtain drops and Buddy appears to welcome us to the Follies. Dressed in plaid pants, a shiny derby and a vibrant-colored jacket, he carries a cutout car and sings an old number (The God-Why-Don't-You-Love-Me-Blues—M Solo with F Needed for Staging). Sally performs as a screen vamp of the thirties (Losing My Mind—F Solo). Phyllis, in a fringed dress, tells a love story (The Story of Lucy and Jessie—F Solo and M Chorus). Ben enters in top hat with cane to perform (Live, Laugh, Love—M Solo and Mixed Chorus). Each of the songs is an ironic parallel to their respective feelings and situations. However, Ben can't go through with his. He stumbles, forgets the words, and anxiously calls to the conductor for the lyrics as he frantically tries to keep going.

The curtains rise, one by one, and the show abruptly ends with Ben becoming frenzied and the chorus continuing as if nothing were wrong. Ben rushes to various groups, screaming and yelling at his past, but collapses and cries out for Phyllis.

The lights change and Ben, Phyllis, Buddy and Sally reunite in the now half-demolished, crumbling theatre. Buddy helps Sally off while Phyllis helps Ben to regain his dignity before they exit. Their counterparts, who have watched the scene from the shadows, slowly move downstage and the young men call softly to the young girls as the curtain falls.

NOTES ON THE PRODUCTION

Tony Awards, 1972—Best Actress (Alexis Smith), Score, Direction, Choreography, Sets, Costumes, and Lighting.

The work is a magnificent and challenging theatrical endeavor with interesting and well-drawn characters. There are many strong female roles which will give older community theatre actresses something more exciting than the usual character chorus parts.

The score varies from simple vaudeville to vocally complex. The younger principal counterparts should all sing well.

The costumes are period or present-day evening clothes. The "Follies Girls" sequence costumes are extremely lavish as are the "Loveland" ones. They will probably need to be rented for they must have an opulently theatrical look that isn't easy to whip up by home seamstresses with limited fabric selection.

The set is that of an old theatre, but the "Follies" sequence is reminiscent of the twenties and thirties and probably will require at least one painted drop with some painted wing pieces. There are companies listed in the *Simon's Directory* that rent drops quite inexpensively.

Follies requires a quality director and choreographer who must work closely together to achieve a strong unity in production. This is a show that needs more than blocking to make it work. The director and actors must examine the character relationships and re-create with clarity and understanding the ugliness, bitterness and love that exist among these couples. The show will not survive without motivated actors who have the emotional maturity to portray these middle-aged characters who have lost so much.

The show is excellent, complex, challenging and worth the effort. It is one that should be seen more often. Do not let the cast size be a deterrent. Many of the characters only have a few lines and one featured song, which means the early rehearsals can be broken up into smaller sections.

SONGS OF SPECIAL INTEREST

"Broadway Baby," vaudeville style, gutsy, good for revue. Alto, showstopper for big-voiced woman.

"Could I Leave You?," bitter, dramatic, angry, character-oriented. Good for developing different ways to portray anger. Alto.

"I'm Still Here," semicomic, strong character, little movement, emphasis on lyrics, low alto.

"The Right Girl," good for class study, lots of transitions, movement, anger, drama, tenor.

"The Road You Didn't Take," introspective, dramatic, good for class study and character, baritone.

Instrumentation: 5 reeds, 3 trumpets, horn, 3 trombones, violins, viola, cello, bass, harp, percussion, piano/conductor.
Script: Random
Score: Hansen
Record: Capitol
Rights: MTI

FUNNY GIRL

Book: Isobel Lennart (Based on an original story by Miss Lennart)
Music: Jule Styne
Lyrics: Bob Merrill

ORIGINAL PRODUCTION

Winter Garden Theatre, March 26, 1964 (1,348 perf.)
Director: Garson Kanin
Musical Numbers Staged by: Carol Haney
Musical Director: Milton Rosenstock
Production Supervisor: Jerome Robbins
Principals: Fanny Brice—Barbra Streisand—mezzo; Mrs. Brice—Kay Medford—alto; Eddie—Danny Meehan—tenor; Nick Arnstein—Sydney Chaplin—baritone; Mrs. Strakosh—Jean Stapleton—mezzo; Mrs. Meeker—Lydia S. Fredricks—VTI; Mrs. O'Malley—Joyce O'Neil—VTI; Ziegfeld Tenor—John Lankston—tenor; Florenz Ziegfeld, Jr.—Roger De Koven—VTNE; Emma—Royce Wallace—VTNE; Keeney—Joseph Macaulay—VTNE
Chorus and Smaller Roles: 8M/12F.

SYNOPSIS

The scene opens in the dressing room, where Fanny Brice is lost in thought and waiting for her husband Nick Arnstein to return from prison. Her thoughts flash to 1910 and her mother's home where Mrs. Brice and three neighbors, Mrs. Strakosh, Mrs. O'Malley and Mrs. Meeker, are playing cards and discussing the homely and awkward Fanny's decision to go into show business (If a Girl Isn't Pretty—Sc to F Quartet).

Still reminiscing, Fanny remembers her first audition at Keeney's Music Hall. The scene shifts to the audition; Fanny has just been thrown out because of her looks. Eddie, her friend and the theatre's choreographer, shows her to the door (If a Girl Isn't Pretty [Reprise]—M Solo) but she begs him to give her another chance (I'm The Greatest Star—L To F Solo).

Early that morning, in Fanny's backyard, Eddie patiently rehearses Keeney's dance routine with Fanny.

The scene moves to Keeney's Music Hall where Fanny auditions with a comic song about a woman who plays second fiddle to her husband's cornet (Cornet Man—F Solo and Mixed Chorus). Backstage, an enthusiastic Fanny clowns around on her hands and knees and crawls right up to Nick Arnstein, a handsome gambler. She covers her embarrassment by acting like a dog and introduces herself. The dashing Nick congratulates her, predicts that she will one day be a star and talks Keeney into paying Fanny $110 a week. After he leaves, Fanny vows to see him again.

In the Brices' kitchen, Mrs. Brice and Eddie talk about Fanny's forthcoming audition for the Ziegfeld Follies; both claim success for teaching her the gimmicks that made her famous (Who Taught Her Everything She Knows?—Sc to M/F Duet).

At the New York Theater, Fanny impresses Ziegfeld but rejects his idea that she portray a glamorous young bride in the finale. She boldly performs the number as if she is nine months pregnant, and the effect is hilarious (His Love Makes Me Beautiful—F Solo to F Chorus). Ziegfeld forgives his outrageous star, and Nick Arnstein appears to congratulate her and ask her for a date (I Want to Be Seen with You Tonight—Sc to M/F Duet). He accompanies her to a neighborhood block party.

At her house on Henry Street, the neighbors discuss the successful people in their neighborhood, especially Fanny (Henry Street—Mixed Chorus). When Nick and Fanny are at last alone, they both discover they are lonely people and need each other desperately (People—Sc to F Solo).

Fanny goes on tour with the Follies and is surprised to discover Nick is in Baltimore. He takes Fanny to an intimate restaurant and overwhelms her with his charm (You Are Woman—Sc to M/F Duet).

At the Baltimore train terminal the company is waiting for the Chicago train when Fanny decides to follow Nick to Europe. Eddie tries to dissuade Fanny and Ziegfeld is furious at her unprofessional behavior, but she insists on making her own decisions (Don't Rain on My Parade—Sc to F Solo).

Act II opens in Long Island, where Mrs. Brice and the neighborhood friends await the arrival of the honeymooners at their newly purchased home. Fanny reveals that she is pregnant and comments on her married status (Sadie, Sadie—Sc to F Solo to Mixed Chorus).

In Mrs. Brice's saloon, Mrs. Strakosh and Eddie encourage Mrs. Brice to go out and find a man of her own. Although she feels too old for dating she is interested in a new life (Find Yourself a Man—Sc to 2F/M Trio).

At the New Amsterdam Theater, Fanny has returned to the Follies and Nick has plans to open a casino in Florida that Fanny financially backs. Eddie, who has always had a romantic interest in Fanny, is doubtful about Nick's stability, but Fanny angrily tells him to stay out of her personal life and exits to rehearse (Rat-Tat-Tat-Tat—Mixed Chorus). The rehearsal quickly turns into a full-scale number which stars Fanny.

After the opening night, in Fanny's dressing room at the New Amsterdam Theater, Fanny angrily confronts Nick, who missed her performance. He confesses that he has lost her investment and accuses her of treating him like a child. Fanny begs him not to leave (Who Are You Now?—Sc to F Solo).

At the Arnstein home, Nick, tired of Fanny's attempts to give him financial assistance, defiantly becomes involved in a crooked bond deal.

On a bare stage at the New Amsterdam, Mrs. Brice interrupts a rehearsal to inform Fanny that Nick has pleaded guilty to embezzlement and is to spend eighteen months in jail. Fanny sings a song which reflects the hurt she feels (The Music That Makes Me Dance—F Solo).

The time returns to the present and Fanny in her dressing room. Nick arrives to tell her they must separate before they cause each other any more pain. Fanny sadly prepares for the performance in the Follies, vowing to pick up the pieces of her life (Don't Rain on My Parade [Reprise]—F Solo).

NOTES ON THE PRODUCTION

The story of Follies comedienne Fanny Brice made Barbra Streisand a star. It was her second Broadway musical; her first was *I Can Get It for You Wholesale*. The play opened in the same season as *Hello, Dolly!*, which won most of the 1964 Tony Awards.

Funny Girl is a vehicle for a company of talented performers as well as a talented actress/comedienne who can handle the comic and dramatic aspects of the role. Fanny's songs require a strong voice to be effectively performed, but the characterization should be emphasized more than the singing. Readers who are only familiar with the movie should know that most of the non-Fanny character songs and musical numbers that rounded out the Broadway script were cut from the film.

The set and costume requirements make this an extremely expensive show. Florenz Ziegfeld was a lavish producer and any show that deals with performances in "his Follies" must reflect the opulence of the man and the era. Some of the scenes take place backstage, which means the actual wall of the theatre may be used, but the remaining sets include a dressing room, an exterior of the music hall, Henry Street, the Brice home, a private dining room, and the Arnstein home. Some of these may be partial sets, but it is nearly impossible to cut any of the sets or transfer them to different locations.

The show requires extremely tight lighting in order to maintain the pace this production requires as it zooms from scene to scene and location to location. The overall work involved in a production of this script is well worth the effort if one has excellent performers and a Fanny worthy of a showcase.

SONGS OF SPECIAL INTEREST

"Don't Rain on My Parade," dramatic, defiant, determined, driving rhythm. Mezzo.

"Find Yourself a Man," comic timing, reaction and strong characterization stressed. 2F/M Trio.

"I'm the Greatest Star," comic, up tempo, high energy, possible cutting for audition. Mezzo.

"Who Taught Her Everything She Knows?," some dance, vaudeville style, interrelationship. Tenor/alto.

"Who Are You Now?," dramatic, introspective, club potential. Mezzo.

Instrumentation: violins, cello, bass, 5 reeds, horn, 3 trumpets, 3 trombones, 2 percussion, guitar/banjo, piano/celeste/conductor
Script: Random
Score: Chappell
Record: Capitol
Rights: TW

A FUNNY THING HAPPENED ON THE WAY TO THE FORUM

Book: Burt Shevelove and Larry Gelbart (Based on the comedies of Plautus)
Music and Lyrics: Stephen Sondheim

ORIGINAL PRODUCTION

Alvin Theatre, May 8, 1962 (964 perf.)
Director: George Abbott
Choreography and Musical Staging: Jack Cole
Musical Director: Harold Hastings
Orchestration: Irwin Kostal and Sid Ramin
Principals: Pseudelos—Zero Mostel—Baritone; Hysterium—Jack Gilford—Tenor; Senex—David Burns—Baritone; Lycus—John Carradine—Baritone; Domina—Ruth Kobart—Soprano; Philia—Preshy Marker—Soprano; Hero—Brian Davies—Tenor; Miles—Ronald Holgate—Baritone; Erronius—Raymond Walburn—VTNE
Chorus and Smaller Roles: 6F/3M (two of the girls should look like twins).

SYNOPSIS

The chorus sings the opening number, which introduces the cast of characters and sets the mood (Comedy Tonight—Mixed Chorus).

Hero's parents, Senex and Domina, planning to be away on a trip, leave him in the charge of Hysterium, chief slave. Hysterium is upset to see the young innocent staring at the house next door, for he knows it is a house of prostitution. Hero assures Hysterium he knows about Lycus and about love (Love I Hear—M Solo). Two citizens enter dragging Pseudelos, Hero's slave, who has been caught cheating at dice. When Hero reprimands him the slave bargains to gain his freedom. Hero agrees on the condition that Pseudelos get him the girl Hero has recently seen in Marcus Lycus's house (Free—Sc to M Duet).

Pseudelos, discovering that Hero's love is a virgin courtesan who has just arrived from Crete, negotiates to buy her from the crafty Lycus. Pseudelos is introduced by Lycus to his various girls (The House of Marcus Lycus—M Solo) but insists he wants to buy Philia. When Lycus informs him she has been sold to a Roman military captain, Pseudelos convinces Lycus that there is a plague on Crete and Philia might infect the others. He magnanimously offers to guard the girl in Senex's house until the captain arrives. Philia, left alone with Hero, confesses she isn't very bright, but Hero doesn't care (Lovely—Sc to M/F Duet).

Pseudelos, knowing his freedom is at stake, tries to entice Philia to escape with Hero and creates a lovely picture of their life together (Pretty Little Picture—2M/F Trio). Philia, who would love to go, is honor bound to wait for her captain. She enters the house to wait. Meanwhile, Senex unexpectedly returns and Pseudelos recklessly tells him Philia is the new maid he has hired. The two sing of the joy of having a maid. Hysterium and Lycus join them in a number that begins as a duet, moves to a trio and ends as a quartet (Everybody Ought to Have a Maid—M Quartet).

Senex, anxious to be alone with Philia, decides to avoid Hero by meeting the girl in his neighbor's house, which he is watching while the man is off looking for his stolen children. Hysterium, convinced Senex will discover his part in the masquerade, tries to remain calm (I'm Calm—L to M Solo). Erronius, the absent neighbor, suddenly returns to his house but is sidetracked by Pseudelos, who plays the part of a soothsayer and sends the old man around the hills of Rome seven times. He guarantees that Erronius will find his children on the seventh trip.

Hero becomes suspicious of Philia's attention to Senex; Senex is suspicious of her attention to Hero. Each wonders what could be transpiring between Philia and the other man (Impossible—Sc to M Duet).

Captain Miles Gloriosus arrives to take Philia (Bring Me My Bride—M Solo with Mixed Chorus) and announces that he will burn the house of Lycus if Philia is not produced. Pseudelos calls for an intermission.

In Act II Domina, Hero's mother, returns home because she suspects Senex is carrying on with someone. She greets Hysterium, who attempts to keep her from discovering Philia (That Dirty Old Man—Sc to F Solo). Domina warns Hysterium that she plans to disguise herself, and then exits.

Philia tells Hero that though she will go with the captain she loves Hero. When she is kissing the captain, she will think of Hero (That'll Show Him—F Solo). This promise is little consolation to the lovestruck youth.

Pseudelos, desperate for his freedom, convinces Hysterium to disguise himself as Philia and pretend he is dead (Lovely [Reprise]—M Duet). Miles and the company prepare for the funeral (Funeral Sequence—Mixed Chorus), which goes as planned until Hysterium discovers that the captain plans on burning the body. He rushes off, followed by the captain and the company.

After a lengthy comic chase with Philia, Domina and Hysterium all costumed alike, the company discovers that Philia and Miles are really brother and sister. They are reunited with their father, Erronius, who has just completed his seventh jog around Rome. Pseudelos gains his freedom. Philia and Hero are pledged and the play ends happily (Finale—Mixed Chorus).

NOTES ON THE PRODUCTION

1963 Tonys: Musical, Supporting Actor (David Burns), Actor (Zero Mostel), Book, Direction, Producer.

This comedic show is easy to produce as there is only one set that consists of the exterior of three Roman houses. Philia in the original was often seen on the rooftop, but she could be seen in an upper window. The costumes, one per actor plus Domina and Hysterium's disguises, are period Roman. Miles is in Roman armor but his entourage may be costumed as servants if necessary.

The music is in keeping with the comedy and should be played cleanly and broadly. The actors and director need to have a solid background in comedy and be versed in standard comedic bits of business. The script is witty and calls for a knowledge of "playing the audience."

SONGS OF SPECIAL INTEREST

"Comedy Tonight," excellent for opening a revue or showcase presentation.

"Free," exciting scene to duet for baritone/tenor. Good interaction and relationship exercise for class situation.

"Everybody Ought to Have a Maid," comic male quartet. Number builds, almost actor-proof. Good for revue.

"I'm Calm," tenor comedic solo, possible for audition, works well in characterization exercise for class situation.

"Impossible," baritone/tenor duet. Emphasis on age and character contrasts. Excellent for revue. Good for playing an audience.

Instrumentation: 5 reeds, 3 trumpets, 3 trombones, percussion, 3 violins, viola, cello, bass, harp, 2 drums. Smaller arrangement available
Script: Dodd, Mead, Chappell (London)
Score: Chappell
Record: Capitol
Rights: MTI

G

GEORGE M!

Book: Michael Stewart and John and Fran Pascal
Music and Lyrics: George M. Cohan
Lyric and Musical Revisions: Mary Cohan

ORIGINAL PRODUCTION

Palace Theatre, April 10, 1968 (435 perf.)
Director and Choreographer: Joe Layton
Musical Director: Jay Blackton
Orchestration: Philip J. Lang
Principals: Jerry Cohan—Jerry Dodge—baritone; Josie—Bernadette Peters—soprano; Nellie—Betty Ann Grove—alto; George M—Joel Grey—tenor; Fay Templeton—Jacqueline Alloway—soprano; Ethel—Jamie Donnelly—mezzo; Agnes Nolan—Jill O'Hara—alto; Sam Harris—Harvey Evans—VTNE
Chorus: 8M/8F minimum, 2M children who look age three and ten.

SYNOPSIS

Act I opens on a stage in Providence, Rhode Island, in 1878. An actor begins to tell the life of George M. Cohan. The doctor, who has just delivered George, arrives on the scene and sends two girls to get Jerry Cohan, who is currently performing Irish songs and dances on the vaudeville stage (Always Leave Them

Laughing—M Solo). Jerry wonders what his new son will be like and decides that he will be introduced to the stage as soon as he can walk.

Onstage, George is seen learning to walk and dance at the same time, as Jerry coaches him along. A quick vignette shows the four Cohans with ten-year-old Georgie, who quickly becomes a young adult. The Cohans sing about the various cities they have visited in their performances, and close with a tap dance (Tap Dance Finish—Dance Quartet).

At the Colombia Theatre in Cedar Rapids, George issues his soon-to-become-a-trademark thanks to the audience. He is already directing the company and ordering the stagehands around. Famed vaudeville producer E. F. Albee arrives to make a contract with the family, but George insists that he see their act first. Jerry, Nellie, and George perform a song and dance about the enchanting role of the moon in all stories (Musical Moon—Sc to 2M/1F Trio). George then introduces his sister, Josie, to Albee, who sings a short love song (Oh, You Wonderful Boy—F Solo to Mixed Chorus). Then George introduces himself as the most talented kid to ever play New York (All Aboard for Broadway—2M/2F Quartet). As they finish this last song, Albee tells them he is only interested in Josie. Josie declines, however, explaining that it is a four-person act. Jerry is willing to make changes in the act in order to be hired by Albee, but George refuses and warns Albee he will regret not hiring the Cohans. Jerry warns George that he is too ambitious, but George has to make it to the top on Broadway. The four Cohans stride out of the theatre and into the street, confident that they will someday be successful.

As the Cohans are marching in the streets, George conveys an ambitious and proud image which the family and town citizens notice (Musical Comedy Man—Mixed Chorus).

In the dining room of Madame Grimaldi's boardinghouse, an assembly of various theatrical people gather for their Friday dinner. George audaciously announces that he and his family will soon be going to New York with their new act, "The Twentieth Century Kid." He later justifies this lie by writing the sketch for "The Twentieth Century Kid" and proposing that the family go to New York and perform for one week without pay. The family agrees to his scheme.

En route to New York, the Cohans and the various people from the boardinghouse sing and act out their individual performances (All Aboard for Broadway [Reprise]—Mixed Chorus). When they finally get to Broadway, they are awed by its lights and glamour (Broadway Tag—Mixed Chorus).

At the Adams Street Theatre, Ethel Levey, an aspiring young performer, continues to sing the Broadway medley. George presents her to Producer Behmen, who has signed the act, and asks if their contract can be altered from four Cohans to five Cohans. George assumes that Ethel will marry him, although he hasn't even proposed to her. When Ethel expresses her need to be wooed, George courts her in eleven short steps. As time passes, the family changes their costumes and the five of them perform their description of modern-day love (Twentieth Century Love—Sc to 2M/3F). The act is completed and the family takes a bow.

George sings a solo about his respect for Manhattan (My Home Town—M Solo), but the people are unresponsive. He begins to write the book, music and lyrics for *Little Johnny Jones*, a story of an American jockey in England. Ethel tries to get him to slow down and spend more time with her, but George is too busy.

On a bare stage, George observes Agnes, an actress from Worcester, Massachusetts, who auditions for his show (Billie—Sc to F Solo). He rushes her off the stage and orders Ethel and some girls to rehearse their latest number (Push Me Along in My Pushcart—F Trio). While they are singing, George orders a stagehand to paint the Eiffel Tower in the middle of a London backdrop. The astonished painter does as he is told, and George asks for another rehearsal of a new song that will be in the show (A Ring to the Name of Rose—M Quartet). George bustles around directing the rehearsals and demands another number to be practiced (Popularity—Dance). After all the practicing, George admits to Jerry that his arrogance is only a facade to hide his fear. Jerry assures him that the show will be a success.

The show begins on a dock in England with George playing the title role. He is a smash, performing his song about Broadway (Give My Regards to Broadway—M Solo to Mixed Chorus), and the show is a hit.

When Act II opens, George is a successful producer and in partnership with Sam Harris. He blatantly announces that their first collaboration will star Fay Templeton, a famous actress who is outraged at his presumption. George daily sends her new songs, hoping to interest her. He sings in his office and she sings the melody in her apartment (Forty-Five Minutes from Broadway—M/F Linear Duet). Fay's manager tries to talk her into joining Cohan, but Fay adamantly resists. George sends her a second number to entice her (So Long Mary—Sc to 3M/2F Quintet) and her mother and manager urge her to listen, but Fay is so angry with her manager that she threatens to fire him. After she receives another song (Down by the Erie Canal—F Trio and Mixed Chorus), she finally agrees.

On opening night in the New Amsterdam Theatre, Fay sings George's next great hit (Mary's a Grand Old Name—F Solo). George's reputation continues to flourish, but he is so caught up in it that he neglects his marriage. On New Year's Eve in 1907, Ethel tells George she wants a divorce and George responds in typical Cohan fashion, saying life must go on. The company celebrates their success and friendship (All Our Friends—M Solo and Mixed Chorus) in a song that counters the news about the marriage. Nellie, Jerry and Josie arrive and read several telegrams, one of which announces that George is splitting all assets with his family (Jolly Good Fellow—Chorus). And one of them is from Ethel, telling of their divorce (Ethel Exit—F Solo). George insists that the party go on as he quietly slips out a side door. He meets Agnes, the girl from Worcester, and on their way home he opens his heart to her.

During the years till 1919, George and his company continue to prosper. They inspire a patriotic spirit with their shows (Yankee Doodle Dandy—1M/3F Quartet and Mixed Chorus). Agnes is now George's wife, supporting him in whatever he attempts. He devises a new show about a beautiful girl called Little Nellie Kelly whose father is a cop (Nellie Kelly—2M/2F Quartet and Mixed Chorus).

Josie announces that she will be getting married and must leave the show to be with her husband. George, who cannot accept her leaving for personal reasons, argues with Jerry during a performance (Harrigan—Sc to 4M Quartet). After the song is over, Harris enters and tells George that Jerry has died. George and Nellie sing a tribute to the deceased Jerry and to the American flag (Over There; You're a Grand Old Flag—1F/1M Duet and Mixed Chorus).

The acting company decides to form a union and strike (Strike—Mixed Chorus). George refuses to go along with the actors' demands and will not comply with the strike. He doesn't want the old Broadway to change (The Man Who Owns Broadway—M Solo to Mixed Chorus).

George's power on Broadway declines and he retires to Midtown, New York. In February 1937, Agnes gives George a letter from Harris, who offers him a part in a musical. He agrees (Park Incidental—Orchestra).

Onstage at the Alvin Theatre, George is playing the role of a president (I'd Rather Be Right—M Solo) but is very old style. Walt, the stage manager, is given the task of telling George he must adapt his presentational style to the more realistic modern theatre. After Walt leaves, George crumples the director's notes, refusing to believe that Broadway has changed (Give My Regards to Broadway [Reprise]—M Solo to Mixed Chorus). Agnes arrives and tries to console George, who vows not to change. He and Agnes leave to retire in Worcester, Massachusetts (Yankee Doodle Finale—M/F Duet). (Finale—Mixed Chorus).

NOTES ON THE PRODUCTION

George M!, based fairly accurately on the life of the famous showman, is a fast-paced, song-loaded musical. The book is occasionally confusing, for it covers a long history, but a slick performance by a talented company can compensate for any flaws in the script.

The theatrically oriented sets should traditionally be drops and smaller units. There are a lot of costumes, at least three per cast member and ideally many more. The costumes also reflect the changing times and must be visually accurate.

The minimum chorus for a smaller theatre would seem to be sixteen extremely good dancers and singers. If the stage is large, the size of the company needs to be increased to give a more exciting look to the production. If the tap-dancing talents of a company are limited, it is advisable to have a large cast who know at least eight tap steps. The larger choruses take a longer amount of time to enter and the massive sounds of tapping feet in different physical configurations compensate for limited experience.

The show is popular among school groups because the music is familiar and catchy and the story interesting.

SONGS OF SPECIAL INTEREST

"All Aboard for Broadway," good for opening of revue of period choreography, quartet to chorus.

"Yankee Doodle Dandy," "You're a Grand Old Flag," "Over There," "Give My Regards to Broadway," "I Want to Hear a Yankee Doodle Tune," "Harrigan"—all are Cohan classics and work well in a revue situation or in shortened form as a medley and may be performed in any configuration.

Instrumentation: 2 violins, viola, cello, bass, 4 reeds, horn, 3 trumpets, 2 trombones, percussion, piano/conductor
Script: NP
Selections: Marks
Record: Colombia
Rights: TW

THE GOLDEN APPLE

Book and Lyrics: John Latouche (Based on Homer's Legend of Ulysses)
Music: Jerome Moross

ORIGINAL PRODUCTION

Phoenix Theatre, March 11, 1954 (48 perf.); moved to Alvin Theatre, April 20, 1954 (123 perf.)
Director: Norman Lloyd
Choreographer: Hanya Holm
Musical Director: Hugh Ross
Principals: Helen—Kaye Ballard—mezzo; Lovey Mars—Bibi Osterwald—alto; Penelope—Priscilla Gillette—soprano; Ulysses—Stephen Douglass—baritone; Paris—Jonathan Lucas—dancer—VTNE; Hector—Jack Whiting—bass; Menelaus—Dean Michener—tenor; Mrs. Juniper—Geraldine VTI—mezzo; Miss Minerva Oliver—Portia Nelson—soprano; Mother Hare—Nola Day—alto
Chorus: mixed, minimum 14 males if Ulysses troop is trimmed to 8 (need 4 dancers, 4 excellent singers, 2 of which are tenors), 10 women. This minimum configuration should only be used if the stage and auditorium are small.

SYNOPSIS

The first act takes place in Angel's Roost, a small town in the state of Washington at the edge of Mt. Olympus. It is 1900.

The curtain rises on a romantic, sexy young woman of twenty who is seated atop a ladder singing of the boredom she feels (Nothing Ever Happens in Angel's Roost—F Solo to F Trio). She bemoans the fact that a small town of 751 residents has little to offer a young girl, especially when the men are off fighting the

Spanish American War. Three of the female citizens extoll the "blessedness" of the town.

Mother Hare, a cross between a witch and a small-town psychic beatnik, enters. She is cheerful but definitely offbeat, as is evident when she produces a crystal ball and reels off a list of predictions. She prophesizes that Helen will go off with a stranger and Mrs. Juniper and Minerva will argue with Lovey Mars, which will result in a split in the town (Mother Hare's Séance—F Solo to F Quartet). The ladies pay her little heed for they are more concerned with determining the length of the war than with what Helen will do; Mother Hare rechecks her crystal ball and tells them the war will last for years.

Penelope, an effervescently attractive girl in her twenties, enters with the aged Sheriff Menelaus, who announces the end of the Spanish American war. The ladies are excited that the war is ended and the troops will soon be home; they turn to berate Mother Hare, who warns them to heed her words and huffily exits. The Sheriff takes his dreamy wife, Helen, home to put her under lock and key before the men return home.

Penelope, left alone, dreams about Ulysses's return (My Love Is on the Way—F Solo). She dances off as the townspeople enter to exclaim their joy about the boys' returning home (The Heroes Come Home—Mixed Chorus). They proceed to decorate the town for a turn-of-the-century homecoming, complete with bunting, flags, and banners. The returning victors and Ulysses are greeted by the townsfolk, who present a small pageant to commemorate their return. The men thank everyone for all the letters and presents, but the young girls interrupt and ask them to tell of their adventures. The men, led by Ulysses, respond, with tongue-in-cheek humor, by describing the "love" all the natives felt toward them, yet wondering why these "loving" natives were so brutal (It Was a Glad Adventure—M Solo to M Chorus).

Lovey Mars interrupts the festivities to request that the girls tell about the plans for the evening (Come Along, Boys—Mixed Chorus). The chorus dances off, leaving Ulysses and Penelope alone to warmly embrace and tell of their longing for each other (It's the Going Home Together—M/F Duet).

The sky suddenly changes color as Mother Hare enters to welcome Ulysses home and force the happy couple to look into the dismal future (Mother Hare's Prophecy—2F/1M Trio). They face a desert where there once were trees. Mother Hare outlines the achievements man will make as the scientific achievements of the twentieth century are projected on a screen. As Ulysses wonders if people will be happier, Penelope turns on Mother Hare, for she fears the woman is entwining them in some sort of spell, but Mother Hare waves her hand, comments that life needs evil for man to grow, and exits. An anxious Penelope urges Ulysses to resist Mother Hare's predictions, but he promises to always be by her side.

As they exit, six of the young veterans enter looking for Helen, whom they remember as high-spirited, fun-loving, and always willing (Helen Is Always Willing—M Chorus). When Helen enters to tell them she has quieted down and married Sheriff Menelaus for his money, the boys begin attacking the old sheriff; Ulysses breaks up the fight and forces them to give their word to protect Helen from others who might take her from Menelaus. They give the Boy Scout salute in agreement.

The townsfolk appear carrying a picnic table laden with food, and the scene changes to represent a church social complete with various flags and posters. The dancers demonstrate the various races and events that were commonplace at a 1900-style country fair (The Church Social—Mixed Chorus).

The sudden appearance of a hot air balloon decorated with flashing electric lights advertising Paris Notions, Inc., startles the villagers. Mr. Paris, a handsome young man, is posed in the basket as the balloon lands. It turns out he is a traveling salesman who dances his thoughts, for he does not speak. The townsmen read an advertising flyer describing his wares as Paris demonstrates (Introducin' Mr. Paris—M/F Mixed Chorus). Everyone is excited by all the different items for sale and they buy up most of what he has to offer.

Lovey Mars, Mrs. Juniper and Miss Minerva enter with their baked goods, but are greeted by an angered Mother Hare, who accuses them of neglecting her advice now that the men are home. When they halfheartedly apologize, she brings forth a golden apple to give to the winner of the baking contest. The three women, certain one of them will be the winner, argue over who will get the award and demand that an impartial judge be summoned. Their wish is granted as an unsuspecting Paris dances on (The Judgement of Paris—F Trio with M Needed for Staging). The three ladies leave him alone with the entries but gradually sneak on, one by one, to bribe the young man. Lovey Mars, who offers him a lucky key charm guaranteed to win him any girl he desires, is declared the winner.

Lovey introduces Paris to Helen, who is immediately attracted to him and serenades him in a sultry voice (Lazy Afternoon—F Solo). Paris responds by dancing his proposal that they leave; she agrees and they hastily ascend in the balloon. An unsuspecting Menelaus enters, perturbed to see Helen in a balloon with someone he doesn't know.

Menelaus and the old men of the town urge Ulysses and his young soldiers to make war on Rhododendron, the town where Paris lives (The Departure for Rhododendron—Mixed Chorus). The women, led by Penelope, are appalled by the thought of another war and urge them to stay home, but Ulysses and the boys set off with Menelaus as the curtain falls.

In Act II the curtain rises on the busy metropolis of Rhododendron, where Helen and Paris are viewing the sights. A group of admiring, elegantly dressed men are following the couple and Helen is excited by her new life (My Picture in the Papers—F Solo with M Chorus). Her happiness is cut short by Ulysses and his men, who urge her to come back before there is trouble. She stubbornly refuses and the townsfolk protect her when Ulysses tries to take her by force.

The boys desire to return home and leave Helen with Paris, but Ulysses is impressed by the wonders of the town and excited by the prospect of controlling it. He quickly divides the town by creating an issue over the morality of keeping Helen. The city folk, who are quick to join a cause, divide in two groups and begin fighting. Mayor Hector arrives to urge a compromise and devises a system to settle the issue by a single fight between Ulysses and Paris. Ulysses wins, restores Helen to Menelaus and the two depart for Angel's Roost, leaving Ulysses and the boys to wonder what the fight was about (The Taking of Rhododendron— M Chorus).

They don't consider the war for very long because Hector invites them to shop for new clothes before going home (Hector's Song—M Solo). They enter a mercantile establishment as Hector tells the audience he will soon have his revenge, for there is nothing the city can't offer the victors and one by one they will succumb to its evil.

A curtain opens to reveal a section of Angel's Roost where Penelope sits sewing a patchwork quilt, surrounded by suitors. Helen and Menelaus enter arm in arm to tell Penelope that Ulysses is probably off on a spree and she may find him greatly changed when he returns. She reassures herself by remembering their wonderful love (Windflowers—F Solo).

The style of the show becomes revue-oriented as Ulysses begins his travels through the city, and each number demonstrates the passing of time.

Ulysses enters, nattily dressed in a new suit (Store-Bought Suit—M Solo to M Chorus); he is joined by his soldiers, who agree to join him on a big spree. Hector arrives to urge them into Madame Calypso's social parlor where everyone looks very familiar, for the characters are played by their counterpart types from Angel's Roost. For example, Madame Calypso is played by Mrs. Juniper.

After an evening with the big-city phony society, who initially are enthralled by the victors but quickly lose interest, Hector guides the scene to an abstract version of the stock exchange where the stockbroker (Menelaus) and Hector perform a parody of a Gallagher and Shean vaudeville number (Scylla and Charybdis—M Duet). An unsuspecting Ajax invests in the market, loses his worldly goods, and leaps through a nearby open window to his death.

Hector quickly passes a flask around and coerces the boys to a volcanic, tropical island amusement area where the siren (played by Lovey Mars) and her sirenettes perform a sultry nightclub number (By A-Goona-Goona Lagoon—F Solo to Mixed Chorus).

During the course of their travels several of Ulysses's crew are shanghaied, but he doesn't discover this until there are only three left. Hector urges Ulysses, Doc and Achilles, the only remaining soldiers, to trust science, and the set is suddenly transformed into a rocket laboratory whose head scientist is a woman (Mrs. Minerva). She outlines the future of the world, which is quite bleak (Doomed, Doomed, Doomed—F Solo to M Chorus).

Her enthusiasm for her latest invention causes Doc to volunteer to be the test pilot. The rocket flies into space as Ulysses discovers that no thought has been given to Doc's return and he is doomed to die.

Ulysses, realizing that only he and Achilles remain, tells Hector he will fight his evil city; Hector's response is to send him to the commanding Circe (Penelope), who introduces herself (Circe, Circe—F Solo to Mixed Chorus). Circe holds out the golden apple to Ulysses and promises him that superpower will be his forever if he goes with her. A jealous Paris, who is enamored of Circe, attempts to stab Ulysses, but Achilles acts as a shield and takes the deathblow. Everyone rushes off, leaving Ulysses alone to question the meaning of life, death, love, faith and hope. A robed chorus led by Mother Hare responds to his questions as if they were part of his mind (Ulysses's Soliloquy—M Solo to F Chorus). During this questioning, the city disappears and Ulysses decides that he can return home much wiser and more capable, for he is his own man.

The set changes to Penelope's house in Angel's Roost where the ladies and Menelaus are commenting that ten years is too long to wait for Ulysses and she must seriously consider someone else (The Sewing Bee—F Solo to F Chorus to M Solo). An exhausted Ulysses arrives, but Penelope's anger causes the townsfolk to hastily disperse and leave the two alone. Knowing she is both upset and relieved at his return, he beseeches her to look at their life together. The two reunite (It's the Going Home Together [Reprise]—Sc to M/F Duet) as the curtain falls.

NOTES ON THE PRODUCTION

In his foreword to the published libretto John LaTouche notes his initial attraction to the Ulysses theme and his attempt to adapt these stories to American life. He wanted the material to evolve from native American situation, history, music, dance and philosophy. He more than achieved his goal, for *The Golden Apple* employs musical theatre, nostalgia, vaudeville, social history, representative characters and attitudes of early twentieth-century America. It is refreshing, brilliantly conceived and unfortunately rarely produced.

The music flows continually through the show with the majority of the dialogue being sung. Each dialogue section scene is a short song of its own, and complete in itself; however, only the complete songs which are titled are named in parenthesis.

The show is unfamiliar to most people, probably due to the fact that it had a short run and the record album has been out of print for a number of years. The musical was originally performed Off-Broadway and received such rave reviews and ticket requests that the producers moved it to Broadway. Unfortunately, the move did not prove to be a wise one; the show, in a larger theatre, lost much of its charm and was unable to survive the summer drop in ticket sales. The original production received the New York Drama Critics and the Donaldson awards as the Best Musical of the Season and is certainly worth consideration by any talented company looking for something unusual, charming and challenging to produce.

The opportunity for character work, for males and more especially for females, is excellent, and colleges and universities looking for quality roles for their female acting students would do well to peruse the full script and score of this musical.

The sets may be trimmed to utilize two basic locations as a backdrop to the overall action. A painted drop or wall of flats denoting Angel's Roost and Rhododendron with small units or cutouts to represent other locations would be sufficient. The costumes are turn-of-the-century period with those in the first act being more small town in flavor than those worn in the second act, which takes place in the city.

SONGS OF SPECIAL INTEREST

"By A-Goona-Goona Lagoon," comedic spoof of South Sea Islands musicals.
"It's the Going Home Together," romantic duet for a baritone/soprano.
"Lazy Afternoon," warm and sentimental, sultry song, mezzo.
"Scylla and Charybdis," vaudeville comic male duet, baritone/bass. Good for revue and class study.

Instrumentation: 3 violins, viola, cello, bass, 5 woodwinds, 2 horns, 2 trumpets, trombone, percussion, harp, piano/celeste, piano/conductor
Script: Random House
Record: Elektra
Rights: TW

GREASE

Book, Music and Lyrics: Jim Jacobs and Warren Casey

ORIGINAL PRODUCTION

Broadhurst Theatre, June 7, 1972 (3,388 perf.)
Director: Tom Moore
Choreographer: Patricia Birch
Musical Direction/Arrangements: Louis St. Louis
Principals: Rizzo—Adrienne Barbeau—alto; Danny Zuko—Barry Bostwick—tenor; Sandy—Carole Demas—mezzo; Kenickie—Timothy Meyers—baritone; Frenchy—Marya Small—soprano; Doody—James Canning—tenor; Marty—Katie Hanley—alto; Jan—Garn Stephens—mezzo; Teen Angel—Alan Paul—high baritone; Roger—Walter Bobbie—high tenor; Johnny Casino—Alan Paul—tenor
Chorus and Smaller Roles: 3M/4F.

SYNOPSIS

The lights rise at a Rydell High School class reunion (Alma Mater—Mixed Chorus). Miss Lynch, the old English teacher; Patty, a former cheerleader; and Eugene Florcayk, former class valedictorian, enter the room. They make short speeches which lead back to the years gone by. The scene switches to 1959, and the greasers parody the school song (Alma Mater—Mixed Chorus).

It is the first day of school. In the cafeteria, the "Pink Ladies" meet Sandy, a typical Sandra Dee type who has moved to town. Patty Simcox, a snobbish honor student, joins the girls and tells them she is running for class vice president.

The lights cross fade to the boys, who eagerly greet Danny, the gang leader, and ask him about his summer. The lights rise on the cafeteria where Sandy is telling the girls about a boy she met over vacation (Summer Nights—M/F Chorus). The two songs are performed in separate areas of the stage but the audience realizes that the different stories are told about the same people. Danny, followed by the boys, sees Sandy and decides to act cool, a drastic change from their summer romance. In the school, Doody, one of the "Burger Palace" boys, shows off his new guitar à la Elvis (Those Magic Changes—M Solo to M Chorus).

The girls, at a slumber party at Marty's, start to smoke and drink. Trying to force Sandy to conform, they pierce her ears but she gets sick. Marty tells the girls about her new boyfriend in the marines (Freddy, My Love—F Quartet). The girls all fall asleep except Rizzo, who climbs out the window to meet her boyfriend.

The scene changes to the gang and Kenickie, who enters driving a beat-up, 1951 Ford convertible. Kenickie sings of the potential greatness of the car (Greased Lightnin'—M Solo and M Chorus). Rizzo enters and drives off with Kenickie.

The scene changes to Sandy, who has made the cheerleading squad and is practicing. Danny enters to invite her to a party, but the two argue about the value of sports. Sandy forces him into joining the track team.

The play moves to a deserted park where the "Pink Ladies" and the "Burger Palace" boys are sitting. Roger, the king of the mooners, sings to Jan about caring for her (Mooning—M/F Duet). Rizzo, upset by all the attention the boys have been giving Sandy, parodies Sandra Dee, the clean-living movie star of the fifties (Look at Me, I'm Sandra Dee—F Solo). Sandy enters and the two girls fight. When Sandy shuns Danny, he spitefully asks Rizzo to the school dance. The rest of the kids pick dates and comment on the way that the "Burger Palace" boys and the "Pink Ladies" go together (We Go Together—Mixed Chorus).

As Act II opens, the greasers and the "Pink Ladies" prepare for the high school dance (Shakin' at the High School Hop—Mixed Chorus), while Sandy sits mournfully at home with her radio (It's Raining on Prom Night—F Solo).

At the dance, Johnny Casino, disc jockey and teen idol, prepares the group for the dance contest (Born to Hand Jive—M Solo and Mixed Chorus). Danny and Cha-Cha, a girl from another school, win the dance contest.

Several days later Frenchy, who dropped out of high school to attend beauty school, drops out of beauty school. She desperately wishes for a guardian angel to advise her. He appears, complete with a chorus of angels (Beauty School Dropout—M Solo and F Choir), and tells her to finish high school.

At the drive-in movie theatre, Danny gives Sandy his ring, which she accepts. He instantly tries to make out with her and she angrily walks home, despite his argument that no one *walks* home from a drive-in. He sits alone in the car and sings (Alone at a Drive-In Movie—M Solo and Mixed Chorus).

At a party in Jan's basement, Roger and Doody perform (Rock 'N Roll Party Queen—M Duet). Everyone learns Rizzo might be pregnant and Sandy privately offers some advice. Rizzo angrily comments on the difference in their life-styles (There Are Worse Things I Could Do—L to F Solo). Sandy decides to change her Sandra Dee image and returns in the final scene dressed as a greaser. Danny is overwhelmed and comments on her new look (All Choked Up—Mixed Chorus).

NOTES ON THE PRODUCTION

Another Off-Broadway musical that found a home on Broadway, the show moved in June 1972 to the Broadhurst Theatre and played to enthusiastic crowds until 1978, when attendance started to fall off. The producers were able to keep the show going by inexpensive ticket prices and low operating costs. The release of the film buoyed attendance, and in 1980 *Grease* surpassed *Fiddler on the Roof* as the longest-running Broadway musical, a record broken on September 30, 1983 by *A Chorus Line*.

The show is popular among high school and community groups as it is a spoof on the greasers of the fifties, inexpensive to costume, and only requires one unit set of platforms and levels to represent various locations. The plot is thin, but the music is catchy and energetic. Although the cast needs are small, some schools wishing to involve more students have added a very large chorus as fillers on the full company numbers.

It is a rock musical and the singers should be miked for the numbers. They may have hand-held mikes with cords, but the choreographer will need fake microphones with cords to use during the rehearsal and staging of the musical numbers. It is possible to have several sets of microphones permanently set, stage left and right, resting on stands. The actors just cross to the instrument when needed and return it when the number is completed.

SONGS OF SPECIAL INTEREST

"Summer Nights," split male/female chorus number, heavily styled in fifties.

"There Are Worse Things I Could Do," dramatic, alto, rock rhythm.

"We Go Together," suitable for revue finale or sing-along with hard jive movements.

Instrumentation: 2 saxophones, 2 guitars, 1 bass, drums, piano/conductor, electric piano (optional)
Script: Winter House, Pocket, Great Rock Musicals, SF
Selections: Morris
Record: MGM
Rights: SF

GUYS AND DOLLS

Book: Abe Burrows and Jo Swerling (Based on Damon Runyon's short story "The Idyll of Miss Sarah Brown")
Music and Lyrics: Frank Loesser

ORIGINAL PRODUCTION

The 46th Street Theatre, November 24, 1950 (1,200 perf.)
Director: George S. Kaufman
Choreographer: Michael Kidd
Musical Director: Irving Actman
Orchestration: George Bassman, Ted Royal
Principals: Sky Masterson—Robert Alda—tenor; Sarah Brown—Isabel Bigley—soprano; Adelaide—Vivian Blaine—alto; Nicely-Nicely—Stubby Kaye—tenor; Nathan Detroit—Sam Levene—baritone; Benny Southstreet—Johnny Silver—baritone; Rusty Charlie—Douglas Deane—bass; Arvide—Pat Rooney, Sr.—tenor; Harry the Horse—Tom Pedi—baritone
Chorus and Smaller Roles: 12M/8F.

SYNOPSIS

The show opens with a brief introduction to the various New York characters which author Damon Runyon depicted in his famous stories. The focus is on Nicely-Nicely, Benny Southstreet and Rusty Charlie, three gamblers with racing forms who try to choose a winner (Fugue for Tinhorns—M Trio). Sarah enters with the mission band (Follow the Fold—Chorus—the two songs are partially sung together) and begins to give a speech about sin, but quickly loses her listeners.

Some men come to Nicely-Nicely and ask if he has seen Nathan Detroit, who earns his living by arranging places for illegal crap games. Brannigan, a tough detective, tells Nicely-Nicely that he is going to close Nathan's crap game down. Nathan enters to comment to Benny and Nicely-Nicely on the difficulties of finding a safe place to hold their forthcoming game (The Oldest Established—Sc to M Trio to M Chorus).

The only place Nathan can find to use is Biltmore's garage, but it will cost $1,000 and Nathan doesn't have that much money. He learns that Sky Masterson, a good-looking gambler in his thirties, is in town looking for some action and decides to con Masterson out of $1,000 by making a can't-lose bet with him.

Adelaide, Nathan's fiancée for the past fourteen years, meets him at the newsstand and tells him she'll be fine as long as he doesn't start a crap game again. Nathan sees Sky approaching and sends Benny and Nicely to take Adelaide to lunch.

Nathan, hoping to get money from Sky, bets $1,000 that he can't get Sarah, the mission group leader, to go to Havana with him the next day. Sky proceeds to the mission and offers Sarah twelve sinners in exchange for accompanying him to Cuba. When she refuses he accuses her of being afraid of romance, so she tells him her imaginings of love (I'll Know—Sc to M/F Duet).

In the Hot Box Nightclub, Adelaide and the dancing girls perform (A Bushel and a Peck—F Chorus). After the show when Adelaide discovers that Nathan is running a crap game her cold grows worse. She begins reading a psychology book and determines that her perpetual cold is caused by Nathan's stalling their wedding date (Adelaide's Lament—Sc to F Solo).

Benny and Nicely observe Sky following Sarah as she performs her mission work and comment on the weakness men have for women (Guys and Dolls—Sc to M Duet).

Outside the mission the discouraged army workers are interrupted by General Cartwright, who informs Sarah she is going to close the mission, which has a poor convert record. Sarah decides to go to Havana with Sky, who has guaranteed her twelve sinners at the next meeting.

On a street corner, the crapshooters, waiting for the game location to be announced, are interrupted by Brannigan, who is certain they are preparing for a game. They quickly announce that they are gathered to honor Nathan, who is marrying Adelaide the next night. Adelaide arrives and is ecstatic to hear the news.

Down in Havana, Sarah and Sky find a place to eat and Sky orders drinks. Sarah soon becomes tipsy and gets involved in a fight. Sky carries her out. Outside, Sarah drunkenly expresses her love (If I Were a Bell—Sc to F Solo).

At 4:00 A.M. outside the mission, Sky tells Sarah it is his favorite time of day (My Time of Day—Sc to M Solo), and they realize they are in love (I've Never Been in Love Before—Sc to M/F Duet). Suddenly a police car is heard, and Nathan and the crapshooters run from the mission. Sarah assumes Sky falsely engineered her absence from New York so they could gamble in the mission. She orders him away as the curtain falls.

When Act II opens, it is the next night in the Hot Box Nightclub. Adelaide and the girls perform (Take Back Your Mink—F Chorus). At the end of the song the lights rise on an empty table, which Sky moves to as Nicely comes in and informs him that the crap game is still on if he wants some of the action. Adelaide, furious that Nathan is running a game, sadly sings (Adelaide's Lament [Reprise]—F Solo).

Out in the street Sarah is walking with her grandfather Arvide, who tries to comfort her with some good wishes (More I Cannot Wish You—Sc to M Solo).

The scene changes to a sewer where the crap game is in progress. Big Jule, a tough gambler from Chicago, has lost and won't let anyone leave until he wins the money back.

Sky arrives at the game and rolls the dice in hopes of winning twelve sinners for Sarah's mission (Luck Be a Lady—M Solo to M Chorus). He wins and the gamblers, including Nathan, head for the mission. When Adelaide spies Nathan, who tells her he is going to a prayer meeting, she accuses him of lying again and walks out (Sue Me—Sc to M/F Duet).

The men enter the mission and begin to tell of their sins. Nicely-Nicely joins in (Sit Down You're Rockin' the Boat—M Solo and Mixed Chorus).

Adelaide and Sarah discuss their mutual problems with men. They decide to marry now convinced it is easier to change a husband (Marry the Man Today—Sc to F Duet). The play ends with both girls getting their guys and changing them to fit their ideal.

NOTES ON THE ORIGINAL PRODUCTION

1951 Tony Awards: Choreography, Direction, Book, Music, Actor (Robert Alda), Musical, Supporting Actress (Isabel Bigley), and Producer.

The show was a blockbuster musical that has since become a classic. Soaringly memorable music, excellent characters and comic treatment make this an assured winner financially and artistically. Although there are numerous set requirements, it is possible to utilize drops and wagons effectively, or a revolving unit set that is manually controlled. The costumes are not complicated and may usually be pulled from attics. The opening sequence depicting various Runyon characters gets somewhat complex insofar as props are concerned, but it is possible to focus attention on the easier portrayals. There are quite a few realistic props which might be time-consuming to obtain.

The gamblers' dance, while brilliantly executed and choreographed on Broadway, is extremely difficult to perform effectively in its entirety by nondancers. Some groups have trimmed the number without losing the mood.

SONGS OF SPECIAL INTEREST

"Adelaide's Lament," showstopper, alto story song, comedic, excellent for character study or revue.

"Fugue for Tinhorns," male trio, tight harmony, good vocal exercise, and strong characters.

"Guys and Dolls," tenor/baritone duet. Contrasting characters, comedic, up tempo, revue material.

"If I Were a Bell," audition potential, requires some movement, shows comedic ability from a soprano.

"I'll Know," strong tenor/soprano duet, romantic and antagonistic, good characters. Much underlies the accompanying scene.

"Marry the Man Today," comic, clever lyrics, needs strong relationships and characters to pull off. Soprano/alto, movement must cover the musical interludes.

"More I Cannot Wish You," tenor, charm song.

"Sue Me," comic scene to duet, requires good timing and strong characters. Alto/baritone.

Instrumentation: 5 reeds, 3 trumpets, trombone, horn, percussion, 4 violins, cello, bass, piano
Script: The Modern Theatre, Vol. 4, Chappell (London)
Score: Frank
Record: Decca, MCA
Rights: MTI

GYPSY

Book: Arthur Laurents (Suggested by the memoirs of Gypsy Rose Lee)
Music: Jule Styne
Lyrics: Stephen Sondheim

ORIGINAL PRODUCTION

Broadway Theatre, May 21, 1959 (702 perf.)
Director and Choreographer: Jerome Robbins
Musical Director: Milton Rosenstock
Orchestration: Sid Ramin and Robert Ginzler
Principals: Rose—Ethel Merman—alto; Louise—Sandra Church—alto; June—Lane Bradbury—mezzo; Tulsa—Paul Wallace—high baritone; Baby June—Jacqueline Mayro—child belt; Baby Louise—Karen Moore—VTNE; Herbie—Jack Klugman—high baritone; Tessie Tura—Maria Karnilova—mezzo; Mazeppa—Faith Dane—alto; Electra—Chotzi Foley—mezzo; Miss Cratchitt—Peg Murray—VTNE
Chorus and Smaller Roles: 6 Hollywood blondes, 8 young males, 4 children, one must be female, 8 character males, 6 showgirls (optional).

SYNOPSIS

The action takes place in the early twenties and thirties throughout various American cities.

The curtain rises on a Seattle, Washington, vaudeville theatre, where Uncle Jocko, the oily MC, is holding auditions for his kiddie shows. The talented Baby June performs with her sister Louise, as their mother, Rose, shouts out directions from the rear of the audience (May We Entertain You—F Ch Duet). Rose enters carrying Chowsie, her little dog, and a very large handbag. Rose is terrifying and demanding as she charms, cajoles and threatens Uncle Jocko into letting the girls finish their performance.

The scene switches to the kitchen of a simple home in Seattle, Washington, where Rose, who has plans for June to headline on the famous Orpheum Circuit, attempts to convince her overly practical father, a retired railroad worker, to give her the money to pay for a new act (Some People—Sc to F Solo). When he refuses to listen, she hocks his gold plaque, honoring fifty years of company service, takes the girls, rounds up three boys for the act and heads for California.

Backstage at a vaudeville house in Los Angeles, Rose is unsuccessfully trying to convince Mr. Weber, the theatre owner, to get her a booking when Herbie, a former agent turned candy salesman, arrives. Rose enlists his aid, which he readily gives. After convincing Weber the act is terrific, Herbie tells Rose he used to be an agent until he developed ulcers and became a candy salesman. When Rose discovers he isn't married but loves children, she wins him over by showing him how they complement each other (Small World—Sc to F Solo). He agrees and the act is booked.

A vaudeville placard announces Baby June and her newsboys as the curtains open on a vaudeville street drop with a newspaper kiosk in front. Three young boys and Louise, dressed as newsboys, loudly perform and introduce Baby June, who tap-dances, sings and performs everything she can before the boys return in military outfits accompanied by Louise, as Uncle Sam. June reenters, dressed as the Statue of Liberty, wearing toe shoes and twirling batons. As she twirls to the big finale, an American eagle pops up over the kiosk and the boys fire their rifles, which display American flags. The audience goes wild and June steps forward for her bow. At the end of the bow the orchestra strikes up, the music builds, a strobe light is turned on and the act seems to dance faster and faster as they move offstage and are gradually replaced by older counterparts. The lights rise on the older group, who takes a final bow before the blackout.

The lights rise on two rooms in a fourth-class hotel. In one of the rooms the boys and Louise are sleeping in various locations, while the other room contains a large bed, a table, and some chairs.

It is Louise's birthday, which everyone celebrates with presents and egg rolls. Rose announces her idea for a new act but is interrupted by Mr. Kringelein, the hotel manager, who smells the food and threatens eviction. Rose throws herself at him, attempting to get him in a compromising situation, but Herbie arrives to smooth things over. He introduces Mr. Goldstone, who has booked the act for the Orpheum Circuit. Rose excitedly offers the overwhelmed man an egg roll and bursts into song as the kids join in (Mr. Goldstone, I Love You—Sc to F Solo to Mixed Chorus). A forgotten Louise, her birthday superseded by the arrival of Goldstone, moves quietly into her bedroom, cuddles her birthday present from Rose, a live lamb, and wistfully sings to the lamb and her stuffed animals (Little Lamb—F Solo).

In a gaudy Chinese restaurant, Rose is scraping leftovers into cartons as Herbie moodily watches. She sends the girls to the hotel and Herbie uses the opportunity to bring up the subject of marriage, the decline of vaudeville and the need for June and Louise to have a home and schooling. Herbie tells Rose he is afraid of losing his temper and walking out, but she confidently promises to marry him after June is a bona fide star (You'll Never Get Away from Me—Sc to F/M Duet).

On the stage of the famous Grantziger's Palace Theatre, Mr. Grantziger's businesslike secretary, Miss Cratchitt, rushed on to answer the stage manager's phone. She tells the impatient Mr. Grantziger, who is in the light booth, that Rose's act is almost ready. The lights dim and the curtains open on a vaudeville-style barnyard and a chorus of farmboys who introduce Dainty June and her dancing cow (Dainty June and Her Farmboys—F Solo and M Chorus). The show resembles the old newsboy show, but the big finish is performed by the farmboys, who now sport top hats, tails and canes that shoot American flags; a train replaces the kiosk and a tap-dancing cow has Louise in the front half. During this splashy ending, Rose has been running around picking up a dropped hat and loudly commenting to Mr. Grantziger about how great everything is. Grantziger phones down to Cratchitt that he likes the act and the surprised secretary takes Rose, Herbie, Louise and June to Grantziger's office to sign a contract.

Louise and June, left alone in the outer office, are excitedly dancing about and playing the piano when Cratchitt enters. Herbie and Rose follow her onstage. Rose is visibly upset that Grantziger is willing to give June free acting lessons if Rose will stay away. Rose angrily refuses to listen to June's pleas and rushes out of the room followed by Herbie and Cratchitt.

Left alone in the office, the two agree that life would be better if Rose married and got out of show business (If Momma Was Married—Sc to F Duet).

Backstage at a Buffalo theatre, Tulsa, the handsomest boy in the act, is practicing a dance routine as Louise watches. As he confides to Louise about the girl he envisions as his partner, he begins to outline and perform the act (All I Need Is the Girl—Sc to M Solo). She becomes involved and it is apparent she likes him very much.

Late one misty night at a train terminal in Omaha, as Yonkers and Angie tell Herbie they are leaving, Louise enters with a note telling Rose that June has married Tulsa. Herbie moves to Rose, who stares in shocked silence. He urges her to marry him and Louise begs her to agree but Rose turns to Louise and vows to make her a star. As her voice rises in determination, she violently bursts into song as Herbie and Louise watch in silence (Everything's Coming Up Roses—L to F Solo).

Act II opens on the Texas desert with a tent on one side of the stage and the back end of a touring car on the other. A rehearsal for Madame Rose's Torea-dorables is in progress. It is a terribly tacky version of the newsboys act, only this time it stars Louise in a blonde wig (Madame Rose's Toreadorables—F Chorus). Herbie enters at the end of the number to tell Rose he has been unable to get a booking, but she is convinced something will turn up. A disheartened Louise, realizing she can never replace June as a performer, confronts her mother, who promises to find something Louise can do well. Rose valiantly tells Louise and Herbie everything will work out as long as they have each other (Together Wherever We Go—Sc to 2F/1M Trio).

Agnes, one of the Toreadorables, enters with the girls' letters home asking for money; when Louise gives her the blonde wig, Herbie decides that the girls should all be blonde, except Louise. They decide to redo the act and book it as Rose Louise and her Hollywood Blondes, a name Herbie is sure will sell.

The scene shifts to the backstage and dressing rooms of a Wichita burlesque house where the girls arrive for their first booking as the new act. Rose is appalled but Louise forces her to realize that they must play out the booking because they are broke and stranded. Herbie enters apologetically, but Rose forgives him and finally admits that vaudeville is dead and there will be no more bookings. She asks Herbie to marry her when they are no longer in burlesque. Herbie goes off to cue the stage manager as Tessie Tura, one of the star strippers who has a background in ballet, enters her dressing room. Rose huffily exits as Cigar, the theatre manager, enters to ask Tessie to play a scene. Tessie refuses but Louise volunteers for the extra salary. Two other strippers, Mazeppa, who "bumps it with a trumpet," and Electra, whose strip is accentuated with lights, enter the dressing room and Tessie introduces them to Louise. The three advise her on the art of burlesque (You Gotta Get a Gimmick—Sc to F Trio).

It is the end of the booking and Rose's wedding day. Herbie is excited and Rose is on edge. When the star stripper gets arrested, Rose volunteers Louise, who is terrified of the prospect but does Rose's bidding. Herbie confronts Rose in a dramatic scene and walks out—he has finally gotten angry and can take no more.

Alone in the dressing room before her entrance, Louise looks into a mirror and realizes she is beautiful and proudly walks to the stage where everyone is waiting to wish her luck. She does a slow burlesque walk to June's "entertain you" number and quietly sings out, ever the lady (Let Me Entertain You—F Solo).

A series of performances follow, which show Louise, now renamed Gypsy Rose Lee, gaining confidence and poise with each booking. The sequence ends at a Christmas holiday show at Minsky's, years later. Backstage at Minsky's, in Louise's opulent dressing room, a French maid, Renée, is straightening up as Rose enters. After an extremely bitter argument with Louise, Rose realizes that she is no longer needed. She crosses onto the empty burlesque stage and soliloquizes. It is as if her entire life parades before her. She is fighting an emotional breakdown and vents her needs, agony and emotions as she parades across the stage of the empty theatre (Rose's Turn—L to F Solo).

Louise quietly enters the stage and Rose smiles in embarrassment and attempts to ease the moment. Rose finally admits she fought for both her kids because of her own need to be noticed. Louise embraces her while admitting she always wanted Rose to notice her and still does. The two exit arm in arm as the curtain falls.

NOTES ON THE PRODUCTION

The majority of 1960 Tony Awards were captured by *The Sound of Music* and *Fiorello!* However, Angela Lansbury received a Tony Award as Best Actress for her portrayal of Rose in the 1975 revival.

The script is excellent, the characters well drawn, the relationships artfully developed, and the music and lyrics are outstanding examples of musical theatre.

Most of the songs were hits and have become standards. The show is more than the story of a stage mother; it is a study in human inter-action and the need for recognition. Developing this script into a fine production requires a strong director who understands human relationships and can help the actors develop their characters into three-dimensional ones. The interdependence between Herbie and Rose must be carefully developed through their unspoken moments and his reactions. It is essential that he be more than the henpecked boyfriend Rose almost marries. Rose must be played on a variety of levels or the final numbers in Acts I and II can never be fully realized.

Gypsy is a technical nightmare, for it requires several vaudeville-style drops, tacky yet showy costumes for Rose's production numbers, a stripper's costume operated by a battery pack that lights up, guns and canes that shoot American flags, two realistic hotel rooms loaded with props which include a live lamb, a touring car, a small pet dog and a variety of wagon sets which represent a Chinese restaurant, a producer's office, a dressing room and a kitchen in Seattle. There isn't much that can be done to combine or cut down on the show's technical requirements if it is presented in a large proscenium theatre. An audience is justified in expecting an elaborate production for this theatrically oriented musical.

SONGS OF SPECIAL INTEREST

"All I Need is the Girl," good for class study for male dancer, requires good movement, high baritone.

"Everything's Coming up Roses," may be performed as a solo but works better in class study if someone portrays Louise. Intensely dramatic, determined, a variety of levels, good for class, revue or club. Alto.

"If Momma Was Married," fun duet, requires strong relationship and understanding of script before staging, character and situation oriented, mezzo/alto.

"Rose's Turn," introspective, powerfully dramatic, intense, character oriented, excellent for class study or showcase, alto.

"Small World," charm ballad for an alto, last verse possible audition if well acted and sung.

"Some People," club, good for class study when combined with scene.

"You Gotta Get a Gimmick," character oriented, requires comedic timing, showstopper, good for class, revue or showcase, movement.

Instrumentation: 3 violins, viola, cello, bass, 4 reeds, 1 horn, 3 trumpets, 3 trombones, 2 percussion, piano/conductor
Script: Random, Theatre Arts (Magazine) 6/62, Ten Great Musicals of the American Theatre.
Score: Chappell
Record: Colombia
Rights: TW

H

HALLELUJAH, BABY!

Book: Arthur Laurents
Music: Jule Styne
Lyrics: Betty Comden and Adolph Green

ORIGINAL PRODUCTION

Martin Beck Theatre, April 26, 1967 (293 perf.)
Director: Burt Shevelove
Dances and Musical Numbers Staged by: Kevin Carlisle
Musical Director and Vocal Arranger: Buster Davis
Orchestration: Peter Matz
Principals: Georgina—Leslie Uggams—soprano; Clem—Robert Hooks—baritone; Mary—Barbara Sharma—mezzo; Prince—Bud West—VTNE; Princess—Carol Flemming—VTNE; Mama—Lillian Hayman—alto; Harvey—Allen Case—tenor; Mr. Charles—Frank Hamilton—VTNE; Mrs. Charles/Mistress/Ethel/Dorothy—Marilyn Cooper—VTNE
Chorus and Smaller Roles: 8F/8M mostly Black—must include two Black male tap dancers.

SYNOPSIS

Georgina, the star of the show, sets up the story line about a young girl's rise to fame. Although the play covers a sixty-year time span from 1900 to 1960, no one ages. As she exits, a 1900-style kitchen rolls on and Mama enters with a laundry basket and urges the offstage Georgina to get to work (Back in the Kitchen—F Solo). The two are employed as servants for wealthy Whites.

Georgina and her mother argue over Georgina's desire to marry Clem, who her mother thinks is a lazy bum and will run off as Georgina's Daddy and Grandpa did. As Mama polishes the silver, Georgina tells her she wants an independent life in her own home (My Own Morning—F Solo).

Clem arrives. He tells her he has won money from some White men in a poker game but a White policeman insisted on his cut and Clem ended up the loser. He brings in four young Blacks to corroborate his story (The Slice—M Solo with M Quartet).

Georgina, resting on the porch outside the kitchen, meets Harvey, a flashily-dressed White who needs a Black actress for the theatre he has just leased. He offers her the job but she knows that Blacks and Whites aren't allowed to appear onstage together. Harvey blithely tells her not to worry as the porch glides off and ''gas'' footlights come on, accompanied by a flat of a Southern plantation.

The next scene depicts Georgina's performance in a Civil War melodrama (Farewell, Farewell—Mixed Chorus). Despite her obvious success in the role, Georgina is fired by Mr. Charles, the nervous theatre owner, who decides it is more prudent to cast a White actor as a Black maid. Harvey advises her to go where there are more opportunities. The men and scenery move off as Georgina tells the audience she is moving up and out.

The scene jumps to a 1920 nightclub where Tip and Tap are headlining and Georgina is performing in the chorus (Feet Do Yo' Stuff-Mixed Chorus). It seems that Harvey manages the prohibition gambling club and has employed Georgina and Clem. The three get fired over a racial issue which centers around Georgina's not being able to sit down with a royal patron.

Georgina wonders where she can find another club job but Clem tells her he doesn't want her performing as a chorus girl because he plans on making big money through bootlegging (Watch My Dust—M Solo). Mama enters carrying a feather duster and she and Georgina start for Mama's new maid job. On the way they meet Clem, who is earning his living as a porter. The three comment on the way Blacks must act in 1920s White America (Smile, Smile—Sc to 2F/M Trio). Unfortunately, the jobs don't last because of the stock market crash.

The scene moves to the heart of the depression and a WPA theatre project where Georgina is playing a witch in a jazzed up *Macbeth* (Witch's Brew—F Trio). The show closes, due to suspected subversive material, but Clem, Georgina, Harvey and Mary, a White performer, look to the future (Another Day—2M/2F Quartet).

Georgina argues with Clem, now a Communist. After he leaves she realizes she preferred the old Clem to this new radical thinker (I Wanted to Change Him—F Solo). Harvey enters to boost her spirits and ends up kissing her, an uncomfortable situation for both of them. Georgina realizes she has to be the best if she is to win in a White folks' world (Being Good Isn't Good Enough—F Solo).

The 1940s. Georgina and Mary are in a USO show and perform at a camp where Clem and Harvey are officers. There is still a tenseness in Clem and Georgina's relationship (Talking to Yourself—2M/1F Trio).

Harvey is furious because Georgina's show is to play separate performances for White and Black audiences. He convinces Georgina to quit and the three friends get on a bus and proceed to sit in the rear. The driver tells them Harvey, who is White can't sit in the back and Georgina, anxious not to miss her train, sends him up front but vows never to be in a position of insult again.

A club in the 1950s with many of the same customers who appeared in the 1920s club scene. The lights dim on the dancing patrons performing the limbo and rise on the stage area where Harvey announces his star attraction, Georgina Franklin in her new act (Hallelujah Baby—F/2M Trio).

Harvey asks Georgina to marry him but she avoids the issue. When Mary enters to tell them Clem, who has become an important civil rights leader, is in the audience, Georgina goes to change. Mary, who has always been attracted to Harvey and senses his mood, asks him to join her at a party but he sadly refuses. Harvey realizes Georgina will never marry him (Not Mine—M Solo). After the song Clem greets Harvey to tell him he wants to stay friends but is going to ask Georgina to marry him. Harvey toasts Clem. Mama enters, still amazed by Georgina's overwhelming talent. She asks the boys about Georgina's performing skills and demonstrates to everyone that Georgina got her talent from her Mama (I Don't Know Where She Got It—F Solo). She exits, song and dance style.

Clem asks Georgina to marry him but accuses her of trying to live in a White world. When the Prince, Princess and hostess enter and address her mother, who has arrived with Georgina's purse, as her maid, Georgina is forced to realize he is right. She has finally grown up. As Mama exits, Georgina vows to become part of the real world (Little Room—F Solo).

The sixties. Partial set pieces reveal a large kitchen. Mary, Mama and Georgina are moving into Georgina's new apartment in an all-White building. They aren't sure they'll be legally accepted until Harvey arrives with official documents. Clem attacks Georgina's dependence on Harvey and urges her to make it on her own. Georgina, realizing she still loves Clem despite the major adjustments they must make in their relationship, leaves Harvey (Now's the Time—Sc to Mixed Chorus).

NOTES ON THE PRODUCTION

Tony Awards: Featured Actress (Lillian Hayman), Best Musical, Producer, Music and Lyrics, Book, and Actress (Leslie Uggams).

The show is a brief history of the change in attitudes toward Blacks from 1900 to 1960. The songs are a showcase for a talented triple-threat performer. At times the script becomes overly didactic to an audience of the eighties that has seen *Roots* and *The Autobiography of Miss Jane Pittman*, but a sensitive director could easily make the "preaching" sections more palatable.

The sets may be made of minimal pieces and should flow quickly on and off to keep the much needed pace of the show. Some scenes may be relocated to trim the sets required by the script; for example, the porch scene in the first act may be played in the kitchen. The costumes span from 1900 to 1960 and many of Georgina's clothes are theatrical and stylish. Probably the bulk of the production budget should be allotted for costumes.

The size of the company is flexible, with mixed Black and White performers. The earlier dance sequences, however, must be performed by Black dancers to depict onstage segregation.

The show will appeal to a relatively sophisticated and open-minded audience. The music is appealing but the book may need to be toned down in order to have more universal interest.

SONGS OF SPECIAL INTEREST

"Another Day," good for Black or White performers in a revue situation, 2M/2F quartet, up tempo, good for beginning choreographer.

"Being Good Isn't Good Enough," strong, determined, soprano.

"I Wanted to Change Him," semidramatic, good range, possible club, soprano.

"I Don't Know Where She Got It," up tempo, song and dance, big voice, showstopper, alto.

"Now's the Time," good for range, up tempo, some movement, soprano/mezzo.

Instrumentation: 5 reeds, 3 trumpets, 3 trombones, 2 percussion, guitar or banjo, violin, cello, bass, piano/conductor
Script: NP
Selections: Chappell
Record: Columbia
Rights: MTI

HELLO, DOLLY!

Book: Michael Stewart (Based on Thornton Wilder's *The Matchmaker*)
Music: Jerry Herman

ORIGINAL PRODUCTION

St. James Theatre, January 16, 1964 (2,844 perf.)
Director and Choreographer: Gower Champion
Musical Direction: Shepard Coleman
Orchestration: Philip J. Lang
Principals: Dolly Levi—Carol Channing—low alto; Horace—David Burns—baritone; Cornelius—Charles Nelson Reilly—tenor; Barnaby—Jerry Dodge—baritone; Irene—Eileen Brennan—mezzo with low belt; Minnie Fay—Sondra

Lee—soprano; Ambrose—Igors Gavon—baritone; Ermengarde—Alice Playten—mezzo; Rudolf—David Hartman—VTI
Chorus and Smaller Roles: 12M/12F minimum. At least six of the male chorus should dance, preferably eight. All should sing.

SYNOPSIS

The musical opens on a New York City street, at the turn of the century, with the neighborhood people talking about widow Dolly Levi, a woman who lives by her wits and serves a variety of needs (Call on Dolly—Mixed Chorus). Dolly, brightly dressed, enters the scene and passes out business cards telling of her varied services, which range from plugging pierced ears to matchmaking. When Ambrose Kemper, a young artist, asks her why she is so interested in everyone's business, she responds in song (I Put My Hand In—F Solo with Mixed Chorus for Staging). She tells Ambrose to buy their ticket for Yonkers where she is going to meet Horace Vandergelder, the wealthy merchant widower, who has hired her as a marriage broker. Dolly is tired of living alone and has plans to marry Vandergelder after she has changed him to a more fun-loving man.

The scene moves to Vandergelder's hay and feed store in Yonkers, New York. Horace Vandergelder, the stuffy shopkeeper, is ordering Cornelius, his chief clerk, and Barnaby, an assistant clerk, to watch the shop when he goes to New York to a meeting with his future wife arranged by Dolly Levi (It Takes a Woman—M Solo with M Chorus). Dolly arrives to convince Horace to let her take his niece Ermengarde to New York, where she intends to help Ambrose and the girl gain Vandergelder's permission to marry. She goes upstairs to help Ermengarde and Ambrose make plans.

When Vandergelder leaves for Manhattan, Cornelius convinces Barnaby to spend the day seeking adventure in New York. The scene ends with Cornelius and Barnaby planning their adventure and Dolly, Ambrose, and Ermengarde preparing to show Vandergelder "they mean business" (Put on Your Sunday Clothes—Sc to 2M Duet to 3M/2F Quintet to Mixed Chorus). The number moves to the Yonkers train station where the chorus continues the song as a train chugs into the station and the principals board for New York.

In widow Irene Molloy's New York hat shop, Irene confides to her naive clerk, Minnie Fay, that she will marry Horace Vandergelder to find a new life. She puts on a "provocative" hat and sings of the beauty she will find in her new freedom (Ribbons down My Back—Sc to F Solo).

When Barnaby and Cornelius see Vandergelder on a New York street, they seek refuge in Mrs. Molloy's hat shop by pretending to be customers. Cornelius becomes infatuated with Irene and she is attracted to him, but an entering Vandergelder forces the two clerks to hide. A shocked Irene tries to keep Mr. Vandergelder from discovering them as Dolly enters to aid Irene in the ruse. Dolly attempts to change the subject by singing about American morals and motherhood. During the number the two men try to find different hiding places while avoiding Vandergelder's suspicious searches. All end up at the end of the song in the same locations (Motherhood March—Sc to 3F Trio with 3M Needed for Staging).

As the song ends, Cornelius, hiding in the closet, sneezes and Irene admits that she is hiding two gentlemen and refuses to discuss the matter further. Vandergelder exits to march in the Fourteenth Street Parade.

Dolly suggests that Cornelius and Barnaby take Irene and Minnie Fay to the Harmonia Gardens Restaurant for dinner. When Cornelius protests that he can't dance, Dolly proceeds to give everyone a lesson (Dancin'—Sc to 2M/3F Quintet to Chorus). The set opens to the street as the chorus dances. Dolly wistfully watches all the young couples enjoying themselves and begs Ephraim, her dead husband, to give her a sign that she can remarry (Before the Parade Passes By— L to F Solo). Dolly exits through the marchers as the parade arrives complete with majorettes, bands, and floats. Dolly returns to tell Vandergelder that the young, wealthy Ernestina Money will meet him later that night outside the Harmonia Gardens Restaurant. He exits and Dolly confides to the audience that he soon will be hers (Before the Parade Passes By [Reprise]—F Solo).

As Act II begins, Cornelius and Barnaby, on a street corner, cleverly convince Irene and Minnie Fay that all elegant people walk to their destinations, and the four set out for the Harmonia Gardens (Elegance—Sc to 2M/2F Quartet; Period). Vandergelder, waiting outside the restaurant, is appalled when an extremely large, boisterous Ernestina arrives. He reluctantly offers his arm and the two enter. They are followed by Ambrose and Ermengarde who hope to win the dance contest and shock Horace into realizing they are serious about marriage.

The In One drop rises to reveal the Harmonia Gardens Restaurant, opulent in tones of red. The waiters, under the watchful eye of Rudolph, the disciplined maitre d', display their varied skills by performing a variety of athletic and acrobatic feats while serving the guests and setting the tables (Waiters' Gallop— M Dance). Irene, Barnaby, Cornelius and Minnie, seated in a private dining room, are overwhelmed by the food, decor and the prices. Vandergelder, in another private dining room, is appalled by the very loud Ernestina Money, whom he tries to keep in order.

Stanley, a waiter, rushes down the long central stairway to announce Dolly's entrance and the waiters and cooks all line up to receive their favorite customer who hasn't visited them in years (Hello, Dolly!—F Solo and M Chorus).

Dolly joins Vandergelder, after signaling Ernestina to exit, and begins serving him luscious foods and discussing marriage. Vandergelder is more upset by each word but she urges him to watch the polka contest. He discovers his clerks, his niece and Ermengarde all dancing and accidentally starts a riot.

The scene quickly shifts to the courtroom where Dolly arrives and hands the judge her counsellor at law card. Dolly turns to Cornelius, who sentimentally expresses his feelings about Irene Molloy (It Only Takes a Moment—L to M Solo to Mixed Chorus). The judge is so moved by Cornelius's story that he frees everyone except Horace.

Vandergelder is taken to jail, where Dolly tells him she is leaving him to his own devices. She takes his hat and cane and gives a vaudeville-style farewell (So Long Dearie—Sc to F Solo).

Vandergelder is released and returns to Yonkers, defeated and alone. Cornelius and Mrs. Molloy arrive to tell him they are opening a hay and feed store across the street; Barnaby demands his back pay, and Ermengarde and Ambrose announce their marriage. They all go into the back room where Vandergelder keeps their money.

Dolly enters and asks Ephraim to please give her the sign. A wallpaper hanger arrives and Vandergelder sends him upstairs to paper the room blue. He tells Dolly the young man is starting in business and he believes in spreading money around. When Vandergelder asks her to marry she agrees, for Ephraim also believed that money should be spread around. She urges Horace to take Cornelius in as a partner and Barnaby as chief clerk so they can all dance at Ermengarde's wedding. He agrees and tells her she is wonderful (Finale—Mixed Chorus).

NOTES ON THE PRODUCTION

The initial success of the show was constantly revitalized by the various stars who performed the title role on Broadway. The actresses included Carol Channing, Ginger Rogers, Martha Raye, Betty Grable, Bibi Osterwald, Pearl Bailey, Phyllis Diller, and Ethel Merman. Jerry Herman had originally written the show with her in mind, but she turned it down, wanting to avoid a long run in a musical. She later accepted the role for a limited engagement which began on March 28, 1970. Two new songs were added and later recorded by Bar-mic.

Hello, Dolly! won 1964 Tony Awards for Best Musical, Actress, Music and Lyrics, Book, direction, Choreography, Producer, musical direction, sets, and costumes.

The show is expensive to produce and should be given a large-scale production, for the success of the vehicle lies in the total look. Without a degree of lavishness, the production never reaches the peaks it had on the New York stage. It survives on pace, lavishness, and gimmicks; each scene overwhelms the previous one, and each new spectacle causes the audience to wonder how anything can be bigger or better. The entrance of Dolly, dressed in red, on the top step of the Harmonia Gardens, is a high point of the show, which is only slightly topped by her curtain call in an unexpected wedding dress. If a company cannot afford to properly mount this lavish production, it should consider *The Matchmaker*, which is the non-musical version.

The original was designed to be performed with a runway, at least two costumes for each chorus member, a full-sized railroad station, five costumes for Dolly and a long stairway for Dolly's entrance to the Harmonia Gardens. On stages with limited wing space, the production can be managed with a Fourteenth Street drop and three eight-by-eight four-sided wagons that revolve for various scenes.

SONGS OF SPECIAL INTEREST

"Before the Parade Passes By," decision making, character-oriented, semi-dramatic, march tempo, alto.

"Elegance," An In One quartet. Emphasis is on relationships and period style. Movement is minimal, though clean and simple.

"Put on Your Sunday Clothes," character-oriented, baritone/tenor duet, short scene to song make it ideal for classroom work.

"So Long Dearie," soft shoe, up tempo with hat and cane, vaudeville style, low alto.

Instrumentation: 3 violins, cello, bass, 4 reeds, 3 trumpets, 2 trombones, 2 percussion, guitar/banjo, piano/celeste/conductor
Script: DBS, Signet
Score: Morris
Record: RCA
Rights: TW

HIGH BUTTON SHOES

Book: Stephen Longstreet and George Abbott (Based on Stephen Longstreet's "The Sisters Liked Them Handsome")
Music: Jule Styne
Lyrics: Sammy Cahn

ORIGINAL PRODUCTION

New Century Theatre, October 9, 1947 (727 perf.)
Director: George Abbott
Choreography: Jerome Robbins
Music Director: Milton Rosenstock
Orchestration: Philip J. Lang
Principals: Harrison Floy—Phil Silvers—baritone; Mama Longstreet—Nanette Fabray—soprano; Oggle Ogglethorpe—Mark Dawson—baritone; Mr. Pontdue—Joey Faye—baritone; Fran—Lois Lee—soprano; Nancy—Helen Gallagher—mezzo; Uncle Willie—Paul Godkin—tenor; Elmer Simpkins—Nathaniel Frey—tenor; Stevie Longstreet—Johnny Stewart—boy soprano; Papa Longstreet—Jack McCauley—baritone
Chorus and Smaller Roles: 12M/12F minimum; a separate singing and dancing chorus of 8M/8F each would be preferred if a tight rehearsal schedule is anticipated.

SYNOPSIS

The play, set in the year 1913, opens with a song by a male quartet introducing the main character, Harrison Floy (He Tried to Make a Dollar—M Quartet). Floy and his sidekick Mr. Pontdue, go through a number of "snake oil" type con games, only to be run out of town in the end by Keystone-style cops. Floy decides to go back to his hometown of New Brunswick, New Jersey, where people remember him as an honest boy. Floy and Pontdue decide that acting successful and refined is the best way to con the townspeople of New Brunswick. So with the police on their tail they flee to New Jersey.

The next scene takes place in the living room of the Longstreet family where Willie, Papa and Stevie are all talking about the "successful" Harrison Floy's return. Mama Longstreet thinks he is a good catch for her sister Fran. During this conversation a football flies through the window and Oggle, the handsome Rutgers football hero, comes in after it. Oggle tells Fran that she should marry him, not Floy, and move to Texas after the wedding (Can't You Just See Yourself—Sc to M/F Duet). Mr. Floy, who has been eavesdropping, cons Papa Longstreet into signing a paper that supposedly gives him an automobile for only $100. They all then go out to see their new car (There's Nothing Like a Model T—Mixed Chorus).

The scene switches to Rutgers's football field where Fran is watching Oggle play. After practice, Oggle confesses to Fran that although he loves her, he loves his home state of Texas more (Next to Texas, I Love You—Sc to M Solo). The Model T is pushed onto the scene by Floy and the rest of the Longstreet family. When Floy asks Fran to go for a walk while her father gets gas, Oggle challenges Floy to a fight. By now, more football players have gathered around for the fight, and Floy tries to calm Oggle by getting all the players to sing Rutgers's alma mater (On the Banks of the Old Raritan—M Chorus). This plan doesn't work, so Floy knocks Oggle out with a pair of brass knuckles, hidden from everyone but the audience. This show of strength impresses Mama Longstreet, who urges Fran to marry Mr. Floy for security (Security—F Chorus).

Uncle Willie and Nancy, the Longstreet's maid, are dancing in the parlor when Mama and the Ladies Walking Society enter (Bird Watcher's Song—F Chorus). Harrison arrives and gives the ladies a pitch for his new real estate con. The women leave determined to have their husbands invest in the real estate swindle.

Outdoors once again, Floy convinces Pontdue that a day away from the city will do him good (Get Away for a Day in the Country—M Solo to Mixed Chorus). The Longstreets and other families that are interested in buying the land show up for a picnic. Mama Longstreet dances with her husband (Papa, Won't You Dance with Me?—F Solo). In the course of the picnic, some of the investors realize they have paid for worthless swampland. Floy plans to skip town, but first he must win over Fran, his appointed treasurer, who refuses to let the money leave her side (Can't You Just See Yourself—M Solo). Fran falls for him, so she, Floy and Pontdue leave town with the investors' cash. Papa Longstreet goes after them in the Model T (Model T [Reprise]—M Solo).

Act II begins with Floy and Fran in a bathhouse in Atlantic City (On a Sunday by the Sea-Mixed Chorus). A hilarious Keystone Kops–style chase involving Fran, Pontdue, a gorilla, and Floy takes place. The police arrest Floy, who manages to escape.

Back in New Brunswick the next day, Fran apologizes to Oggle, who still proclaims his love (You're My Girl—M/F Duet). Floy returns to the Longstreet living room, blames Pontdue for cheating everyone, and promises to return all the money he spent by betting on the Rutgers big game. Papa Longstreet doubts his honesty but Mama is taken in (I Still Get Jealous—M/F Duet).

At the game, Floy meets up with Pontdue, who is upset about taking all the blame for the real estate scheme. Floy assures Pontdue of his loyalty (You're My Boy—M Duet). Pontdue and Floy bet on Princeton over Rutgers, but at half-time Princeton is losing. Floy goes to the Rutgers locker room to get the team not to try so hard to win (Nobody Ever Died for Dear Old Rutgers—M Solo). His plea fails and Rutgers wins.

Back at the Longstreet home, the family waits for the arrival of Harrison Floy with the money he promised to return. Floy tells the now highly skeptical family about using the real estate swampland mud as a new beauty clay product. Oggle is the only one not taken in by this new con game and runs Floy out of the house. The play ends with Harrison Floy and Pontdue selling the mud as beauty clay to the audience until the "Keystone Kops" chase them out of sight (He Tried to Make a Dollar [Reprise]—M Quartet).

NOTES ON THE PRODUCTION

A 1948 Tony Award went to Jerome Robbins for his choreography. In fact those who saw the original production still comment on Jerome Robbins's marvelous "Keystone Kops Chase" ballet, which is fun to re-create.

An excellent vehicle for a male comic and his stooge, the show affords good vignette character opportunities and is an excellent choice for a company looking for a variety of featured roles. In addition to principals there are good roles for the barbershop-style quartet and the ladies bird-watching society.

Although it is a period piece that must be played with an air of charm and innocence, it is not a spoof on the era and shouldn't be camped. In order to maintain the pace modern audiences prefer, the director should not be afraid to edit some of the longer musical and dance-oriented numbers. It is difficult, in an amateur situation, to successfully execute dance numbers that were written for professional dancers. Audiences would rather see a shortened rendition that captures the flavor of the piece than the full song weakly performed.

The sets may be trimmed, combined and kept relatively skeletal to keep the pace flowing. The costumes are period but not complex. The car may be a flat cutout, "driven" on by Uncle Willie. It should be properly proportioned and is necessary to the Model T number. The beach sequence needs dressing "tent" bathouses for the chase sequence to be effective. It should be styled after the original Mack Sennett silent film chases which consisted of running in and out of doors and mistaken identities.

The music is tuneful and varied. Since scenes often require different performers, a director with limited rehearsal time should have a good choreographer for the dance numbers and an assistant director to stage the non–dance-oriented numbers. It is possible to rehearse the separate scenes/songs simultaneously if separate dancing and singing choruses are utilized.

SONGS OF SPECIAL INTEREST

"I Still Get Jealous," M/F duet, middle-aged character number, charm duet, baritone/soprano.

"Papa Won't You Dance With Me?," up tempo, charm, polka, revue potential for middle-aged performers, baritone/soprano.

Instrumentation: 3 violins, cello, bass, 5 reeds, 3 trumpets, trombone, percussion, piano/conductor
Script: NP
Record: Camden
Rights: TW

HIGH SPIRITS

Book, Music and Lyrics: Hugh Martin and Timothy Gray (Based on the Noel Coward play *Blithe Spirit*)

ORIGINAL PRODUCTION

Alvin Theatre, April 7, 1964 (375 perf.)
Director: Noel Coward
Dances and Musical Numbers: Danny Daniels
Vocal Direction and Arrangements: Hugh Martin and Timothy Gray
Orchestration: Harry Zimmerman
Principals: Madame Arcati—Beatrice Lillie—mezzo; Elvira—Tammy Grimes—alto; Charles Condomine—Edward Woodward—baritone; Ruth Condomine—Louise Troy—mezzo; Edith—Carol Arthur—VTNE; Mrs. Bradman—Margaret Hall—VTNE; Dr. Bradman—Lawrence Keith—VTNE
Chorus and Smaller Roles: 4M/4F minimum.

SYNOPSIS

British mystery novelist Charles Condomine and his second wife Ruth are preparing for an evening of research for Charles's latest book, dealing with mediums and seances. They discuss Elvira, Charles's first wife, whom Charles remembers with mixed emotions. When Charles leaves, Ruth wonders about Elvira (Was She Prettier Than I?—L to F Solo).

Madame Arcati, the wacky medium hired to perform the seance at the Condomines' that evening, hurries to the home on her bicycle (The Bicycle Song—F Solo to Mixed Chorus).

At the seance, Dr. Bradman, his wife and the maid Edith are astounded when Madame Arcati makes contact with the other world. Strange happenings occur with increasing intensity until all activity comes to an abrupt halt. Arcati falls to the floor in a dead faint. Charles is appalled to learn that Elvira has returned from beyond. Later that evening, Ruth is upset by Charles's seemingly abusive behavior to her. He is actually berating Elvira, whom Ruth cannot see. Ruth storms from the room. Elvira takes advantage of her time alone with Charles by seductively warning him (You'd Better Love Me—Sc to F Solo).

The next morning, at the terrace breakfast table, Ruth and Charles argue over the previous evening's events (Where Is the Man I Married?—Sc to M/F Duet). Elvira shows up and Charles persuades her to show Ruth some tricks to prove her existence, but Ruth only becomes more upset and seeks out Madame Arcati for assistance in getting rid of the bothersome Elvira. She finds her in her coffee house, "The Inner Circle," surrounded by enthusiastic students (Go into Your Trance—F Solo and Mixed Chorus).

Madame Arcati tells Ruth she has no idea of how to get rid of Elvira, and Ruth angrily accuses Arcati of irresponsibility and leaves.

At home, Elvira and Charles romantically remember their wedding night (Forever and a Day—Sc to M/F Duet). He later promises to take her dancing, which she feels is a positive sign (Something Tells Me—F Solo).

Charles and Elvira visit the Penthouse Club. As Charles remembers her conniving ways, Elvira continually sets him up in high-risk situations, hoping he will eventually "accidentally" kill himself (I Know Your Heart—Sc to M/F Duet). She attempts to teach him how to fly (Faster Than Sound—L to F Solo and Mixed Chorus), and the act ends as Charles climbs to the roof and leaps off with his arms outstretched.

As Act II opens, we discover that Charles has landed on a parapet and suffered only a minor sprain. Ruth manages to convince Charles that Elvira is trying to kill him, and the two decide to enlist Madame Arcati's help in exorcising Elvira. Feeling more in control, they reminisce about Charles's marriage proposal to Ruth (If I Gave You—Sc to M/F Duet).

Elvira tries to manipulate Charles into taking her for a drive, but he tells her Ruth has taken the car and she has a fit of hysterics. Elvira has tampered with the car in an attempt to kill Charles but only succeeds in killing Ruth, whose spirit returns to cause them both trouble.

In her bedroom, Arcati, clad in bathrobe and white bunny slippers, happily caresses her Ouija board (Talking to You—F Solo), which lovingly responds by telling her of Ruth's death. She calls Charles and offers her help.

Elvira, bored by life on Earth, tells Charles about her famous friends on the other side (Home Sweet Heaven—F Solo). When she agrees to go home, she and Charles hurry to Madame Arcati, who is excited by the prospect of entertaining a genuine ectoplasm (Something Is Coming to Tea—F Solo with M Chorus). Madame Arcati vainly tries to dematerialize Elvira (The Exorcism—Mixed Chorus) but only succeeds in materializing Ruth.

At home, the two spirits, not anxious to spend eternity on Earth or without Charles, poison his brandy. When he arrives, they argue and examine their respective marriages (What in the World Did You Want?—Sc to M/2F Trio).

Arcati arrives, and with the help of Edith succeeds in dematerializing both Ruth and Elvira, but as she and Charles toast their success, they succumb to the poisoned brandy. Now all four are locked in the spirit world forever (Faster Than Sound [Reprise]—Mixed Chorus).

NOTES ON PRODUCTION

There are some difficult technical aspects of the production which need to be worked out before the show is chosen—for example, the set falling apart in the final scene and the explosive shaking of the seance table in the first scene. Rigging is required to fly Elvira, but some companies have deleted Elvira's flying sequences.

The music is good, the main characters are extremely well developed, the situation hilarious, the dialogue extremely witty and the evening entertaining. If trimmed in size it is perfect dinner theatre fare and can be successfully performed on a small stage. The most essential sets are the Condomines' parlor and a space for Arcati's tea room.

SONGS OF SPECIAL INTEREST

"Home Sweet Heaven," clever lyrics, rhythm, make this a wonderful number for a revue or showcase situation. Alto.

"Talking to You," strong alto character song, not much range or vocal quality required. Takes a comedienne to make the number successful.

"What in the World Did You Want?," trio, clever lyrics, relationships and characters emphasized. Good for classroom study.

Instrumentation: 3 violins, viola, cello, bass, 5 reeds, 3 trumpets, 3 trombones, 2 percussion, harp, guitar/bass guitar, piano/conductor
Script: NP
Selections: Cromwell
Record: ABC/Paramount
Rights: TW

HOW TO SUCCEED IN BUSINESS WITHOUT REALLY TRYING

Book: Abe Burrows, Jack Weinstock and Willie Gilbert (Based on the book by Shepherd Mead)
Music and Lyrics: Frank Loesser

ORIGINAL PRODUCTION

46th Street Theatre, October 14, 1961 (1,415 perf.)
Directors: Abe Burrows and Bob Fosse
Choreographer: Hugh Lambert
Musical Director: Elliot Lawrence
Orchestration: Robert Ginzler
Principals: J. Pierpont Finch—Robert Morse—baritone; Hedy—Virginia Martin—mezzo; J. B. Biggley—Rudy Vallee—baritone; Frump—Charles Nelson Reilly—tenor; Rosemary—Bonnie Scott—mezzo; Smitty—Claudette Sutherland—alto; Miss Jones—Ruth Kobart—soprano
Chorus and Smaller Roles: 8F/12M minimum. Male chorus must be vocally balanced.

SYNOPSIS

The play opens in front of the Worldwide Wicket Company, where J. Pierpont (Ponty) Finch, an enthusiastic young window washer intent on quick advancement, is studying a book on business (How To—L to M Solo).

In the office lobby, Finch bumps into J. B. Biggley, the president of the Worldwide Wicket Company. When he apologizes and tells Biggley he is looking for a job, the irritated president sends him to personnel. Rosemary, an attractive secretary, offers to introduce Ponty to Smitty, a friend of hers who is secretary to Mr. Bratt, the head of personnel, but Ponty brashly enters Mr. Bratt's office and tells him Biggley sent him for a job. Bratt quickly offers him a job in the mailroom. Smitty soon discovers that her steno pool friend, Rosemary, has personal plans for Finch (Happy to Keep His Dinner Warm—Sc to F Solo).

In the outer office, the office personnel are desperately waiting in line for their morning coffee when they discover the machine is empty (Coffee Break—Mixed Chorus). The group collapses in dramatic agony.

Rosemary encounters Finch, who is delivering mail to the executive offices. He is stopped by the wimpy Bud Frump, Mr. Biggley's nephew, who takes the mail into the offices in hopes of being promoted. Seeing Miss Jones, Mr. Biggley's secretary, Finch introduces himself and flatters her in hopes of getting in her favor. She introduces him to an important man in the company, Mr. Gatch.

Finch quickly befriends the soon-to-be-promoted head of the mailroom, Mr. Twimble, by asking him the key to his success (The Company Way—Sc to M Duet). When Twimble offers him a job, Ponty quickly consults his book and realizes the mailroom is a dead-end job so he suggests Bud Frump. Bud accepts and promises to play it the company way (The Company Way [Reprise]—Sc to M Solo to Mixed Chorus). Bratt, who has witnessed the scene, is so impressed with Finch's integrity that he promotes him to junior executive.

Hedy LaRue, Biggley's sexy, redheaded girlfriend, arrives in the corridor looking for Mr. Bratt, who has been instructed to give her a job in the steno pool. The junior executives, attracted by Hedy's looks, desire her for their secretary but Mr. Bratt reminds them of the secretary code (A Secretary Is Not a Toy—M Solo to M Chorus).

Ponty waits in front of the elevators as Miss Jones walks on with Mr. Biggley and reminds Biggley he is playing golf the next day with the chairman of the board. Ponty pumps Miss Jones for information about Biggley's alma mater, his hobbies and his schedule. Impressed by his interest, she answers his questions and returns to her office.

Smitty and Rosemary arrive at the elevators and Smitty manipulates Ponty into asking Rosemary for dinner (Been a Long Day—Sc to 2F/1M Trio). At the end of the number the elevator doors open, and they enter the elevators as the chorus within completes the song. Bud, seeing Biggley talking to Hedy, blackmails him into a higher promotion (Been a Long Day [Reprise]—M Duet).

On a Saturday morning, Ponty arrives at the office early and sets the stage to look as if he had been working all night. J. B. Biggley is impressed at his enthusiasm and deeply affected when he hums a few bars of J. B.'s alma mater. Biggley, after running through the groundhog cheer with Ponty imitating (Grand Old Ivy—Sc to M Duet), tells Ponty he will remember him when the right job comes along.

The following Monday, Hedy arrives in Ponty's office and announces she has been assigned to him. When she flunks her secretarial skills test, he realizes she is involved with Biggley and sends her to see his boss Mr. Gatch, who invites her out. Gatch is instantly transferred to Venezuela and Ponty to Gatch's job.

Rosemary, the newly promoted advertising manager's secretary, arrives at a company reception dressed in the same exclusive "original" designer dress as the other secretaries (Paris Original—F Chorus).

At the reception a drunken Hedy decides to take a shower in Biggley's private bath. Bud, wanting revenge on Ponty, calls him to Biggley's office and goes to get Biggley. When Ponty discovers Hedy wearing only a towel, he realizes he has been set up. He tries to escape but Hedy kisses him and the sound of choral music sounding Rosemary's name is heard. He realizes he is in love with Rosemary, who enters to tell him Bud and Biggley are on the way. He asks her to marry him and she also hears music (Rosemary—M/F Duet). Biggley arrives but never discovers Hedy. When Ponty points out that the newly hired head of advertising played football against Biggley's alma mater, Biggley has him fired and Ponty promoted.

Ponty asks Rosemary to be his secretary and begins working on his new advertising campaign. He is so involved that he forgets about his proposal (Rosemary [Reprise]—2M/F Trio), much to her disappointment. Bud Frump swears to stop him as the curtain falls.

Act II opens in the outer office. Rosemary tells the secretaries she is quitting, but they urge her to stay in order to prove that a secretary might marry her boss (Cinderella Darling—Sc to F Chorus).

Bud comes to Ponty's office with an idea for an advertising campaign treasure hunt, which Ponty decides to enhance by giving away stock in the company.

Hedy tells J. B., in the privacy of his office, that she is returning to Los Angeles because she isn't having any fun. Biggley tells her he can't live without her and romantically woos her (Love from a Heart of Gold—Sc to M/F Duet). Hedy agrees to stay for one more day.

In the executive washroom the vice presidents are inwardly wondering how to stop Finch, who confidently sings to his mirrored image (I Believe in You— M Solo with M Chorus).

Ponty has concocted a TV treasure stock give away scheme, which backfires when Hedy, the treasure girl, appears nationwide and reveals the hiding place of the treasure as one of the Worldwide Wicket Buildings. The buildings are invaded and destroyed by an enthusiastic public searching for the treasure. In the boardroom, Ponty faces Mr. Womper, the chairman of the board, and tells him he is ready to return to being a window washer. Womper excitedlly tells him that he too began as a window washer and urges him to disclose the entire story. Ponty cleverly shifts the blame and urges Womper not to fire Bud and his uncle, Mr. Biggley (Brotherhood of Man—M Solo to Male Chorus with Miss Jones as a Featured Performer).

The play is quickly resolved as Biggley announces that Womper has married Hedy and made Finch, who has married Rosemary, chairman of the board. Biggley sends a letter to the White House to beware as the company sings (The Company Way—Finale—Mixed Chorus).

NOTES ON THE PRODUCTION

1962 Tony Award for Best Musical, Actor, Supporting Actor, Book, Producer, Musical Director and Direction. It also received the Pulitzer Prize for drama.

The show was warmly received and well performed. Rudy Vallee, a singing star of the twenties and thirties, revitalized his career as an excellent J. B. Biggley. Bobby Morse, a charming, impish type, made all Ponty's conniving quite enjoyable, while Charles Nelson Reilly, who won the Tony Award for Best Supporting Actor, had a melodramatic comedic touch which was perfect for Frump. All three repeated their roles in the musical film version, which should be seen by anyone interested in studying comic timing and clearly defined acting styles.

The male and female leads were supposed to represent the Kennedys and were costumed and hair-styled accordingly. This parallel has been lost in subsequent performances and it is up to the individual director to determine if the show should represent the early sixties or be updated.

The original production had ten large sets and several partial sets and drops. This configuration may prove limiting to theatres with no fly or wing space. It is possible to combine the location of several scenes. In the original production, Ponty sings from atop a scaffolding where he is washing windows. This scene could be performed in a neutral area in front of the main curtain. The corridor scenes and outer office scenes could be combined. In fact, the bulk of the set could be permanently onstage and encompass the outer office with the elevator doors at an angle off left (just out of view of the audience), and Biggley's office stage right, with a space downstage left as an office area to depict the mailroom, Finch's offices, and the television show. The boardroom scene could take place in Biggley's office. If at all possible the washroom sequence should consist of several cartoon-style washbowl cutouts with a large mirror frame in front. This could be rolled on in front of the act curtain or even in front of the outer office set.

SONGS OF SPECIAL INTEREST

"Been a Long Day," nice trio scene for alto, soprano, and baritone. Easy to stage; characters and situation make this a nice showcase number.

"Brotherhood of Man," a showstopper number, big, character-oriented, gospel style. Works well in a revue situation. Need strong vocals for harmony.

"Coffee Break," comic chorus number which is a hit in a revue or class situation. Good for a beginning choreographer as it utilizes a large cast but the characters and situation "make the number."

"The Company Way," good for character study, game and role-playing exercise and interrelationship. Two Baritones.

"Grand Old Ivy," wonderful scene to song, a real showstopper, almost actorproof, two baritones.

Instrumentation: 5 reeds, 3 trumpets, 3 trombones, horn, 2 percussion, guitar, harp, 4 violins, cello, bass.
Script: Frank (London)
Score: Frank
Record: RCA
Rights: MTI

I

I DO! I DO!

Book and Lyrics: Tom Jones (Based on *The Fourposter*, by Jan De Hartog)
Music: Harvey Schmidt

ORIGINAL PRODUCTION

46th Street Theatre, December 5, 1966 (560 perf.)
Director and Choreographer: Gower Champion
Musical Director: John Lesko
Orchestration: Philip J. Lang
Principals: Agnes—Mary Martin—mezzo; Michael—Robert Preston—baritone
Chorus and Smaller Roles: None.

SYNOPSIS

A two-character musical about married life, its happiness and problems. As the play opens, the young couple is preparing for the wedding ceremony, which is quickly enacted in the title song (All the Dearly Beloved/Together Forever/I Do! I Do!).

The newlyweds dress for their wedding night and greet each other as any shy young couple might. Agnes realizes she doesn't know much about Michael and begins to question him about his prior knowledge of women (Good Night—Sc to M/F Duet).

Michael announces to the world that he loves Agnes (I Love My Wife—M

Solo). Time quickly passes and Agnes changes into maternity clothes (Something Has Happened—F Solo). Michael is overcome with false labor pains. Agnes assures him that the baby won't ever take his place in her heart (My Cup Runneth Over—Sc to M/F Duet).

After the baby is born, Michael clutters the household with toys, and Agnes spends most of the day devoted to feedings and diapers. They realize that life is more than love (Love Isn't Everything—M/F Duet). Twelve years pass and certain irritating habits begin to fray on their nerves. One evening as the couple prepare for a party, they bitingly comment on each other's idiosyncrasies and the scene ends on an ugly note (Nobody's Perfect—Sc to M/F Duet).

After the party, Michael tries to explain to Agnes that he loves someone else. He tells her that a forty-one–year–old man is more irresistible than a thirty-nine–year–old woman and it is perfectly normal for a younger woman to find him attractive (A Well-Known Fact—M Solo). Agnes is furious at his pompous manner and privately opens up a storage trunk to produce an $85 hat she has been saving for just such an occasion (Flaming Agnes—L to F Solo). She is in the process of packing to leave when Michael returns home and forces her to unpack. They angrily express their feelings (The Honeymoon Is Over—Sc to M/F Duet). She leaves, but he rushes after her and brings her back. He decides that they still need each other and forgets about the other woman.

In Act II Agnes and Michael, now middle-aged, are in bed celebrating New Year's Eve while waiting for their sixteen-year-old son to return home (Where Are the Snows?—Sc to M/F Duet). Michael discovers a bottle of bourbon in Michael Jr.'s drawer, gets upset and tells Agnes, who suggests they have some tea. Michael takes a swig of bourbon instead and discovers it is an accumulation of all the cod liver oil Junior was supposed to take when he was younger. Michael, upset by his son's deceit, angrily awaits his arrival. The boy arrives home quite tipsy, wearing a top hat, and Michael doesn't have the heart to yell at him. The top hat reminds Michael of marriage, and the couple realize how much their lives will change when the children are married (When the Kids Get Married—Sc to M/F Duet; he plays sax and she plays the violin).

The time has come for their daughter's wedding, which Michael dreads. As he prepares for the wedding, he angrily comments on the man his daughter has chosen (The Father of the Bride—Sc to M Solo). After the wedding, Agnes feels extremely alone and questions the reasons for life (What Is a Woman?—Sc to F Solo). When she tells Michael she is leaving him to discover the meaning of her life, he convinces her that he needs her to inspire him. She is touched (Someone Needs Me—Sc to M/F Duet).

Agnes and Michael are moving out of the house into a small apartment (Roll up the Ribbons—This House—Sc to M/F Duet). As Michael carries Agnes out of their old bedroom, they agree that marriage is a very good thing.

NOTES ON THE PRODUCTION

Robert Preston received the 1967 Tony Award for Best Actor, but *Cabaret* received most of the other Tonys. Mary Martin lost out to Barbara Harris, *The Apple Tree*.

The musical is often performed in summer stock due to its one-set, two-character, low-budget appeal. It can be quite charming but relies heavily on the talents of Agnes and Michael. There are a lot of props which denote the passage of time, and they must be moved quickly on and off to keep the flow of the script.

The show, although originally performed with a full orchestra, works with a smaller combo, which includes a saxophone and violin if the onstage performers do not play those instruments. It may be possible to substitute other instruments, and it is certainly worth searching out actors who play instruments because the "When the Kids Get Married" number "live" is outstanding.

There are different costumes for each scene which depict the period and changing styles. These must be impeccably accurate.

The success of the original was due to its two stars and the talents of director/choreographer Gower Champion, who was a genius at heightening interest in musical numbers. It is important to have an excellent choreographer/director who can keep the flow from scene to song and make the musical numbers heightened reality.

SONGS OF SPECIAL INTEREST

"The Father of the Bride," semidramatic, poignant, good for class, baritone.

"Flaming Agnes," good for getting a stiff actress to have more freedom of movement and abandonment, comic, angry, mezzo.

"Good Night," mezzo/baritone, comic, reaction-oriented, good for showcase, audience pleaser, nearly actor-proof.

"The Honeymoon Is Over," angry, bitter, quarrel, good for class work and reaction, mezzo.

"Nobody's Perfect," excellent, dramatic, angry, biting, good for actors in their thirties; younger performers have trouble with the game playing. Mezzo/baritone.

"What Is a Woman?" introspective, older woman, questioning life, semi-dramatic, mezzo.

Instrumentation: 4 reeds, 2 trumpets, trombone, 2 horns, 2 percussion, 2 pianos, harp, violin, viola, cello, bass, piano/conductor
Script: NP
Score: Chappell
Record: RCA
Rights: MTI

I LOVE MY WIFE

Book and Lyrics: Michael Stewart (Based on the play *Viens Chez Moi* by Luis Rego)
Music: Cy Coleman

Ethel Barrymore Theatre, April 17, 1977 (857 perf.)
Director: Gene Saks
Musical Numbers Staged by: Onna White
Musical Director: John Miller
Orchestration: Cy Coleman
Principals: Cleo—Ilene Graff—mezzo; Monica—Joanna Gleason—alto; Alvin—
Lenny Baker—baritone; Wally—James Naughton—baritone
Chorus and Smaller Roles: 4M vocal backup and onstage musicians.

SYNOPSIS

Act I opens with the cast and musicians onstage in a line. The orchestra conductor enters, a cast member hits a note on the pitch pipe and the small company of eight (four actors, four actor/musicians) burst into an a cappella choral ode to Trenton, New Jersey. This leads into the musically accompanied opening song that tells how all eight grew up together (We're Still Friends—Mixed Chorus). The song ends and the musicians, dressed as moving men, join the stagehands in setting the stage for a diner.

At the diner, Alvin, a moving man by trade, asks his wife's friend Monica about the sex test she is taking from her women's magazine. When he takes the test, he discovers he is thirty years behind the new sexual revolution. He rejoins his fellow movers, who inquire about his carnal feelings toward Monica. Alvin, who has been friends with Monica since childhood, begins to consider the matter (Monica—M Chorus and F Dancer). As the men sing about her, Monica removes her outer jacket, scarf and hat and dances wildly around in jeans and leotard top—the lighting demonstrates it is all in Alvin's imagination.

At the end of the number Monica returns, fully clothed, to her magazine as Wally, her husband, and Cleo, Alvin's wife, enter the diner. The girls go off to finish their Christmas shopping, and the two men discuss Wally's multiple love experiences (By Threes—Sc to M Trio). The piano player is essential to the success of the number because Wally and Alvin mime piano playing during much of the song. Alvin promises Wally he will sound out his wife on the possibility of a multiple love experience with Cleo and Monica.

Alvin and the moving men sing as they set the stage to represent Alvin's bedroom and living room (A Mover's Life—M Solo to M Chorus). Cleo, at first appalled by Alvin's suggestion, begins to consider the proposal as the band enters dressed as devils (Love Revolution—Sc to F Solo). However, when she agrees to play the game with two men instead of two women (she mentions Wally as a possible third), Alvin is shocked.

When Wally and Monica arrive to invite them to a Christmas Eve party, Cleo and Monica, Nashville style, wonder if by limiting themselves to their spouses they missed something (Someone Wonderful I Missed—F Duet).

Wally, Cleo and Alvin decide to invite Monica to join them in a foursome on Christmas Eve. The orchestra enters in togas, and all proclaim they are sexually free as the leads demonstrate a series of confused sex poses (Sexually Free—Sc to 2M/1F Trio).

It is snowing in Act II as the orchestra enters in Santa Claus suits to comment on the proposed evening's event (Hey There, Good Times—M Quartet). They quickly set the stage to Wally and Monica's living/dining room where Wally and Monica, in a comic scene, open their horrible Christmas presents. Monica comments on her feelings for Wally and her favorite holiday (Lovers on Christmas Eve—Sc to M/F Duet); the two perform à la "Fred and Ginger."

When Wally tells Monica about the evening's planned marital exchange, she furiously serves the turkey and slams the food down. The four are uncomfortably seated at the table as the band marches on and advises the four to let loose (Scream—M Quartet).

In an attempt to ease the situation, Wally passes around some $80 hash and the girls proceed to get high. Alvin and Wally later discover it is nothing more than modelling clay and comment on the fact that people turn on to anything (Everybody Today Is Turning On—Sc to M Duet—Period Style).

The four finally strip to their underwear and get into bed, but Alvin is extremely uncomfortable and attempts to play for time. Wally informs Alvin that they are only attempting today's norm and refers to the newspaper's personal section (Married Couple Seeks Married Couple—2M/2F Chorus with Band in Pajamas).

The attempted orgy fails when both men end up next to their wives. The band enters in Santa Claus suits and comments on the lack of excitement in the room. The men proclaim that they love their wives (I Love My Wife—M Duet).

The couples say farewell and agree to meet the next night at the diner—the boys will have a few drinks while the girls return Christmas gifts.

NOTES ON THE PRODUCTION

1977 Tony Awards: Direction—Featured Actor—(Lenny Baker).

This small-cast production needs a male lead in the part of Alvin who has excellent comedic talents and impeccable timing. Since some audience members may find the subject matter distasteful, it is important that the production be well mounted and the leading man have tremendous warmth and charm.

The costumes and sets are minimal, the music mostly contemporary and fun to perform onstage. A good choice for a low-budget, small company or dinner theatre production. The band is costumed in a variety of clothes and must be able to make quick changes offstage. It is important to obtain "performing musicians" who can relate to the action onstage, their music and the audience. The success of the casting of the musicians may affect the success of the entire show.

SONGS OF SPECIAL INTEREST

"Everybody Today Is Turning On," revue or class showcase, modern vaudeville-style number, baritone duet. Possible in revue situation for two females.

"Love Revolution," good for developing abandon in a usually inhibited performer, movement required, mezzo.

"Lovers on Christmas Eve," alto, baritone, extremely funny scene precedes this comic song showcase.

Instrumentation: Onstage musicians: piano/conductor, bass, (acoustic and fender), guitar (banjo/clarinet), drums. Offstage musicians: 2 drums, 2 pianos
Script: SF
Selections: Big 3
Record: Atlantic
Rights: SF

J

JOSEPH AND THE AMAZING TECHNICOLOR DREAMCOAT

Music: Andrew Lloyd Webber
Lyrics: Tim Rice

ORIGINAL PRODUCTION

Royale Theatre, January 27, 1982 (747 perf.); originated Off-Broadway at the Entermedia Theatre
Director/Choreographer: Tony Tanner
Musical Director: David Friedman
Orchestration: Martin Silvestri and Jeremy Stone
Principals: Narrator—Laurie Beechman—mezzo; Joseph—Bill Hutton—tenor; Pharaoh—Tom Carder—baritone; Levi—Steve McNaughton—baritone; Mrs. Potiphar—Randon Li—VTI; Potiphar—David Ardao—baritone; Baker—Barry Tarallo—baritone; Butler—Kenneth Bryan—baritone; Reuben—Robert Hyman—baritone; Napthali—Charlie Serrano—tenor
Chorus and Smaller Roles: 8F/9M.

SYNOPSIS

The spotlight centers on the narrator, who invites the audience to listen to her tale of a dreamer. The curtain opens on a set of various levels of rock formations with a small tepee from which Jacob and his sons enter. As each son is introduced he briefly interacts with Jacob and goes to his respective mother. Joseph, a blue-eyed, handsome, blonde youth, resplendent in white and gold, is the last to enter (Jacob and Sons—Mixed Chorus).

A winged messenger enters on a scooter and hands Joseph's father a package which contains a multicolored coat for Joseph (Joseph's Coat—Mixed Chorus). Joseph looks stunning in his new coat, as is evidenced by the women who flirt with him. The preferential treatment Jacob gives Joseph annoys his brothers but they are more angered by his dreams, which predict that he will someday rule them (Joseph's Dreams—1F/1M to M Chorus).

The brothers plot to kill him (Poor, Poor Joseph—F Solo to Mixed Chorus) but stop when they spy two overly hairy Ishmaelites in Groucho Marx noses leading two sculpted camels on wheels. His brothers sell Joseph to the Ishmaelites, who drag him off in chains, and cover the coat with animal blood as proof that Joseph was killed.

The narrator enters to comment on their audacious behavior, and the scene switches to Jacob in a rocking chair by a western fence. The brothers reenter in ten-gallon hats, with guns and lassos, to tell their father of Joseph's plight (One More Angel in Heaven—M Chorus).

Meanwhile, Joseph and some dancing girls have been taken to Egypt by a slave trader who sells him to Mr. and Mrs. Potiphar. Joseph is an asset to Potiphar's business and quickly rises to a position of leadership. Unfortunately, Mrs. Potiphar seduces the young man and the two are caught by an enraged Potiphar, who sends Joseph to jail (Potiphar—F Solo to Mixed Chorus).

In jail, where Joseph reiterates his belief in Israel, faith and peace, he is joined by a female chorus (Close Every Door—M Solo and F Chorus). The narrator arrives to describe his surroundings and bolster his spirits. Joseph impresses his two cell mates, a baker and a butler, with his interpretations of their dreams, and all comment on the brightness of his future (Go, Go, Go, Joseph—F Solo, 3M and Mixed Chorus).

The Act II curtain opens on the interior of the palace with the narrator bringing on Pharaoh's dais. Joseph enters with his jailers and a crowd of onlookers to question the ruler about his recurring nightmares. Pharaoh leaps from behind the dais wearing a white Elvis Presley–style outfit as the chorus divides into various singing groups to provide musical backup (Poor, Poor Pharaoh/Song of the King—F Solo/M Solo and Mixed Chorus). Pharaoh is so impressed with Joseph's dream interpretation that he picks him as his second in command; the girls present him with a gold cloak (Stone the Crows—F Solo and Mixed Chorus).

Meanwhile, two of Joseph's brothers, Reuben and Jacob, are seen running a French-style cafe in Paris and reminiscing, à la Chevalier, about the good old days in Canaan (Those Canaan Days—M Solo and M Chorus).

The brothers go to Egypt to beg for food but ironically are led to Joseph, who forces them to grovel (The Brothers Came to Egypt/Grovel, Grovel—F Solo, M Solo to Mixed Chorus). He gives them the sacks of grain they request but hides a golden goblet in Benjamin's sack. He pretends to be angered, accuses them of thievery and orders Benjamin to be thrown in jail (Who's the Thief?— M Solo to Mixed Chorus).

The brothers beg for mercy in a calypso rhythm as the dancing girls enter with large fruit hats and perform à la Carmen Miranda. Led by Napthali, they offer to take the blame if Benjamin can be freed (Benjamin Calypso—M Solo to M Chorus). Joseph is impressed by his brothers' magnanimity and makes his true identity known (Joseph All the Time—F Solo, M Solo, and Mixed Chorus).

Jacob and his wives arrive in Egypt (Jacob in Egypt—F Solo) to be greeted by Joseph, who enters on a chariot-style Rolls Royce. The family is reunited (Any Dream Will Do—M Solo to Mixed Chorus). Jacob hands Joseph his colored coat as the company soars through the finale which quickly reviews the story (May I Return to the Beginning?—Mixed Chorus).

NOTES ON THE PRODUCTION

This interesting production is suitable for all ages and tours extremely well. The story theatre–style show may be kept to a technical minimum. The narrator must be multitalented, able to relate well to an audience, have a voice that projects well and a personality that exudes charismatic warmth. It is important to have an excellent director as there are many creative moments that can be added to enhance audience enjoyment.

The original play was written for schoolboys to sing and subsequently was expanded. The entire production runs about an hour and has a seven-minute curtain call. The shortness of the play makes it a perfect middle school theatre piece.

The costumes are a mixture of period biblical, modern overalls in various colors, and Carmen Miranda. It is an open-ended production, and the chorus may be increased or decreased. It is possible to use a unisex cast in most of the parts, thereby allowing the brothers to be played by girl altos. If the unisex approach is used, it must be established in the beginning and maintained throughout.

SONGS OF SPECIAL INTEREST

The songs in the production are an integral part of the show and as such are difficult to perform out of context. Most of the numbers in the show are memorable, for they have different musical modes and performance styles.

Instrumentation: piano, trombone/tuba, trumpet, 2 reeds, guitar, bass guitar, drums, percussion
Script: Holt, Rinehart, Winston
Score: Novello
Record: MCA, Chrysalis
Rights: MTI

K

THE KING AND I

Book and Lyrics: Oscar Hammerstein II (Based on the book *Anna and the King of Siam*, by Margaret Landon)
Music: Richard Rodgers

ORIGINAL PRODUCTION

St. James Theatre, March 29, 1951 (1,246 perf.)
Director: John Van Druten
Choreographer: Jerome Robbins
Musical Director: Frederick Dvonch
Orchestration: Robert Russell Bennett
Principals: Anna—Gertrude Lawrence—mezzo; The King—Yul Brynner—baritone; Lun Tha—Larry Douglass—tenor; Tuptim—Doretta Morrow—soprano; Louis—Sandy Kennedy—boy soprano; Lady Thiang—Dorothy Sarnoff—soprano; Prince—John Juliano—boy soprano; The Kralahome—John Juliano—VTNE; Sir Edward Ramsay—Robin Craven—VTNE
Chorus: 14F/8M, 12 children.

SYNOPSIS

The play opens in Bangkok Harbor on the deck of a ship. The English captain is greeted by Louis Leonowens, the young son of Anna Leonowens, a British widow, who has been hired to teach English to the King of Siam's children.

Anna enters, anxious to see the capital city of Siam. It is the early 1860s and this thirty year-old woman and her son nervously try to keep up their spirits and hide their real fears (I Whistle a Happy Tune—F Solo to F/M Duet).

The ship docks and the two are greeted by the Kralahome, the prime minister, who gruffly informs Anna she is to live in the palace. It is obvious that he has little respect for her. Anna, determined to succeed, follows with Louis.

In the palace, two weeks later, the Kralahome informs the King he has been disciplining Anna by making her wait two weeks before gaining an audience. The King agrees to see her, but before the Kralahome leaves to get Anna, Lun Tha, a handsome young envoy from Burma, enters with the beautiful English-speaking Tuptim, a gift from the King of Burma. The King declares he is pleased. Lun Tha leaves after exchanging a worried look with Tuptim. Left alone, Tuptim is bitter that she is to be a concubine and angrily sings (My Lord and Master—F Solo).

The King returns to greet Anna and introduce her to Lady Thiang, his first and favorite wife. The King asks Anna to teach English to his wives and children and to help him with his foreign correspondence. She agrees, but becomes angry when the King absolutely refuses to give her a house. He says she will teach and live in the palace or do neither. The King exits with Tuptim as the King's favored wives gather around Anna and Lady Thiang. They discuss women's positions in society and love.

Anna tells them of her love for her husband, Tom (Hello, Young Lovers—Sc to F Solo). The King enters to introduce the children (March of the Siamese Children—Orchestra March—Children) who graciously aand formally greet the King and Anna. Anna is so charmed that she glances at the King and slowly unties her bonnet, thus signifying she will stay. The children all run to embrace her.

While walking on the palace grounds, the adolescent Prince Chulalongkorn, heir to the throne, questions the King about his newfound learning. He is confused because he has been taught the world rides on the turtle's back, yet Anna has told him the world is round. He turns to the King for help, but the King has been questioning his own beliefs and tells the boy he believes the world is round. He abruptly orders his son to leave and slowly admits to himself he isn't sure of anything (A Puzzlement—Sc to M Solo).

In the classroom, Anna teaches the students an alma mater (The Royal Bangkok Academy—Mixed Chorus). During a geography lesson, Anna confesses to the children and wives that she likes them a great deal and has learned much about Siam (Getting to Know You—Sc to F Solo to Chorus).

Anna and the children get into a classroom discussion about snow which they have never seen. They are very rowdy until the King enters to tell Anna he does not want this uproar and that as a servant, she should obey him. Infuriated at his attitude, she angrily tells him she is leaving if she does not get her promised house and more polite treatment. She and Louis leave the room; the wives and children are upset and call after her to stay. The King, disturbed by this outbreak of emotion, dismisses the class and slowly exits feeling very much alone.

Tuptim quietly returns to the empty schoolroom where her lover, Lun Tha, secretly joins her. Tuptim tells him that Anna has fallen into disfavor and they will probably not be able to meet in the schoolroom anymore. Lun Tha wishes they could openly declare their love (We Kiss in a Shadow—M/F Solos). Lady Thiang quietly enters the room, sees the lovers and quickly leaves. Tuptim, certain they have been discovered, urges Lun Tha to leave and finishes the song.

Louis and Chulalongkorn meet in the palace corridor and apologize for almost fighting. They can't figure out why grown-ups are very uncertain about many things (A Puzzlement [Reprise]—Sc to Ch Duet).

Alone in her bedroom, Anna vents her anger at the King's refusal to give her the house she was promised (Shall I Tell You What I Think of You?—F Solo). Lady Thiang enters and urges Anna to see the King and help him. She explains that certain politicians in England, feeling the King is a barbarian, are determined to make Siam a protectorate of Great Britain. She movingly convinces the concerned Anna (Something Wonderful—Sc to F Solo).

In the corridor Lady Thiang tells the Kralahome that Anna has agreed to see the King. The Kralahome takes the cue and goes to ask the King to see her.

Anna arrives at the King's study and the King tricks her into apologizing. He eventually admits to her that the British think he is a barbarian and cleverly seeks Anna's advice. She tells him to hold an elaborate dinner for the arriving British dignitary, Sir Edward Ramsay, and prove that Siam is a modern country. They decide to dress everyone English-style and have a fine European style evening, complete with dancing and a theatrical entertainment Tuptim has written based on *Uncle Tom's Cabin*. The wives and children arrive as the King instructs them in the preparations that must be made. He leads them in prayer to Buddha and promises Buddha he will give the unworthy schoolteacher a brick house per their agreement. Anna looks in wonder.

In Act II the schoolroom, quickly converted into a dressing room for the ladies, is bustling with activity. Lady Thiang enters wearing a western bodice and a Siamese Penang skirt, and the wives comment on the oddity of the western dress (Western People Funny—F Solo to Chorus).

Anna inspects the wives and realizes that they don't have the proper undergarments, but the British have arrived and there is no time to repair the oversight. When Sir Edward, wearing his monocle, wanders into the schoolroom by mistake, the wives screamingly exit, terrified by his "evil eye." After a short discussion they are called for dinner. Anna and Ramsay stay behind, and Ramsay reminds her that he still cares for her. They begin to dance and Sir Edward hints at a marriage between them, but the King interrupts, irritated at the closeness of Anna and Ramsay.

In the courtyard Lady Thiang sees Tuptim and tells her she knows about her relationship with Lun Tha, which is why she has made arrangements to send Lun Tha home to Burma. She exits as Lun Tha hurries on to ask Tuptim to escape with him after her play is performed (I Have Dreamed—Sc to M/F Duet). Anna comes to tell Tuptim it is time for the performance and wishes them luck (Hello, Young Lovers [Reprise]—F Solo).

In the theatre pavilion, the play (Small House of Uncle Thomas—Mixed Chorus Ballet), a cleverly disguised Siamese-style performance about slavery, is enacted. Tuptim, who narrates, begins to draw the parallel between the play and her own life but is stopped by the sound of a gong.

In the King's study Sir Edward tells Anna and the King that the play is a success and promises to send glowing reports about Siam to Queen Victoria. After he exits, Anna tries to explain love to the King (Shall We Dance—Sc to M/F Duet) and teaches him the polka and the waltz. Their romantic mood is broken when the Kralahome enters followed by the guards and Tuptim. The King threatens to beat her, but Anna accuses him of being a barbarian and angrily stands to watch. Unable to proceed in Anna's presence, the King leaves the throne room. The Kralahome tells Anna he wishes she had never come to Siam and she agrees.

On the palace grounds, Captain Orton, who has come to take Anna and Louis to Singapore, learns that the King is ill and Chulalongkorn, coming by in a procession, is told to go immediately to the palace.

In Anna's house, which is nearly empty of all her furniture, Lady Thiang and Chulalongkorn wait anxiously for Anna and Louis. When Anna enters, Lady Thiang delivers a letter from the King, which is a note of thanks for all she has done for Siam and for him. The letter upsets Anna, who goes to the palace.

Anna enters the King's study where the King lies on his bed surrounded by Lady Thiang, Chulalongkorn, and the Kralahome. Anna sits at the foot of the bed. The King orders her to wear a ring he gives her and summons the children, who cluster around begging her not to leave. She sends Louis to tell Captain Orton to return their things to the house. The King questions Chulalongkorn about the changes he will make when he is King. The frightened boy begins a series of proclamations which include fireworks and boat races for the New Year's celebration. He hesitantly bans kowtowing but asks the King if it angers him. The King orders him to act like a King. As the boy continues his proclamations, the King dies, unnoticed by all but the Kralahome, who bows, and Anna, who kisses his hand.

NOTES ON THE PRODUCTION

Tonys: 1952 Best Musical, Book, Music, Best Actress, Supporting Actor, Sets, Producer, and Costumes.

Yul Brynner, a relative unknown at the time of his audition, went on to become a star for his excellent portrayal of the King. He may be seen in the film where he acted opposite Deborah Kerr's delightful Anna and Marnie Nixon's singing voice.

The show is probably the best constructed of Ooscar Hammerstein's librettos. The plot develops in an interesting and dramatic manner, and the *Uncle Tom's*

Cabin sequence, which parallels the Siam situation with the famous Stowe novel, is a brilliant example of how dance can further dramatic plot. A choreographic masterpiece, it is one of Jerome Robbins's most innovative numbers, and should be studied by anyone considering re-creating the choreography.

The songs were written for Gertrude Lawrence's limited range, so the female role should feature an *actress* who sings. Casting the two leads requires two excellent actors who can honestly react off each other. The role of the King, so often associated with Brynner, is extremely complex and has to be handled with believability or it becomes a comic caricature which destroys the overall mood and charm of the play.

The entire production is large and lavish and must be budgeted accordingly. The period costumes require yards of fabric while the court costumes of Siam have a rich look of brocaded and jeweled silk. The sheer number of sets, actors, and costumes possibly accounts for the reason the show isn't performed by more local groups. It is worthy of more productions as the script is humorous, dramatic, poignant, charming and sad. Given the right production, good performers and a quality director/choreographer, the show would be a highlight in any theatre's memory book.

SONGS OF SPECIAL INTEREST

"Hello, Young Lovers," ballad, not much range required, mezzo.

"I Whistle a Happy Tune," lighthearted, movement-oriented, possible for audition, mezzo.

"A Puzzlement," dramatic, introspective, baritone solo.

"Shall I Tell You What I Think of You?" dramatic, mezzo, angry, excellent lines to song character study for class situation. Good acting required to make the transitions work.

"Shall We Dance," charm scene/song, dance number, good for revue or class study, baritone/mezzo.

"Something Wonderful," possible soprano audition song, shows off a legit voice.

Instrumentation: 4 violins, cello, viola, 5 reeds, 2 horns, 3 trumpets, 2 trombones, harp, percussion, piano/conductor
Script: Six Plays by Rodgers and Hammerstein
Score: Williamson
Record: Decca
Rights: R & H

KISMET

Book: Charles Lederer and Luther Davis (Based on the play by Edward Knoblock)
Music and Lyrics: Robert Wright and George Forrest (Based on music by Alexander Borodin)

ORIGINAL PRODUCTION

Ziegfeld Theatre, December 3, 1953 (583 perf.)
Director: Albert Marre
Choreographer: Jack Cole
Musical Director: Louis Adrian
Orchestration: Arthur Kay
Principals: Hajj—Alfred Drake—baritone; Caliph—Richard Kiley—tenor; Marsinah—Doretta Morrow—soprano; Wazir—Henry Calvin—baritone; Lalume—Joan Diener—alto
Chorus and Smaller Roles: 6F/6M minimum, much doubling.

SYNOPSIS

Iman, an old man in Baghdad, sets the scene for the morning marketplace where the beggars of the city prepare for work (Sands of Time—M Solo). A poet enters selling rhymes (Rhymes Have I—Sc to M Solo). When the poet sits on the steps of the mosque in begger Hajj's place, he is astonished to receive coins and comments on the turn of events (Fate—L to M Solo). Mistaken for Hajj, he is carried off to a desert encampment by villains of Jawan, who plan on torturing him until he removes a curse that Hajj has placed on Jawan. He agrees to remove the curse if the villains will pay the sum of 100 gold pieces.

It seems that Jawan's only son was stolen from him fifteen years ago, immediately after Hajj's curse. The poet promises Jawan he will find his son that day in Baghdad. Since Jawan is a robber, he is not safe entering the city but does so in hopes of finding his heir.

In Baghdad, at the palace, the Wazir's wife, Lalume, sings of the enchantment of the city to three homesick princesses (Not Since Nineveh—F Solo to Mixed Chorus) who have arrived at court. The princesses are the daughters of the Sheik of Ababu, to whom Lalume has promised wealthy mates for the princesses in return for a loan to enrich the Wazir's treasury.

The poet meets his lovely daughter Marsinah in the bazaar, gives her the gold, and urges her to buy some pretty things and the house she has always wanted. She is immediately surrounded by merchants who display a variety of trinkets (Baubles, Bangles and Beads—F Solo to Chorus).

The poet is captured by the Wazir's police, who see him carrying a moneybag bearing the insignia of a family that was robbed. When he mistakenly mentions Jawan's name, they take him to the Wazir.

Marsinah is followed to the garden of a house she wants to own by the young Caliph, who is fascinated by her (Stranger in Paradise—Sc to M/F Duet). They agree to meet the next night, even though neither knows the other's true identity.

Later that day at the palace, the Caliph orders Omar, his servant, to send away his concubines and prepare for him to marry the girl he has met in the garden (He's in Love—Mixed Chorus).

The poet is brought before the Wazir, who wants the poet's right hand cut off, the usual punishment for theft, but Hajj plays on Lalume's sympathies and convinces them to give him a hearing (Gesticulate—M Solo and Mixed Chorus) before passing sentence. Jawan, dragged on by the police, curses Hajj for being a fake, but spying an amulet hanging from the Wazir's neck, he realizes he has found his son, and praises Hajj's skills as a prophet. The Wazir panics at this news, for Hajj has cursed him moments before. He begs Hajj to remove the curse and agrees to raise him to an Emir if he will stop the young Caliph's wedding to the unknown girl from the garden.

The Caliph is on his way to meet Marsinah (Night of My Nights—M Solo and Mixed Chorus), but she never arrives, for Hajj, fearing they may be killed when he is unable to stop the Caliph's wedding, has hidden her in the harem. The Caliph brokenheartedly returns to the palace and the Wazir is overjoyed to discover that his new Emir is really a wizard (Was I Wazir—M Chorus).

Lalume and the harem girls entertain the new Emir (Rhadlakum—F Solo to F Chorus). Hajj comforts Marsinah as she describes her lost love; while in another part of the palace, the Caliph describes Marsinah to the Wazir (And This Is My Beloved—Split 3M/1F Quartet).

Hajj and Omar exchange some poetic verses (The Olive Tree—M Solo).

The Wazir, discovering that Marsinah is in his harem, prepares to marry her before the Caliph realizes her true identity. He will do this in order to guarantee the Caliph's marriage to one of the Sheik's daughters.

When the Wazir, not realizing Marsinah is Hajj's daughter, tells him he is going to marry her and have her poisoned, Hajj drowns him in the palace pool. Marsinah and the Caliph are united, and Lalume and the poet agree to spend the rest of their days on a desert oasis.

NOTES ON THE PRODUCTION

This musical fantasy, which won most of the season's Tonys, was unusual because it was based on an old play and utilized much of Alexander Borodin's music. Tonys: Best Actor, Musical, Producer, Book, Music and Musical Direction.

The musical was revived as an all-Black musical on March 1, 1978, at the Mark Hellinger Theatre (243 perf.) and renamed *Timbuktu*. It was produced by author Luther Davis and directed by Geoffrey Holder. The show starred Eartha Kitt, Melba Moore, Ira Hawkins and Gilbert Price, but was unable to sustain a long run despite the lavish production and added music.

This fantasy is still an audience pleaser and an interesting treatment of the late-night, nonmusical film. The show is refreshing because the Arabian Nights setting is so unusual. It is good summer stock and community fare and may be performed within four basic sets which are interchangeable: the bazaar area with the mosque as a background wall, the interior of the palace, the house and garden, and the desert. In spaces with no fly space and little offstage storage, foldover flats have been utilized to specifically define areas. These flats which might open, similar to folding screens, allow for one permanent set to be utilized. The foldouts have different walls that denote specific location.

The chorus may be cut to the bare minimum, but this is only advisable in touring situations where cost might be a problem.

The costumes should show the rising opulence of Hajj's station and should reflect the Arabian Nights location. Props are not extensive, choreography is not difficult and the entire production may be quickly mounted. The show does require an excellent leading man and two romantic leads with superior voices.

SONGS OF SPECIAL INTEREST

"And This Is My Beloved," good class exercise and showcase piece. Emphasis on vocal and timing. Marsinah's ending section good for audition.

"Gesticulate," certain verses have audition potential for a strong baritone.

"Night of My Nights," audition for quality tenor voice.

Instrumentation: 5 reeds, 3 trumpets, horn, 2 trombones, tuba, 4 violins, viola, cello, bass, harp, percussion, piano/conductor
Script: Chappell (London), Random
Score: Frank
Record: Columbia
Rights: MTI

KISS ME, KATE

Book: Bella and Samuel Spewack (Based on *The Taming of the Shrew*, by Shakespeare)
Music and Lyrics: Cole Porter

ORIGINAL PRODUCTION

New Century Theatre, December 30, 1948 (1,077 perf.)
Director: John C. Wilson
Choreographer: Hanya Holm
Musical Director: Pembroke Davenport
Orchestration: Robert Russell Bennett
Principals: Petruchio/Fred—Alfred Drake—baritone; Lucentio/Bill—Harold Lang—baritone; Kate/Lilli—Patricia Morison—soprano; Bianca/Lois—Lisa Kirk—mezzo; 1st Man—Harry Clark—baritone; 2nd Man—Jack Diamond—baritone; Baptista/Harry—Thomas Hoier—VTI; Hattie—Annabelle Hall—alto; Paul—Lorenzo Fuller—baritone
Chorus: 8M/8F minimum and 3M jazz dancers.

SYNOPSIS

In a Baltimore theatre the company has just finished the final rehearsal of *The Shrew*, based on Shakespeare's famous comedy. Fred Graham, leading actor and director, gives some last-minute notes which irritate Lilli Vanessi, his ex-wife and leading lady. As he stages the curtain call, she privately curses him and stalks off. He gives a morale-boosting speech to the company and exits as Hattie and the ensemble prepare for the show (Another Op'nin', Another Show—F Solo to Mixed Chorus).

Lois is on the phone in a backstage corridor. She is trying to locate her gambler boyfriend fellow actor, Bill Calhoun, who enters as she hangs up the phone. He tells her he has signed director Fred Graham's name to a $10,000 IOU, which upsets her because she is afraid that Mr. Graham will be bumped off before he can make her a star on Broadway. She asks him why he constantly gambles (Why Can't You Behave—Sc to F Solo).

The scene shifts to two adjoining dressing rooms with a connecting door. Lilli's room is ornate, while Fred's is stale and dilapidated. The two are arguing from their own rooms. They are still in love but both are temperamental and self-centered, so they constantly fight. Lilli shows off her engagement ring from her wealthy boyfriend, Harrison Howell, and Fred seethes with jealousy. As they talk, the mood changes and Lilli reminds him of the crazy things they did together when they were married. He joins in the nostalgic game and they relive a romantic moment (Wunderbar—Sc to M/F Duet). They kiss and Lilli asks whose fault it was they divorced; there is no answer and Fred returns to his room to prepare for the performance.

Two gunmen have come to collect on the $10,000 IOU that bears Fred's signature. Fred denies any knowledge of the phony signature and dismisses the men, who urge him to pay up and promise to return.

In Lilli's room she receives flowers that Fred intended for Lois, his newest flirtation. She mistakenly assumes he wants to rekindle his love (So in Love—Sc to F Solo).

Fred discovers that the flowers for Lois have been sent to Lilli and rushes into Lilli's dressing room, hoping she hasn't read the card and discovered the flowers were for Lois. Lilli puts the unread card in her bosom and the two go to prepare for their entrances.

The opening number of *Shrew* begins (We Open in Venice—Small Mixed Chorus), and the plot quickly unfolds. It seems that Bianca cannot wed until after her elder, quick-tongued sister, Katherine, is betrothed. Three suitors urge Bianca to marry one of them (Tom, Dick or Harry—Small Chorus, 3M/1F Trio).

Petruchio, an old friend of Lucentio who loves Bianca, arrives in Padua to find a wife (I've Come to Wive It Wealthily in Padua—L to M Solo with M Chorus), and it seems that Kate may be an excellent choice for this confident, handsome suitor.

Katherine, extremely unhappy because her father and all men favor Bianca, expresses her angry feelings (I Hate Men—F Solo). Petruchio bargains with Kate's father for her hand and he implores Kate to let him glimpse her face, but she tells him it is like anyone else's. He attempts to woo her (Were Thine That Special Face—M Solo).

Katherine exits, as Petruchio finishes the song. She later appears holding Lilli's flowers, which she hurls at Fred; she has obviously read the note. He urges her to remember they have an audience. The play continues with Lilli slugging him partially in character but mostly for her own vengeance. The scene ends as Fred takes her over his knee and spanks her.

Backstage, Lilli confronts Fred, who doesn't deny that the flowers were intended for Lois. The two bicker throughout and the scene finally ends as the two leave for their dressing rooms.

Lilli phones Harrison and promises to marry him immediately and begins packing but is stopped by Fred, who can't believe she would walk out in the middle of a show. She scoffs and sends him back to his room where the two hit men are waiting. Fred decides to get the hit men to persuade Lilli not to leave the show and admits signing the IOU but promises to pay once the show is a success. When the men understand that Lilli's sudden departure could cause the show to close, they enter her dressing room and attempt to flatter her into staying. They eventually show her their guns as the lights black out.

In front of the *Shrew* curtain, the chorus performs a filler number to allow time for a set change (I Sing of Love—Mixed Chorus).

The curtain opens to reveal the exterior of the church, where Kate has just married Petruchio. Couples are dancing happily and the wedding guests comment on the bizarre ceremony. Petruchio enters carrying a whip, followed by Kate and the two gunmen, costumed in *Shrew* garb. When Kate refuses to kiss her husband, Petruchio and the company urge her to comply with this simple request (Kiss Me, Kate—Mixed Chorus). He carries her off as the curtain falls on Act I.

Act II begins by the stage door where the actors are cooling off and watching Fred's dresser Paul and his friends perform a jazz number (Too Darn Hot—M Solo with M Trio).

Fred comes from behind the *Shrew* curtain to announce to the audience that the mule-riding scene will not be performed because Miss Vanessi can't ride the mule. Thus they will perform the following scene, which takes place in Petruchio's house. Petruchio, to force Kate to realize how badly she has treated her own servants, begins ordering and kicking his servants about. He complains about everything while she urges moderation. His plan seems to be working, but she locks the door to their bridal chamber and refuses him admission. He thinks of his many former girlfriends (Where Is the Life That Late I Led?—L to M Solo).

Backstage, Harrison Howell, a Washington bigwig, arrives to save Lilli from Fred, but Fred and the two gunmen convince him that Lilli is under emotional stress and might say anything. They exit for their onstage entrance as Lois enters and recognizes Howell as a former lover. He begs her to be discreet, to which she agrees. He then leaves for Lilli's dressing room.

Bill, who has overheard their conversation, asks Lois about their relationship. She responds that she will always love him, but Bill doubts her and exits. She continues the song which explains her philosophy (Always True to You in My Fashion—L to F Solo).

Lilli greets Harrison with the story that she is being held at gunpoint, but he thinks she is merely being temperamental and ignores her pleas for help. Fred and Harrison describe the life Lilli will lead as Harrison's wife, a picture of quiet social gatherings with stuffy statesmen. Lilli angrily orders Fred and his thugs from the dressing room.

A messenger and several men arrive with a package for Lois from admirers and the chorus girls tease Bill, who sings about his love (Bianca—M Solo and F Chorus). As he sings, the girls sing and tap-dance. After they all dance off in kick-line style, the gangsters enter to phone their boss, who they discover has been bumped off. Ordered to report to their new boss, they say farewell to Fred and Lilli. When Lilli realizes she is free to go, Fred urges her to stay, but she exits to a waiting cab. Fred is left alone (So in Love [Reprise]—Sc to M Solo).

The two gunmen, in their street clothes, attempt to leave the theatre but become confused and wind up onstage where they happily break into song (Brush up Your Shakespeare—M Duet).

At Baptista's house, Bianca and Lucentio's wedding party is beginning, but Fred and the company are afraid that Lilli has left and the play will end a fiasco. When Kate dutifully enters to obey Petruchio's every wish (I Am Ashamed That Women Are So Simple—F Solo), the actors are jubilant, the play is a success, and Lilli and Fred are reunited (Finale—Mixed Chorus).

NOTES ON THE PRODUCTION

1949 Tony Awards for Best Musical, Music, Book, Producers and Costumes.

The musical is well constructed with a clever book by Sam and Bella Spewack, and tuneful music and witty lyrics by Cole Porter. However, the leading roles require vocal and emotional maturity to make the game-playing/argument sequences believable and enjoyable. It is essential that all the "fight" sequences, both in the Shakespeare play between Kate and Petruchio and in the backstage sequences between Fred and Lilli, be played as a sincere game. The audience must always know that they are setting each other up or the play can become uncomfortable and vicious. Much rehearsal time and improvisation work should be set aside to accomplish this, for if the leading characters don't understand the relationship and enjoy the "game," the play can never achieve the brittle wittiness and fun inherent in the libretto.

The costumes are modern and "Shakespearean medieval," and are usually obtainable from classical companies or those who have performed *Once upon a Mattress* or *Camelot*. The essential sets are the connecting dressing rooms and the backstage corridor. It is ideal to have an outdoor alley for "Too Darn Hot."

If companies have limited funds and space, the Shakespeare play sequences may be permanent set pieces with all scenes being played in front of the same basic location.

The cast may be expanded to fit the size of the stage. It was traditionally performed with a separate singing and dancing chorus, but these may be combined if singers who move well are used and the longer dance numbers are trimmed.

SONGS OF SPECIAL INTEREST

"Another Op'nin', Another Show," opening number for revue or club, works well for beginning choreographer, simple movement, needs effective staging.

"We Open in Venice," may be done as quartet, revue potential, dance may be kept simple.

"I Hate Men," strong vocal, angry, clever lyrics comic in tone, good for character work and learning to play to an audience, soprano.

"Too Darn Hot," dance-oriented, jazz style, slick. Good for revue or nightclub.

"Where Is the Life That Late I Led?" lots of specifics, good for audition when trimmed, strong vocal, baritone.

"Brush up Your Shakespeare," vaudeville style, clever lyrics, diction and interrelationship emphasized, baritone duet.

"Always True to You in My Fashion," good for movement and presentation work, sexy character with charm, alto/mezzo.

Instrumentation: 2 violins, viola, cello, bass, 5 reeds, horn, 3 trumpets, trombone, percussion, harp, piano/celeste, guitar/mandolin, piano/conductor
Script: Knopf, Ten Great Musicals of the American Theatre, Theatre Arts (Magazine) 1/55
Score: Harms
Record: Columbia
Rights: TW

L

L'IL ABNER

Book: Norman Panama and Melvin Frank (Based on the Al Capp comic strip)
Music: Gene de Paul
Lyrics: Johnny Mercer

ORIGINAL PRODUCTION

St. James Theatre, November 15, 1956 (693 perf.)
Director/Choreographer: Michael Kidd
Musical Director: Lehman Engel
Orchestration: Philip J. Lang
Principals: Daisy Mae—Edith "Edie" Adams—mezzo; Mammy Yokum—Charlotte Rae—VTNE; L'il Abner—Peter Palmer—tenor; Appassionata—Tina Louise—VTNE; General Bullmoose—Howard St. John—baritone; Marryin' Sam—Stubby Kaye—tenor; Earthquake McGoon—Bern Hoffman—bass; Evil Eye Fleagle—Al Nesor—VTNE; Senator Jack S. Phogbound—Ted Thurston—VTNE; Pappy Yokum—Joe E. Marks—VTNE; Dr. Finsdale—Stanley Simmonds—baritone; Dr. Smithborn—George Reeder—baritone; Dr. Krogmeyer—Ralph Linn—baritone; Dr. Schleifetz—Marc Breaux—baritone
Chorus and Smaller Roles: 6M/6F minimum (the three scientists may be in dogpatch scenes as townsfolk).

SYNOPSIS

The curtain rises on the hillbilly town of Dogpatch, USA, as the residents introduce themselves (A Typical Day—Mixed Chorus). They are preparing for the annual Sadie Hawkins Day race, where the Dogpatch women marry any man they capture in the race.

At the fishing hole, L'il Abner tells his friends he doesn't plan on letting Daisy Mae, his girlfriend, catch him on race day because he enjoys his freedom (If I Had My Druthers—Sc to M Solo with M Chorus). Daisy arrives to summon the boys to the town meeting in Cornpone Square.

At the meeting, Marryin' Sam tells the story of the square's namesake and illustrious Civil War hero (Jubilation T. Cornpone—M Solo with Mixed Chorus).

Senator Jack S. Phogbound arrives with Dr. Finsdale to tell the people that Dogpatch has been chosen by the U.S. Government as the most unimportant place in the country and will be honored by being blown up during an atom bomb test. The Dogpatchers are excited to be recognized by the government (Rag Offen the Bush—Mixed Chorus). Since the town will be obliterated before Sadie Hawkins day, the citizens must return to the code of the hills, whereby next of kin may arrange the marriage of an eligible female. When Mammy Yokum discovers that a distant relative has promised Daisy to the odorous Earthquake McGoon, she urges the people to find something necessary so the townsfolk can have the Sadie Hawkins Day race. Away from the crowd, Abner promises to let Daisy catch him and assures her she deserves something better than Earthquake (Namely You—Sc to M/F Duet).

Back in Cornpone Square, the residents despair of finding something to make the town necessary. They try to explain to Dr. Finsdale how they feel (Unnecessary Town—Mixed Chorus). They are saved when the government discovers that Mammy's Yokumberry tonic produces supermen like Abner. The government orders Abner and a group of male Dogpatchers to Washington for tests.

In Washington, three radio towers and commentators flash out the news that the tests are underway. Pappy assures the President of the United States that he intends to donate the fruit from the Yokumberry tree to the U.S. government.

General Bullmoose, a business tycoon, is seen in his Washington office enlisting the help of Senator Phogbound in securing the tonic for himself. His male secretaries agree that what is good for the U.S. is good for Bullmoose (What's Good for General Bullmoose—M Chorus). He offers Abner $1,000,000 for the rights to the tonic, but Abner turns him down and returns to Dogpatch.

The Dogpatchers eagerly greet Abner (There's Room Enough for Us—Mixed Chorus) with the news from Washington. They assure the crowd that the country is doing fine (The Country's in the Very Best of Hands—M Duet with Mixed Chorus). Abner tells Daisy he is going to do his darndest to let her catch him in the afternoon Sadie Hawkins Day race.

General Bullmoose, furious that Abner has refused him, sends Appassionata Von Climax, his mistress, and Evil Eye Fleagle to trap Abner in the Sadie

Hawkins Day race. Fleagle has the ability to paralyze people with his eyes and promises to freeze Abner until Appassionata can claim him.

In Dogpatch the race begins (Sadie Hawkins Day Ballet—Mixed Chorus Dance). Appassionata claims Abner, and Fleagle and Bullmoose take Abner back to Washington while Daisy and the family sadly bid him farewell.

Act II opens in a Washington government test lab, where Drs. Finsdale, Smithborn, Krogmeyer, and Schleifetz are wrapping up their tests on the Yokumberry tonic. The results delight them (Oh Happy Day—L to M Quartet).

Back in Dogpatch, Daisy worries about her lost youth and confides to Marryin' Sam that she is getting old (I'm Past My Prime—Sc to M/F Duet). When Mammy has a vision that Abner is going to be killed by General Bullmoose immediately after he marries Appassionata, Daisy agrees to marry Earthquake if he will go to Washington and help her save Abner's life. Daisy, Earthquake, Mammy, Pappy, Sam and the other Dogpatchers set out for Washington to save Abner.

General Bullmoose, running out of time to get the formula for Yokumberry tonic from Abner, hires Evil Eye Fleagle to put a truth whammy on Abner at an engagement party he's planned for Abner and Appassionata. Daisy tries to convince Abner to run away with her (Love in a Home—Sc to M/F Duet), but he feels honor bound to marry the girl who caught him in the race no matter what the outcome is. Daisy and the Dogpatch crowd decide to crash the party to try to save Abner.

In a corridor of the Bullmoose mansion, Bullmoose, fearing a scandal, tells his secretaries to let the Dogpatchers in. When urged to consider his dignity, he complains of the problems of modern life (Progress Is the Root of All Evil—L to M Solo).

In the ballroom the Dogpatchers rescue Abner when Earthquake grabs a tray and reflects Evil Eye's whammy to General Bullmoose, who tells about his crimes and is arrested. Daisy thanks Earthquake and tells him she is ready to marry him.

In a corridor, Bullmoose, accompanied by a policeman, bemoans his capture (Progress Is the Root [Reprise]—M Solo).

Meanwhile, the government experiments have been deemed a failure because the men have all become cold, unfeeling, self-centered creatures—just like Abner. The wives beg the government scientists to return their husbands to their normal selves (Put 'Em Back—F Chorus). The Dogpatchers arrive but are informed by the scientists that Abner and the men must stay for more tests. Daisy sadly bids Abner farewell (Namely You [Reprise]—F Solo) and exits. Pappy takes Abner and the boys aside and tells them they can solve their problems by taking Cornpone's Powerfully Potent Romanticizing Potion, which makes all men, including Abner, capable of love. The boys agree to try it and Pappy sends a telegram to Dogpatch to stall the wedding.

In Dogpatch, the wedding of Earthquake McGoon and Daisy is slowly proceeding as Daisy, Mammy and Sam stall until Pappy and Abner arrive from Washington. Sam describes the problems of marriage to the repulsive Earthquake

(The Matrimonial Stomp—M Solo with Mixed Chorus). By the end of the number Earthquake is convinced that marriage isn't for him and gives Daisy to Abner. The husbands return to their normal selves, eagerly greeted by their wives (Put 'Em Back—[Reprise]—F Chorus) as Dr. Finsdale enters and orders evacuation to begin. The citizens, refusing to leave without their statue of Jubilation T. Cornpone, discover a letter inside signed by Abraham Lincoln proclaiming the statue a national shrine. This unexpected news means the town is saved (Finale—Mixed Chorus).

NOTES ON THE PRODUCTION

Because of the political humor, the musical is extremely dated. A successful production is much more likely if the humor is updated to reflect the present political climate. Unless the show is quickly paced it may seem overburdened with overly long musical numbers. A director may want to examine the possibility of editing numbers that rely too heavily on creative staging and exuberant dancing. It is also possible through careful streamlining to reduce the cast size by reassigning dialogue.

During casting, care should be taken that the performers chosen look as much as possible like the characters they are portraying. A study of old comic books and anthologies of the Abner Sunday funnies will help with makeup and costume suggestions.

The set should be cartoon in style and may utilize the same basic exterior of ground rows and trees for the Dogpatch sequences and Washington. Most companies try to have two sets, one with Cornpone's statue and the exterior of a Dogpatch shack, and one with a background that represents Washington. Specific delineation of location is provided by props, i.e., desks, barrels, etc.

SONGS OF SPECIAL INTEREST

"Jubilation T. Cornpone," foot-stomping chorus number, spirited, suited for revue. Tenor featured.

"Progress Is the Root of All Evil," vaudeville style solo, may be done as a duet in a club situation.

"Put 'Em Back," F chorus, spirited, showcase potential.

"Rag Offen the Bush," mixed chorus, energetic, hillbilly sound, thigh slapping, simple choreography required as emphasis on energy.

Instrumentation: 2 violins, viola, cello, bass, 2 trumpets, 3 trombones, percussion, guitar/banjo, 5 reeds, piano/conductor
Script: NP
Score: Commander
Record: Columbia
Rights: TW

LITTLE MARY SUNSHINE

Book, Music, and Lyrics: Rick Besoyan

ORIGINAL PRODUCTION

Orpheum Theatre, November 18, 1959 (1,143 perf.)
Director: Ray Harrison and Rick Besoyan
Choreographer: Ray Harrison
Musical Direction: Jack Holmes
Orchestration: Rick Besoyan
Principals: Captain Jim—William Graham—baritone; Corporal Jester—John McMartin—tenor; Little Mary—Eileen Brennan—soprano; Nancy—Elmarie Wendel—alto; Mme. Ernestine—Elizabeth Parrish—soprano; Oscar—Mario Siletti—baritone; Fleet Foot—Robert Chambers—VTNE; Chief Brown Bear—John Aniston—VTNE
Chorus and Smaller Roles: 5M/5F.

SYNOPSIS

The house lights dim and a spotlight focuses on a young woman in a turn-of-the-century costume "lighting the footlights" in a turn-of-the-century theatre. As she works she invites the audience to come back in time to the innocence and fun of the operettas of Strauss, Friml and Herbert. She exits and the scene opens on the exterior of Little Mary's Inn, in the mountains of Colorado. A group of forest rangers, led by handsome Captain Big Jim Warrington, are returning from maneuvers and sing about their achievements (The Forest Rangers—M Solo to M Chorus).

At the end of the song Captain Warrington promotes Corporal Billy Jester to second in command and exits, leaving a befuddled Billy, who quickly refers to his Ranger's Rule Book. He begins to lecture on courage but is interrupted by Chief Brown Bear of the Kadota tribe, who tells the rangers that Little Mary, his adopted daughter, is coming to greet them. He leaves as the rangers sing a tribute to her (Little Mary Sunshine—M Chorus and F Solo).

Mary invites the rangers to a garden party with some visiting young ladies and Billy accepts for the group. When he mentions her present difficulty, she is undaunted that the U.S. Government plans to foreclose on her property for back taxes (Look for a Sky of Blue—F Solo and M Chorus). Captain Jim enters, salutes Mary and dismisses the men. He confides his desire to be more than friends but can't commit himself further because his life is threatened by an evil band of marauding Indians. When he asks if she knows his guide, Fleet Foot, she excitedly responds that he saved her life when she was a child and is her adopted father's friend. She asks him to stroll in her garden.

The garden drop comes in as Captain Jim expresses his feelings to Mary by comparing her to the garden itself (You're the Fairest Flower—Sc to M Solo).

At the end of the number a female operatic voice is heard, and Little Mary recognizes the Germanic voice of the plump Mme. Ernestine, who grandly greets them. Mary introduces Mme. Ernestine, an opera singer and frequent visitor to Little Mary's Inn, and Mary and Captain Jim leave the opera singer to reminisce about her youth in Bavaria (In Izzen Schnokken on the Lovely Essen Zook Zee—Sc to F Solo).

At the Inn, Cora, Maud, Gwendolyn, Henrietta and Mabel, five wealthy young ladies from Eastchester Finishing School, are passing the time (Playing Croquet—F Chorus). They soon get bored with croquet and find amusement on their swings but are surprised by the entrance of the forest rangers (Swinging/How Do You Do?—F and M Chorus).

The girls, except Cora, are eager to flirt. As two of the girls slip off with a ranger, Cora, Henrietta and Gwendolyn agree to answer Ranger Pete's question regarding their beauty (Tell a Handsome Stranger—Mixed Chorus). As they exit, Nancy Tweakle, the overly friendly maid who welcomes attention from men, enters with several rangers. A jealous Billy dismisses them as Nancy rushes to kiss him. He refuses to accept her outlandish behavior until she promises never to look at another man (Once in a Blue Moon—Sc to M/F Duet).

Captain Jim, alone onstage, rehearses his proposal scene, but is interrupted by an arriving Billy. Jim commands Billy to disguise himself as an Indian brave and go into the enemy camp if Captain Jim's mission fails. Billy nervously exits as Mary enters with an almost blind, ancient Indian who keeps walking into things and toppling over. It is Fleet Foot. Captain Jim tries to get the old fellow to draw a map, but he insists on accompanying Jim and exits to prepare for the journey.

When Captain Jim tells Mary that the Indian they seek is Yellow Feather, who is Chief Brown Bear's son, Mary fears that the Chief's shame will be great, for she told him his errant son died trying to save her life. Jim promises to keep the truth from the old Chief and falls to his knees to ask Little Mary to marry him when he returns (Colorado Love Call—Sc to M/F Duet). She agrees and they exit in different directions.

Yellow Feather's call is heard and Little Mary is frightened by a singing Mme. Ernestine, who comforts her (Every Little Nothing—Sc to F Duet). Mary hears Yellow Feather's call and screams. The ensemble appears to find out what is upsetting her (What Has Happened?—Mixed Chorus), and Little Mary tries to remain optimistic (Finale—F Solo to Mixed Chorus).

When Act II opens, the young ladies and the forest rangers are engaged in a party (Such a Merry Party—Mixed Chorus) when Oscar Fairfax, a retired wealthy general, arrives. He is quite enamored of all the ladies, and after sending the rangers off to find Captain Jim, he gives the girls jewelry and urges them to think of him as their uncle (Say "Uncle"—M Solo and F Chorus).

In front of Brown Bear's tepee, Billy gets Indian lessons and clothes from Chief Brown Bear, who adopts him as his son. Billy is pleased at the honor (Me a Heap Big Injun—Sc to M Solo). In front of Brown Bear's tepee the ladies are saddened by the absence of the forest rangers, but Nancy is too busy disguising herself to notice their depression. Mary, discovering Nancy's plan to help Billy, admonishes her for her headstrong, careless ways (Naughty, Naughty, Nancy— F Solo and F Chorus).

After Mary exits, Nancy enters dressed like Theda Bara and excites the girls with her tales of the most famous of women spies (Mata Hari—F Chorus). As the song ends she climbs out the window on a rope of sheets.

Mme. Ernestine is exercising in the garden when Oscar backs on with a pistol. The two happily discover they were both in Vienna at the same time; he to sell his paintings, and she to study opera—they reminisce (Do You Ever Dream Of Vienna?—Sc to M/F Duet).

At the Inn, Mary is sadly waiting for Captain Jim's return when a cuckoo bird brightens her thoughts (Coo Coo—F Solo). Yellow Feather captures Mary, but Captain Jim arrives in time to save her (Colorado Love Call [Reprise]—M/ F Duet). The rangers take Yellow Feather off before Brown Bear can discover that his son lives. Oscar Fairfax, on behalf of the U.S. Government, awards Brown Bear one quarter of the State of Colorado. The old Chief gives Mary the Inn and grounds and the remainder of his newly acquired land to Billy for a National Park. Fleet Foot arrives as the company bursts into song (Finale— Mixed Chorus).

NOTES ON THE PRODUCTION

This small musical spoof on the operetta productions of Friml, Strauss and Herbert, has a delightful script, and is perfect for school, summer theatre or community productions. The music is lilting, the lyrics true to the period, and the dialogue humorous. It is important to have an excellent director who understands the operetta form and is able to spoof the production with loving sincerity. The show only requires three main settings, the Inn exterior, the garden, and the bedroom. Brown Bear's tepee may be onstage throughout as if in a separate area. It may be possible to play the bedroom scene on the porch of the house, but it will take some readaptation of dialogue.

There are two costumes each for the younger females. The Mounties are in uniform and the Indians are appropriately dressed. Three Indian costumes must be identical for a confusion chase with Nancy, Billy and Yellow Feather.

SONGS OF SPECIAL INTEREST

"Colorado Love Call," heavily stylized spoof of Jeanette McDonald/Nelson Eddy movies. Overdone, good for revue or period study, soprano/baritone.

"Do You Ever Dream of Vienna?" charm, older-character duet, good for revue, soprano/baritone.

"Mata Hari," small F chorus which gives a student director a chance to work on developing characterizations and staging contrasts of solo to choral.

"Once in a Blue Moon," Charm duet for young comedian and soubrette, alto/tenor.

Instrumentation: 5 reeds, 2 trumpets, 2 horns, trombone, percussion, 2 violins, viola, cello, bass, harp, piano/conductor. Duo piano arrangement also available
Script: Theatre Arts (Magazine) Dec 60, SF
Score: Valando
Record: Columbia
Rights: SF

LITTLE ME

Book: Neil Simon (Based on a novel by Patrick Dennis)
Music: Cy Coleman
Lyrics: Carolyn Leigh

ORIGINAL PRODUCTION

Lunt-Fontanne Theatre, November 17, 1962 (257 perf.)
Director: Cy Feuer
Choreographer: Bob Fosse
Musical Director: Charles Sanford
Orchestrations: Ralph Burns
Principals: Noble/Val du Val/Mr. Pinchley/Prince Cherney/Otto Schnitzler/Fred Poitrine—Sid Caesar—baritone; Young Belle—Virginia Martin—mezzo; Patrick Dennis—Peter Turgeon—VTNE; Old Belle—Nancy Andrews—alto; George— Swen Swenson—baritone; Benny Buchsbaum—Mort Marshall—baritone; Bernie Buchsbaum—Joey Faye—baritone
Chorus and Smaller Roles: 6M/6F minimum.

SYNOPSIS

Patrick Dennis, noted author, arrives at Belle Poitrine's lavish drawing room, prepared to write the famous woman's memoirs. He waits with her butler as the large, flamboyant Belle enters, followed by her three hairdressers from New York. Patrick insists that she tell him all the facts and intimacies of her life (The Truth—F Solo to Small M Chorus).

As she begins her story the scene flashes back to Venezuela, Illinois, the town where sixteen-year-old Belle is growing up in poverty.

Belle is an extremely attractive, sexy young girl who only has eyes for the wealthy, handsome captain of the football, baseball, debating and tumbling teams, Noble Eggleston.

Noble first meets Belle when he and his friends give her family some food. As he gives her the basket, their hands touch and the music crescendos. He asks her to his sixteenth birthday party and exits. Belle yearns to marry Noble and change her life (The Other Side of the Tracks—Sc to F Solo).

At the party the rich kids dance (The Rich Kids Rag—Dance—Mixed Chorus). When Noble's mother discovers her son has invited a girl from Drifter's Row to the party, she insists that he marry an equal, someone with navy blue blood. Belle enters in her mother's red working dress and Noble tells her of his mother's mandate, yet confesses that he loves her (I Love You—Sc to M/F Duet with Mixed Chorus in an Echo Effect).

Realizing she must achieve wealth and social position in order to marry Noble, Belle sets out to achieve her life's desire (The Other Side of the Tracks [Reprise]—F Solo). George Musgrove, a boy from Drifter's Row who is attracted to Belle, bids her farewell and promises help if she ever needs it.

The lights rise on an older Belle narrating her story to Patrick Dennis. As she continues, the lights cross fade to the interior of a small-town bank owned by the cranky eighty-eight–year–old Amos Pinchley, who is wheeled on by his nurse. He terrorizes his son Junior and the people of Drifter's Row who have come to ask him not to evict them. Belle calls him a rotten man and forces him to realize that no one loves him. She tries to demonstrate the way he can change his image (Deep down Inside—Sc to M/F Duet to Mixed Chorus). During the number Pinchley tears up the mortgages on Drifter's Row and befriends everyone. The new Pinchley is overjoyed and sets Belle up in Peoria where she tries to gain culture and refinement.

Older Belle tells Patrick that the gossipmongers were upset that Pinchley spent every weekend in Belle's hotel room and proceeds to describe the event that caused a tremendous sensation.

The lights rise on the hotel room where Belle practices her poise and diction exercises while waiting for Pinchley to arrive. Pinchley dances on, excited that he can walk, and asks Belle to marry him. She agrees when he promises to leave her all his money. They embrace and Pinchley's gun, in his breast pocket, accidentally goes off, killing the old man.

Belle is tried, acquitted, and booked into vaudeville by the Buchsbaum Brothers, Bernie and Benny, who comment on her obvious talent (Be a Performer—Sc to 2M/F Trio). Belle triumphantly performs with four policemen (Dimples—F Solo and M Quartet).

Lights rise on an older Belle sculpting a clay figure of Patrick Dennis in a tiger skin. She tells him her vaudeville career suddenly ended when the Buchsbaum Brothers dropped her for Peaches Browning, who killed her millionaire husband at the wedding. Belle found work as a photographer in a nightclub.

In the nightclub, Belle is taking pictures of the patrons when Noble, his mother, and his fiancée Ramona, a childhood friend, appear. Belle is crushed that Noble didn't wait for her, but he blames it on his mother. As they exit, Val Du Val, an egotistical star, is introduced by three French coquettes. Val enters with his partner Collette, who emphasizes his lyrics with her drum, and the girls sing backup (Boom-Boom—M Solo to F Trio).

At the end of the number Val takes his bows and exits backstage to discover the heartbroken Belle preparing to leap from a window's edge. He dissuades her by telling her the story of his last love and leaves her with a tall, handsome man who turns out to be George Musgrove from Drifter's Row. As the club empties, George ignores the fact that Belle still loves Noble and invites her to his downstairs apartment (I've Got Your Number—Sc to M Solo). War is declared, and Belle succumbs.

Older Belle in the middle of a ballet lesson continues to tell her story. It seems George joined the Navy and unknowingly left her pregnant while Noble was shipped overseas before he could marry Ramona.

The scene shifts to a small World War I apartment party which the six-months pregnant Belle is attending. Her friends introduce her to Fred Poitrine, a thickly bespectacled wimpy individual who is simplistically happy. He offers to marry Belle because she reminds him of his mother, who is also "fat." She tells him the truth, but he is oblivious to her condition and insists that everyone get married before leaving for the front. The preacher arrives to marry everyone and Fred admits to Belle that he has never kissed a girl (Real Live Girl—Sc to M Solo).

A series of lights rise on various girls reading letters from the front while their husbands are shown in fighting conditions. As Belle reads, the lights rise on Fred, who is typing orders. A letter arrives that Fred has died from wounds received while typing. Hearing that Noble has been shot down, she leaves her daughter with her mother and goes to France to find him.

In a French base hospital the soldiers learn that Belle and her girls are coming (Real Live Girls—Small M Chorus). Belle arrives and discovers Val Du Val suffering from amnesia. As the cannons sound in the distance, she helps him regain his memory and promises never to leave him. As he goes to evacuate his orchestra, Noble arrives and begs her to marry him. She agrees and Noble exits into the hospital as Val Du Val enters. When she tells Val she is going to marry Noble, the amnesia returns and he exits. Afraid that her departure will cause a permanent relapse, she bids the entering Noble farewell. Noble exits and Val Du Val returns. She agrees to the wedding and the troops move out.

Act II opens with older Belle in a steam bath continuing her memoirs. It seems she and Val booked cruise tickets on the SS *Gigantic*.

The scene shifts to the ship's decks where Belle is greeted by the Buchsbaum Brothers who have become Broadway producers. Noble is also on board, now a famous judge, doctor, husband and father. When the ship hits an iceberg, Noble takes over the ship and tirelessly saves everyone except Val, who drowns when his amnesia returns and he forgets how to swim.

Older Belle finishes telling the story to Patrick on a massage table. It seems that Belle sued the steamship company for two million dollars and Mrs. Eggleston had Ramona and Noble's marriage annulled when she discovered that Ramona's family lost their money in the stock market crash. Belle, knowing Mrs. Eggleston won't accept her without culture, contacts the Buchsbaum Brothers.

Young Belle becomes a partner to Bernie and Benny and tells of the loneliness of being a Hollywood starlet. As she sings, various theatre marquees and variety headlines are displayed with letters of her various hits (Poor Little Hollywood Star—F Solo).

In Bernie and Benny's office, the three are desperately searching for a director when an elderly delivery boy arrives with their lunch. They discover that the delivery boy is none other than Otto Schnitzler, a former German film director who has hit bottom. The filming begins. As Schnitzler is demonstrating the knife scene, he accidentally stabs himself with a real knife and Belle is forced to direct the picture, which is a financial flop but a cultural smash according to the *Harvard Lampoon*.

Older Belle tells Patrick after a game of tennis that she discovered oil on the studio back lot and became one of the world's wealthiest women but still had no social position. She sings with young Belle (Little Me—F Duet).

In the casino at Monte Carlo Belle meets Prince Cherny, who has come to win money for his bankrupt kingdom. At the last minute Belle switches his bet and he loses the last of his royal treasury. He collapses, but Belle, determined to minister to his needs, moves into his bedchamber for two weeks. The weakened Prince rallies enough to bid his subjects farewell (The Prince's Farewell—Sc to M Solo). The number builds into a rousing dance in the Russian style. When Belle arrives to give the Prince a check to save his kingdom, he gives her a title and dies. She returns to the United States with wealth, culture, and social position.

Noble is sworn in as Governor of North and South Dakota and asks Belle to marry him. The future looks rosy until Belle urges him to join her in a celebration drink, then he becomes an alcoholic.

Older Belle continues her story. The drunken Noble, disgraced and impeached, disappears and she returns to her estate to await his return.

One night Belle and her friends are gathered to toast the occasion (Here's to Us—F Solo to Mixed Chorus) when Noble, now a bum, arrives, takes George Musgrove aside and confides he is going to the South Seas to kick the habit.

Years later, Noble returns after Belle's daughter and Junior Eggleston have become engaged and Belle has married George. As he enters Belle's home, Mrs. Eggleston enters with a gun to kill Belle, but kills George instead. At last Noble and Belle are free to be with each other (Finale).

NOTES ON THE PRODUCTION

The show ran opposite *A Funny Thing Happened on the Way to the Forum* and *Oliver!*, two shows that took most of the Tony Awards. However, Bob Fosse's choreography won an award.

The script is extremely humorous and fun for a community theatre, high school or college, for it can be performed by a small cast. Much of the enjoyment is derived from the fact that the leading male performer plays many roles and must constantly run offstage as one character and return a few seconds later in a different part. The chorus plays a variety of parts and is always busy either offstage changing costumes or onstage performing. The use of a smaller chorus makes the show more fun for the audience, who usually enjoy seeing the same performers in a variety of scenes.

There are quite a few costumes, a different one for each scene and each character in the scene. The story covers a wide time frame, and this must be reflected in the costumes. The set may be comprised of small pieces which establish location; a unit set of levels would be the most adaptable.

SONGS OF SPECIAL INTEREST

"Be a Performer," trio, good for revue situation and for beginning choreographer as the two men must move a lot in the vaudeville style. Good character relationship important.

"I've Got Your Number," baritone, soft shoe, suave, good for class and playing an audience.

"The Other Side of the Tracks," mezzo solo, shows off voice, good for audition, spunky, up tempo, some belt.

Instrumentation: 3 violins, cello, bass, 5 reeds, 2 trumpets, 3 trombones, 2 percussion, harp, banjo, piano/conductor
Script: Collected plays of Neil Simon Volume Two
Selections: Hansen
Record: RCA
Rights: TW

A LITTLE NIGHT MUSIC

Book: Hugh Wheeler (Based on *Smiles of a Summer Night*, a film by Ingmar Bergman)
Music and Lyrics: Stephen Sondheim

ORIGINAL PRODUCTION

Shubert Theatre, February 25, 1973 (601 perf.)
Director: Harold Prince
Choreographer: Patricia Birch
Musical Director: Harold Hastings
Orchestration: Jonathan Tunick
Principals: Mme. Armfeldt—Hermione Gingold—alto; Desiree—Glynis Johns—alto; Fredrika—Judy Kahan—soprano; Petra—D. Jamin Bartlett—mezzo; Fredrik Egerman—Len Cariou—baritone; Henrik—Mark Lambert—tenor; Anne—Victoria Mallory—soprano; Charlotte—Patricia Elliott—mezzo; Count Carl Magnus—Laurence Guittard—high baritone
Chorus and Smaller Roles: 4M/5F—includes the vocal quintet comprised of 2M/3F; must blend well together and be able to move with style.

SYNOPSIS

The play opens with the quintet vocalizing and singing of what is to come and what has passed (Remember?—2M/3F Quintet).

The plot revolves around Anne Egerman, a pretty eighteen-year-old virgin bride of eleven months: Henrik, Fredrik's nineteen-year-old son; Fredrik, a lawyer in his forties; Desiree Armfeldt, a popular actress; the Countess Charlotte and her husband, Carl Magnus, Desiree's lover.

Fredrik arrives home with tickets to the theatre as Anne excitedly rattles on about the day's events. He wonders if he should nap or attempt to consummate their marriage (Now—M Solo with F Lines). He decides to nap.

Henrik, the melancholy nineteen-year-old Bible scholar and cellist, son of Fredrik, is in the parlor below, reading, when Petra, the easygoing young maid, sexually teases him. Henrik attempts to kiss her, but she breaks away, promising—later. Henrik angrily wonders when later is (Later—M Solo). Meanwhile, in the bedroom Anne looks at the sleeping Fredrik and promises that soon she will be his (Soon—F Solo). The three, unaware of each other, sing in unison.

The scene switches to Desiree's mother's house where Fredrika, Desiree's thirteen-year-old daughter, plays scales on the piano (Ordinary Mothers—F Solo). Desiree enters in a flurry to talk with her mother and daughter as the quintet comments (Ordinary Mothers—Mixed Chorus).

The Egermans arrive at the performance in which Desiree is starring. The actress enters the stage and obviously recognizes Fredrik. Two of the quintet comment on the moment (Remember?—M/F Duet) while Anne, who is upset, rushes from the theatre.

Meanwhile, in the Egerman parlor, Henrik quickly puts on his trousers and laments his failure to seduce Petra. She is busy comforting him as Anne and Fredrik enter. The Quintet highlights the moment (Remember?—3F/2M Quintet). While Anne sleeps, Fredrik seeks out Desiree in her apartment and uncomfortably tries to explain his reason for coming to see her (You Must Meet My Wife—Sc to M/F Duet). Desiree is shocked that Anne hasn't allowed her husband to make love to her, and realizing Fredrik's needs, she ushers him into the bedroom. The scene switches to Mme. Armfeldt, who sings (Liaisons—F Solo).

When Desiree's present lover, a count in the dragoons, unexpectedly arrives in the dressing room, Fredrik and Desiree fabricate a story to convince the count that she has not been unfaithful. He is doubtful (In Praise of Women—L to M Solo).

Carl Magnus forces his wife, Charlotte, to visit Anne and tell her about Fredrik in Desiree's apartment. The two lament the problems of love (Every Day a Little Death—Sc to F Duet).

Desiree, anxious to be with Fredrik, convinces her mother to send a weekend invitation to Fredrik and his family. When Petra excitedly delivers the invitation to Anne, who is appalled, Charlotte convinces her to go and tells Carl about the invitation. He informs her that they will also visit Desiree, and the groups set off (A Weekend in the Country—Mixed Chorus).

Act II begins with the quintet setting the mood for the weekend visit on the estate (The Sun Won't Set—3F/2M Quintet).

As Fredrik and Carl Magnus wait for Desiree on the lawn in front of the estate, each sings his inner thoughts (It Would Have Been Wonderful—Sc to M Duet).

The guests enter the dining room as the women from the quintet sing (Perpetual Anticipation—F Trio). The dinner is a shambles with the Countess trying to infuriate Carl Magnus by flirting with Fredrik, Henrik rushing off because of the phoniness of the people present, and Anne hastening to find Henrik. Fredrik and Desiree both admit they wanted to recapture time, and Desiree comments on their foolishness (Send in the Clowns—Sc to F Solo).

Anne finally discovers Henrik in the garden attempting suicide; they embrace and tell each other of their love. Nearby, Anne's maid, Petra, has finished a night of lovemaking with Fred, a servant. As Fred sleeps, Petra dreams of her future (The Miller's Son—F Solo).

Henrik and Anne leave together as Charlotte tells Fredrik she really loves her husband. Carl Magnus jealously accuses her of infidelity and challenges Fredrik to Russian roulette. A shot is heard and Fredrik is carried on with a grazed ear. Carl Magnus and Charlotte leave—she has achieved her aim.

Desiree and Fredrik are left to each other. The play ends with the lovers waltzing with their respective partners (Finale—Mixed Chorus).

NOTES ON THE PRODUCTION

Tonys, 1973: Director, Score, Book, Actress, Featured Actress, Musical and Costumes.

The show is a charming one and is a musical pastiche that captures the flavor of turn-of-the-century Sweden. The actors must be superb or the show shouldn't be considered. It is musically quite difficult and there are quite a few period costumes for each character, including formal dinner wear. The sets may be simplified by using the wing and border system if the stage is proscenium. In fact, the sets aren't as important as the performances or the costumes.

The production must be extremely fluid, and the movement must be smooth and flowing. While there are no "dance numbers" per se, a choreographer should be utilized to train the performers in the art of movement and period decorum. In order for the show to be successful and interesting, the audience must experience the "evening" as an entire believable theatrical entity.

SONGS OF SPECIAL INTEREST

"Every Day a Little Death," mezzo-alto/soprano duet, relationship, lyric and underlying emotion of importance, good for drama and pain.

"Liaisons," older character woman, philosophic number, class work only, low alto without much vocal quality.

"The Miller's Son," mezzo, movement possible but not necessary; emphasis is on lyric and emotion. Character study.

"Send in the Clowns," bittersweet, now a standard, good for character study when coupled with scene before and "You Must Meet My Wife." Takes a mature and charming actress to make the number work.

"You Must Meet My Wife," clever lyric and underlying story makes this an excellent number for relationship development. Baritone/alto.

"A Weekend in the Country," vocal work emphasized, good for showcase or revue. Characters are important; movement is necessary. Good for beginning choreographer. Small chorus.

Instrumentation: 5 reeds, 3 horns, 2 trumpets, trombone, percussion, harp, celeste/piano, 3 violins, viola, cello, bass, piano/conductor
Script: Dodd, Mead, Great Musicals of the American Theatre, Volume Two
Score: Revelation
Record: Columbia, RCA
Rights: MTI

LITTLE SHOP OF HORRORS

Book and Lyrics: Howard Ashman (Based on the film by Roger Corman)
Music: Alan Menken

ORIGINAL PRODUCTION

Orpheum Theatre, July 27, 1982 (still running)
Director: Howard Ashman
Musical Staging: Edie Cowan
Musical Direction/Vocal Arrangements: Robert Billig
Instrumental Arrangements: Robby Merken
Puppets: Martin P. Robinson
Principals: Chiffon—Marlene Danielle—VTI; Crystal—Jennifer Leigh Warren—VTI; Ronnette—Sheila Kay Davis—VTI; Mushnik—Hy Anzell—baritone; Audrey—Ellen Greene—mezzo; Seymour—Lee Wilkof—tenor; Orin/Bernstein/Snip/Luce and Others—Franc Luz—baritone; Audrey II—Martin P. Robinson and Ron Taylor—bass
Chorus and Smaller Roles: There is no chorus in the production; Chiffon, Crystal and Ronnette act as a Greek chorus by commenting on the action. Their vocal types are interchangeable.

SYNOPSIS

After a godlike voice thunders out a pronouncement of danger, à la a grade B science fiction film, the lights rise on Crystal, Ronnette and Chiffon, three street urchins who exemplify the 1960s singing groups (Little Shop of Horrors—F Trio).

The act begins as the three move downstage to sit on a stoop, where a wino sleeps, to read monster magazines. Upstage, the shop lights rise on the interior, which is dismally decorated with a large clock which revolves to show the passage of time. Mr. Mushnik, the owner of this very faded, unpopular shop in the skid row area, comments on the poor business to his two shop clerks, Seymour, a balding wimp in his mid-twenties, and Audrey, a well-built not very bright, bleached blonde. He yells at the three urchins on the stoop to go out and better themselves, but they retort on the impossibility of their situations. The wino, Mushnik, Audrey and Seymour add in their own reasons for living in the seedy section of town (Skid Row—Mixed Chorus).

The clock slowly ticks off the hours and stops at six; no one has been in the shop all day. The defeated Mushnik announces the closing of the business, but Seymour and Audrey, convinced that the addition of exotic plants would help business, beg him to renovate his stock to highlight the unusual. Seymour rushes into the workroom and reenters with a weird plant he has romantically named Audrey II. Within seconds after the plant is placed in the window, a customer arrives to inquire into the history of the plant. Seymour relates the story of the purchase of Audrey II as the urchins, outside the store, vocally back him (Da Doo—M Solo/3F Trio).

The customer buys $100 worth of roses and Mushnik deliriously invites his clerks to dinner. Audrey sadly refuses, for she has a date with her sadistic boyfriend, and a sudden drooping of the plant forces Seymour to stay behind to discover the problem. Mushnik exits, leaving Seymour alone with Audrey II; he begs her to grow (Grow for Me—L to M Solo). When Seymour accidentally pricks his finger, the plant perks up; it dawns on him that Audrey II needs blood to stay healthy. He gives the hungry plant a few more drops and begs it to grow. As he exits, the plant grows several sizes before the lights black out.

Mushnik, Crystal, Chiffon, and Ronnette are seated outside the shop listening to a radio interview in which Seymour discusses his new plant. Mushnik is amazed at the sudden popularity of Audrey II and Seymour. As he announces his astonishment to the urchins, Seymour enters to extol in his new found fame (Don't It Go to Show Ya Never Know—Sc to 2M Solo to 3F Trio). The plant, which Seymour carries in a medium-size pot, becomes extremely involved in the number by attempting to take nibbles out of the urchins. Seymour rushes Audrey II off as Audrey enters with a black eye.

The urchins urge Audrey to dump her creepy boyfriend and take up with Seymour. She is touched to think that Seymour could care for her and dreams of a place where they could be happy together (Somewhere That's Green—L to F Solo).

One week later, Mushnik, Seymour and Audrey are busy renovating the shop (Closed for Renovations—2M/1F Trio). At the end of the song Audrey II is revealed; she has reached five feet in height and has sprouted spiked leaves. Audrey is impressed with Seymour and offers to help him choose new clothes for his garden club lectures and television interviews. They are obviously in love, but Audrey has a date with her motorcyclist boyfriend, whom she is afraid to leave.

On the street, the urchins meet Orin Scrivello, Audrey's boyfriend, and immediately attack him for his awful treatment of her. He nonchalantly explains that he has always loved the pain of others, which is why he became a dentist (Dentist—Sc to M Solo with F Trio).

Orin enters the shop and begins telling Seymour to sell Audrey II to another florist shop at top price. Mushnik overhears this and ponders his life without Seymour. After Audrey and Orin exit, Mushnik asks Seymour to be his son, and Seymour agrees (Mushnik and Son—Sc to M Duet).

Mushnik leaves Seymour alone to consider his good fortune but Seymour's thoughts are interrupted by the plant, which begs for food. Seymour, whose fingers are bandaged, has nothing more to give, for he has become anemic. Audrey II orders him to get blood and reminds him that his recent success is due to her (Git It! Git It!—Sc to M/Puppet Duet). Audrey II cunningly suggests that Seymour should consider how many evil people deserve to die, and Seymour agrees that Orin Scrivello, the sadistic dentist, would be an excellent candidate.

The scene shifts to a small, antiquated dentist office where Seymour arrives, gun in hand, to shoot Orin, but the dentist quickly takes the gun away and decides to pull one of Seymour's teeth without the benefit of a painkiller. He exits to give himself some laughing gas, so he can have a more memorable experience, and reenters wearing an enormous clear plastic bubble on his head with a hose extending to the gas line. He is hysterical with laughter but panics when he discovers he is unable to remove the mask. Seymour watches as Orin laughingly begs him to remove the mask (Now—It's Just the Gas—Sc to M/F Duet); Orin drops to the floor dead as Seymour returns to feed the hungry plant.

In Act II the lights rise on Audrey II, who takes up approximately one-third of the shop. Business is booming, as evidenced by the increase in phones and the constant phone calls (Call Back in the Morning—Linear M/F Duet). At six they close the shop and Audrey hesitantly reveals her past to an understanding Seymour. She is overjoyed that he loves her (Suddenly Seymour—Sc to M/Duet with F Trio).

Mushnik enters to find them embracing, sends Audrey home and confronts Seymour with his suspicions concerning the dentist's death. The plant, in the background, hints that it is hungry (Suppertime—2M Scene Interspersed with Plant Solo). Mushnik wants Seymour to go to the police and proclaim his innocence, but Seymour tells Mushnik they had better not leave the cash receipts, which are in the plant. Mushnik enters the plant, which greedily swallows him.

Seymour leaves the shop but is instantly surrounded by the urchins, who represent teenage fans. He is subsequently approached by Bernstein, a high-spending, fast-talking television producer who offers him a contract for a TV gardening show; the wife of the editor of *Life*, who wants his picture on the cover; and a slick talent agent who wants him to sign for lecture tours. Seymour is overwhelmed at the possibilities but nervous about the outcome of the continued feeding of Audrey II (The Meek Shall Inherit—2M Solo and 3F Trio).

One stormy night Seymour is in the shop with the starving plant when he decides he must kill the plant. He exits feeling very satisfied and relieved.

Later that same evening Audrey reenters the shop looking for Seymour. The hungry plant grabs her, and Seymour arrives in time to pull her crushed body from its tentacles. He confesses to Audrey that Orin and Mushnik are inside the plant and she lovingly begs him to feed her to her namesake; she would like nothing better than sacrificing herself for Seymour's continued fame. As a sunset appears in the background, Seymour dramatically feeds the dead Audrey to the waiting plant.

Seymour's sadness is interrupted by yet another opportunist, Patrick Martin, who wants to take cuttings of the exotic creature and sell them across the country. After Martin exits, Seymour turns to the plant and realizes that the plant was sent to conquer the world. He shoots the plant, he tries poison and in desperation he picks up a machete and climbs into the plant to hack at its insides. The creature's jaws close around Seymour and reopen to toss the machete to the floor.

Martin reenters with the urchins, whom he has hired to take cuttings of the plant. They move downstage, as the shop screen closes, to tell of the horrible fate of the world as entire towns were eaten by Audrey II's offspring.

The screen opens to reveal a nine-foot-tall Audrey II complete with four blood-red flowers containing the faces of the dead Seymour, Mushnik, Audrey and Orin. They urge the audience not to feed the plants (Finale-Mixed Chorus).

NOTES ON THE PRODUCTION

This wonderful small-cast spoof of horror films is a delight for audiences and performers alike. It is best produced in smaller theatres, for the audience should feel they are in danger of being swallowed by the plant. Many of the reviewers who saw productions in both New York and on the road felt the show lost a great deal by being performed in larger theatres.

The costumes are few and simple. The set is primarily a one-set location with the shop interior upstage left, a step unit stage right, representing a stoop, and an entryway to the shop's exterior downstage left. There should be a curtain or folding door arrangement to conceal the "growing" plant.

The major problem in producing the show revolves around the different puppets which represent Audrey II. The excellence of the puppets is what makes the play so much fun, so the show should not be attempted by a company without a good puppet maker and manipulator. Audrey begins as a small hand puppet in a small pot, is later seen, and operated, in a medium-size pot, and finally consumes entire human beings. The enormous Audrey also moves around in dance style, and this must be considered when staging the "Feed Me" number. Companies planning a production of *Little Shop* should have the puppets completed by the time rehearsals begin.

SONGS OF SPECIAL INTEREST

"Dentist," may be done as a baritone solo in a classroom situation, characterization and laughter important.

"Mushnik and Son," strong character-oriented duet, good for class study, baritone/tenor.

"Skid Row," good small chorus, representative of the sixties-style singing groups, characterization work.

"Somewhere That's Green," wonderful lyrics make this an excellent number for a musical revue or class situation. Characterization believability and sincerity important. Mezzo/tenor.

Instrumentation: piano/conductor, percussion, guitar (6 string electric, 6 string acoustic), keyboards (synthesizer, organ, electric piano), bass
Script: Nelson, Doubleday
Selections: Menken
Record: Geffen
Rights: SF

M

MACK AND MABEL

Book: Michael Stewart
Music and Lyrics: Jerry Herman

ORIGINAL PRODUCTION

Majestic Theatre, October 6, 1974 (66 perf.)
Director and Choreographer: Gower Champion
Musical Director and Vocal Arrangements: Donald Pippin
Orchestration: Philip J. Lang
Principals: Mack Sennett—Robert Preston—baritone; Mabel Normand—Bernadette Peters—mezzo; Frank Wyman—Jerry Dodge—VTI; Lottie Ames—Lisa Kirk—mezzo; Mr. Kleiman—Tom Batten—VTI; Wally—Robert Fitch—VTI; Eddie—Stanley Simmonds—baritone
Chorus and Smaller Roles: 6F/6M with a great deal of doubling.

SYNOPSIS

The play opens in Brooklyn in 1938 on the eve of Mack Sennett's unwilling departure from his film studio. He is a large man in his late fifties who soliloquizes about the future of films and reminisces about the past (Movies Were Movies—L to M Solo).

The soundstage comes to life and the scene flashes to 1911, where a young Mack Sennett is busy shooting a silent film. Mabel Normand, a waitress from

the nearby delicatessen, enters with an order which the leading lady takes—
without paying. Her behavior so infuriates Mabel's Irish temper that she angrily
berates everyone on the set. Mack, who is still filming, decides to keep her in
the film and orders her back the next day. She initially refuses but looks up and
is amazed to see herself on the screen (Look What Happened to Mabel—L to
F Solo with Mixed Chorus).

Mack decides to move from Brooklyn to California, where he can make more
films in larger, better studios. Ella, the piano player; Frank, one of the unpaid
actors; Mabel, who has just discovered that movie stars get paid; and Lottie, all
enter to urge Mack to get the financial backing necessary. Everyone awaits the
arrival of Kleiman and Fox, who will help finance the move to California. When
the two arrive and meet the staff, they suspiciously ask to meet the writers,
whom Mack has just fired. He quickly hires the *New York Times* delivery boy
and introduces him as their chief writer. They get the backing, and the company
begins packing (Big Time—Mixed Chorus).

On the observation platform of the train, Mabel is admiring the desert by
moonlight and making up a poem when Mack overhears her and interrupts.
Mabel, attracted to this demanding director, invites him into her compartment
for dinner, but Mack insists that she knows the rules he lives by, which don't
include marriage (I Won't Send Roses—Sc to M Solo). The train arrives in
California and Mack rushes off, promising Mabel nothing. She wistfully watches
him leave but realizes that she loves him and is willing to play the game his
way (I Won't Send Roses [Reprise]—F Solo). In front of Los Angeles's Union
Station, Kleiman and Fox, who see the successful D. W. Griffith pass, urge
Mack to make Griffith-type extravaganzas, but he only wants to direct comedies
(I Wanna Make the World Laugh—L to M Solo). As the song continues, a
screen composite of early Sennett films is shown.

One year later in the new studio paid for by Mack's extremely successful
films, Frank, the writer, attempts to convince Mabel she is an actress, not just
a comedienne. Mabel seems to ignore him, but when Mack and the actors enter
for the day's shooting, Mabel begins asking for her motivation. Mack tells her
that he is her motivation, which so angers her that she throws a pie in his face.
The rest of the company join in the melee (I Wanna Make the World Laugh
[Reprise]—Mixed Chorus).

The scene shifts to the Orchid Room of the Hollywood Hotel where Mabel
is dancing with William Desmond Taylor, a melodramatic director she admires.
When he informs her that he has asked Mack to loan her to him for several
pictures, she is surprised. Mack enters and cold-shoulders Taylor, who gives
Mabel his card and urges her to call. Mabel verbally attacks Mack for thinking
she is only good enough for two reelers. As he walks out she tells him she is
determined to become a respected actress (Wherever He Ain't—Sc to F Solo).

Later that day, at the studio gate, where everyone is packing for the day's
shooting, Mabel informs Mack she is finished with him and with two reelers.
He tells her off in front of the company and forces her to walk out. Everyone

urges him to get her back at any cost but his pride won't let him; he is convinced that he can train anyone to replace her. A hot dog vendor starts on and the scene shifts to Santa Monica Beach, which is full of bathing beauties, all potential Sennett stars (Hundreds of Girls—Sc to M Solo to F Chorus). He adds the bathing beauties to his films but realizes that he misses Mabel (I Won't Send Roses [Reprise]—M Solo).

When Act II opens, Mabel has been making dramatic films for five years. Kleiman and his friends urge Mack to get her back because the public is beginning to tire of the Sennett bathing beauties. Mack finally agrees; Mabel returns to the studio and is warmly greeted by Eddie, the watchman, and the company (When Mabel Comes in the Room—M Solo to Mixed Chorus). Mack arrives, obviously glad to see her back. The two dance and everything appears to be going smoothly until Mack decides to clown up the film he is directing by adding the Keystone Kops. While everyone is in their dressing rooms he describes the action to Kleiman and Fox as the Kops enter and the business begins (Hit' Em on the Head—Sc to M Trio to M Chorus). Mack becomes so involved with shooting his two-reeler Kops films that he never gets around to directing Mabel's serious film and she leaves for the east coast and a trip to Europe.

Mack finds Mabel on the New York pier preparing to sail for Europe with Taylor. He enters carrying a box of roses and tries to tell her he loves her, but she realizes he can never change and says good-bye. Mack, to cover his real emotions, begins clowning and exits without giving her the flowers. Taylor tries to get Mabel to forget about Mack by giving her a snort of cocaine, and Mabel wonders if anything can make her stop loving Mack (Time Heals Everything— Sc to F Solo).

In a solo spot, Mack tells the audience that all his friends and company members have deserted him for bigger studios and talking movies. As he talks, the various characters walk by, including Mabel, who unsteadily weaves on supported by Taylor. He finishes his story by mentioning Lottie, his tap dancer, and her dancers, who give an example of the newest movie musicals (Tap Your Troubles Away—F Chorus).

When Mack is told by Frank that Mabel is finished in pictures because of the scandalous murder of her lover Taylor and the public knowledge that she is a heroin addict, Mack vows to star her in a serious picture. He goes to her room and promises to change her life (I Promise You a Happy Ending—L to M Solo). During the number the lights fade on Mabel, and Mack continues the story. It seems the film's producers refused to release the movie, certain that Mabel's name was too notorious to merit the promotional expense. Mabel died in 1930. Mack, however, can never admit that Mabel's story ended so tragically and will always remember her as she was. He calls everyone onstage and rewrites the ending of her life, the way he would have wished it, complete with Mabel in a wedding gown surrounded by the Kops, the bathing beauties and the preacher with a pie in the face.

NOTES ON THE PRODUCTION

The show, although short-lived, works well in summer stock and dinner theatre situations for the company size may be adjusted to meet the stage requirements. The story is interesting; the character-oriented songs enhance the plot and are varied enough to maintain audience interest. If a small company is employed they will have many opportunities to demonstrate individual talents.

The set requirements need not be overpowering, for Mack usually narrates either the endings or beginnings of scenes. Since lines often establish location, the set may consist of small reference pieces to enhance the action.

Modern audiences that may not have a silent film frame of reference possibly are not familiar with Sennett's work. Companies unable to afford specific film sequences to use in "I Wanna Make the World Laugh" may want to utilize slides of still photographs during the song. A brief history/picture sequence in the lobby or program would help younger audiences' understanding.

The costumes are period 1911 to 1930 and each character has several outfits. All should be true to the Sennett films, i.e., Kops, Bathing Beauties. The Kops' costumes may need to be rented as the uniforms are often time-consuming to make and not often needed in the company's wardrobe.

Special film clips for the production are available from Killiam Shows, Inc., 6 E. 39th St., New York, New York (212) 679–8230.

SONGS OF SPECIAL INTEREST

"I Won't Send Roses," semidramatic, charm, poignant, baritone, sung several times in a variety of moods.

"Look What Happened to Mabel," good character song for a two-song character study, demonstrates comic abilities, mezzo. Possible for audition as it shows strong focus, excitement, energy and some movement.

"Movies Were Movies," good as a baritone solo audition piece for it enables the actor to show off movement, comic sense and a variety of characters. Also works well in a revue situation with the ensemble staged in as various film sequences.

"Time Heals Everything," dramatic, good for club. Possible audition, mezzo. Excellent character study when combined with "Look What Happened. . . . "

"Wherever He Ain't," angry, possible audition, strong vocal, mezzo dramatic.

Instrumentation: 4 reeds, 3 trumpets, 2 trombones, 2 percussion, 3 violins, viola, bass, cello, guitar/banjo, piano/conductor
Script: SF
Selections: Morris
Record: ABC
Rights: SF

MAME

Book: Jerome Lawrence and Robert E. Lee (Based on the novel by Patrick Dennis and the play *Auntie Mame*, by Lawrence and Lee)
Music and Lyrics: Jerry Herman

ORIGINAL PRODUCTION

Winter Garden Theatre, May 24, 1966 (1,508 perf.)
Director: Gene Saks
Dances and Musical Numbers: Onna White
Musical Director and Vocal Arranger: Donald Pippin
Orchestration: Philip J. Lang
Principals: Mame Dennis—Angela Lansbury—mezzo; Agnes Gooch—Jane Connell—soprano; Vera Charles—Beatrice Arthur—alto; Gloria Upson—Diana Walker—VTNE; Beauregarde—Charles Braswell—baritone; Patrick (Age 29)—Jerry Lanning—baritone; Dwight Babcock—Willard Waterman—VTNE; Pegeen Ryan—Diane Coupe—VTNE; Patrick (Age 10)—Frankie Michaels—boy soprano; Ito—Sab Shimono—baritone
Chorus and Smaller Roles: 9M/8F who sing and move well, a mixture of ages, minimum.

SYNOPSIS

The time is 1928; the place, New York City.

Agnes Gooch, the dowdy nanny to recently orphaned Patrick Dennis, is taking the boy, age ten, to live with his Auntie Mame. Agnes, a rather plain, religious girl, is terrified of New York and prays for safe delivery (St. Bridget—Sc to F/Ch Duet).

At Mame Dennis's elaborate residence on Beekman Place, Mame is giving one of her famous parties complete with noted celebrities, caviar, booze, flappers and gangsters (It's Today—F Solo To Chorus). Ito, Mame's Japanese houseboy, enters with the terrified Gooch, who decides that Beekman Place is no place for Patrick. Patrick has other ideas and sets out to find out which of these wild people is his dear aunt. Patrick's arrival surprises Mame, who was expecting him a day later, but she invites him to have some caviar and join in the fun.

Two weeks later, in Mame's bedroom, Patrick awakes his hung over aunt, who has defied the provisions of her late brother's will by enrolling Patrick in an experimental school in Greenwich Village called "The Laboratory of Life." The school is run by one of Mame's friends, whose students spend their time at school in the nude. Mame tells Patrick she is going to open his eyes to the world and all life has to offer (Open a New Window—Sc to F/Ch Duet to Mixed Chorus). The number quickly moves to the streets of New York where Patrick is introduced to various characters. He is followed by an angry Mr. Babcock, the conservative banker in charge of Patrick's trust fund.

Babcock arrives at the apartment, which is now calmly decorated and filled with religious art. The angered banker, upset at Mame's failure to place Patrick in a proper school, enrolls the boy in St. Boniface, a boarding school in Massachusetts. Mame is brokenhearted at losing Patrick.

As Patrick prepares to leave for St. Boniface, Mame receives the news from her broker that she has lost everything in the stock market crash. She has absolutely no means to support her extravagant life-style, so her best friend Vera Charles, a famous actress, insists that Mame perform in her newest play about a woman astronomer. Mame is cast as the moon lady. As Vera is describing the operetta, the set drops in and the performance begins (The Man in the Moon—L to F Solo). Mame is late for her entrance and as a result doesn't secure herself properly to the lowering moon. As it begins to drop in, Mame loses her balance and ends up hanging underneath the moon, totally upstaging Vera, who is still singing.

Backstage, Mame valiantly tries to make amends but accidentally gets her jewelry caught on Vera's costume and is forced to join Vera when she goes out to take her bow. Mame is promptly fired. Patrick arrives backstage to tell Mame she was the best thing in the show (My Best Girl—Sc to Ch/F Duet).

Mame is forced to take a job as a manicurist in a fancy hair salon. While working on her first customer, Beauregarde Burnside, a very handsome member of the rich Southern aristocracy, she becomes so enthralled that she forgets what she is doing, cuts his fingers to shreds and is instantly fired. Beau tries to console her as she is leaving.

Mame returns to Beekman Place to discover that Patrick is home for Thanksgiving. When Agnes and Ito try to ease her troubles by assuring her that they won't leave, she decides they all need an early Christmas to bolster their morale (We Need a Little Christmas—Sc to Mixed Quartet). Beauregarde appears at the door, upset that he was the cause of Mame's being fired, and offers to take them all to dinner. They set out, arms linked and singing.

Beauregarde invites Mame and Patrick to his plantation to meet the family. At a lawn party outside the plantation, a crowd has gathered to meet Beau's Yankee friend. Among them is Sally Cato, Beau's ex-girlfriend, who forces Mame into joining in a fox hunt, and Mother Burnside, a Yankee hater who makes sure Mame is riding Lightnin' Rod, a killer horse. The chorus comments on the ride as Patrick yells for Mame to fall off (The Fox Hunt—Mixed Chorus). When Mame manages to catch the fox rather than see him killed, Beau realizes just how fond he is of this crazy lady and asks her to marry him. The chorus continues the tribute to Mame as the curtain rings down, closing Act I (Mame—Mixed Chorus).

Act II opens with Patrick writing a letter to Mame to tell her everything that's happening in his life. As one verse ends and another begins, young Patrick is replaced by an older Patrick, who still writes his dear aunt every chance he gets (The Letter—Ch/M Solo). When Patrick receives the news that Uncle Beau has fallen off an Alp while skiing with Mame, he quickly phones to remind her that she still has him (My Best Girl [Reprise]—M Solo).

Six months later, at Beekman Place, Vera is waiting to greet the bereaved Mame and the two become friends again—a friendship that only two sophisticated, biting women could understand (Bosom Buddies—Sc to F Duet).

Vera and Mame, appalled to discover that Agnes has never had a date, decide to change her frumpy image. They begin the make-over, which Agnes initially rejects but eventually enjoys. She amazes them by slinking in wearing a sexy red dress ready to set the world on fire.

It is six months later and the apartment is full of books, for Mame is writing her memoirs and always immerses herself in her projects. It seems Agnes disappeared the night they remade her and has only sent one postcard . . . from a motel in Pennsylvania.

Agnes, extremely hesitant, embarrassed and six months pregnant, returns home to seek help. Mame listens to her story (Gooch's Song—Sc to F Solo) and insists that Agnes stay with her, a fact that upsets Patrick, who has become extremely snobby since he met Gloria Upson, his social-climbing girlfriend.

Patrick takes Mame to meet Gloria's parents at the Upsons' family home in Connecticut. She is quickly bored by the Upsons, and totally disgusted with the food they serve as hors d'oeuvre, but thoroughly enjoys the young college students who are visiting (That's How Young I Feel—F Solo to Mixed Chorus).

The Upsons let slip that Patrick and ''Glory'' are planning to be wed soon and they are giving them the lot next door as a wedding present. Mame is overwhelmed. When she and Patrick argue about the snobbery of the Upsons, Patrick angrily leaves a questioning Mame to wonder if she was too lenient in raising him (If He Walked into My Life—Sc to F Solo).

Mame, determined to save Patrick from Gloria, devises a lavish party for the Upsons at her apartment. With the aid of an attractive interior decorator, Pegeen Ryan, she has modernized the apartment. Despite Patrick's instructions not to visit the party, Agnes comes down in all her pregnant glory. When Mame sees the reaction that Agnes's unwed motherhood brings to the Upsons, she announces that she has bought the property in Connecticut adjoining theirs, for a home for unwed mothers. The family leaves in a huff and Patrick, realizing their bigotry, thanks Mame for saving him from a disastrous marriage (My Best Girl [Reprise]—M Solo).

The show closes as Patrick and his wife Pegeen leave their son, Peter, at the Beekman Place apartment with Auntie Mame, who promises to broaden his horizons (Open a New Window [Finale]—Mixed Chorus).

NOTES ON THE ORIGINAL PRODUCTION

1966 Tony Awards for Best Actress (Angela Lansbury), Featured Actress (Beatrice Arthur), and Featured Actor (Frankie Michaels).

The sets need not be complex, but the set decorations and props in the Beekman

Place apartment are constantly changing and should always be filled with artwork demonstrating Mame's lavish tastes.

The major budget allocation should be given to the costumes, which span from 1928 to 1946, and involve glitzy evening clothes, hunting outfits, Southern antebellum and the theatrical "Moon Lady" costumes. It is an extremely heavy costume show, a fact that should be carefully weighed before attempting a production of this lavish musical. A company with limited funds should seriously consider the play *Auntie Mame*, which is less costly and less involved.

SONGS OF SPECIAL INTEREST

"Bosom Buddies," comic, biting, reaction and lyrics important, strong relationship. Requires maturity and comic timing, alto/mezzo.

"Gooch's Song," character-oriented, comedic sincerity and honesty, mezzo/soprano range.

"If He Walked into My Life," good for club, strong, dramatic and intense, alto.

"Open a New Window," alto featured to chorus, good for class work and revue, marching-type choreography.

"We Need a Little Christmas," small scene to quartet, some movement, high energy, strong relationships.

Instrumentation: 2 violins, viola, cello, bass, 5 reeds, 3 trumpets, 3 trombones, percussion, harp, guitar and banjo, piano/celeste, and optional tuba
Script: Random
Score: Morris
Record: Columbia
Rights: TW

MAN OF LA MANCHA

Book: Dale Wasserman (Based on the novel *Don Quixote*, by Miguel de Cervantes y Saavedra)
Music: Mitch Leigh
Lyrics: Joe Darion

ORIGINAL PRODUCTION

ANTA Washington Square Theatre, November 22, 1965, later moved to Martin Beck (2,329 perf.)
Director: Albert Marre
Choreographer: Jack Cole
Musical Director: Neil Warner
Musical Arrangements: Music Makers, Inc.

Principals: Don Quixote/Cervantes—Richard Kiley—baritone; Sancho/The Manservant—Irving Jacobson—tenor; Innkeeper/Governor—Ray Middleton—baritone; Padre—Robert Rounseville—tenor; Dr. Carrasco/The Duke—Jon Cypher—
baritone; Aldonza—Joan Diener—alto; Antonia—Mimi Turque—soprano;
Housekeeper—Eleanor Knapp—mezzo; The Barber—Gino Conforti—tenor; An-
selmo—Harry Theyard—VTNE
Chorus and Smaller Roles: 8M/2F.

SYNOPSIS

Setting: Seville, Spain, at the end of the sixteenth century.

A stairway is lowered into a dingy, prison common room full of prisoners
awaiting trial under the Spanish Inquisition. A tall, thin, stately man in his late
forties, followed by a chubby servant carrying a straw trunk, descends. The
man, Miguel Cervantes, an aristocratic poet, is approached by the prisoners'
leader, the Governor, who orders him to stand trial by his fellow prisoners.
Cervantes agrees to their judgment if they will portray the characters in his newly
written manuscript.

Sancho, the manservant, brings forth the costumes and the props as Cervantes
describes the leading character in his book, Don Quixote. He physically begins
to take on the characteristics of the man as he applies his makeup (Man of La
Mancha—L to M Duet).

Quixote and Sancho begin their adventures (after jousting a windmill) by
stopping at an inn that Quixote imagines is a castle. Cervantes drops character
to set the stage for an inn and to cast the prisoners in their roles.

As the scene of the story is set, a female prisoner is chosen to portray Aldonza,
the rough kitchen wench abandoned by her mother soon after her birth. In the
poor inn, Aldonza serves a group of hungry muleteers, who make lewd advances.
She spurns them and contemptuously comments on the emotional deadness of
her life (It's All the Same—F Solo).

Quixote and his artless servant Sancho arrive at the inn, which Quixote imagines is the castle where he will find his lady. The innkeeper humors him because
he believes that madmen are the children of God and it is obvious to him that
Quixote is a crazed old man. Quixote, who insists Aldonza is his lady Dulcinea,
declares his love (Dulcinea—Sc to M Solo). She harshly ridicules him for his
insanity. The muleteers scoff at Quixote and mimic his warmhearted love song
(Dulcinea [Reprise]—M Chorus).

The lights shift to the prison where Cervantes describes the Quixote household,
composed of his selfish niece, Antonia, and a worried housekeeper. The two
women confide to the local Padre that their only thoughts are of Quixote's safety,
and he responds as any good confessor would (I'm Only Thinking of Him—Sc
to 2F/M Trio). Dr. Carrasco, Antonia's fiancé, embarrassed by the thought of
a madman in his family yet determined to marry Antonia for her future inher-
itance, goes with the Padre to turn Quixote from his insanity (I'm Only Thinking
of Him [Reprise]—Sc to 2M/2F Quartet).

Cervantes shifts the scene to the inn, where Sancho is trying to give Aldonza a missive from his master. Sancho, unable to read, has memorized the message which describes Dulcinea as the fairest of the pure. She has no understanding of Quixote and even less of Sancho, a man who would follow a madman. He delightfully explains that he doesn't have a very good reason, he just wants to (I Really Like Him—Sc to M Solo). Aldonza ponders this after he leaves (What Does He Want of Me?—F Solo).

The lights cross fade to the exterior of the inn where the muleteers are harmoniously singing a mocking song to Aldonza as she enters to get water from the well (Little Bird, Little Bird—M Chorus).

Dr. Carrasco and the Padre arrive at the inn to discover that although Quixote recognizes them, he is still obviously quite mad because he insists that he is a knight who has a lady named Dulcinea. When Quixote hears singing offstage and sees a traveler with a bowl on his head, he urges Sancho to hide. The merry barber enters (Barber's Song—M Solo). Quixote attacks the man with his sword and insists that the barber give him his shaving basin, which Quixote imagines is a golden helmet (Golden Helmet—Sc to M Trio). The Padre agrees to crown him in a mock coronation as the chorus of muleteers join in. As the others exit, the Padre feels that Quixote is either very insane or very wise. Believing that everyone needs a dream, he poignantly sings (To Each His Dulcinea—M Solo).

Aldonza, on her way to meet one of the muleteers, stops to demand what Quixote wants of her, for she cannot understand why he believes in knighthood. He tries to explain that he hopes to better the world and has a quest that must be followed (The Quest—Sc to M Solo). At the end of the song, Pedro enters and accuses Aldonza of keeping him waiting. He slaps her, which outrages Quixote who, in a comedic choreographed scene with Aldonza and Sancho, beats off the muleteers, who limpingly exit (The Combat—Dance).

The innkeeper, nervous that the muleteers will ruin the inn, asks Quixote to leave as soon as possible, but Quixote asks to first be dubbed a knight and given a new name. After studying Quixote's face the innkeeper devises a name that suits the bruised old man (Hail Knight of the Woeful Countenance—Sc to M Solo to 2M/F Trio) as Sancho and Aldonza join him in tribute. The innkeeper exits, leaving a tired Aldonza, Quixote and Sancho.

Quixote, ever the gracious knight, prepares to treat the muleteers' wounds but Aldonza, worried for his safety, volunteers to go in his stead. She goes to the angry muleteers, who beat, ravage and carry her off (The Abduction—Dance). Quixote, unaware of her plight, ponders on the luck of the muleteers who know the healing hand of his lady.

The scene is abruptly cut as the inquisition men descend the stairs to fetch someone. Cervantes fears his time has come and the Duke berates him for cowardice when another is taken. Cervantes describes life as he has seen it; as a man, as a soldier and as a poet. He philosophizes on the meaning of madness.

The orchestra underscores the next scene, where Sancho and Quixote are on the open road surrounded by Moors who bilk them and rob them of their belongings (Moorish Dance—Dance). The two are forced to return to the inn, where Quixote is confronted by Aldonza, who has returned bruised and in rags. She dramatically tells him the ugly story of her life (Aldonza—Sc to F Solo).

A trumpet call brings forth Dr. Carrasco, disguised as the Knight of Mirrors. He and Quixote duel in a dramatic movement piece where Quixote sees his own reflection in Carrasco's and his attendants' shields (The Knight of the Mirrors—Dance). The aged knight falls broken and weeping to the floor. Carrasco removes his helmet and apologizes as Aldonza sadly walks toward her fallen knight. The mood is broken by the captain of the inquisition, who tells Cervantes he is soon to be called. Cervantes turns to his fellow prisoners to tell them that the story has ended, but they force him to improvise an ending.

He summons the actors who portrayed the scene in Quixote's household and continues the story at the manor where the old man lies ill in bed. Sancho tries vainly to cheer his dying friend (A Little Gossip—Sc to M Solo) but Dr. Carrasco, infuriated at his mention of jousting windmills, stops him.

As Quixote prepares to make his will, Aldonza forces her way into the room and dramatically implores him to remember her, his past dreams (Dulcinea [Reprise]—F Solo) and his quest (The Quest [Reprise]—Sc to 2M/F Trio). For a moment he remembers his past glory, but the excitement is too much and he drops exhausted to the floor where the priest gives the final blessing (The Psalm—M Solo). Aldonza, determined that Quixote will always live, urges Sancho to believe and call her Dulcinea.

The drums of the inquisition are heard, and the captain and his men descend to take Cervantes to trial. The prisoners return his manuscript and encourage him as he climbs the stairs to face his real trial (Finale—The Quest—Mixed Chorus).

NOTES ON THE PRODUCTION

The show received the following Tony Awards: Best Actor, Musical, Direction, Music and Lyrics, and Set Design.

The show was one of the first "Goodspeed Opera House" original musicals to become a successful Broadway hit. The most famous "Goodspeed Opera House" musical to date is *Annie*. The description and history of the theatre at East Haddam, Connecticut, is detailed in the Martin Charnin *Annie* book. In 1980, the theatre received a special Tony Award for outstanding contributions to the American theatre.

Man of la Mancha is often performed by amateur groups and remains a popular choice for revivals and stock companies. The show is well written, the music memorable, and the moments range from charmingly comedic to intensely dramatic. It is a show well worth producing but does require a strong choreographer to stage the Abduction, the Combat, and the Mirrors numbers.

The play traditionally requires one set and a limited number of props and costumes. The success of the production calls for excellent actors who sing well to portray the demanding major roles. Mood lighting, with a lot of instruments to specify various areas, is required. The production expenses that are saved by a unit set and limited costumes should be used for lighting rental.

SONGS OF SPECIAL INTEREST

"Aldonza," powerfully dramatic and intense, excellent for class study, alto.

"Dulcinea," unusually pleasant ballad that doesn't require a young romantic lead, baritone.

Final sequence from "Dulcinea" to "The Psalm," highly dramatic and intense, emotional, musical scene, excellent acting exercise for class work.

"I Like Him," comic, charm, character study, tenor.

"It's All the Same," good to show character development and contrast in a two-song character study for class, bitter, matter-of-fact. Underlying emotion is important, alto.

Instrumentation: 5 reeds, 2 horns, 2 trumpets, 2 trombones, string bass, 2 guitars, timpani, 2 percussion, piano/conductor
Script: Dell, Great Musicals of the American Theatre Volume Two
Score: Fox
Record: Kapp
Rights: TW

THE MOST HAPPY FELLA

Book, Music and Lyrics: Frank Loesser (Based on Sidney Howard's *They Knew What They Wanted*)

ORIGINAL PRODUCTION

Imperial Theatre, May 3, 1956 (676 perf.)
Director: Joseph Anthony
Choreographer: Dania Krupska
Musical Director: Herbert Greene
Orchestration: Don Walker
Principals: Doctor—Keith Kaldenberg—baritone; Tony—Robert Weede—tenor; Cleo—Susan Johnson—alto; Herman—Shorty Long—tenor; Roseabella—Jo Sullivan—soprano; Marie—Mona Paulee—soprano; Joe—Art Lund—baritone; Postman—Lee Cass—tenor; Guiseppe—Arthur Rubin—VTI; Pasquale—Rico Froehlich—VTI; Ciccio—John Henson—VTI
Chorus and Smaller Roles: 12M/12F, 3 children.

SYNOPSIS

The play opens in a San Francisco middle-class restaurant at closing time. The year is 1927.

Cleo, a waitress in her mid-thirties, wearing one shoe and carrying the other on a tray, limps out and sings (Ooh My Feet—F Solo). The cashier makes a pass at Cleo's friend, who slaps him, despite his threats to fire her. The girl turns to clean her table and spies a man's tiepin and a note from the bashful customer calling her Roseabella and asking her to write because he wants to marry her (Recitative—Sc to F Duet). Cleo warns her against corresponding with an unknown man who writes in broken English, but her friend is interested and tells Cleo that she wants to be needed and this man may be the one (Somebody, Somewhere—L to F Solo).

Several months later, on a street in a Napa Valley town, the postman, delivering the mail to the townsfolk, presents Tony, a middle-aged wine producer, with a letter from Roseabella. The town is interested in the mail-order romance of Tony and Roseabella, so he shows her picture around (The Most Happy Fella—M Solo). Tony's older sister, Marie, comes to take Tony home, but he intends to have his photograph taken to send to Roseabella. Marie is against this infatuation, but Tony defends his relationship (I Don't Know Nothin' about Her—Sc to M Solo). Eventually, he decides Marie is right about sending a picture of himself and he gloomily exits, passing some of his workers, who stand on a corner to watch the girls go by (Standing on the Corner—M Quartet). When Joe, Tony's handsome young foreman, tells him that he feels like moving on (Joey, Joey, Joey—M Solo), Tony asks for a picture of Joe (Soon You Gonna Leave Me, Joe—Sc to M Duet), and Joe laughingly agrees. Tony confesses to his dead mother that he is going to send Joe's picture to Roseabella (Roseabella—L to M Solo).

Everyone in Tony's household is anxiously awaiting the arrival of his mail order sweetheart. Pasquale, Ciccio and Guiseppe, the three Italians responsible for organizing the party, are checking over the food and extravagant decorations (Abbondanza—M Trio). Tony happily looks at everyone, especially the children, and imagines his future with his wife (Plenty Bambini—M Solo). Tony drives to the station to pick up Roseabella as the townsfolk arrive for the party (Sposalizio—Mixed Chorus). When Roseabella enters with the postman (Special Delivery—M Solo), Pasquale, Ciccio, Guiseppe and Joe line up to greet her (Benvenuta—M Trio). Roseabella turns to Joe and asks if he is happy she has come to marry him (Aren't You Glad?—Sc to F Solo). He is bewildered until she shows him his picture, which forces Joe to explain that Tony must have sent Joe's picture because Tony thinks he is too old for her. When Joe explains that he helped Tony write the letters, Roseabella is outraged and tries to leave. A scream is heard and some men carry in Tony, who has just been hurt in an auto accident. Roseabella is trapped and doesn't know where to go (Laughing—F Solo).

When Tony, afraid of losing her, requests that she marry him immediately, she consents to the marriage to save her pride.

Joe waits outside the house and hears the wedding vows. As the ceremony ends, Roseabella descends from the house crying and Joe attempts to comfort her (Don't Cry—M Solo), but she breaks away. Joe grabs her and the two succumb to their emotions, passionately embrace and slowly exit together as the curtain closes.

Act II opens one week later. The vineyard workers are busy working (Fresno Beauties—M Chorus). Joe and Roseabella are enduring the guilt of their brief affair and have not been together since the fateful night. Tony enters with the doctor, who tries to ease the strain of Roseabella and Tony's relationship (Love and Kindness—Sc to M Solo). Tony convinces Roseabella to start over and she begins to teach Tony English (Happy to Make Your Acquaintance—Sc to 2F/M Trio). Cleo arrives in the middle of the song and Roseabella is overjoyed that Tony has sent for her. When Tony's lonely sister, Marie, takes Cleo aside to convince her that Tony and Roseabella are not right for each other, Cleo takes an instant dislike to Marie (I Don't Like This Dame—Sc to F Duet). As Marie exits, Herman, a young, friendly worker, passes Cleo, who instantly recognizes his Dallas, Texas accent. The two realize they have a common ground (Big D—Sc to M/F Duet To Mixed Chorus).

Roseabella and Tony enjoy each other's company (How Beautiful—Sc to 3F/M Quartet) but Marie, realizing she has been replaced, laments and Joe, who has promised to stay until Tony recovers, yearns to leave for New Mexico.

One month later, while the vineyard workers are dancing with Roseabella, Marie attempts to convince Tony that he is old and inept (Young People—M/F Duet) but Roseabella, sensitive to his feelings, tells him how much she cares for him (Warm All Over—Sc to F Solo). Nonetheless, Tony is trapped by the wheelchair and comments on his inability to physically join in the fun (Old People—M Solo).

Inside the barn, as Herman teaches Cleo how to label grape boxes, Pasquale enters and orders Herman around. Cleo, in a fury, asks Herman why he takes everyone's guff and he responds in his usual cheery manner (I Like Everybody—Sc to M Solo).

Roseabella confides to Cleo that she really loves Tony (I Love Him—F Solo), and Cleo urges her to "tell him" and exits. When Roseabella convinces Tony that she loves him more than in a platonic nature (Like a Woman Loves a Man/My Heart Is So Full of You—Sc to M/F Duet), Tony invites everybody to a Sposalizio. Roseabella collapses and the doctor takes her inside for a checkup.

Roseabella, realizing she is going to have Joe's baby, asks Cleo's advice, but for once her friend has no answers. Tony is ecstatic that Roseabella loves him and sings to his dead mother (Mama, Mama—M Solo), telling her how happy he is. It is a heartrending moment, for the audience knows the hurt that Tony must face.

As Act III opens, Pasquale, Ciccio and Guiseppe are preparing for the Sposalizio (Abbondanza [Reprise]—M Trio). Cleo, who has packed her suitcases, stops by the barn to say good-bye to Herman, but she can't make him understand that they may never meet again (Good-bye Darlin'—Sc to M/F Duet).

At the Sposalizio (Song of a Summer Night—Chorus), Doc urges everyone to leave Tony and Roseabella alone for a few moments, which gives Roseabella the opportunity to tell Tony she is pregnant, and is leaving because she knows what his reaction will be. He is hurt and angry and orders her to go. She sadly returns his tiepin and tells him, once more, that she loves him (Please Let Me Tell You—F Solo). Tony orders Pasquale to tell Joe he is fired, but Pasquale tells him Joe has left to take the train out of town. Tony, thinking his wife has gone off with Joe, gets a gun and leaves for town, determined to kill Joe.

Tony arrives at the bus station to discover that Joe has left town alone. Realizing Roseabella has told him the truth, he begins to understand what her life will be like without him and decides to bring her back (She's Gonna Come Home with Me—L to M Solo). Marie, happy that Tony will again be dependent on her, tries to stop Tony from seeing Roseabella by taking his cane. Cleo struggles with Marie, grabs the cane, and hands it to Tony, who goes to Rose-abella. Marie lunges at Cleo and the two fight. When Pasquale separates the two women, forcing Cleo to fall to the ground, Herman strikes him, which astounds both Cleo and Herman, who can't believe he really hit someone (I Made a Fist—Sc to M/F Duet). They exit happily.

Tony convinces Roseabella that he wants her to stay and that no one need know the paternity of the child. She is afraid, but he persuades her to start all over again. As she agrees, the chorus enters (Finale—Mixed Chorus).

NOTES ON THE PRODUCTION

The musical, a work of exceptional merit, deserves a thorough study by any student of musical theatre. The characters are well drawn, the music challenging and the acting opportunities excellent. The show, revived in 1979, was video-taped for public television. It deserves more productions but should not be attempted without a strong dramatic director and four excellent singers who act. The part of Marie is extremely difficult to cast, for the audience must be aware that the reason she appears so negative is an outgrowth of her fear of being shut out.

The set need not be complex because the emphasis is on the singing, acting, characterizations and story line. Much of the show takes place in Tony's barn, front yard and vineyards, and these scenes may utilize a single location. Smaller scenes occur in the San Francisco restaurant, on Main Street and at the bus station; the latter two sets may be combined.

The play may be updated but should take place before World War II when society was more innocent and people weren't as mobile. It needs the aura of naivete to believably capture its charm.

SONGS OF SPECIAL INTEREST

"Abbondanza," comic Italian, two tenor/baritone trio. Demands tight vocals and strong story line, good for revue; characterizations important to humor of number.

"Big D," alto/tenor, Texas-style dance duet. Works well for class situation or revue. Both performers must dance and have strong relationship.

"Don't Cry," scene to song, good acting exercise for class study; difficult, dramatic scene with lots of opposites, subtext and reaction work, tenor, soprano.

"Happy to Make Your Acquaintance," charm song, light, concentrates on interrelationship and reactions, tenor, soprano, alto.

"I Don't Like This Dame," clever scene to alto/soprano duet, training in use of aside and reaction to other performer, subtext important.

"Ooh My Feet" into "Recitative" into "Somebody, Somewhere," scene character study song for advanced musical theatre class. Requires comedic and dramatic abilities, strong relationship and reactions, soprano, alto.

"She's Gonna Come Home with Me" through "I Made a Fist," heavy dramatic, difficult acting sequence. For class or studio work.

"Standing on the Corner," vocally tight M Quartet, characterizations important to the comedy, good for revue.

Instrumentation: 5 reeds, 2 trumpets, 2 trombones, 3 horns, harp, accordion, 2 violins, viola, cello, 2 basses, 2 percussion
Script: Theatre Arts (magazine) 10/58, Included in score
Score: Frank
Record: Columbia
Rights: MTI

THE MUSIC MAN

Book, Music, Lyrics: Meredith Willson (based on a story by Willson and Frank Lacey)

ORIGINAL PRODUCTION

Majestic Theatre, December 19, 1957 (1,375 perf.)
Director: Morton Da Costa
Choreographer: Onna White
Musical Director: Herbert Greene
Orchestration: Don Walker
Principals: Harold Hill—Robert Preston—baritone; Marian Paroo—Barbara Cook—soprano; Mayor Shinn—David Burns—baritone; Mrs. Paroo—Pert Kel-

ton—alto; Winthrop Paroo—Eddie Hodges—boy soprano; Marcellus—Iggie
Wolfington—tenor; Eulalie Shinn—Helen Raymond—soprano
Chorus and Smaller Roles: 8F/10M plus 8B/4G.

SYNOPSIS

The play opens on the interior of a train where some salesmen are discussing
business and playing cards. Their dialogue is patterned to fit the rhythm of the
train clacking along the tracks (Rock Island—M Chorus). During the rhythm
song, the men comment on the notorious Harold Hill, a traveling salesman who
concentrates on selling band instruments and uniforms to enthusiastic parents.
During their conversation, one player with his back to the audience, who is
winning all the money, says nothing. As the train arrives at the station, Harold
Hill bids everyone good-bye and descends onto Main Street of River City on
July 4, 1912.

The town is celebrating the festive day and remarks on the peculiarity of
Iowans (Iowa Stubborn—Mixed Chorus). Hill meets his old partner, Marcellus
Washburn, and tells him of his latest musical instrument scheme. Marcellus,
who has given up con games, warns Hill that he will have problems with the
town's librarian and music teacher, Marian Paroo. Hill isn't concerned and begins
to tell the townsfolk of the trouble they have in their town due to the new pool
table. In a quickly paced patter song, he describes the evil that will befall the
town's youth. The townsfolk soon agree (Ya Got Trouble—Sc to M Solo to
Mixed Chorus).

Marcellus points out Marian to Hill, who attempts to strike up a conversation.
She brushes him off and enters her house, where her Irish-born mother is cleaning
and overseeing Amaryllis's piano lesson. When Marian tells Mrs. Paroo that a
strange man has tried to pick her up, Mrs. Paroo advises her to give the young
man a chance. The ensuing song develops the character of both mother and
daughter and clearly defines their differing philosophies (Piano Lesson/If You
Don't Mind My Saying So—Sc to F Duet).

When Winthrop, Marian's nine-year-old brother with a lisp, sullenly enters,
Amaryllis asks him to a party. He refuses and exits to his room. Amaryllis tells
Marian she loves Winthrop and hopes to marry him but fears she'll be an old
maid like Marian. Marian looks out the window as Amaryllis continues practicing. She begins to realize that she is tired of being the town's much gossiped
about unmarried female and secretly yearns for someone to love (Goodnight,
My Someone—Sc to F Solo).

At the high school gymnasium, a Fourth of July pageant circa 1912 is being
presented by the townspeople (Columbia the Gem of the Ocean—Mixed Chorus).
The idiosyncrasies of the various townspeople are pointed up in the pageant,
which deteriorates into a discussion of the local pool table. Hill reiterates (Ya
Got Trouble [Reprise]—M Solo) and convinces the townspeople they need a
boys band to keep the youngsters off the streets. In a rousing patriotic style he

captures the spirit of the town (Seventy-Six Trombones—M Solo to Mixed Chorus).

The Mayor, astounded by Hill's spellbinding methods, instructs the school board to get his credentials. They attempt to follow orders, but Hill hoodwinks them by pointing up their hidden vocal talents and turning them into a barbershop-style quartet (Sincere—Sc to M Quartet).

On a street in front of the library Marcellus congratulates Hill on his flamboyant demonstration at the gym and frankly admits he is astounded by Hill's most recent scheme. He offers to introduce him to a Sunday school teacher in town, but Hill rejects the idea for he doesn't want any unnecessary complications (The Sadder But Wiser Girl—Sc to M Solo).

The ladies of the town are overwhelmed by the professor and eagerly congratulate him on his speech in the gym. He discovers that the Mayor's wife, Mrs. Shinn, is reticent, so he makes her the chairman of the "Ladies Auxiliary for the Classic Dance." She accepts and is won over. When he asks about Marian, the women gossipingly fill him in and are joined by the newly formed male quartet in the background (Pick-a-Little, Talk-a-Little/Goodnight, Ladies—Sc to F Chorus to M Quartet).

Hill decides to approach Marian in the library and cons her into listening to his plea (Marian, the Librarian—Sc to M Solo). He kisses her; she slaps him but misses and hits Tommy, a teenager Hill has named as his assistant.

On the Paroo porch, Mrs. Paroo is taken with Hill, who convinces her that her son Winthrop, who hasn't spoken more than three words since his father died, can play in the band. Marian is furious with Hill and determined to expose him for the fraud he is. Mrs. Paroo cautions her against turning away all men who express an interest and accuses her of setting her sights too high. Marian assures her that she isn't waiting for a man in white armor (My White Knight—Sc to F Solo).

The Mayor enters the town square berating his wife for her nightly rehearsals when Marian rushes on carrying a large book which proves that Hill lied about his credentials. She is interrupted by the excitement of the arrival of the band instruments (The Wells Fargo Wagon—Mixed Chorus). When Winthrop is so overwhelmed that he verbalizes his emotions, something he hasn't done since his father died, Marian tears the incriminating page from the book and turns to Hill in gratitude as the curtain falls.

Act II opens in the gymnasium where the Ladies Auxiliary is rehearsing (Eulalie's Ballet into It's You—Mixed Chorus) for the ice cream social. The rehearsal ends abruptly as the social begins with the new dance the professor has taught the town's teens (Shipoopi—Mixed Chorus). During a confrontation with the Mayor in which Harold defends Tommy, whom the Mayor considers a troublemaker, Marian confesses her belief in Hill. The ladies gossip on the new events and invite Marian into their circle (Pick-a-Little [Reprise]—F Chorus).

The following week, on the hotel porch, the school board, under the orders of the Mayor, sends Hill to his hotel room to get his credentials or be arrested.

He hastily segues into the name Lida Rose and the quartet begins to sing (Lida Rose—M Quartet). The lights come up on Marian on her porch steps thinking of the effect Hill has had on her life (Will I Ever Tell You—F Solo). The quartet counterpoints.

Mrs. Paroo, insisting that Marian tell Harold her real feelings, is interrupted by Winthrop, who enters to tell of his fishing trip with the professor. He excitedly sings the song with hardly any S's that Hill has taught him (Gary, Indiana—L to B Solo to Trio) and runs off to visit Amaryllis.

Charlie Gowell, a salesman, stops by to inform the town of Hill's music fraud. He starts to leave word with Marian, who decides to protect Hill by vamping Gowell and stalling for time. Gowell, realizing too late that Marian is under Hill's spell, runs to catch his train.

Marian agrees to meet Hill at the footbridge and tells him she doesn't expect anything from their relationship but is grateful for everything he has done for her family ('Til There Was You—Sc to F Solo). Hill starts to tell her the truth about himself but discovers she already knows. He is astounded when she kisses him and hastily exits.

Mayor Shinn has received convincing proof that Hill is a crook. He orders him tarred and feathered, but the atrocious sound of the boys band playing the Hill Think-System Minuet in G causes the town to forget their intent and cheer wildly as Marian and Hill embrace (Finale—Mixed Chorus).

NOTES ON THE PRODUCTION

The show won the coveted Tony Award for Best Musical; Robert Preston, in his Broadway debut, received the Best Actor Award; David Burns, Featured Actor; and Barbara Cook, Featured Actress. The show also received awards for Book, Producer, Music and Musical Direction.

The production needs a charming yet villainous leading man in order to succeed. Without an appealing Hill it becomes unbelievable and uninteresting. Since its 1958 production it has often been performed by high schools, community and professional theatres to sellout crowds. This is a show that benefits from a large cast of children and adults, the larger the better, for it means more people to sell tickets, make costumes and work on sets and props.

An imaginative designer can trim the sets or use cutout silhouettes to represent various locations. Nothing need be terribly complex, for the homespun quality is more necessary than an over-produced lavish look.

There should be approximately two costumes per person, which includes the band sequence, the pageant and the Fourth of July finery.

The members of the male quartet should have excellent, tight harmonizing voices and be able to portray specific yet varied characters. In fact, the emphasis in this musical is on characterization, especially among the chorus.

SONGS OF SPECIAL INTEREST

"My White Knight," soprano, nice opportunity for transition work and pointing up specific images, ballad.

"Piano Lesson/If You Don't Mind My Saying So," comic, fast-paced, character song for alto/soprano. Excellent diction emphasized. Argument song, class work.

"Pick-a-Little . . . /Goodnight, Ladies," revue or showcase. Good number for beginning musical director and choreographer. Characterizations among chorus are important, minimal movement. Vocal emphasis.

"The Wells Fargo Wagon," good chorus number for class; simple staging, excitement and energy make it nearly actor-proof. Nice exercise for beginning choreographer.

Instrumentation: 4 reeds, 2 trumpets, 3 trombones, 3 violins, cello, bass, percussion, piano/conductor
Script: Putnam, Frank (London)
Score: Frank
Record: Capitol
Rights: MTI

MY FAIR LADY

Book and Lyrics: Alan Jay Lerner (Based on *Pygmalion*, by George Bernard Shaw)
Music: Frederick Loewe

ORIGINAL PRODUCTION

Mark Hellinger Theatre, March 15, 1956 (2,717 perf.)
Director: Moss Hart
Choreographer: Hanya Holm
Musical Director: Franz Allers
Orchestration: Robert Russell Bennett and Philip J. Lang
Principals: Mrs. Pearce—Philippa Bevans—VTNE; Henry Higgins—Rex Harrison—baritone; Eliza Doolittle—Julie Andrews—soprano; Colonel Pickering—Robert Coote—baritone; Alfred P. Doolittle—Stanley Holloway—baritone; Mrs. Higgins—Cathleen Nesbitt—VTNE; Freddy Eynsford-Hill—John Michael King—tenor; Mrs. Eynsford-Hill—Viola Roache—VTNE
Chorus and Smaller Roles: 12M/12F minimum, half of whom dance well.

SYNOPSIS

The curtain opens on the exterior of the Royal Opera House in Covent Garden, London. A wealthy audience emerges from the theatre, some searching for taxis, others standing by the columns of St. Paul's Church. On the opposite side of the stage, the costermongers are warming their hands around a small fire. Three buskers rush on to perform acrobatics and dances, hoping for money from the departing audience. Mrs. Eynsford-Hill, a domineering British matron, enters with her son, Freddy, who bumps into Eliza Doolittle, a poor flower girl. Eliza angrily accuses Freddy of ruining her violets and attempts to get him to pay, but his mother, ignoring the girl, sends him off in search of a taxi. Eliza turns to Colonel Pickering, a well-dressed, middle-aged military man, who gives her some money to pay for her ruined flowers.

Eliza, warned that a stranger has been taking down everything she says, appeals to Pickering, who comes to her aid. The man turns out to be Henry Higgins, a dialectician whom Pickering has come to London to meet. Higgins launches into a discourse on the problem of the English language (Why Can't the English?—Sc to M Solo with Extras for Staging).

Higgins, pleased that Pickering has come to London, invites this expert on Indian dialects to stay at his house on Wimpole Street. The two exit after Higgins buys Eliza's entire basket of flowers. She counts her good fortune and dreams of a better life as she warms her hands at the costermongers' fire (Wouldn't It Be Loverly—Sc to F Solo with M Trio).

The scene changes to a tenement section of Tottenham Court Road, where Eliza's coarse but charmingly roguish father, Alfred P. Doolittle, and his two friends, Jamie and Harry, are being evicted from a local pub for lack of payment. Doolittle is convinced that something is bound to turn up when he sees Eliza on her way home; he convinces her to give him some money and jubilantly celebrates with Jamie and Harry (With a Little Bit of Luck—M Trio).

The scene shifts to Higgins's study in Wimpole Street, where Higgins is playing voice recordings to Colonel Pickering, who is growing weary of the constant guttural sounds spewing forth from the recorder. When Eliza appears as a customer for speech lessons, Higgins boasts to Pickering that in six months he can pass her off as a duchess at the Embassy Ball. Pickering, intrigued by Higgins's boast, agrees to pay the expenses. Mrs. Pearce, the warmhearted housekeeper, expresses concern for Eliza's future but Higgins insists he knows what is best, and Mrs. Pearce takes Eliza for a thorough cleaning and some new clothes. Pickering expresses his apprehensions to Higgins and wonders if Higgins lacks character in his relations with women. Higgins assures Pickering that he is a simple man and a confirmed bachelor (I'm an Ordinary Man—Sc to M Solo).

In a local pub, when Alfred Doolittle is told that Eliza has gone to live with two gentlemen on Wimpole Street, he begins to see a way to make a little money from her good fortune (With a Little Bit of Luck [Reprise]—M Solo to Mixed Chorus).

Doolittle goes to Higgins's home to ask him for reimbursement for the use of his daughter as a "guinea pig" for Higgins's whims. Higgins and Pickering are appalled by Doolittle's lack of morals, but Higgins is also intrigued by his philosophy and offers him ten pounds, to which Alfie responds that he only needs five and that's all he wants. Higgins is amused and readily gives him the five pounds.

Higgins proceeds to drill Eliza in a series of exercises which she soon grows to detest. She expresses her hatred of her teacher in a humorous song where she imagines all the evil things she will do to Higgins when she is a lady (Just You Wait—Sc to F Solo).

The scene progresses with a variety of exercise vignettes and a chorus of servants who urge Higgins to quit. When Eliza finally says her exercises to Higgins's satisfaction, Pickering, Higgins and Eliza exuberantly sing (The Rain in Spain—Sc to 2M/F Trio).

Eliza is so excited by her achievement that she is unable to agree with Mrs. Pearce's attempts to have her sleep on the couch in the study (I Could Have Danced All Night—Sc to F Solo with Small F Chorus).

Higgins decides to test Eliza's decorum at the annual Ascot Opening Day Horse Race where his sixty-year-old mother is entertaining her society friends. The chorus, elegantly costumed in black and white, demonstrates the staid manner of the upper-class British by their obvious lack of enthusiasm (The Ascot Gavot—Mixed Chorus).

A nervous Higgins, Pickering and Eliza arrive at Ascot to be greeted by the charmingly tolerant Mrs. Higgins. Eliza's conversation, which by necessity only concerns health and the weather, captivates Freddy Eynsford-Hill, a guest of Mrs. Higgins. Freddy gives her a ticket, assuring her that she will enjoy the race much more if she has a horse to cheer for. Eliza proceeds to scream her horse to victory by urging him to move his "bloomin' arse." Her language causes several of the ladies to faint and Higgins to roar with laughter.

The scene shifts to the front of Higgins's house where Freddy asks Mrs. Pearce to announce him to Eliza. He is obviously infatuated with her (On the Street Where You Live—Sc to M Solo).

Six weeks later, at the Embassy Ball (The Embassy Waltz—Mixed Chorus Dance), Eliza manages to astound everyone by her decorum, charm and beauty. The highlight of the evening occurs when a phony dialectician, Zoltan Karpathy, declares Eliza's English to be too good for someone who spoke it from birth. He declares to everyone present that she is no less than a Hungarian princess.

Act II opens with Higgins and Pickering congratulating themselves to Mrs. Pearce and the servants (You Did It—Sc to M Duet to Small Mixed Chorus). As everyone retires to bed, Eliza furiously throws Higgins his slippers and expresses doubts about her abilities to live and work in the world she left behind. Higgins tries to mollify her but she informs him she is leaving, and he loses control for the first time in their relationship.

Eliza packs a suitcase and leaves the house. She runs into Freddy, who is still waiting in front of the house. While actually venting her anger at Higgins, she confronts Freddy and instructs him on how to behave (Show Me—Sc to F Solo).

Eliza returns to her past surroundings but realizes she can never go back to her old life. When she meets her father, he tells her of an American millionaire who, upon Higgins's recommendation, left Alfie 4,000 pounds a year for being the most original moralist in England. He is on his way to marry Eliza's step-mother, depressed that he must maintain a certain level of respectability. Eliza leaves as the chorus of friends return to take Alfie to his wedding (Get Me to the Church on Time—M Solo to Mixed Chorus).

At Wimpole Street, Higgins, incredulous that Eliza has left, questions Mrs. Pearce and Colonel Pickering on the behavior of women (A Hymn to Him—Sc to M Solo).

Henry storms off to his mother's house, where he finds Eliza calmly having tea with Mrs. Higgins in the conservatory. After an unpleasant scene with Higgins, Eliza realizes she can get along without him (Without You—Sc to F Solo to M Solo). When he changes moods at the end of her song and tells her that he is proud she has become a strong woman, Eliza leaves. He is confused by her behavior and calls out to his mother, who cheers Eliza for besting him.

He returns home in a rage, furious that he has grown so attached to a woman. As he reaches his front door he realizes he will honestly miss Eliza (I've Grown Accustomed to Her Face—L to M Solo).

He enters the house, where he proceeds to turn on the recorder to hear Eliza's voice. As he sits and listens, Eliza softly enters the room, turns off the gramophone and finishes her own words. Higgins is overjoyed but, in typical fashion, refuses to acknowledge his inner emotions, and responds by asking her where his slippers are; she smiles in understanding as the curtain falls.

NOTES ON THE PRODUCTION

1957 Tony Awards for the Best Actor, Direction, Musical, Book, Producer, Music, Musical Direction, Scenic and Costume Design.

The show is one of the finest shows ever written. It has an excellent book, memorable music and brilliant lyrics. The characters are well drawn and the roles worthy of the best actors and actresses the musical theatre has to offer.

The original production had eleven different scenes, several of which took place in full stage settings. It is possible to combine locations. For example, the ballroom of the embassy and the outside hall often use the same setting; the upstairs hall scene may be set in the study; the Covent Garden exterior and the flower market may be combined, as can the two Ascot scenes. This means that the entire show would need a Covent Garden exterior, Higgins's study, a ten-ement section, an Ascot area, an embassy ballroom, Mrs. Higgins's conservatory (sometimes utilizes the embassy ballroom drop with different furniture), and the outside of Higgins's house, for a total of six different settings. Covent Garden, the tenement, the Ascot scene, the ballroom and the exterior of Higgins's house may be rented drops. It is extremely important to the overall look that the production have lavish sets and costumes. If a company is going to have trouble financially achieving a quality look to the production, it might be better to present the nonmusical version.

The costumes are many and varied. The period is 1912, London, and costumes range from evening clothes to those of the Covent Garden poor. Each chorus member should have at least one costume for the opera opening, which may be used again without the outer wear for the embassy ball; one costume for the Covent Garden scenes, which may also be used in the Doolittle pub sequences; separate outfits for the Ascot scene, and possibly working-class clothes for "Get Me to the Church. . . . " Eliza needs five costumes, Higgins three, Pickering three, Doolittle two, Mrs. Higgins two, and the house servants need at least one.

For further reading about the original production, see Alan J. Lerner's book *The Street Where I Live*.

SONGS OF SPECIAL INTEREST

"Get Me to the Church on Time," good chorus number, excellent directing and choreographing exercise for class situation.

"I've Grown Accustomed to Her Face," essential as final number in a character study for it shows an unusual side of Higgins.

"Just You Wait," excellent acting exercise, story-style song with lots of actable specifics, class work.

"On the Street Where You Live," strong vocal quality needed, nice movement exercise for awkward actor, possible tenor audition.

"With a Little Bit of Luck," fun male trio, requires strong characterization and audience relationship.

"Without You," difficult and challenging scene to duet, lots of emotional levels, excellent example of change in a relationship.

"Wouldn't It Be Loverly," lots of actable images, simple dance, classroom study.

Instrumentation: 3 violins, cello, bass, 5 reeds, 2 horns, 3 trumpets, 2 trombones, tuba, percussion, harp, piano/conductor
Script: Coward-McCann Signet
Score: Chappell
Records: Columbia
Rights: TW

N

NO STRINGS

Book: Samuel Taylor
Music and Lyrics: Richard Rodgers

ORIGINAL PRODUCTION

54th Street Theatre, March 15, 1962 (580 perf.)
Director and Choreographer: Joe Layton
Musical Director: Peter Matz
Orchestration: Ralph Burns
Principals: David Jordan—Richard Kiley—baritone; Barbara Woodruff—Diahann Carroll—soprano; Jeanette Valmy—Noelle Adam—mezzo; Comfort O'Connell—Bernice Massi—mezzo/alto; Mike Robinson—Don Chastain—baritone; Luc Delbert—Alvin Epstein—baritone; Louis de Pourtal—Mitchell Gregg—baritone; Mollie Plummer—Polly Rowles—alto
Chorus and Smaller Roles: 6M/8F.

SYNOPSIS

Time: The present. Place: Paris, Monte Carlo, Honfleur, Deauville, and St. Tropez.

The play begins in prologue, when the lights rise on Barbara, an attractive, vibrant, American expatriate, who yearns for the sound of love (The Sweetest Sounds—F Solo Accompanied by a Flute). As the lights fade on her they come up on David, a handsome man of thirty with the same desire (The Sweetest Sounds—M Solo Accompanied by a Clarinet). The lights rise on both, still unaware of each other, who sing the final chorus and move into the darkness.

The actual story begins in a photography studio in Paris, where Jeanette, a young Parisian coquette, is assisting Luc, her photographer boyfriend, in preparing a layout for *Vogue*. Mollie, editor of the famous magazine, awaits the arrival of preferred model Barbara Woodruff. David Jordan, a moderately known American writer friend of Luc's, relates to Mollie his philosophy regarding women (How Sad—Sc to M Solo).

Barbara comes in to prepare for her modelling session and immediately shows her distaste for Americans by attacking David's writing. She later apologizes and agrees to let him escort her home. As the scenery is changing, the musicians appear and some Parisians walk by. As Barbara and David walk, Barbara explains to David what she wants from life (Loads of Love—Sc to F Solo). David suspects she is involved with someone when she doesn't allow him in her apartment. He wanders off in the crowd as the scene changes to her apartment.

Louis, a stylishly handsome Frenchman in his fifties, greets Barbara, whom he hopes will someday become his mistress. She is the only thing he has been unable to buy, and he is willing to wait until she agrees (The Man Who Has Everything—M Solo).

The scene suddenly switches to the Monte Carlo auto races where David has gone for some enjoyment. Mike Robinson, a friend of David's who makes his living as a gigolo, brings Comfort, his most recent rich American conquest, to meet David and Luc. They decide to throw a party at Luc's studio in Paris paid for by Comfort's wealth (Be My Host—Sc to F Solo to M Trio). Luc makes a pass at Gabrielle, a French girl he has met, but hastily bids her good-bye when Jeanette appears. The two explain their unusual relationship to the audience (La-La-La-La-La—Sc to M/F Duet).

Back in Paris, at Luc's studio, the party is in full swing when Barbara arrives with Louis. David takes her aside and confesses he cannot stop thinking about her, but Barbara tries to avoid the issue. When he accuses her of staying with Louis to be safe from real involvement, she orders him to stop analyzing her motives (You Don't Tell Me—Sc to F Solo). She exits with Louis, and David storms out of the room leaving Comfort and Mollie to express their viewpoint (Love Makes the World Go—Sc to F Duet).

Later that evening, in Barbara's sitting room, David invites her to join him on a trip to the coast. She initially refuses, for she hates his empty life-style, but later accepts when he assures her that her influence will help him return to serious writing (Nobody Told Me—Sc to M/F Duet).

In Act II David and Barbara are in Normandy and very much in love (Look No Further—Sc to M/F Duet). They reminisce about their childhoods; he comes from a small village in Maine, and she from a New York City ghetto (Maine—Sc to M/F Duet). The mood is too good to last. David becomes angered because he feels he can't write anything good, the two argue, and David runs off to be with his fun loving friends so he won't have to concern himself with writing.

When Barbara returns to Paris seeking advice from Mollie, the older woman tells her to send David back to America, where he will have to work to write a novel worthy of a Pulitzer Prize. Louis invites her back, but she refuses. He wishes her luck and leaves her alone to soliloquize on the stupidity of her relationships (An Orthodox Fool—F Solo).

Comfort, on the beach with Mike and David, begs Mike for some action (Eager Beaver—F Solo to M/F Duet). When she later discovers Mike with another woman, she informs him he is through. This confrontation forces David to realize that Barbara is right about his wasted life. He returns to Paris where he finds her in Luc's studio and they reaffirm their love (No Strings—Sc to M/F Duet). She urges him to go home to Maine. He agrees expecting her to go with him, but she is afraid to trade the safe modelling world of Paris for a quiet life in New England. Realizing she is right, he urges her to stay in Paris while he goes to Maine. He promises to be back, but until he returns they agree to live their lives as if they had never met. They both sing as in the opening, passing each other and moving into the darkness.

NOTES ON THE PRODUCTION

Tony Awards: Actress, Composer, and Choreography. Most other awards went to *How to Succeed in Business without Really Trying*.

This was the only full-length production for which Richard Rodgers served as composer and lyricist. The show had many innovations: the actors moved parts of scenery; the orchestra, which contained no string section, was backstage and occasionally appeared onstage.

The musical is extremely fluid with scene pieces flowing into place accompanied by onstage musicians. The scenery need not be complicated or large, but the lighting must be very tight for the locations to be properly delineated.

The two leads must be excellent actors and singers who have the maturity to handle the romantic love scenes as well as the angry dramatic arguments. Without sensitive actors and a superior artistic staff, the play runs the risk of falling flat.

The book is an interesting, original text and the songs are worth studying for they are not over-performed; some may be suited for auditions or nightclubs. Although there is no specific mention in the script that Barbara is Black, there must be some reason she is insecure about returning to America with David. Of course, many of the problems a Black Barbara would have faced in the America of the early sixties are not as severe in an America of the eighties. If a non-Black actress is used, it is suggested that the play be updated to the eighties and that some strong characterization questions regarding being born "up north of Central Park," her hatred of Americans, and her uniqueness as a model in Europe be answered in the early rehearsal stage.

SONGS OF SPECIAL INTEREST

"Love Makes the World Go," 2 altos, some movement, presentational, brassy.

"Nobody Told Me," baritone audition performed as a solo.

"An Orthodox Fool," semidramatic soprano, audition potential, shows range and emotion.

"Loads of Love," soprano up tempo, includes some movement, nice upbeat tempo.

Instrumentation: 4 reeds, trumpet, trombone, percussion, bass, piano, conductor
Script: Random
Score: Williamson
Record: Capitol
Rights: R & H

O

OKLAHOMA!

Book and Lyrics: Oscar Hammerstein II (Based on Lynn Riggs's *Green Grow the Lilacs*)
Music: Richard Rodgers

ORIGINAL PRODUCTION

St. James Theatre, March 31, 1943 (2,212 perf.)
Director: Rouben Mamoulian
Choreographer: Agnes de Mille
Musical Director: Joseph Schwartzdorf (Jay Blackton)
Principals: Aunt Eller—Betty Garde—alto; Curly—Alfred Drake—baritone; Laurey—Joan Roberts—soprano; Will Parker—Lee Dixon—baritone; Jud Fry— Howard Da Silva—baritone; Ado Annie—Celeste Holm—alto; Ali Hakim— Joseph Buloff—tenor; Gertie Cummings—Jane Lawrence—VTNE; Ike Skidmore—Barry Kelley—baritone; Andrew Carnes—Ralph Riggs—VTNE
Chorus and Smaller Roles: 12M/12F, at least half of whom should dance.

SYNOPSIS

The play opens, in front of Laurey and Aunt Eller's farmhouse, on a lovely summer day in the Oklahoma territory. The time is the early 1900s. Aunt Eller Murphy, a kind, elderly woman, is busy churning butter as a male voice is heard in the distance (Oh What a Beautiful Morning—M Solo).

Curly has come to ask Aunt Eller's niece, Laurey, to a party and teases her into believing he has a new buggy for the event (The Surrey with the Fringe on the Top—Sc to 1M/2F Trio). Aunt Eller and Laurey become involved in Curly's dream. When Laurey realizes Curly has no such rig, she leaves in a spiteful mood. Aunt Eller tells Curly that her niece likes him but Curly isn't so sure. He exits to hitch up Aunt Eller's big wagon to take people to the box social.

Will Parker, a local cowhand, home from a rodeo in Kansas City, eagerly tells Aunt Eller and a group of men about the wonders of the city (Kansas City—L to M Solo with M Chorus) and confides that he has come home to marry Ado Annie, his flirtatious girlfriend. Ado's father promised Will he could marry Annie if he had fifty dollars, which Will just won in a roping contest.

As the boys leave, Curly asks Aunt Eller who Laurey really likes; he is unwilling to believe it is himself. Aunt Eller leads him on, even tells him it might be Jud, the hired hand. They see Jud disappear into the house, then return with Laurey, saying he is taking her to the party. Curly asks Aunt Eller to accompany him to the party and exits. A frightened Laurey begs Aunt Eller to ride with her in Jud's wagon but is interrupted by Ado Annie, who enters talking to peddler Ali Hakim. Earlier he sold Aunt Eller an eggbeater and Eller takes him into the house to complain. Ado Annie confides to Laurey that she has difficulty choosing a favorite beau because she likes them all (I Cain't Say No—Sc to F Solo).

Aunt Eller and the peddler return, after settling their dispute. Laurey buys a magic elixir, guaranteed to help her solve her problems. As Annie asks Ali if he really wants to marry her, Will enters and explains that he and Annie can get married because he has won the fifty dollars her father required. Annie kisses Will as the party guests arrive. Curly is among them and escorts a simpering Gertie Cummings.

Pretending she isn't jealous of Curly's new preoccupation with the giggling Gertie, Laurey tells the girls of her refusal to pine over men (Many a New Day—F Solo to F Chorus).

Mr. Carnes rejects Will's proposal since he has spent the fifty dollars on presents for Annie and no longer has the cash. When Mr. Carnes discovers that Ali Hakim has been toying with his daughter, he insists that the peddler's attentions to Ado Annie justify a proposal. Ali, furious at being trapped, vocally vents his anger (It's a Scandal! It's an Outrage—M Solo to M Chorus).

Curly and Laurey, alone on the porch, challenge each other with reasons why everyone assumes they are stuck on each other (People Will Say We're in Love—Sc to M/F Duet). At the end of the song Curly asks her to refuse Jud, but she will not agree to do so. Curly goes to the smokehouse to see why Jud is so fascinating to her.

Curly enters the smokehouse where Jud lives and apprises him of how people would mourn if he, Jud, were to die. Jud fantasizes the event with him (Pore Jud Is Daid—Sc to M Duet). When Jud warns Curly to stay away from Laurey, Curly gives Jud an example of his gun-firing expertise. The others hear the gunshot and run to the smokehouse to find out what has happened. Discovering the shooting was accidental, everyone leaves but Ali, who attempts to sell Jud some of his wares. When Jud asks if Ali has a Little Wonder kaleidoscope, which has a knife blade hidden inside that releases when activated, Ali says he doesn't handle such things.

Jud, left alone, contemplates his empty life in a chilling number that forces the audience to see him as a three-dimensional character who is determined to have Laurey no matter what the price (Lonely Room—L to M Solo).

Laurey, seated in a grove on her farm, takes a whiff of the "magical potion" she bought from Ali Hakim and envisions her future (Out of My Dreams—Dream Ballet Sequence). In her dream the leading characters are portrayed by three dancers who substitute for Jud, Laurey, and Curly. (In productions where Jud's size makes it unfeasible to double, it is possible for him to play the dance role.) During the dream Jud kills Curly and Laurey is carried off. She awakens from this nightmare to find Jud standing before her, ready to take her to the box social. Afraid to reject him, she sadly gazes at Curly, who has hopefully entered, and hesitantly takes Jud's arm and exits.

Act II opens at the Skidmore Ranch, where the party is going strong. Aunt Eller urges the groups of ranchers and farmers to intermingle (The Farmer and the Cowman—Mixed Chorus).

Will offers to sell the presents he bought for Ado Annie to an anxious Ali Hakim, who quickly agrees. Still needing more money, an unsuspecting Will sells his Little Wonder to Jud, who knows it is a weapon and not an amusing toy. Jud and Curly both bid for Laurey's basket, which Curly wins by selling everything he owns, including his saddle and gun. Jud pretends that there are no hard feelings, and tries to show him the Little Wonder, intending to kill Curly by releasing the safety device on the hidden knife. Ali, knowing what lies in store, tells Aunt Eller, who saves Curly's life by asking him to dance.

Will, who is dancing with Ado Annie, takes the opportunity to tell her that she must behave and not mess around with any other men (All 'Er Nothin'—Sc to M/F Duet).

The scene shifts to Jud and Laurey in front of the Skidmores' ranch house. When Jud tries to embrace her she pulls away. He becomes enraged, but she fires him and tells him to leave immediately. He promises revenge. Curly arrives and asks Laurey to marry him (People Will Say We're in Love [Reprise]—Sc to M/F Duet).

Will discovers Ali amorously saying good-bye to Annie. The peddler comments that it is a traditional Persian good-bye and exits. Will tells Ado Annie she must become used to Oklahoma hellos and kisses her passionately.

At Laurey's house, it is Curly and Laurey's wedding day and everyone is gathered at the farm to celebrate the marriage and the admission of the territory to statehood (Oklahoma—Chorus).

Gertie enters the celebration, introducing everyone to her new husband, Ali Hakim. Will, trying to make Ali mad, gives Gertie an Oklahoma hello, but the only one who gets angry is Annie. A brawl starts between Annie and Gertie, which ends with Gertie being chased offstage by Ado Annie.

Jud arrives at the farm on the pretext of kissing the bride. When he grabs Laurey, Curly pulls him off and a fight ensues in which Jud pulls a knife. Jud falls on his own knife and is instantly killed. Curly is tried and declared innocent. He and Laurey depart for their honeymoon in a beautiful surrey as the company sings (Finale—Mixed Chorus).

NOTES ON THE PRODUCTION

Oklahoma! was a landmark musical that integrated music and dance into a plausible book with three-dimensional characters. It was Rodgers and Hammerstein's first collaboration and began a new trend in musical theatre by becoming a model form for subsequent musicals. In 1944, the authors received a special award from the Pulitzer Prize board; no regular prize for drama was awarded that year. On December 13, 1979, the show was revived on Broadway and starred Christine Andreas, who made Laurey into more than a lovesick two-dimensional ingenue. People who had seen stereotypical productions of *Oklahoma!* for the past thirty six years were totally enchanted by this refreshing production.

For any production of *Oklahoma!* it is essential that the director spend a lot of time working with the actors on character understanding and development. The production needs well-rounded characterizations if the audience is to empathize with the leads and be fearful of Jud. Too many productions portray Laurey and Curly as egotistical, self-centered teenagers who are picking on Jud, a mentally retarded man who isn't responsible for his actions. Jud Frye is a terrifying menace to society and must be played as such. His soliloquy demonstrates his dreams and aspirations, but the transitions within the song are more frightening because the audience knows what he will do.

The time of the show is the turn of the century, which is not a difficult period to costume. There are four full sets and two partial sets—the smokehouse and the Skidmore's porch—which usually employ wagons. However, on stages with limited wing space, the wagons may be cut and simple props substituted. It is possible to perform the show with the front of Laurey's farmhouse and the Skidmore ranch as the only full sets.

SONGS OF SPECIAL INTEREST

"All 'Er Nothin'," comic scene to duet, good for class study or showcase. Alto/baritone.

"I Cain't Say No," character-oriented, story song. Alto, deceptively simple. Emphasis must be placed on the problem of the character, not on action. Too many young performers forget what the song is about and dance it through.

"Kansas City," performed as a baritone solo, good for audition or character movement study. A joy for beginning performers as there are lots of actables.

"Lonely Room," dramatic, introspective solo that gives an audience an understanding of Jud's character. Baritone.

"People Will Say We're in Love," charm, romantic duet. Good first romantic song for hesitant performers. The emphasis is on the "game" and the relationship, soprano/baritone.

"Pore Jud Is Daid," comedic scene to baritone duet, good character/situation song. Wonderful in intimate revue or showcase production.

Instrumentation: 5 reeds, 2 horns, trumpet, trombone, percussion, 4 violins, viola, cello, bass, guitar, piano/conductor. Two-piano arrangement available
Script: Random, Six Plays By Rodgers & Hammerstein
Score: Williamson
Record: Decca, RCA
Rights: R & H

OLIVER!

Book, Music, and Lyrics: Lionel Bart (adapted from Charles Dickens's *Oliver Twist*)

ORIGINAL PRODUCTION

Imperial Theatre, July 6, 1963 (774 perf.)
Director: Peter Coe
Musical Director: Donald Pippin
Orchestration: Eric Rogers
Principals: Fagin—Clive Revill—baritone; Widow Corney—Hope Jackman—alto; Mr. Bumble—Willoughby Goddard—tenor; Nancy—Georgia Brown—alto; Bill Sikes—Danny Sewell—baritone; Oliver—Bruce Prochnik—boy soprano; Dodger—David Jones—tenor; Mr. Sowerberry—Robin Ramsey—baritone; Mrs. Sowerberry—Helena Carroll—mezzo; Bet—Alice Playten—mezzo; Mr. Brownlow—Geoffrey Lumb—VTNE; Dr. Grimwig—John Call—VTNE; Mrs. Bedwin—Dortha Duckworth—VTNE
Chorus and Smaller Roles: 8 children (usually boys), 6M/4F.

SYNOPSIS

The scene is a dingy workhouse dining room, where the starving orphans yearn for better fare to fill their stomachs (Food, Glorious Food—Ch Chorus). Oliver, a small workhouse boy of thirteen, asks the parish beadle, Mr. Bumble, a large, pompous fifty–five–year–old man, for more of the disgusting gruel they are eating. Mr. Bumble and Widow Corney, the headmistress of the workhouse, are appalled at Oliver's insolence and direct the boys to join in the chase (Oliver!—Sc to Mixed Chorus).

The widow locks Oliver up and settles down to a cup of tea with Mr. Bumble in her sitting room. Mr. Bumble, who is hoping to make his partnership with the widow a little more substantial, is flirting with the sharp-tongued, domineering woman who is harsh with everybody but Bumble. As Bumble makes advances to Widow Corney, she politely refuses, hoping he will get the idea that she wants to get married (I Shall Scream—Sc to M/F Duet). After the song, the Widow advises Bumble to take Oliver out and sell him for a good price. Bumble begins his sales pitch (Boy for Sale—M Solo).

Oliver is bought by undertaker Sowerberry, whose dour expression is matched by his extremely melancholy temperament. Sowerberry intends to make Oliver a coffin boy to follow the funerals of children. Mrs. Sowerberry rejects the idea but finally agrees and comments along with Bumble and her husband about undertaking as a profession (That's Your Funeral—Sc to 2M/F Trio).

Mrs. Sowerberry nightly locks Oliver in the coffin room; he desperately yearns for the love he knows must exist somewhere (Where Is Love?—B Solo).

Oliver escapes the Sowerberrys into the bustling city of London where he is picked up by the Artful Dodger, a young, dirty, worldly street urchin, who invites Oliver to join him (Consider Yourself—Sc to B Duet).

Dodger takes Oliver to the Thieves Kitchen, run by Fagin, an elderly man (still quite agile) who makes his living off the goods he receives from the children he trains as pickpockets and thieves. Fagin welcomes the new lad by teaching him the art of pickpocketing (You've Got to Pick a Pocket or Two—L to M Solo).

The next morning, Nancy, a street girl, former protégé of Fagin's who is now the girlfriend of the local villain Bill Sikes, arrives with her young friend Bet. The two meet Oliver and poignantly comment on their hard but happy life-styles (It's a Fine Life—Sc to F Duet to B Chorus). Dodger, Nancy, Oliver, and Bet demonstrate the life-styles of the rich (I'd Do Anything—Sc to B/F Duets with B Chorus).

Fagin sends the boys off to pick some pockets, but urges them to be careful and hurry back (Be Back Soon—M Solo and Mixed Chorus).

The scene moves to the street, where Oliver, mistakenly accused of stealing from Mr. Brownlow, a wealthy gentleman, is captured by the police.

Act II opens in a tavern, where Nancy is urged by the drinking clientele to sing (Oom Pah-Pah—F Solo to Mixed Chorus). As she finishes, Bill Sikes enters in a swaggering manner, boasting about himself (My Name—M Solo). While Fagin is talking to Bill (another of his ex-students), an exhausted Dodger enters to tell Fagin that Oliver has been accused of pickpocketing but released to a wealthy man who feels responsible for falsely accusing the boy. Nancy is reluctantly convinced by Bill to go after Oliver and bring him back to Fagin for safekeeping. She desperately loves Bill and expresses her feelings (As Long As He Needs Me—F Solo).

Oliver has been ''adopted'' by Mr. Brownlow, and moved into Brownlow's mansion, where he awakens to the sound of street vendors hawking their wares (Who Will Buy?—3F/1M Quartet to Ch Solo to Mixed Chorus).

Oliver, on an errand for Mr. Brownlow, is kidnapped by Nancy and Bill, who return him to Fagin's where the old man is considering his life-style (Reviewing the Situation—L to M Solo).

At the workhouse, Bumble and Corney, now wed, are approached by an old woman who confesses to stealing a locket from Oliver's dying mother. The locket points to a wealthy family. Bumble, sensing an opportunity, takes the locket to Mr. Brownlow, who recognizes the picture of the girl in the charm as his long-lost niece Agnes and surmises that Oliver is his grandnephew. He admonishes Bumble and promises to have him evicted from his post.

Nancy secretly arrives at Brownlow's estate to tell Brownlow she wants to save Oliver from growing up as a thief. She arranges to bring the boy to London Bridge at midnight.

It is a dark night as Nancy leads Oliver to London Bridge to meet Mr. Brownlow. They are followed by an angry Bill Sikes, who brutally kills Nancy and takes Oliver to Fagin's. Bill is pursued by the police, who finally kill him at the entrance to the Thieves Kitchen. Fagin is alone in the world (Reviewing the Situation [Reprise]—M Solo), and Oliver is reunited with his family (Finale—Mixed Chorus).

NOTES ON THE PRODUCTION

Most of the season's Tony Awards went to *A Funny Thing Happened on the Way to the Forum*; however, *Oliver!* received awards for Music and Lyrics, Musical Direction and Scenic Design.

The action may be placed in front of a backdrop of London and utilize a variety of levels for various locations. Too many set changes slow the place of the second act; a single set with limited props to denote location helps alleviate this weakness in the script.

The costumes are one per actor, unless there is quite a bit of doubling. The period is Charles Dickens mid–1800s.

The major problem in the show involves finding a talented Dodger and Oliver, who both sing well. The adult characters are broadly drawn and easily cast, but a company planning a production of the show would be wise to know there were several talented youngsters who could play the leading roles. Too often the show is chosen with a young boy in mind, and by the time the season gets underway, sometimes eight months later, the child's voice has changed from a soprano to baritone.

SONGS OF SPECIAL INTEREST

''As Long As He Needs Me,'' slow, sustained song that demands that the actress be able to portray strong emotions effectively. She must play torment, strength and pathos well. Alto solo.

"I Shall Scream," comic tenor/alto duet with emphasis on strong characters and relationships.

"Reviewing the Situation," introspective, comic monologue set to music. Good for character development. Baritone, a bit on the high side.

Instrumentation: 2 violins, viola, cello, bass, 4 reeds, horn, trumpet, 2 trombones, percussion, piano/conductor
Script: NP
Score: Hollis
Record: RCA
Rights: TW

ONCE UPON A MATTRESS

Book: Jay Thompson, Marshall Barer and Dean Fuller
Lyrics: Marshall Barer
Music: Mary Rodgers

ORIGINAL PRODUCTION

Phoenix Theatre, May 11, 1959 (460 perf.)
Director: George Abbott
Choreographer: Joe Layton
Orchestra Direction: Hal Hastings
Orchestration: Hershy Kay, Arthur Beck and Carroll Huxley
Principals: Winifred—Carol Burnett—alto; Dauntless—Joe Bova—baritone; Queen—Jane White—alto; King—Jack Gilford—VTNE; Lady Larkin—Anne Jones—soprano; Sir Harry—Allen Case—tenor; Jester—Matt Mattox—baritone; Minstrel—Harry Snow—tenor; Wizard—Robert Weil—baritone
Chorus: 6M/6F minimum.

SYNOPSIS

The play begins in prologue when the Minstrel appears singing and playing his lute. His story is pantomimed by the actors (Many Moons Ago—Minstrel and Mixed Chorus). The play moves to the "true" story of "The Princess and the Pea" where the Queen is conducting a quiz to see if princess number twelve is suitable for her son, Dauntless. The Court is anxiously hoping the princess will pass because no one in the land may marry until Dauntless is wed.

The court, disappointed when the twelfth princess fails the Queen's ridiculous examination, laments (An Opening for a Princess—Sc to Mixed Chorus).

Lady Larken explains to Sir Harry, her lover, that she is pregnant and will be forced to leave the Kingdom unless they can wed. He promises to find a princess and the two anticipate their future (In a Little While—Sc to M/F Duet).

The Queen, an overbearing, dominant mother and wife, scolds Dauntless for dawdling as they walk down a castle corridor. When King Sextimus passes them chasing a girl, she proceeds to scold him for not setting a proper example for the rest of the court. Dauntless hesitantly suggests to his mother that she does not really want him to get married. The Queen dramatically goes into a fit of rage (The Mamalogue). Sir Harry enters to gain permission from the Queen to seek a princess from the marshland and she grudgingly concedes.

Sir Harry, after a perilous three-week search, returns to the Kingdom accompanied by Princess Winifred, who enters sopping wet. It seems she was so excited to meet Dauntless that she swam the moat. Winifred, in a very large voice, urges the prince to step forward and greet her without being shy (Shy— F Solo). The Queen stammers that she could never consider Winifred for her daughter-in-law, but Harry presents proof that she is a real princess and the Queen is forced to test her.

The King mimes his news to the Jester and Minstrel, who must guess his thoughts, for the King is unable to speak until "the mouse devours the hawk." He tells them Larken is pregnant and begs them to keep the secret. They agree but wonder if he can be trusted. He signals that he can't communicate without them and the three sing of their reliance on each other (The Minstrel, the Jester and I—Sc to M Trio).

In a corridor, the Queen confers with the Wizard, a slimy, conniving individual, to find a test which the seemingly crude Winifred will fail (Sensitivity— Sc to M/F Duet). She decides on the scheme of placing a pea under twenty mattresses, a test that requires the sensitivity which Winifred certainly lacks.

In her dressing room, where Winifred has changed from her wet clothes, she tells three ladies in waiting and Dauntless about her home on the Bog (The Swamps of Home—Sc to F Solo with F Trio Backup). This seems to explain her unique character.

Lady Larken enters Winifred's room and finds her alone on her hands and knees mopping the floor. She mistakes her for a maid and doesn't discover her error until Harry introduces them. She is mortified. She and Harry argue and Larken bids him an angry good-bye.

Later that evening Lady Larken prepares to leave the Kingdom but the King, Minstrel and Jester try to convince her that the other side of the castle wall is terrifying if one goes alone. They advise that she journey with them to Normandy (Normandy—Sc to Trio).

The Great Hall is decorated for a celebration dance which the Queen is holding in Winifred's honor. She hopes to get the girl so tired that she cannot possibly feel the pea under the mattresses (Spanish Panic—L to F Solo to Dance Chorus). After the dance, everyone collapses in exhaustion except Winifred, who is ready for more.

Winifred asks Dauntless what sort of test she should expect, and he outlines previous tests the Queen has given. He tells Winifred how wonderful she is and how much he likes her (Song of Love—Sc to M/F Duet and Chorus). As he sings Winifred acts out his ideal and becomes more and more exhausted as the number progresses.

In Act II the Queen insists on absolute quiet and the court is whispering (Opening Act II) while setting up the mattresses for Winifred's test. The Queen discovers Larken, disguised as a boy, running away with the Minstrel and angrily orders her to wait on Winifred and orders the Minstrel banished.

In Winifred's room Dauntless helps her study for the test they think is the next day. A downhearted Larken enters and Winifred convinces her to patch up her differences with Harry. Larken leaves in excitement and Dauntless follows, leaving Winifred to sleep. Unable to rest, for she fears she will fail the test, Winifred yearns to be like the other princesses in the fairy tales (Happily Ever After—L to F Solo).

When the Jester and Minstrel convince the King to have his "talk" with Dauntless, he embarrassingly confronts his son. He mimes his information and Dauntless slowly begins to understand the secret of a man and woman (Man-to-Man Talk—Sc to M Duet).

The Minstrel and Jester try to trick the Wizard into revealing the Queen's test by reminding him of the good old days when they were all friends. The Minstrel arranges to meet the Wizard later to split a bottle of wine. The Jester pays tribute to his father, who played the "Palace" in 1492 (Very Soft Shoes—L to M Solo/ Dance).

Later on Larken and Harry patch up their differences (Yesterday I Loved You—Sc to M/F Duet).

Upstairs in Fred's chamber, the Queen, who has been desperately attempting to get Winifred to sleep, resorts to a sleeping potion. Winifred still tosses about the tall lumpy bed and passes the test. When the Queen begins to berate Winifred, Dauntless tells her to shut up and the Queen is dumbstruck. The Jester realizes that the age-old prophecy of the Kingdom has come true: "the mouse has swallowed the hawk." The King finally speaks and orders Queen Agravain about; the Court is overjoyed (Finale—Mixed Chorus).

NOTES ON THE PRODUCTION

The musical is an enjoyable one that is suited for family audiences and small theatres; it was originally produced Off-Broadway. The sets should be kept simple and the show is best performed on a unit with limited props. The same costumes may be worn throughout except where specifically noted in the synopsis. It is a low-budget vehicle that needs a strong chorus and good comic featured performers. The show is easily toured, for medieval banners and tapestries may be used to delineate specific areas where desired.

The story is comedic, the characters enjoyable, the treatment creative and the score extremely actable. A choreographer and director need only examine the lyrics for ideas on staging the musical numbers. The show can be easily broken down for rehearsing separate numbers simultaneously.

It is a good "first" show for a young theatrical group for it affords a variety of individual performers a chance to showcase their talents, is low-budget and has an expandable chorus with memorable songs.

SONGS OF SPECIAL INTEREST

"Happily Ever After," comedic alto solo, story song, lots of actable specifics, problem song.

"Very Soft Shoes," soft-shoe dance, vaudeville style, emphasis on total performance, charming number, baritone.

"Song of Love," comic song, good for beginning director to work on for staging may be simple, character song for F, small chorus. Good for class situation.

"Man-to-Man Talk," good for class, relationship and mime stressed, charm song, baritone. Possibility for showcase.

"Sensitivity," character song for loud, brazen alto, relationship with the oily wizard makes this good for class work.

Instrumentation: 4 reeds, 2 trumpets, 3 trombones, horn, percussion, 3 violins, viola, 3 cellos, bass, harp, guitar, piano
Script: Theatre Arts 6/60
Score: Chappell
Record: Kapp
Rights: MTI

110 IN THE SHADE

Book: N. Richard Nash (Based on the play *The Rainmaker*, by N. Richard Nash)
Music: Harvey Schmidt
Lyrics: Tom Jones

ORIGINAL PRODUCTION

Broadhurst Theatre, October 24, 1963 (330 perf.)
Director: Joseph Anthony
Dances and Musical Numbers Staged by: Agnes de Mille
Musical Director: Donald Pippin
Orchestration: Hershy Kay
Principals: Starbuck—Robert Horton—baritone; File—Stephen Douglass—baritone; Snookie—Lesley Warren—mezzo; Lizzie—Inga Swenson—mezzo; H.C.—Will Geer—baritone; Noah—Steve Roland—baritone; Jimmy—Scooter Teague—tenor
Chorus and Smaller Roles: 4M/4F.

SYNOPSIS

At the railroad station of a western town, the townsfolk are waiting for the train and commenting to Sheriff File about the long drought (Another Hot Day—Mixed Chorus). The townsfolk exit as the enthusiastic, youthful Jimmy Curry rushes on to see if his sister Lizzie's train has arrived. His father H.C. and stern older brother Noah appear and sing of their feeling for her (Lizzie's Comin' Home—M Trio).

Lizzie greets her family warmly. She is a plain, bright and matter-of-fact girl in her late twenties who has traveled to her relatives to find a prospective suitor. She informs them she didn't meet any man she could consider marrying. H.C., concerned for her future, decides to invite the sheriff to a picnic. Lizzie, who likes File, is embarrassed but hopes he will consider their offer (Love, Don't Turn Away—L to F Solo).

At the sheriff's office, the three men discuss Lizzie's attributes and enter into a card game, hoping to get File to the picnic (Poker Polka—Sc to M Quartet). File, realizing they are planning a match, refuses to become involved. H.C. accuses File of having a chip on his shoulder because his first wife ran out. File attempts to deny their accusations, but H.C. forces him to realize that the whole town knows the truth. The men depart as the scene shifts to the picnic grounds.

Lizzie and the women prepare for the picnic (Hungry Men—Mixed Chorus). Lizzie, realizing that File isn't coming, attempts to cover her disappointment by pretending nothing is wrong. Her emotions quickly switch to interest as Bill Starbuck, a strong, virile and energetic man, arrives in their midst. He introduces himself as a rainmaker and boldly announces he can save the crops (Rain Song—L to M Solo to Mixed Chorus). Although Lizzie and Noah urge their father not to risk his money, H.C. gives Starbuck $100 and lodging in exchange for rainy weather in twenty-four hours.

A crowd gathers around Starbuck's wagon and he begins giving directions. Jimmy is to beat a drum when he gets the feeling, H.C. is supposed to draw an arrow with a special white paint and Noah is to tie the hind legs of a mule together. Lizzie is infuriated that her family is going along, but H.C. tells her one must not be afraid to take a chance in life. Starbuck is impressed by H.C.'s confidence and promises he will get his money's worth. After everyone leaves, Lizzie accuses Starbuck of being a con man, and he accuses her of not being a woman. In a dramatic scene/song the two express their anger, but there is an underlying physical attraction driving the tension (You're Not Foolin' Me—Sc to M/F Duet).

Starbuck leaves a shattered Lizzie, who quietly rethinks his words. Noah, Jimmy and H.C. return. Starbuck's influence has begun to affect Jimmy, who realizes he isn't as dumb as Noah makes him believe. The two brothers exit as Lizzie asks her father how to take lessons in being a woman. He scoffs but she is serious and begins parodying the various sexy, mindless girls around town (Raunchy—Sc to F Solo).

File arrives at the picnic as Lizzie ends the number. He abruptly tells her that he and his first wife were divorced and he has a bitter outlook on marriage. Lizzie shows him that relationships need not be ugly and bitter (A Man and a Woman—Sc to M/F Duet). They seem to be close, but Lizzie discovers that File's pride wouldn't let him ask his wife to stay and calls him a fool. He rushes off in anger as the family runs on to question her. Lizzie, left alone after a confrontation among Starbuck, Jimmy and Noah, ponders Noah's prophecy that she will be an old maid (Old Maid—Sc to F Solo).

In Act II the townspeople are celebrating and dancing at the pavilion (Everything Beautiful Happens at Night—Mixed Chorus). Lizzie seeks out Starbuck at his wagon. He tries to get her to believe in herself (Melisande—L to M Solo) and flashily creates a new image for her but Lizzie prefers little things (Simple Little Things—Sc to F Solo).

Realizing her need to be beautiful, he embraces her, unpins her hair and urges her to say over and over that she is pretty. She begins to believe the words as Starbuck gently kisses her and forces her to realize the words are true.

In another part of the picnic grounds, Noah and H.C. search for Jimmy, who enters to tell them he has spent the night with his girlfriend Snookie, whom Noah considers ditsy and conniving. He and Snookie describe the innocence of the evening (Little Red Hat—M/F Duet). File interrupts to question them about Starbuck's whereabouts but they feign ignorance and File searches elsewhere. Noah reproaches H.C., who tells him that Lizzie needs to be with a man who can make her feel important—even for one night.

The scene shifts to Lizzie and Starbuck seated by the wagon. Lizzie asks Starbuck if she has changed (Is It Really Me?—Sc to M/F Duet). He admits he is a fake and would consider leaving his world to be with her. Overjoyed, she goes to share the news with the family but File returns to arrest Starbuck. After File is convinced to let Starbuck go, Starbuck tries to persuade Lizzie to leave with him. This action forces File to ask Lizzie to stay and be his wife (Wonderful Music—Sc to 2M/F Trio). As Lizzie decides to stay with File, it begins to rain. For the first time Starbuck's miracle has worked (Finale-Mixed Chorus).

NOTES ON THE PRODUCTION

This musical, although not one of the more frequently performed, is excellent for dramatic study and characterization work. The script seems to be locked between the large-scale Broadway musicals of the sixties and the smaller Off-Broadway ones that often focused on drama and story line. The power of the piece lies in the scenes that are closely connected to the straight play. When the play "opens up" to become a large musical, suitable for Broadway theatre-goers of the sixties, the story line loses importance.

It has been rumored that Schmidt and Jones are going to redo the show and delete the larger numbers, but to date this hasn't been done. A company con sidering a production may want to obtain permission to turn it into a small 5M/ 2F show.

The characters are well drawn, the family relationship true to life and the situation dramatically strong.

SONGS OF SPECIAL INTEREST

"Love, Don't Turn Away," simple lyric, crying out with drama, shows off voice and acting, mezzo.

"Melisande," lots of actable specifics, story song, strong character required, baritone.

"Old Maid," dramatically gripping song. Introspective, frightening, heart-rending. Powerful mezzo number. Excellent for character study.

"Poker Polka," M quartet, good for class study, comic dance, nice choice for beginning choreographer.

"Raunchy," comic song, shows vocal range and characterization ability. Movement required but need not be graceful or coordinated. Good song to loosen up a stiff soprano.

"You're Not Foolin' Me," dramatic scene to baritone/soprano duet, good for relationship, tension, subtext, song deals with two people who are attracted to and terrified of each other.

Instrumentation: 6 reeds, 2 horns, 3 trumpets, trombone, 2 percussion, guitar, harp, 4 violins, 2 cellos, contra bass, piano/conductor
Script: NP
Score: Chappell
Record: RCA
Rights: TW

ON THE TWENTIETH CENTURY

Book and Lyrics: Betty Comden and Adolph Green (Based on plays by Ben Hecht, Charles MacArthur and Bruce Millholland)
Music: Cy Coleman

ORIGINAL PRODUCTION

St. James Theatre, February 19, 1978 (460 perf.)
Director: Harold Prince
Musical Staging: Larry Fuller
Musical Director: Paul Gemignani
Orchestration: Hershy Kay
Principals: Owen O'Malley—George Coe—baritone; Letitia Primrose—Imogene Coca—mezzo; Oliver Wells—Dean Dittman—baritone; Bruce Granit—Kevin

Kline—tenor; Oscar Jaffee—John Cullum—baritone; Lily/Mildred—Madeline
Kahn—soprano; Max Jacobs—George Lee Andrews—VTNE
Chorus and Smaller Roles: Minimum 8F/8M who sing well; four of the men
should tap-dance.

SYNOPSIS

The musical opens during a mediocre performance of *The French Girl*, a
terrible production about Joan of Arc. Since the entire audience has walked out
by the middle of the show, the play closes and the actors sing of their common
problem—out of work and no money to get home (Stranded Again—M Solo to
Mixed Chorus). During the song the set is struck to reveal Owen O'Malley, the
show's fast-talking, hard-drinking press agent, and Oliver Webb, the easily
angered, overweight business manager. The company surrounds the two, demanding to know where Oscar Jaffee, their egotistical producer/director, has
gone. Owen and Oliver send the actors to search the roof as Oscar, disguised
as a knight in full armor, hands them a note to meet him on the Twentieth
Century Ltd. in Drawing Room A. The set changes to the Chicago station
platform where the conductors, passengers and porters are introduced to the
audience as they laud the famous train (On the Twentieth Century—M Duet to
Mixed Chorus).

The scene is transformed to the interior of the train, showing Drawing Room
A and the Observation Car. Oliver and Owen manage to get the Drawing Room
by threatening to expose the occupants, a congressman and his mistress, who
quietly move elsewhere. They wait in the Observation Car as the train moves
out, certain that Oscar has been unable to escape the angry actors. As they talk
they discover Oscar hanging outside their window, furious that they are not in
the car he ordered. As they pull him in, he vows not to let this recent financial
setback daunt his spirits (I Rise Again—Sc to M Trio).

Oscar plans to be saved by enlisting the aid of Lily Garland, the famous
Hollywood star whom he discovered, trained and fell in love with.

The scene flashes back to an empty stage, where a klutzy piano player named
Mildred Plotka is accompanying and correcting an operatic star who is auditioning
for Oscar's play (Indian Maiden's Lament—F Solo). The temperamental off-
key singer, humiliated by this treatment, fires the girl, who angrily demands her
twenty-cent carfare. She terrorizes the poor woman, who meekly gives her
twenty-five cents, urges her to keep the change and begs someone to help her
to a cab. Oscar cleverly decides the pianist is star material, changes her name
from Mildred Plotka to Lily Garland, and vows to make her an international
sensation. As he describes the plot of his new play to the confused girl, the
scene shifts to the production featuring Lily Garland (Veronique—F Solo to M
Chorus). During the number she is transformed from a dull Mildred to the
sparkling Lily through Oscar's coaching and direction.

The scene returns to Drawing Room A, where an anxious conductor bursts
in to inform Jaffee that he is an aspiring playwright who has written a script

about life on a train (I Have Written a Play—M Solo). Oscar agrees to look at it and pushes him out the door. Meanwhile, in the Observation Car, the conductor informs Mrs. Letitia Primrose, a wealthy and frequent customer, that there is a religious nut on the train; she smilingly nods, turns to her Bible and pastes a religious sticker on the desk.

The train stops at the edge of Chicago as the passengers excitedly anticipate Lily Garland's entrance (Together—Mixed Chorus). Lily enters through the gaping crowd of passengers followed by her sturdy maid, Agnes, and her current boyfriend, Bruce Granit. After giving Bruce a syrupy farewell, she collapses in Drawing Room B and bursts into tears. Her maid, who cynically reminds her she has been wanting to ditch Bruce for months, is interrupted by the returning lover, who refuses to leave her alone on the train. She embraces him as Owen and Oliver enter to tell her that Oscar needs her. Furious to hear that Oscar is on the train, she refuses to have anything to do with the man or his schemes (Never—2M/F Trio). She ends the number musically screaming her rejection as Oliver and Owen beat a hasty retreat.

Lily sits in Bruce's lap to reassure him that Oscar Jaffee never meant anything to her. The lights rise in Drawing Room A to reveal Oscar. Both Lily and Oscar reminisce and begin singing to each other as if in a memory (Our Private World— M/F Duet). At the end of the number they return to their drawing rooms to think.

The Observation Car is crowded with angry passengers pulling religious stickers from their luggage and clothing. The conductor assures the wealthy Mrs. Primrose he will find the religious extremist and everyone clears the car. As Letitia looks out the windows of the train, she urges everyone to change their wicked ways (Repent—F Solo).

Oscar sees a repent sticker on Oliver's coat, which gives him the idea to have Lily play Mary Magdalen in a play he will produce. He sends Owen and Oliver out while he quickly changes to meet Lily. As he dresses he looks into a mirror which faces Drawing Room B. Bruce, on the other side of the wall, is studying himself in the mirror facing Oscar in Drawing Room A. As they preen in front of their mirrors, it looks as if they are singing to each other, but in reality they are singing to themselves (Mine—M Linear Duet).

Owen, in the Observation Car, discovers that Mrs. Primrose is interested in artistic endeavors. He sees a way to get Oscar out of debt and excitedly calls Oliver.

Oscar barges into Lily's room, interrupting a passionate moment, which ends with Lily throwing the jealous Bruce out and ordering Oscar to leave as well. She tells him she needs no one (I've Got It All—Sc to M/F Duet), but he retorts that she has gone stale as an actress and needs something more challenging. She scoffs, for she is going to be in a production of his archenemy, Max Jacobs. At the mention of the name, Oscar begins shouting and exits in a fury as Lily throws a champagne bottle at the door.

Oscar threatens Oliver and Owen with annihilation, but their news about Letitia Primrose investing in the arts so excites him that he graciously escorts Mrs.

Primrose into his room. The conversation is interrupted by the congressman, who has written a play about life on the hog market committee (I Have Written a Play—M Solo). Oliver and Owen hastily escort the congressman out and mime to Oscar that Mrs. Primrose is a Baptist. He quickly uses this information to his advantage and strikes a bargain with her as the passengers sing that luck may be changed by riding the train (On the Twentieth Century [Reprise]—Mixed Chorus).

In the entr'acte, four tap-dancing porters perform a number correlating life and a train (Life Is Like a Train—M Quartet).

Act II opens in Oscar's room, where Letitia writes a check, much to the excitement of Owen, Oliver, and Oscar (Five Zeros—3M/F Quartet). They are interrupted by a Dr. Johnson, who bursts into the room to inform Oscar she has written a play about life in a hospital (I Have Written a Play—F Solo). Oscar, who is preparing to meet Lily, tells her he is too busy. She exits in a huff, warning him not to expect any medical assistance from her, for she will certainly be too busy.

Oscar rushes to Lily's room to outline a play about Mary Magdalen. As he describes it, she enacts the role. When Lily doubts the authenticity of Letitia Primrose, Oscar quickly ushers her next door, where everyone urges Lily to sign the contract. Bruce enters as she is deciding and vehemently opposes her involvement with Oscar (Sextet—4M/2F Sextet). Lily almost relents but can't give up Hollywood for a long-term contract. Oscar promises to give her the film rights if she will agree to a short Broadway run, and Mrs. Primrose agrees to put up three million dollars for Lily's own film company. Lily is interested and goes to read the contract.

In the Observation Car where Oliver is relaxing, the conductor, a porter and two officers from a rest home enter searching for Mrs. Primrose. Word quickly spreads throughout the train as the passengers search for the crackpot (She's a Nut—Mixed Chorus). Oscar, Oliver and Owen are terribly upset by the news, Bruce is overjoyed and Lily is once again furious at Oscar.

Max Jacobs, Oscar's rival, enters; he has flown in to tell Lily he has a wonderful play for her. She and Max leave Oscar and go to Drawing Room B, where Lily begins reading Max's script. As she reads she becomes caught up in the story line and begins to act out the entire production (Babette-Lily—L to F Solo; Mixed Chorus Needed for Staging). She agrees to star in the production.

Oscar enters the Observation Car to tell his drunken cohorts he is committing suicide (The Legacy—L to M Solo). They seem uninterested in his last wishes so he exits, followed by Mrs. Primrose. A shot is heard offstage; it seems Mrs. Primrose shot Oscar while trying to take his gun away. He staggers in as the attendants take Mrs. Primrose off. He decides to use the shooting incident to his advantage and promises the doctor he will read her play if she will help him convince Lily he is dying. Lily enters and the two enact an operatic death scene (Lily/Oscar—M/F Duet). She grants his last request to sign a contract for his new play. He falls back, seemingly dead, as Max Jacobs rushes on. Oscar rises in triumph, certain he has beaten his archrival by getting Lily's name on a contract, but she tells him she knew he was faking and signed Peter Rabbit to the contract. The two laugh and fondly embrace as the musical ends.

NOTES ON THE PRODUCTION

The musical won Tony Awards for Actor (John Cullum), Featured Actor (Kevin Kline), Book, Score, and Set Design.

The show is extremely funny when directed and acted as a stylized spoof on the 1930s films. The production calls for superb acting and singing on the part of Lily, Oscar and Bruce. Most of the stylization notes are included in the acting version of the play and should be followed quite closely if the director has limited experience in directing period-style musicals. The chorus may be expanded in size; in fact, a larger company would add more to the vocals and general look of the piece. The work has been successfully presented by smaller summer stock companies and by high schools with enormous stages to fill. The play breaks down very nicely for ease in rehearsals as there is little choral work and few choreographic demands. The stage director could be working on scenes with the principals while the musical director is working with the chorus in a separate area. When the choreographer prepares to stage the larger musical numbers, the director and musical director could work with the smaller vocal numbers.

The set is not too complex. Usually the Observation Car and Drawing Room A are on a large wagon which can come onstage from the right or be pushed downstage, and Drawing Room B is on a smaller wagon which comes from the left side. It simplifies matters if one has access to drops for the opening sequence and "Babette," but small pieces can be used if there is lack of fly space. There is a scene with Mrs. Primrose on the cowcatcher of the train and another with her in the caboose to demonstrate the passing of time, but the emphasis can be on lighting and not construction. The costumes are period 1930s, Joan of Arc, and 1930s formal attire. Most of the passengers have two costumes, one for daytime and one pair of pajamas. Lily has quite a few costumes, and Oscar can change his look from a suit to a smoking jacket.

The show is a fairly complicated prop show due to the fact that everything must be period 1930s or earlier. The props are relatively common, i.e., carpet sweeper, pens, muskets, sword, trunk, cameras, typewriter; but many items from the period now qualify as antiques and it may be difficult finding people who will loan expensive items to a theatre.

SONGS OF SPECIAL INTEREST

"I Rise Again," comic male trio, heavily stylized, presentational.
"Never," angry, overdone comedic song which features a soprano.
"Repent," comic mezzo, characterization more important than vocal.

Instrumentation: 5 reeds, 2 horns, 2 trumpets, 2 trombones, 3 violins, viola, cello, bass, harp, 2 percussion, piano/conductor
Script: SF, DBS
Selections: Big Three
Record: Columbia
Rights: SF

OVER HERE!

Book: Will Holt
Music and Lyrics: Richard M. and Robert B. Sherman

ORIGINAL PRODUCTION

Shubert Theatre, March 6, 1974 (341 perf.)
Director: Tom Moore
Musical Director: Joseph Klein
Musical Numbers and Dances Staged by: Patricia Birch
Orchestration: Michael Gibson and Jim Tyler
Principals: Mitzi—Janie Sell—alto; June—April Shawhan—soprano; Bill—John Driver—tenor; Paulette De Paul—Patty Andrews—mezzo; Pauline De Paul—Maxene Andrews—mezzo; Utah—Treat Williams—tenor; Sam—Samuel E. Wright—baritone; Norwin Spokesman—Douglass Watson—VTI
Chorus and Smaller Roles: 4M/3F

SYNOPSIS

The scene opens at a train station in the beginning of World War II. Norwin Spokesman, who portrays Sarge, the train conductor, and serves as a narrator throughout the play, talks about the effects of the war. All the old memories are relived as pictures of FDR and various popular stars of the 1940s are shown. He and the rest of the company introduce the wartime atmosphere and capture the loneliness a soldier feels without his "gal" (Since You're Not Around—Mixed Chorus).

As the train whistle blows, the civilians board the train. They consist of a mother and a father who represent model middle-aged American parents; Mr. Rankin, a prosperous businessman wartime profiteer; Donna, a local waitress; Maggie, a wealthy debutante on her way to Wellesley; and Mitzi, a Nazi spy who uses her lipstick and compact as a secret transmitter and camera.

Spokesman talks about the draft as two American boys, Lucky and Utah, head for the train. Utah's character is very similar to his name—the honest cowboy with a strong belief in his country. Lucky, the wise kid from the city, puts on a tough act, but underneath it all he is both patriotic and sensitive. Next to arrive on the scene are June and Bill, high school sweethearts still attired in their prom outfits. The draftees are inducted and Spokesman is transformed into a hard and overbearing Army Sergeant.

Pauline and Paulette De Paul, a singing sister duo who are looking for a third singer to complete their act, arrive to boost morale. They sing about working together as a team for the good old U.S.A. (Over Here!—Sc to F Duet to Mixed Chorus). The train door finally closes as Sam and Spokesman yell "All aboard for Victory!" (Buy a Victory Bond—Mixed Chorus).

The train sets off and the various lives of the travelers are revealed in typical forties style. June tells Bill she loves him but cannot sleep with him until they are married (My Dream for Tomorrow—Sc to F Solo).

June meets up with the De Pauls, and they allow her to bunk with them if she will help them out by serving doughnuts at the canteen. Donna and Maggie join in as the troop enters the canteen. Lucky and Maggie are reminded by Pauline that romance can happen anywhere (Charlie's Place—Sc to Mixed Chorus—Jitterbug). June and Bill are still debating their relationship. Bill wants to live for today, June hopes for the future, and Mother and Father supervise. Father talks to Bill about his younger days in World War I and the difference between a "good girl" and a "good time girl." Rankin and spokesman join in and reminisce about the French girls in World War I (Hey Yvette—Sc to M Trio).

Mother, Father, and the rest of the civilians intervene in Bill and June's dilemma and explain that there are larger issues at hand. She should stop thinking of herself and get involved in helping the boys. June decides to collect lipstick tubes and donate them to make munitions.

The Sarge gives the boys a lecture on hygiene and disease which the De Pauls reinforce (The Good Time Girl—Sc to F Duet and F Chorus).

When Paulette asks Mitzi to join the canteen activities, Mitzi agrees, thinking she will be able to get information. Mitzi tries to convince Bill not to wait until he marries June since he may not make it back from the war (Wait for Me Marlena—F Solo and M Chorus). June accidentally collects Mitzi's secret transmitter lipstick, so Mitzi is left unable to communicate with the Germans. In a sudden stroke of luck Pauline and Paulette ask her to join their group, which will be broadcasting over the radio (We Got It—Sc to F Trio and Mixed Chorus).

In Act II Mitzi devises a song for the trio to sing which is actually the Morse code signal for "ship leaving twelve midnight." Various relationships develop as the train speeds along. As usual, June and Bill are discussing sex but Bill decides to wait until they are married. The De Pauls sing about wartime marriages (Wartime Wedding—Sc to F Duet and Mixed Chorus). The company prepares for the wedding.

Sam, the Black porter, caught up in the wartime enthusiasm, considers enlisting but Spokesman reminds him, in racist tones, to remember who he is. Sam retaliates in his own lingo (Don't Shoot the Hooey to Me, Louie—Sc to M Solo).

The civilians try to get off the train, which is temporarily stopped, but are ordered by Spokesman to stay put. The company grows more and more annoyed; Lucky and Utah start fighting and even Paulette gets discouraged (Where Did the Good Times Go?—Sc to F Solo). Pauline manages to lift her sister's spirits by getting her to knock some sense into the company. Everyone ends up taking out their frustrations by hitting each other, but the effect is positive. All are in better spirits. All ponder on their own dreams (Dream Sequence—Dance). The number culminates as Utah fantasizes about being a famous drummer (Dream Drummin'—Sc to M/F Solos and Mixed Chorus).

Paulette, Pauline, and Mitzi perform on the radio, singing Mitzi's hidden code song (The Big Beat—F Trio). Lucky recognizes the Morse code in the song and figures out that it is a message to Hitler. After the trio is quizzed, Mitzi is dragged off as a Nazi spy. Bill and June complete their wedding ceremony. The train finally arrives at the last stop and everyone promises there will be no farewells (No Good-byes—Sc to F Duet, Mixed Chorus).

NOTES ON THE PRODUCTION

Janie Sell won the 1974 Tony for Best Supporting Actress in a musical.

The production script differs from the Broadway original and the cast has been slightly minimized, which should appeal to smaller companies. The music is tremendous fun and should be appreciated by audiences of all ages. It is very forties and works quite well in the context of the show.

The dialogue is quite wordy and could benefit from some trimming, but the musical numbers when combined with an excellent cast would make this a show worth seeing. The women who play the De Pauls are obviously a carbon copy of the Andrew Sisters and must have tremendous performing confidence in tight microphone-style singing. If a company has three excellent female singers and a top "big band," this show can be rewarding. Without the combination of vocal blend, musical sound and singing style, the production is risky. There are some memorable vignette roles that are important to the overall quality of the show.

The primary set is a train with separate cars for the military, civilians and the canteen. The canteen could be a neutral area between the civilians and the military. The De Pauls are supposed to enter on a military Jeep, but this may be impossible in theatres with no backstage. All attempts should be made to focus attention on their entrance if a Jeep isn't used. Projections may be used to familiarize younger audience members with familiar figures from the forties. They also enable some variety to be added to the set and more firmly establish the nostalgic element of the piece.

Costumes may be the same throughout. Technically, the show is relatively inexpensive to produce. It is assumed that the bulk of the budget will go to pay the musicians. It is perfectly acceptable to have the band onstage as the music is extremely important and may be further highlighted.

SONGS OF SPECIAL INTEREST

"The Big Beat," good period-style trio in Andrews Sisters' style. 2 mezzos, alto. Good for revue with full orchestra.

"Don't Shoot the Hooey to Me, Louie," good stylized movement number, bitter humor, Black actor/dancer necessary, baritone.

"Over Here," good period duet in the Andrews Sisters' style, good for class or revue, 2 mezzos.

"Where Did the Good Times Go?" good for club or semidramatic for class study, alto/mezzo range.

Instrumentation: 5 reeds, 4 trumpets, 4 trombones, 2 percussion, cello, bass, guitar, piano/conductor
Script: SF
Selections: Hansen
Record: Columbia
Rights: SF

P

PACIFIC OVERTURES

Book: John Weidman
Music and Lyrics: Stephen Sondheim
Additional Material: Hugh Wheeler

ORIGINAL PRODUCTION

Winter Garden Theatre, January 11, 1976 (193 perf.)
Director: Harold Prince
Choreographer: Patricia Birch
Orchestration: Jonathan Tunick
Musical Director: Paul Gemignani
Principals: Reciter—Mako—baritone; Abe—Yuki Shimoda—baritone; Manjiro—Sab Shimono—baritone; Kayama—Isao Sato—baritone
Chorus: 9F/12M who play a variety of roles; original was performed by an all-male cast.

SYNOPSIS

The play begins in a quiet Japanese fishing village in 1853 during the Tokugawa era when most of Japan was outlawed to foreigners and the Japanese were prisoners of their homeland. The Reciter, in Kabuki/Bunraku style, narrates the story by conveying the history and the advantages of isolation (The Advantages of Floating in the Middle of the Sea—M Solo to Mixed Chorus).

The Reciter introduces the Shogun's Court where the counselors are meting out sentence on Manjiro, a young sailor who was shipwrecked, taken to Massachusetts and recently returned to Japan to announce the impending arrival of the Americans. The counselors are enraged that he suggest they contemplate trade with the approaching Westerner barbarians.

Next to arrive at the Shogun's Court is Kayama Yesaemon, a minor Samurai who mistakenly cast his fishing nets in a stream belonging to the Shogun. Kayama is elevated to the position of Prefect Policeman and ordered to greet the approaching Americans and send them away.

As Kayama tells his wife Tamate of this impossible task, two singers appear onstage, one to sing her thoughts, and one to tell about her. During the song, Tamate mimes her emotions, for she knows that failure of this important task will mean dishonor for the family and thus suicide (Is There No Other Way?— F Duet). As the touching scene ends, an enormous bell rings signaling the arrival of the Americans. Various villagers comment on their ideas of the warship. A fisherman hears this bell and perceives the four battleships to be four black dragons, spitting fire. A merchant realizes that the arrival of the battleships will endanger his family and attempts to move elsewhere before being destroyed by "foreign dogs." And lastly, a thief sees the battleships and thinks they are four volcanoes spitting fire. Each villager reacts with fear and shock as the USS *Powhatan* disturbs their peaceful isolation (Four Black Dragons—Trio to Mixed Chorus).

Kayama dutifully rows to the warship, but is shamefully sent away by the Americans, who demand that a high official receive their message. The Council decides to disguise the English-speaking Manjiro as a high official and the two manage to gain six days' reprieve for the country. At the end of six days, if the Shogun hasn't personally met with Commodore Perry on Japanese soil, the American warships will level the town of Uraga. Manjiro and Kayama are left with the task of both satisfying the demands of the Americans and respecting the sacred decree that will not allow a foreigner to set foot on Japan.

The isolation of the Shogun and his refusal to deal with the changing outside world are seen in the Shogun's quarters, when the ruler repeatedly ignores his mother, who urges him to negotiate with the Americans. She gradually poisons him, for she feels that no Shogun is better than a weak one (Chrysanthemum Tea—F Solo and Small M Chorus).

Kayama, with the help of Manjiro, proposes that a special treaty house be built and the ground be covered with tatami mats, which can be burned when the Americans leave, thereby keeping Japanese soil sacred. The Council immediately raises him to Governor of Uraga with Manjiro as his assistant. Manjiro is grateful to Kayama for saving him from the death sentence usually given to men who have left and then return to Japan. He tells Kayama that America is a land of equality and liberty. As Manjiro sings of Boston, Kayama idealizes his wife Tamate. Both the city and the woman embody life's glorious journey to Manjiro and Kayama. They reveal these feelings through poems on the way to Kayama's home (Poems—Sc to M Duet).

Manjiro waits for Kayama, who discovers his wife, Tamate, has committed suicide because she was certain her husband would fail the Shogun. Kayama leaves with Manjiro, who doesn't notice Kayama's disguised grief. Manjiro excitedly imagines the great advancements America can bring to Japan.

The scene shifts to a madam and her young girls, who await a boost in business when the sailors arrive. The madam instructs her charges on behavior and hands out "instructional" fans which contain erotic drawings. The young girls are both frightened by the arrival of the "barbarians" and excited at the prospects of a booming business. The madam hopes to satisfy the American sailors so that they will not destroy Uraga (Welcome to Kanagawa—L to F Chorus).

Though no written Japanese record survives of the treaty meeting, the narrator is interrupted by an old man and a warrior who outline their memories of the event (Someone in a Tree—M Duet). The treaty is signed, the Americans leave and the Japanese burn the mats and try to forget the unpleasant incident.

In Act II the Americans have left the village and Abe, a former counselor, is elevated to the position of Shogun by a Bunraku "puppet" emperor. The fact that the emperor is portrayed by a puppet implies his powerlessness and inability to make decisions. In actuality, it is the priests who are running Japan, since they manipulate the emperor. Kayama is raised to the position of Governor of Uraga and Manjiro is elevated to Samurai. The priest talks for the emperor and congratulates the saviors of Japan.

The quiet does not last and soon the British, Dutch, Russians and French join the Americans by sending envoys to make treaty demands (Please, Hello—Small M Chorus).

The peaceful island is soon complete with booming businesses and factories. Kayama as Governor is interested in progress, while Manjiro, now a Samurai, is studying the ancient customs. The next song covers a ten-year time span and shows how Kayama has adapted to Western ways (A Bowler Hat—L to M Solo).

The arrival of the Westerners, who have been relegated to the Yokohama and Nagasaki areas, causes problems. One instance occurs when some British sailors, lonely for companionship, enter a private garden, mistake a young girl for a geisha and attempt to buy her attention (Pretty Lady—M Trio). The girl, terrified, calls her father, who kills one of the sailors and causes an international incident. Abe, now Shogun and interested in pleasing the foreigners, suggests they punish the Samurai who killed the sailor.

As Lord Abe and Kayama are journeying on a road discussing the murder of the sailor, they are attacked by a Samurai and Abe is killed. Kayama recognizes Manjiro and is shocked when he is forced to fight his former friend. Kayama is killed by Manjiro, who seeks to have the puppet emperor Meiji in power and the foreigners expelled.

As Manjiro and the Samurais carry the puppet emperor to victory, the puppet comes to life and announces that the Japanese must become westernized, and sets about to rule; it is the start of the Meiji era. The scene jumps to modern times, and the Japanese, in western dress, comment on their changes. They look to the future (Next—Mixed Chorus).

NOTES ON THE PRODUCTION

Tony Awards: Set and Costume Design. Most of the other awards went to *A Chorus Line*.

The show is more interesting than its short run indicates. In the original production, all the roles were played by men, for the director wanted to stylize the show in the Kabuki manner. This is unnecessary and would normally be detrimental to the quality of any American production because it takes years of training for a male to accurately portray a female in the traditional Japanese theatre. In fact, in America the final product would appear *more* accurate if the female roles were played by females.

The music is challenging and the show worthy of study if the director has some knowledge of Japanese dance, theatre and manners.

The costumes include court brocades, peasant Yukatas, modern costumes, and 1860s period European military. The visual style is maintained through the costumes and they should be accurate and designed for stylized movement.

Sets may be comprised of small pieces or presented on a very large scale, depending on the director's needs and the budget allowed. The acting and the style are more essential in creating the mood than the sets.

SONGS OF SPECIAL INTEREST

"A Bowler Hat," development of character throughout, good for developing Japanese character, baritone.

"Chrysanthemum Tea," clever, strong characterization for the mother. Interesting number for class project, alto.

"Please, Hello," excellent number for class study, various nationality characters, characters important.

Instrumentation: 5 reeds, 2 horns, 2 trumpets, trombone, harp, keyboard-RMI celeste, 2 percussion, viola, cello, bass, shamisen (onstage), Oriental percussion (onstage)
Script: Dodd, Mead
Score: Revelation
Record: RCA
Rights: MTI

PAINT YOUR WAGON

Book and Lyrics: Alan Jay Lerner
Music: Frederick Loewe

ORIGINAL PRODUCTION

Shubert Theatre, November 12, 1951 (289 perf.)
Director: Daniel Mann
Choreographer: Agnes de Mille
Musical Director: Franz Allers
Orchestrations: Ted Royal
Principals: Ben Rumson—James Barton—baritone; Julio—Tony Bavaar—tenor;
Jennifer—Olga San Juan—alto; Elizabeth Woodling—Marijane Maricle—VTI;
Jacob Woodling—Joshua Wheeler—baritone; Steve Bullnack—Rufus Smith—
VTI; Sarah Woodling—Jan Sherwood—VTI
Chorus and Smaller Roles: 6F/8M.

SYNOPSIS

The play is set in 1853 when Californians had gold fever and any speculation of gold caused people to rush to the area of the strike.

One evening, while Ben Rumson is eulogizing at the burial of a dead miner friend, Ben's sixteen-year-old daughter, Jennifer, discovers a piece of gold. Ben quickly finishes his prayer and triumphantly stakes a claim.

On a trail somewhere in California, Steve Bullnack, a handsome young man, decides to head north to Ben Rumson's claim. Other men are on various roads leading to Rumson (I'm on My Way—M Chorus).

The men arrive in the rapidly growing mining camp of Rumson, whose main attraction is Salem's store. The various characters are introduced and sing about their dreams of wealth (Rumson—M Chorus). Jennifer, the only woman in Rumson, wonders why the men avoid her (What's Going on Here?—Sc to F Solo). She doesn't realize they stay away lest they lose control and get themselves in trouble with her father. When Julio Valveras, a young Mexican, arrives outside Salem's store for some foot medicine, Mike and Sandy, two miners, question him about the legend of the lake of gold. He tells them that several of his friends died looking for the gold but later explains to Jennifer that he fears if he finds the gold, the men will jump his claim because he is a Mexican with no rights. Julio confides his dream of learning to read and write (I Talk to the Trees—Sc to M Solo).

The men warn Jennifer to stay away from them, and they try to keep their minds off the wind, which calls through the hills, by telling stories about the women they left behind (They Call the Wind Maria—M Chorus).

In front of Rumson's cabin, the men urge Ben to send Jennifer back East for school, but he hesitates because he will be lonely without her. She urges him to tell her about her mother (I Still See Elisa—Sc to M Solo), whom Jennifer never knew, and Ben decides it is time for Jennifer to get some proper schooling. She tries to talk him out of it because of Julio, but he insists (How Can I Wait?—F Solo).

On a hill near Rumson, Jacob, a Mormon, is seated with Elizabeth and Sarah, his two quarreling wives. The three pray (Trio—2F/1M Trio) for happiness.

Ben declares it is illegal for a man to have two wives and orders Jacob to sell one of them. Ben worries that Elizabeth would mind marrying someone she didn't know, but she figures anyone would be better than her present husband. Ben tells her about himself (In Between—M Solo), and goes out to win the bidding (Whoop Ti Ay—M Chorus). Jennifer hears that Ben is going to marry someone he hardly knows and runs off to find Julio. Julio sensibly convinces her to go to school (Carino Mio—M Solo) and promises they will be together in a year. She says good-bye and leaves for the coach which will take her East.

The men, anxious for female companionship, fervently await the arrival of a group of Fandango girls (There's a Coach Comin' In—M Chorus). Steve tells Julio his claim has dried up, and Julio realizes that all the veins will soon be depleted and the town will go bust. He sadly looks off in Jennifer's direction and wonders if he will see her again.

Act II opens one year later, at the music hall. The men and Fandangos are having a great time (Hand Me Down That Can o' Beans—Mixed Chorus), but the atmosphere quickly changes when the girls realize the men have no cash to spend because the town has dried up.

Mike prods Julio to take him to the frozen lake so he can strike a claim, but Julio refuses, fearing he will be killed if Mike finds gold. He finally realizes that the only way to achieve his dream is to trust Mike and the two set off (Another Autumn—M Solo).

Out at the diggings the men are packing up (Movin'—M Chorus).

Jennifer, who has been gone a year, returns to the cabin in hopes of marrying Julio. She tells Elizabeth that the only reason she left was because Julio wanted her to (All for Him—Sc to F Solo). Ben greets Jennifer with the news that he is moving out to search for new claims and Julio has gone (Wand'rin Star—M Solo). Jennifer resigns herself to patiently wait for Julio's return.

Later that night, Ben, hoping to raise money, goes to Jake's and sells Elizabeth to Jamey the gambler for three thousand dollars. When the two discover she has run off with Crocker, Jamey attempts to get a refund but is laughed away. There is news of another strike forty miles off (Strike!—M Chorus) and the men head out. Jennifer decides to wait for Julio, and Ben discovers he is unable to leave the town named after him.

The following spring, the store is partially boarded and the population has dropped to six. Julio, on his way to Mexico, returns to inquire about Jennifer. He learns she is in town waiting for him and asks Ben how she knew he would come back. Ben responds that everyone needs a dream. When Jennifer enters, Julio is overwhelmed by the change in her. They embrace (Finale—Mixed Chorus).

NOTES ON THE PRODUCTION

The musical stage play bears no resemblance to the movie adaptation, which shouldn't be used to judge the merits of the production. The script in its published form is somewhat slow but the music is exceptionally good. One may want to consider obtaining the rights to perform this show in capsulized version with shortened scenes into the musical numbers. The songs are certainly worthy of presenting and the basic idea of the show is workable. Because of the lack of action, amateur groups may find it difficult to keep the audience interested without judicious editing of the existing script.

The scenes may be combined or trimmed to include Rumson's cabin, Salem's store, Jake's and a street. The chorus may have one costume per actor, but Jennifer and Elizabeth should have at least two.

SONGS OF SPECIAL INTEREST

"I Talk to the Trees," beautiful, lilting melody, ending possibly suited for audition, tenor.

"I Still See Elisa," poignant love song for a character actor who sings about his departed wife. Baritone.

"What's Going on Here?" comic lyrics, situation, make this a humorous song for an alto. Lots of actable specifics, problem song.

Instrumentation: 3 violins, viola, cello, bass, 5 reeds, 3 trumpets, 2 trombones, percussion, guitar/banjo, piano/conductor
Script: Theatre Arts (magazine) 9/52 Chappell (London), Coward-McCann
Score: Chappell
Record: RCA
Rights: TW

THE PAJAMA GAME

Book: George Abbott and Richard Bissell (Based on the book 7½ Cents by Richard Bissell)
Music: Richard Adler and Jerry Ross

ORIGINAL PRODUCTION

St. James Theatre, May 13, 1954 (1,063 perf.)
Directors: George Abbott and Jerome Robbins
Choreographer: Bob Fosse
Musical Director: Hal Hastings
Orchestration: Don Walker
Principals: Hines—Eddie Foy, Jr.—baritone; Sid—John Raitt—baritone; Babe Williams—Janis Paige—mezzo; Prez—Stanley Prager—tenor; Gladys—Carol Haney—alto; Mabel—Reta Shaw—alto; Poopsie—Rae Allen—VTI; Hasler—Ralph Dunn—VTNE; Mae—Thelma Pelish—VTI; Brenda—Marion Colby—VTI; Pop—William David—VTNE
Chorus and Smaller Roles: 8M/8F.

SYNOPSIS

The play opens sometime in the 1950s in a small town in Iowa. Hines, a time-study man, stands in front of the curtain, a composite of pajama fabric swatches, and introduces the audience to the Sleep-Tite pajama factory (The Pajama Game—L to M Solo).

The curtain opens on the interior of the pajama factory where girls are busy sewing, inspecting, and sorting pajamas. As Hines continues to narrate, Prez, the union president, a stocky, glasses-wearing, wise-mouthed individual, tells everyone there will be a strike if the seven and a half cent raise doesn't come through. Mr. Hasler, Hines's boss, enters yelling for everyone to economize and dictates a letter to his secretary, Gladys, to refuse the proposed raise. He orders Hines to keep things going and exits (Racing with the Clock—F Chorus).

The girls break for lunch as Sid Soroken, the ambitious, handsome new superintendent, enters with two belligerent helpers, one of whom he shoves aside for being slow. The helper leaves to complain to the grievance committee and Sid sends the other off. He comments on the atmosphere both in the town and among the workers but is convinced he can overcome the obstacles (A New Town Is a Blue Town—M Solo). Brenda, Mae, and Babe Williams, of the workers' grievance committee, meet Sid, who convinces them that he treats the workers fairly. He tells Babe she is the cutest grievance committee head he has ever encountered and hopes they can discuss matters further.

In a factory hallway, Mae, Brenda, Poopsie, Virginia and Martha encounter Babe and accuse her of being in love with Sid, but she denies any interest (I'm Not at All in Love—Sc to F Solo to F Chorus).

In the superintendent's office, Mabel, Sid's stylishly stout secretary, sits at her desk typing while Poopsie asks Hines if he is going to do his knife-throwing act at the annual company picnic. Hines, noticing Gladys putting a note on Sid's desk, jealously accuses her of playing around. He is ashamed to discover it is only a payroll statement. Mabel tests Hines, who vows he is cured of his jealousy (I'll Never Be Jealous Again—Sc to F/M Duet). Mabel and Hines exit. When Sid hears from Babe that the grievance committee is dropping the workers' complaint, he tries to date her. Doubting the wisdom of becoming involved with someone in management, she refuses. Left alone, he talks to his dictaphone (Hey There—M Solo with His Voice Mechanically Echoed).

On the road to the company picnic, Prez, a married man, makes a play for Gladys (Her Is—Sc to M/F Duet).

At the picnic, denoted by a banner, picnic tables, and beer kegs, Hines is throwing his knives at a practice target. The workers sing the company anthem (Sleep-Tite—Mixed Chorus), and Babe nearly gets herself killed during the inebriated Hines's knife-throwing act. Sid takes Babe aside, kisses her, announces his love and bursts into song. The chorus enters and joins in (Once a Year Day—M Solo to Mixed Chorus).

On the way back from the company picnic, Prez makes a play for the overweight Mae (Her Is [Reprise]—M/F Duet).

Babe, at home in the kitchen, attempts to force Sid to realize that the seven and a half cent proposed raise will cause their relationship problems, but he refuses to listen (Small Talk—Sc to M/F Duet).

At the factory, the girls have noticed Babe's infatuation with Sid and hope she can handle it. Babe and Sid greet each other warmly and Sid tells her how much he loves her (There Once Was a Man—Sc to M/F Duet). The workers, with Babe's knowledge, stage a slowdown (Racing with the Clock [Reprise]— Slower Tempo F Chorus), which is stopped when Sid insists they speed up before he fires everyone. When Babe purposely jams a machine and stops the line, Sid fires her and clears the area until he can fix things. As he begins to work on the machine, he realizes that the problems at work have affected his personal life (Hey There [Reprise]—M Solo).

Act II opens at a union meeting; the members are being entertained with a song and dance by Gladys and two men (Steam Heat—Dance Trio, 2M/1F).

Sid arrives at Babe's to tell her he loves her despite their problems, but she exits into her room, leaving Sid with Pop and his stamp collection. In her bedroom, she tearfully sings (Hey There [Reprise]—F Solo).

Hines, who can't stand to see time wasted, reproaches the girls involved in the factory slowdown. He feels personally attacked and tries to explain his emotions (Think of the Time I Save—M Solo to Chorus).

In Sid's office, Mabel and Sid are greeted by an angry salesman and Hines. It seems the factory workers have only been putting two threads in the buttons, so when the pajama models demonstrate, the pajamas fall off. Sid, who has become suspicious of Hasler's refusal to give the workers their raise, invites Gladys to a dark restaurant to try to obtain the key to the company's ledgers (Hernando's Hideaway—M/F Solo). During the song, the scene switches to Hernando's Chop Suey Restaurant, where it is pitch dark. Matches are lit showing individual patrons.

At the end of the number the lights rise to full. Gladys, on her way to becoming very tipsy, gives Sid the key to Hasler's accounts. A drunken Hines arrives carrying a knife and threatens Gladys, who berates him. Hines slumps in the booth and imagines what life would be like married to her (Jealousy Ballet— Comic Dance Sequence).

The next morning in the office, Sid asks Charlie, Joe, Babe and Prez to keep the union rally going until he gets there. As they exit, Gladys runs on seeking help; it seems Hines is chasing her around with a knife. As she speaks, a knife hits the wall near Sid's head and several others hit near Hasler. Sid overpowers Hines and sends him with Gladys for medical aid. Sid tells Hasler he has discovered that Hasler gave the workers their raise on the books, six months ago, and threatens to expose him unless he comes through with the raise. Hasler agrees.

Meanwhile, on a street near the park, Prez and Babe tell the striking workers that they have figured out the overall profit rate of the proposed raise; the members are thrilled (Seven-and-a-Half Cents—Mixed Chorus). Sid arrives to tell them they can have their raise and the workers run off to celebrate. Babe and Sid deliriously reaffirm their love (There Once Was a Man [Reprise]—M/F Duet).

Hines, as the narrator, invites the audience to a joint union/management party at Hernando's Hideaway, which is decorated for a pajama party. A pajama fashion show curtain call is performed (Finale—Mixed Chorus).

NOTES ON THE PRODUCTION

Tonys: Featured Actress (Carol Haney), Best Musical, Producers, Book, Music, and Choreography.

The show is enjoyable and well suited for school groups and communities as there are a variety of characterization opportunities and well-known songs. The production is easily costumed but not readily updated due to the "Seven and a Half Cents" lyric requirement which allows for $1,705.48 to buy a foreign car, and $3,411 to be real wealth. There are various dialogue sections which refer to wages of eighty cents an hour.

The part of Gladys requires an excellent dancer/comedienne while the roles of Prez, Hines, Mabel, and Mae demand comedic character actors who move well. The "Steam Heat" number requires two excellent male jazz dancers and the leading players, Babe and Sid, need dynamism and powerful voices.

The sets may be trimmed and the "Pajama Sampler" drop used to replace certain of the In One scenes or used as a background throughout with set pieces placed to establish definite location.

All in all, it is a fun show worthy of more productions.

SONGS OF SPECIAL INTEREST

"I'll Never Be Jealous Again," comic, soft shoe, lots of actable specifics, good for focus work. Alto/baritone.

"I'm Not at All in Love," vocally strong alto, shows off voice, suitable for revue or beginning choreographer.

"Small Talk," alto/baritone male romantic duet, class study.

"Steam Heat," 1F/2M classic dance number, works well for revue or dance concert.

Instrumentation: 5 reeds, 3 trumpets, 3 trombones, 4 violins, viola, cello, bass, guitar, percussion, piano
Script: Theatre Arts (magazine) 9/55, Random
Score: Frank
Record: Columbia
Rights: MTI

PAL JOEY

Book: John O'Hara
Music: Richard Rodgers
Lyrics: Lorenz Hart

ORIGINAL PRODUCTION

Ethel Barrymore Theatre, December 25, 1940 (374 perf.)

REVIVAL PRODUCTION

Broadhurst Theatre, January 3, 1952 (542 perf.)
Director: David Alexander and Robert Alton
Choreographer: Robert Alton
Musical Director: Max Meth
Orchestration: Don Walker and Hans Spialek
Principals: Joey—Harold Lang—baritone; Gladys—Helen Gallagher—mezzo/
alto; Vera Simpson—Vivienne Segal—soprano; Melba—Elaine Stritch—alto;
Linda—Patricia Northrop—soprano
Chorus and Smaller Roles: 8M/8F minimum.

SYNOPSIS

The show is set in Chicago, late thirties. At a cheap nightclub, Joey is auditioning for an MC/singer job (Chicago—M Solo). Joey is a smooth talker in
his early thirties who loves to exaggerate his talents and personal accomplish-
ments. Through his convincing conversation with Mike, the nightclub owner,
he manages to get himself hired for a week's engagement. Joey meets the girl
dancers and immediately tries to charm them, but his charm tactics lead him
nowhere. He rehearses with the girls (You Mustn't Kick It Around—L to M
Solo).

Later that evening Joey notices Linda English talking to a small dog in a pet
store window. He engages her in conversation by fabricating incredible tales of
a wealthy upbringing and a sudden loss of finances. She is touched that he
confided in her and Joey thanks her for inspiring him (I Could Write a Book—
Sc to M/F Duet).

In the nightclub while the girls are performing (Chicago—F Chorus), Mrs.
Vera Simpson, a very wealthy married woman, enters with some friends and
beckons Joey to her table. His rudeness, which both intrigues and irritates her,
causes her to leave. Mike, the owner, fires him, but Joey persuades Mike to
wait for two days—he is convinced Vera will be back. Gladys and the girls
perform the next song (That Terrific Rainbow—F Solo to F Chorus).

Joey calls Vera, accuses her of getting him fired, tells her to go to hell and
hangs up. His behavior interests her (What Is a Man?—F Solo). She appears at

the club at closing time and, warning him not to cross her, tells him to get his hat and coat. He goes to get his things and tells the dancers he is only temporarily out of circulation (Happy Hunting Horn—M Solo).

Vera picks out fabric in a tailor shop for Joey's custom-made suits and admits to herself that she is in love with him (Bewitched, Bothered and Bewildered—F Solo). When she discovers that Joey cares for Linda English, who is employed at the shop, she jealously causes Linda to believe she is Joey's second wife. Linda, shocked to hear that Joey is married, angrily tells him off, but Joey is unmoved (Pal Joey—M Solo).

In Act II Vera backs Joey in a nightclub venture and hires Mike and the girls to spruce the place up. The group rehearses as Louis, the tenor, sings (The Flower Garden of My Heart—Mixed Chorus). Melba Snyder, a famous newspaper reporter, comes to the club to interview Joey. She realizes the stories of his background are all lies and tells him her best interview was with Gypsy Rose Lee. She proceeds to describe the classy stripper's dialogue (Zip—F Solo).

A man named Ludlow Lowell comes into the club and makes Joey a proposition: he will be Joey's agent and guarantee Joey $50,000 a year if Joey signs a contract. Joey signs without reading it, and Gladys cosigns as a witness. Joey agrees to send his paychecks directly to Lowell for deposit into a special account, not realizing he is being set up. A rehearsal number with Gladys and the ensemble begins (Plant You Now, Dig You Later—F Solo to Mixed Chorus).

Later that evening, in Joey's apartment which Vera is paying for, Joey reads the opening night reviews and is upset that he wasn't highlighted. Vera reassures him (In Our Little Den of Iniquity—Sc to M/F Duet).

Linda, waiting at the club to deliver a package for Joey, overhears Gladys and Lowell (who are boyfriend and girlfriend) talking about their plan to blackmail Vera through Joey. Linda leaves and Gladys goes to rehearse a number that Mike has created (Chicago Morocco—M Solo).

When Linda phones Joey to warn him that Gladys and her boyfriend, Lowell, are planning on blackmailing Vera, Vera insists on talking to Linda in the apartment. Joey attempts to assure her that he hasn't seen Linda, but Vera is skeptical because Joey is such a liar. She accuses him of doing everything the hard way. He comments on her suspicions (Do It the Hard Way—M Solo). After Vera hears Linda's story, she questions why Linda is so concerned about someone she hasn't been involved with and urges Linda to take Joey (Take Him—Sc to F Duet). Linda replies that Vera should keep Joey for she isn't interested.

Lowell and Gladys enter to get $20,000 in exchange for not revealing Joey and Vera's affair to Mr. Simpson. Vera isn't upset, for she is friends with police commissioner Jack O'Brien, who arrives to escort Lowell and Gladys out of town. When Vera informs Joey their affair is over and closes his bank account, Joey orders her to leave his apartment.

Linda finds Joey in front of the pet store—apparently Vera sent her. He rejects her offer of supper and tells her he is leaving for New York. She realizes he can't get involved in a meaningful relationship and they exit in opposite directions.

NOTES ON THE PRODUCTION

The original show, which starred Gene Kelly, was short-lived, primarily due to the subject matter and the antihero quality of Joey. It opened to mixed reviews and wasn't popular among prewar audiences who wanted more lighthearted musicals. The revival in 1952 was warmly received and won the following Tony Awards: Musical Direction, Choreography and Featured Actress (Helen Gallagher).

The show is not expensive to mount as most of the action takes place in two nightclubs; the first in Mike's lower-class club and the second in Chez Joey, which may be an upgraded version of Mike's. Secondary sets are the pet shop exterior, a phone booth, a tailor shop, and Vera's boudoir, which could consist of a phone table and an elegant side chair tightly lit. Special attention must be given to Joey's apartment for several scenes and songs take place there. If offstage storage space is a problem for wagon use, it may be possible to have a section of the nightclub revolve to be the apartment.

The play was originally set in the thirties but may be upgraded if costumes of that period are a problem. There are quite a few nightclub show costumes for the chorus girls and Vera must be opulently dressed in a new outfit per scene. Tuxedos for the men are a requirement for the Chez Joey sequences.

The tempos on the Harold Lang record seem slow for a modern-day audience and may have to be brighter to hold the musical and dramatic interest. The music is popular and much of it is well-known. Those familiar with the movie will realize that the songs in the club were more familiar Rodgers and Hart melodies than those originally written for the stage play. Companies may want to consider writing for permission to use more familiar songs in order to maintain audience enthusiasm.

Vera, played by Vivienne Segal in the original and the revival, is a soprano role, which is unusual by modern standards. Most of the modern-day, older "leading-lady sophisticate" shows seem to be written for altos. In light of this, companies considering a production may want to cast someone who can sing the part down, or in cases of a smaller orchestra, rewrite the role for the lower range.

The show is worthy of more productions and is a quality vehicle for companies that have women who need good roles. It is an appealing university show, for the parts are challenging and require good acting. The role of Joey, a despicable character originated by Gene Kelly, is difficult to portray. He must be a charming rogue who can appeal to women of all ages, yet be talented enough to act as a mediocre singer/dancer. Vera is a perfect counterpoint to Joey, but their scenes must be tightly directed to be believable.

SONGS OF SPECIAL INTEREST

"Bewitched," although written for a soprano, seems more to fit the older woman alto voice, good for character study.

"I Could Write a Book," romantic duet, lovely melody, charm song.

"Take Him," F duet, two sopranos; Vera's part could be sung down for more variety. Tempo may need to be faster than record for modern-day interest. Good situation and scene into song for class study.

"That Terrific Rainbow," alto, up tempo, large volumed, club style.

Instrumentation: 5 reeds, horn, 3 trumpets, trombone, percussion, 3 violins, cello, bass, piano/conductor
Script: Random House, Popular Library
Score: Chappell
Record: Columbia
Rights: R & H

PIPPIN

Book: Roger O. Hirson
Music and Lyrics: Stephen Schwartz

ORIGINAL PRODUCTION

Imperial Theatre, October 23, 1972 (1,944 perf.)
Director and Choreographer: Bob Fosse
Musical Director: Stanley LeBowsky
Orchestration: Ralph Burns
Principals: Leading Player—Ben Vereen—tenor; Pippin—John Rubenstein—tenor; Charles—Eric Berry—baritone; Lewis—Christopher Chadman—baritone; Fastrada—Leland Palmer—mezzo; Berthe—Irene Ryan—alto; Catherine—Jill Clayburgh—mezzo; Theo—Shane Nickerson—VTI
Chorus and Smaller Roles: 5M/5F.

SYNOPSIS

The show opens with the Leading Player and his "Players" informing the audience of the action that will occur (Magic to Do—M Solo and Mixed Chorus). The Leading Player tells the audience that the subject of their tale is the story of Pippin, son of Charlemagne, and sets up the play within a play effect.

Pippin appears on the scene promising not to waste his life in ordinary tasks (Corner of the Sky—M Solo).

The Leading Player magically transforms the scene to the royal court of Charles the Great. Pippin arrives home from his studies in Padua and converses with his father about power. The Leading Player introduces Lewis, Pippin's half-brother, whose pumped-up ego matches his physique. Lewis boasts of his magnificent war record and vows to slaughter even more Visigoths, who will soon be at war with Charlemagne's Holy Roman Empire. Fastrada, Pippin's devious step-mother, is next to welcome Pippin home. Her one ambition is to see her son,

Lewis, in control of the throne. After Fastrada criticizes Pippin's posture, she and Lewis depart, leaving Charles alone again with his son. The welcoming talk between father and son is awkward and leaves Pippin unsatisfied (Welcome Home—Sc to M Duet). Charlemagne's words confuse Pippin, who is left with the feeling that life has no direction.

When he sees the country preparing for war, Pippin asks his father if he can join in the battle. Charles agrees.

In a tent near the battlefield Charles lectures his army on the science of war (War Is a Science—M Solo and Mixed Chorus). The inexperienced Pippin constantly interrupts his father in his enthusiasm to learn. Annoyed and worried at Pippin's inexperience, Charles views his son disapprovingly, but Pippin assures him he will do well.

As Lewis, Pippin and Charlemagne, along with the soldiers, leave to wage war, the Leading Player enters and sings of the glory of war as various battle scenes are acted out (Glory—M Solo and Mixed Chorus). Glory becomes grotesque as limbs and bodies litter the stage and Pippin reflects upon the necessity of war. Finding a severed head, he converses with it and realizes that war is not what he is searching for.

The Leading Player comments on Pippin's life as the set changes to the country (Simple Joys—M Solo). Pippin visits Berthe, his spry grandmother, who is surrounded by four young male admirers. She advises Pippin to get fresh air, home cooking and some fun with women (No Time at All—F Solo and M Chorus). Pippin temporarily occupies himself with several girls (With You—M Solo to Mixed Chorus Dance). He finds sex unfulfilling and turns to politics.

The Leading Player mischievously manipulates Pippin into starting a revolution. Pippin's action immensely pleases Fastrada, who has plans for her son Lewis to gain the throne; she sings of her philosophy to Lewis (Spread a Little Sunshine—Sc to F Solo; Lewis Needed for Staging).

Fastrada informs Charles of Pippin's disloyalty and suggests that Charles go to church to pray. She later informs Pippin, and Pippin, disguised as a priest, confronts Charles at a church in Arles. When Pippin accuses Charlemagne of slaughtering peasants, Charlemagne, recognizing his son, explains it is necessary to shed blood to preserve order. Pippin stabs his father and becomes King (Morning Glow—Mixed Chorus).

The Act II curtain opens on the same scene that closed Act I (Morning Glow [Reprise]—Mixed Chorus). The Players congratulate the new king, Pippin, who gives land to the peasants, abolishes taxes, and dissolves his army. This idealistic government, however, is short-lived; upon hearing of an attack on his country, Pippin remobilizes his army and taxes the lords. The lords take the land away from the peasants in order to have tax money, and Pippin's reign collapses. He then begs Charlemagne to take back the crown. Surprisingly, with a little magic, Charles comes to life and Pippin apologizes to his father.

The discouraged Pippin still longs for meaning in his life and the Leading Player tells him he is headed in the right direction (On the Right Track—Sc to

M Duet). Ironically, as the Leading Player gets more and more encouraging, Pippin sinks deeper and deeper into despair. His disillusionment causes him to collapse in a heap, where he is found by Catherine, a wealthy widow, and her small son Theo, who has a pet duck.

As an act of charity, Catherine nurses Pippin back to health. When he is well enough, she introduces herself as an ordinary but terrific girl (Kind of Woman—L to F Solo with F Choral Backup). Catherine convinces Pippin to stay and work on her estate but he soon tires of manual labor and feels there is something more (Extraordinary—M Solo). He is preparing to leave when Theo's pet duck gets sick. Pippin prays for the animal (Prayer for a Duck—M Solo) in vain, for the duck dies. Theo is heartbroken, and Pippin goes to extremes to raise the boy's spirits. Catherine is pleased to see him trying so hard and the two fall in love (Love Song—M/F Duet). The love spell is soon broken when Pippin realizes how ordinary his life has become and he decides to leave. Catherine quietly comments on his idiosyncrasies (I Guess I'll Miss the Man—F Solo).

Pippin greets the Leading Player, who invites Pippin to join in the finale, a magic trick of fire that will supposedly give Pippin glory with a flash. The other players rush on the set with a fire box and try to lure him to achieve his final perfection (Finale—Mixed Chorus). Mesmerized by the chanting and the trickery, Pippin is almost conned into obeying their will, but he realizes that he does not want this grand finale. He concludes that he must have ties to give meaning to his life. At this point, Catherine and Theo appear and the three stand together, hand in hand. The players leave in disgust as Pippin sings happily without music, stage lights or elaborate costumes.

NOTES ON THE PRODUCTION

Tonys: Best Actor—Ben Vereen, Director—Bob Fosse, Choreography, Lighting and Scenic Design.

The musical, performed in the commedia style, was imagintively directed and choreographed by Bob Fosse and deftly performed by the talented Ben Vereen.

Because the success of this show relies so heavily on the talents of the Leading Player, companies may want to consider dividing the Leading Player part into two characters. This division allows for more musical variety and staging, as it leaves room for trios and duets in a show that is solo heavy.

The production may be as sparse or elaborate as a company can afford because it requires few sets and only one costume per player with add-on pieces. Because of minimal set requirements—an opening curtain, a drop or cutout section for the church, a bed that doubles as a tree or table, a war map and a fire box—it is necessary to have extremely tight lighting and elaborate props for the special effects. The show is supposed to be highly theatrical in tone and needs to have a consistent "look" in order for the audience to remain caught up in the performing style.

It is a crowd pleaser and fun for the performers, who must all sing and dance competently. Plan on extra weeks of rehearsal with the choreographer, for there are a lot of dance numbers. In the show's original form, a few of the more sensually oriented numbers become overly uncomfortable for some audience members. It is possible to style this production for more of a family tone, if desired, without losing the music, story or result.

SONGS OF SPECIAL INTEREST

"Corner of the Sky," tenor, introspective, searching, can use movement.

"I Guess I'll Miss the Man," pleasant ballad for mezzo/alto, lyrics allow for sensitive acting performance, possible audition piece.

"Magic to Do," small chorus, good for revue opening.

"No Time at All," alto character solo, especially when tempo is slowed so lyrics are more easily understood, adaptable to one-woman show on aging.

"On the Right Track," solid, movement-oriented, male tenor/high baritone duet, up tempo, showcase and class use.

Instrumentation: 8 reeds, horn, trumpet, trombone, guitar, violin, viola, cello, harp, harpsichord, organ, percussion, drums, electric bass
Script: Bard, DBS
Selections: Jobete
Record: Motown
Rights: MTI

PLAIN AND FANCY

Book: Joseph Stein and Will Glickman
Music: Albert Hague
Lyrics: Arnold B. Horwitt

ORIGINAL PRODUCTION

Winter Garden Theatre, January 27, 1955 (461 perf.)
Director: Morton Da Costa
Dances and Musical Numbers: Helen Tamiris
Musical Director: Franz Allers
Orchestration: Philip J. Lang
Principals: Ruth Winters—Shirl Conway—alto; Emma Miller—Nancy Andrews—alto; Dan King—Richard Derr—baritone; Peter—David Daniels—tenor; Katie Yoder—Gloria Marlowe—soprano; Papa Yoder—Stefan Schnabel—baritone; Ezra Reber—Douglas Fletcher Rodgers—baritone; Hilda Miller—Barbara Cook—soprano
Chorus and Smaller Roles: 12M/12F/2F children minimum.

SYNOPSIS

Dan King, a worldly New Yorker whose grandfather has left him a farm in the Amish country of Pennsylvania, travels with his girlfriend Ruth Winters to inspect the area. The two become totally confused by the road signs that lead to Bird-in-Hand and inquire at a local gas station for directions (You Can't Miss It—M/F Duet to Mixed Chorus).

Papa Yoder and his daughter Katie, returning from Lancaster, pass their Amish neighbors working in the fields. Katie, who is to be married in two days, marvels at the beauty of the countryside (It Wonders Me—Sc to F Solo to Mixed Chorus). As Papa Yoder and Katie exit, Dan and Ruth enter still looking for the Yoder farm. Dan receives more directions and he and Ruth wearily walk off.

In the Yoder yard, everyone is preparing for the coming wedding and commenting on the bountiful crops that grow on their lands (Plenty of Pennsylvania—Mixed Chorus). Dan and Ruth are greeted by Hilda, an attractive, easily impressed girl, who takes them to meet her Uncle Jacob Yoder.

Peter, a headstrong Amish boy in love with Katie since childhood, has been sent to his aunt's for fighting. When he hears about Katie's impending marriage to his brother Ezra, he returns to tell her he still loves her (Young and Foolish—Sc to M Solo). Katie, who still loves Peter, is afraid to get involved and runs off.

Ruth and Dan are invited into the parlor, introduced to the family members and asked to stay in the house until Dan's farm can be sold. They are escorted to their rooms. When the men ask Ezra how he feels about Katie, he tells them his only interest is in marrying someone attractive, who can cook and raise children (Why Not Katie?—Sc to M Chorus).

Dan finds Katie outside the house and asks her for directions to his farm. She volunteers to take him.

The scene shifts to show the outside of Dan's barn where Peter is painting a bluebird for Katie. Dan leaves, realizing the two need to be alone. Katie promises to convince her father that she should marry Peter (Young and Foolish [Reprise]—Sc to F/M Duet to Mixed Dance Chorus).

Ruth, whose bedroom is far from Dan's, realizes she isn't adjusting well to life without drinking, smoking or indoor plumbing. She sings about the stupidity of her affair with Dan (It's a Helluva Way to Run a Love Affair—F Solo). Hilda, curious to know more about Dan, enters to talk to Ruth. When Ruth goes to wash up in the kitchen, Dan enters and asks Hilda about Peter and Katie. Hilda, infatuated with Dan, assumes when he gives her a brotherly kiss that they are in love (This Is All Very New to Me—Sc to F Solo to F Quartet). As she sings the scene shifts to the Yoder yard and a trio of girls sing with her.

The guests are arriving for tomorrow's wedding. Dan discovers that Mr. Yoder wants to buy Dan's grandfather's farm as a wedding present for Katie and Ezra. He tells Mr. Yoder that since Katie loves Peter, it is wrong to force her to marry

Ezra. Yoder angrily responds that it is the Amish way (Plain We Live—M Solo with M Chorus).

Dan is approached by Peter, who wants to buy the farm, but Ezra interrupts and needles Peter into fighting. Peter is blamed for starting the fight and is shunned by the community when lighting strikes Dan's barn. Papa Yoder is convinced that Peter's hex sign on the barn was meant to bring disaster to Ezra and Katie. The act ends with Peter alone onstage.

As the curtain rises on Act II, the Amish build a new barn, demonstrating the swift results of community effort (How Do You Raise a Barn?—Mixed Chorus). After everyone leaves, Peter arrives to tell Katie he is leaving the community and privately begs her to go with him (Follow Your Heart—Sc to M Solo). She runs to Hilda, who agrees with Peter that Katie would be happier marrying for love (Follow Your Heart [Reprise]—F Duet).

Meanwhile, in the Yoder kitchen, Ruth, determined to manipulate Dan into marriage by learning how to cook his favorite dishes, gives up in confusion. Emma and the girls comment on the difference between city girls and country girls (City Mouse, Country Mouse—F Solo to Small F Chorus).

Hilda, finding Dan alone on the porch, begins to talk about marriage. Dan gently attempts to tell her she must marry someone from the same background, not a city person. She is brokenhearted and rushes off crying.

Ezra helps Ruth unlock her hatbox, where she keeps her liquor supply, and begins drinking. In a matter of seconds he is totally drunk. Hilda is appalled to discover a very drunk Ezra in Ruth's bedroom. Ezra decides to go to the carnival in Lancaster and see some girlie shows. Ruth follows him out as Hilda decides Lancaster is a good place to become citified. In a humorous song, she dresses in Ruth's clothes and attempts to look like a woman of the world (I'll Show Him!—Sc to F Solo).

In front of a landscape traveler, Ruth finds Peter and tells him about Ezra. Peter agrees to bring his brother home before he shames the family and Katie.

At the fair, various midway shows are on view (Scranton Sally—F Chorus and Dance). Hilda and Ezra get their fill of city ways when they get involved in a fight with Mambo Joe and a sailor. Peter overcomes Mambo Joe, who has a knife at Ezra's throat, and Hilda escapes for home.

Meanwhile, outside the Yoder kitchen, Ruth has just finished making one of Dan's favorite Amish dishes. Dan, realizing at last that she has always worked to please him, admits he loves her and wants to marry her. Hilda tells Dan and Ruth about the carnival and her future plan to marry an Amish boy. They urge her to choose wisely (Take Your Time and Take Your Pick—Sc to 2F/M Trio).

Early the next morning, a drunken Ezra enters and Papa Yoder refuses to let Katie marry a drunk. When Peter arrives escorted by a policeman who arrested him for fighting at the carnival, Papa Yoder discovers that Peter fought to save his brother from shame. Peter, now owner of Dan's farm, asks permission to marry Katie. Papa Yoder agrees and the wedding procession begins (Finale—Mixed Chorus).

NOTES ON THE PRODUCTION

The show is an enjoyable one that relies on character contrasts for much of its humor. There are quite a few good parts for women, especially the roles of Ruth, Hilda, Katie, and Emma. The dance requirements are minimal although the barn-raising sequence in the second act relies heavily on a clever set designer. It is a show worth examining and an excellent choice for high schools searching for something charming and unusual.

The original production had a great many sets, but these are easily combined to simplify the scenic costs. The major sets necessary for the production are the Yoder yard with the porch of the house, a section of the road, the barnyard of Dan's farm, Ruth's bedroom, kitchen of the Yoder house, the carnival. If backstage space is limited, the kitchen scene could be moved to the yard area, if there is an area for outside cooking. For those wanting to minimize set movement, it would be possible to angle the Yoder house, stage right, and have a section of it revolve to be Ruth's room, and later a section of the kitchen. In this manner the barn could move on from stage left and be delineated as a separate farm by lighting. The parlor scenes could all be played on the porch area.

The costumes, except for Ruth's, may be the same throughout.

SONGS OF SPECIAL INTEREST

"City Mouse, Country Mouse," class potential, small F chorus, comic lyrics, good for beginning director.

"I'll Show Him!," comic, determined, soprano, needs props to work in class situation, ending good for audition as it shows range and isn't overdone.

"It Wonders Me," F soprano, shows off range, possible for audition ballad.

"It's a Helluva Way to Run a Love Affair," alto, comic, lots of specifics, problem number.

"This Is All Very New to Me," possible audition for soprano, up tempo, movement potential, abandon, shows off voice.

"Take Your Time and Take Your Pick," alto, soprano, baritone trio, up tempo, good exercise for beginning director.

Instrumentation: 5 reeds, 3 trumpets, horn, 2 trombones, percussion, 4 violins, viola, cello, bass, harp, piano/conductor
Script: Random, Theatre arts (magazine) 7/56, SF
Score: Chappell
Record: Capitol
Rights: SF

PORGY AND BESS

Book: Dubose Heyward (Based on the play *Porgy* by Dorothy and Dubose Heyward)
Music: George Gershwin
Lyrics: Dubose Heyward and Ira Gershwin

ORIGINAL PRODUCTION

Alvin Theatre, October 10, 1935 (124 perf.)
Director: Rouben Mamoulian
Musical Director: Alexander Smallens
Choral Director: Eva Jessye
Orchestration: George Gershwin
Principals: Sportin' Life—John W. Bubbles—tenor; Crown—Warren Cole-
man—bass; Porgy—Todd Duncan—baritone; Serena—Ruby Elzy—alto; Bess—
Anne Brown—soprano; Clara—Abbie Mitchell—soprano
Chorus and Smaller Roles: 20M/16F necessary for vocal quality.

SYNOPSIS

In Catfish Row, a waterfront ghetto in Charleston, South Carolina, Clara, a young mother, is soothing her baby with a lullaby (Summertime—F Solo). The men are shooting craps on a nearby stoop and Serena is in a window above urging her man Robbins not to join the game.

The crapshooters, discussing their day's work, are caught up in the game when Jake takes the baby from Clara and sings (A Woman Is a Sometime Thing—M Solo to M Quartet). At the end of the song Clara takes the baby inside as one of the men opens the outside gate for the crippled Porgy, who enters on his goat cart to join the game. The men begin to get serious about their gambling but are warned to wait for Crown, the bad-tempered bully of the area. The drunken Crown and Bess arrive as the women, led by Serena, negatively comment to each other about Bess's wanton ways. Crown tells Sportin' Life, the area pusher-pimp, to give him some "happy dust" to sober him up. The game begins in earnest but Crown, who is losing, gets nasty and kills Robbins with a cotton cutting hook (Crap Game Fugue—M Chorus). Serena screams and catches the dying man in her arms as Bess urges Crown to escape. A police siren is heard and everyone but Sportin' Life rushes into hiding. He cleverly promises to hide Bess if she will accompany him to New York, but she isn't ready to let any man pimp for her and refuses his offer. She runs to various doors along the row, but Porgy's door is the only one that opens.

The police have come and gone and the chanting of a funeral procession is heard as the lights rise (Gone, Gone, Gone—Mixed Chorus). Porgy leads the people of the Row in a money-raising rhythmic gospel song (Overflow—Mixed Chorus). A White detective arrives and questions everyone about the murder but no one has anything to say. He takes old Peter as a witness, promising to return him when Crown is captured. The people comment on injustice as Serena, the widow, reveals how empty her life is without Robbins (My Man's Gone Now—F Solo to Mixed Chorus).

The undertaker agrees to bury the body on credit and Bess leads the mourners in a song of inspiration (Leavin' fo' de Promis' Lan'—F Solo and Mixed Chorus).

The next morning, as the fishermen prepare their nets for the day's catch (It Takes a Long Pull to Get There—M Chorus), Porgy examines the working men and just laughs because he is content with having nothing (I Got Plenty O' Nuttin'—M Solo to Mixed Chorus).

Porgy, deeply in love with Bess, who has been living with him since Crown's escape, observes Sportin' Life trying to lure her back to her cocaine habit and warns him to keep away. Porgy urges Bess to join the women on the picnic and attempts to boost her spirits (Bess, You Is My Woman Now—Sc to M/F Duet). The women stop by to urge Bess to join them, for they notice how she has changed since living with Porgy. Sportin' Life leads the group to the picnic (Oh, I Can't Sit Down—Mixed Chorus) and Bess joins in.

In Act II, on Kittiwah Island, there is spontaneous gaiety as Sportin' Life sings to the group (I Ain't Got No Shame—M Solo to Mixed Chorus). When Maria and Annie accuse him of Sodom and Gomorrah behavior, he responds by telling them not to believe everything the Bible tells them (It Ain't Necessarily So—M Solo).

The boat whistle sounds and everyone starts for shore. Bess is secretly grabbed by Crown, who keeps her from leaving. She tries to discourage him (What You Want with Bess?—Sc to M/F Duet), but he keeps her with him, telling her that no cripple is ever going to take Crown's woman.

One week later, Bess, who has been out of her mind with delirium since her return from the island, begins screaming. Porgy, who is afraid she may be dying, urges Serena, who has great healing powers, to help the woman he loves. Serena comes to pray for Bess (Time and Time Again—Sc to M/F Duet and Mixed Chorus) and promises Porgy she will be cured by five o'clock. As Porgy waits, the street vendors peddle their wares (Street Cries—F Solo/M Solo). At five o'clock, Bess recovers and implores Porgy to save her from Crown (I Loves You, Porgy—Sc to M/F Duet).

A hurricane breaks out and the residents gather to pray in Serena's room (Oh, De Lawd Shake de Heaven—Mixed Chorus). Crown breaks in and mocks God as the people beg the Lord to strike him down (A Red-Headed Woman—M Solo to Mixed Chorus). The storm stops, and Clara runs to the window and spies her husband Jake's overturned boat. Leaving her baby with Bess, Clara runs out in the storm to find her fisherman husband. She is followed by Crown, who promises to bring her back, but he fails and Clara is lost to the sea.

Act III opens later that same night as the people pray for the dead Clara and Jake (Clara, Don't You Be Downhearted—Mixed Chorus), Porgy sits at his window waiting for Crown to return. Sportin' Life, who waits in the shadow, tells Maria who wants to know why he is hanging around, that he is waiting for Bess. He knows that Bess is soon going to be ready to go with him, for one of her men will be killed and the other jailed. As he waits in the shadows he sees Crown enter Porgy's room with a knife. The fight ends in the street as Crown is killed with his own knife. As Bess leads Porgy inside the men come to remove Crown's body.

The next morning the police choose Porgy to identify Crown's body. He is terrified because Sportin' Life has convinced him that the police will know he killed Crown when the dead man's wounds begin to bleed. Porgy is forcibly taken off.

Sportin' Life slyly tells Bess that Porgy will be in jail for at least two years and offers her some happy dust. He enticingly sings (There's a Boat Dat's Leavin' Soon for New York—M Solo) and offers to set her up as a highly paid prostitute. She agrees and goes off with him.

Porgy comes back a week later with presents for his friends and Bess but realizes that something is wrong (Buzzard—M Solo). He inquires as to Bess's whereabouts (Where's My Bess?—M Solo) and is told she has gone back to happy dust and to New York with Sportin' Life. Although everyone urges him to forget her, Porgy asks where New York is and prepares to follow (I'm on My Way—M Solo). Everyone waves good-bye.

NOTES ON THE PRODUCTION

The first New York production of *Porgy and Bess* was performed during the depression, a period when people wanted escapism, not drama, in theatrical entertainment; hence, a limited run for this Gershwin masterpiece. On October 10, 1935, after an international tour, *Porgy and Bess* had a nine-month New York run. The show had Cab Calloway and Leontyne Price as the leads. In 1942, Cheryl Crawford revived the now musically familiar opera, which was warmly received and widely toured.

The Gershwin estate, seeking to maintain the quality of this classic, maintains licensing control and usually only allows performance rights to professional companies. Anyone considering a production should write for permission before announcing their theatrical season.

The music is vocally demanding and requires superb singer/actors. The lines, somewhat simplistic, can seem almost racist if not properly handled. The answer to Porgy's question, that "New York is up North, beyond the courthouse," may seem ridiculous if the tone of the entire production hasn't established the period, mood and style of the piece.

The costumes represent a poor but proud 1935 Black community and include everyday wear and Sunday best. There is no specialized choreography; the large numbers are more gospel in style and require simple movement. Sportin' Life is traditionally played by a performer who moves well and dances soft shoe.

The sets should be "practical" for they must hold a large company. The exterior of the Catfish Row buildings contain windows with operable shutters and should have entrances at a variety of levels to create visual interest. Serena's room, where everyone waits out the storm, is often constructed by a wall that folds back to show the interior. The island sequences can be a drop in front of Catfish Row.

Lighting must re-create a hurricane and be able to properly enhance the dramatic highlights.

Porgy and Bess is a classic that should be performed more often. It is worth trying to obtain the rights.

SONGS OF SPECIAL INTEREST

"Bess, You Is My Woman Now," heartrending baritone/soprano duet, happy, exciting and dramatic, excellent for showcase and class.

"Summertime," shows incredible range and control, good for audition if soprano can effectively sing it.

"There's a Boat Dat's Leavin' Soon for New York," character-oriented, good for class study, tenor.

"It Ain't Necessarily So," good for revue, shows character, movement-oriented, solo section may be done for audition, tenor.

"I Got Plenty o' Nuttin'," up tempo, shows range, happy mood, possible club, baritone.

Instrumentation: 5 reeds, 2 trumpets, 2 trombones, 3 violins, viola, cello, bass, percussion, piano/conductor
Script: Ten Great Musicals of the American Theatre
Score: Chappell
Record: Odyssey, RCA
Rights: TW

PROMISES, PROMISES

Book: Neil Simon (Based on the screenplay *The Apartment*, by Billy Wilder and I.A.L. Diamond)
Music: Burt Bachrach
Lyrics: Hal David

ORIGINAL PRODUCTION

Shubert Theatre, December 1, 1968 (1,281 perf.)
Director: Robert Moore
Musical Numbers Staged by: Michael Bennett
Musical Director: Harold Wheeler
Orchestration: Jonathan Tunick
Principals: Chuck—Jerry Orbach—baritone; Eichelberger—Vince O'Brien—VTI; Vivien—Donna McKechnie—VTI; Fran—Jill O'Hara—alto; Sheldrake—Edward Winter—baritone; Miss Polansky—Margo Sappington—VTI; Marge—Marian Mercer—alto; Miss Wong—Baayork Lee—VTI; Mr. Dobitch—Paul Reed—VTI; Dr. Dreyfuss—A. Larry Haines—baritone; Kirkeby—Norman Shelly—VTI; Peggy Olson—Millie Slavin—VTNE
Chorus and Smaller Roles: 4M/4F is an ideal minimum but some dinner theatres with small stages have negated the chorus and utilized the principals in choral sections.

SYNOPSIS

In his office at Consolidated Life, an insurance company, Chuck Baxter, a rather nondescript but likable young man, is telling the audience about his lifelong problem of not being noticed. He yearns to figure out what is wrong (Half as Big as Life—L to M Solo).

On his way home he stops at an East Side bar, where he meets Mr. Dobitch, an executive at his office. Dobitch, on the pretext of helping a woman recover from a sudden illness, convinces Chuck to loan him his apartment for about an hour. Before long he is loaning out his apartment on Tuesday nights to Mr. Dobitch, on Wednesday nights to Mr. Kirkeby, and on Thursday nights to Mr. Eichelberger. All are executives who promise him advancement.

Outside the apartment, waiting for the last executive to leave, Chuck explains his predicament (Upstairs—L to M Solo). He is unexpectedly visited by Vanderhoff, another executive, who promises him a promotion in exchange for using the apartment for one night. Chuck is forced to stand out in the rain until his apartment is free. His neighbor, a friendly doctor, hears the nightly noises from Chuck's apartment and warns him to slow down.

The next morning, Chuck, who has a horrible head cold and temperature, waits in the company medical office for treatment. Fran Kubelik enters with a case of hiccups. He tells her that hiccups are psychosomatic and urges her to take her mind off whatever is distressing her. She thinks of taking up a hobby or seeking new companionship (You'll Think of Someone—Sc to M/F Duet). The nurse tells Chuck that Mr. Sheldrake in personnel has asked to see him. He rushes off certain that his two months of key loaning has paid off.

In his office, Sheldrake, director of personnel, reads Chuck all the glowing reports he has received and demands to know what is going on. Chuck, convinced he is about to be fired, explains his innocence in the key lending. When Sheldrake offers him two tickets to the basketball game, he realizes that Sheldrake himself wants the key to his apartment. Sheldrake swears him to secrecy (Our Little Secret—Sc to M Duet).

Chuck waits in the lobby for Fran and asks her if she is interested in basketball. When she replies "yes," he invites her to the game. She tells him she is meeting someone but promises to be there in time for the second game. He is ecstatic (She Likes Basketball—L to M Solo).

Fran goes to a Chinese restaurant, where she meets Mr. Sheldrake, whom she has been having an affair with. Upset that he hasn't called her in six weeks, she wants to end their relationship but can't. When he goes to make a phone call, she berates herself for not leaving (Knowing When to Leave—F Solo). During sections of Fran's song, the spot comes up on Chuck waiting outside Madison Square Garden and making excuses for her failure to show. It is obvious that he is very naive about women. Sheldrake returns to the table, tells Fran he is going to get a divorce and convinces her to go to Chuck's apartment with him.

The lights come up on Kirkeby, Dobitch, Vanderhoff and Eichelberger bemoaning the fact that Chuck won't loan his key anymore (Where Can You Take a Girl?—Sc to M Quartet). They enter the executive dining room, where Fran is a waitress. When Chuck, who has been promoted, enters, Fran apologizes for standing him up and tells him she isn't worthy of him. The four executives confront Chuck and ask for some gratitude (Where Can You Take a Girl? [Reprise]—M Quartet). Chuck goes to the executive sun deck to return a compact he found in the apartment and Sheldrake comments on Chuck's bachelor life. When Chuck exits, Sheldrake contemplates the reason why he wants things that he can't have (Wanting Things—M Solo).

Outside an elevator, the night of the office Christmas party, a tipsy Miss Olson, Sheldrake's secretary, corners Fran and tells her she was once Mr. Sheldrake's girlfriend and lists the other girls Sheldrake has been involved with. Fran denies everything and hastily exits.

On the nineteenth floor, the company party is in full swing, with Vivien, Miss Polansky, and Miss Wong, three of the office girls, singing and dancing (Turkey Lurkey Time—F Trio). Chuck asks Fran's opinion of his newly purchased homburg. She assures him that he looks good and offers him her compact so he can see for himself. He recognizes the broken compact and disheartenedly hands it back. She leaves as the phone rings, and he tells Mr. Sheldrake the apartment is ready for tonight.

As Act II opens, Chuck is in a seedy bar on 8th Avenue when he is approached by Marge, a lonely woman who hasn't heard from her husband in two years. She talks to Chuck in a teasing manner—she is still in love with her husband and Chuck is interested in Fran, but since neither of them is available, they realize something is better than nothing (A Fact Can Be a Beautiful Thing—Sc to M/F Duet—Mixed Chorus). The patrons join in and Chuck and Marge exit.

At Chuck's apartment, where Fran is confronting Sheldrake about his wife and his thoughtlessness where she herself is concerned, he apologizes and gives her a hundred dollars as a Christmas present. She suddenly feels very cheap and urges him to leave before he misses his train. She looks at a photograph of them together, and wonders why he looks different to her (Whoever You Are—F Solo). She sees some pills and stares at them as the lights fade.

Marge and Chuck, who are quite tipsy, enter the apartment. Chuck sees Fran, fully dressed, in a deep sleep and is unable to wake her. Realizing she has attempted suicide, he rushes next door to get the doctor and sends Marge on her way. Chuck and the doctor walk Fran around the apartment for several hours, while the doctor, who assumes the attempted suicide is because of Chuck's behavior, berates the worried man. He agrees not to file an attempted suicide report and leaves to get some sleep. Chuck calls Mr. Sheldrake to tell him the details, but Sheldrake seems only interested in not getting involved.

The next morning, the doctor returns to check up on Fran and finds her depressed that he saved her. He and Chuck give her some advice (A Young Pretty Girl Like You—Sc to M Duet). The doctor leaves Fran and Chuck. When Fran asks why he isn't married, he explains he was in love once, but the girl married his best friend and he contemplated suicide. They both realize they have similar love problems (I'll Never Fall in Love Again—Sc to M/F Duet).

The doorbell rings and Fran's brother, Karl, comes in to take Fran home. When the doctor enters to check her, Karl discovers that Fran has taken an overdose of sleeping pills and hits Chuck, despite Fran's protests.

Outside the apartment building, the three executives are happy because they have discovered a new single man in the office who has his own apartment.

At the office, Miss Olson tells Mr. Sheldrake she is quitting, and if he is worried about his wife finding out about his affair, he can continue to worry.

Mr. Sheldrake meets Chuck in the Chinese restaurant to inform him that he and Mrs. Sheldrake have split up. He asks Chuck for the key to the apartment so he can continue to see Fran. Chuck gives him the key to the executive washroom and walks out, promising to change his life (Promises, Promises—M Solo).

Back at the apartment Chuck is busy packing when the doctor enters for some ice. He can't believe Chuck has no date for New Year's Eve, but Chuck assures him it's so and offers him some champagne. He thanks the doctor and tells him good-bye. Fran arrives to tell him that she and Sheldrake are through for they don't have very much in common; he doesn't even like basketball. She begins to deal the cards as the curtain falls.

NOTES ON THE PRODUCTION

Some excellent monologues are in this script. Tonys went to Jerry Orbach and Marian Mercer.

The show is popular among community theatres, for the setting may be simple and the roles are good showcases for the performers. The Neil Simon book is comedic and charming and the leading character is extremely likable.

Publicity directors find the show easy to advertise since it is based on the movie *The Apartment*, which is often seen on television. The costumes are modern-day and the production may be kept quite simple and inexpensive. It is a good fund-raising show for a company that wants a popular, yet not overdone, inexpensive show.

An excellent leading man is required. The leading actor, although not a dancer, must be able to move well. The basketball number calls for a lot of stylized movement and high energy. The other roles are primarily character-oriented and require actors rather than strong singers.

SONGS OF SPECIAL INTEREST

"Knowing When to Leave," semidramatic, mezzo solo.

"Promises, Promises," decision making, strong baritone solo.

"She Likes Basketball," baritone audition potential, allows for movement, character and shows off vocal quality.

"You'll Think of Someone," M/F duet, charm, relationships, scene is necessary for class study.

Instrumentation: 2 violins, 2 cellos, 4 reeds, horn, 3 trumpets, 2 trombones, 2 percussions, 2 guitars, piano/electric conductor
Script: The Comedy of Neil Simon, Random House
Score: Morris
Record: United Artists
Rights: TW

PURLIE

Book: Ossie Davis, Philip Rose and Peter Udell (Based on the play *Purlie Victorious*, by Ossie Davis)
Music: Gary Geld
Lyrics: Peter Udell

ORIGINAL PRODUCTION

Broadway Theatre, March 15, 1970 (688 perf.)
Director: Philip Rose
Choreographer: Louis Johnson
Musical Director: Joyce Brown
Orchestration and Choral Arrangements: Garry Sherman and Luther Henderson
Principals: Purlie—Cleavon Little—baritone; Church Soloist—Linda Hopkins—soprano; Lutiebelle—Melba Moore—mezzo; Missy—Novella Nelson—alto; Gitlow—Sherman Hemsley—baritone; Charlie—C. David Colson—tenor; Idella—Helen Martin—VTNE; Ol' Cap'n—John Heffernan—baritone
Chorus and Smaller Roles: 3M/2F minimum.

SYNOPSIS

The curtain rises on Big Bethel, a small church somewhere in Georgia. A Black congregation, led by self-appointed Reverend Purlie Victorious, is joyfully singing at the funeral of Ol' Cap'n, the man who profited from their labors in the cotton fields (Walk Him Up the Stairs—Mixed Chorus).

The scene flashes back to a shabby yet cozy shack, the home of Aunt Missy, Purlie's sister-in-law. Purlie tells the young, innocent Lutiebelle, whom he has brought from Alabama, that he wants to unite the Blacks in their own church, with him as their preacher (New-Fangled Preacher Man—L to M Solo).

Purlie reveals to Missy his plan to pass off Lutiebelle as his Cousin Bee. Purlie needs the aid of his brother, Gitlow, the only Black Ol' Cap'n trusts, to help him gain the deceased Cousin Bee's $500 inheritance. Gitlow refuses to get involved and plans on continuing his "Step N Fetch It" manner. He and three field hands demonstrate (Skinnin' a Cat—M Solo to 3M Trio). After Gitlow leaves, Missy promises to persuade him to Purlie's side and Purlie exits, excited at the prospects of a church for Blacks.

Over a slice of potato pie, Missy hints to Lutiebelle that Purlie could use a good wife. The lovestruck Lutiebelle bursts into song (Purlie—Sc to F Solo). When Purlie urges Missy to beat some sense into Gitlow, the spunky woman takes a baseball bat and hurries out. Purlie gives Lutiebelle a pep talk and makes her proud of being Black (The Harder They Fall—Sc to M/F Duet). Purlie asks Lutiebelle to be his disciple and they seal their convictions with a kiss as Gitlow is persuaded to talk to Ol' Cap'n about the $500.

The set changes to a commissary, where food and clothing supplies are sold to the Blacks at outrageous prices. Charlie, Ol' Cap'n's twenty-five–year–old revolutionary son, is getting a hot poultice put on his swollen eye by Idella, a tough little Black woman. She talks to Charlie about his subversive songs which go against the traditional beliefs of the Old South (Barrels of War/Unborn Love—M Solo). Ol' Cap'n, positive his only son is a Communist, arrives at the commissary to convince him that the old ways, with the White man dominating the Black, are best (Big Fish, Little Fish—M Duet to Mixed Chorus). Ol' Cap'n, overwhelmed by Charlie's behavior, begins having heart palpitations, which Gitlow's subservient manner gradually alleviates.

Lutiebelle arrives with Purlie, prepared to meet Ol' Cap'n as Cousin Bee. She is very positive and feels she can conquer the world (I Got Love—Sc to F Solo). Lutiebelle fools Ol' Cap'n with the aid of Purlie, Gitlow, and the other plantation workers, who present him with a scroll of gratitude in typical "shufflin' " style (Great White Father of the Year—Mixed Chorus).

At the end of the song Ol' Cap'n requests Lutiebelle to sign a receipt, but she mistakenly signs her real name and the money is lost. Ol' Cap'n orders Charlie and Gitlow to go after Lutiebelle and Purlie, but they purposely fall over each other and the two escape.

Two days later Purlie and Missy, in the humble shack, are frustrated and dejected. Purlie yearns for the freedom of the North, but Missy contradicts his every lyric, saying the South is far nicer (Down Home—Sc to M/F Duet).

Gitlow, convinced that he can get the money from Ol' Cap'n, leaves Lutiebelle serving dinner to the lecherous old man and tells Purlie and Missy of his certain success. Lutiebelle arrives at the cabin, disheveled and furious. Purlie stomps off to get revenge upon the man who made advances to the woman he loves.

As the Act II curtain rises, the plantation workers are reclining and thinking of what they will do Monday (First Thing Monday Mornin'—Mixed Chorus).

At the shack Missy tries to convince Lutiebelle that Purlie will come back unharmed, with her honor restored (He Can Do It—L to F Solo). Gitlow arrives to announce that Purlie is running and it is better to survive than to be brave. The women are furious that Gitlow has so little faith in his brother (The Harder They Fall—2F/1M Trio).

Purlie arrives with Ol' Cap'n's whip and a tall tale about how he conquered this tyrant. Ol' Cap'n threatens to jail Purlie, but Charlie rushes in and informs his father that he has bought Big Bethel and put the deed in Purlie's name. He asks to be a member of the congregation (The World Is Comin' to a Start—Mixed Chorus). Ol' Cap'n, who finally realizes his son has foregone the ways of the Old South, dies.

The final scene, in Big Bethel, is a completion of the opening number (Walk Him up the Stairs [Reprise]—Sc to Mixed Chorus).

NOTES ON THE PRODUCTION

The show, a foot-stomping, humorous one, made stars of Melba Moore and Cleavon Little, who received Tony Awards for their performances.

Purlie has minimal set, costume, and cast requirements and would be a good "first" show for a company to attempt. The music is tuneful, the leading characters well-defined and sincere. There is a particularly excellent scene in the second act where Purlie describes his imagined confrontation with Ol' Cap'n that is good material for competition. The chorus is easily adapted to large or small casts, which is good in school situations where a choir director may want to involve the entire chorus.

Purlie must be performed as a "period piece," pre–civil rights movement, and be sincerely portrayed in order to be true to the author's intent.

SONGS OF SPECIAL INTEREST

"Purlie," exciting, up tempo, full volumed, shows off the voice, audition potential, mezzo.

"The Harder They Fall," foot-stomping, convincing, up tempo, revue possibility.

"I Got Love," up tempo, vibrant, audition, vocally demanding, mezzo.

"Down Home," alto/baritone, character and lyric contrasts, character and mood change.

Instrumentaion: 5 reeds, 3 trumpets, 2 trombones, percussion, drums, 2 violins, viola, cello, bass, 2 guitars, piano, organ, piano/conductor
Script: SF
Selections: Mourbar
Record: Ampex
Rights: SF

R

REDHEAD

Book: Herbert and Dorothy Fields, Sidney Sheldon and David Shaw
Music: Albert Hague
Lyrics: Dorothy Fields

ORIGINAL PRODUCTION

46th Street Theatre February 5, 1959 (452 perf.)
Director and Choreographer: Bob Fosse
Musical Direction: Jay Blackton
Orchestration: Philip J. Lang and Robert Russell Bennett
Principals: Essie—Gwen Verdon—mezzo; Maude Simpson—Cynthia Latham—alto; Sarah Simpson—Doris Rich—alto; Tom—Richard Kiley—baritone; George Poppett—Leonard Stone—tenor; Sir Charles—Patrick Horgan—VTNE; Tenor—Bob Dixon—tenor; Howard—William LeMassena—VTNE
Chorus and Smaller Roles: 8M/8F with high energy who dance well.

SYNOPSIS

The play opens on a prologue vignette of a young actress being strangled by a redheaded, bearded man. The music the girl has been singing underscores the opening of the play, the exterior of the Simpson Sisters Wax Museum. The new exhibit, "The Strangler and the Dancing Girl," is popular with the turn-of-the-century Londoners. The inspector, who thinks the killer might visit the waxworks on opening day to witness his likeness, plans to observe the crowds that await the museum's opening (The Simpson Sisters—Mixed Chorus).

In the main salon of the museum, various exhibits enhance the dimly lit space. The people anxiously await the unveiling of the new exhibit when Essie, the Simpsons' niece, enters to tell Aunts Maude and Sarah that she has had another vision of a handsome man who will enter her life. Maude accuses her of not being realistic and not hunting for a real man to marry, but Essie disagrees and sings of her hopes for marriage (The Right Finger of My Left Hand—L to F Solo). She hurries to the unveiling where she meets Tom Baxter, a strong, handsome American actor who wants the exhibit to close because the murdered girl was his partner. He draws the curtain and orders that no one reopen it. When Maude defies him by pulling the curtain, everyone notices that the scarf is gone and assumes the murderer is in the museum. Pandemonium breaks loose.

While the inspector is searching Essie's workroom for the killer, Tom tells Essie about his ideal girl. Essie obviously doesn't fit the role, but as he and his coworker George start to exit, she fabricates wild stories to elicit their attention and sympathy. The two men, appalled by her tales, urge her to get out and live (Just for Once—Sc to 2M/F Trio). Tom and George leave for the theatre, promising to see Essie again. She feels wonderful (I Feel Merely Marvelous—F Solo). Essie tells Sarah she is in love but worries that she may never see Tom again. She decides to tell Tom that she knows what the killer looks like and her aunt, ever the romantic, agrees to help her in her lie that the killer has attempted to strangle Essie. Maude, taken in by Essie's story, insists they go to Scotland Yard and the three set out.

On a foggy street Essie confuses her Aunt Maude and the three make their way to the Odeon Theatre.

At the theatre, the show is in rehearsal as George leads the group in a tribute to ragtime (The Uncle Sam Rag—M Solo and Mixed Chorus). Essie meets Tom, who is onstage rehearsing, and tells him she has seen the strangler and is certain he will kill her unless Tom protects her. Since she needs to be around lots of people, George invites her to stay at the theatre but Howard, the manager, is opposed. Essie quickly assures him she can perform and demonstrates with an old music hall song (Erbie Fitch's Twitch—F Solo). The number is a disaster, but Tom valiantly suggests that Howard just use her in the finale. George, an expert at makeup, takes her to begin the transformation from Essie to chorus girl.

Sir Charles Willingham, nobleman and friend of the dead girl, has overheard Essie's story and asks to speak to her but Tom begs off until later. George accuses Tom of being in love with Essie, but Tom denies that she is the right girl for him (She's Not Enough Woman for Me—Sc to M Duet).

Outside the dressing room a few hours later, Essie enters, a glowing beauty, and Tom asks her to dinner before exiting; he is surprised at her transformation. Maude and Sarah, hearing the news, try to prepare her for the event. Sarah urges fun and Maude urges caution (Behave Yourself—Sc to F Duet, Essie Needed for Staging). As Essie goes on the date the aunts, on one side of the stage, offer words of wisdom to Essie, who mistakes their advice; the scene becomes a study in opposite manners.

Later that night, in Tom's apartment where Essie has moved under the chaperonage of her aunts, Tom tells her he loves her (Look Who's in Love—Sc to M/F Duet). As he leaves he urges her to make a wax head of the murderer, and Essie is forced to go into one of her trances in an attempt to envision the killer. While she is in the trance Sir Charles opens the door of the apartment and she sees him briefly before he exits. She is aghast but quickly starts working on a wax replica of the head.

In front of the wax museum, which is temporarily closed, Tom spies a picture of Essie and tells everyone she is his girl (My Girl Is Just Enough Woman for Me—M Solo).

A terrified Essie is backstage waiting to go on when Tom enters and tells her she is gorgeous enough to be a star. She imagines herself as a fabulous dancer (Essie's Vision—Mixed Chorus Dance). As her vision ends, she is brought back to reality and the performance (Two Faces in the Dark—M Solo—Mixed Chorus for Staging). Essie is totally messing up the number with forgotten choreographic movement when she sees Sir Charles seated in a box. She runs to Tom and tells him she has seen the killer. He can't believe it is Sir Charles, his best friend and the fiancé of the dead girl. When he discovers that her stories have all been lies and she only saw Sir Charles in a vision, he leaves in disgust. Essie goes to call Scotland Yard, but the phone goes dead and Sir Charles approaches.

Act II opens in Tom's apartment. George arrives to warn Tom that the stage doorman saw Essie leave with Sir Charles and she could be in trouble. Tom isn't concerned and renounces his feelings for her (I'm Back in Circulation—M Solo).

On a street Sir Charles is escorting Essie to his apartment to question her about the killer. She manages to escape when she recognizes May and Tillie, two streetwalkers she met previously. The three enter a pub where she tells the patrons she is finished with lying. David and May cheer her (We Loves Ya Jimey—M/F Duet—Mixed Chorus). The dance ends in a fight, and the police arrive and arrest everyone.

In jail the following evening, Aunt Maude and Sarah come to visit Essie and arrange for her release. George arrives and tells Essie he is going to help her trap the killer by having Sir Charles come to the museum and confront Essie. George promises that Tom will be on hand to save her, so she agrees. Essie devises a plan to get out of jail by seducing the guard into a dance and pickpocketing the key (The Pick Pocket Tango—F/M to F Chorus Dance).

Backstage at the theatre George attempts to convince Tom to go to the waxworks, but Tom is certain he doesn't care about Essie's schemes. He begins to reject her but realizes he still loves her (Look Who's in Love [Reprise]—M Solo) and runs off to the museum. George's dressing room door opens and George walks out disguised as Sir Charles.

Tom tells Essie he loves her and the two agree to correct their flaws (I'll Try—Sc to M/F Duet). Tom goes to wait for Sir Charles and Essie discovers that George is disguised as Sir Charles. He confesses the murder and his plan to get even with Sir Charles by making the police think the aristocrat is the killer. As he starts to strangle her, the real Sir Charles interrupts and the chase is on, complete with the two redheaded bearded men, some police, Essie, Howard and Tom.

The play concludes happily with Tom and Essie united and Howard putting Essie and her aunts in the show (Finale—Mixed Chorus).

NOTES ON THE PRODUCTION

Tony Awards: Choreography, Costumes, Book, Musical, Music, Producer, Actress (Gwen Verdon) and Actor (Richard Kiley).

An excellent though seldom done musical which is exciting and fun in the hands of a talented director, choreographer and versatile performers. A variety of smaller vignette roles make this ideal for smaller companies wishing to give everyone a chance.

The basic sets include the waxworks exterior and interior which may include Essie's workroom, a stage, a street, backstage, Tom's apartment, a pub and jail cell. Usually the street drop or the exterior of the waxworks is used to change from the larger sets. It is possible to combine the street and waxworks.

SONGS OF SPECIAL INTEREST

"Behave Yourself," F duet with third F for staging, character-oriented, two elderly women with different points of view.

"Erbie Fitch's Twitch," mezzo, music hall oriented, period.

"I'm Back in Circulation," strong baritone, possible audition, extremely masculine number.

"Just for Once," trio, up tempo, character of F strongly established, interrelationships important.

"Merely Marvelous," mezzo, up tempo, movement-oriented.

"The Right Finger of My Left Hand," mezzo ballad, poignant, good for two-song character study.

"The Uncle Sam Rag," chorus number, music hall style, good for revue.

Instrumentation: 5 reeds, 2 trumpets, 2 trombones, horn, percussion, guitar, harp, 3 violins, viola, cello, bass, piano/conductor
Script: NP
Score: Chappell
Record: RCA
Rights: MTI

S

SEESAW

Book: Michael Bennett (Based on the play *Two for the Seesaw*, by William Gibson)
Music: Cy Coleman
Lyrics: Dorothy Fields

ORIGINAL PRODUCTION

Uris Theatre, March 18, 1973 (296 perf.)
Director and Choreographer: Michael Bennett
Musical Director: Donald Pippin
Orchestration: Larry Fallon
Principals: Gittel Mosca—Michele Lee—mezzo; Jerry Ryan—Ken Howard—baritone; David—Tommy Tune—baritone; Sophie—Cecilia Norfleet—VTI; Sparkle—La Monte DesFontaines—tenor; Julio—Giancarlo Esposito—tenor
Chorus and Smaller Roles: 5F/3M, all must tap-dance.

SYNOPSIS

The curtain rises on a projection of New York City. The chorus, costumed in white, introduces the title song about the ups and downs of life (Seesaw—Mixed Chorus).

As the number ends, Jerry Ryan, a lonely, attractive man from Nebraska, is propositioned by the neighborhood girls as he waits to use the phone (My City—

Onstage F Chorus to Mixed Offstage Chorus). A policeman enters and disperses the girls as Jerry enters the booth to phone Gittel Mosca, a girl he met at a party. As he dials, the scene switches to a dance studio where Gittel, a kookie New Yorker, is working out. When she answers the phone, she doesn't know how to react and makes a mess of the conversation. They both hang up. Gittel is furious at herself and berates her ineptness (Nobody Does It Like Me—L to F Solo). When Jerry calls back and asks her to dinner, she agrees to meet him at 46th and Broadway.

They go to a Japanese restaurant where she orders a Japanese meal for him and a tuna on rye for herself. She is a character study in contrasts and he is a WASP lawyer from Nebraska with marital problems. The two hit it off—Gittel is impressed by his manners and education and he enjoys her stories and New York Jewishness. They rise and leave the restaurant as projections fade up depicting the fountain at Lincoln Center.

They stop outside Lincoln Center and begin mime conducting to the accompaniment of an offstage chorus. The onstage and offstage voices counterpoint each other (In Tune—Sc to M/F Duet with Mixed Chorus Backup). She takes him to see her friend Sophie's performance in a street theatre Spanish version of *Hamlet*. As the play ends, the audience begins to leave, commenting in mixed Spanish and English. Jerry asks Gittel if the language is Spanish or English and Julio, a spectator, calls it Spanglish. Sophie and some other spectators join in (Spanglish—2M/2F Quartet to Mixed Chorus).

They return to Gittel's apartment and Jerry makes a pass. She rejects his advances because she never sleeps with anyone on the first date. He apologetically explains it is his birthday and Gittel melts (Welcome to Holiday Inn—Sc to F Solo, M Needed for Staging).

The next morning Jerry tells Gittel he is getting divorced because his father-in-law and wife dictate his life. He feels like taking care of someone and would like it to be Gittel. Deeply touched, Gittel decides to fix up Jerry's apartment and enlists the aid of her gay friend and dance partner, David.

The projections show Jerry's neighborhood and apartment, which Gittel and David have decorated. Jerry, excited by the change, announces that he is going to work in New York and will finance a dance showcase for Gittel and David. Gittel, ever the pessimist, wonders when her world will begin to fall apart, but Jerry loves her crazy ways and assures her it won't (You're a Lovable Lunatic—Sc to M Solo). A phone call from Jerry's separated wife brings them back to reality, but Jerry begs Gittel to need him and promises to be important in her life.

In Gittel's apartment, Gittel, readying for a fancy party in the East 60's with wealthy friends of Jerry's, gets an ulcer attack. She convinces herself to go, despite the pain, and starts out the door as the projection screens depict New York.

On the way to the dinner, she contemplates her relationship with Jerry (He's Good for Me—L to F Solo), knowing that he is good for her but wondering what she can offer him. As the song ends Gittel enters the Banana Club where

Sophie performs and David and Oscar hang out. She orders a drink, lights a cigarette and informs everyone she never got to the party. They try to stop her from drinking but the floor show of Sparkle and the Sparklettes begins and Sophie rushes onstage. The Sparklettes do the latest dance as the patrons join in (Ride out the Storm—M Solo to Mixed Chorus).

Gittel returns to her apartment in great pain and calls the doctor, who is out on call. As she hangs up Jerry enters, furious with her at missing the party. She tries to get him to leave by convincing him she's not his type of person, but he realizes her ulcer is acting up and calls the hospital. As Gittel clings desperately to him the curtain falls.

In Act II Jerry arrives at the hospital with a plastic pink flamingo for Gittel. He tells her he is trying to pass the New York bar exam and has booked a theatre for her and David's showcase. He tells her they are a great couple (We've Got It—Sc to M Solo). Gittel is overjoyed that she is loved and expresses her feelings after Jerry leaves (Poor Everybody Else—F Solo).

Jerry is in the studio watching a rehearsal and trying to learn statutes he needs to pass the bar. David tells him it's easier to learn in rhythm and demonstrates as Gittel counterpoints (Chpt. 54, Number 1909 to Poor Everybody Else—2M/F Trio and Mixed Chorus). The entire company taps out the rhythm.

Gittel is moving into Jerry's apartment when the phone rings. It is Jerry's wife, Tess, who is in New York to have Jerry sign the final divorce papers. Upset that Jerry neglected to tell her the divorce was nearly final, Gittel confronts him with the facts, telling him his wife still loves him. He tries to calm her by promising to meet her after the dance concert.

At the concert the sound of applause is deafening and David is overjoyed when a famous choreographer asks him to be his assistant on a Broadway show (It's Not Where You Start—L to M Solo to Mixed Chorus). Gittel congratulates David, who vows to include her in his plans. She realizes he is on his way to being a big-name choreographer and she no longer has the drive to make it. She bids him farewell and returns to her apartment.

Jerry, who missed the concert because he was seeing his wife off at the airport, phones to tell Gittel he'll be around as long as she needs him. She sends him home to Omaha to live life on his own terms and thanks him for helping her gain some confidence in herself. The two say good-bye and Gittel is left to rethink her life. She dashes out onto the street as the projections of New York come up, realizing she is better prepared to enter new relationships because of Jerry (I'm Way Ahead—F Solo).

NOTES ON THE PRODUCTION

Tony Awards: Choreographer, Featured Actor—Tommy Tune. There are many monologues worth studying for possible audition material, but there are more in the straight play. In fact, the ''opening up'' of the two-character straight version to make a large, splashy-feeling musical destroyed some of the dramatic impact inherent in the two-character play. The Gittel/Jerry scenes are heightened by the musical numbers, and a good cutting of the show to approximately one hour would make it ideal for community theatre play contests. Permission must be obtained.

The script in its present form is most suitable for dinner theatres as it has splash, pizzazz, and drama. Traditionally, dinner theatre audiences are not overly bothered by slight inconsistencies in tonal quality, and dinner theatres are often better suited to technically smaller versions of musicals.

The costumes are modern-day and easy to obtain. The show is designed to have locations quickly established by use of projected scenes for exterior locations. Slides for the show are available from Sheppard Kerman, Suite 1700, 204 Lexington Avenue, New York, NY 10016.

SONGS OF SPECIAL INTEREST

"He's Good for Me," club potential, mezzo/alto, torchy sound, big volume.

"I'm Way Ahead," up tempo, mezzo, good acting and vocal number.

"It's Not Where You Start," baritone, audition potential as it shows excitement, character, strong voice and movement ability.

"Nobody Does It Like Me," alto/mezzo problem song, needs specifics added by the actress to show characterization.

"Welcome to Holiday Inn," Sc to F Duet, mezzo, good for sexy and open movement, relationship with other character is extremely important.

Instrumentation: 4 reeds, 3 trumpets, 2 trombones, 2 percussion, drums, violin, viola, cello, bass (fender, acoustic), guitar, piano/conductor
Script: SF
Selections: Notable
Record: Buddah
Rights: SF

1776

Book: Peter Stone
Music and Lyrics: Sherman Edwards

ORIGINAL PRODUCTION

46th Street Theatre, March 16, 1969 (1,217 perf.)
Director: Peter Hunt
Musical Numbers: Onna White
Musical Director: Peter Howard
Orchestration: Eddie Sauter
Principals: John Hancock—David Ford—VTI; Benjamin Franklin—Howard Da Silva—baritone; Martha Jefferson—Betty Buckly—mezzo; Thomas Jefferson—

Ken Howard—baritone; John Adams—William Daniels—tenor; Abigail Adams—Virginia Vestoff—soprano; Edward Rutledge—Clifford David—high baritone; Richard Henry Lee—Ronald Holgate—high baritone; Robert Livingston—Henry LeClair—tenor; Roger Sherman—David Vosburg—tenor
Chorus and Smaller Roles: 19M. All have specific single characters that are essential to the production.

SYNOPSIS

The Continental Congress, on a hot day in May of 1776, urges John Adams to stop making speeches about independence (Sit Down, John—M Chorus). John, the congressman from Massachusetts, in his fiery manner, refuses to give up his belief in independence and comments on the inability of his colleagues to make decisions on anything requiring action (Piddle, Twiddle and Resolve—L to M Solo). In the midst of Adams's fuming, Abigail Adams appears. She is speaking to him through her letters from their Braintree home. Abby is interested in having John home, but he feels too committed to the creation of a new country to give up. They express their love, though they're miles apart (Till Then—Sc to M/F Duet).

Outside the Congress, John approaches Ben Franklin, who is getting his portrait painted, on the matter of getting Congress to discuss independence. Franklin, in his urbane fashion, explains to John that the members of Congress will not listen to him since he is "obnoxious and disliked" and from New England, but perhaps they would pay heed to someone else, for instance, Virginia's Richard Henry Lee. Lee enters, and Franklin entices him to return home to convince his constituents to formally declare independence. Lee, ever the endearing, egotistical aristocrat, agrees as he comments on his prestigious lineage and certain success (The Lees of Old Virginia—Sc to M Trio).

In the chambers, it is now early June. McNair, the chamber custodian, is greeted by the newly appointed delegate from Georgia, Dr. Lyman Hall, who is coerced by the Conservatives to oppose independence. He is, however, somewhat unsettled in making this decision. Hancock takes his place at the president's desk and the meeting begins but is interrupted by Lee, who bursts in with the news that Virginia has sided with independence. A tally is taken and the topic of independence debated. Hancock appoints a declaration committee composed of Adams, Franklin, Sherman, Livingston and Jefferson, and recesses the Congress.

The five men try to avoid writing the document as they pass a quill from man to man (But Mr. Adams—L to M Quintet). Jefferson, who desires to return home to his new wife, is forced to accept the task of writing the declaration.

In his room, the angry Jefferson curses the tenacious Adams and begins writing but is unable to concentrate. Adams sends for Jefferson's wife, Martha, in hopes that after Jefferson has seen her he will get on with his writing. This act forces Adams to realize how much he misses his own wife and in his imagination he addresses her (Yours, Yours, Yours—Sc to M/F Duet).

Outside Jefferson's apartment, Franklin and Adams greet Martha, who tells them about herself and her quiet husband (He Plays the Violin—Sc to 2M/F Trio). When Adams and Martha waltz together, Franklin is astonished to find that the staid Adams can actually dance.

The time progresses to June 22. The Conservatives are convinced that the fight against the British is futile but Adams takes Chase, a Conservative from Maryland, to see the American militia in action. If Chase is impressed he will change his vote. Dickinson and the Conservatives are pleased by the sudden quiet caused by the absence of Adams and the other Radicals (Cool, Cool Considerate Men—M Chorus).

After the Conservatives leave, McNair, the Leather Apron, and a courier from Washington's headquarters are left alone in Congress. The courier tells them of the tragedies of the war (Momma Look Sharp—Sc to M Trio, Tenor Essential).

During the reading of the newly written Declaration, Franklin, Adams and Jefferson are in the anteroom, pacing in anticipation. They parallel it with an egg—the birth of a new nation—and choose, after some debate, the eagle as its representative bird (The Egg—Sc to M Trio).

After all deletions and alterations are agreed upon, except the freedom of slaves, Rutledge, a wealthy, South Carolina slave owner, accuses both the North and the South of needing slaves for economic reasons (Molasses to Rum—L to M Solo). The Southern delegates refuse to vote for independence if the slavery clause remains. The meeting ends in shambles. Adams sends McKean to bring back a cancer-ridden and dying Caesar Rodney from Delaware in case there is a chance. The others leave, convinced the proposal will fail, but Adams will not give up. He asks Abigail, in his imagination, for advice; however, his thoughts are interrupted by a shipment of gunpowder ingredients that Abigail has sent from Braintree. He happily thanks her (Yours, Yours, Yours [Reprise]—Sc to M/F Duet). A dispatch from George Washington arrives. Its message touches Adams, who wonders if anyone else in Congress cares about America's need for independence (Is Anybody There?—M Solo). Near the end of Adams's questioning, Lyman Hall of Georgia enters the dark chamber and announces that he is voting with Adams.

July 4 dawns and everyone returns, including Caesar Rodney. Since one Nay vote will defeat the motion, there is tension in the room. Rodney shifts Delaware's vote to Yea and Maryland's Chase, after seeing the Continental soldiers on the battlefield, votes Yea and New York, as usual, votes to abstain. The issue finally comes down to Rutledge of South Carolina, who forces Jefferson to remove the passage about freedom for slaves. Franklin sways Wilson, from Pennsylvania, to change his vote to Yea in order for this meek man to maintain his anonymity. The Declaration is signed by all, and the play ends with actors frozen as in the Pine Savage Engraving of the historic event.

NOTES ON THE PRODUCTION

Tony Awards: Best Musical, Ron Holgate—Featured Actor, Direction, Book, Music and Lyrics.

The show was an unexpected success at a time when audiences needed to renew belief in their country. It chalked up a long run and is often revived by larger stock companies.

The show is usually performed on a set that is a replica of the Continental Congress with slatted screens pushed in front for the smaller scenes. The costumes are lavish, period 1776. The representatives to Congress were wealthy men, and their financial status needs to be demonstrated through the fabric of the costumes.

The play requires four excellent actors for Adams, Franklin, Lee and Rutledge and two superb singers, a tenor for "Mama Look Sharp" and a high baritone for Rutledge.

The most difficult moments in the show occur when Abigail, who is in Braintree, and Adams, in Philadelphia, have scenes. Under no circumstances should their scenes be given a readers theatre treatment where each actor focuses on a spot on a wall behind the audience. The scenes must be portrayed as if the two were actually in the same room; they should relate honestly as if in conversation. The distance is established by the fact that they never touch but yearn to physically relate; this adds to the dramatic impact of their scene/songs.

SONGS OF SPECIAL INTEREST

"But Mr. Adams," M quintet, good for examples of individual characterizations in a small chorus number, comic situation.

"The Egg," up tempo, fun, character contrasts, good for revue, M trio.

"Is Anybody There?," semidramatic, completes Adams's character study. It is recommended that the music be from the original production as the vocal selections are incomplete.

"Molasses to Rum," dramatically biting high baritone solo, strong, requires good voice.

"Piddle, Twiddle and Resolve," establishes character, resolute, angered frustration, tenor.

"Till Then," charming tenor/soprano duet, helps round out Adams's character and should be combined with "Piddle, Twiddle and Resolve" for characterization work.

Instrumentation: 4 reeds, trumpet, horn, 3 trombones, percussion, harp, harpsichord, violin, viola, cello, bass, piano/conductor
Script: Ten Great Musicals of the American Theatre, Random
Selections: Schirmer
Record: Columbia
Rights: MTI

SHE LOVES ME

Book: Joe Masteroff (Based on the play *Parfumerie* by Miklos Laszlo and the film *The Shop around the Corner*)
Music: Jerry Bock
Lyrics: Sheldon Harnick

ORIGINAL PRODUCTION

Eugene O'Neill Theatre, April 23, 1963 (302 perf.)
Director: Harold Prince
Musical Numbers Staged by: Carol Haney
Musical Director: Harold Hastings
Orchestration: Don Walker
Principals: Amalia Balish—Barbara Cook—Soprano; Georg Nowack—Daniel
Massey—baritone; Ilona Ritter—Barbara Baxley—mezzo; Kodaly—Jack Cas-
sidy—high baritone/tenor; Sipos—Nathaniel Frey—baritone; Arpad—Ralph
Williams—tenor; Maraczek—Ludwig Donath—baritone; Waiter—Wood Ro-
moff—tenor/high baritone
Chorus and Smaller Roles: 4M/4F.

SYNOPSIS

The play opens in front of Maraczek's Parfumerie in a European city, on a
beautiful summer day in the early 1930s. During the opening song, the clerks
of the Parfumerie greet each other. There is Sipos, an agreeable yet dull man
in his forties; Arpad, a bright teenage delivery boy who hopes to own the
Parfumerie; Miss Ilona Ritter, a thirty-year-old who has experienced life; Mr.
Kodaly, the handsome, shallow lover of Ilona; and Georg Nowak, a soft-spoken,
personable thirty-year-old (Good Morning-Good Day—4M/F Quintet).

Mr. Maraczek, the owner, age sixty, unlocks the door, and the front of the
shop revolves to the store interior, with a workroom to the right and Maraczek's
office to the left. Sipos, Georg and Kodaly successfully sell products to three
women customers (Sounds While Selling—Mixed Chorus).

As Georg is telling Sipos that he has received another lonely hearts letter from
his "dear friend," Mr. Maraczek enters and tells Georg he should really settle
down. Georg tries to explain that he leads a quiet life, but Maraczek remembers
his own bachelorhood (Days Gone By—L to M Solo—Georg Needed for Staging).
Arpad brings in some musical cigarette boxes Mr. Maraczek ordered; Georg is
unsure of their appeal, so Maraczek bets him they will sell at least one in the
next hour.

Amelia Balish, an attractive, personable young girl in her twenties, enters
looking for a job. Georg refuses to give her an interview but this doesn't stop
the determined Amalia, who proceeds to sell a music box as a functional candy
box (No More Candy—L to F Solo). Maraczek is so pleased that he hires her
on the spot. She smiles triumphantly at Georg, who coldly stares back as the
clerks line up to bid the customer farewell.

Georg, on a bench to one side of the shop, reads a letter to his dear friend;
his letter writing is interspersed with the passing of the season and problems
with Amalia. On a cold winter day, Amalia enters reading one of Georg's letters
concerning their upcoming rendezvous (Three Letters—L to M/F Solo). They

are not aware they are writing to each other. In fact, it appears they dislike each other as they constantly argue.

In the shop, Georg confides to Sipos his fears about meeting his girl of the letters (Tonight at 8—L to M Solo). Amalia and Ilona are busy in the workroom wrapping Christmas packages. Ilona, shocked to discover Amalia has a date with a man she has never met, imagines all sorts of horrible things. Amalia convinces her she knows about him from his letters and Ilona considers meeting someone other than Kodaly (I Don't Know His Name—Sc to F Duet).

The lights come up on the interior of the shop, where Mr. Maraczek is berating Georg in an irrational manner. Unbeknown to anyone, Maraczek suspects Georg of carrying on an affaiar with his wife. He orders all the employees to stay late, but Georg refuses. An argument ensues, which Sipos ends by dropping all the music boxes. Sipos admits he doesn't want Georg to leave (Perspective—M Solo), but Maraczek's needling continues and Georg is forced to resign. Ilona, Sipos, Kodaly and Arpad wish him farewell (Goodbye, Georg—Mixed Chorus).

Amalia exits, dressed for her date, and wonders if the letter writer will like what he sees (Will He Like Me?—L to F Solo).

In the shop, as the clerks are busy decorating, Kodaly plays up to Ilona (Ilona—M Solo), who weakly agrees to spend the evening with him. When Kodaly unexpectedly breaks his date with her to be with someone else, she is furious and tells Sipos that she is going to change her ways and not be so easy (I Resolve—Sc to F Solo).

As Sipos leaves the shop, Georg, who is waiting outside, begs him to take a letter to his date, saying he was called out of town, but Sipos insists that Georg accompany him to the cafe.

Mr. Keller, a private investigator, meets Mr. Maraczek in the empty shop to inform him that Mrs. Maraczek has been having an affair with Kodaly. The news upsets and surprises him because he wrongly suspected Georg. Maraczek shakily enters his office determined to kill himself, but Arpad stops him as the lights black out.

The scene shifts to the Cafe Imperiale, a romantic cafe with candles and wine, and lovers seated at the tables. An inept busboy, a snobby head waiter and a roving violinist attempt to create a serene atmosphere (A Romantic Atmosphere—M Solo with Mixed Chorus for Staging).

Sipos, recognizing Miss Balish, urges Georg, who is convinced her presence is a mistake, to talk to her. Amalia, confused and angered by his arrival, tries to get him to leave. An argument ensues, much to the chagrin of the head waiter, and Georg warns her she could be in danger from this man she's never met (Tango Tragique—L to M Solo). She accuses Georg of being pompous and verbally attacks him; he leaves, quite upset. Amalia sadly wonders what has happened to her letter date (Dear Friend—F Solo).

In Act II, Arpad visits Mr. Maraczek, recuperating in the hospital, to tell him how things are going at the shop. He urges Mr. Maraczek to think of him as a potential salesman, not a mere delivery boy (Try Me—S to M Solo). Arpad leaves Maraczek to apologize to Georg and make him head of the store. Georg, hearing from Arpad that Amalia is ill, stops by her room to visit.

Amalia, resting in bed, discovers that Georg is now head of the shop and rushes to get dressed (Where's My Shoe?—Sc to M/F Duet). He manages to calm her by telling her he spoke to her friend, who was unable to meet her because of an emergency business appointment. Georg promises to see her at the shop when she feels better, and happily exits. She starts to write a letter to her "dear friend," but keeps thinking of Georg, who was thoughtful enough to bring her vanilla ice cream as a get-well present (Ice Cream—L to F Solo).

Georg jauntily walks to the shop, overjoyed that Amalia cares for him, even though she doesn't know it (She Loves Me—M Solo).

In Maraczek's office Georg is congratulated by Sipos and Ilona on his promotion. When Georg leaves to fire Kodaly, Ilona describes the meeting of her new optometrist boyfriend to Sipos (A Trip to the Library—Sc to F Solo).

Kodaly leaves (Grand Knowing You—L to M Solo), and three carolers remind everyone there isn't much time left until Christmas. Their song is interspersed with groups of shoppers rushing into the parfumerie. The song ends on Christmas Eve as the store closes for the night (Twelve Days Till Christmas—Mixed Chorus). Maraczek returns from the hospital to treat everyone to champagne and take Arpad to dinner. Sipos goes home to his family, and Ilona is met by her boyfriend, Paul. As Georg and Amalia leave the shop, he quietly tells her that he is her dear friend. They embrace as the shop window Christmas tree lights up and the snow begins to fall (Ice Cream [Reprise]—Sc to M/F Duet). (Finale—Mixed Chorus.)

NOTES ON THE ORIGINAL PRODUCTION

Tony Awards: Featured Actor (Jack Cassidy); other awards that year tended to go to *Hello, Dolly!*. The show is charming and worthy of character/class studies and public performance. Especially timely for Christmas production dates.

The music is well written and strongly character oriented. It adds a richness and texture to the dialogue by rounding out the characters. The show is a charming pastiche and the evening a memorable one if the characters are honestly portrayed and the relationships clearly defined.

It is not a heavy costume or set show, as it requires only the shop exterior and interior (usually revolving), a wagon for Amalia's bedroom, a wagon for the restaurant, and possibly two smaller wagons for the workroom and Maraczek's office. These last two sets could be reduced to a rolling table with two stools for the workroom and a desk for the office area.

Although not often performed, the show is a favorite among Broadway theatregoers who were lucky enough to see the original. The PBS, Hal Prince–directed London version of the show has allowed it to become known by a wider audience.

SONGS OF SPECIAL INTEREST

"Ice Cream," up tempo, shows off the voice, good for audition or class study, soprano. Freely moving and vocal range.

"I Don't Know His Name," complex female duet, vocally demanding, strong character orientation, mezzo/soprano.

"I Resolve," character-oriented, comic song, mezzo/alto range.

"She Loves Me," character study, up tempo, movement-oriented number for a more gentle baritone. Awkward movement is OK, which may make it a feasible audition song for a male who doesn't move like a dancer.

"A Trip to the Library," comic, story song for character actress, good for revue, alto/mezzo range.

Instrumentation: 3 violins, viola, cello, bass, 5 reeds, trumpet, trombone, harp, accordion/celeste, percussion, piano/conductor
Script: Dodd, Mead
Selections: Hansen
Records: MGM
Rights: TW

SHENANDOAH

Book: James Lee Barrett, Peter Udell and Philip Rose (Based on the original screenplay by James Lee Barrett)
Music: Gary Geld
Lyrics: Peter Udell

ORIGINAL PRODUCTION

Alvin Theatre, January 7, 1975 (1,050 perf.)
Director: Philip Rose
Choreographer: Robert Tucker
Musical Director: Lynn Crigler
Orchestration: Don Walker
Principals: Charlie Anderson—John Cullum—baritone; Anne—Donna Theodore—mezzo; James—Joel Higgins—VTI; Jenny—Penelope Milford—alto; Jacob—Ted Agress—VTI; Nathan—Jordan Suffin—VTI; John—David Russell—VTI; Henry—Robert Rosen—VTI; Sam—Gordon Halliday—VTNE; Gabriel—Chip Ford—boy soprano; Robert—Joseph Shapiro—boy soprano
Chorus and Smaller Roles: 8M/3F (see Notes).

SYNOPSIS

In Prologue, the male chorus is seen on opposite sides of the stage, half in Confederate gray, half in Union blue. As the song continues, the two sides confront each other and mime in silhouette the horrors of the war (Raise the Flag of Dixie—M Chorus).

The play opens inside the Anderson house on a Sunday morning as Charlie Anderson, a Virginia farmer, tells his seven children, Jacob, James, Nathan, John, Henry, Jenny, and Robert, and James's pregnant wife Anne, that he refuses to have any member of his family involved in the Civil War. He tells them that the war doesn't concern them for they are first and foremost Andersons living on Anderson land. He is against war that men wage for their honor (I've Heard It All Before—Sc to M Solo).

In church the minister is advocating supporting Virginia in the war when the Andersons tramp in and interrupt. The minister comments on their tardiness and continues his sermon on duty to the State. The congregation sings hymn number 228 (Pass the Cross to Me—Mixed Chorus).

Moments later, on a country road, Jenny, accompanied by three of her brothers, is stopped by her shy suitor, Sam, who nervously asks her if he can stop by later. She agrees and exits with the others as Robert arrives with his Black friend Gabriel on their way to the fishing hole. The two discuss the differences in their lives (Why Am I Me?—Sc to 2M Ch Duet).

In the farmyard, which consists of a barn and well, Sergeant Johnson and his patrol try to forcibly enlist the Anderson sons into the army, but Charlie convinces them it would be unwise as the boys have a natural love for fighting. After the patrol leaves, the boys roughhouse (Next to Lovin'—M Quintet).

Later that evening Charlie and Robert are seated on the porch watching Sam, who is having a difficult time verbalizing his thoughts to Jenny. She is convinced she will be an old woman before he asks her to marry him (Over the Hill—Sc to F Solo—M Needed for Staging).

While Charlie and Robert watch Sam and Jenny go off, Charlie explains the courting procedure in song (The Pickers Are Coming—Sc to M Solo). A lieutenant arrives to inform Charlie that Johnson and his patrol were wiped out on the edge of the farm. This news upsets James, who tells his father they are involved whether they want to be or not. Charlie goes to visit his wife's grave and sort out his thoughts about the war (Meditation I—L to M Solo). When Charlie returns to the parlor, Sam asks him for permission to marry Jenny. Charlie gives the nervous suitor some incomprehensible advice about women and agrees.

Moments before the wedding, as Anne is helping Jenny dress, she tells Jenny about married life (We Make a Beautiful Pair—Sc to F Duet). The two leave the bedroom and descend the steps for the outside ceremony. After the wedding (Violets and Silverbells—Mixed Chorus), Sam is ordered to leave for the front and Anne's delivery pains start. As everyone rushes for water and the doctor, Charlie imagines a grandson (It's a Boy—M Solo). The baby is a girl. The happy mood is broken when Gabriel reports to the family that Robert was taken by the Yankees because he was wearing a Confederate cap. Charlie tells the family that the war now concerns them and everyone but Anne and James leaves to find Robert.

The act ends as Charlie goes to Anne's room to say farewell to her and the baby, who has been named Martha in honor of Charlie's wife.

Act II opens weeks later in the farmyard, where Gabriel recounts to Anne the scene on the plantation when the Yankees freed the slaves (Freedom—Sc to F/M Ch Duet). Gabriel bids her good-bye, telling her he intends to look for his parents, who are somewhere in Georgia and Mississippi. James enters and he and Anne plan their future (Violets and Silverbells [Reprise]—M/F Duet). She exits into the house and he is soon killed by three scavengers, who enter the house to rape and pillage.

In a wooded area near a railroad track, the Andersons wait to stop another Yankee train and search for Robert. As they wait, Charlie reaffirms his belief that they will find Robert (Papa's Gonna Make It Alright—Sc to M Solo). The train stops and the weary prisoners descend; among them is Sam, who embraces Jenny and tells the prisoners to go home, for their war is over. As they exit, a corporal sings (The Only Home I Know—M Solo to M Chorus).

Later that evening two Confederate soldiers mistake Jacob for a soldier and kill him. When they discover their mistake, one runs off and the other apologizes to Charlie, who shoots him several times. The children are appalled at their father's vengeance, and he sadly realizes they must go home and bury Jacob beside Martha.

They arrive home to discover that Anne and James have been murdered and only the Reverend's visit saved baby Martha from starvation. Charlie feels that if they had stayed on the farm, everyone would still be alive. He leaves to visit his wife's grave and explain. At the grave he tells her of the bitterness and the hatred, and confesses he feels Robert is dead (Meditation II—L to M Solo). He hears the church bells and the family sets off to pray.

Inside the church the hymn is interrupted by the Andersons' entrance and the Reverend happily greets them and begins again. Robert hobbles in and slowly walks to the family as the music swells.

NOTES ON THE PRODUCTION

Tony Awards: Best Book and Actor.

The show was effectively produced and made a powerful antiwar statement during a time when American sentiments were in agreement with Charlie Anderson. If one has a strong singer/actor in the leading role, the show is worth doing. Without an excellent Charlie, the show quickly falls apart.

The cast is male-oriented, which is unfortunate for companies with predominantly female members. There should be some women in the church sequence, but the original production utilized some of the male chorus dressed as women in the hymnal sections.

There are quite a few sets which may be easily trimmed. The interior of the home meal scene may take place outside, as if picnic style; the porch of the house and the well may be combined with the barn and parlor sequences. Anne's bedroom may be placed to one side and delineated with tight lighting. The war scene may take place in a darker area or on a country road.

The costumes, many of which are military in style, may need to be rented, which could be a major financial consideration.

SONGS OF SPECIAL INTEREST

"I've Heard It All Before," strong, high baritone vocal and character. Good for developing transitions and acting motivation.

"Meditations I and II," excellent dramatic high baritone solos, thought-provoking, lots of actable specifics, good for two-song character study.

"The Pickers Are Coming," poignant baritone solo, strong male lead demonstrates sensitivity. Good for mood and transition work.

Instrumentation: 3 reeds, 2 trumpets, 2 horns, trombone, percussion, 3 violins, viola, cello, bass, harp, guitar/banjo, harmonica, piano/conductor
Script: SF
Selections: Morris
Record: RCA
Rights: SF

SHOW BOAT

Book and Lyrics: Oscar Hammerstein II (Based on the novel by Edna Ferber)
Music: Jerome Kern

ORIGINAL PRODUCTION

Ziegfeld Theatre, December 27, 1927 (572 perf.)
Directors: Oscar Hammerstein II and Zeke Colvan
Choreographer: Sammy Lee
Musical Direction: Victor Baravalle
Orchestration: Robert Russell Bennett
Principles: Cap'n Andy—Charles Winninger—baritone; Parthy Ann—Edna May Oliver—VTNE; Magnolia—Norma Terris—soprano; Gaylord Ravenal—Howard Marsh—baritone; Julie LaVerne—Helen Morgan—mezzo; Joe—Jules Bledsoe—bass; Steve—Charles Ellis—VTNE; Queenie—Tess Gardella—alto; Frank Schultz—Sammy White—tenor/high baritone; Ellie May Chipley—Eva Puck—alto; Sheriff Vallon—Thomas Gunn—VTNE

Chorus and Smaller Roles: 12M/12F, 1 White child, 2 Black children. A much better configuration is a mixed chorus of Blacks and Whites that totals 18M/18F, 3 children.

SYNOPSIS

The time is 1890. As the river show boat *Cotton Blossom*, owned by jovial Cap'n Andy and his sharp-tongued wife, Parthy Ann, docks on the levee in Natchez, Mississippi, the company of actors are greeted by the stevedores and townsfolk. The actors are introduced: Julie Lavern, the leading lady, married to the untalented leading man, Stephen Baker; Frank, the villain with a comic touch, who dances with Ellie, the comic soubrette (Cotton Blossom—L to Mixed Chorus). The happy mood ends when Pete, who is attracted to Julie, angrily confronts her for giving his present to one of the Blacks. Steve orders him away and the two fight. Cap'n Andy tries to persuade the crowd it was just a staged fight to drum up interest in the performance. The chorus exits as Cap'n Andy has Pete thrown off the boat.

Gaylord Ravenal, a handsome riverboat gambler looking for a quick passage to the next town, is a traveling man with a zest for life (Who Cares If My Boat Goes Upstream?—Sc to M Solo). He meets Magnolia, Andy and Parthy's daughter, and urges her to pretend they are lovers who have just met (Only Make Believe—Sc to M/F Duet). Ravenal, standing on the dock, kisses the hand Magnolia extends from the rail of the ship. Ravenal exits to talk to the Judge as Joe, a stevedore, enters carrying a sack of flour and comments to Magnolia about the wisdom of the Mississippi (Ol' Man River—M Solo—M Chorus).

In the kitchen pantry, Magnolia asks Queenie, the cook, and Julie about love. Julie tries to explain why she loves Steve (Can't Help Lovin' Dat Man—Sc to F Solo to Mixed Chorus). When Queenie's husband, Joe, enters, Queenie reprises the song and Joe and two Black children join in.

In the auditorium Cap'n Andy is rehearsing Julie, Rubberface, and Steve, accompanied by Magnolia on the piano. Ellie interrupts the rehearsal to quietly tell Steve and Julie that Sheriff Vallon plans to arrest Julie for being Black and married to a White. Steve cuts Julie's finger and sucks the wound so that he has Black blood. When the sheriff accuses them of miscegenation, Steve announces that he has Black blood and everyone present swears it is true. Before exiting, Vallon tells Cap'n Andy he won't arrest anyone but doesn't want any mixed blood performers in the show.

Andy has Magnolia perform in Julie's place and hires Gaylord Ravenal, who is still looking for passage out of town, as his leading man. As Joe watches the rehearsal, he senses that Ravenal will bring problems (Ol' Man River [Reprise]—M Solo). The rehearsal ends as Ravenal passionately kisses Magnolia.

On the ship's deck, five starstruck girls enter to buy tickets to the show. When they are overwhelmed by the supposed glamour of Ellie's life, she quickly fills them in on the realities of show business (Life upon the Wicked Stage—Sc to

F Solo to F Chorus). Parthy, worried about Magnolia's infatuation with Ravenal, informs Andy she is going to find out about Ravenal's past.

That night, during the performance, two backwoodsmen become so antagonized by Frank, portraying the villain, that they pull a gun and prepare to shoot. Frank fearfully rushes from the stage and Cap'n Andy is forced to bring down the curtain and detail the remainder of the story to the audience. In a comic monologue, he single-handedly enacts all the roles.

On the moonlit deck of the *Cotton Blossom*, Ravenal asks Magnolia to marry him (You Are Love—Sc to M/F Duet). She eagerly accepts. The next day Cap'n Andy, taking advantage of the free publicity, invites the show boat customers to the wedding (Finale—Mixed Chorus). As the wedding carriage is drawn onstage, a scream is heard offstage and Parthy enters with Vallon and Pete claiming that Ravenal is a murderer. When Andy finds out it was self-defense, he tells Parthy to come along to the wedding. She promptly faints as the bridal couple enter the carriage and the curtain falls.

When Act II opens, it is 1893 and the Chicago World's Fair is in full swing (At the Chicago World's Fair—Mixed Chorus). Magnolia is showing her parents the sights. Cap'n Andy is enthralled, Parthy appalled, by the cooch dancers and low life. Ravenal enters and invites them to an evening on the town but Parthy refuses, and she and Andy return to the hotel. Magnolia and Ravenal reaffirm their love (Why Do I Love You?—Sc to M/F Duet). As they exit, the Dahomey savages from the wild west show enter and perform (In Dahomey—Mixed Chorus).

It is 1904. Frank and Ellie, who have become partners in a vaudeville dance act, enter to look at a room in a second-class boardinghouse whose former tenant is being evicted. They are shocked to discover that Magnolia is the one who is being evicted; it seems Ravenal has fallen on hard times and left Magnolia and their eight-year-old daughter, Kim. His final correspondence included $200 and the suggestion that Magnolia return to the *Cotton Blossom*. The two tactfully leave but urge her to consider the possibility of working at the Trocadero nightclub where they are employed.

Two weeks later at the Trocadero, Julie, the featured singer, depressed, drunk and alone since Steve left, is finishing a rehearsal (Bill—F Solo). Magnolia, not realizing Julie is at the club, arrives to audition. She is about to be rejected when the doorman quietly tells the boss that Julie has left to get drunk but has recommended that Magnolia be hired in her place.

Later that evening, the comedy team of Shultz and Shultz (Ellie and Frank) performs (Goodbye, My Lady Love—M/F Comic Period Duet). A terrified Magnolia appears onstage and is nearly hissed off by the patrons, but Cap'n Andy, who happens to be carousing at the club, helps her out by urging the patrons to sing along (After the Ball—F Solo to Mixed Chorus).

It is 1927. Andy has convinced Ravenal to return to Magnolia and the *Cotton Blossom*. He greets Magnolia, who embraces him happily as the curtain falls.

NOTES ON THE PRODUCTION

Most historians cite *Show Boat* as the beginning of musical theatre. It was not an operetta in the Viennese style nor a lighthearted musical comedy in the popular vein. This was the first attempt to integrate a sensitive story with music and lyrics, the first time miscegenation was mentioned in a musical and it was unique in its treatment of the leading lady, who begins the show as an ingenue and ends nearly forty years later as a mature woman. Oscar Hammerstein II and Jerome Kern took a tremendous risk in thus pursuing their goal to achieve a cohesive, dramatic evening in the theatre. The fact that the show is so often revived attests to their success.

Edna Ferber, the author of the novel, was astounded that Jerome Kern wanted to musicalize this lengthy and complicated story. She considered musical theatre as lighthearted comedy and couldn't imagine *Show Boat* being successfully adapted to the musical stage of the 1920s. Even more astounding, in retrospect, is the fact that the show was produced by Florenz Ziegfeld, usually noted for his glorification of the American girl.

The show is extremely difficult to properly produce, as it has a very large chorus of both Blacks and Whites who are essential to the overall tone of the production. Much of the emotional impact is derived from the Black reaction to things that happen on the riverboat.

The acting version that is available for production is based on the 1946 revival. Much of the material, important in 1946, may be slightly tedious to modern-day audiences. Some scenes that were included to allow for set changes may not be totally necessary to modern productions.

Show Boat should not be attempted in strictly theatrical form if a company does not have the financial means to support a lavish production. It would be better to perform it as a concert piece with certain scenes being enacted prior to the songs. The music is memorable, notable, and well worth being enacted. When considering a concert version, the company should mention that to the licensing agency when applying for the rights.

SONGS OF SPECIAL INTEREST

"Bill" (lyrics by P. G. Wodehouse), poignant, club style. Deceptively simplistic, takes a special personality to perform with quality, mezzo.

"Can't Help Lovin' Dat Man," semidramatic, club potential, mezzo.

"Goodbye, My Lady Love," vaudeville style, up tempo duet, alto/baritone.

"Life upon the Wicked Stage," female chorus, good exercise for beginning director/choreographer. Good for revue or class situation.

"Only Make Believe," romantic, charm duet, where lovers never touch, soprano, baritone.

"Ol' Man River," sensitive, poignant, Black bass solo. Shows off vocal and acting.

Instrumentation: 4 violins, viola, cello, bass, flute, oboe, 2 reeds, 2 trumpets,
2 horns, bassoon, banjo/guitar, percussion, piano/conductor
Script: Cimino, Chappell (London)
Score: Harms
Record: RCA
Rights: R & H

SOMETHING'S AFOOT

Book, Music and Lyrics: James McDonald, David Vos and Robert Gerlach
Additional Music: Ed Linderman

ORIGINAL PRODUCTION

Lyceum Theatre, May 27, 1976 (61 perf.)
Director and Choreographer: Tony Tanner
Musical Director: Buster Davis
Orchestration: Peter Larson
Principals: Lettie—Neva Small—mezzo; Flint—Marc Jordan—tenor; Clive—
Sel Vitella—VTI; Hope Langdon—Barbara Heuman—mezzo soprano; Dr. Gray-
burn—Jack Schmidt—VTI; Nigel Rancour—Gary Beach—baritone; Lady Grace
Manley-Prowe—Liz Sheridan—alto; Col. Gillweather—Gary Gage—VTI; Miss
Tweed—Tessie O'Shea—mezzo; Geoffrey—Willard Beckham—tenor
Chorus and Smaller Roles: None.

SYNOPSIS

The curtain rises on a large entrance hall of the 1935 country estate of Lord
Rancour, situated on an island in the middle of a lake. The hall has several
doorways leading to a library, a study, a kitchen and the outside. There are
stairs which lead to an upstairs landing that has at least two doors to bedrooms
opening onto it. Lettie, a young woman, enters, sets down her suitcase and
surveys the room. She removes the dustcover from the desk and chair and
surprises Flint, the caretaker, who is asleep under the dustcover. Her screams
bring Clive, the butler.

The guests arrive (A Marvelous Weekend—Mixed Chorus) and include Hope
Langdon, the typical ingenue; Dr. Grayburn, the family doctor; Nigel Rancour,
the disgruntled nephew; Lady Grace Manley-Prowe, a typical English matron;
Col. Gillweather, the retired Army colonel; and Miss Tweed, the elderly amateur
detective. The song is interspersed with dialogue and ends as the guests come
to dinner dressed in their finery.

The visitors are drinking sherry as Clive enters from Lord Rancour's room to
announce that Lord Rancour is dead. Throughout his speech he slowly steps

down the stairs until he announces dinner is served and steps on the last stair, which instantly explodes, killing him. The guests momentarily freeze, then become hysterical, for they realize someone in the room is a killer (Something's Afoot—Mixed Chorus).

Everyone wants to leave, but the roads are flooded. While the men remove Clive, Dr. Grayburn descends from Rancour's room to explain that Rancour was shot with a revolver at close range. At first everyone suspects Clive, but they ascertain he didn't do it.

The men leave to see if there is any way off the island and the women, left alone, valiantly vow to carry on (Carry On—Sc to F Duet to F Quartet). As the song ends there is a clap of thunder and a flash of lightning. The door flies open and Geoffrey, a young, handsome man, appears. The women automatically suspect him of the two murders and tie him up. The men return and find a gun in his backpack. Geoffrey explains he's a member of the college crew team whose boat capsized, and the gun is their starting gun. Miss Tweed, who has taken his gun and substituted it for one with blanks, fires it at him and he is declared innocent.

They try the telephones, but discover the wires have been cut. Mysteriously, a phone rings and Dr. Grayburn finds it hidden in the desk. As he answers, a pink gas emerges from the receiver, killing him instantly. The men remove the body to the library; Tweed, Lettie and the Colonel go to the kitchen for some tea; and Lady Grace goes to her room to rest, leaving Hope and Geoffrey to get to know one another (I Don't Know Why I Trust You—M/F Duet).

Nigel, alone in the main room, searches through the desk but is spied by Lady Grace, whom he confronts with the fact that she was once married to Lord Rancour. She confesses and promises to help Nigel find the missing will by stalling everyone while he searches the rooms.

The Colonel comes out and she learns that he is Shirley, the man she had an affair with twenty-six years before. They think over those happy times (The Man with the Ginger Moustache—Sc to F Torch Song). She tells him she and Lord Rancour had a child she never saw because Lord Rancour took it from her, promising to raise it as his heir. Nigel enters and the three start to argue.

Tweed, Hope and Geoffrey enter with the gun they found on Clive's body. As they go to put the gun with the telephone, they find the shears responsible for cutting the phone wires. They gaze at each other and move away (Suspicious—Sc to Mixed Chorus). Thunder booms and the lights go out. As Lady Grace finds the light switch, the electricity courses through her body, killing her.

Act II opens and there is just enough light onstage to make out the action. Lady Grace is being dragged into the library; Miss Tweed enters with a candle, notices the body, and tugs at the other end. She cries out, the lights go on and the Colonel is revealed holding Lady Grace.

Nigel, left alone, earnestly begins searching the room for the will (I Don't Know What I'm Looking For—M Solo). During the song he finds the missing document and learns that he is not the heir. The sconce attached to the post at the bottom of the stairs suddenly falls, kills him, and returns to its orignal position.

The Colonel enters, finds Nigel and begins to read the will. A shrunken head with a blowgun appears and shoots a poisoned dart at the Colonel, who judges he has five minutes left to live. Miss Tweed enters and reads that Hope Langdon is the daughter of Grace Rancour Manley-Prowe. The Colonel dies as she hides the will in her pocket and exits.

Hope sings of her love for Geoffrey while she is standing under a chandelier. As she sings, the chandelier begins to descend, but when she moves away it stops (You Fell Out of the Sky—F Solo). The chandelier finally falls, narrowly missing her. Geoffrey comforts her as everyone enters. They put the chandelier back up and everyone goes off but Flint and Lettie. Flint tells Lettie he remembers there is a boat they can escape in and the two prepare to run away without the others (Dinghy—Sc to M/F Duet). As Flint goes to look for oars, Lettie finds a note in her pocket saying that Lord Rancour has hidden money in the four-foot-tall Ming vase. She jumps into the vase, which totally engulfs her. The others return to the room, find the note and one of Lettie's shoes and realize one more person is gone.

Flint goes to the kitchen to light the stove but is killed by a gas explosion. They realize that Flint must be the murderer because he was the only one whose death was accidental. Tweed tells the couple that Hope is the adopted daughter of Rancour and therefore the legal heir. The girl is amazed by her deductions, and she and Geoffrey beg her to tell them how she does it, to which Tweed responds she owes everything to all the famous mystery writers of the day (I Owe It All—F Solo to 2F/M Trio).

Hope goes to pack and Tweed decides to paint Geoffrey. As she works she realizes that Flint didn't commit the murders and starts to announce the killer when a spear wraps around her muffler and strangles her to death.

Hope comes downstairs and accuses Geoffrey of killing Tweed. They argue but he tries to make her realize that she is wrong and he loves her. She backs to the fireplace where a portrait falls, revealing a record player. They turn it on and the voice of the late Lord Rancour explains that she is his heir and he killed everyone so they wouldn't contest his will. He also explains he has taken his own life because he convicted himself of the murders he had committed. As the record continues, Hope and Geoffrey look out the front door at the sunlight (New Day—M/F Duet). The record ends as Rancour says he killed Flint by lacing the wine with arsenic. Unfortunately, Hope and Geoffrey don't hear this because they are toasting the new day with that very wine and drop to the floor, dead (I Owe It All—Finale—Mixed Chorus).

NOTES ON THE PRODUCTION

The play is extremely enjoyable and charming. It is a musical spoof of the Agatha Christie murder mysteries of the thirties and must be played honestly. The songs are reminiscent of a variety of period tunes and help establish character.

Technically, the play survives on visual effects, which are carefully outlined in the French acting version. The action takes place in a single setting, but the visual aids are essential to the production and must be carefully handled.

The show did not survive the summer months and had a short Broadway run, so few people have heard of it. It is funny, charming, exciting and certainly worthy of companies that can handle the technical requirements, which are complicated but important to the script.

SONGS OF SPECIAL INTEREST

"Carry On," female quartet, spirited kick-line ending.
"I Owe It All," may be performed as a solo, clever lyrics, character-oriented, mezzo/alto.

Instrumentation: 2 reeds, trumpet, trombone, 2 percussion, bass, guitar/banjo, piano/conductor
Script: SF
Selections: New York Times
Rights: SF

THE SOUND OF MUSIC

Book: Howard Lindsay and Russel Crouse (Suggested by *The Trapp Family Singers*, by Maria Augusta Trapp)
Music: Richard Rodgers
Lyrics: Oscar Hammerstein II

ORIGINAL PRODUCTION

Lunt-Fontanne Theatre, November 16, 1959 (1,443 perf.)
Director: Vincent J. Donehue
Musical Numbers Staged by: Joe Layton
Musical Director: Frederick Dvonch
Orchestration: Robert Russell Bennett
Choral arrangements: Trude Rittman
Principals: Maria—Mary Martin—mezzo; Abbess—Patricia Neway—soprano; Cpt. Von Trapp—Theodore Bikel—baritone; Liesl—Lauri Peters—mezzo; Rolf—Brian Davies—tenor; Elsa Schraeder—Marion Marlow—alto; Max—Kurt Kaznar—baritone; Sister Berthe—Elizabeth Howell—alto; Sister Sophia—Karen Shepard—soprano; Sister Margaretta—Muriel O'Malley—mezzo
Chorus and Smaller Roles: 4F/2M children, 8F/6M.

SYNOPSIS

The play opens in the interior of the Salzburg, Austria, Honnberg Abbey where the nuns are singing and praying (Preludium—F Chorus). When Sister Berthe discovers that someone is missing, calls for Maria fill the hall. On a mountainside near the Abbey, Maria is seen at the base of a large tree, viewing the countryside around her (Sound of Music—F Solo).

In the sparsely furnished office of the Mother Abbess, the Mother Superior discusses with Sisters Berthe, Margaretta, and Sophia the merits of the postulants and the problems of Maria (Maria—F Quartet).

The Mother calls for Maria, who begs forgiveness for her bad behavior, especially her constant singing. The Abbess asks her for the lyrics of a long-forgotten children's song and Maria obliges (Favorite Things—F Duet). The Abbess informs Maria she is temporarily sending her to Captain Von Trapp's home to be governess to his seven children. Maria resigns herself to leave for the Von Trapp home.

In the living room of the Von Trapp estate where French windows open onto a terrace, and a circular staircase rises to the second floor hall, Captain Von Trapp enters and blows several signals on his boatswain's whistle. When his housekeeper Fraulein Schmidt and butler Franz enter, he informs them that he has a new governess from the Abbey and will soon be leaving for Vienna. After he leaves the two reveal they are pro-Nazis and waiting for some information about Hitler's takeover of Austria.

The doorbell rings and Maria is greeted by Captain Von Trapp, who terrifies her, for he is an overbearing, strong disciplinarian with a different whistle call for every member of the household. She talks with the children alone and is appalled to discover that they don't know how to sing. She teaches them the notes of the scale (Do Re Mi—Sc to Mixed Chorus) and an accompanying song.

Later that day outside the villa, near a stone wall and bench, sixteen-year-old Liesl meets seventeen-year-old Rolf, her pro-German boyfriend, who tells her she knows so little of the world that he will have to take care of her (You Are Sixteen—Sc to M/F Duet). In Maria's bedroom, with a wardrobe on one side, a large window nearby, and a hall door on the opposite side, Maria sees Liesl climbing through the bedroom window and attempts to win her friendship. When the rest of the children gradually seek refuge from the sounds of a thunderstorm, she entertains them with a song (The Lonely Goatherd—F Solo to Mixed Chorus).

A month later, on the terrace of the Von Trapp home, the Captain is entertaining Elsa Schraeder, an attractive woman in her late thirties, and Max Detweiler, a clever, witty, middle-aged man searching for a music group to enter in the Salzburg Festival. When the Captain exits to search for the children, Elsa confesses to Max that she plans on marrying Von Trapp. The Captain returns and Max pushes Elsa to him (How Can Love Survive?—M/F Duet with Captain Needed for Staging).

The children enter with Maria, and the Captain is appalled by their play clothes, which Maria has made from her old bedroom drapes, and by their lack of discipline. He complains to Maria, who tells him he should learn more about his children. He orders her to return to the Abbey but is interrupted by the children singing to Frau Schraeder. The Captain realizes she is right, asks her to stay and joins Maria and his family in song (The Sound of Music—M/F Duet with Mixed Children's Chorus).

In the living room, Captain Von Trapp's party to introduce Frau Schraeder to his friends is interrupted by an argument between a pro-Nazi and a pro-Austrian. The Captain invites everyone to the terrace to cool down as Kurt and Maria enter the living room and begin an Austrian folk dance. The Captain interrupts to show Kurt how the dance should be done, but when the Captain dances with Maria, the children realize they are in love. They tell Maria, who is horrified to find anything that conflicts with her desire to be a nun. The Captain insists that she join them all for dinner and sends her to her room to change, and Elsa begs him to have the children perform their goodnight song for the guests. As the children say good-bye (So Long, Farewell—Mixed Chorus) to the guests, Maria sadly leaves for the Abbey.

The Mother Abbess sends Maria back to the Von Trapps to discover her true feelings and urges her to search for the life she was meant for (Climb Ev'ry Mountain—Sc to F Solo).

When Act II opens, Max is on the terrace encouraging the children to sing, but they are upset by Maria's absence and the announcement that their father is to marry Frau Schraeder. Cheered by Maria's voice, they excitedly finish the song, greet her (Favorite Things [Reprise]—Mixed Children's Chorus), and relay the news that Frau Schraeder is to be their stepmother. Von Trapp asks her why she left, but she assures him the reason no longer exists. She exits to be with the children.

Max and Frau Schraeder, worried about Germany's possible invasion of Austria, urge the Captain to play along as insurance on his property and wealth (No Way to Stop It—2M/F Trio). Frau Schraeder, realizing that the Captain will not bend to the Germans, calls off the wedding. As she goes to pack, the Captain and Maria confess their love for each other (An Ordinary Couple—Sc to M/F Duet). The two are married at the Abbey to the accompaniment of a chorus of nuns cloistered beyond (Processional to Maria—F Chorus). The Captain and Maria, whose honeymoon is interrupted by the Anschluss, return to discover that nearly everyone around them is pro-Nazi. Liesl, in love with Rolf, who is an admitted Nazi, asks Maria about love and Maria tries to explain (You Are Sixteen—Sc to F Duet). Rolf brings a telegram, ordering Captain Von Trapp to join the German Navy, and begs them to join the Germans or leave Austria. The Germans arrive to take Von Trapp to accept his commission but Maria bids for time, insisting that they must sing in the music festival. Because the Germans want things to appear unchanged, they allow the performance.

The family performs on the stage of the Salzburg Concert Hall (Edelweiss, So Long Farewell—Mixed Chorus), and escapes while the judges decide the winner. They flee to the Abbey and are followed by the Germans. In the garden of the Abbey, Rolf sees the Captain and starts to betray him, but when he sees Liesl, he cannot. The Germans leave and the family begins the climb to Switzerland and safety (Climb Every Mountain [Reprise]—Finale, Mixed Chorus).

NOTES ON THE PRODUCTION

The Sound of Music was Rodgers and Hammerstein's final collaboration, for Hammerstein died during the run of the show. The show tied with *Fiorello!* for the following Tony Awards: Best Musical, Book, Producer, Composer, and singly won for Musical Direction, Scenic Design, Actress, and Supporting Actress (Patricia Neway).

Little need be said about this show; the success of the stage play followed by the triumph of the Julie Andrews movie makes it a familiar musical around the globe. The story is romantic and hopeful, the songs melodious and familiar, the casting requirements a dream, for it is one of the few scripts that primarily feature women.

The costumes, mostly nuns' habits, may be difficult to obtain since many nuns have discarded the traditional garb for modern wear. Unless a group has access to the old-style black habits, they will have to be rented.

The set for the Von Trapp house is quite large and ideally structural, but it is possible to cut the stairway and upper hall by assuming the stairs are offstage.

It may be best when undertaking this show to have a nun as an advisor to the actors and director. There will be many Catholics in the audience who have been educated in parochial schools and will be aware of certain arm and hand positions, demeanor and decorum that are associated with the older nuns.

SONGS OF SPECIAL INTEREST

"An Ordinary Couple," baritone/mezzo, older, charm, romantic duet.

"How Can Love Survive?" baritone/alto sophisticate, humorous duet.

"Maria," F quartet, specific characterizations make this an ideal number for class study.

"You Are Sixteen," F mezzo duet, difference in age and wisdom are important in the reprise. The original is a movement-oriented, love tenor/mezzo duet.

Instrumentation: 4 reeds, 2 horns, 2 trumpets, 2 trombones, tuba, percussion, 3 violins, viola, cello, bass, harp, guitar, piano/conductor
Script: Random House
Score: Williamson
Record: Columbia
Rights: R & H

SOUTH PACIFIC

Book: Oscar Hammerstein II and Joshua Logan (Adapted from James A. Michener's *Tales of the South Pacific*)
Music: Richard Rodgers
Lyrics: Oscar Hammerstein II

ORIGINAL PRODUCTION

Majestic Theatre, April 7, 1949 (1,925 perf.)
Book and Musical Numbers Staged by: Joshua Logan
Musical Director: Salvatore Dell'Isola
Orchestration: Robert Russell Bennett
Principals: Nellie Forbush—Mary Martin—mezzo; Emile De Becque—Ezio Pinza—bass; Bloody Mary—Juanita Hall—alto; Luther Billis—Myron McCormick—baritone; Lt. Cable—William Tabbert—tenor; Liat—Betta St. John—VTNE; Cpt. Brackett—Martin Wolfson—VTNE; Cmdr. Harbison—Harvey Stephens—VTNE; Lt. Buzz Adams—Don Fellows—VTNE
Chorus: M/F Eurasian children, 14M/8F minimum.

SYNOPSIS

At Emile De Becque's plantation, on an island in the South Pacific during World War II, two Eurasian children, Ngana, an eleven-year-old girl, and Jerome, her eight-year-old brother, are playing (Dites Moi—M/F Ch Duet). Henry, De Becque's servant, interrupts their play and escorts them inside as De Becque's voice is heard.

De Becque, a handsome, middle-aged French planter, enters with Nellie Forbush, a young American nurse from Little Rock, Arkansas. She is overwhelmed by the beauty of the place and Emile's life-style. She tells him about her optimistic outlook on life (A Cockeyed Optimist—L to F Solo) but becomes self-conscious. Emile tactfully offers her some cognac and the two soliloquize about their possible future together (Wonder How I'd Feel—L to M/F Solos). Emile admits to Nellie that he cares for her even though he has only known her for two weeks (Some Enchanted Evening—Sc to M Solo). When Henry tells them Nellie's Jeep has arrived to take her back to camp, Emile tells her that he left France because he killed an evil bully. Nellie accepts his explanation, promises to consider his proposal and exits. Emile happily greets his children and the three sing (Dites Moi [Reprise]—2Ch/M Trio).

In an intermediate area along the beach the Seabees serenade an older Tonkonese woman, who is busy selling cheap souvenirs (Bloody Mary—M Chorus).

The scene shifts to the edge of a palm grove near the beach with Luther Billis's Laundry on one side and Mary's Straw Shop on the other. Mary sells Billis her Bali Hai boar's tooth bracelet, and the men study the mysterious off-limits island where the French planters have sent their women (There Is Nothin' Like a Dame—Sc to M Chorus).

When Lieutenant Cable, a handsome young officer, enters, seeking information about De Becque, Bloody Mary tries to entice him to visit Bali Hai. She hauntingly describes the calling of the island (Bali Ha'i—L to F Solo). She exits, leaving a spellbound Cable. Billis, seizing the opportunity to be part of a trip to the island, tries to convince the officer to let him requisition a boat but Cable refuses, for he has to see the commander. Billis sends the "professor" to escort Cable to the commander's office, but Commander Harbison arrives accompanied by Captain Brackett to order Bloody Mary off government property. The Seabees and Mary pick up her things and exit. Cable introduces himself to the two officers and explains that his mission entails setting up a coast watch from the Japanese-held islands. The two officers look worried until they find out that Cable has plans to take De Becque with him. They agree to meet in Brackett's office to discuss the matter. Lieutenant Cable, left alone, looks at the island and begins to remember Bloody Mary's haunting song; the lights fade.

In an intermediate area Billis tells Cable, who is on his way to Brackett's office, that he has requisitioned a boat for the trip to Bali Hai. Cable tells him to forget it and exits, but Billis vows to get Cable and himself on that island.

In the commander's office Brackett, Cable and Harbison question Nellie. She leaves promising to find out more about De Becque.

Nellie and Cable, in an intermediate scene, discuss differences in ages and cultures, and Cable warns her that she doesn't know much about De Becque.

On the beach several nurses are relaxing, while others are washing clothes. There is a sign advertising Luther Billis's "showerbath." When Nellie enters to wash her hair, the nurses ask her why she is so preoccupied. She tells them she is going to break off the relationship with Emile before she gets too involved (I'm Gonna Wash That Man Right Outa My Hair—F Solo to F Chorus). At the end of the song, Emile appears and the girls exit, leaving Emile and Nellie alone. He asks her to a party at his home in her honor, but she begins questioning him about his former life. He explains why he came to the islands and asks her to marry him. Nellie agrees to meet his friends the following Friday (Some Enchanted Evening [Reprise]—Sc to M/F Duet). When Emile waves good-bye, the girls, who have been listening offstage, taunt Nellie, who defiantly sings (A Wonderful Guy—L to F Solo to F Chorus).

In Brackett's office, when Cable is unable to convince Emile to help him spy on the Japanese, the disappointed lieutenant leaves for Bali Hai with Billis.

On the island the French and native girls greet the boat, and Bloody Mary takes Cable to the interior of a native hut where a seventeen-year-old, slight-framed Tonkonese waits. She introduces her as Liat, and leaves. Cable and Liat embrace and the lights fade as projections come up behind. When the lights rise, Cable is bare chested and Liat's hair is undone. He is obviously enthralled by this delicate girl and shocked to discover she is Bloody Mary's daughter. The boat whistle is heard in the distance but he ignores it and sings of his feelings (Younger Than Springtime—Sc to M Solo).

Billis is waiting for Cable on the dock. As the young man walks to the boat he ignores the groups of waving girls, and Mary happily tells everyone he is going to be her son-in-law.

On the terrace of Emile's home, Henry and another servant enter to clean up the residue of the party that has preceded. Nellie is overjoyed and a little tipsy. In a charming scene Emile and Nellie show their enjoyment of each other (Twin Soliloquies, Cockeyed Optimist, Wash That Man [Reprise]—Sc to M/F Duet). Emile's two Eurasian children enter to say good night and Nellie is obviously charmed. When Henry leads them off, Nellie asks Emile if they are Henry's and Emile tells her the children are his. She assumes he is joking until he tells her their mother is dead. Horrified by the fact that he lived with a non-White woman, she quickly excuses herself, promising to call him when she is free. She rushes off in tears. Emile fears she may not return but vows to do all he can to keep her.

Act II opens during the Thanksgiving Follies; the nurses and Seabees are performing (Soft Shoe—Dance). At the end of the number the scene shifts to backstage, where Emile appears with flowers for Nellie and learns that she has asked for a transfer to another island. Cable appears anxious to visit Liat. Mary and Liat arrive to inform Cable that unless he marries Liat, she will be forced to marry a drunken, repulsive French planter. Mary cleverly paints a picture of Liat and Cable's life together (Happy Talk—Sc to F Solo) and promises that they will have beautiful babies. This last forces Cable to realize that his upbringing will not allow him to marry anyone non-White. When he explains to Mary that he can't marry Liat, she drags the girl off; Cable sadly watches.

At the Thanksgiving Follies, while Nellie sings, Luther enacts the showstopper of the evening (Honey Bun—F Solo—F Chorus).

Emile finds Nellie and demands to know why she asked for a transfer. She tries to explain her reasons but leaves Cable to finish (You've Got to Be Taught—M Solo). Feeling he has nothing to live for (This Nearly Was Mine—L to M Solo), Emile agrees to go on the mission with Cable.

In the communications office Brackett and a radio operator are listening to sounds from the island where Cable and De Becque are spying on the Japanese. Brackett comments on the stupidity of Billis, who cost the government more than $600,000 to rescue him from the Japanese fighter planes. It seems Billis stowed away on the drop-off plane and fell out. Billis enters with pilot Buzz Adams, who says that Billis's action may have bought more time for the men on the island. When Billis looks pleased, Brackett throws him out.

Two weeks later Nellie, who has been to De Becque's house to apologize for her earlier behavior, learns that Cable and Emile are behind enemy lines. In the radio room, she hears Emile's voice telling everyone that Joe has been killed and De Becque is in danger. Nellie, realizing she may lose Emile forever, runs to the beach and call to him to please come back so she can tell him that nothing matters but their being together. She is interrupted by Mary, who enters with Liat. It seems Liat refuses to marry anyone but Cable. Nellie tearfully comforts the forlorn girl.

The company street is crowded with the men who are ready to move out. Billis questions Commander Harbison on the whereabouts of De Becque, but no one knows if he got off the island alive.

The scene switches to Emile's plantation, where Nellie spends all her free time with Emile's children. Emile surprises her and joins in the song (Dites Moi—Finale—Mixed Quartet), knowing that all is well.

NOTES ON THE PRODUCTION

Tony Awards: Actor, Actress, Featured Actor (Myron McCormick), Featured Actress (Juanita Hall), Direction, Musical, Producer, Music and Book.

South Pacific is a classic musical. The story deals with the subject of the meaning of life and the growing up of a young nurse during World War II. The music is wonderful; there isn't a bad song in the entire score; most of it is familiar, extremely actable and memorable. The book is poignant, romantic, dramatic and emotional. It is a musical well worth trying, but unfortunately it often suffers from bad direction.

Anyone considering a prouction of this show must spend a great deal of rehearsal time getting the actors to understand the relationships, emotions and background of the characters they will portray. The honesty and sincerity of the principals are essential to retain the charm and drama of the piece. Too often Nellie is played as a mindless, happy-go-lucky girl, and audiences are left wondering why the character is so unbelievable. Nellie is an educated, optimistic nurse during one of the worst wars in modern history. She has dealt in life and death, sometimes on a daily basis, yet her hope for the future keeps her going. Both she and De Becque are lonely and isolated people, for they do not fit into any "crowd" of friends. They are meant for each other, despite the difference in their ages.

There are quite a few sets in the show, five of which traditionally are full stage settings. It is possible to trim the number of sets and substitute standard curtains for the Thanksgiving show sequences. Most companies use a backdrop of Bali Hai throughout.

The costumes are primarily sailor-type uniforms and are not expensive to obtain.

The leading role requires a strong male voice and some age. In the case of a high school production it may be advisable to find an older actor for the role. Bloody Mary, a character that can seem vicious, conniving and very corrupt, needs to be played with a comedic touch. She also requires an excellent voice to sing the haunting "Bali Ha'i," a song that must evoke mood.

SONGS OF SPECIAL INTEREST

"A Cockeyed Optimist," up tempo, mezzo, requires movement, good to free up a beginning performer.

"A Wonderful Guy," good for audition and for movement, up tempo.

"There Is Nothin' Like a Dame," actor-proof, male chorus number, specific characterizations help, good for beginners, revue.

Instrumentation: 4 violins, viola, cello, bass, 5 reeds, 3 trumpets, 2 trombones, 3 horns, tuba, harp, drums, piano/conductor
Script: Six plays by Rodgers and Hammerstein, Random
Score: Williamson
Record: Columbia
Rights
R & H

STOP THE WORLD—I WANT TO GET OFF

Book, Music, and Lyrics: Leslie Bricusse and Anthony Newley

ORIGINAL PRODUCTION

Shubert Theatre, October 3, 1962 (556 perf.)
Director: Anthony Newley
Choreographer: John Broome. Restaged by: Virginia Mason
Musical Director: Milton Rosenstock
Orchestration: Ian Frasier, David Lindup, Burt Rhodes, Gordon Langford
Principals: Littlechap—Anthony Newley—baritone; Evie, Anya, Ilse, Ginnie—Anna Quayle—mezzo; Jane—Jennifer Baker—VTI; Susan—Susan Baker—VTI
Chorus and Smaller Roles: 5F/1 Boy

SYNOPSIS

There need not be any specific set, for the locations shift as Littlechap goes in search of himself. The play opens with the chorus as younger children singing a child's song (ABC Song—Mixed Chorus). Littlechap sets out to find his way in the world and the chorus grows up. The games turn from those of childhood to mimed work that adults perform, for example, production line. Littlechap is older and tries to pick up Evie, a secretary who is waiting for her bus. Flattered by his attempts, she laughs and leaves him alone at the bus stop, where Littlechap decides she would be interested if he had money (I Wanna Be Rich—M Solo to Mixed Chorus).

At the end of the number he remeets Evie and a voice from the chorus, acting as narrator, comments on her attempts to ignore him. Evie professes she has been properly raised and is very upper-class (Typically English—F Solo with M Comments). At the end of the number she exits with Littlechap as the narrator comments on how accidents sometimes happen when twenty-five-year-old men become involved with seventeen-year-old women.

Littlechap goes to meet the boss of his company, who is unseen and represented by music. Littlechap's monologue and reactions to the music are the only way the audience understands the boss's comments. Littlechap promises never to see Evie again; he had no idea that she was the boss's daughter.

He confronts Evie, who tells him she is pregnant. The wedding proceeds, but Evie exits in the middle with a wave of nausea. Littlechap tells the audience he has been forced into a marriage he did not intend (Lumbered—M Solo to F Chorus). Time passes and Evie enters to tell him she is pregnant again. When he tells her he has been lumbered again, she says she has the same feeling (Lumbered [Reprise]—M/F Duet).

Realizing he is going to need a larger salary to raise another child, Littlechap goes to see Evie's father, who proposes to send him to their Northern Office in Sludgepool. The three arrive in the very cold, very ugly climate and are welcomed by the disgruntled workers (Welcome to Sludgepool—F Chorus). He sends her off to look at their house while he goes to examine the factory. He greets the workers, who are extremely slow, and tells them he has aspirations for their factory. As he sings they are skeptical but gradually become excited (Gonna Build a Mountain—L to M Solo to F Chorus).

Evie informs him she is pregnant for the third time and Littlechap needing a larger salary goes to see his father-in-law, who sends him to Russia as a delegate to the International Trade Festival. He arrives in Moscow and immediately makes a play for Anya, the tour guide, who tells him about her upbringing (Glorious Russian—F Solo to F Chorus). Anya takes him to her flat on the seventeenth floor and tells him she would like a little boy; Littlechap agrees and the two imagine the joys of a son (Meilinki Meilchick—Sc to F/M Duet). The little boy dies and Littlechap screams for the world to stop.

In England years later his two daughters, now in their teens, comment on the coldness between their parents as Littlechap and Evie, from opposite sides of the stage, dig at each other (Family Fugue—Sc to M/3F Quartet). Littlechap goes to see his father-in-law, who asks him to sit down and offers him a cigar. It seems the boss is fond of him.

Evie hires Ilsa, a German servant girl, who tells Littlechap she is not a Nazi and her father was cleared during the Nuremberg trials. She is extremely militaristic and tells him about her upbringing (Typische Deutsche—Sc to F Solo with Mixed Chorus).

Littlechap and Evie continue to bicker (Nag! Nag! Nag!—Mixed Chorus). The act ends on an ominous tone as Littlechap tells Ilsa he loves her. Ilsa twists his arm, tells him Germany will rise again, and she has no time to waste on him. Evie confronts him with his constant philandering and moves his things into the spare room. They both yell that they have been lumbered as the lights black out.

Act II opens with Littlechap's father-in-law sending him to New York City with his family (Once in a Lifetime—M Solo). He arrives in New York and the chorus mimes various New York City events. Littlechap goes to the Chocolate Box Club where Ginnie, an extremely dumb girl, is performing (All American—F Solo). After the show she takes him to a Chinese restaurant and he tells her he loves her. In the middle of the scene he hears his daughter Susan call out and rushes home to find out that his unmarried daughter is going to have a baby. His whole life rushes by and he wants to stop the world, but he becomes the father of the bride and gives her away.

Back in England Littlechap goes to see his father-in-law, who tells him he should run for Parliament (Once in a Lifetime [Reprise]—M Solo). The number segues into the campaign speeches (Mumbo Jumbo—Mixed Chorus). Littlechap wins.

Littlechap is in Parliament when he has a heart attack. He decides to take it easy. The chorus portray retirees at a wealthy institution (Welcome to Sunvale—F Chorus). Evie enters on Littlechap's arm and he quietly asks her why she stayed by him for the past thirty-five years (Someone Nice Like You—Sc to M/F Duet). As the number ends, she dies.

He goes to visit his father-in-law's grave and tells him he is probably going to be made a lord and an honorary doctor, and be given the key to Sludgepool. All his successes are meaningless for he has lost Evie, who was dearest to him. As he begins his memoirs all his various girlfriends reappear, but he is at last able to admit he was only in love with one person in his life and that was himself. He berates himself for his foolishness (What Kind of Fool Am I—M Solo with F Chorus). The play ends as his grandson appears and takes his hand.

NOTES ON THE PRODUCTION

This small-cast show is a good choice for smaller companies that have an excellent male and female for the leading roles. Anna Quayle won a well-deserved Tony Award for her characterization in the show. It is a duo-star vehicle but is also demanding for the chorus. The charm of the show is in its smallness, and the chorus should be kept to a minimum and in one basic costume throughout. The grandson may be played by a female chorus member, and Jane and Susan may also be in the chorus.

Many of the songs require chorus backup to heighten the vocal and physical interest. This requires an imaginative choreographer and a cast with mime abilities.

The subject matter is extremely serious but there is balance between the comic and the serious. There are some very touching scenes which may be a surprise to audiences expecting a lighthearted comedy.

The leading female role requires a singer with a large voice and a broad range. She must be able to do accents, and handle the comedy and dramatic demands of the role.

SONGS OF SPECIAL INTEREST

"Once in a Lifetime," dramatic, club style, strong voice, shows off acting and singing. Baritone.

"Typically English," humorous number if the actress's attitude is typically upper-class. At the end of each verse she tells of her boredom. Mezzo.

"What Kind of Fool Am I?" strong, vocally dramatic baritone song.

Instrumentation: 5 reeds, 2 trumpets, bass, 2 trombones, percussion, piano/conductor
Script: NP
Selections: TRO
Record: London
Rights: TW

STREET SCENE

Book: Elmer Rice (Based on Elmer Rice's Pulitzer Prize play of the same name)
Music: Kurt Weill
Lyrics: Langston Hughes and Elmer Rice

ORIGINAL PRODUCTION

Adelphi Theatre, January 9, 1947 (148 perf.)
Director: Charles Friedman
Musical Director: Maurice Abravanel
Orchestrations: Kurt Weill
Principals: Abraham Kaplan—Irving Kaufman—tenor; Mrs. Fiorentino—Helen Arden—high soprano; Mr. Olsen—Wilson Smith—bass; Emma Jones—Hope Emerson—mezzo; Olga Olsen—Ellen Repp—contralto; Henry—Creighton Thompson—high baritone; Willie Maurrant—Peter Griffith—boy soprano; Anna Maurrant—Polyna Stoska—dramatic soprano; Sam Kaplan—Brian Sullivan—tenor; Frank Maurrant—Norman Cordon—bass/baritone; George Jones—David E. Thomas—baritone; Lippo Fiorentino—Sydney Rainer—tenor; Harry Easter—Don Saxon—baritone; Daniel Buchanan—Remo Lota—tenor; Steve Sankey—Lauren Gilbert—VTNE; Rose Maurrant—Anne Jeffreys—soprano
Chorus and Smaller Roles: 11M/8F, 4Ch—2M/2F.

SYNOPSIS

The play takes place on the exterior of a walk-up apartment house in a tenement section of New York City. Various apartment dwellers are seen at their windows and walking by the building. Emma Jones, Mrs. Fiorentino, and Mr. Olsen, who are outside, comment on the heat, while inside, Abraham Kaplan's daughter, Shirley, serves her father a cup of tea (Ain't It Awful, the Heat—Mixed Chorus).

Henry, the happy-go-lucky janitor, comes from the cellar with the garbage (I Got a Marble and a Star)—M Solo).

Willie Maurrant, a young boy on roller skates, yells up to his mother for some money for ice cream. Mrs. Fiorentino and Mrs. Olsen invite Anna, Willie's mother, to come and visit. While they wait, the two gossip about Steve and Anna's affair, shocked that both are married (Get a Load of That—F Duet). Daniel Buchanan, whose wife is about to have a baby, nervously enters with a bag of oranges and greets the three women. He tells them having a baby is also difficult for the man (When a Woman Has a Baby—3F/M Quartet). His wife's voice interrupts him and he hurries off, certain her time has come.

Frank Maurrant, an abrupt man, enters complaining about the heat and berates his wife about not knowing where their working daughter is. George Jones, Mrs. Fiorentino, Emma Jones, and Mr. Olsen witness his anger. After he leaves, Mrs. Maurrant tells the women she regrets that love sometimes disappears and hopes a brighter day will come (Somehow I Never Could Believe—F Solo).

When Steve Sankey, the collector for the milk company, happens by, Anna makes an excuse to go off with him. Everyone feels certain her husband will discover their affair and kill them (Get a Load of That [Reprise]—2F/2M Quartet). Mrs. Olsen, returning from the drugstore, announces that she has seen Steve and Anna together in an alleyway. Lippo Fiorentino enters with ice cream cones for everyone; Henry reenters (Ice Cream—M Solo to Mixed Chorus). Maurrant, a physically violent man, argues with Kaplan, a philosopher with pro-Communist leanings, and starts to go after him but is stopped by the men on the stoop. He is angry at the changes in the world (Let Things Be Like They Always Was— M Solo).

A group of graduates enter, and Jenny expresses how excited she is to have a diploma (Wrapped in a Ribbon and Tied in a Bow—F Solo to Mixed Chorus). The people of the neighborhood join in the merriment, but the mood is broken when Willie, who has been fighting, enters. As he and Anna go upstairs, Frank announces he is going to shoot pool. The women's gossip is interrupted by Sam, who is in love with Rose Maurrant. Later, when the street is deserted, he studies the quiet house (Lonely House—M Solo).

Rose enters with Harry Easter, a married coworker who tries to kiss her. He tells her she belongs in show business and promises to arrange things (Wouldn't You Like to Be on Broadway?—Sc to M Solo), but she doesn't want to get involved with a married man (What Good Would the Moon Be?—Sc to F Solo). Her thoughts are interrupted by Daniel Buchanan, who sends her for the doctor.

Mae, a flirtatious type, and Dick, a rake, enter. The two drunkenly express their emotions (Moon-Faced, Starry-Eyed—Sc to M/F Duet).

Rose returns from phoning the doctor and Vincent Jones tries to grab her, but Sam jumps out the window to her rescue. When the two are alone, Rose asks Sam if it is true about her mother and the milkman, but he lets Rose draw her own conclusions. They both yearn to get away from the tenement and have a better life (Remember That I Care—Sc to M/F Duet).

When Act II opens, it is early morning. The children are the first ones seen (Catch Me If You Can—Ch Mixed Chorus). Rose tries to talk to her father about being nicer to her mother, but he takes a drink and tells her to mind her own business. When his wife returns from helping Mrs. Buchanan with the baby, he suspiciously questions her and tells her to look after her own home (There'll Be Trouble—Sc to 2F/M Trio). He leaves and Willie enters on his way to school. His mother tells him she loves him and has high aspirations for his future (A Boy Like You—F Solo).

Vincent crudely comments to Rose as Sam appears to make sure she isn't being bothered. The two dream of running away (We'll Go Away Together—F/M Duet).

The street empties as Steve Sankey appears and Anna waves to him to come up. Sam witnesses this last exchange and worriedly sits on the stoop and waits. The marshal enters to evict a family and various street salesmen pass. Maurrant enters, sees the shade drawn in his apartment, thrusts Sam aside and rushes upstairs. Two shots are heard, the neighbors all rush to the sidewalk, the police arrive and Maurrant runs off. Rose returns in time to see her mother carried out on a stretcher (The Woman Who Lived up There—Mixed Chorus).

Later the same day, two nurses wheeling baby carriages enter to look at the house where the murders occurred. They sing a lullaby as they gossip (Lullaby—F Duet). Two policemen enter with Maurrant, who begs for a moment to tell Rose that he really loved Anna (I Loved Her, Too—M/F Duet to Mixed Chorus). Sam offers to go away with Rose but she insists that they get to know themselves before making a lifetime commitment. They say good-bye (Don't Forget the Lilac Bush—F/M Duet) and Rose exits, leaving the neighbors to gossip.

NOTES ON THE PRODUCTION

The emphasis is on the mood acting and singing in this dramatic piece. There is a one-unit set with practical windows and the costumes may be styled either thirties or forties. It is important to capture the flavor of the neighborhood and characters, which would not exist in their ethnic configuration much past World War II. The roles are balanced between males and females and the characters are definitive, well drawn and excellent to portray. It is a challenging show well worth the effort of a talented company.

The musical requirements may have to be trimmed in quantity of instruments per part, especially the string section.

SONGS OF SPECIAL INTEREST

"A Boy Like You," soprano, lovely melody, charming lyric that expresses mother love.

"Lonely House," tenor solo, may be done in a revue situation by alto. Poignant, dramatic driving number.

"When a Woman Has a Baby," a predominantly tenor solo, comic, may be sung without the operatic quality and kept simplistic. Problem song. Charm.

"Wouldn't You Like to Be on Broadway?" baritone, up tempo, dance beat to "What Good Would the Moon Be?" soprano. Good scene character study, contrasting opinions.

Instrumentation: 2 piano/celeste, 6 reeds, 2 trombones, 2 horns, 2 trumpets, 2 percussion, 11 violins, 4 viola, 3 cellos, 2 bass, conductor
Script: (in Score)
Score: Chapell
Record: Columbia
Rights: R & H

THE STREETS OF NEW YORK

Book and Lyrics: Barry Alan Grael (Based on Dion Boucicault's play *The Sidewalks of New York*)
Music: Richard B. Chodosh

ORIGINAL PRODUCTION

Maidman Playhouse, October 29, 1963 (318 perf.)
Director: Joseph Hardy
Choreographer: Neal Kenyon
Musical Director: Jack Holmes
Principals: Gideon Bloodgood—Ralston Hill—baritone; Badger—Barry Alan Grael—baritone; Alida Bloodgood—Barbara Williams—mezzo; Mark Livingstone—David Cryer—baritone; Lucy Fairweather—Gail Johnson—soprano; Mr. Puffy—Don Phelps—tenor; Mrs. Fairweather—Margot Hand—alto; Mrs. Puffy—Janet Raymond—mezzo
Chorus and Smaller Roles: 3F/5M (who double as needed).

SYNOPSIS

The prologue begins twenty years before the actual play in banker Gideon Bloodgood's office. As a mob is heard outside, Bloodgood, a young widower with a baby daughter, prepares to desert the bank with all his customers' money. He justifies himself by claiming he is only stealing the money for his poor motherless child, Alida (Prologue—L to M Solo to M Duet). Badger, a bank clerk, learning of Bloodgood's intentions, promises to keep quiet if Bloodgood offers him a percentage of the take. As they are about to make their getaway, a customer, Captain Fairweather, arrives through a side door to deposit his life's savings for his young daughter, Lucy. Bloodgood readily grabs the money as Fairweather has a heart attack and drops dead. Badger takes the Captain's receipt and rushes off to California to dig for gold.

Twenty years later, on Wall Street, a group of tourists are sightseeing outside

Bloodgood's bank. As they observe the harsh cruelty inflicted on the poor, the tourists negatively comment on the city of New York (Tourist Madrigal—Sc to Mixed Chorus). As the tourists exit, Bloodgood enters and sees Puffy, a chestnut seller. The heartless Bloodgood reminds him that he will foreclose if the note isn't paid. A messenger enters to tell Bloodgood his twenty-three–year–old daughter Alida is upset because she is not accepted by society. He rushes home to console her, shoving the tourists out of the way as he leaves.

In the drawing room of the mansion, Alida devises a plan to marry someone poor with a respectable name. She wants a marriage in which she can dominate (He'll Come to Me Crawling—Sc to F Solo). Bloodgood is followed by a well-respected gentleman, Mark Livingstone, who has come to ask for another loan. Alida, realizing that this is her chance to acquire a good name and have infinite power, plots her own version of "The Bloodgood Squeeze" (He'll Come to Me Crawling [Reprise]—F Solo).

Later that afternoon, in Mme. Victorine's dress shop, Lucy Fairweather, the daughter of the late Captain Fairweather, is sewing a dress for Alida. The girls tease her about her boyfriend, Mark Livingstone (If I May—Sc to F Solo and F Chorus). Mark nervously enters the shop. Lucy and he awkwardly talk about their past relationship, which was broken off because of their economic differences. Now Mark has squandered his wealth and wishes to befriend Lucy again. Lucy is unaware of Mark's financial difficulties and the two make plans to see each other Saturday for lunch at the Puffys' where Lucy and her mother are lodging. As Lucy and Mark touch hands, Alida bustles into the shop. She manages to make everyone uncomfortable by flaunting her wealth. After Mark leaves, Alida offers to secure a job for Lucy on a far-off isolated island, claiming that she is fond of Lucy and wants to be her benefactress. It is obvious that Alida only wants to get rid of Lucy so she can take advantage of Mark. When Lucy declines Alida's offer, Alida has her discharged.

The set changes to a street. It is Saturday and Mark contemplates his love for Lucy (If I May [Reprise]—M Solo).

In the Puffy home, Lucy and Mark sit and look at views of India on a stereopticon; they romanticize about life there, as Mrs. Fairweather comments on the cold (Aren't You Warm?—M/2F Trio). Mark offers to give the Fairweathers aid whenever they should need it. Everyone joins in a toast, claiming that the rich and the poor are equal in the great USA (Where Can the Rich and the Poor Be Friends?—3F/2M Quintet). When Bloodgood and some of his men barge in, Mark flees, unable to save his friends from Bloodgood's cruel eviction.

At home Alida and her father gloat over their cruelty to Lucy and her family. As father and daughter admire themselves, Badger, the former bank clerk, arrives accompanied by some Mexican friends. When Badger reminds Bloodgood of his promise to meet him in California, he and the Mexicans sing a song which tells the tale of Bloodgood robbing Captain Fairweather (California—Sc to M Chorus). Badger threatens to find Fairweather's heirs if Bloodgood doesn't pay him a large sum. In the midst of these dealings, Lucy enters to beg for employment but is told that Alida and Mark are to be wed. When Mark arrives, Lucy, hurt and shocked by Mark's supposed betrayal, renounces her love and leaves in tears. Alida proposes that she and Mark marry. Bloodgood has Badger and his friends escorted to jail, but fears exposure (Finale—Mixed Chorus).

When Act II opens, it is nearing Christmas and the Puffys are trying to sell chestnuts outside a high-class restaurant. They ironically sing joyfully about their skimpy Christmas feast (Christmas Carol—Mixed Chorus). Mr. Puffy meets Mark, who gives Puffy a card for Lucy; he intends to find out where she lives by following Puffy. Badger makes plans to meet Bloodgood at Badger's apartment to discuss the price of the receipt. Badger lives in the same building as Lucy and her mother.

Inside Delmonico's Mark announces to Alida that he plans to find Lucy. Deserted at her own engagement party, Alida jokes about her predicament to the guests (Laugh after Laugh—F Solo to Mixed Chorus).

In front of her shabby apartment on Cross Street, Lucy forlornly wishes for Mark (Arms for the Love of Me—F Solo and Mixed Chorus). Lucy returns to the apartment where her mother waits in the cold. Badger is seen in the next room drinking. Lucy and Mrs. Fairweather decide to end their lives by the noxious fumes in the heating stove. Bloodgood goes to confiscate the receipt from Badger, but Badger is armed and insists on fifty thousand dollars. Bloodgood leaves to get the money, as Lucy and Mrs. Fairweather hope that death will erase the pain they have suffered (Close Your Eyes—F Duet). Mark and Mr. Puffy valiantly save the suffocating Lucy, Mrs. Fairweather and Badger who has also inhaled the fumes. Mark offers everyone a place to live in his home.

While Lucy, Mrs. Fairweather, and Badger are recovering in Mark's cottage, Bloodgood, certain the receipt is in Badger's apartment, buys the building, intending to burn it.

At Mark's cottage, Mark discovers and freely expresses his love for Lucy (Love Wins Again—Sc to M/F Duet). Badger, deeply moved, tells the truth about Captain Fairweather's death and Bloodgood's fortune. Mrs. Fairweather offers a large reward for any proof of Bloodgood's thievery and everyone hurries to the apartment, which is now in flames. Badger manages to get the receipt in the nick of time.

At Bloodgood's mansion, the bridesmaids excitedly comment on the supposed wedding of Mark and Alida. Mark enters with Lucy, the Puffys and Mrs. Fairweather to tell Alida the marriage is off. Mrs. Fairweather informs Bloodgood she is aware of his swindle, and Badger enters accompanied by the police and the Mexicans to charge Bloodgood with arson, theft and murder. Alida is shocked at the extent of her father's guilt. Just as Bloodgood is being carried off to prison, Mrs. Fairweather tears up the receipt and lets father and daughter begin life anew. Mark and Lucy are united in marriage (Finale—Mixed Chorus).

NOTES ON THE PRODUCTION

This musical melodrama is fun for community theatres that have had successful productions of *Little Mary Sunshine* and *The Boy Friend* and are looking for something different. The show was originally performed in a small theatre Off-Broadway and utilized a revolving turntable which had a three-level set in skeletal form. The actors were able to revolve the set and place props (many of which doubled from scene to scene), eliminating the need for a large technical crew. Less elaborate, yet successful productions have simplified this to minimal flats on the stage floor.

The show needs to be produced in the tongue-in-cheek melodrama style but is a refreshing change from the usual nonmusical melodramas. The script is well worth perusing.

SONGS OF SPECIAL INTEREST

"He'll Come to Me Crawling," evil, character-oriented, mezzo solo.

Instrumentation: 2 pianos
Script: SF
Rights: SF

SUGAR

Book: Peter Stone (Based on Billy Wilder's screenplay *Some Like It Hot*)
Music: Jule Styne
Lyrics: Bob Merrill

ORIGINAL PRODUCTION

Majestic Theatre, May 6, 1972 (505 perf.)
Director and Choreographer: Gower Champion
Musical Director and Vocal Arrangements: Elliot Lawrence
Orchestration: Philip J. Lang
Principals: Jerry (Daphne)—Robert Morse—baritone; Osgood Fielding, Jr.—Cyril Ritchard—baritone; Bienstock—Alan Kass—VTNE; Joe (Josephine)—Tony Roberts—tenor; Sugar Kane—Elaine Joyce—mezzo; Spats Palazzo—Steve Condos—baritone; Knuckles Norton—Dick Bonelle—VTNE; Sweet Sue—Sheila Smith—alto
Chorus and Smaller Roles: 6F/8M.

SYNOPSIS

The lights rise on the stage of the Chicago Theatre where Sweet Sue, the leader of an all-girl band, is announcing the sexy vocalist ukulele player, Sugar Kane. Sugar begins singing (When You Meet a Girl in Chicago—F Solo with

F Chorus). After the number Sue tells the audience they have a booking at a Miami Beach resort hotel (Turn Back the Clock—F Chorus).

Backstage, Sue berates manager Bienstock for not finding a new sax and bass player. She stalks off to pack as Joe and Jerry, two quick-witted saxophone and bass players, enter to apply for the job. Bienstock tells them he needs girl musicians but will hire them to deliver the band's orchestrations to Dearborn Street Station for ten dollars.

The boys agree to get Beinstock's car from the Clark Street Garage and deliver the music, if nothing better turns up. They proceed to the Chicago Musicians Union where they join the job line (Penniless Bums—Sc to M Duet to M Chorus). Since there are no jobs, they decide to deliver the music.

As they exit, four gangsters enter with violin cases and meet Spats Palazzo, a nattily dressed gang leader who constantly tap-dances. Spats and the boys tap over to the Clark Street Garage to wipe out Knuckles Morton.

At the Clark Street Garage, a poker game is in progress with Knuckles Norton, three hoods and a garage mechanic. Jerry and Joe stumble upon the gangland killing and narrowly escape with their saxophone and bass. Spats orders his gang to find them and rub them out. In a patter song, he orders and dances the message to find the saxophone and bass player (Tear the Town Apart—Small M Chorus).

At the train station, Sweet Sue is waiting for Bienstock to deliver the two girl musicians. Jerry and Joe arrive, disguised as Daphne and Josephine—it is their only means of escape from Spats. It may help the reader keep the disguised men straight by remembering that Joe is the abbreviation for Josephine. They display their talent (The Beauty That Drives Men Mad—Sc to M Duet) in a humorous movement-oriented number which ends with them playing their sax and bass.

In the Pullman car, which contains berths and a private lounge, Jerry and Joe enter complaining to each other about high heels and skirts. They walk to the lounge and meet Sugar, who is sneaking a bottle of bourbon from her ukulele case. Jerry is attracted to her but Joe warns him of the consequences. Sue discovers Sugar's flask and threatens to fire her, but Jerry takes the blame.

Later that night, Sugar climbs into "Daphne's" berth for a chat and proceeds to drive Jerry wild (We Could Be Close—Sc to M/F Duet). When Dolores, Rosella and Mary Lou join the party, Sugar goes to the lounge for more cups.

Joe is shaving in the lounge, but quickly cleans his face when Sugar enters. She confides that she will be glad to get to Miami to snare a millionaire with a yacht, for she is tired of poor saxophone players.

Next morning, the conductor announces the arrival in Miami and the girls, in choreographic sequence, pop their heads out of the curtained berths and sing (Sun on My Face—Small F Chorus).

On the veranda of the Seminole-Ritz Hotel, Sir Osgood Fielding, an elderly millionaire, announces to the other elderly millionaires that his divorce has come through. He spies Daphne among the girl musicians, introduces himself and comments on her shapely ankle. Jerry hits him with his bass fiddle and exits as

Osgood and a group of fellow octogenarians comment on youth (November Song—M Solo with Small M Chorus).

In Josephine and Daphne's hotel room, the two discuss their interest in Sugar. Joe tells Jerry that Sugar wants a millionaire who wears glasses and owns a yacht; he convinces Jerry to help her achieve her dream (Sugar—Sc to M Duet). After Jerry exits, Joe removes his wig and disguises himself in a pair of glasses and a yachting outfit.

Act II opens on the beach, where Sugar notices Joe disguised as her dream millionaire. He introduces himself as Junior, tells her his family is Shell (Shell Oil—M Solo) and returns to his *Wall Street Journal*. Sugar imagines herself married to a millionaire (Hey, Why Not!—Sc to F Solo with Small M Chorus). During the number a male chorus, dressed like Joe, enters, followed by a line of girl dancers dressed like Sugar. As the number ends, Daphne enters followed by Osgood, who asks Joe to have Daphne meet him on his yacht so they can be alone for the evening.

Later that night, aboard the yacht, Joe tells Sugar he has a mental block about sex. She sympathizes and puts forth her best effort (What Do You Give to a Man Who's Had Everything?—Sc to M/F Duet).

The next morning, Jerry dressed in an evening gown, enters the hotel room acting like Hildegarde (Magic Nights—M Solo). When Joe enters, Jerry announces that he plans on marrying Osgood, hoping for a large financial settlement when his true identity is discovered. Sugar knocks on the door and they put on their wigs as she enters to tell them she's in love. After she leaves, Joe admits to himself he is a heel (It's Always Love—M Solo).

The lights fade and the sound of tapping feet is heard. Spats and his gang have arrived at the nightclub, and Sue dedicates her next number to the "boys" from Chicago (When You Meet a Man in Chicago—L to F Solo with Mixed Chorus). During the number, Jerry and Joe recognize Spats and hastily exit. Spats suspiciously follows them into the corridor. The ensuing wild chase through the kitchen swinging doors involves Spats, his henchmen, Sugar, Joe and Jerry. During the confusion, Joe tells Sugar he isn't Josephine and he isn't a millionaire. She isn't upset for she loves him and begs to go with him. Spats is mistakenly killed by his own men but tap-dances his way to his end in a hilarious death spoof. On board the yacht with Joe, Sugar and Osgood, Jerry tells Osgood he can't marry him because he is a man. Osgood shrugs and comments that nobody's perfect.

NOTES ON THE PRODUCTION

The show, which is built on a gimmick, doesn't have a great amount of dramatic sustaining ability, thus the success of the production depends on its leads and should not be attempted without an extremely strong Joe, Jerry, Osgood, Sugar and Spats.

It is good summer stock fare and appeals to audiences who enjoy *The Best Little Whorehouse in Texas*. The sets may be simplified to save expenses. Some companies have combined all the hotel sequences, other than the bedroom, and placed them on the veranda/nightclub.

The costumes are period thirties. Jerry and Joe need a wide variety of girls' outfits, which usually need to be sewn because of the large size required. There is a section where the chorus appears dressed as Sugar/Joe look-alikes, but it isn't absolutely necessary to the script and may be edited if desired.

SONGS OF SPECIAL INTEREST

"It's Always Love," semidramatic, questioning, lots of transitions, good for class study, tenor.

Instrumentation: violin, cello, bass, 4 reeds, horn, 3 trumpets, harp, 2 trombones, guitar/banjo, 2 percussion, piano/celeste/conductor
Script: NP
Record: United Artists
Rights: TW

SWEENEY TODD: THE DEMON BARBER OF FLEET STREET

Book: Hugh Wheeler (Based on a version by Christopher Bond)
Music and Lyrics: Stephen Sondheim

ORIGINAL PRODUCTION

Uris Theatre, March 1, 1979 (557 perf.)
Director: Harold Prince
Dance and Movement: Larry Fuller
Musical Director: Paul Gemignani
Orchestration: Jonathan Tunick
Principals: Anthony Hope—Victor Garber—tenor; Beggar Woman—Merle Louise—soprano; Sweeney Todd—Len Cariou—baritone; Judge Turpin—Edmund Lyndeck—baritone; Mrs. Lovett—Angela Lansbury—mezzo; The Beadle—Jack Eric Williams—tenor; Johanna—Sara Rice—soprano; Tobias—Ken Jennings—tenor; Pirelli—Joaquin Romaguera—tenor
Chorus and Smaller Roles: 8M/8F.

SYNOPSIS

The play takes place in nineteenth-century London, around the area known as Fleet Street. As the audience enters, the organ plays funeral music while two gravediggers start to dig. When the play is ready to begin, a factory whistle is heard and the stage plunges into darkness. This whistle is effectively used throughout the production to heighten dramatic tension.

The lights rise on the company, who ominously invite the audience to listen to the tale of Sweeney Todd (The Ballad of Sweeney Todd—Mixed Chorus). Graveside action accompanies the song, which ends with Sweeney rising from the grave.

The scene switches to the docks. It is early morning. A young, romantic sailor, who has saved Todd from drowning, joins the forty-year-old embittered man in expounding their different views of London. A half-crazed beggar woman, demonstrating the coarser side of the town, interrupts them (No Place Like London— Sc to 2M/F Trio).

Anthony, realizing that Todd is distraught, offers him aid, but is quickly rebuffed by the angered man, who relates a story about the class-structure filth of London (The Barber and His Wife—Sc to M Solo). The two say good-bye and Todd heads for Fleet Street, where Mrs. Lovett, the slatternly, conniving owner of a grubby meat pie shop, is busy shooing flies away from her main source of income. She is overjoyed to see a customer, but warns Todd that hers are the worst pies in London (The Worst Pies in London—F Solo). When he asks her about renting a vacant room upstairs over her shop, she tells him the story of the former residents, an unfortunate barber and his wife (Poor Thing— Sc to F Solo). When Sweeney reacts strongly to the story, Mrs. Lovett recognizes him as the barber, Benjamin Barker. He assures her he is no longer Benjamin Barker, but Sweeney Todd, who has returned, after fifteen years of transportation to Australia, to gain his revenge. Mrs. Lovett offers to let him have the upstairs room and gives him his barber equipment, which she had safely stored for his return. Sweeney eyes the sharp razors and an idea begins to take its bloody shape (My Friends—Sc to M/F Duet).

The scene moves to Judge Turpin's home, where Johanna, Sweeney's daughter, was taken at age one to be raised by the lecherous Judge, who had raped Sweeney's wife in front of a group of party guests. Johanna at sixteen is beautiful and naively unaware of the Judge's evil lechery. She appears at the balcony and mournfully compares her life to that of a caged bird (Green Finch and Linnet Bird—F Solo).

Anthony, who happens by, is instantly enamored, but Johanna is frightened inside by the sudden appearance of the beggar woman (Ah, Miss—M/F Sc to Duet), who warns Anthony to avoid the house of Judge Turpin. Ignoring her advice, Anthony gives a bird to Johanna, who shyly offers her hand as the Judge enters and calls her inside. The Judge orders Anthony away and the Beadle adds to the warning by strangling the bird. As the two exit into the house, Anthony vows to steal the unhappy girl from the evil Judge (Johanna—M Solo).

At a nearby marketplace, a fraudulent Italian barber, Aldolfo Pirelli, has set up his cart for his weekly Thursday haircuts and bald-remedy sales. He is announcing his latest elixir, with the help of his young assistant, Tobias, when Sweeney and Mrs. Lovett arrive (Pirelli's Miracle Elixir—M Solo to Mixed Chorus). Sweeney challenges the egotistical barber to a shaving contest (The Contest—M Solo), which he easily wins. His reputation is assured when the Beadle promises to visit his shop within the week.

In his shop, as Sweeney impatiently awaits the arrival of the Beadle, Mrs. Lovett urges patience (Wait—Sc to F Solo). Anthony bursts in to ask Sweeney for the use of the shop as a resting place for Johanna, whom he intends to steal from Judge Turpin. Sweeney happily agrees, and the lad rushes from the shop.

Pirelli interrupts Mrs. Lovett and Todd and asks to speak to Todd alone. Mrs. Lovett takes Tobias into the pie shop as Pirelli, who has recognized Todd as Benjamin Barker, attempts blackmail. Todd slashes his throat and stuffs the dead Pirelli in a nearby trunk. Three tenors from the chorus comment.

Meanwhile, Johanna confides to Anthony that she will kill herself if the Judge pursues his desire to marry her. He assures her that he will save her (Kiss Me—Sc to M/F Duet).

The Judge, on his way home after a long day of passing unjust sentences, confides to the Beadle his desire for Johanna. The Beadle directs him to Sweeney's shop (Ladies in Their Sensitivities—Sc to M/Solo to 3M/F Quartet). Anthony outlines his plan for escape as Turpin decides to visit the now-famous barber.

The Judge arrives at Sweeney's and Sweeney prepares to slit the Judge's throat (Pretty Women—Sc to M Duet), but Anthony bursts in to announce his marriage to Johanna. The Judge exits, promising to move Johanna from Anthony's reach, and Todd orders Anthony from his sight. Mrs. Lovett enters to hear Sweeney's vow of vengeance (Epiphany—Sc to M Solo). He vows to practice his killing until the Judge returns. He is beginning to grow demented, but Mrs. Lovett forces him back to the reality of disposing of Pirelli's body. When she decides that burial would be a waste of a potentially good filling for her pies, the two spiritedly connive (A Little Priest—Sc to F/M Duet).

In Act II, Mrs. Lovett's pie shop is so successful that she has added an outdoor dining area to seat the newly acquired customers. Tobias, Pirelli's former slow-witted assistant who waits for his master to return, helps dish up the pies (God, That's Good!—Mixed Chorus).

Anthony is searching the streets for Johanna, whom Turpin has incarcerated in a mental asylum; Sweeney is testing his newly designed barber chair, which slides the victims to the kitchen below; and the beggar woman is screaming a warning about Mrs. Lovett's pies (Johanna—2M/2F Quartet).

At the end of the day, Todd rests in the parlor while Mrs. Lovett counts her money. She tries to take Todd's mind from the Judge by verbally painting a vacation spot the two of them could enjoy (By the Sea—Sc to F Solo) in married comfort.

Anthony interrupts to tell Todd he has found Johanna in a mental asylum. Todd quickly devises a plan to disguise Anthony as a wigmaker, who can easily gain admission to purchase human hair from the inmates (Wigmaker's Sequence—M Duet). When Anthony leaves, he drafts a note to the Judge stating that Johanna will soon be at his shop. He vows that the Judge will not escape his vengeance again (The Letter—M Solo).

Tobias tells Mrs. Lovett that he appreciates her kindness and will protect her from any danger (Not While I'm Around—Sc to M/F Duet). During their conversation, he discovers that Todd has killed his former boss, but Mrs. Lovett lures him to the baking cellar and quickly locks him in before he can alert the police.

When she enters the house, she finds the Beadle in the parlor and joins him in some songs, hoping that Todd will return (Parlor Songs—Sc to M/F Duet). At last Todd arrives and escorts the Beadle upstairs to slit his throat. Tobias, in the bake-house below, hears a noise from above as the Beadle's bloody body is deposited down the chute. He screams in terror, for he has at last realized the exact ingredients of Mrs. Lovett's pies.

Anthony rescues Johanna, who shoots her captor. As they run off, the inmates tear down the wall and escape to the street (City on Fire!—Mixed Chorus).

The musical builds to the climax as Tobias escapes and Todd kills the beggar woman, whom he later discovers is his long-lost wife. He fulfills his plan for vengeance by killing the Judge and gains revenge on Mrs. Lovett, who let him believe his wife was dead, by throwing her into the oven (Final Sequence—Mixed Chorus). As Todd mourns his dead wife, Tobias, who has gone stark raving mad, emerges from the cellar, seizes the razor and slits Todd's throat.

The company comments as the actors return for their bows (The Ballad of Sweeney Todd—Mixed Chorus).

NOTES ON THE PRODUCTION

This unusual musical theatre offering received many well-deserved Tony Awards: Actor, Actress, Musical, Director, Book, Score, Set Design, and Costume Design.

It is a musically demanding show whose cast requirements include four tenors in leading roles and a vocally talented chorus. The set requires no drops and may be performed with the pie shop, usually a revolve from exterior to interior, and a location for Judge Turpin's home. The costumes are period, Industrial Revolution, England. It is possible for each cast member to have one costume although it gives more visual variety if Mrs. Lovett has several.

The trick barber chair must be rigged and timed to allow the bodies to fall, via a trapdoor, to the area below. It is an extremely important part of the action which must be smoothly controlled. Another consideration is the handling of the throat-slashing sequences and the use of blood pellets, or squirter, either on the razor or hidden on the actors' necks. The costume crew must be prepared for daily laundering.

Both Todd and Tobias visually deteriorate through the show, as each grows more and more insane. Some backstage help should be waiting to assist the performers in the makeup changes.

The show is extremely exciting and can be occasionally seen on cable TV. It would help a company considering the show to purchase or rent the Lansbury touring tape.

SONGS OF SPECIAL INTEREST

"Kiss Me," comic soprano, good for relationships, vocally demanding.

"Epiphany," transition from anger to madness makes this an excellent baritone acting song.

"A Little Priest," diction, character relationship and interaction highlight this mezzo or alto/baritone song.

Instrumentation: 5 reeds, 2 trumpets, horn, 3 trombones, 2 percussion, harp, organ, violin, viola, cello, bass
Script: Dodd, Mead
Score: Valando
Record: RCA
Rights: MTI

SWEET CHARITY

Book: Neil Simon (Based on an original screenplay by Fellini, Pinelli and Flaiano)
Music: Cy Coleman
Lyrics: Dorothy Fields

ORIGINAL PRODUCTION

Palace Theatre, January 29, 1966 (608 perf.)
Conceived, Staged and Choreographed by: Bob Fosse
Musical Director: Fred Warner
Orchestration: Ralph Burns
Principals: Charity—Gwen Verdon—alto; Nickie—Helen Gallagher—mezzo; Vittorio Vidal—James Luisi—baritone; Daddy Brubeck—Arnold Soboloff—baritone; Helene—Thelma Oliver—alto; Ursula—Sharon Ritchie—VTNE; Oscar—John McMartin—baritone; Herman—John Wheeler—tenor; Rosie—Barbara Sharma—VTNE
Chorus and Smaller Roles: 6M/6F.

SYNOPSIS

Charity's theme is heard as a spotlight picks up Charity Hope Valentine, a romantic dance hall hostess, who is dancing about the stage. A sign drops in, reading "The Adventures of Charity," followed by a second, third and fourth that reads: "The Story of a . . . Girl Who Wanted to Be . . . Loved." The lights rise to full on a park with the orchestra pit representing a lake. Charity happily greets her young, greaser-type boyfriend, who is wearing a black leather jacket and dark glasses, and begins to tell him how wonderful he is (You Should See Yourself—L to F Solo).

When she informs him she has brought her savings, enough for a down payment for some furniture, he grabs her purse and pushes her into the lake. A sign appears reading "Splash!" followed by another reading "The Rescue." As Charity yells for help, several passersby ignore her, not wanting to get involved. A crowd gathers and comments, in typical New York fashion, before a man finally rescues her.

A sign appears reading "Fan-Dango Ballroom . . . that night" and the scene shifts to the dressing room of the Fan-Dango. Charity tells her story to several of the dance hall hostesses, who urge her to forget him. The girls leave Charity, who is still dressing, to enter the ballroom.

In the ballroom, the girls line up to greet the customers (Big Spender—F Chorus). Several of the girls go to the booths with the male customers as Charity tells her problems to her friends Nickie and Helene. She explains how she got involved (Charity's Soliloquy—Sc to F Solo).

Charity, on her way home, passes the Pompeii Club as Ursula, fiancée of famous actor Vittorio Vidal, angrily walks out followed by Vidal. A sign drops in reading "A Stroke of Luck." Vidal sees Charity and asks her to join him.

In the club, which is lavishly decorated, five couples dance (Rich Man's Frug—Mixed Dance Chorus) but stop and gossip as Vidal and Charity enter. He orders dinner and the two begin to dance, but the starving Charity faints in his arms. Vidal wonders what to do until Charity raises her head and hints that he should take her home.

In Vidal's apartment, which is a combination bed/sitting/dressing room, Vidal arrives with Charity, who is no longer hungry but does accept a drink. As the two talk, Vidal finds Charity enchanting. She begs him for a souvenir and he exits to autograph a picture. Charity imagines the reactions of her friends at the ballroom (If My Friends Could See Me Now—F Solo with M/F Scenes Interspersed). At various points during the number, Vidal gives her a photograph, walking stick and top hat, all props from his films. Ursula arrives and demands to be seen. Manfred, Vidal's servant, stalls her while Charity hides in the closet. During the next scene, the lights rise on Charity in the closet, who reacts to everything she sees. Vidal woos the jealous Ursula (Too Many Tomorrows—Sc to M Solo) and Charity watches. The lights fade on the bed and a sign appears: "A New Day." Ursula is asleep and Vidal tiptoes to the closet to say good-bye to Charity, who waves in return.

In the dressing room of the Fan-Dango, Charity tells Nickie and Helene about her night with Vidal. The two girls think she is stupid for not demanding more, but all three realize they are stuck with their fate. The three sing of their aspirations for a better life (There's Gotta Be Something Better Than This—Sc to F Trio). Herman, the manager, enters and orders the girls to work.

Charity refuses to dance and a sign drops in: "A Big Decision." She leaves, determined to get some culture as a sign appears: "The 92nd Street 'Y' " (an institution noted for its wide variety of self-improvement classes and lectures). Charity follows a shy young man in his mid-thirties onto the "Y" elevator, which proceeds to get stuck between floors. It turns out the man is Oscar Madison, who has claustrophobia. Charity tries to calm him (I'm the Bravest Individual—Sc to F/M Duet), but the plan fails when the lights go out. A sign appears: "To Be Continued."

Act II opens on a sign reading "Meanwhile Back in the Elevator . . . "; the lights are on and the elevator is on the bottom floor. Oscar invites Charity to the Rhythm of Life Church, which meets under the Manhattan Bridge. The two exit as the scene shifts to a garage which has been converted to a church. The service, a hash party led by Big Daddy, is in progress (The Rhythm of Life—M Solo to Mixed Chorus) but is soon raided by the police. Everyone stamps out their cigarettes and rushes off.

Two weeks later, Helene and Nickie, in the apartment, humorously enact Charity's dreams of marriage, a house and children. Both agree they would like the wish for themselves (Baby, Dream Your Dream—Sc to F Duet).

A sign reading "Coney Island" appears and the lights rise on Charity and Oscar midway up and stuck on the famous parachute jump. When Oscar discovers that Charity has a fear of heights and needs him, he realizes he loves her (Sweet Charity—Sc to M Solo). Charity attempts to tell him the truth about her job, but he expresses his love of her innocent purity and she is afraid to continue. They declare their love (Sweet Charity [Reprise]—Sc to M/F Duet). In the Fan-Dango Ballroom, where there are no customers, a bored Nickie and Helene greet a new young girl, named Rosie, who only plans on working a few weeks. Charity enters and urges Rosie to get out. A customer arrives and Nickie urges Charity to look busy but she retorts that she is through. She moves downstage and soliloquizes (Where Am I Going?—F Solo).

Charity enters a phone booth to send a telegram to Oscar urging him to meet her at a chili restaurant later that night.

A sign appears, "The proposal," and the lights rise on the Eighth Avenue chili restaurant. There are two booths against the wall—Oscar is in one as Charity enters and sits in the booth behind; they are back to back. She tries to tell him she works in a dance hall, but he already knows and asks her to marry him. As Oscar outlines their future Charity walks from the scene, overwhelmed that someone loves her (I'm a Brass Band—Sc to F Solo).

At the Fan-Dango, the girls, waiters, three regular customers and Herman give Charity and Oscar a wedding party. Herman, their usually tough boss, breaks down at the thought of their future happiness (I Love to Cry at Weddings—M Solo to Mixed Chorus).

A sign appears reading "plans" and the lights come up on Oscar and Charity in the park. Oscar tells her he is unable to marry her because he can't forget her past and urges her to leave him. He pushes her into the lake, apologizes and runs off. Charity, quite wet, climbs from the pit. Realizing she still has her purse, she comments that things are better. A light picks up a Good Fairy, who tells Charity her dreams will come true. A sign drops in as Charity begins dancing: it reads "She lived . . . hopefully . . . ever after."

NOTES ON THE PRODUCTION

Tony Award for Best Choreography. Most of the other awards went to *Man of La Mancha*.

Anyone considering this show must have an excellent triple-threat performer to play Charity. The part was specifically written for Gwen Verdon, whose naivete, yet warm-hearted sexual quality charmed audiences of both sexes.

The musical numbers are relatively easy to stage and need not be as intricate as Mr. Fosse's. There is room for variety and new choreographic interpretation.

The script is humorous. The characters, portrayed in the movie as extremely hard, may be given a lighter touch that might appeal more to regional audiences.

The major sets are the ballroom, the hostess room at the ballroom, the Pompeii Club, Vidal's apartment, Charity's apartment, and the Chili House. It is possible to utilize the same flats for Charity's and Vidal's apartments by changing the set decorations and props. The hostess room could be a permanent section on the ballroom. It is also possible to turn the ballroom into the Pompeii Club and possibly the Chili House. The remaining scenes in the park and the garage, at the Y and Coney Island, may be delineated by lights and a simple set piece. It would be helpful to have a New York street drop, but this isn't absolutely necessary.

The costumes are period middle 1960s and could be updated, but the Rhythm of Life Church sequence doesn't work as well because it is so obviously sixties. The costumes are inexpensive. The show is a gem for schools and communities that are looking for excellent roles for women, good songs, humorous situations and witty dialogue. A guaranteed crowd pleaser.

SONGS OF SPECIAL INTEREST

"Big Spender," good number for a musical theatre beginning class and inexperienced choreographer, allows for specific characterizations. Effective for loosening stiff performers.

"If My Friends Could See Me Now," vaudeville-style song and dance, good for character study or club. Mezzo.

"There's Gotta Be Something Better Than This," excellent 2 alto/mezzo trio, specific stories, relationship development is stressed.

"I'm the Bravest Individual," humorous scene/song. Requires strong characterization, comic timing, reactions.

"Rhythm of Life," simple chorus song for beginning choreographer, allows for free-style improvisation from performers. Drug orientation may be deleted. Class or revue.

"Baby, Dream Your Dream," change of character alto duet, actable specifics.

"Charity's Soliloquy," introspective song, semidramatic for young alto or mezzo.

Instrumentation: 3 violins, cello, bass, 4 reeds, 4 trumpets, 2 percussion, synthesizer, 2 guitars, piano/conductor
Script: Random
Selections: Notable
Record: Columbia
Rights: TW

T

THEY'RE PLAYING OUR SONG

Book: Neil Simon
Music: Marvin Hamlisch
Lyrics: Carole Bayer Sager

ORIGINAL PRODUCTION

Imperial Theatre, February 11, 1979 (1,082 perf.)
Director: Robert Moore
Musical Numbers Staged by: Patricia Birch
Musical Direction: Larry Blank
Orchestration: Ralph Burns, Richard Hazard and Gene Page
Principals: Vernon—Robert Klein—baritone; Sonia Walsk—Lucie Arnez—mezzo
Chorus of Alter Egos: 3M/3F

SYNOPSIS

This semiautobiographical story revolves around Vernon Gersh, a successful composer, and Sonia Walsk, an eccentric lyricist, who meet in Vernon's apartment to decide if they are able to artistically work together. Vernon plays a song (Fallin'—L to M Solo). They decide to attempt the collaboration and set a date for their next work session.

Sonia arrives for the meeting at Vernon's studio one day and twenty minutes late, frazzled by her breakup with her lover, Leon. When they finally start working, Vernon sets one of her lyrics to music and they are joined by their three-person chorus alter egos (Workin' It Out—Sc to M/F Duet and M/F Chorus).

Sonia tells Vernon they must get to know each other on a personal level in order for their professional work to become cohesive. As Vernon phones for reservations at a club, she wishes he knew her better (If He Really Knew Me—F Solo). When she leaves, Vernon expresses the same feelings (If She Really Knew Me—M Solo).

At "Le Club," Sonia shows up late because she has been trying to ease Leon's anguish. Sonia and Vernon settle down to enjoy the evening, but Vernon hears his first hit playing over the sound system and bursts into song (They're Playing My Song—M Solo). After the number ends, Sonia hears her first big hit played and urges him to listen (They're Playing My Song—F Solo). They hear a different song which Vernon proclaims as theirs (They're Playing Our Song—Sc to M/F Duet).

They arrange to meet at her tiny, disheveled apartment later that evening, after she gets rid of Leon. When Vernon arrives, she urges him to play psychiatrist and listen to her problems; as she talks he thinks (If She Really Knew Me—M Solo). When he starts to tell about himself, her mind wanders and she comments (If He Really Knew Me—F Solo).

Vernon convinces her to join him for the weekend at a Long Island beach house and leaves to pack while she and her alter egos consider the decision (Right—F Solo/F Trio).

The trip to the island, taken in Vernon's small sports car, is fraught with wrong turns, no gas, etc. They finally arrive at the house, but a phone call from Leon interrupts their romantic embraces. Determined to concentrate on Vernon, she tells Leon she can't help and hangs up (Just for Tonight—F Solo).

In Act II Sonia manipulates her way into Vernon's apartment by telling him she has no place to stay since Leon is still living at her place. He helps her with her bags and they eagerly embrace (When You're in My Arms—Sc to M/F Duet). Her relationship with Vernon begins to crumble because of her inability to send Leon away. Vernon interrupts a recording session to suggest that they break off their relationship and then he leaves, but Sonia stays long enough to cut their new song (I Still Believe in Love—F Solo).

A few months later, while Vernon is in a Los Angeles hospital, Sonia arrives unexpectedly with a child's tiny red piano as a get-well gift. Vernon and his alter egos compose (Fill in the Words—M Solo and M Trio).

Months later, in New York, Vernon arrives at Sonia's apartment to tell her he wants to try again. She agrees.

NOTES ON THE PRODUCTION

This show is a popular one on the winter and summer stock circuits, due to its slick book, rhythmic music, and small cast. Although it had a long run on Broadway, it lost out on the Tony Awards, the majority of which went to *Sweeney Todd*. It has a small cast, minimal costumes, simple sets and memorable music.

The theme and dialogue must be carefully considered because the plot revolves around the dilemma of mixing personal and professional lives. There are also several mildly sexual scenes which may not be suitable for all audiences.

The dialogue is full of laughs; therefore, the leading characters must know how to play comedy and hold for laughs. It is nearly an actor-proof and director-proof script; however, it may become dated in time.

SONGS OF SPECIAL INTEREST

"They're Playing Our Song," exuberant and energetic showstopper. Although a duet, it may be performed in larger configuration in a revue situation, suited for all voices.

"I Still Believe in Love," romantic, club style, suited for all voices.

Instrumentation: 3 reeds, 2 trumpets, 2 trombones, percussion, drums, violins, viola, cello, harp, 2 guitars, fender bass, keyboard, piano/conductor
Script: SF, Random
Selections: Chappell
Record: Casablanca
Rights: SF

THE THREEPENNY OPERA

Original Book and Lyrics: Bertolt Brecht
English Book and Lyrics: Marc Blitzstein
Music: Kurt Weill

ORIGINAL NEW YORK PRODUCTION

Theatre DeLys, opened March 10, 1954 (95 perf.), reopened September 20, 1955 (2,611 perf.)
Staged by: Carmen Capalbo
Orchestration: Kurt Weill
Musical Director: Samuel Matlowsky
Principals: Macheath—Scott Merrill—tenor; Peachum—Leon Lishner—baritone; Mrs. Peachum—Charlotte Rae—mezzo; Polly Peachum—Jo Sullivan—soprano; Tiger Brown—George Tyne—baritone; Lucy Brown—Beatrice Arthur—alto; Jenny Oliver—Lotte Lenya—alto; Street Singer—Gerald Price—baritone
Chorus and Smaller Roles: 4M/4F.

SYNOPSIS

In Soho, England, a beggar gives his introduction to the opera, describing Macheath and his unlawful deeds. Macheath is a true villain in every sense of the word. He murders, thieves, rapes, and has no conscience (Ballad of Mack the Knife—M Solo).

The set opens on Jonathan Peachum's store for beggars. Peachum, a fraud who uses the poor for his own profit, greets the new day (Peachum's Morning Anthem—M Solo). Filch enters Peachum's wardrobe and exchanges his old rags for new ones. Peachum assigns the lad to a street corner to beg and demands 50 percent of all of Filch's earnings. Mr. and Mrs. Peachum bemoan daughter Polly's involvement with the villain Macheath (Instead of Song—Sc to M/F Duet).

In an unoccupied stable, Macheath announces to Polly that they are to be wed. Initially upset that he is starting their married life receiving stolen wedding gifts, she grows less shocked as the ceremony goes on (Wedding Song—M Chorus). Polly contributes to the singing and celebrating by telling a narrative about a poor washer girl who gets revenge on her oppressors by having them shot when her pirate ship comes in (Pirate Jenny—F Solo).

When Sheriff Brown enters the barn, the thieves are surprised to learn that Macheath's old Army buddy is there to pay respects to the bride and groom (The Army Song—Sc to M Duet). He tells his cronies about the system where Macheath gives Brown 30 percent of his profits earned from stealing. The wedding guests depart and Polly and Macheath reaffirm their love (Love Song—Sc to M/F Duet).

At Peachum's establishment, an excited Polly tells her parents of her recent marriage (Barbara Song—F Solo). Peachum decides to threaten Brown with exposure if he doesn't arrest Macheath, and sends Mrs. Peachum to Macheath's former whores, certain they will help in his capture. They comment on the evilness in the world which hinders human hopes (The World Is Mean—Sc to M/2F Trio).

In Act II, Polly rushes to the stable to warn Macheath to escape but makes him promise to be true. Polly, now in charge of managing the gangster business, forces the men to accept her as their leader. When Macheath, impressed by her handling of his gang. tells Polly he plans on being faithful, she is certain he will not be caught whoring and neglects to warn him about her mother's plan (Melodrama—Sc to M/F Duet to Polly's Song—F Solo).

Mrs. Peachum offers Macheath's favorite whore, Jenny Diver, money if she reports his whereabouts to the police. Mrs. Peachum then comments on Macheath's promiscuity which will ultimately lead to his downfall (The Ballad of Dependency—Sc to F Solo).

Macheath breaks his promise and visits his harlot friends. As Macheath reminisces with Jenny, she signals the sheriff and Mrs. Peachum (The Ballad of the Fancy Man—M/F Duet). The sheriff takes him to prison.

In the Old Bailey prison, when Macheath gives Brown the cold shoulder, the guilt-ridden Brown cries. Macheath pays Smith, a jailer, to release his handcuffs and comments on the easy life (The Secret of Gracious Living—M Solo).

An angry Lucy Brown, obviously pregnant, accuses Macheath of betraying his promise to her by marrying Polly. Macheath, in order to coerce Lucy into freeing him, denies his marriage and swears allegiance to Lucy. When Polly enters, the two women argue and fight (Jealousy Duet—Sc to 2F Duet). Mrs. Peachum enters and drags Polly out as Lucy helps Macheath escape. Peachum threatens Brown, who sends a search party after his friend. Macheath sings a song about the art of survival; he is joined by Jenny (How to Survive—M/F Solo to Mixed Chorus).

Act III opens on Peachum's wardrobe room, where he and Mrs. Peachum instruct the beggars on how to disrupt Victoria's coronation by evoking pity in the wealthy aristocrats. Brown and his constables burst in to arrest Peachum for trying to disrupt the coronation, but Peachum points out they would have to arrest all of the poor and handicapped. Peachum remarks about human failures and inability to attain goals (Useless Song—Sc to M Solo).

Jenny, in front of a curtain, contemplates various famous historical persons whose best attributes seemed to cause their downfall. She concludes that wisdom, beauty, bravery, inquisitiveness, and emotion are hindrances to humanity (The Song of Solomon—Sc to F Solo).

In Lucy's attic bedroom, Polly seeks information on Macheath. They are sincerely sympathetic to each other when they realize that neither knows his whereabouts. Lucy reveals that her pregnancy was a fraud to get Macheath to marry her. Mrs. Peachum arrives to announce Macheath's capture, and tells her daughter to prepare to be a widow.

One hour before Macheath is to be hanged and two hours before the coronation, Macheath desperately asks two of his gangsters to buy his freedom (Call from the Grave—M Solo). Everyone enters to say good-bye and Macheath forgives them all (Call from the Grave—M Solo).

At the last minute, a mounted messenger arrives (The Mounted Messenger—Mixed Chorus) with the notice that Macheath is to be released, raised into the ranks of nobility and given 10,000 pounds a year by the Queen of England. Peachum comments that noble messengers only too rarely appear.

NOTES ON THE PRODUCTION

Tony Award: Featured actress (Lotte Lenya).

The show, originally performed in Berlin in 1928, was adapted from John Gay's 1728 ballad opera, *The Beggar's Opera*. It was extremely successful during its 1955 New York run, and many communities have mounted productions since then.

It is possible to update the production costume-wise to the mid-thirties for it is similar in tone to *Cabaret*. The setting may be a unit set with locations made more specific through use of props. The show is vocally demanding and requires strong voices and broad characterizations. There are quite a few featured roles of various sizes which make it an ideal show for schools and communities. The chorus may be expanded as necessary to give more performing experience.

The music is dissonant in tone and a first-time listener may not appreciate the often harsh and strident sound. The satire of the melodrama is hard to pull off, but if put in the thirties style it is much more palatable and understandable to modern audiences.

The above synopsis is based on the Grove Press text, which differs from the Off-Broadway original cast recording. In order to avoid total confusion for those who are considering the show and trying to correlate it with the record, the names of the songs have been adjusted somewhat to fit those of the recording.

The major musical differences in the Off-Broadway version and the Grove Press version are as follows: Off-Broadway—"Pirate Jenny" sung by Jenny Diver, Grove—by Polly; Off-Broadway—"Barbara Song" sung by Lucy Brown, Grove—by Polly.

SONGS OF SPECIAL INTEREST

"The Army Song," baritone/tenor duet, blustering, bravado, militaristic, good for strong characters.

"Barbara Song," soprano, interesting lyrics, story song.

"Pirate Jenny," dramatically bitter song, many levels and lots of specifics, good for acting, alto sound is best.

"Jealousy Duet," F duet, good for alto/soprano, angry yet comedically dark, good for class study, insult contest.

Instrumentation: 2 reeds, 2 trumpets, trombone, percussion, guitar/banjo, piano/celeste, conductor
Script: Grove
Score: Universal
Record: MGM
Rights: TW

TWO BY TWO

Book: Peter Stone (Based on *The Flowering Peach*, by Clifford Odets)
Music: Richard Rodgers
Lyrics: Martin Charnin

ORIGINAL PRODUCTION

Imperial Theatre, November 10, 1970 (343 perf.)
Director and Choreographer: Joe Layton
Musical Director: Jay Blackton

Orchestration: Eddie Sauter
Principals: Esther—Joan Copeland—mezzo; Noah—Danny Kaye—tenor; Shem—
Harry Goz—baritone; Leah—Marilyn Cooper—alto; Ham—Michael Karm—
baritone; Rachel—Tricia O'Neil—soprano; Japheth—Walter Willison—tenor;
Goldie—Madeline Kahn—soprano
Chorus and Smaller Roles: None.

SYNOPSIS

The time—before, during and after the Flood. Outside his house, 900-year-
old Noah is trying to write his memoirs, when the voice of God informs him
the world is coming to an end. Noah calls for his wife, Esther, who usually puts
up with his ideas and prattlings but can't accept this one. Noah can't understand
why he has been chosen to be saved, but after considering the other men in town
he realizes there is no other choice (Why Me?—L to M Solo).

When he tells his two oldest sons, Ham and Shem, of God's pronouncement,
they ridicule him. Ham, Shem and Shem's wife Leah decide he is crazy and
should be sent to a mental home (Put Him Away—2M/F Trio). Japheth, the
youngest son, claims that Noah isn't crazy, God is.

The earth grows very still as everyone looks out and realizes the animals are
waiting calmly, two sheep next to two lions. As the biblical Gitka, the creature
with the most beautiful voice, begins its haunting song, the family kneels at the
well to pray for strength. Japheth begs God not to strike (Something, Somewhere—M Solo). While the women start to pack and the men set out to build
the ark, an angry Japheth asks Noah why the rudder wasn't included, to which
Noah responds that God probably didn't want one. The three sons urge him to
reconsider, but he stubbornly refuses (You Have Got to Have a Rudder on the
Ark—M Quartet).

As the men are off building, Esther and Ham's wife Rachel pack their things.
Esther questions Rachel about her unhappy relationship with Ham, and Rachel
sadly admits that something is missing (Something Doesn't Happen—Sc to F Solo).

Japheth tells his father he isn't going to build the ark and runs off to town.
A disturbed Noah, knowing he can't build anything without Japheth's youthful
energy, sadly walks off. The children comment on Noah's attitude and Esther
forces them to understand old age (An Old Man—L to F Solo).

At the end of the song a spry young man of ninety appears; it is Noah; God
has made him young so he can finish the building. He shocks his family as he
cavorts with Esther (Ninety Again—M Solo).

Japheth returns to the family and is shocked to see his father looking so
ridiculous, but Noah is more concerned that Japheth mate with someone. The
family urges him to find a wife (Two by Two—Mixed Chorus). As the song
ends, Goldie, a scantily dressed temple priestess who has met Japheth earlier,
enters and Noah invites her along, assuming that she will fall in love with Japheth.

Rachel begs Japheth to come with them, and he tells her he can't because he
loves her and she is Ham's wife (I Do Not Know—Sc to M Solo). She is

confused, but goes to get Esther to convince Japheth to join them. When the storm begins, Noah knocks Japheth out and has him carried on board. Noah takes a last look at the darkening world and sadly leaves the Gitka, who has no mate. He begs the Lord to reconsider, but the storm crescendos and he exits up the ramp to the ark (Something, Somewhere [Reprise]—M Solo).

Act II opens forty days and nights later. The rain has stopped. Everyone gazes out on an empty land. Noah philosophizes that it will be terrific when it dries but Japheth believes the sins of man will continue (When It Dries—Mixed Chorus).

There is tremendous tension on board. Ham, who finds Goldie exciting, is constantly chasing her around the ark; Rachel has moved into Esther's room to avoid Ham, and Esther feels too old for her young husband, Noah. She attempts to keep the family problems from Noah but confesses her own feelings of inadequacy. He assures her he needs her to cheer him (You—M Solo).

After Ham confides to Goldie that he has never had anything of his own and wants her, she agrees to perform her temple song for him (Golden Ram—F Solo). Noah discovers them in a compromising position and orders Goldie to marry Japheth immediately. Japheth refuses and openly declares his love for Rachel. Esther further upsets Noah by agreeing with the children. In the middle of this tense scene, the boat lists and Japheth and the boys rush to get the rudder they have stowed on board. Noah orders them to have faith in God (Poppa Knows Best—M Solo), but the boat starts to sink and a defeated Noah orders Japheth to use the rudder.

Weeks later, Shem and Leah, the two most despised, Shem for his laziness and Leah for her miserliness, declare their acceptance of each other (As Far As I'm Concerned—Sc to M/F Duet).

Noah, who hasn't spoken to anyone in weeks, appears to send the dove off in search of dry land. Japheth urges him to visit Esther, who is ill, but he is too ashamed. She enters and urges him to marry the children before she dies. The dove returns with an olive branch and Noah shows it to Esther, protesting that God won't let anything happen to her. He begs her to get well (Hey Girlie—M Solo), but she dies in his arms and he tearfully grants her last request by asking God to sanctify the children's marriages.

Atop Mt. Ararat, the children sadly leave the ark and say good-bye to Noah. Noah, left alone, bargains with God for a sign that the world will be left in man's hands (The Covenant—L to M Solo). A rainbow appears as the curtain falls.

NOTES ON THE PRODUCTION

Two by Two has a well-written book which can be exciting when performed by a good acting ensemble. The moods shift quickly and include comedic, anger, and tense drama. The subject matter covers a broad spectrum which includes the meaning of life and death. In order to capture the sensitivity of the piece, it is essential that Noah be a three-dimensional character played by a strong actor.

There are two sets, the exterior of the house with a well to allow for movement variety, and the upper level of the ark. The final scene may be played with the ark in the background and a ramp to enable the actors to perform on "dry land." A peach tree and rainbow are also required for the final scene.

There may be as few as one costume per actor with two costumes for Noah: one when he is older and one when he is younger. Props are quite simple and easily obtained.

The animal sequences, left to the imagination on Broadway, have occasionally been given a more artistic treatment through the use of marionettes, shadow puppets or live actors with masks. It is easier to choreograph the title song if there is some sort of visual accompaniment, than if the entire song is left for seven actors to perform.

The character of the Gitka needs to be animated. There is a strong dramatic impact on an audience who sees Noah leave a tangible, living creature behind. The Gitka may be portrayed by a birdlike marionette whose operator is fully seen, similar to the master puppeteer in the Japanese Bunraku. The audience soon accepts the convention, and it greatly enhances the final scene of Act I.

The small size of the company and the relationships within the family must be believable both in acting and reacting. In order to achieve this reality, the director would do well to spend a certain number of rehearsals utilizing improvisational techniques as a family unit and in pairs.

SONGS OF SPECIAL INTEREST

"An Old Man," mezzo dramatic, sensitive, lyrics, philosophical teaching song, strong.

"As Far As I'm Concerned," relationship, baritone/alto, comic character-oriented duet.

"The Covenant," semidramatic, strong acting, doesn't require a great voice as it may be talk sung, tenor.

"Put Him Away," comic trio with Noah needed for staging.

"Something, Somewhere," ending possible for audition as the musical build shows off range and pitch. Beginning is intensely dramatic.

Instrumentation: 3 reeds, 2 trumpets, trombone, 2 percussion, 2 violins, viola, cello, bass, piano/conductor
Script: NP
Score: Williamson
Record: Columbia
Rights: R & H

U

THE UNSINKABLE MOLLY BROWN

Book: Richard Morris
Music and Lyrics: Meredith Willson

ORIGINAL PRODUCTION

Winter Garden Theatre, November 3, 1960 (532 perf.)
Director: Dore Schary
Musical Numbers Staged by: Peter Gennaro
Musical Director: Herbert Greene
Orchestration: Don Walker
Principals: Molly Tobin—Tammy Grimes—mezzo; Shamus Tobin—Cameron Prud'Homme—VTNE; Johnny "Leadville" Brown—Harve Presnell—tenor; Christmas Morgan—Joseph Sirola—VTI; Johnny (Matinees)—James Hurst—tenor; Mrs. McGlone—Edith Meiser—VTNE; Prince DeLong—Mitchell Gregg—baritone; Roberts—Christopher Hewett—VTNE; Grand Duchess—Patricia Kelly—VTI
Chorus and Smaller Roles: 12M/12F.

SYNOPSIS

The play opens in the early 1900s with Molly, a feisty Irish girl in her teens, and her rowdy brothers involved in a typical wrestling match. Molly refuses to cry "uncle" as Shamus Tobin watches his defiant daughter, who yearns for a better life (I Ain't Down Yet—F Solo and M Chorus). Molly, determined to marry a wealthy man, decides to head for Denver. Shamus advises her to keep her religion, sense of humor and "never say die" attitude.

Molly reaches Leadville, Colorado, stops in the Saddle Rock Saloon and convinces owner Christmas Morgan to hire her as a piano player and singer. After he sees a display of Molly's Irish ambition, Christmas gives her the job and a place to sleep. Molly rehearses all night until the miners arrive for their morning drink. She successfully performs (Belly up to the Bar Boys—F Solo to Mixed Chorus).

After the miners leave, Molly imitates the prostitutes who were dancing promiscuously with the miners but is interrupted by Johnny "Leadville" Brown. He tries to dance with her, but she crashes a chair over his head and flounces out.

In the saloon three weeks later, Johnny asks Molly to marry him, but she refuses because she wants a man who can give her enough money to take care of her like a lady. He warns her that he is going to win her (I've A' Ready Started In—M Solo to M Chorus).

A month later, Johnny shows Molly a rather crude but solid log cabin he has built for her and her father. He promises to give her anything she asks for (I'll Never Say No—Sc to M Solo). Molly is so touched by the brass bed she has always wanted (My Own Brass Bed—Sc to F Solo) that she agrees to the marriage.

Three weeks later, Molly is alone in the cabin and dejected, for she hasn't seen Johnny since their wedding. He arrives with $300,000 as a wedding present and she is overwhelmed. He exits to buy a round of drinks at the saloon and Molly hides the money in the wood stove. Johnny returns home, lights a fire in the stove, and incinerates their fortune. He goes back out to discover "Little Johnny," the richest mine in the United States.

Six months later, she and Johnny have built a mansion in the most exclusive section of Denver, where the police comment on the ease of their job (The Denver Police—M Trio).

Molly yearns to be a part of the beautiful Denver society, but her neighbors represent second-generation wealth and feel uncomfortable with the rough and rugged Browns, who remind them of their parents. Molly unwittingly crashes the wealthy Mrs. McGlone's party and is overly awed at the beautiful decor and French-speaking Americans (Beautiful People of Denver—L to F Solo). In a conversation with the Monsignor, Molly discovers that the affluent people of Denver haven't donated to the church building program. In a revival spirit, she rallies them to contribute (Are You Sure—F Solo to Mixed Chorus). Mrs. McGlone has Molly ushered out and Molly, not knowing she has been snubbed, invites everyone to her housewarming party in a month.

In her red parlor, decorated for the party, Molly realizes she has been given the cold shoulder when no one but the Monsignor comes to her housewarming. The Monsignor tells Molly that perhaps she ought to travel to Europe and get cultured. She is anxious to take his advice, but Johnny is against hobnobbing with the Denver society. She reminds him of his promise to never say no (I'll Never Say No [Reprise]—F Solo) and he relents. Molly is certain of eventual acceptance (I Ain't Down Yet [Reprise]—F Solo).

Act II opens at the Browns' lavish salon in Paris, where the crowned heads of Europe are giving Molly a surprise party (Happy Birthday, Mrs. J. J. Brown—Mixed Chorus). Molly, determined to outdo Denver society, is involved in the study of music, art and foreign languages. She demonstrates her language expertise as the Prince quizzes her (Bon Jour—M/F Duet to Mixed Chorus). Molly invites her royal friends to Denver and announces to Johnny that they are going home. Johnny is worried by Molly's motives and wonders what makes her tick (If I Knew—M Solo).

Back home in Denver, Molly, assisted by Roberts, Mrs. McGlone's ex-butler, is preparing a grand party to introduce her royal friends to Denver. Johnny tells her he has dressed his friends from Leadville as waiters and assures her that everything will be fine (Chick-a-Pen—Sc to M/F Duet). The odd combination of guests causes the fete to end in a brawl. Molly heads back to Europe, but Johnny refuses to go with her and leaves for Leadville.

On the street in front of the Saddle Rock Saloon, Johnny and the boys are enjoying themselves with the local women (Keep A'Hoppin'—Mixed Chorus). Johnny soon loses interest because he can't forget about Molly (Leadville Johnny Brown's Soliloquy—M Solo).

It is 1912, in Monte Carlo. Molly has become superficial and jaded, a wealthy American who parties nightly with the Prince, who constantly asks her to marry him (Dolce Far Niente—I May Never Fall in Love with You—Sc to M/F Duet). Molly happens to meet Mrs. McGlone and attempts to embarrass her. Realizing how shabby she has become, she tells the Prince she is going home. She returns to the United States on the ill-fated *Titanic*; her spirit and energy save a boatload of people.

Molly returns to Denver a heroine who is finally satisfied, accepted by society, and reunited with Johnny (Finale—Mixed Chorus).

NOTES ON THE PRODUCTION

Tammy Grimes got the Tony Award for Featured Actress.

This is a large-scale production with good roles for character actors, lots of lavish scenery, costumes and props. It is expensive to produce and requires a strong singer to effectively portray Leadville Johnny. The rest of the roles are not as vocally demanding. It is a good choice for an organization looking for a lavish show, with humor, drama and strong moral values. There are quite a few dance sequences in the production which will require innovative choreography and possibly a separate dance chorus.

The production needs an opulent look to reflect turn-of-the-century Denver, and the chorus members will need several sets of costumes that range from 1900 to 1912. Each chorus member plays a variety of roles throughout; it would be conservative to suggest three costumes per person.

SONGS OF SPECIAL INTEREST

"Leadville Johnny Brown's Soliloquy," dramatic, tearful yet strong, tenor, vocally difficult.

Instrumentation: 5 reeds, 2 trumpets, 2 trombones, 3 horns, violin, cello, bass, percussion, piano/conductor
Script: Theatre Arts (Magazine) 2/63 Putnam
Score: Frank
Record: Capitol
Rights: MTI

W

WEST SIDE STORY

Book: Arthur Laurents (Based on Shakespeare's *Romeo and Juliet* and an idea by Jerome Robbins)
Music: Leonard Bernstein
Lyrics: Stephen Sondheim

ORIGINAL PRODUCTION

Winter Garden Theatre, September 26, 1957 (732 perf.)
Director and Choreographer: Jerome Robbins
Co-Choreographer: Peter Gennaro
Musical Director: Max Goberman
Orchestration: Leonard Bernstein, Sid Ramin and Irwin Kostal
Principals: Riff—Mickey Calin—baritone; Bernardo—Ken LeRoy—baritone; Tony—Larry Kert—tenor; Maria—Carol Lawrence—soprano; Anita—Chita Rivera—alto; Chino—Jamie Sanchez—VTNE; Doc—Art Smith—VTNE; Anybodys—Lee Becker—Dancer—VTNE
Chorus and Smaller Roles: 10M/8F and 2M adults.

SYNOPSIS

The scene opens on two rival New York street gangs: the Jets, whose leader is Riff and whose members are American, and the Sharks, whose leader is Bernardo and whose members are Puerto Rican. Because of the difference in backgrounds, there is much hostility and prejudice, and frequent wars over territories.

One late afternoon Bernardo and the Sharks corner A-rab, a Jet member, and proceed to beat on him until the rest of the Jets arrive. A free-for-all ensues but gets broken up by a big, goonlike cop, Krupke, and plainclothesman, Schrank. They advise the two groups to leave each other alone.

The Jets, determined to hold their turf, plan a rumble against the Sharks. In counting up their available fighters they decide to enlist the help of Tony, a former member-founder who hasn't been with the gang for a while. Leader Riff assures them that once someone is a Jet they are always loyal to the group (Jet Song—M Chorus).

When Riff finds Tony at the drugstore where he works, he asks Tony to join him at the dance to fight the Sharks. Tony reluctantly agrees, for Riff is like a brother, yet Tony yearns for something different (Something's Coming—M Solo).

Tony meets Bernardo's sister, Maria, at the dance and realizes she is what he has been waiting for (Dance at the Gym/Maria—M Solo with Mixed Chorus Background). He goes to Maria's home and climbs the fire escape to see her. The two express their mutual feelings (Tonight—Sc to M/F Duet).

The Sharks and their girls are in the street arguing about the virtues of Puerto Rico. When the boys leave to plan the war council, the girls comment on Puerto Rico; Rosalia, fantasizing the island's beauty, while Anita, Bernardo's girlfriend, and the girls prefer the USA (America—F Chorus).

The Jets are in the drugstore planning their rumble strategy despite Doc's comments on the pointlessness of fighting. He calls them hoodlums, which angers the boys, but Riff wisely counsels them to save their energy for the Sharks (Cool—M Solo with M Chorus).

Bernardo and the Sharks arrive at the drugstore to settle the details of the rumble. They agree to meet the next night under the highway and prove which gang is best by a fistfight between each gang's best man.

Tony secretly meets Maria in the dress shop after she finishes work. Using dressmaker dummies to represent their families, they dramatize what their lives should be like. The mood draws serious as they enact their make-believe wedding ceremony (One Hand, One Heart—Sc to M/F Duet).

In various areas of the neighborhood, the Jets, Sharks, Anita, Maria and Tony prepare for the evening (Tonight—Mixed Chorus).

The rumble begins with Bernardo and Diesel, the two best fighters, surrounded by the other gang members. They are interrupted by Tony who, keeping his promise to Maria, tries to stop the fight. Bernardo, recognizing him as the boy who danced with his sister, taunts Tony in an attempt to fight him. Riff, seeing that Tony will not fight back, strikes out at Bernardo, and both Riff and Bernardo pull knives. Tony draws Riff's attention away from the fight, which enables Bernardo to kill him. Seeing this, Tony grabs Riff's switchblade and kills Bernardo. He stands there stunned as the gang members all begin fighting. The sound of police sirens drives everyone off, but Tony stands staring at the two bodies and cries Maria's name. Anybodys, a tomboy who yearns to join the Jets, darts on and pulls him away as the cruiser lights comb the area.

When Act II opens, Rosalia and Consuelo, two Puerto Rican girls, are in Maria's bedroom, discussing what they will do after the rumble, when Maria announces that there will be no rumble and she feels wonderful for it is her wedding night. The girls think she is crazy (I Feel Pretty—F Trio) and tell her that one gets married before the wedding night. As Chino, her Puerto Rican former boyfriend, enters, the girls leave. Chino tells her there has been a fight and Maria reveals she is worried about Tony. Chino tells her that Tony has killed Bernardo and slams the door leading to the parlor. He stops before leaving and picks up Bernardo's gun.

Tony enters through the bedroom window to tell Maria he has killed her brother. She pleads with him not to leave her and the two, in an imaginary dance sequence, visualize their utopian world. As an offstage voice sings (Somewhere—F Solo, M/F Duet), the walls of the apartment move off, and the Sharks and Jets enter with their girls. Everyone dances happily together. The lights suddenly become harsh, and the dream turns into the real nightmare with the reenactment of the knife fight. At the end of the number Tony and Maria are back in the bedroom holding one another and finishing the song.

In an alley, the Jets, in hiding from Officer Krupke, comment on the officer and his treatment of them (Gee, Officer Krupke—M Chorus). Anybodys enters to tell them that Chino is out to get Tony, and the gang spreads out to warn and protect Tony.

Anita enters Maria's room seeking comfort and discovers that Tony has been there. She tells Maria that Tony is no good, but Maria forces Anita to understand that her love for Tony is as great as Anita's for Bernardo (A Boy Like That/I Have a Love—Sc to F Duet).

Officer Schrank enters to question Maria, who asks Anita to deliver a message to the drugstore. When Anita arrives at the drugstore, the Jets, believing she is there to find Tony, push her around in a dramatically stylized dance (The Taunting—Dance), which is stopped by the arrival of Doc. Anita tells the Jets to tell Tony that Chino has shot Maria and storms out of the drugstore.

Doc goes into the cellar to give Tony money for his escape and informs Tony that Maria is dead. Stunned, Tony runs out into the streets yelling for Chino to kill him. As he enters the street, he sees Maria and starts toward her, but Chino shoots him. Tony dies in Maria's arms and Maria, enraged and saddened by Tony's death, grabs the gun from Chino and threatens both Jets and Sharks with death. She collapses in tears but recovers herself and stretches out her arms to both gangs, who gently carry Tony's body off.

NOTES ON THE PRODUCTION

Tony Awards: Set Design, Choreography; most other awards went to *The Music Man*.

The show was lyricist Stephen Sondheim's Broadway debut, and was a brilliantly dramatic treatment of the Romeo and Juliet theme. The music and lyrics are familiar to modern audiences and enhance the book's dramatic action.

The production is extremely demanding, as it requires triple-threat performers capable of excellent dancing, singing and acting. The dancing is a high point and amateur groups will need a lot of work on these action-oriented numbers to avoid the risk of being hurt. Do not attempt to perform this musical without excellent dancers, a quality choreographer, and a lot of rehearsal hours.

The larger dance numbers require full stage space to perform, which usually means drops to set the location of the gym, the alley, the highway, and the street. It may be possible to combine the street sequences and possibly even include the rumble in front of the street drop. Other scenes occur in the bedroom/parlor, the bridal shop, the drugstore and the cellar. Some groups may find it technically feasible to have the drugstore and cellar placed in the same location, and have Tony enter the drugstore from a separate entrance after the Jets leave. The important element in designing the sets is to keep the stage action flowing from scene to scene.

The company members, except Anybodys, Doc and the policeman, usually have two costumes, one for the dance and one for everyday.

SONGS OF INTEREST

"A Boy Like That/I Have a Love," excellent scene/song duet for alto and soprano, dramatic, powerful. Excellent for class study.

"Gee, Officer Krupke," comic male chorus number. Many actable specifics, and solo selections. Good for showcase or class study.

"I Feel Pretty," female trio, interreaction, reaction stressed.

"One Hand, One Heart," romantic soprano/tenor duet, excellent scene, transitional emphasis.

"Something's Coming," quality tenor number, exciting, up tempo, good for audition.

Instrumentation: 5 reeds, 3 trumpets, 2 trombones, 2 horns, percussion, guitar, piano, 2 violins, cello, bass, piano/conductor
Script: Ten Great Musicals of the American Theatre, Theatre Arts (Magazine) 10/59, Dell, Random.
Score: Schirmer, Chappell
Record: Columbia
Rights: MTI

THE WIZ

Book: William F. Brown (Adapted from *The Wonderful Wizard of Oz*, by L. Frank Baum)
Music and Lyrics: Charlie Smalls

ORIGINAL PRODUCTION

Majestic Theatre, January 5, 1975 (1,672 perf.)
Director: Geoffrey Holder
Choreographer: George Faison
Musical Director: Charles H. Coleman
Orchestration: Harold Wheeler
Principals: Tinman—Tiger Haynes—baritone; Lion—Ted Ross—bass; Scare-
crow—Hinton Battle—baritone; Addaperle—Clarice Taylor—alto; Dorothy—
Stephanie Mills—mezzo; Glinda—Dee Dee Bridgewater—mezzo; The Wiz—
Andre De Shields—tenor; Aunt Em—Tasha Thomas—mezzo; Evillene—Mabel
King—alto
Chorus and Smaller Roles: 5F/9M.

SYNOPSIS

The curtain opens on a small, ramshackle farmhouse in Kansas where Dorothy,
a bright, energetic young teenager, is being scolded by her Aunt Em, a farm
wife who is disappointed that Dorothy isn't ready to accept the adult responsi-
bilities necessary to life on a farm. Despite her strict manner, it is obvious that
Aunt Em cares very much for the girl (The Feeling We Once Had—F Solo).

The Tornado, played by a colorful mass of dancers (Tornado Ballet—Mixed
Chorus Dance), sweeps up Dorothy's house and carries it to the strange, mystical
and magical land of Oz, where it kills the wicked witch of the East. The witch's
death causes quite a stir among the Munchkins and the good witch of the North,
Addaperle, an extremely zany comic character. When Dorothy asks the Munchkins and Addaperle how she is to get back to Kansas, they advise her to visit
the great Oz (He's the Wizard—F Solo to Mixed Chorus).

A yellow brick road appears, played by four men in yellow and orange squared
costumes, but Dorothy is frightened of the journey she must take (Soon as I Get
Home—L to F Solo). Her fears are alleviated by a friendly scarecrow, perched
on a pole in a cornfield, whom she frees. Accompanied by three crows, he tells
her about his dream to have brains (I Was Born on the Day before Yesterday—
L to M Solo to 2M/F Trio). Dorothy tells the Scarecrow that the Wiz could
probably help him, and the two join forces with the "road" on their way to the
Emerald City (Ease on Down the Road—M/F Duet to M Chorus).

In a small patch of woods along the yellow brick road, they find a rusted
tinman who begs for some oil (Slide Some Oil to Me—Sc to M Solo to 2M/F
Trio) and tells the two he wants a heart to make his life complete. They ask him
to join them and the three set out (Ease on Down the Road [Reprise]—Mixed
Chorus). Their journey is interrupted by the Cowardly Lion, who tries to convince
them of his ferocity (I'm a Mean Ole Lion—M Solo). He turns out to be under
the psychiatric care of an owl and decides to go to Oz in hopes of finding courage
(Ease on Down the Road [Reprise]—Mixed Chorus). When the Lion shows his

cowardice in a fight with the Kalidahs, a frightening witchlike gang (Kalidah Battle—Mixed Chorus Dance), Dorothy comforts him (Be a Lion—Sc to F Solo).

The four find themselves in a poppy field. Dorothy, remembering the warning that Addaperle gave her about the dangerous Poppies, warns everyone to run, but the Lion succumbs to the treacherous aroma. Luckily a paddy wagon containing four mice from the Mice Squad comes in and rescues the four travelers.

After many trials and tribulations, the group arrives in the futuristic Emerald City with its exotically and exquisitely dressed inhabitants. All the citizens wear green glasses as part of their apparel (Emerald City Ballet—Mixed Chorus Dance).

The four eventually meet the Wiz, who makes a fantastic entrance riding in on a set piece that looks like a giant tongue. He strikes a magnificent pose which overwhelms everyone. The Wiz theatrically introduces himself to the travelers, who are thoroughly frightened by what they have just witnessed (So You Wanted to Meet the Wizard—M Solo). The Wiz listens to their problems, and though he appears very harsh with everyone's requests, he is deeply moved by the Tinman's song (What Would I Do If I Could Feel—L to M Solo). He agrees to grant their wishes if they kill Evillene, the wicked witch of the West and the most powerful witch of Oz.

Act II opens in Evillene's perfectly dreadful castle where a large ugly throne is rolled on covered with carcasses. The large, grotesque witch harshly instructs her slaves, the Winkies, not to bother her for she is in a bad mood (Don't Nobody Bring Me No Bad News—F Solo). When an unfortunate messenger has the bad luck to report on the presence of Dorothy and her friends, the angry witch kills the messenger and summons the winged monkeys. The scene shifts to another part of the stage where the monkeys do a wild dance which includes the capture and eventual kidnapping of Dorothy (Funky Monkeys—Mixed Chorus Dance).

At Evillene's castle about a week later, when Evillene starts victimizing the Lion, Dorothy hurls a bucket of water on the unsuspecting witch, who promptly shrieks in horror, begins to melt and is reduced to a pile of smoldering cloth on the floor. The Winkies shout with joy at the death of their despicable witch (Everybody Rejoice—Mixed Chorus).

The four return to Emerald City and discover the Wiz is a fake (Who Do You Think You Are?—Mixed Quartet). The Wiz reveals to Dorothy and the others that he is a nobody from Omaha, Nebraska, whose hot air balloon got swept up in a big storm and landed in the middle of a ladies' social in Oz. These women, having never seen a hot air balloon before, expected him to do another miracle so he devised the green glasses that everyone wears. The four friends are puzzled until he explains that the miracle behind the glasses is what you allow yourself to see (If You Believe—Sc to M Solo).

The Wiz reaches into his magic storage chest and begins to hand out his miracles: a box of all-bran sprinkles for the Scarecrow, which he dubs "all brain"; a large, red satin heart for the Tinman; a whiskey bottle marked O & Z which he throws together in a chalice and has the Lion drink for courage, and he promises to take Dorothy to Kansas in the balloon he arrived in.

At a farewell launching where the citizens are bidding their leader good-bye (Y'All Got It—L to M Solo and Mixed Chorus), the balloon accidentally ascends without Dorothy. Dorothy throws a temper tantrum which is interrupted by a puff of smoke and a dazed Addaperle, who tells the foursome that her sister, Glinda, the good witch of the South, is on her way. She arrives in a large tent with an escort of four Quadlings. She tells Dorothy to rest her body and her mind (A Rested Body—F Solo) and tells her she can go home if she believes in herself (If You Believe [Reprise]—Sc to F Solo).

Dorothy begins to sing of her home (Home—F Solo) and is reminded by her friends that she can return to Oz by clicking her silver shoes and thinking of her friends. During the song the members of the Oz fantasy disappear, leaving her alone onstage at the end of the song. Toto her dog appears and she realizes that she's home. Curtain.

NOTES ON THE PRODUCTION

Tony Awards: Supporting Actor (Ted Ross), Supporting Actress (Dee Dee Bridgewater), Musical, Direction, Score, Choreography, Costumes and Set Design.

This show was an extremely innovative production with marvelous dancing and theatrical staging. Audiences who enjoyed it most were the ones that didn't compare it to the Garland film.

The show is an interesting one to produce, for much of its success lies with a creative director/choreographer. The company may be relatively small, with the chorus portraying a variety of different parts, or large, with the chorus work not as involved. In the case of community theatres, who may have singers with limited dance training, it would be best to have a larger cast and several dance captains. This would enable the choreographer to stage a number and have the dance captain polish it while the choreographer goes on to stage another number with a different group of people.

The costumes are many; each group of people mentioned in the synopsis needs extremely different costumes, i.e., the Winkies, the citizens of Oz. It is a heavy costume show and while much is creative and can be inexpensively achieved, the fact remains that there are a lot of costumes.

The production, for younger children of kindergarten through third grade, is approximately thirty minutes too long as they grow very restless in the slower, less visually exciting moments. A director may want to consider minor editing if there will be a lot of younger children in the audience.

The show has quite a few props, usually oversized. It is suggested that the director of props be a fun-loving, imaginative person in order to guarantee the consistent look the production calls for.

The notes in the published French version are quite detailed and well worth following. The play is a challenge to any group and can best be performed under the auspices of a creative director and a strong choreographer.

SONGS OF SPECIAL INTEREST

"Ease on Down the Road," small chorus number, good for revue or class situation, requires movement.

"Don't Nobody Bring Me No Bad News," comic alto, character development. Good study for performers who have trouble bringing strong characters to life.

Instrumentation:2 percussion, guitar, bass, drums, 4 reeds, horn, 3 trumpets, 2 trombones, cello, 2 violins, and piano
Script: SF Great Rock Musicals
Selections: Fox
Record: Atlantic
Rights: SF

WONDERFUL TOWN

Book: Joseph Fields and Jerome Chodorov (Based on the play *My Sister Eileen*, by Joseph Fields and Jerome Chodorov, and the stories of Ruth McKenney)
Music: Leonard Bernstein
Lyrics: Betty Comden and Adolph Green

ORIGINAL PRODUCTION

Winter Garden Theatre, February 25, 1953 (559 perf.)
Director: George Abbott
Choreographer: Donald Saddler
Musical Director: Lehman Engel
Orchestration: Donald Walker
Principals: Ruth—Rosalind Russell—alto; Eileen—Edith (Edie) Adams—soprano; Robert Baker—George Gaynes—baritone; Wreck—Jordan Bentley—baritone; Frank—Chris Alexander—VTI; Chick—Dort Clark—VTI; Appopolous—Henry Lascoe—VTNE
Chorus and Smaller Roles: 12M/12F; all males must sing well, dance is helpful; a small ensemble of policemen who sing tight harmony is included in the 12M.

SYNOPSIS

The setting is New York City in the 1930s. At the play's opening, a guide is showing a group of tourists the sights of Greenwich Village (Christopher Street—Mixed Chorus). In the course of this fast-paced number various members of the community are introduced: Mr. Appopolous, a dynamic and explosive artist; Lonigan, the cop whose beat is Christopher Street; Wreck, a football player; and his girlfriend Helen. At the end of this number, a scream is heard offstage, and Ruth Sherwood and her sister Eileen enter claiming that someone has stolen their typewriter. Appopolous, who has ended up with the typewriter in question, returns it. When the sisters, newly arrived from Ohio, tell Appopolous that they need a place to stay, he offers to let them see an apartment he owns that was just vacated.

The scene shifts to an absolute horror of an apartment, which sits below street level and contains two daybeds, a fake fireplace and one barred window that looks out onto the street. The girls are forced to take the apartment. When a man walks in the front door looking for Violet, the former tenant who was a prostitute, the girls call for help. Wreck, a neighbor, enters and scares the man off. Later that night Ruth, an aspiring writer, and Eileen, an aspiring actress, begin to regret their decision to rent the apartment (Ohio—Sc to F Duet).

A pantomine shows the sisters' struggles to make it in their respective fields. Wherever Ruth goes with her manuscripts no one is interested, and wherever Eileen goes for theatre jobs the people are interested in her but not as an actress. The girls are very discouraged (Conquering New York—Dance).

A few weeks later, on the street, Eileen has managed to accumulate quite a group of helpful men: the floor manager of the supermarket, who gives food samples; Speedy Valenti, owner of the Village Vortex, a local nightclub, who might hire Eileen if he knew her a little better; and Frank, the manager of Walgreen's drugstore, who gives her free lunches. Ruth is amazed at Eileen's innocent ability to attract men and comments on her own problems with the opposite sex (One Hundred Easy Ways—L to F Solo).

At the "Manhatter" office of editor Robert Baker, Ruth attempts to convince the skeptical Baker to read some of her stories. He and two of his editors advise her to return to Ohio and comment on the waste of talented people in New York (What a Waste—M Trio). Baker finally reads three of Ruth's stories, all containing sophisticated heroines in wordly situations. As Baker, on one side of the stage, reads, Ruth, on another side, acts out the vignettes with herself as the heroines (Story Vignettes—Mime with 4M/1F).

Frank, on his way to work, meets Eileen on the street and gives her a box of candy. She reminds him of their dinner date and imagines herself in love (A Little Bit in Love—Sc to F Solo).

Wreck and Helen, who live upstairs from Ruth and Eileen, have convinced the girls to let Wreck live in their kitchen during Helen's mother's visit. Wreck, in the garden of the apartment, brags to the delivery boys about his college career as a football hero (Pass the Football—M Solo).

Eileen has invited three men, including Bob Baker from the "Manhatter," to dinner at the apartment. Everyone tries to ease the tension resulting from their not having anything to discuss (Conversation Piece—2F/3M Quintet).

After Bob Baker tells Ruth she has talent, but must stop writing about situations she hasn't experienced, a stormy argument ensues, and she leaves. Baker yearns for a long lasting relationship with someone quiet and gentle (A Quiet Girl—Sc to M Solo).

Chick Clark, a newspaperman admirer of Eileen's, desiring to be alone with her, sends Ruth to Brooklyn on a phony assignment. At the naval yard, Ruth attempts to interview a group of Brazilian cadets, but they are more interested in the conga. Every time she asks their opinion they break into a wild conga and force her to join in (Conga!—F Solo to M Chorus). The men conga Ruth all the way back to her apartment. The wild party that follows is raided by the police, who arrest Eileen as part of a prostitution ring.

Act II opens at the Christopher Street Police Station where Eileen has become the darling of the force (My Darlin' Eileen—M Trio). She is visited by Ruth, who marches around with an electric "Village Vortex" sign. Ruth returns to the street to drum up business (Swing—F Solo with Mixed Chorus).

Ruth takes Baker's advice and writes about something she has experienced, namely, the Brazilian cadets and her sister's arrest. Baker argues with his editor, who refuses to publish it, and gets fired. He tries to convince Eileen it was a matter of principle, but she tells him he's upset because he loves Ruth (It's Love—Sc to M/F Duet). The story hits the front page and Chick Clark's editor offers Ruth a job, and Speedy Valenti offers Eileen a singing job at his club.

The scene shifts to the Village Vortex, where Ruth and Eileen perform a period duet, stylized à la 1913 vaudeville (Wrong Note Rag—2F Duet with Mixed Chorus). Bob admits he loves Ruth (Finale—Mixed Chorus).

NOTES ON THE PROUDCTION

Tonys: Best Musical, Book, Music, Sets, Choreography, Musical Direction Producer and Actress (Rosalind Russell).

This wonderfully funny show isn't produced often enough, possibly because it has long been forgotten. Both high schools and community theatres would benefit greatly from a production of this hit musical. The music is memorable, the characters enjoyable, the dialogue witty and the chorus emphasis on characterization and situation.

Ruth should sing, dance and have good audience presence to effectively perform the conga number and "One Hundred Easy Ways." Eileen needs an excellent voice that blends with Ruth's.

The show was originally set in the 1930s but some companies have updated it to the late fifties for costume reasons. It could probably be set in the present although the Village Vortex scenes wouldn't work as well as the Greenwich Village street types of today might not create as amusing an evening. The script is totally innocent and charming, and the setting and time frame should be kept in a similar era.

The sets aren't complicated; much of the action takes place on the street, the garden, and the apartment, with addditional settings in the jail, Baker's office, the navy yard and the Village Vortex. It is possible to utilize more scenes, in front of the street drop, and just add props for the garden, Christopher Street and the Village Vortex exterior. For those with limited offstage space and fly space, it is possible to have one drop of the street and a turntable revolve which shows the other locations.

SONGS OF SPECIAL INTEREST

"Conversation Piece," good for class study or revue, complicated timing, musically difficult, quintet.

"Ohio," comic, tight harmony number, good for class study with scene work, alto/soprano.

"One Hundred Easy Ways," comic, character song, lists specifics, good for audience contact, alto.

"What a Waste," actable due to the specifics in varying stories, nice harmony for male trio; all men have solo section.

Instrumentation: 6 violins, 4 woodwinds, 3 trumpets, 2 trombones, viola, cello, bass, percussion, piano/conductor
Script: Random, Great Musicals of the American Theatre Volume Two
Selections: Chappell
Record: Decca
Rights: TW

Y

YOU'RE A GOOD MAN, CHARLIE BROWN

Book: John Gordon (Based on the comic strip *Peanuts*, by Charles M. Schulz)
Music, Lyrics and Adaptation: Clark Gesner

ORIGINAL PRODUCTION

Theatre 80, March 7, 1967 (1,597 perf.)
Director: Joseph Hardy
Musical Supervisor: Joseph Raposo
Assistant Director: Patricia Birch
Principals: Charlie Brown—Gary Burghoff—tenor; Schroeder—Skip Hinnant—
baritone; Lucy—Reva Rose—alto; Linus—Bob Balaban—baritone; Patty—Karen
Johnson—soprano; Snoopy—Bill Hinnant—tenor
Chorus and Smaller Roles: None.

SYNOPSIS

The play is a series of vignettes in an average day of Charlie Brown's life.
Charlie Brown is a rather simple soul who is considered to be stupid, clumsy
and destined for failure by his friends Patty, Linus, Schroeder, Lucy and his
dog Snoopy.

The lights rise to full as the company sings the title song, which attempts to
make Charlie feel good about himself (You're a Good Man, Charlie Brown—
Mixed Chorus).

Charlie, left alone clutching his lunch bag, soliloquizes on the contents of his lunch and the little redheaded girl he wants to speak to. As he builds his courage, he realizes she is watching him and puts his lunch bag over his head. Lucy and Patty enter discussing a dress and proceed to draw a design on Charlie's bag without noticing him. He stands, speaking through the bag about his dilemma. He finally removes the bag and sadly walks off as Beethoven's "Moonlight Sonata" is heard and the lights rise on Schroeder, who is sitting at a box which resembles a piano. He is absorbed in his playing and Lucy tries to get him to manifest some interest in her (Schroeder—F Solo).

Various characters comment on events in their daily lives; Lucy greets Snoopy but is unable to kiss him because she is repelled by the thought of kissing a dog; Linus questions the meaning of happiness; and Lucy asks a disturbed Schroeder how he would feel about selling his piano to buy saucepans for their future kitchen. Schroeder collapses as Snoopy imagines he is a fierce animal. Charlie Brown tells Snoopy he will be back with his supper and Snoopy thinks about his winning personality (Snoopy—M Solo).

Charlie Brown enters with his paper bag, talking about introducing himself to the little redheaded girl. He realizes it's impossible and exits. Snoopy looks up to grimly face the fact that he is a dog and can't advance further.

Linus sits to watch TV while clutching his blanket. He gradually overcomes his dependency and casually walks away, only to return to his blanket (My Blanket and Me—M Solo). Lucy enters, forces her brother to change channels and tells him she is going to be a queen when she grows up. He attempts to tell her that queen is an inherited title but she angrily retorts it's undemocratic and she will find a loophole. Charlie enters with an invisible kite and struggles to get and keep it airborne (Kite Song—M Solo).

Everyone is exchanging valentines and Charlie is upset to discover that Snoopy has received a ton of valentines while Charlie hasn't even received one. In desperation, he seeks help from Lucy, who considers herself an amateur psychiatrist (The Doctor Is In—Sc to M/F Duet). Feeling much better, Charlie thanks Lucy for her friendship. She responds by charging him five cents for her advice.

Schroeder, Linus, Lucy and Charlie Brown enter with pencils and notebooks and sit in various places around the stage as they prepare to write their homework (Book Report—3M/1F Linear Quartet).

The Act II lights rise on Snoopy atop his doghouse, dressed as a World War I flying ace in search of the Red Baron (The Red Baron—M Solo). Patty enters and orders Snoopy to join her in a rabbit hunt. He goes through the motions but falls in front of her in feigned exhaustion. She congratulates him for his spirited effort and exits.

Charlie, the manager of the baseball team, attempts to give the group the desire to win, despite Lucy's disparaging remarks (The Baseball Game—Sc to Mixed Chorus). Charlie Brown, the last man at bat, sees the little redheaded girl and strikes out, as the team sadly leaves.

Schroeder tells Lucy, as a favor, that she has a crabby personality. She is quite angry but decides to take a personality rating poll. She corners Charlie Brown to ask his opinion. He is extremely uncomfortable and attempts to evade her questions but responds with nebulous answers in order to stave off Lucy's wrath. Linus ranks her 95 percent on crabbiness and she slugs him, but she has regrets and begins to admit her personality is terrible. She is lamenting her inadequacies when Linus tells her he loves her. She happily bursts into tears and the two exit.

Schroeder waits for everyone for choir practice but an argument ensues and he is unable to keep order (Glee Club Rehearsal—Sc to Mixed Chorus). Several vignettes follow. Lucy enters with Linus to undertake the job of teaching him about life (Little Known Facts—Sc to F Solo/2M Needed for Staging) but she is interrupted by Charlie Brown, who is appalled at her lack of honesty.

Snoopy imagines that Charlie Brown has forgotten to feed him and dramatically soliloquizes. When his supper finally arrives, he bursts into song (Suppertime—L to M Solo).

At the end of the day the group relaxes and gives their own definition of happiness (Happiness—Mixed Chorus).

NOTES ON THE PRODUCTION

A good first show for a newly formed theatre group as it is usually performed on a bare stage with set pieces in the shape of large children's blocks. These colorful blocks represent a piano, Snoopy's house, chairs and tables, and may be moved as needed. There are very few props or extra costume pieces. The cast is small, although some companies have enlarged the larger production numbers to include more performers.

Because the show consists of many unrelated vignettes, it is essential that lighting be as controlled as possible. Much of the flow of the production comes from the ability of the audience to move their attention from one segment to another. This can only be achieved by area lighting that allows performers to enter and exit quickly without pulling unnecessary focus.

SONGS OF SPECIAL INTEREST

It is best to avoid performing these songs at an audition as they have tricky rhythms and are difficult for an audition accompanist to sight-read.

"The Baseball Game," character-oriented, small chorus, action and energy essential.

"The Doctor Is In," good for actors in beginning musical theatre class, not vocally demanding, interaction and listening exercise, alto/baritone or tenor.

"Little Known Facts," good for part of character study for Lucy, alto.

"Suppertime," vaudeville styled, soft shoe, shows movement ability and style, tenor.

Instrumentation: 2 violins, viola, cello, bass, 5 reeds, horn, 2 trumpets, trombone, percussion, piano, celeste, toy piano, melodica, guitar (combo score as heard on record is also available)
Script: Random, Fawcett
Score: Jeremy
Record: MGM
Rights: TW

Z

ZORBA

Book: Joseph Stein (Adapted from *Zorba the Greek*, by Nikos Kazantzakis)
Music: John Kander
Lyrics: Fred Ebb

ORIGINAL PRODUCTION

Imperial Theatre, November 17, 1968 (305 perf.)
Director: Harold Prince
Choreographer: Ron Field
Musical Director: Harold Hastings
Orchestration: Don Walker
Principals: Leader—Lorraine Serabian—alto; Nikos—John Cunningham—tenor; Zorba—Herschel Bernardi—baritone; Pavli—Richard Dmitri—VTI; Widow—Carmen Alvarez—mezzo; Mme. Hortense—Maria Karnilova—mezzo; Mavrodani—Paul Michael—VTI; Mimiko—Al De Sol—VTI
Chorus and Smaller Roles: 9M/5F.

SYNOPSIS

The story takes place in Piraeus, Greece, and the Island of Crete in 1924.

The play opens on a bare stage with the entire company seated in two semi-circles, bouzouki style. Each of the company members has an instrument of some sort with which they accompany the other members of the chorus. As the company decides to do a narration of the Zorba story (Life Is—F Solo to Mixed Chorus), they begin to set the stage to represent a cafe in Piraeus. Nikos enters carrying a coat, valise and a carton of books. He is uneasy for he is not the type of person who usually is found in such a cafe. Zorba, a lusty man in his late sixties, enters, spies the stranger and strikes up a conversation; Zorba's manner of interrogation into Nikos's affairs is more an attempt at inflicting his own beliefs than an honest attempt to listen to Nikos's problems. Zorba explains his philosophy of life to Nikos (The First Time—M Solo).

When Nikos tells Zorba that he is going to take over a mine that he recently inherited, Zorba insists that he too go along because "mining is his speciality." He gives the impression that everything is his "speciality." Nikos agrees rather halfheartedly.

The scene shifts to the exterior of a cafe in Crete where the men are playing games, drinking, and discussing the new owner of the mine. The village is extremely poor, backward and superstitious. When Zorba and Nikos arrive, they are urged to stay with certain villagers and agree to move in with an old man who starts demanding extra payment for various services. However, Mimiko, a nineteen-year-old simpleton, entices them to the house of the "Frenchwoman." The chorus tells them about Mme. Hortense (The Top of the Hill—Mixed Chorus).

Nikos and Zorba go to a shabby inn where they are greeted by Mme. Hortense, a flirtatious, faded coquette in her fifties who still dresses and acts in a youthful manner. An interested Zorba charms her as she relates her experiences to him (No Boom Boom—L to F Solo). While Zorba is carrying Mme. Hortense to her bedroom the chorus comments (Vive la Différence—Mixed Chorus), and Zorba romantically calls Mme. Hortense his virgin. She is pleased and confesses she has been a virgin many times, but never married. Her deepest wish is to marry before she dies. Zorba answers "perhaps" and begins to caress her.

The men are gathered at the mine to sign in for work. Mimiko enters only to be berated by Manolakas, the younger brother of Mavrodani. Zorba stands up for the boy as an attractive widow enters with Mimiko's lunch. The widow is a woman in her late twenties with an air of mysterious tragedy about her. Most of the men in the village are attracted to her—especially Pavli, Mavrodani's son. Having no interest in any of them, she ignores them. Zorba urges Nikos to follow her but Nikos refuses. The chorus and Nikos comment on not rushing things (The Butterfly—Mixed Chorus).

The next day as Zorba leaves to buy items for the mine, Hortense offers Zorba a farewell basket of fruit and worries that he will forget her while he is away (Goodbye, Canavaro—Sc to M/F Duet). She tells him she would like a ring when he returns.

The scene opens with Nikos reading a letter from Zorba, which flashes back to a cafe in Khania. The song is acted out by Zorba in another part of the stage and tells of Zorba's failure to spend Nikos's money on anything but women and good times. He mentions nothing about Hortense (Grandpapa—M Solo to Chorus). Nikos tells her that Zorba is bringing her a present when he returns. She excitedly tells him she knows it is a ring and that Zorba will marry her. Nikos is uneasy, but she is ecstatic (Only Love—F Solo).

The chorus approaches Nikos, leading him to the widow's house (Bend of the Road—Chorus). She opens the door and they embrace. Pavli sees them embrace and runs off in agony.

Act II opens at a dance in the village square, which is interrupted by a mourning song. The priest and townsfolk enter, carrying the body of Pavli, who has drowned himself. The town blames the widow for driving him to suicide.

Zorba returns to Hortense's garden and lyingly says he has ordered the rings. When Hortense shows him the wedding rings she has, he is forced to agree to the engagement. The chorus and Nikos solemnize the occasion (Y'assou—Mixed Chorus) in a mock marriage ceremony.

On the road, Nikos tries to assure the widow that everything will be fine, but she is unable to express her feelings (Why Can't I Speak?—M/F Duet). As he tries to draw her out, a young girl stands behind the widow, expressing the widow's innermost thoughts, and they sing together.

On the steps of the church, Mavrodani, in a dramatic and captivating scene, decides to revenge his son's death by stabbing and killing the widow. He does kill her.

At the entrance to the mine, a priest is chanting blessings. Nikos, still distraught over the death of the widow, can't condone Zorba's compliance in letting Mavrodani live, but Zorba philosophizes that revenge only brings more revenge. Zorba and Manolakas go down in the mine to try a sample blast, but a huge explosion occurs and the mine is declared useless. Its timbers are rotting and it isn't operational. Mimiko enters to tell the men that Mme. Hortense is very ill and wants Zorba.

They arrive at Hortense's home to discover the chorus gathered around her like vultures (The Crow—F Chorus) waiting for her death so they can take her things.

Zorba enters, pushing the women out, and tells her he has come. She confesses to him of her past and her sixteenth birthday—the action freezes as she walks downstage and sings as if she were a young girl (Happy Birthday—F Solo). At the end of the song, she collapses on the bed and dies in Zorba's arms. Zorba is overcome with grief and Nikos, fearing Zorba will go mad if he doesn't vent his sorrow, begins a Greek dance, which Zorba finally joins.

The baggage is packed and Zorba and Nikos are ready to leave. Nikos suggests that he might join Zorba, but Zorba knows Nikos really isn't able to do that, for only Zorba is able to risk all that he has (I Am Free—M Solo). The two men say good-bye. The play closes as it began, with the chorus singing (Life Is [Reprise]—Mixed Chorus).

NOTES ON THE PRODUCTION

Tony Awards: Set Design. The show was revived in 1983 and Lila Kedrova received the Best Actress award.

Written by Kander and Ebb, the show has some excellent musical numbers that allow for solid characterizations. It is very simple to stage, for the premise is that a group of people gather to perform a retelling of the Zorba story. The stage is more interesting if there are levels but the production works quite well on the stage floor. The actors may set their own props in full view of the audience, which helps if there is a limited technical crew available.

The actors need one costume throughout the production, although Hortense should have at least two as it is more fitting for her character.

The script is exciting and interesting but greatly dependent on an excellent actor to play Zorba and a charming, comedic actress to play Hortense.

SONGS OF SPECIAL INTEREST

"Life Is," good choice for musical revue, or as a solo nightclub performance, alto.

"No Boom Boom," comedic story song, character-oriented, should have a small male chorus but works quite well as a mezzo solo in a classroom situation.

"I Am Free," strong, robust, baritone, some movement.

"Goodbye, Canavaro," nice scene to duet character-oriented, charm number, character study in class situation, mezzo/baritone.

"Why Can't I Speak?," effective female duet where one character can't express emotions and another character does. Pretty ballad, effective number for showcase, mezzo.

Instrumentation: 2 bouzouki/mandolin, 4 reeds, 4 trumpets, French horn, 2 trombones, 2 percussion, 2 violins, viola, cello, bass, guitar, accordion. Electric harpsichord/conductor (piano may be substituted)
Script: Random, SF
Selections: Valando
Record: Capitol
Rights: SF

CONCEPT, ROCK, NOSTALGIA
AND OTHERS

A

ALL IN LOVE

Book and Lyrics: Bruce Geller (Based on Sheridan's *The Rivals*)
Music: Jacques Urbont

ORIGINAL PRODUCTION

Martinique Theatre, November 10, 1961 (141 perf.)
Director: Tom Brennan
Musical Director: Jacques Urbont
Orchestration: Jonathan Tunick
Principals: Lucy—Christina Gillespie—soprano; Mrs. Malaprop—Mimi Randoph—alto; Jack Absolute—David Atkinson—baritone; Sir Anthony Absolute—Lee Cass—bass; Lydia Languish—Gaylea Byrne—soprano; Sir Lucius O'Trigger—Michael Davis—baritone; Bob Acres—Dom Deluise—tenor
Chorus: 6M/5F. Three of the men form a trio and must vocally blend well as bass, baritone and tenor.

SUMMARY AND NOTES

The play takes place in 1775 in Bath, England, where the upper crust go for amusement. Sir Anthony wishes his son, Jack Absolute, to marry Lydia Languish, the flighty Mrs. Malaprop's niece, but Lydia yearns to marry someone poor. Jack, knowing of Lydia's desire, disguises himself as Ensign Beverly and, with the aid of her maid Lucy, woos Lydia. Meanwhile, Sir Lucius O'Trigger, once wealthy but fallen on hard times, decides Lydia's wealth and beauty make her the ideal wife. After a great deal of confusion caused by maid Lucy's deliberate tampering with messages, several comic chase sequences and witty character development which pokes fun at the British, the play reaches its climax.

Bob Acres, Jack's foppish friend who is in love with Lydia, prepares to duel Ensign Beverly, actually Jack, and O'Trigger prepares to duel, first Jack and later Sir Anthony. Everyone arrives at the duelling grounds and things are quickly resolved: Lydia agrees to marry Jack; Lucy, who has gained great wealth from carrying messages, marries O'Trigger; and Mrs. Malaprop is paired with Bob Acres.

There were quite a few sets in the original, but scene locations may be switched without affecting the meaning of the script. The scene at the baths and the exterior of the brothel may possibly be played at the exterior of the baths. It is possible to do the show on a three-sided revolve, one side for Mrs. Malaprop's home, one for the exterior of the baths, and the third for Jack's room.

The costumes are period, somewhat complex and costly in terms of fabric yardage. However, the cast is small and most may wear the same costumes throughout. Lucy should have several costumes, each demonstrating her rising financial status.

The show is worth considering for a company that is looking for something different, musically interesting and humorous. The script plays much better in a smaller theatre.

SONGS OF SPECIAL INTEREST

"A More Than Ordinary Glorious Vocabulary," comic duet, alto/bass diction and character emphasized. Good for class scene study. Sung by Mrs. Malaprop to Sir Anthony in response to his feeling that women should not have an education.

"What Can It Be?," mezzo or soprano, up tempo, movement-oriented, for comic soubrette. Lucy sings in response to an earlier kiss by O'Trigger and wonders if she could be in love with this roguish man.

Instrumentation: piano, bass, drum
Script: NP
Record: Mercury
Rights: MTI

THE AMOROUS FLEA

Book: Jerry Devine (Based on Molière's *School for Wives*)
Music and Lyrics: Bruce Montgomery

ORIGINAL PRODUCTION

78th Street Playhouse, February 17, 1964 (93 perf.)
Staged by: Jack Sydow
Musical Director: Ted Simons
Orchestration: Lou Busch
Principals: Arnolphe—Lew Parker—baritone; Chrysalde—David C. Jones—baritone; Alain—Jack Fletcher—baritone; Georgette—Ann Mitchell—alto; Agnes—Imelda De Martin—mezzo; Horace—Philip Proctor—tenor
Chorus and Smaller Roles: None.

SUMMARY AND NOTES

Arnolphe, a self-centered older man, has decided to marry Agnes, his orphaned ward, whom he has been grooming to be a subservient wife since she was four. Raised in a convent, Agnes is now conveniently living in a courtyarded house and is watched by Arnolphe's two comic servants, Alain and Georgette. Arnolphe continues to keep her away from all suitors. However, Horace, the son of one of Arnolphe's friends, confides that he has seen a lovely girl and plans on marrying her. Arnolphe is apoplectic when he discovers the girl is Agnes. He confronts the girl, who innocently hopes she can soon marry Arnolphe so she can sin with Horace. The play continues, with much of Arnolphe's teaching being misinterpreted by the girl and a great deal of chicanery on the part of the servants.

The play is resolved when Horace's father arrives with Agnes's father to announce that a marriage has been arranged between Horace and Agnes. Apparently Agnes was never an orphan. There is great rejoicing from everyone but Arnolphe, who stands alone.

The show is enjoyable to produce and perform, the music pleasant, the situations humorous and the characters fun to portray. It is a nice ensemble show which is relatively easy to tour and may prove a good choice for groups wishing to provide a sampling of period theatre for junior and senior high school students.

The play is inexpensive to produce, the royalty is reasonable, there are few props, and the actors need only one costume each. The original production employed a full set and utilized a ground row with a background of houses on a street. The main house has a window with practical shutters and curtains. There is usually a platform to enable Agnes to stand at her window. A hinged wall unit was attached to the house and could be opened or closed to represent the garden or the street. Groups that wish to tour the production or have limited technical expertise could simplify this set through the use of portable flats to represent the house, a cutout tree with prop bench to establish the garden, a street flat set downstage right and a ladder for Agnes to stand on to establish her room.

SONGS OF SPECIAL INTEREST

"Lessons on Life," comic situation baritone/mezzo duet with stylized period movement à la Molière. Character contrast and imitation add to the humor. Arnolphe, worried about Agnes's involvement with Horace, decides to give her some lessons on married decorum. She misinterprets his teachings and he constantly tries a new approach.

Instrumentation: piano, percussion
Script: DPS
Selections: Saunders
Record: NP
Rights: DPS

B

THE BOYS FROM SYRACUSE

Book: George Abbott (Based on Shakespeare's *Comedy of Errors*)
Music: Richard Rodgers
Lyrics: Lorenz Hart

ORIGINAL PRODUCTION

Alvin Theatre, November 23, 1938 (235 perf.)
Director: George Abbott
Choreographer: George Balanchine
Musical Director: Harry Levant
Orchestration: Hans Spialek
Principals: Dromio of Syracuse—Jimmy Savo—baritone; Luce—Wynn Murray—alto; Antipholus of Syracuse—Eddie Albert—baritone; Adriana—Muriel Angelus—mezzo; Dromio of Epheseus—Teddy Hart—tenor; Luciana—Marcy Westcott—soprano; Antipholus of Epheseus—Ronald Graham—baritone; Courtesan—Betty Bruce—alto; Tailor's Apprentice—Burl Ives—baritone
Chorus and Smaller Roles: 6M/6F.

SUMMARY AND NOTES

The play revolves around the twins Antipholus, lost at birth, and their twin servants, the Dromios. The confusion begins when Antipholus of Syracuse and his servant Dromio arrive in Epheseus and are mistaken for their married twin brothers who live in the town. After a great many comical mix-ups caused by mistaken identities, everything is resolved by the arrival of the Antipholus boys' father. Interspersed with witty dialogue, comedic business and a marvelous score, the show still proves to be entertaining.

It was successfully revived Off-Broadway on April 15, 1963, and ran for 502 performances. The 1963 script was revised by Fred Ebb and contains many directorial and choreographic notes, a detailed ground plan, costume plots, technical notes and property lists.

It is basically a four-set show that takes place in a square, inside the house of Antipholus, on a street outside the house of Antipholus and in the house of the courtesans. It is possible to combine the street and the square into one unit, and possibly the two interiors into one interior.

The action must be broadly played and quickly paced in order to keep the confusion comedic. Many of the musical numbers are popular standards and will be a good selling point.

SONGS OF SPECIAL INTEREST

"Oh, Diogenes," comic, alto solo, witty lyrics, not often performed, good for revue. Sung by the courtesan who has just been seemingly lied to by Antipholus. She comments to the chorus that all men are crooks.

"Sing for Your Supper," female trio, tight harmony, potential showstopper, good for revue. Adriana, Antipholus of Syracuse's wife, and Luce, her servant, try to comfort Luciana (Adriana's unmarried sister), who has just fallen in love with Antipholus (actually of Epheseus), who she believes is her sister's husband. Adriana tells the women it is best to please the men in your life.

"This Can't Be Love," nightclub standard, originally a soprano/baritone duet sung by Antipholus of Epheseus upon meeting Luciana. As the song progresses, Luciana finds she is falling in love with the man she believes to be her sister's husband, and hastily exits.

Instrumentation: 3 reeds, trumpet, trombone, 2 percussion, 2 violins, cello, bass, harp, piano/conductor
Script: NP
Score: Chappell
Record: Columbia, STET–1963 version
Rights: R & H

C

CELEBRATION

Music: Harvey Schmidt
Words: Tom Jones

ORIGINAL PRODUCTION

Ambassador Theatre, January 22, 1969 (109 perf.)
Director: Tom Jones
Choreographer: Vernon Lusby
Musical Director: Rod Derefinko
Orchestration: Jim Tyler
Principals: Potemkin—Keith Charles—baritone; Orphan—Michael Glenn Smith—tenor; Rich—Ted Thurston—baritone; Angel—Susan Watson—mezzo
Chorus and Smaller Roles: 5M/5F.

SUMMARY AND NOTES

The story, told by a narrator, aided by a chorus of revelers and musicians, revolves around a young orphan who hopes to create a lovely garden on the site of the now demolished orphanage. He meets Potemkin, a sleazy con artist, played by the narrator, who takes the youth to meet Mr. Rich, the owner of the property.

As the play progresses, it explores the themes of corrupt money, the world belonging to the young, and the yearning of the old to recapture their past. Mr.

Rich attempts to regain his youth through Angel, a rock singer the orphan loves. In the end Rich dies in the arms of the youthful orphan.

The impact of the show rests on the tight visual meshing of the choreograpic and design elements. The chorus is involved throughout and enhances the overall theatricality of the piece. The company may be kept at a minimum or expanded without detriment to the show.

The costumes of the chorus members may be basic, but many add-on pieces will be required for special movement sequences.

This play is an unusual though interesting choice for college groups wishing to give audiences a thought-provoking, often exciting production.

SONGS OF SPECIAL INTEREST

"Somebody," alto/mezzo solo, audition potential. Sung by teen rock singer who yearns for stardom. Driving tempo, some movement necessary.

"Celebration," mixed chorus, baritone soloist featured. Good for revue, has an aura of mystery. The show's opening song, which invites the audience to join in the celebration of the evening's events.

Instrumentation: 2 pianos, percussion, guitar, bass, harp, electric piano
Script: Drama Books
Score: Portfolio
Record: Capitol
Rights: MTI

A CHORUS LINE

Conceived by: Michael Bennett
Book: James Kirkwood & Nicholas Dante
Music: Marvin Hamlisch
Lyrics: Edward Kleban

ORIGINAL PRODUCTION

Shubert Theatre, July 25, 1975 (still running 1986)
Director/Choreographer: Michael Bennett
Co-Choreographer: Bob Avian
Musical Director: Don Pippin
Orchestration: Bill Byers, Hershy Kay, Jonathan Tunick
Principals: Sheila—Carole Bishop—Alto; Val—Pamela Blair—Mezzo; Mike—Wayne Cilento—Baritone; Maggie—Kay Cole—Soprano; Richie—Ronald Dennis—Baritone; Zach—Robert LuPone—VTI; Cassie—Donna McKechnie—Mezzo; Al—Don Percassi—Tenor; Kristine—Renee Baughman—Alto; Bebe—Nancy Lane—Mezzo; Diana—Priscilla Lopez—Mezzo; Paul—Sammy Williams—VTI
Chorus: 7M/7F who should also act as understudies or alternates.

SUMMARY AND NOTES

A Chorus Line won the 1976 Pulitzer Prize for Drama, and captured the following Tony Awards: Best Musical, Director, Book, Score, Choreography, Actress (Donna McKechnie), Featured Actor (Danny Williams), Featured Actress (Carole Bishop) and Lighting Designer. On September 30, 1983, it surpassed the record for longest running show, previously held by *Grease* (3,388 perf.). Michael Bennett celebrated the occasion by a special performance featuring 332 of the dancers who once appeared in the show. At that time the show had grossed more than $75 million.

This innovative musical opens with director/choreographer Zach, auditioning twenty-six dancers. The first cut leaves nine women and eight men for the final audition sequences. Zach, seeking to know more about these dancers asks them to tell about themselves and how they became interested in dance.

The audience is introduced to the various performers: Sheila, the aging chorine, who, along with Bebe and Maggie, escaped her childhood problems at the dance studio; Val, who has undergone plastic surgery to improve her looks; Cassie, Zach's former lover, begging for a chance to be in the chorus; Diana, who always wanted to be an actress; Paul, who at last understands his manliness and his homosexuality; Kristine, a capable dancer who is unable to carry a tune despite her husband Al's assistance and the rest of these talented performers.

As the play progresses, the dancers' personalities and problems are enacted, often in monologue. The moments are interspersed with dance and end in tragedy when Paul falls on an already injured knee. Zach asks the auditioners what they will do when they have to give up dancing. The answers are different but all agree that everything they went through to become dancers was an act of love. The show ends as Zach makes his final cut and the entire company comes out for their bows in white tuxedos.

The costume requirements are dance outfits and excellent fitting tuxedos for the finale. The major theatrical emphasis must be on the lighting, acting, dancing and singing. The original Broadway version utilized mirrors for Cassie's solo, but this may be left to individual directors.

Companies excited about the availability of this low-budget musical should ensure they have an excellent choreographer and a talented company of male and female triple threat performers before attempting this show. Many audience members familiar with the original will be justifiably alienated by a weak production of this classic show.

SONGS OF SPECIAL INTEREST

"At the Ballet," Alto, Mezzo, Soprano trio. Wonderful number for three dancer/actresses. Dramatic, moving. Works well in a class or revue situation. Each girl has a solo section which explains why she chose dance to escape the reality of her childhood.

"Dance: Ten; Looks: Three," Mezzo Solo. Story of a girl who discovers, after an audition, that her dance excels but her physical attributes are hindering employment. The song is the story of her visit to the plastic surgeon and the subsequent changes in her life. Biting, comedic tone. Character oriented.

"Nothing," Mezzo/Alto story solo. Revolves around girl who wants to be a dancer but is put down by her teacher at the high school of Performing Arts. Poignant ending.

"I Can Do That," Tap oriented, Baritone solo. Overdone as an audition piece but works well in a class situation. Young man shows off his talents while telling the story of how he began dance classes.

Instrumentation: 4 reeds, 3 trumpets, 3 trombones, 2 keyboards, guitar/banjo, fender bass, bass, percussion, drums, harp
Script: NP
Score: Morris
Record: Columbia
Rights: TW

CURLEY MCDIMPLE

Book: Robert Dahdah and Mary Boylan
Music and Lyrics: Robert Dahdah

ORIGINAL PRODUCTION

Bert Wheeler Theatre, November 22, 1967 (931 perf.)
Director: Robert Dahdah
Musical Numbers Staged by: Lonnie Evans
Musical Director: Robert Atwood
Musical Arrangers: Keith McClelland and Robert Atwood
Principals: Jimmy—Paul Cahill—high baritone; Bill—George Hellman—baritone; Sarah—Helen Blount—alto/mezzo; Miss Hamilton—Norma Bigtree—VTI; Alice—Bernadette Peters—mezzo; Mr. Gillingwater—George Galvin—VTI; Curley—Bayn Johnson—child mezzo
Chorus and Smaller Roles: None.

SUMMARY AND NOTES

This musical spoof of the Depression era Shirley Temple films is a nice small-cast musical for smaller companies that have a talented and not obnoxious child for Curley.

The play takes place in Sarah's theatrical boardinghouse where Curley, an endearingly optimistic eight-year-old, arrives looking for a mother and father to adopt her. She wisely settles on Jimmy and Alice, two boarders who room next to each other and who fall in love at first meeting. The boarders come to the aid of Sarah, whose mortgage is about to be foreclosed, by producing a vaudeville benefit. During this, an evil social worker, who looks quite like the wicked witch of the West, takes Curley to an orphanage in New Jersey. Curley escapes and performs in the show, aided by Miss Hamilton and the wealthy banker Mr. Gillingwater. The show is booked on Broadway, Curley discovers that Gilling-water is her grandfather and a former sweetheart of Sarah's, and Jimmy and Alice marry.

Not technically difficult, the music is enjoyable, the story charming, and the roles good for versatile performers. The principals all take part in a playland jamboree dream and a large sequence where they appear as fairy-tale characters. The costumes, period thirties, dream sequence, and fairy tale can usually be pulled from a company's costume collection.

SONGS OF SPECIAL INTEREST

"The Meanest Man in Town," mezzo solo spoof, torch song.

Instrumentation: piano
Script: SF
Score: Chappell
Record: Capitol (2 songs)
Rights: SF

G

GIRL CRAZY

Book: Guy Bolton and John McGowan
Music: George Gershwin
Lyrics: Ira Gershwin

ORIGINAL PRODUCTION

Alvin Theatre, October 14, 1930 (272 perf.)
Director: Alexander Leftwich
Choreographer: George Hale
Musical Director: Earl Busby
Orchestration: Robert Russell Bennett
Principals: Molly Gray—Ginger Rogers—mezzo; Kate—Ethel Merman—alto;
Churchill—Allen Kearns—tenor
Chorus and Smaller Roles: 7M/4F minimum.

SUMMARY AND NOTES

This musical classic revolves around Kate, a down-on-her-luck cabaret singer, and her pianist ex-husband, Zoli, who happen upon friend and former TV star Johnny Churchill, owner of a failing Arizona cattle ranch.

Molly, the local postmistress, whom Johnny is attracted to, goads him into opening a dude ranch and running for sheriff. Meanwhile, Kate is coerced by Johnny's agent into trying to woo Johnny back to television and away from

Molly's influence. Johnny wins the election, but believing that Molly is involved
with his agent, Johnny follows her to Mexico with Kate. The Mexican adventure
ends with an explosion of fireworks and everyone returning to town much wiser.
Kate remarries Zoli, and Molly marries Johnny, who has rid the town of all
outlaws.

The musical made a star out of club performer Ethel Merman, and the memorable music, humorous dialogue and interesting characters add much to the
revised script.

The show is more enjoyable if the chorus is kept to a minimum and the
production is "obviously" low-budget where everybody does everything—a sort
of "let's do a musical" à la Garland/Rooney films of the thirties.

The sets are relatively simple and consist of the dude ranch, the hotel lobby
(some combining possible) with an easily cut election headquarters. Costumes
may be limited to two or three for the women, one for the male chorus and two
for the principals.

SONGS OF SPECIAL INTEREST

"Bidin' My Time," M quartet, sung by four cowboys with very tight harmony.
Good for a revue.

"But Not for Me," F alto solo, poignant love ballad about everyone being
romantically involved but her.

"Strike up the Band," M solo to Mixed Chorus, up tempo, patriotic fervor,
originally from *Of Thee I Sing*, but added to the revised script. Good for revues.

"Treat Me Rough," M/F duet, comic, up tempo song between Zoli and Kate
where she tells him she will tell the man when to treat her rough.

Instrumentation: 3 violins, viola, cello, bass, 4 reeds, horn, trumpet, trombone,
percussion, piano/conductor
Script: NP
Score: New World
Record: Columbia
Rights: TW

GODSPELL

Book: John-Michael Tebelak
Music and Lyrics: Stephen Schwartz

ORIGINAL PRODUCTION

Cherry Lane Theatre, May 17, 1971 (2,118 perf. Off-Broadway); moved to
Broadway, June 22, 1976 (527 perf.)
Director: John-Michael Tebelak

Musical Director: David Lewis
Orchestration: Stephen Schwartz
Principals: John/Judas—David Haskell—baritone; Jesus—Stephen Nathan—tenor
Chorus and Smaller Roles: 3M/5F.

SUMMARY AND NOTES

A small company of ten reenacts familiar biblical parables and the teachings, betrayal, death and resurrection of Jesus Christ. The women's vocal types are in the alto/mezzo range and the male roles are divided into baritone, high baritone, and tenor.

The performers need one basic costume, usually pulled from stock and not representing any specific period of time. The minimal set needs make the show an easy one for school groups to tour. Although based on a biblical theme, the show is not uncomfortably religious or preachy. The chorus may be expanded if desired although the charm rests in demonstrating the varied talents of a small company.

SONGS OF INTEREST

"All for the Best," tenor duet, vaudeville style, soft shoe required. An excellent study in diction and speed.

"Turn Back O Man," alto, torch song, movement and sensuality necessary. Good for combining sensuality and humor.

Instrumentation: Pit band: Piano/organ, guitars, bass (electric), drums. Onstage: recorder, 2 tambourines, 2 acoustic guitars, Vibra-slap, various toy instruments—usually played by the performers
Script: NP
Score: Hansen
Record: Bell
Rights: Max

H

HAIR

Book and Lyrics: Gerome Ragni and James Rado
Music: Galt MacDermot

ORIGINAL PRODUCTION

Biltmore Theatre, April 29, 1968 (1,742 perf.)
Director: Tom O'Horgan
Choreographer: Julie Arenal
Musical Director: Galt MacDermot
Principals: Claude—James Rado—tenor; Sheila—Lynn Kellogg—alto; Berger—
Gerome Ragni—tenor; Dionne—Melba Moore—mezzo; Crissy—Shelley Plimp-
ton—mezzo; Hud—Lamont Washington—baritone; Woof—Steve Curry—
baritone
Chorus and Smaller Roles: 6M/6F.

SUMMARY AND NOTES

The play opens at a hippie tribe gathering, complete with incense and psychedelic trappings. The various members of the group are musically introduced.
The individual and chorus songs reflect the tribal life-style, generation differences, and the philosophy of the youth of the late sixties.

The rather thin plot revolves around Berger, a social activist; Claude, Berger's
best friend, who gets drafted; and Sheila, an antiwar activist who loves Berger

but is having Claude's baby. The first act ends at a traditional Be-In where the tribe gathers in a park to embrace the Hare Krishna and symbolically burn their draft cards. Claude, who dearly loves his country despite things he feels are politically wrong, is unable to burn the card. The play ends as Claude goes off in uniform, and Berger and Sheila part, leaving a section of their lives behind.

The tribal rock musical that captured the mood of the era for which it was intended was hailed as spontaneous, fresh and original. The show took young New York audiences by storm and ran until 1972. An August 1978 revival, lasting 108 performances, demonstrated that the fervor of the sixties had receded and the show had become passé.

There is some wonderful music in the score that is still worthy of production, but a director considering the show must have a fun-loving, talented cast and be prepared to do some judicious editing, for example, the nude scene. The scene is totally unnecessary to the script and was only utilized for shock value.

Hair only works as a period piece and in fact it has almost become a study on the stereotypes of the period. If a company approaches the show with that attitude and can recapture the vitality of the original, the production should do well at the box office.

SONGS OF SPECIAL INTEREST

''Aquarius,'' mixed chorus, good for opening of a revue section of the sixties; modern dance style open movement combined with disco makes this visually interesting. The hit song from the show.

''Easy to Be Hard,'' Rock ballad sung by Sheila, who is disgusted that her boyfriend wants to loan her to his best friend.

''Frank Mills,'' charm song, mezzo ballad, story song about a girl who is waiting for a hippie boy she met once and hopes to find again. Simplistic character-oriented lyrics.

''Hair,'' mixed chorus, rock beat, good for revue and beginning choreographer as it utilizes disco steps.

Instrumentation: reed, 2 trumpets, electric bass, drums, percussion, 2 guitars (electric, acoustic, bass), electric piano/conductor
Script: Pocket, Great Rock Musicals
Selections: Big Three
Record: RCA
Rights: TW

THE HAPPY TIME

Book: N. Richard Nash (Suggested by characters in stories by Robert L. Fontaine)
Music: John Kander
Lyrics: Fred Ebb

ORIGINAL PRODUCTION

Broadway Theatre, January 18, 1968 (286 perf.)
Director and Choreographer: Gower Champion
Musical Director: Oscar Kosarin
Orchestration: Don Walker
Principals: Jacques Bonnard—Robert Goulet—high baritone; Bibi—Mike Rupert—tenor; Grandpère—David Wayne—baritone/tenor; Laurie—Julie Gregg—soprano
Chorus and Smaller Roles: 8F/2M, 4M teenagers.

SUMMARY AND NOTES

Jacques Bonnard, a photographer who is also the narrator, invites the audience to return to the memory of his home in French Canada. He sets the stage and introduces his family, consisting of two brothers, their wives and daughters, his adolescent godson Bibi, and the sprightly Grandpère. No one but Bibi is happy that Jacques has returned, for he was always the black sheep of the family. As the play progresses, Jacques and Grandpère introduce Bibi to some dance hall girls and life, and Jacques remeets Laurie, his former girlfriend and music teacher at Bibi's school. Laurie, who knows Jacques's restless nature, urges Jacques not to hurt Bibi, who idolizes him. Jacques is forced to admit to Bibi that he returned because he was on a photographic assignment, not because he wanted to see the family. Bibi cries in misery as Jacques heartlessly snaps his picture to use in a national magazine. The play ends with Jacques concluding the story, in narrative form, and relating the death of Grandpère, Jacques's eventual marriage and the birth of a son.

The play has the potential to be charming, but the original Broadway production employed photographs and large-chorus dance numbers. If the show is kept small and the technical requirements trimmed to enable the audience to become involved in the reflective tone of the piece, it should be particularly appreciated by audiences over thirty years of age. The nieces' roles may be combined, the dance chorus eliminated and the adolescent boys choir and friends of Bibi trimmed to four.

The music is sparkling, quality Kander and Ebb; the story absorbing, family-oriented and thought-provoking. It is not a blockbuster musical and would best be produced by a company looking for a more intimate vehicle or for a workshop production of a little known show.

Tony Awards: Actor, Director, Choreographer.

SONGS OF SPECIAL INTEREST

"Catch My Garter." Six dance hall girls of different characters and vocal types perform in a vaudeville show. F Chorus.

"The Happy Time," opening high baritone/tenor solo, sets the stage and introduces various characters, exciting and nostalgic. Similar in tone to "Try to Remember," from *The Fantasticks*.

"The Life of the Party." Grandpère, in a red top hat, has the solo section of this showstopper. Vaudeville, audience-oriented baritone solo to mixed chorus.

"Please Stay," young tenor solo, Bibi tries to convince his uncle to stay in town but tries to be worldly by telling him he realizes there are obstacles. Song operates on two emotional levels; attention must be paid to subtext throughout.

"Seeing Things," soprano, tenor duet. Lovers' confrontation when they realize their different philosophies will never allow them a permanent relationship. At the end of the song they say good-bye. Semidramatic, vocally demanding, good for class study.

Instrumentation: strings, piano/conductor, 4 reeds, 2 trumpets, 3 trombones, percussion, harp
Script: DPC
Selections: Valando
Record: RCA
Rights: DPC

I

I'M GETTING MY ACT TOGETHER AND TAKING IT ON THE ROAD

Book: Gretchen Cryer
Music: Nancy Ford
Lyrics: Gretchen Cryer

ORIGINAL PRODUCTION

Public/Anspacher Theatre, June 14, 1978 (1,165 perf.)
Director: Word Baker
Choreographer: Tina Johnson
Orchestration: Nancy Ford and The Band
Principals: Joe—Joel Fabiani—VTNE; Heather—Gretchen Cryer—mezzo; Alice—Margot Rose—alto; Cheryl—Betty Aberlin—mezzo; Jake (guitar)—Don Scardino—tenor
Chorus and Smaller Roles: 4 onstage musicians

SUMMARY AND NOTES

Successful rock singer, thirty-nine–year–old Heather Jones, astounds Joe, her manager and friend, when she privately showcases her new act. The material demonstrates a new direction for Heather, her backup singers Alice and Cheryl, and the male band. All want to make a statement about women and their relationships with men. Joe urges her to tone things down, but Heather is determined to present herself as she really is, not as her audience would like to see her. Jake, her young acoustical guitarist, supports her and convinces her that he loves her.

The show is dramatically powerful, the music energetic and the lyrics and dialogue thought-provoking. A quality cabaret show with few costume and set requirements that would be best produced on a college campus where an audience could accept, understand and appreciate the issues at hand.

Microphones, atmospheric lighting and a strong band backup are necessary to the success of the show.

SONGS OF SPECIAL INTEREST

"Dear Tom," dramatic, comedic, and poignant when coupled with monologue. Story about a woman who was Mrs. Perfect and her failing relationship with her husband. Demonstrates a range of emotions. Good to work on in a class situation, possible audition.

"Old Friend," charm, ballad, about two people of the opposite sex who are close friends.

"Put in a Package and Sold," F trio, strong statement, solid, emphatic song about women who want to be noticed for what lies inside.

"Smile," strong alto/mezzo number, F featured, mixed trio backup. May be done as a solo. Dramatically powerful. Story song about a young woman trained from childhood to be nice to men. Traces her life from smiling for her father to pleasing her husband, and through her subsequent divorce. Transitions and emotions are essential.

Instrumentation: guitars (acoustic, electric), drums, percussion, bass, piano/conductor (synthesizer and fender piano optional)
Script: SF
Selections: Valando
Record: CBS
Rights: SF

IRENE

Book: Hugh Wheeler and Joseph Stein (from an adaptation by Harry Rigby, based on the original play by James Montgomery)
Music: Harry Tierney
Lyrics: Joseph McCarthy (Additional lyrics and music by Charles Gaynor, Jack Lloyd, Wally Harper, Otis Clements)

ORIGINAL PRODUCTION

Vanderbilt Theatre, November 18, 1919 (670 perf.)

REVIVAL PRODUCTION

Minskoff Theatre, March 13, 1973 (605 perf.)
Director: Gower Champion
Musical Numbers Staged by: Peter Gennaro
Musical Director: Jack Lee
Orchestration: Ralph Burns
Principals: Mrs. O'Dare—Patsy Kelly—character alto; Jane Burke—Janie Sell—character alto; Irene O'Dare—Debbie Reynolds—mezzo; Helen McFudd—Carmen Alvarez—character mezzo; Emmeline Marshall—Ruth Warwick—soprano; Ozzie Babson—Ted Pugh—tenor; Madame Lucy—George S. Irving—baritone; Donald Marshall—Monte Markham—baritone
Chorus and Smaller Roles: 8M/8F who sing and dance well.

SUMMARY AND NOTES

New York City, 1919. Irene O'Dare, a Ninth Avenue Irish-American who runs a piano store, is called to the home of snobby and wealthy Mrs. Marshall to tune her piano. Irene meets the Marshall's son Donald and the two fall in love. Donald, anxious to help Irene and give her enough social standing so his mother will approve of their marriage, becomes involved in Cousin Ozzie's latest venture. Cousin Ozzie wants to promote Madame Lucy's designer fashions in the United States, and Donald agrees to add financial backing if Irene can manage the stores. Irene agrees and hires her friends Jane and Helen to model. Madame Lucy turns out to be none other than an eccentric male with a European flair who once was romantically involved with Irene's mother.

Irene, under a phony title and complete with European accent, is accepted by Society and Mrs. Marshall but returns to Ninth Avenue, determined to be herself. All ends well as Donald returns to Irene, admitting he loves her the way she is, and Mrs. O'Dare renews her old romance with Madame Lucy.

This tuneful, nostalgic hit show, both in 1919 and 1973, is a wise choice for community groups looking for a vehicle that will appeal to all ages. The large number of featured female roles, which include Irene, her two comedic friends, Mrs. O'Dare, and Mrs. Marshall, is a strong consideration.

SONGS OF SPECIAL INTEREST

"I'm Always Chasing Rainbows," shows senstivity, nice contrast piece. Ballad, possible for an alto/mezzo audition. Poignant standard.

"The Great Lover Tango," 2 mezzo/alto, baritone trio. The young male lead is convinced by the two character friends of his girl that he can break out and be like the film lover Valentino. They lead him through this comedic tango, which he finally learns. Good to loosen up a stiff male singer. Interactions and style important.

"They Go Wild over Me," baritone solo. Male dressmaker, madame Lucy, eccentric character. Character introduction song, good for flamboyant and co-medic movement.

Instrumentation: 5 reeds, 2 trumpets, 3 trombones, 2 percussion, harp, guitar/banjo, organ/piano, 2 violins, cello, bass, piano/conductor
Script: NP
Selections: Big Three
Record: Columbia
Rights: TW

J

JESUS CHRIST SUPERSTAR

Music: Andrew Lloyd Weber
Lyrics: Tim Rice

ORIGINAL PRODUCTION

Mark Hellinger Theatre, October 12, 1971 (711 perf.)
Director: Tom O'Horgan
Musical Director: Marc Pressel
Orchestration: Andrew Lloyd Weber
Principals: Judas—Ben Vereen—tenor; Jesus—Jeff Fenholt—tenor; Mary Magdalene—Yvonne Elliman—mezzo; Pilate—Barry Dennen—baritone; Herod—Paul Ainsley—tenor
Chorus and Smaller Roles: 12M/12F.

SUMMARY AND NOTES

A musical based on the last days in the life of Jesus Christ. The show is vocally demanding, especially the roles of Judas and Christ. The musical when well done is exciting and energetic. The Broadway version, which was technically overblown, has possibly kept some theatre groups from attempting a production. The technical needs are not great. In fact, one of the most vital professional productions of this show was in Los Angeles in an enormous open-air amphitheatre and performed on a unit set.

The show is dramatic, introspective, character-oriented and gives meaning to Judas's betrayal. The music is well-known and must be "miked." For companies with limited resources, it is possible to use microphones with wires for the principals, but their use must be choreographed in during the early rehearsals.

SONGS OF SPECIAL INTEREST

"I Don't Know How to Love Him," mezzo solo, Mary Magdalene relates her confusion about her relationship with Christ. A woman primarily used to physical love, she is in a quandary and examines the different methods of playing the love game. The song is much more than a ballad and needs to be acted and interpreted in order to reflect the character.

"King Herod's Song," vaudeville, soft-shoe style, tenor. Herod confronts Christ and, using the words he has heard about this God, mocks him. Underneath his superficial exterior there is a confused fear which is in direct opposition to the musical style of the piece.

"Pilate's Dream," introspective baritone. Pilate examines his dream about the last days of Christ and becomes fearful of the role he must play in Christ's death.

Instrumentation: electric and acoustic guitar, bass guitar, 2 trumpets, piano/organ, drums/percussion, trombone, French horn, 4 reeds. May add 2 violins, cello and viola if desired.
Script: Great Rock Musicals
Selections: Leeds
Record: Decca
Rights: MTI

M

MAN WITH A LOAD OF MISCHIEF

Book: Ben Tarver (Adapted from a play of the same name by Ashley Dukes)
Music: John Clifton
Lyrics: John Clifton and Ben Tarver

ORIGINAL PRODUCTION

Jan Hus Playhouse, November 6, 1966 (240 perf.)
Director: Tom Gruenewald
Choreographer: Noel Schwartz
Musical Director: Sande Campbell
Orchestration: John Clifton
Principals: The Innkeeper—Tom Noel—baritone; His Wife—Lesslie Nicol—
alto/mezzo; The Lord—Raymond Thorne—baritone; Charles—Reid Shelton—
tenor; The Lady—Virginia Vestoff—mezzo; The Maid—Alice Cannon—soprano
Chorus and Smaller Roles: None.

SUMMARY AND NOTES

At an early nineteenth-century inn run by an elderly couple, a small group of
people arrive, the direct result of a coach breakdown. The guests, who are forced
to stay overnight, are a Lord and his manservant Charles, and a Lady and her
maid. The Lord, eager for a dalliance with the Lady, who is the mistress of the

Prince, is cleverly refused by the Lady. Seeking his own form of revenge, he orders his servant to make love to her.

Charles discovers the Lady is really a lady with a sensitive heart and soul. She relates the sad story of her life and the two realize they have the same philosophical viewpoint. The maid becomes involved with the Lord only to be later hurt by his urging her to forget the evening. As the play ends the Lady and Charles profess their love and go off together to make a new life.

This small-cast, one-set show is ideal for small companies as the musical numbers are spread out among all the cast members. The dialogue is witty and the music is lovely. Easy to tour.

SONGS OF SPECIAL INTEREST

"Man with a Load of Mischief," touching song about a woman of the world who explains her past. Soprano.

"Make Way for My Lady," lovely tenor solo, nice vocal build. Shows off voice. Possible for audition.

"Once You've Had a Little Taste," the maid comments on how difficult it is to give up riches and wealthy men after you've experienced them. Spunky character, sprightly music.

"Little Rag Doll," nice melody, poignant and touching song by the maid, who yearns for her youthful innocence.

Instrumentation: reed, cello, piano/conductor (celeste/harpsichord)
Script: NP
Selections: NP
Record: Kapp
Rights: SF

THE ME NOBODY KNOWS

Book: Herb Shapiro and Stephen M. Joseph (Spoken text written by children ages seven to eighteen in New York City schools)
Music: Gary William Friedman
Lyrics: Will Holt

ORIGINAL PRODUCTION

Orpheum Theatre, May 18, 1970, moved to Broadway December 18, 1970 (587 perf.)
Director: Robert H. Livingston
Choreographer: Patricia Birch
Musical Director: Edward Strauss
Orchestration: Gary William Friedman
Company: 6M/6F teenagers.

SUMMARY AND NOTES

The show, one of the earliest concept musicals, deals with the problems of interracial school-age children who grow up in a large metropolitan area. The themes sensitively and dramatically explored involve drugs, poverty, death, suicide and the dream everyone has of escaping the ghetto. The script utilizes many of the words of actual school children; the experiences are all true.

The youthful, energetic and talented cast combined with refreshing music and innovative choreography made this a captivating show.

The production needs no specific setting; it may be performed on a gymnasium floor or on a unit set consisting of various levels. Each actor needs one costume, modern, teenage in style.

The nature of the material calls for a talented and sensitive company and directorial staff. It is suggested that the rehearsal period involve a great deal of discussion of the feelings of the characters and the parallel with the actors' emotions. Although the actors' environments may differ from those of an inner-city ghetto, the emotional problems are quite similar.

An effective and dramatic show well worth perusing by high schools with talented performers.

SONGS OF SPECIAL INTEREST

"Flying Milk and Runaway Plates," mixed chorus, good for class situation and beginning choreographer. Deals with teenagers at school lunch, lots of action and energy.

"How I Feel," two teens, on separate sides of the stage, totally unrelated to each other, contemplate suicide. Baritone/mezzo, linear duet. Dramatic and powerful.

"If I Had a Million Dollars," mixed chorus with solos interspersed, tells of various children's dreams and what the children would do with untold wealth. Touching, good for revue on teenagers. Possible as a solo audition if a single actor is able to play three different voices and types, shows versatility but needs to be edited.

"Let Me Come In," mixed chorus, crying out of children who yearn for a better life, love and nurturing. Good for closing of a revue on teenagers.

"Light Sings," a hopeful song about a new day dawning, good for the opening of a revue. Mixed chorus. Rock beat.

"The Tree," touching story, set to music but not requiring a good voice, about a man waiting for an apple tree to bear fruit and preparing to chop it down when it fails to do so. A fog prevents him from cutting the tree and the next time he looks at the tree, there is an apple. Good for children's theatre audition.

Instrumentation: reed, trumpet, trombone, cello, bass, guitar, drums, piano/conductor
Script: NP

Selections: Sunbeam
Record: Atlantic
Rights: SF

MERRILY WE ROLL ALONG

Book: George Furth (Based on the play by George S. Kaufman and Moss Hart)
Music and Lyrics: Stephen Sondheim

ORIGINAL PRODUCTION

Alvin Theatre, November 16, 1981 (16 perf.)
Director: Harold Prince
Choreographer: Larry Fuller
Musical Director: Paul Gemignani
Orchestration: Jonathan Tunick
Principals: Franklin Shephard—Jim Walton—tenor; Mary Flynn—Ann Morrison—alto/mezzo; Charley Kringas—Lenny Price—tenor; Beth Spencer—Sally Klein—soprano/mezzo; Gussie—Terry Finn—mezzo; Joe—Jason Alexander—baritone
Chorus and Smaller Roles: 7F/13M.

SUMMARY AND NOTES

The musical begins in 1980 at a graduation ceremony where the class expresses in song their hopes for the future. The song was written by former graduate and guest speaker, Franklin Shepard. As he speaks, warning the students about the harsh realities of life, the graduates become the characters in the play, Franklin Shepard's associates and friends.

The scene moves to Franklin Shepard's California home at a party to celebrate his new film. As the story progresses backwards from 1979 to 1955, the audience discovers that Frank and Charley, best friends, dream of forming a songwriting team and making it in the big time. During their rise to fame the two meet Mary, who wants to write. The three decide to put together a revue and hire Beth, a young singer who becomes pregnant and marries Frank, much to the disappointment of Mary. The two writers are produced on Broadway in 1964. Beth divorces Frank for adultery with Gussie, a producer's wife.

The two writer/friends have a falling out. Mary, who still loves Frank, is now a famous critic with a caustic tongue. She is forced from his life by Gussie, whom he has married. The show ends as it began, at graduation where Frank begins his 1955 graduation speech about his hopes and aspirations. It is a brutal reality. The curtain slowly falls, leaving the audience to rethink the script.

There are quite a few locations, which include the graduation area, a roof of a New York apartment, a nightclub, an elegant apartment, the steps of a courthouse, a television show, a hotel lounge, and a California home. It is probably best to perform the entire show on various levels and specify location by minimal props.

Many people felt the major problem with the show was due to the reverse order. The audience never got to know the characters as nice, hopeful youngsters before events changed them into disillusioned, bitter adults. There were also complaints that the youthful cast did not have the maturity to portray the older roles; they just didn't understand the depth of the roles. In view of the latter criticism it is recommended that the roles be portrayed by people no younger than twenty-five, preferably thirty, who have the ability to physically portray youth and emotionally portray age. There is a note in the MTI catalogue disallowing order change as a violation of copyright.

SONGS OF SPECIAL INTEREST

"Not a Day Goes By," tenor solo that Frank sings to his wife, who has just accused him of infidelity. He reaffirms his love. Beautiful melody, shows off range.

"Opening Doors," 2F/2M quartet, scene song that lasts approximately seven minutes. Good for class study. The story of Franklin, Charley, Mary, in their early twenties and living in New York; their aspirations, work, disappointments and subsequent meeting with Beth and their first produced revue.

"Our Time," youthful energy and hope make this an excellent song for a revue closing. May be done in entirety as a 2M/F trio but addition of chorus makes it more exciting.

Instrumentation: 5 reeds, 2 trumpets, trombone, tuba, horn, 3 cellos, electric bass, guitar, 2 keyboards (synthesizer), 2 percussion
Script: Dodd, Mead
Selections: Valando
Record: RCA
Rights: MTI

N

NO, NO, NANETTE

Book: Frank Mandel and Otto Harbarch (Readapted by Burt Shevelove for 1971 revival)
Music: Vincent Youmans
Lyrics: Irving Caesar and Otto Harbach

ORIGINAL PRODUCTION

Globe Theatre, September 16, 1925 (321 perf.)

REVIVAL PRODUCTION

46th Street Theatre, January 19, 1971 (861 perf.)
Production Supervisor: Busby Berkley
Director: Burt Shevelove
Choreographer: Donald Saddler
Musical Director: Buster Davis
Orchestration: Ralph Burns
Principals: Pauline—Patsy Kelly—alto; Lucille Early—Helen Gallagher—mezzo; Sue Smith—Ruby Keeler—alto; Jimmy Smith—Jack Gilford—light baritone; Billy Early—Bobby Van—tenor; Tom—Roger Rathburn—high baritone; Nanette—Susan Watson—mezzo; Flora—K. C. Townsend—mezzo; Betty—Loni Zoe Ackerman—mezzo; Winnie—Pat Lysinger—soprano
Chorus and Smaller Roles: 8M/8F who sing and dance well.

SUMMARY AND NOTES

This three-act hit musical charmed audiences of the twenties and the seventies. It is an energetic show, with colorful costumes, a youthful chorus, memorable songs, and marvelous character roles for the principals. Tony Awards went to Patsy Kelly and Helen Gallagher; Costumes and Choreography were also honored.

The story revolves around Jimmy and Sue Smith and their adopted daughter of marriageable age, Nanette. It seems that Jimmy, a wealthy publisher of Bibles, has become involved with three young girls, from various sections of the country, and sends his friend and lawyer, Billy Early, to buy them off. Nanette's fiancé, Tom, and Billy decide to expedite matters by meeting the three girls in Atlantic City at the Smiths' usually vacant weekend cottage. Meanwhile, Nanette, yearning for adventure before she settles into marriage, begs her mother to let her have a fling with her friends in Atlantic City. Sue refuses, insisting it isn't proper unless she is chaperoned. Jimmy, who can't stand to see a young girl depressed, unknown to Sue escorts Pauline and Nanette to Atlantic City. Sue and Lucille, Billy's wife, have nothing to do for the weekend and decide to travel to Atlantic City.

The remainder of the play deals in fun and confusion as the three girls arrive at the cottage and refuse to be bought off, Nanette discovers Tom, and Sue and Lucille confront their husbands. Everything is tunefully resolved, much to the delight and amusement of the audience.

The revival, fraught with production and personality problems, is detailed in *The Making of No, No, Nanette* by Don Dunn. This book should be read by anyone planning a career in the professional theatre; it is full of horror stories which involve the presentation of this production.

Tony Awards: Actress - Helen Gallagher, Supporting Actress - Patsy Kelly, Choreographer, Costumes.

The costumes are period twenties, everyday, evening and bathing suits. Each female cast member needs three costumes. Ideally the men should also have three. There are three different sets: the interior of the Smiths', the exterior of the Atlantic City cottage, and the living room of the cottage; both interiors must be large enough to hold the dancing chorus for large-scale production numbers.

The production requires a lot of choreography and a company that dances well. The revival had a beach ball number with the girls walking on weighted beach balls. This effect is detailed in the Dunn book and requires hours of rehearsal.

SONGS OF INTEREST

"I've Confessed to the Breeze," tenor/soprano romantic duet, lovely melody. Tom proposes marriage to Nanette, who admits she loves him.

"I Want to Be Happy," tenor, older man solo, originally performed by Jimmy, who gives Nanette $200 to enjoy herself in Atlantic City. The chorus enters and the number becomes a large-production tap number with everyone playing the ukulele. It is later reprised in Atlantic City with Jimmy and his three gold-digging friends.

"Tea for Two," dance, romantic, charm song when Tom and Nanette imagine their future together in their own little cottage.

"You Can Dance with Any Girl at All," mezzo/baritone duet, good example of stylized Astaire/Rogers musical theatre number. Good period piece with scene prior for class study. Lucille tells her lawyer husband that she trusts him to come home to her. Good class exercise in playing scene/song to partner and audience. Number ends with a fast fox-trot.

Instrumentation: 5 reeds, horn, 3 trumpets, 2 trombones, percussion, guitar/banjo/ukulele, 2 violins, viola, cello, bass, piano/conductor
Script: NP
Score: Harms
Record: Columbia
Rights: TW

O

OF THEE I SING

Book: George S. Kaufman and Morrie Ryskand
Music: George Gershwin
Lyrics: Ira Gershwin

ORIGINAL PRODUCTION

Music Box Theatre, December 26, 1931 (441 perf.)
Director: George S. Kaufman
Choreographer: Georgie Hale
Musical Director: Charles Previn
Orchestration: Robert Russell Bennett and William Daly
Principals: Diana Devereaux—Grace Brinkley—alto; Mary Turner—Lois Moran—soprano; Alexander Throttlebottom—Victor Moore—baritone; John P. Wintergreen—William Gaxton—baritone
Chorus and Smaller Roles: 15M/11F.

SUMMARY AND NOTES

This was the first Broadway musical to win a Pulitzer Prize. It is a multiset show which originally had a large chorus whose size may be trimmed.

The story opens on a political rally where everyone is shouting for Wintergreen to be President. He is easily nominated as his party's candidate. The action moves to the hotel and National Committee headquarters where three electioneers are planning out their strategy. Everyone is excited about the Presidential choice but can't seem to remember the name of his running mate. This forgetting the Vice Presidential candidate is comically used throughout the show. The group decides to run the candidates on a ticket of love and concoct a scheme where a panel of judges will meet in Atlantic City to choose the most beautiful girl in America as the wife for their candidate.

The scene shifts to Atlantic City where Southern beauty Diana Devereaux is chosen the winner, but Wintergreen refuses to marry her. It seems he has fallen in love with the attractive Mary Turner, a homebody who makes corn muffins without any corn.

After Mary and Wintergreen are married, he is elected and they are living in the White House, the French Ambassador interrupts their nuptial bliss by insisting that the only way to save French honor is for the marriage to be annulled and the President to marry Diana. It seems the poor girl is the illegitimate daughter of a relative of Napoleon and it is time she was legitimized.

The Senate plans to impeach Wintergreen, but Mary's announcement that she is going to have a baby turns their anger into joy and they stop the proceedings. France demands the baby as retribution and threatens to sever ties with the United States. The arrival of twins and the subsequent announcement that the Vice President, who must act for the President in emergencies, will marry Diana, saves the honor of France.

Revivals of this 1931 musical have attempted to update it by changing the political humor, but most have failed. It is best performed as a period piece but needs two tremendously comedic and talented leading men for Throttlebottom and Wintergreen. These two must be good actors as well as reactors. In fact, many critics believe that much of the success of the original was due to the comedic talents of the principals.

There are approximately two costumes per actor, although the men may stay in one suit throughout if financially necessary. The female chorus needs to appear in bathing suits for the Atlantic City section as it is a spoof of the Miss America pageant. However, if figures of the company are not compatible with this, evening gowns would suffice. The male chorus, originally much larger, has been trimmed to the barest minimum, which means that many of the politicians who have smaller roles will have to double as chorus.

SONGS OF SPECIAL INTEREST

"Love Is Sweeping the Country," up tempo, mixed chorus, easy to move to and good for a beginning choreographer as it requires stage pictures and marching-style movement more than dance steps. Good in a revue.

"Who Cares?," baritone/soprano, carefree, movement-oriented duet, now a solo standard often performed in nightclubs. Wintergreen and Mary tell the world they don't care about the nation's worries as long as they have each other.

Instrumentation: 3 reeds, 2 trumpets, trombone, 3 violins, viola, cello, bass, piano/conductor
Script: Ten Great Musicals of the American Theatre
Score: Chappell
Record: Columbia
Rights: SF

ON A CLEAR DAY YOU CAN SEE FOREVER

Book: Alan J. Lerner
Music: Burton Lane
Lyrics: Alan J. Lerner

ORIGINAL PRODUCTION

Mark Hellinger Theatre, October 17, 1965 (280 perf.)
Director: Robert Lewis
Choreographer: Herbert Ross
Musical Director: Theodore Saidenberg
Orchestration: Robert Russell Bennett
Principals: Daisy Gamble—Barbara Harris—mezzo; Dr. Mark Brockner—John Cullum—baritone; Edward Moncrief—Clifford David—high baritone; Themistocles Kriakos—Titos Vandis—baritone; Warren Smith—William Daniels—baritone
Chorus and Smaller Roles: 12M/8F.

SUMMARY AND NOTES

This unusual themed musical revolves around Daisy Gamble, an offbeat character who yearns to give up smoking by hypnosis. She attends a lecture at psychiatrist Mark Bruckner's clinic and finds herself often hypnotized. Mark discovers her extrasensory powers, which include making plants grow, and agrees to help her stop smoking if he can discover how she developed her powers. He is astounded to discover that she lived in the eighteenth century and becomes intrigued by her hypnotic recollections of her life as Melinda Wells. Melinda, a very attractive and sought-after young woman, had to constantly evade a variety of suitors but did fall for, and subsequently marry, the handsome and wealthy Edward Moncrief, a painter and rake whom she eventually left.

After several hypnosis sessions, Mark realizes that he believes Daisy's stories and has fallen in love with her former self, Melinda. Scoffed at by the psychiatrists, Mark finds further proof from Themistocles Kriakos, a wealthy Greek, who believes in reincarnation and proves the existence of Edward Moncrief, a little-known eighteenth-century painter.

Daisy overhears some tapes in the office and realizes that Mark is in love with Melinda, not Daisy. She ponders the past and dramatically wonders what she was like to make her so appealing. She runs off, refusing to see Mark anymore, but he forces her back through his extrasensory powers. She isn't certain of his feelings and decides to head for California. At the airport she succumbs to her feelings that the plane, named *Trelawney*, will crash. It seems that Melinda was killed centuries ago on a boat by the same name. She returns to Mark.

The costumes, often complicated, are period eighteenth century and modern day. There are several sets but many of these can be combined or relocated without detriment to the script. There are several scenes on the apartment rooftop, and the remainder can take place at Bruckner's and the airport.

The difficulty with the script lies in the fact that the show revolves primarily around a single character, which doesn't allow for much variety. The role is difficult and requires an extremely talented actress/singer. High school directors might find the need for judicious editing in order to give Daisy a breather and to tighten the script.

SONGS OF SPECIAL INTEREST

"Come Back to Me," baritone, strong male solo in which the psychiatrist concentrates on getting his extrasensory powers to bring Daisy back so he can tell her he loves her.

"Hurry! It's Lovely up Here," mezzo solo. Daisy, who has extrasensory powers, demonstrates in Dr. Bruckner's office her ability to make plants grow. Charm song, good as part of a character study to help student actress work on focusing attention at the plant, the psychiatrist and the audience.

"She Wasn't You," ending sixteen bars good for an audition for high baritone/tenor as it shows range and isn't overdone, ballad. Edward falls in love with Melinda.

"Wait Till We're Sixty-Five," mezzo/baritone duet. Daisy and her old boyfriend Warren, on the roof of the tenement, are excited about his job's retirement plan. He outlines all the fun he and Daisy will have when they are old. Up tempo. Best used in a revue about old age, dance and movement enhance this number.

"What Did I Have That I Don't Have?," mezzo, semidramatic, questioning, good for club. Daisy discovers that Mark is really in love with Melinda and she wonders why she is so different in the twentieth century.

Instrumentation: 5 reeds, 3 violins, viola, cello, bass, 2 horns, 2 trumpets, trombone, percussion, piano, celeste, harpsichord, piano/conductor
Script: Random
Score: Chappell
Record: RCA
Rights: TW

ONE TOUCH OF VENUS

Book: Ogden Nash and S. J. Perelman (Suggested by F. Anstey's *The Tinted Venus*)
Music: Kurt Weill
Lyrics: Ogden Nash

ORIGINAL PRODUCTION

Imperial Theatre, October 7, 1943 (567 perf.)
Director: Elia Kazan
Choreographer: Agnes de Mille
Musical Director: Maurice Abravanel
Orchestration: Kurt Weill
Principals: Whitelaw Savory—John Boles—baritone; Molly Grant—Paula Laurence—alto; Rodney Hatch—Kenny Baker—baritone; Venus—Mary Martin—mezzo; Mrs. Kramer—Helen Raymond—VTI; Gloria Kramer—Ruth Bond—VTI; Stanley—Harry Clark—tenor; Taxi Black—Teddy Hart—tenor
Chorus and Smaller Roles: 12F/12M, at least half of whom dance well.

SUMMARY AND NOTES

A charming musical with excellent character roles for men and women, witty dialogue, exceptional lyrics and supporting music. The plot involves wealthy Whitelaw Savory, an eccentric art collector, teacher with a barbed tongue and wit to match, who has sent the shady Taxi Black to find a famous missing statue of Venus. When Taxi returns with the statue which is shrouded in mysterious events and deaths, Savory is ecstatic and Molly, his Eve Arden–type girl Friday, wonders what the statue has that she hasn't.

Rodney Hatch, a young barber who is substituting for Savory's real barber, happens to see the statue and puts the engagement ring intended for his girlfriend on the statue's outstretched hand. The statue comes to life and Rodney's troubles begin. Venus, ever devoted to love, follows him to his flat and is confused by the modern-day morality which seems to reject physical love.

Venus goes to Radio City, where she gets caught up in the lunchtime melee of shoppers and becomes interested in obtaining some clothes off a store mannequin. The manager calls the police, but Whitelaw Savory and Molly pay them off. Whitelaw tells Venus he loves her for she reminds him of a lost flame, but she spurns him and announces that love is only for the present. The enamored Whitelaw promises her anything and vows to make her care.

At the bus depot, Stanley and Taxi, under orders from Whitelaw, spy on Rodney, who awaits the arrival of his girlfriend Gloria Kramer and her overbearing mother. Venus arrives and watches Rodney try to explain the loss of Gloria's ring to the haughty beauty. Gloria, goaded on by Venus, leaves Rodney with a vow to end their relationship if he doesn't produce the ring in twenty-four hours.

Whitelaw, certain that Rodney has stolen his statue, goes to his barbershop where Taxi and Stanley are waiting to search the place. When Gloria unexpectedly arrives, the boys, who suspect her of being an accomplice, tie her up and leave Rodney unconscious in the basement. Venus interrupts the search, discovers Gloria and magically sends her out of Rodney's life to the North Pole. Venus and Rodney declare their love.

Rodney is picked up by the police for the theft of the statue, and Mrs. Kramer accuses Venus and Rodney of murdering Gloria and disposing of the body. The two are taken to jail but escape with the aid of Venus's magic powers. Venus produces Gloria while Rodney, realizing he would have been miserable married to such an overbearing woman, reiterates his feelings for Venus and paints a picture of their married life. The scene segues into an Ozone Heights Ballet sequence which depicts Venus's duties as a suburban housewife. As the number ends she realizes she wouldn't be happy and transforms herself back into a statue.

Back in the museum Rodney gazes at the statue, upset that she never said good-bye. He notices a girl who looks like Venus, discovers she comes from Ozone Heights and introduces himself as the curtain falls.

A show definitely worthy of more productions. The necessary sets include the Savory Foundation, Radio City, a bus terminal, the barbershop and the apartment. Other scenes may be moved to these locations or played In One with a prop piece to establish location. The costumes are everyday wear. The period may be moved to the present to keep costume costs down.

The characters are well drawn and the number of women's leading roles and vignette parts makes this a show to be perused. Rodney need not be a handsome leading man, and all the other male roles are definitely character types. Recommended for colleges and community theatres as an outstanding choice.

SONGS OF SPECIAL INTEREST

"Speak Low," mezzo solo, standard. Good for clubs.

"That's Him," mezzo solo, comic charm, ballad. Possible audition, not overdone.

"The Trouble with Women," male quartet. Taxi, Stanley, Savory and Rodney, four extremely different types of men, comment on their experience with women. Clever lyrics. Each man has a solo section which resolves around a problem with women.

Instrumentation: 3 reeds, 2 horns, trumpet, trombone, 2 violins, viola, cello, bass, harp, percussion, piano/conductor
Script: Little, Ten Great Musicals of the American Theatre
Score: Chappell
Record: Decca
Rights: TW

ON THE TOWN

Book: Betty Comden and Adolph Green (Adapted from the Bernstein/Jerome Robbins ballet *Fancy Free*)
Music: Leonard Bernstein
Lyrics: Betty Comden and Adolph Green

ORIGINAL PRODUCTION

Adelphi Theatre, December 28, 1944 (463 perf.)
Director: George Abbott
Choreographer: Jerome Robbins
Musical Director: Max Goberman
Orchestration: Leonard Bernstein, Hershy Kay, Don Walker, Ted Royal
Principals: Gabey—John Battles—tenor; Hildy—Nancy Walker—alto; Ozzie—Adolph Green—baritone; Claire—Betty Comden—mezzo; Chip—Cris Alexander—baritone; Ivy—Sono Osato—soprano
Chorus and Smaller Roles: 12M/12F at least 8M and 8F who dance extremely well.

SUMMARY AND NOTES

The show is a difficult one to properly mount because so much of the plot is furthered through dance. It is possible to edit the length of the numbers, but even with editing this still remains a difficult dance show. It is actually to the production's benefit to have a large chorus and several dance captains to ease the rehearsal pace.

The story concerns three sailor friends, on twenty-four–hour leave in wartime New York. The three all have the same interest, to find the one special girl during their leave. They hop on a subway and Gabey's eyes fall on a poster of the subway glamour girl of the month, Miss Turnstiles, Ivy Smith. Determined to find her, the three set off in different directions. Chip meets Hildy, a cabdriver recently fired for sleeping on the job, who entices him to her apartment. Ozzie meets Claire, a wealthy anthropologist who is writing a book on ancient man and is struck by the similarity Ozzie bears to the Neanderthal. Ozzie and Claire discover they have much in common, for they both succumb to their emotions, often in an unruly vein. Gabey finds Ivy in Carnegie Hall Studios in the middle of a voice lesson taught by her overpowering soprano teacher Madame Dilly. She agrees to meet him later at Nedick's, an orange drink and hot dog place at Times Square.

When Ivy fails to show up because Madame Dilly has forced her to perform as a cooch dancer in Coney Island, Claire, Ozzie, Hildy and Chip decide to cheer Gabey by showing him New York's nightlife. They go to a series of clubs, the tab for which is picked up by Claire's wealthy, snobby and over-used boyfriend Pitkin. They finally find Ivy at Coney Island, and the three girls say farewell to the boys at the navy yard, twenty-four hours later.

The leads in the show do not have to be terribly good-looking, just average types, which is a definite strong point. There are several smaller character roles, namely Hildy's sneezing roommate, Flossie, a New York girl whose boss is on the make; Pitkin; and an extremely prim tour guide, called Figment. The chorus is comprised of definite types, which makes the show easy to cast as far as singers go. A large chorus with a separate one for dancing is recommended. Much time must be allotted for the dance rehearsals.

There are quite a few sets and set pieces: a subway train, taxicab, museum, Carnegie Hall corridor, various nightclubs, Nedick's, Claire's and Hildy's apartments and Coney Island. Many of these may be pieces, but all are necessary to the flow of the show. The costumes are period forties and consist of sailor uniforms, workman uniforms, everyday clothes and evening wear. Specialty dance costumes for various club and Coney Island sequences are also necessary.

It is a big show to tackle but well worth the effort if a company has dancers and a quality choreographer. A definite audience pleaser, partially because it isn't often performed, but mostly because the music is wonderful.

SONGS OF SPECIAL INTEREST

"Carried Away," baritone/mezzo comic duet. Takes place in the Museum of Natural History between Ozzie and Claire. They discover that they both are the type to go wild over things that intrigue them. Specific examples are outlined in the lyrics. Very good for class study and characterization.

"I Can Cook Too," fast-paced, alto/mezzo solo, broad characterization, movement potential. Hildy has enticed Chip to her apartment and outlines her attributes, besides cooking.

Instrumentation: 5 reeds, 3 violins, viola, cello, bass, horn, trumpet, trombone, percussion, piano/conductor
Script: DBS
Selections: Warner
Record: Columbia
Rights: TW

P

PIPE DREAM

Book and Lyrics: Oscar Hammerstein II (Based on *Sweet Thursday*, by John Steinbeck)
Music: Richard Rodgers

ORIGINAL PRODUCTION

Shubert Theatre, November 30, 1955 (246 perf.)
Director: Harold Clurman
Musical Director: Salvatore Dell'Isola
Orchestration: Robert Russell Bennett
Principals: Doc—William Johnson—baritone; Millicent—Jayne Heller—VTNE; Suzy—Judy Tyler—mezzo with low belt; Hazel—Mike Kellin—baritone/bass; Mac—G. D. Wallace—baritone; Fauna—Helen Traubel—mezzo; Jim Blaikey— Rufus Smith—baritone
Chorus and Smaller Roles: 6F/10M.

SUMMARY AND NOTES

The play opens at the Western Biological Lab, where Doc lives and works on his experiments. This California coastal town, whose main industry was a recently closed cannery, is extremely poor. Mac, a friend of Doc's, introduces Suzy, a homeless, pretty girl of twenty-one with an abrasive and outspoken nature. Fauna, the warmhearted manager of the Bear Flag Cafe across the way, offers Suzy a job and a place to live with her and her "girls." Throughout the play various characters are introduced. There are the boys at the flophouse where Hazel, Doc's kind but slow-witted assistant, lives, and the various girls in Fauna's establishment. All are concerned about Doc and interested in the growing relationship between Doc and Suzy. It seems that Suzy has goaded Doc into writing a paper and the boys at the flophouse raise money for a new microscope for Doc's experiments.

Fauna manipulates Doc to ask Suzy for a date and bolsters the girl's confidence in herself. Suzy is enthralled and Doc enchanted by her awkward charm. Suzy decides to leave Fauna's and make her home in an empty boiler that an elderly couple has abandoned. She gains her independence and belief in herself, and Doc is forced to realize that their relationship has changed both of them. He declares his love and asks to marry her, much to the delight of the town.

This unusual show is not as familiar as many of the other Rodgers and Hammerstein productions but may be growing in popularity due to the recent TV airing of *Cannery Row*. The characters are interesting and one can quickly become wrapped up in the story of Doc and Suzy. The secondary characters are real "character" roles and would be good for an older company with good performer/actors.

SONGS OF SPECIAL INTEREST

"All at Once You Love Her," lovely ballad, now a standard. Baritone solo sung by Doc as an interpretation of a Mexican song.

"Everybody's Got a Home but Me," standard ballad, good for club, lovely melody, haunting lyrics, potential tearjerker. Suzy sings a factual song. Suited for any vocal type. Alto, audition potential.

"The Man I Used to Be," charm song, some soft shoe, nice up tempo higher-voiced song, breezy tempo, possible for a second song in an audition situation where a strong singer is trying to show lightheartedness and movement. Baritone.

"The Next Time It Happens," baritone/mezzo or alto, scene to duet, good for class study. Suzy and Doc say good-bye to each other. Strong subtext of two people who want to stay together saying good-bye.

Instrumentation: 3 reeds, 2 horns, trumpet, trombone, percussion, 2 violins, viola, cello, bass, piano/conductor
Script: Viking Press
Score: Williamson
Record: RCA
Rights: R & H

R

RAISIN

Book: Robert Nemiroff and Charlotte Zaltzberg (Based on the play *A Raisin in the Sun*, by Lorraine Hansberry)
Music: Judd Woldin
Lyrics: Robert Brittan

ORIGINAL PRODUCTION

46th Street Theatre, October 18, 1973 (847 perf.)
Director: Donald McKayle
Choreographer: Donald McKayle
Musical Director: Howard A. Roberts
Orchestration: Al Cohn and Robert M. Freedman
Principals: Walter Lee Younger—Joe Morton—high baritone; Ruth Younger—Ernestine Jackson—mezzo; Lena Younger (Mama)—Virginia Capers—alto; Joseph Asagai—Robert Jackson—baritone; Beneatha Younger—Deborah Allen—mezzo; Travis Younger—Ralph Carter—boy mezzo range; Karl Lindner—Richard Sanders—VTNE
Chorus and Smaller Roles—4F/4M Blacks.

SUMMARY AND NOTES

Tony Awards: Virginia Capers—Best Actress, Best Musical.
Set in a Black ghetto area of Chicago in the 1950s, this musical concerns the Younger family, comprised of Mama, daughter Benetha, son Walter Lee, his wife

Ruth, and their son Travis. The Youngers, cramped in their tenement apartment and stifled by the neighborhood streets which are filled with pushers, prostitutes and drunks, yearn to better their position in life. Walter Lee, a chauffeur, dreams of a more successful career while his Mama wants to get the family into a home of their own. In Chicago of the fifties, that means a White one.

Mama, recently widowed, awaits the arrival of her husband's $10,000 insurance check, which will enable them to move. Walter, who now considers himself the man of the family, also awaits the check; he plans on going into partnership in a liquor store, an investment Mama is against. Benetha, a college student who Mama hopes will be a doctor, wants to escape to Africa with her boyfriend, Asagai, an African exchange student.

The check arrives and Mama announces that she has bought a house in a White neighborhood. Walter crumbles, accuses his wife Ruth of not standing by him and goes on a druken binge. Three days later, Mama finds him in a bar, gives him the money, minus the small down payment for the house, makes him promise to keep $3,000 for Benetha's schooling and allows him the responsibility of the rest. He is touched by her love and trust but makes the mistake of turning over the cash to one of his partners, who promptly leaves town.

A defeated Walter Lee decides he can get the money back by allowing the White neighborhood association to buy them out of the house. Mr. Lindner had approached them earlier to convince them not to move into the neighborhood. Mr. Lindner arrives and Mama forces Travis, Walter's young son, to watch his father negotiate with the White man. Walter's pride in his parents and in himself will not allow him to take the money, and he refuses the offer. The family is overjoyed. As the show ends the moving men begin emptying the apartment.

This powerful drama, originally an award-winning play, is a study in human relationships, character growth and development. There are many dramatic points, especially the confrontation scenes between Walter and Mama and Walter and Ruth, and many touching moments, for example, when young Travis says good-bye to the sidewalk tree that grows on the block, and Mama's demonstration of her love and belief in Walter Lee.

The show may be performed on a unit, multileveled set with set props adjusted for the various scenes, the nightclub, the church, the kitchen. The costumes should be 1950s style with a different costume per performer for each Act.

SONGS OF SPECIAL INTEREST

''Not Anymore,'' 2F/M trio, comic trio that occurs after a White man representing the neighborhood association comes to plead with the Youngers not to move into the neighborhood. Walter, Ruth and Benetha try to relate to Mama the tone of the conversation. Foot-stomping, tongue-in-cheek, movement- and lyric-oriented song. Requires clever choreography which is outlined in the script.

Instrumentation: 2 keyboards, 4 reeds, 2 trumpets, horn, 2 trombones, tuba, 3 percussion, 3 violins, viola, cello, bass, guitar
Smaller Orchestration: keyboard, reed, trumpet, trombone, guitar, bass, 2 percussion
Script: SF
Selections: Blackwood
Record: Columbia
Rights: SF

THE ROAR OF THE GREASEPAINT—THE SMELL OF THE CROWD

Book: Leslie Bricusse and Anthony Newley
Music: Leslie Bricusse
Lyrics: Anthony Newley

ORIGINAL PRODUCTION

Shubert Theatre, May 16, 1965 (232 perf.)
Director: Anthony Newley
Choreographer: Gillian Lynne
Musical Director: Herbert Grossman
Orchestration: Philip J. Lang
Principals: Sir—Cyril Ritchard—baritone; Cocky—Anthony Newley—tenor; The Kid—Sally Smith—mezzo; The Negro—Gilbert Price—tenor; The Girl—Joyce Jillson—soprano; The Bully—Murray Tannenbaum—VTNE
Chorus and Smaller Roles: 8F urchins.

SUMMARY AND NOTES

An allegory about those who get and those who do not, the establishment versus the status quo. At the opening of the show Sir, who represents wealth and success, meets Cocky, who represents those who can never get ahead, for "The Game." They must play by Sir's rules, and when Cocky starts to get ahead, Sir merely changes the rules. Midway through, Cocky, tired of being bested, revolts. To appease Cocky, Sir allows him to be crowned King and have a few rewards, namely a girl he loves. Cocky's dreams, however, are short-lived when Sir replays the game and wins the girl away. A downtrodden Black enters, even more unfortunate than Cocky, and wants to play. Cocky treats him as badly as Sir had treated Cocky, proving he is as unfit as Sir to rule.

As the game goes on, Cocky gains confidence and forces Sir to play the game by his rules. The two have come full circle; neither is good alone, and they must work together to create a new beginning.

A simple show to produce because it requires no special set, and is performed in "pulled" costumes, Victorian in tone. Often the first show in a summer stock season because of the small technical requirements, it is fun for the chorus, which has a great deal of performance exposure, but vocally demanding for the two principals.

The female chorus may be expanded as needed. Often a larger chorus is used for choreographic variety. The music is familiar and absorbing. The character of Cocky, although a tenor, need not be played by a typically romantic tenor; he is definitely an offbeat romantic. Sir is a character actor, usually with a theatrical flair and experience in "playing an audience."

SONGS OF SPECIAL INTEREST

"Feeling Good," Black, soulful, wonderful imagery makes this good for class study. Actor must see the images and feel the emotions. Vocally soaring, tenor. Audition.

"The Joker," tenor solo, good for nightclub, semidramatic, gripping, soulful.

"My First Love Song," tenor/mezzo or soprano duet. This romantic song between an attractive girl and an offbeat character is especially good in a class situation as it gives atypical males a chance to experience love duets without feeling overly self-conscious.

"Who Can I Turn To?," tenor solo. A desperate Cocky cries out for someone or something. Semidramatic, good for vocal styling and reaching out gestures. Could be F solo if taken from context. Club.

Instrumentation: 4 reeds, 2 horns, 2 trumpets, 2 violins, cello, bass, percussion, harp, guitar/banjo, piano/conductor
Script: NP
Selections: TRO
Record: RCA
Rights: TW

THE ROBBER BRIDEGROOM

Book and Lyrics: Alfred Uhry (Based on a novella by Eudora Welty)
Music: Robert Waldman

ORIGINAL PRODUCTION

Biltmore Theatre, October 9, 1976 (145 perf.)
Director: Gerald Freedman
Choreography: Donald Saddler
Orchestration: Robert Waldman
Principals: Jamie Lockhart—Barry Bostwick—baritone; Clemment Musgrove—

Stephen Vinovich—baritone; Rosamund—Rhonda Coullet—mezzo; Salome—
Barbara Lang—alto; Little Harp—Lawrence John Moss—baritone; Goat—Trip
Plymale—baritone
Chorus and Smaller Roles: 6M/5F.

SUMMARY AND NOTES

An empty stage is in view as the audience enters. A narrator describes the
small town of Rodney, Mississippi. Many of the town citizens gather around to
reflect upon the good old days of the buffalo and Natchez Indians. Each character
focuses on a famous ancestor as they engage in a country dance. The character
of Jamie Lockhart is pictured as the man with two faces, one very honest and
clean-cut, the other like a villain. The story begins to unfold as Salome, the
wicked and selfish stepmother; Musgrove, Rosamund's wealthy father; and Little
Harp and Big Harp, two incorrigible robbers, are described.

The time flashes back. Two robber brothers, Big Harp, the head who does
the thinking, and Little Harp, the manpower behind the scheming bandits, who
carries his brother's head in a trunk, attempt to murder and rob Musgrove, a
wealthy man. Jamie Lockhart, another villain, saves Musgrove's life and wins
the trust of this plantation owner. Musgrove promises to give him his daughter
as a reward.

Salome, Musgrove's scrawny, conniving second wife, hates his daughter Rosamund and hires Goat, a half-wit, to push her into a ravine. He is thwarted by
the surprise arrival of Jamie, dressed as a robber. Jamie saves Rosamund but
steals her clothes and sends her home. Her father decides to send his new friend
Jamie Lockhart after the bandit, not knowing that the man who saved his life
and the bandit are one and the same.

The next day Jamie arrives, handsomely dressed, but he doesn't recognize
Rosamund, nor she him. He promises to consider marriage but can't get his
mind off the girl he met in the woods. He remeets his wood nymph and after a
fight with Little Harp, discovers that Rosamund is the girl he loves. Fearing that
her wealth will destroy his real feelings, he runs off but changes his mind and
decides he really wants Rosamund. After nine months of searching, as Rosamund
is swelling in motherhood, they find each other in New Orleans and Rosamund
delivers twins.

Barry Bostwick won the Tony Award for Best Actor.

The show is easy to produce, for it has limited scenery and few costumes. It
is stylized in the story theatre musical mode, so the ensemble can be onstage
throughout. This enables the actors to position set pieces or just establish location
by means of physical formation. This style show needs excellent, versatile and
tight lighting since areas must be readily delineated to keep the action fluid.

The subject matter is far fetched and farcical, and the music, country/folk.
There are many sexual references which cannot be altered as they are part of
the plot. This probably limits its appeal to high school groups.

The songs are not easily pulled from context and as much are not well suited to classroom study or revues.

Instrumentation: 3 violins, 2 guitars, bass, banjo
Script: DBS
Selections: Schirmer
Record: Columbia
Rights: MTI

RUNAWAYS

Words and Music: Elizabeth Swados

ORIGINAL PRODUCTION

Plymouth Theatre, May 13, 1978 (199 perf.)
Directed and Staged by: Elizabeth Swados
Arrangements: Improvised by the Musicians
Company: May be performed by a company of 8M/8F ranging in age from twelve to twenty. Some combining of roles necessary if the minimum configuration is used.

SUMMARY AND NOTES

The play opens in a fenced in area with bleachers. It may represent a playground. A group of adolescents, all runaways, play typical children's games. They finally come together and perform the opening number, which asks the question "Where do people go when they run away?" The remainder of the production deals with the desperateness of these children who didn't want to leave but had no other options.

The problems of the runaways are shown in music, through mimes, and in powerful monologues; the child prostitute, kept on drugs by her pimp and still dreaming of a better life; the boy with a flair for theatre, searching for a hero; the boy who escapes his home problems by playing basketball; the addict who dies despite the efforts of another runaway to get him to kick the habit; and the girl who is senselessly raped and murdered. These are the children who are forced to seek shelter on the playground, who are comfortable with each other; whose nights are a constant nightmare and whose days are filled with dreams of revenge on those who have hurt them.

The group learns about survival and violence. After one of the girls becomes victimized, the rest mock the punk rock stars who sang of a happy ending. All beg to be allowed to enjoy their youth.

This musicalized comment on the deterioration of the family as the backbone of life is charged with energy and emotion. It is a powerful, touching and horrifying collage of the feelings of runaways.

An excellent vehicle for touring as it requires no specific settings. The costumes are everyday, present adolescent style. The piece requires a sensitive director who can relate the problems of the script to a talented group of adolescent-appearing actor/singers. The French acting version is broken into 11M/9F, but this size may be abbreviated or expanded to fit the stage space.

SONGS OF SPECIAL INTEREST

"Let Me Be a Kid," mixed chorus, a crying out of children who want to be children while they still have time. Good for a revue on youth. Requires movement.

"Where Are Those People Who Did Hair?," M/F duet, baritone, alto to mixed chorus. Rock tempo, questioning what happened to the rock stars of the previous generation who promised to change the world, became millionaires and are no longer concerned.

Instrumentation: string bass, percussion, drums, 2 reeds, guitar, 2 horns/trumpets, piano/conductor
Script: SF
Record: Columbia
Rights: SF

S

THE SECRET LIFE OF WALTER MITTY

Book: Joe Manchester (Based on the story by James Thurber)
Music: Leon Carr
Lyrics: Earl Shuman

ORIGINAL PRODUCTION

Players Theatre, October 26, 1964 (96 perf.)
Director: Mervyn Nelson
Choreographer: Bob Arlen
Musical Director: Leon Carr
Orchestration: Ray Ellis
Principals: Walter Mitty—Marc London—baritone; Agnes Mitty—Lorraine Serabian—mezzo; Peninnah—Christopher Norris—child mezzo; Willa de Wisp—Cathryn Damon—alto; Harry—Rudy Toronto—baritone
Chorus and Smaller Roles: 6F/6M who play a variety of roles. Need one tenor minimum.

SUMMARY AND NOTES

The play is the musicalized version of the famous story of Walter Mitty, the everyday man who daydreams romantic visions of what his life could be. Walter begins his typically average day, but as he shaves, his dreams come alive and he is the man who cleverly outwits the firing squad. His dreams are interrupted by his wife, who constantly reminds Walter of everything he forgets. The forty-year-old Walter yearns for freedom and youth and easily relates to his daughter Peninnah, whom he adores.

As the play progresses, it jumps from Walter's reality to his dreams. In his real world he goes to his favorite bar where Harry, the owner, and Willa De Wisp, a nightclub singer, urge him to have confidence in himself. He wants to run off with Willa and leave Agnes, but when the moment of decision is at hand he is unable to make the final break. Agnes sadly wonders what happened to their lives but knows Walter needs her to get through life. She stands by him because she really cares. He realizes that things aren't going to change but appreciates the fact that he has much more than those lonely individuals at the bar because he has a family. Besides, if life gets to be too unbearable he always has his dreams.

The musical rapidly switches from reality to daydreams, which keeps the action moving and the tone comedic. A charming and lovable actor is needed to play Mitty; and an excellent actress, who can round out Agnes's character and make her less one-sided and shrewish, is required to make the show honestly sympathetic to both leads. It is fun for a company of performers to present for all have roles in the dream sequences. The set may be cartoon in style with location established by props and lighting. There are quite a few costume pieces as the company portrays many parts, but most of these are quite easily obtained and modern-day. Best suited for community theatres.

SONGS OF SPECIAL INTEREST

"Aggie," touching song that Walter sings about the change in his relationship with his wife. On his fortieth birthday he looks back on his life and wonders what has become of the woman he married. Baritone solo.

"Marriage Is for Old Folks," may be performed as an alto solo. Reflects free-thinking nightclub singer's attitude about life. Good for freeing an inhibited performer.

Instrumentation: 3 reeds, 2 trumpets, percussion, 2 violins, viola, cello, bass, harp, piano/conductor. Smaller Orchestration: Reed, bass, percussion, piano/conductor
Script: SF
Record: Columbia
Rights: SF

SUGAR BABIES

Sketches: Ralph G. Allen
Music: Jimmy McHugh
Lyrics: Dorothy Fields and Al Dubin
Additional Music and Lyrics: Arthur Malvin

ORIGINAL PRODUCTION

Mark Hellinger Theatre, October 8, 1979 (1,208 perf.)
Staged and Choreographed by: Ernest Flatt
Musical Director: Glen Roven
Orchestration: Dick Hyman
Principals: Mickey, First Comic—Mickey Rooney—tenor; Ann—Ann Miller—
mezzo; Jack—Jack Fletcher—baritone; Scot—Scot Stewart—tenor; Sid—Sid
Stone—VTNE
Chorus and Smaller Roles: At least 6F for burlesque beauties, must sing and
dance, M quartet, and 3M for comics and straight men.

SUMMARY AND NOTES

A long well-deserved run on Broadway for this tribute to burlesque from the
early 1900s through 1930. Much of the success of this historical musical was
due to the talent and energy of its stars, Ann Miller and Mickey Rooney. While
many of the sketches are too risqué for some audiences, the historical reenactment
of one of the greatest eras of show business more than compensates. America's
greatest comics received their training in burlesque before moving to vaudeville,
Broadway, films and television. The show pays tribute to such famous stars of
the genre as Sally Rand and Ed Wynn, and reenacts old burlesque sketches like
The Little Red Schoolhouse, Meet Me 'round the Corner, and The Minstrel.

The script provides for casting flexibility and reassigning of roles to utilize
each cast member to best advantage.

The production numbers and the specialty burlesque tributes call for elaborate
settings and specialty costumes. These numbers will be the major budgetary
expense of the show.

SONGS OF SPECIAL INTEREST

"Good Old Burlesque Show," opening number tribute to burlesque, begins
as male solo and goes into a company number. Good for tribute revue and class.

"I'm Just a Song and Dance Man," dance-oriented, showstopping number,
great voice not required, tenor, although music is available in baritone range.

"On the Sunny Side of the Street," up tempo, movement-oriented mezzo/
tenor (baritone) duet, good for relationship to each other and the audience. Also
works as a solo for any voice range.

Instrumentation: 5 reeds, 3 trumpets, horn, 3 trombones, 2 percussion, 3 violins,
cello, bass, harp, guitar/banjo, piano/celeste, piano/conductor
Script: SF
Selections: Jimmy McHugh Music
Record: B'Way Entertainment
Rights: SF

T

TWO GENTLEMEN OF VERONA

Book: Adapted by John Guare and Mel Shapiro (Adapted from Shakespeare's play of the same title)
Lyrics: John Guare
Music: Galt MacDermot

ORIGINAL PRODUCTION

St. James Theatre, December 1, 1971 (627 perf.)
Director: Mel Shapiro
Choreographer: Jean Erdman
Additional Musical Staging: Dennis Nahat
Musical Supervision: Harold Wheeler
Principals: Thurio—Frank O'Brien—tenor; Valentine—Clifton Davis—baritone; Proteus—Raul Julia—baritone; Julia—Diana Davila—alto; Lucetta—Alix Elias—mezzo; Silvia—Jonelle Allen—alto; Eglamour—Alvin Lum—baritone; Duke—Norman Matlock—baritone; Launce—John Bottoms—VTI; Speed—Jose Perez—VTI
Chorus and Smaller Roles—11M/8F who sing and move well.

SUMMARY AND NOTES

The play opens with Thurio, a funny, shrill-voiced character who joins the ensemble in setting the tone of the musicalized version of Shakespeare's play. As he exits, Cupid enters, zaps everyone with an arrow and the ensemble freezes, with Proteus and Valentine frozen in struggle. Valentine breaks the freeze and the play begins.

Valentine asks his friend Proteus what he wants to do with the rest of his life. Proteus, who has never considered the subject before, answers that he would like to live for Julia's love. Valentine would rather rule the world and so their characters evolve: Valentine the emperor/seeker and Proteus the romantic.

Valentine goes with his servant Speed to the city of Milan to find excitement and fame while Proteus stays home and successfully woos Julia. Sent by his father to Milan, he exchanges rings with Julia as a token of affection, and leaves with his servant Launce.

Julia, who waits in Verona, discovers she is pregnant and decides that she and her maid Lucetta will disguise themselves as men and follow Proteus to Milan.

Valentine, newly arrived in the colorful city, sees Silvia, the Duke's daughter, who is unwillingly bethrothed to the nebulous Thurio. Valentine falls hoplessly in love. Silvia arrives at Valentine's Letter Writing Shoppe to send a letter to her true lover Eglamour, begging his assistance. Valentine offers to save her from Thurio and arranges to help her escape. She declares her love for Valentine and embraces him as Proteus enters, sees them and desires the girl for himself. Proteus anonymously sends the Duke word of their escape plan. As Proteus announces his love for Silvia, Julia and Lucetta arrive, introduce themselves as Sebastian and Caesario, and are hired into Proteus's service.

Meanwhile, the Duke has thwarted Valentine's plan and drafted him into the Army but Eglamour arrives and steals Silvia away. They are discovered by Proteus, who declares desire for Silvia. Valentine returns, followed by Julia, who announces her true identity and her pregnancy. Proteus regains his senses and declares his love for Julia; the Duke knights Valentine and decides he is a good match for Silvia; Thurio and Lucetta fall in love and all ends happily.

No synopsis can do justice to this 1972 Tony Award winner for Best Book and Best Musical; it must be seen to be appreciated. The songs, choreography, characterizations and creative treatment of this tale successfully bring Shakespeare to life. Originally produced as part of Central Park's summer tour, the musical was so well received by the inner-city population that it was moved to Broadway.

The show is best performed on a unit set, preferably multileveled for choreographic variety. The script will be appreciated in larger metropolitan areas and on college campuses where the sometimes off-color language, sexual innuendos, and antiwar comments may not be detrimental to the audience's enjoyment.

The musical numbers are diverse and require a choreographer versed in a variety of dance styles. The cast needs to move well and be able to make modernized Shakespearean dialogue understandable.

SONGS OF SPECIAL INTEREST

The songs are integral to the show and don't work well out of context.

Instrumentation: bass, 2 guitars, percussion, drums, reed, 2 trumpets, 2 trombones, 2 violins, viola, cello, piano/celeste/conductor
Script: Great Rock Musicals
Selections: Holt
Record: ABC
Rights: TW

V

VERY GOOD EDDIE

Book: Guy Bolton (Based on the play *Over-Night*, by Phillip Bartholomae)
Music: Jerome Kern
Lyrics: Schuyler Greene

ORIGINAL PRODUCTION

Princess Theatre, December 23, 1915 (341 perf.)

REVIVAL PRODUCTION

Booth Theatre, December 21, 1975 (307 perf.)
Director: Bill Gile
Choreographer: Bill Gile
Musical Director: Russell Warner
Orchestration: Russell Warner
Principals: Mrs. Elsie Lilly—Cynthia Wells—soprano; Mr. Dick Rivers—David Christmas—tenor; Mr. Eddie Kettle—Charles Repole—high baritone; Mrs. Elsie Darling—Virginia Seidel—soprano; Mr. Percy Darling—Nicholas Wyman—baritone; Mrs. Georgina Kettle—Spring Fairbank—VTNE; Mme. Matroppo—Travis Hudson—alto; Steward—James Harder—VTNE
Chorus and Smaller Roles: 6M/4F.

SUMMARY AND NOTES

This charming revival was one of the original Princess Theatre musicals especially written for the intimacy of the 299-seat house. The idea behind the productions was to develop musicals limited to two sets, a small cast and orchestra. This was extremely innovative in 1915 as musicals of the day tended to be revue, operetta, nearly plotless and mounted on a large scale.

Revived in 1975 by the Goodspeed Opera, a professional theatre in East Haddam, Connecticut, which seasonally produces two revivals and a new musical, the show subsequently moved to Broadway where it received three Tony nominations.

This two-set musical opens on the deck of the *Hudson River Liner* which is stopped in Poughkeepsie. The year is 1915. Dick Rivers, a wealthy young man in town for the boat races, happens to see Elsie Lilly, a young singing student of Mme. Matroppo, on board and falls in love. Determined to meet the girl, he boards the boat and convinces Matroppo he is a reporter desiring to interview her prize student. Various honeymoon couples arrive on board, including the diminutive Eddie Kettle and his tall and overbearing wife Georgina. They are followed by the overblown, unromantic Percy Darling and his petite wife Elsie. It is obvious from the start that the couples are mismatched.

Eddie, a college acquaintance of Percy, is left on board with Elsie, as Percy and Georgina go off to complete some last-minute business. The boat sets off without the spouses, and Elsie and Eddie, in order to avoid a scandal, pretend they are married to each other.

The two gradually fall in love but are terrified of the outcome and try to avoid the issue. The boat docks at the Honeymoon Inn and despite their efforts to find a way back to Poughkeepsie, there is no way out until morning; they are forced to register for the night. They do manage to obtain separate rooms when Eddie explains they need one for the luggage.

Later that evening, in oversized pajamas, Eddie has Elsie distract the desk clerk while he spills ink on the register to obliterate their names. Elsie screams there is a mouse in her room and everyone rushes out from all the rooms. A confused chase occurs, with all the characters running off and on and the main characters searching for each other: Mme. Matroppo attempts to seduce a visiting Frenchman, and Dick Rivers begs Elsie Lilly to marry him. When she refuses because he is too much of a sport with an eye for the women, he sends her some roses and a note declaring his love.

Percy and Georgina arrive after everyone has retired for the night. To save their reputation they are forced to register as husband and wife and check into the same room. The next morning Percy and Georgina confront Elsie and Eddie, who profess their innocence and accuse their spouses of also registering as husband and wife. The desk clerk comes on with a telegram from the minister who married everyone, announcing that his license had expired and none of the ceremonies were legal. The couples are relieved, pair off with the partners that best suit their size and temperament and the play ends happily.

The dialogue is witty, the characters well drawn and the situation hilarious. The production needs a chorus of good singer/dancers and principals with impeccable timing. The character roles of the Frenchman, the steward, who also acts as the desk clerk, and Mme. Matroppo are excellent vignettes that add greatly to the delight of the show. An excellent vehicle for any group with a good director/choreographer who can time the comic chases and recapture the style of the Pre–World War I dances.

SONGS OF SPECIAL INTEREST

"I've Got to Dance," mixed chorus, could be a mixed quartet for class study. Period 1915 dance number staged as Vernon and Irene Castle, spirited tempo.

"Thirteeen Collar," high baritone solo sung by Eddie, who has married a domineering woman. Song of the downtrodden, meek and small-in-size husband. Problem charm song, character-oriented.

Instrumentation: 2 violins, viola, cello, bass, 2 reeds, trombone, trumpet, percussion, piano/conductor
Script: NP
Score: Harms
Record: DRG
Rights: TW

W

WHERE'S CHARLEY?

Book: George Abbott (Based on *Charley's Aunt*, by Brandon Thomas)
Music and Lyrics: Frank Loesser

ORIGINAL PRODUCTION

St. James Theatre, October 11, 1948 (792 perf.)
Director: George Abbott
Choreographer: George Balanchine
Musical Director: Max Goberman
Orchestration: Ted Royal, Hans Spialek and Philip J. Lang
Principals: Charley—Ray Bolger—baritone; Amy—Allyn Ann McLerie—mezzo; Kitty—Doretta Morrow—soprano; Jack—Byron Palmer—tenor; Sir Francis—Paul England—baritone; Dona Lucia—Jane Lawrence—soprano; Spettigue—Horace Cooper—VTNE
Chorus and Smaller Roles: 8M/8F.

SUMMARY AND NOTES

Oxford England, 1892. Charley and Jack, two Oxford students, are entertaining two young ladies, Amy and Kitty, who have come to visit them. The girls are properly upset to discover that Charley's aunt hasn't arrived to chaperone, but the boys assure them she will be on the next train. Jack suggests that Charley pose as his own aunt in the costume he is to wear in the drama club production. He is forced to agree in order to appease Kitty's guardian, and Amy's uncle, Mr. Spettigue. Spettigue, an opportunist who has heard the aunt is extremely wealthy, considers marrying her for her money. Charley, as Dona Lucia Alvadorez, leads him on a merry chase.

The real Dona Lucia arrives, an extremely attractive, stylish woman. She is greeted by Jack's father, Sir Francis, whom she recognizes as the soldier she was infatuated with twenty years before. She decides to disguise her true identity until she has talked to Charley, so she announces herself as Mrs. Beverly-Smythe and renews her acquaintance with Sir Francis.

The play resolves when Charley, as Dona Lucia, to agrees marry Spettigue if he gives his written consent that Kitty and Amy may marry Jack and Charley. Spettigue doesn't mind losing their money (which he controls until they marry) since he is going to gain more wealth by marriage to Dona Lucia. Spettigue announces his agreement to the marriages of his niece Kitty and his ward Amy to the boys. A humorous scene of Charley rushing back and forth to change from himself to Dona Lucia follows. His disguise is unveiled, but the couples are still to be wed for they have the letter of agreement. Charley meets his real aunt, who declares her love for Sir Francis, and the musical ends on a happy note.

Tony Award: Ray Bolger, who nightly stopped the show with the charming "Once in Love with Amy," soft-shoe solo where he invited the audience to sing along.

Because the dance requirements are limited, the show is an ideal one for school groups with large choirs who want to give everyone a singing opportunity. The chorus is expandable. There are several dance sections but these may be trimmed in length and are set in the Victorian period, where style is more important than tricky steps. The principals need excellent singing voices, and Charley must be a high-energy comedian who dances.

The costumes, although period ones, also include some Spanish-styled ones for a movement sequence involving Dona Lucia's background. Charley's costume, traditionally representing Whistler's Mother, needs to be designed for quick changes. It is advised that extreme care be given to cast a Charley with a sense of humor and a certain masculine charm. Without this the transvestite sections may become uncomfortable.

SONGS OF SPECIAL INTEREST

"Make a Miracle," baritone/soprano, up tempo, duet between Charley and Amy about prospective inventions. Charley wants to talk about their future but Amy is more enthralled with modern technology. Unusual lyric about love, with definite actables.

"Once in Love with Amy," charm song. Charley expresses his love for Amy by cavorting in soft shoe and song around the stage. Baritone.

Instrumentation: 5 reeds, 2 trumpets, trombone, horn, 3 violins, viola, cello, bass, percussion, piano
Script: French (London)
Score: Frank
Record: Monmouth/Evergreen
Rights: MTI

WHOOPEE

Book: William Anthony McGuire (Adapted from *The Nervous Wreck*, by Owen Davis)
Music: Walter Donaldson
Lyrics: Gus Kahn

ORIGINAL PRODUCTION

New Amsterdam Theatre, December 4, 1928 (379 perf.)
Revival Production: ANTA Theatre, February 14, 1979 (204 perf.)
Director: Frank Corsaro
Choreographer: Dan Siretta
Musical Director: Lynn Crigler
Orchestration: Russell Warner
Principals: Bob—Nicholas Wyman—baritone; Mary Custer—Bonnie Leaders—alto; Sally Morgan—Beth Austin—mezzo; Henry Williams—Charles Repole—tenor; Wanenis—Franc Luz—high baritone; Harriet Underwood—Catherine Cox—mezzo
Chorus and Smaller Roles: 11M/5F.

SUMMARY AND NOTES

Sally Morgan, about to be wed to Sheriff Bob, a man who saved her father from financial ruin, declares her love for Wanenis, an Indian she has known since childhood. When the Sheriff threatens to kill Wanenis, she runs off with Henry Williams. Henry, a confirmed hypochondriac without one ounce of bravery, sets out across the desert, partially to aid the girl and partially to escape from his nurse, Mary Custer, who wants to trap him into marriage.

Out of gas in the desert, Henry discovers that Sally has left a note announcing that she has eloped with him. Realizing that the angry Sheriff will kill him, he stops the touring car of the wealthy Jerome Underwood, holds him at gunpoint and demands extra gasoline.

Early the next morning Sally and Henry seek refuge at a cattle ranch that they later find out belongs to Underwood. They disguise themselves as cooks but are soon discovered. During the course of events Sheriff Bob and Harriet, Underwood's man-hungry daughter, fall in love, Henry decides to throw away his pills and propose to Mary, and a clash of thunder from the gods above decrees it is all right for the white and red races to unite. Wanenis and Sally are accepted by the Indians and her father.

The show, set in Arizona in the later 1920s, has several sets that are usually Mission Rest, four different In One scenes that occur on roads or in the wilderness, the ranch, and the reservation. The interior of the ranch set consists of a kitchen with an oven large enough to hold Henry. There are also two period automobiles, one a touring car, the other a sportier model; these may be cutouts. The costumes are period ones and western outfits. The chorus members should have two each for visual variety.

The script is extremely funny, and the role of Henry requires a superb comic with impeccable timing. The roles are broadly written and comedic, which makes it excellent for summer stock fare or for organizations looking for something witty and refreshing.

SONGS OF SPECIAL INTEREST

"Love Me, or Leave Me," F alto solo, now a standard, good for club. Sung by Mary, who is Henry's nurse and hurt that he doesn't return her affection.

"Makin' Whoopee," high baritone solo to mixed chorus, clever lyrics that describe the different things that happen to men when they get married. Sung by Henry, who hopes to remain single. Strongly associated with Eddie Cantor, who originated the role.

"Yes, Sir, That's My Baby," M baritone solo, sung by Henry, who realizes he loves his nurse Mary and is ready for marriage. He is joined by the company.

Instrumentation: 3 violins, viola, cello, bass, 4 reeds, trumpet, trombone, banjo, piano, percussion
Script: NP
Score: Schirmer
Record: Smithsonian
Rights: TW

WORKING

Book: Studs Terkel, Stephen Schwartz, and Nina Faso
Music and Lyrics: Craig Carnelia, Micki Grant, Mary Rodgers, Susan Birkenhead, Stephen Schwartz, and James Taylor

ORIGINAL PRODUCTION

46th Street Theatre, May 14, 1978 (25 perf.)
Director: Stephen Schwartz
Musical Staging: Onna White

Musical Director: Stephen Reinhardt
Orchestration: Kirk Nurock
Principals: Cleaning Woman—Lynne Thigpen—alto; Lovin' Al—David Langston Smyrl—baritone; Newsboy—Matthew McGrath—boy mezzo; Teacher, Millworker—Bobo Lewis—alto; Waitress—Leonora Nemetz—alto/mezzo; Joe—Arny Freeman—baritone; Fireman—Matt Landers—VTNE; Housewife—Susan Bigelow—mezzo
Chorus and Smaller Roles: 3F/4M.

SUMMARY AND NOTES

It is impossible to capture the scope of this musical in synopsized form simply because it deals with so many characters. The individual monologues are absorbing, the music and lyrics impressive in the messages they convey, yet the entire show lacks an overpowering emotional impact. It is a show about individuals who work, a show with excellent monologues worth studying, and gripping songs worth singing. An easy musical to rehearse because there are so few sequences with more than one character.

The production opens to a jazzy theme song, complete with working sound effects. As the show unfolds, the various characters tell about themselves: the garage man, who takes great pride in all the cars he parks: the stonemason, who builds his walls to last; the frightened office vice president; the newsboy; the elderly schoolteacher, trying desperately to adapt to the new system; the phone operators; the migrant workers whose life is one of severe hardship; the housewife who enjoys her job and resents those who look down on her; the widowed millworker who barely ekes out a living by endless production-line labor; the retiree who still enjoys life; the waitress; the truckers; the firefighter; and the cleaning woman who works so her children will have a better future.

The show may be performed anywhere with props to designate specific location. Lighting should be tight in order to keep the flow. The company may vary in size, although the show has more impact with a smaller company because the audience is impressed by the acting versatility of the performers.

SONGS OF SPECIAL INTEREST

"Cleanin' Women," alto/mezzo solo. Soul sound, ambitious woman who wants her daughter to achieve. Requires a powerful voice. Usually performed by a Black.

"It's an Art," waitress solo, mezzo. A waitress who has a theatrical flair describes her love for her job. Good character-oriented song.

"Joe," baritone/tenor talk sung by a retiree who reminisces and tells about his days. Poignant and charming. Strongly character-oriented, deceptively simplistic. Good for class or a revue about aging.

"Just a Housewife," mezzo solo sung by the housewife whose full-time job is taking care of her family. Made to feel unimportant by television, she defends herself. Strong subtext. Dramatic. Character-oriented.

"Millwork," mezzo solo with trio backup. A story about a widowed mill-worker who despises her job but accepts the necessity of feeding her family. She reminisces about her past. Transitions, many specifics and mood changes make this excellent for class study.

"Nobody Tells Me How," mezzo/alto solo. Sung by the older schoolteacher. Dramatically powerful with some comic overtones in the monologue. Excellent for characterization development and transition from story to song.

Instrumentation: 2 keyboards, guitar, bass, drums, percussion
Script: NP
Selections: Valando
Record: Columbia
Rights: MTI

Y

YOUR OWN THING

Book: Donald Driver (Suggested by Shakespeare's *Twelfth Night*)
Music and Lyrics: Hal Hester and Danny Apolinar

ORIGINAL PRODUCTION

Orpheum Theatre, January 13, 1968 (937 perf.)
Staged by: Donald Driver
Musical Director: Charles Schneider
Orchestration: Hayard Morris
Principals: Olivia—Marion Mercer—alto; Viola—Leland Palmer—mezzo; Orson—Tom Ligon—baritone; Sebastian—Rusty Thacker—tenor
Chorus and Smaller Roles: 4M/1F.

SUMMARY AND NOTES

As the show opens, a shipwreck is in progress and Viola and her twin brother Sebastian, both rock performers, are arguing about who should save their orchestrations. Viola lands in Illyria, a city not unlike New York, disguises herself as a boy, and finds work as a tenor with the rock quartet Apocalypse, who lost one of its members to the draft.

Sebastian finds his way to Illyria and is mistakenly hired into the Apocalypse by Orson, the booking agent, who doesn't realize he has hired twins and proceeds to use both as messengers to deliver notes to his love, Olivia.

Olivia is attracted to the youthful Charlie/Sebastian, who she imagines are the same, but Charlie is attracted to Orson and attempts to tell him how to woo a girl. Orson, realizing he loves Charlie, fears he is a homosexual and begins reading about famous male friends in history. When he confesses his love to Charley, she ecstatically tells him she's a girl.

Olivia and Sebastian's relationship is faltering, due to the mistaken identities, but both urge the other to stay. The musical closes with the Apocalypse, now a trio, urging everyone to follow their feelings and "do their own thing."

It was the first Off-Broadway show to win the New York Drama Critics Circle Award, usually reserved for Broadway productions. Tony Awards, as of 1984, are not given to Off-Broadway shows.

The show is an interesting theatre event of the late sixties but obviously dated by the references to political happenings of the day. A director would need to make a decision to maintain the period or update it. The original production utilized screens as a visual part of the set and had slides and films constantly aiding the action and pace. Without the visuals the show may lose its impact. It is important that the audience be caught up in the experience and not be given any time to think about what is going on. It must be a quickly paced, enjoyable presentation.

SONGS OF SPECIAL INTEREST

"Be Gentle," mezzo, baritone duet. Viola, who Orson believes is a boy, advises him on wooing a girl. Strong subtext for Viola.

"I'm on My Way to the Top," tenor solo sung by Sebastian after finding a job in Illyria. The ending section shows off high tenor range and is particularly good for a rock audition.

Instrumentation: electric organ, 2 guitars (electric fender bass and electric), percussion
Script: Dell, Great Rock Musicals
Selections: Shayne
Record: RCA
Rights: TW

APPENDIXES

Appendix A

Song Charts

The following Song Charts, categorized into solos, duets, trios/quartets and small chorus numbers, are designed as a workshop and class aid for teachers, directors and students. It is a ready reference to representative songs that are most suited for class study and auditions. Each song is defined in more detail in the *Songs of Special Interest* section at the end of each show.

This study chart makes some modifications from the original shows; that is, some songs suited for auditions appear in the Solo Song Charts even though the song may have originally been performed in a different manner. Another change from the original is in vocal typing. Because the chart is intended for class study, some of the vocal types have been altered to fit the available music. Full Scores are usually printed as the original Broadway show was performed but Selections are usually more geared for ease to a piano player and for group sing-alongs, hence the vocal ranges have been altered. In the charts, songs sung by the same characters may be listed as requiring different vocal types. This reflects the variety within any given role. Even though a soprano or tenor is required to sing an entire score, certain songs they perform may be sung by a lower vocal type.

The abbreviations that follow are the most readily understood by theatre people and are the easiest way to quickly peruse the charts.

ACT—Acting, refers to transition and mood changes. Used when emphasis is also placed on visualizing lyric images.

ANGER—Anger.

AUD—Audition.

BITT—Bitter.

CHAR—Character is emphasized.

CHM—Charm, or poignant.

CLUB—Suited for nightclub performances.

COM—Comic.

DANCE—Dance.

DICTION—Emphasis is on language and verbal clarity, usually fast paced.

DR—Dramatic.

ERG—Energy; high energy is required. Often these numbers are presentational, but sometimes they require strong acting focus.

LYR—Lyric or diction emphasis.

MOOD—Mood. This must be interpreted with the tempo. If the song is a ballad the emphasis is usually on the romantic, but with an up tempo the emphasis may be on fun.

MOVMT—Movement, usually simple, nonstylized or specialized dance.

PERIOD—refers to songs that reflect the period they represent, for example, the 20's. The numbers are best performed in the style suitable to the era. Usually Period songs require stylized movement and these are most often combined with presentational.

PRE—Presentational; requires strong eye contact with the audience. More often these are ''sell'' songs.

PROB—Problem. Often these songs are comedic to an audience because they focus on a specific problem i.e. ''Adelaide's Lament.''

REL—Relationship.

ROCK—Rock and roll sound.

ROMANT—Romantic.

STORY—Story or descriptive numbers. Usually the easiest for a beginning performer because they are loaded with specifics.

STRONG—Strength, sometimes vocal, sometimes character.

STYL—Style. Most often broadly played.

V—Vocal. These numbers require an excellent voice as they usually have a broad range.

All the songs are performed by those under the age of forty unless otherwise noted by the following terms. One must remember that age includes chronological, physical and attitude.

MID—Forties to sixties.

OLD—Sixty-five and up.

Vocal ranges are listed by the type that best suits the number. There are certainly cases when a high baritone can sing a tenor song without too much difficulty. Mezzo's can often sing alto and soprano songs, especially if the selections are used rather than the full score.

A—Alto.

Br—Baritone.

Bs—Bass.

M—Mezzo.

VTI—Vocal type interchangeable.

VTNE—Not essential.

S—Soprano.

T—Tenor.

SOLOS

SHOW AND SONG	VOCAL	TEMPO	TYPE/EMPHASIS
ALL IN LOVE			
What Can It Be?	M	Up	Movmt, Romant
ALLEGRO			
The Gentlemen Is a Dope	A	Med	Chm, Anger
ANNIE			
Little Girls	A	Med	Com, Char, Mid
Something Was Missing	Br	Slow	Chm, Mid
ANNIE GET YOUR GUN			
I'm a Bad, Bad Man	Br	Med	Strong, Char, V
I'm an Indian Too	A	Med	Com, Aud, Erg
Moonshine Lullaby	A	Slow	Aud, Char, Chm
You Can't Get a Man . . .	A	Up	Com, Prob, Story
ANYONE CAN WHISTLE			
Anyone Can Whistle	M	Slow	Act, Chm, Lyr
Everybody Says Don't	Br	Med	Anger, Dr, Strong
Me and My Town	A	Up	Movmt, Char, Mid
See What It Gets You	M	Up	Anger, Dr, Strong
There Won't Be Trumpets	M	Med	Anger, Strong
ANYTHING GOES			
Be Like the Bluebird	Br	Med	Com, Char, Pre
I Get a Kick Out of You	A	Med	Club, Romant
APPLAUSE			
But Alive	A	Up	Club, Mid, Pre
One Hallowe'en	M	Med	Dr, Story, Act
Welcome to the Theatre	A	Med	Char, Mid, Lyr
Who's That Girl?	A	Up	Movmt, Mid, Pre

SHOW AND SONG	VOCAL	TEMPO	TYPE/EMPHASIS
APPLE TREE, THE			
Eve	Br	Up	Chm, Lyr, Act
Forbidden Fruit	Br	Med	Movmt, Com, Char
Here in Eden	M	Med	Chm, Lyr, Story
It's a Fish	Br	Up	Story, Com, Prob
I've Got What You Want	M	Med	Movmt, Hard Char
Movie Star to Gorgeous	M	Up	Char, Aud, Pre
Tiger, Tiger	M	Up	Movmt, Hard, Char
What Makes Me Love Him?	M	Slow	Chm, Mid, Lyr
BABES IN ARMS			
Johnny One-Note	A	Up	Story, Aud
The Lady Is a Tramp	A	Med	Club, Char, Lyr
My Funny Valentine	M	Slow	Club, Chm
Way Out West . . .	A	Up	Pre, Movmt, Lyr
BALLROOM			
Fifty Percent	A	Med	Dr, Strong, Mid
Somebody Did All Right . . .	A	Med	Char, Mid, Pre
A Terrific Band . . .	A	Med	Semi Dr, Act, Mid
BARNUM			
Thank God I'm Old	A	Up	Old, Erg, Pre
There Is a Sucker Born . . .	Br	Up	Pre, Erg, Movmt
BELLS ARE RINGING			
I Met a Girl	T	Up	Movmt, V, Romant
I'm Going Back	A	Med	Club, Pre, Movmt
Is It a Crime?	A	Med	Story, Char, Com
It's a Perfect Relationship	A	Med	Com, Prob, Pre
The Party's Over	A	Slow	Aud, Chm, Lyr
BEST LITTLE WHOREHOUSE IN TEXAS, THE			
The Bus from Amarillo	A	Slow	Mid, Chm, Char
Doatsey Mae	A	Med	Char, Semi Dr
The Sidestep	Br	Med	Mid, Movmt, Com
BOYS FROM SYRACUSE, THE			
Oh, Diogenes	A	Up	Com, Movmt, Pre
BRIGADOON			
I'll Go Home with Bonnie . . .	T	Up	Aud, Romant, V
The Love of My Life	A	Med	Com, Story, Char
My Mother's Wedding Day	A	Up	Com, Lyr, Diction
Waitin' for My Dearie	S	Med	Aud, V, Romant
BYE BYE BIRDIE			
How Lovely to Be a Woman	M	Med	Chm, Char, Lyr
One Last Kiss	T	Up	Pre, Styl, 50's

SHOW AND SONG	VOCAL	TEMPO	TYPE/EMPHASIS
Put on a Happy Face	Br	Med	Movmt, Chm, Club
Spanish Rose	A	Med	Movmt, Pre, Strong
CABARET			
Cabaret	M	Med	Club, Pre, Movmt
What Would You Do?	A	Med	Dr, Strong, Mid
Why Should I Wake Up?	T	Slow	Romant, Aud, V
CALL ME MADAM			
The Best Thing for You . . .	A	Slow	Chm, Aud, Mid
Hostess with the Mostes'	A	Up	Pre, Mid, V, Erg
Marrying for Love	A	Slow	Aud, Mid, Chm
CAMELOT			
Camelot	Br	Med	Chm, Act, Char
C'est Moi	T	Med	V, Char, Aud
I Wonder What the King . . .	Br	Med	Char, Lyr, Act
Seven Deadly Virtues	Br	Up	Char, Movmt, Pre
Where Are the Simple Joys . . .	?S	Med	Lyr, Com, Chm
CANDIDE			
Glitter and Be Gay	S	Med	Aud, Com, Styl
I Am Easily Assimilated	A	Med	Com, Char, Mid
CARNIVAL			
Everybody Likes You	Br	Med	Char, Act
Her Face	Br	Med	Dr, Romant, Act
I Hate Him	S	Med	Dr, Strong, V
Mira	M	Med	Chm, Story, Char
She's My Love	Br	Slow	Dr, V, Pre
CAROUSEL			
Geraniums in the Window	T	Med	Chrm, Char, V
Soliloquy	Br	Med	Dr, Act, V, Char
What's the Use of Wond'rin'	S	Med	Semi Dr, Lyr
When I Marry Mr. Snow	M	Med	Story, Chm
CELEBRATION			
Somebody	M	Up	Aud, Movmt, Pre
CHARLIE AND ALGERNON			
Charlie	T	Med	Dr, Aud, V
Charlie and Algernon	T	Up	Com, Erg, Styl
Hey, Look at Me!	T	Up	Aud, Pre, V
The Maze	T	Med	Semi Dr, Act
CHICAGO			
All That Jazz	A	Med	Club, Movmt, Pre
Mister Cellophane	Br	Med	Chr, Styl, Char
Razzle Dazzle	Br	Med	Club, Pre, Styl

SHOW AND SONG	VOCAL	TEMPO	TYPE/EMPHASIS
Roxie	M	Med	Story, Movmt, Pre
When You're Good to Mama	A	Med	Pre, Mid, Char
CHORUS LINE, A			
Dance: 10; Looks: 3	M	Up	Pre, Lyr, Char
I Can Do That	Br	Up	Movt, Dance, Erg
Nothing	A	Med	Story, Pre, Char
COMPANY			
Being Alive	T	Med	Aud, Club, V
The Ladies Who Lunch	A	Slow	Mid, Char, Act
CURLEY MCDIMPLE			
The Meanest Man in Town	M	Slow	Pre, Styl, Com
DAMES AT SEA			
Wall Street	A	Up	Movmt, Styl, Pre
DAMN YANKEES			
A Little Brains, a Little . . .	M	Med	Char, Movmt, Pre
Those Were the Good Old . . .	Br	Med	Styl, Pre, Aud
A DAY IN HOLLYWOOD/A NIGHT IN THE UKRAINE			
The Best in the World	M	Med	Club, Pre
Nelson	S	Med	Styl, Pre, Com
DO I HEAR A WALTZ?			
Bargaining	T	Med	Aud, Char, Act
Someone Woke Up	M	Up	Pre, Romant
DO RE MI			
All of My Life	Br	Med	Dr, Act, Strong
I Know about Love	T	Med	V, Aud, Strong
The Late, Late Show	Br	Med	Char, Com, Aud
EVITA			
Another Suitcase in . . .	S	Slow	Chm, Char
FADE OUT-FADE IN			
I'm at the Dangerous Age	Br	Med	Mid, Aud, Char
The Usher from the . . .	A	Up	Pre, Erg, Char
FANNY			
Fanny	T	Slow	Romant, Aud, V
Panisse and Son	T	Up	Mid, Erg, Story
FANTASTICKS, THE			
Much More	S	Med	Pre, Aud, Char
Try to Remember	Br	Slow	Club, Chm
FIDDLER ON THE ROOF			
Far from the Home I Love	S	Slow	Dr, Chm, Act

SHOW AND SONG	VOCAL	TEMPO	TYPE/EMPHASIS
If I Were a Rich Man	Br	Med	Story, Mid, Pre
Miracle of Miracles	Br	Up	Aud, Movmt, Act
Tevye's Monologue	Br	Med	Act, Char, Mid
FINIAN'S RAINBOW			
How Are Things in Glocca Mora?	S	Slow	Aud, Romant
When I'm Not Near . . .	Br	Up	Com, Movmt, Chm
FIORELLO!			
I Love a Cop	A	Med	Prob, Char, Story
Marie's Law	M	Med	Char, Strong
The Very Next Man	M	Med	Lyr, Strong, Pre
When Did I Fall in Love?	S	Slow	V, Romant, Aud
FLOWER DRUM SONG			
Like a God	T	Med	Aud, V, Strong
Love Look Away	S	Slow	Aud, V, Semi Dr
FOLLIES			
Broadway Baby	A	Slow	Pre, Styl, Old
Could I Leave You?	A	Med	Dr, Anger, Mid
I'm Still Here	A	Slow	Story, Mid, Lyr
The Right Girl	T	Med	Mid, Dr, Act
The Road You Didn't Take	Br	Med	Mid, Dr, Act
FUNNY GIRL			
Don't Rain on My Parade	M	Med	Dr, Strong, Anger
I'm the Greatest Star	M	Up	Com, Erg, Aud
Who Are You Now?	M	Slow	Semi Dr, Club
FUNNY THING HAPPENED ON THE WAY TO THE FORUM, A			
I'm Calm	T	Med	Char, Aud, Act
GEORGE M!			
Give My Regards to Broadway	Br	Up	Pre, Styl, Movmt
GIRL CRAZY			
But Not for Me	A	Slow	Chm, Club, Romant
GODSPELL			
Turn Back O Man	A	Slow	Club, Movmt, Pre
GOLDEN APPLE, THE			
Lazy Afternoon	M	Slow	Styl, Mood, Club
GREASE			
There Are Worse Things . . .	A	Slow	Dr, Act, Lyr
GUYS AND DOLLS			
Adelaide's Lament	A	Med	Story, Pre, Com

SHOW AND SONG	VOCAL	TEMPO	TYPE/EMPHASIS
If I Were a Bell	S	Med	Aud, Movmt, Com
More I Cannot Wish You	T	Slow	Chm, V, Aud
GYPSY			
All I Need Is the Girl	B	Med	Dance, Aud
Everything's Coming Up Roses	A	Up	Dr, Act, Club
Rose's Turn	A	Med	Dr, Act, Pre
Small World	A	Slow	Aud, Chm
Some People	A	Med	Club, Act, Char
HAIR			
Easy to Be Hard	A	Slow	Rock, Club, Dr
Frank Mills	M	Slow	Chm, Char, Lyr
HALLELUJAH, BABY!			
Being Good Isn't Good . . .	S	Slow	Strong, Aud
I Don't Know Where She . . .	A	Up	Char, Styl, Pre
I Wanted to Change Him	S	Med	Semi Dr, V, Club
Now's the Time	S	Up	Movmt, V, Erg
HAPPY TIME, THE			
Happy Time, The	Br	Up	Chm, Romant, V
Life of the Party, The	T	Up	Pre, Styl, Movmt
Please Stay	T	Slow	Act, Char, Chm
HELLO, DOLLY!			
Before the Parade . . .	A	Med	Semi Dr, Club
So Long Dearie	A	Up	Styl, Pre, Movmt
HIGH SPIRITS			
Home Sweet Heaven	M	Med	Lyr, Pre, Char
Talking to You	A	Med	Char, Com
I DO! I DO!			
The Father of the Bride	Br	Med	Mid, Semi Dr
Flaming Agnes	M	Up	Movmt, Com, Anger
What Is a Woman?	M	Slow	Mid, Semi Dr
I LOVE MY WIFE			
Love Revolution	M	Med	Movmt, Pre
I'M GETTING MY ACT TOGETHER AND TAKING IT ON THE ROAD			
Dear Tom	M	Slow	Aud, Dr, Com, Act
Old Friend	M	Slow	Chm, Club
Smile	M	Med	Story, Act
IRENE			
I'm Always Chasing Rainbows	M	Slow	Club, Chm, Aud
They Go Wild over Me	Br	Med	Char, Com, Movmt
JESUS CHRIST SUPERSTAR			
I Don't Know How to Love Him	M	Slow	Act, Char

SHOW AND SONG	VOCAL	TEMPO	TYPE/EMPHASIS
King Herod's Song	T	Up	Pre, Styl, Movmt
Pilate's Dream	Br	Slow	Semi Dr, Act
KING AND I, THE			
Hello, Young Lovers	M	Slow	Chm, Romant, Mood
I Whistle a Happy Tune	M	Up	Pre, Movmt
A Puzzlement	Br	Med	Semi Dr, Prob, Mid
Shall I Tell You . . . ?	M	Med	Act, Pre, Anger
Something Wonderful	S	Slow	Romant, V, Aud
KISMET			
And This Is My Beloved	S	Slow	Aud, Romant, V
Gesticulate	Br	Med	Aud, Mid, V
KISS ME KATE			
Always True to You . . .	M	Up	Char, Story
I Hate Men	S	Med	Lyr, V, Act
Where Is the Life That . . . ?	Br	Med	V, Act, Aud
L'IL ABNER			
Progress Is the Root . . .	Br	Med	Styl, Mid, Movmt
LITTLE ME			
I've Got Your Number	Br	Med	Dance, Pre
The Other Side of the . . .	M	Up	Aud, V, Pre
Real Live Girl	Br	Med	Char, Com, Romant
LITTLE NIGHT MUSIC, A			
Liaisons	A	Slow	Char, Lyr
The Miller's Son	M	Med	Story, Char
Send in the Clowns	A	Slow	Semi Dr, Act, Lyr
LITTLE SHOP OF HORRORS			
Dentist	Br	Med	Char, Com, Pre
Somewhere That's Green	M	Slow	Char, Com, Chm
MACK AND MABEL			
I Won't Send Roses	Br	Slow	Char, Semi Dr
Look What Happened to Mabel	M	Up	Story, Pre, Char
Movies Were Movies	Br	Up	Aud, Story, Erg
Time Heals Everything	M	Slow	Semi Dr, Club, V
Wherever He Ain't	M	Up	Anger, Dr
MAME			
Gooch's Song	M	Med	Story, Com, Char
If He Walked into My Life	A	Med	Mid, Club, Dr
MAN OF LA MANCHA			
Aldonza	A	Med	Dr, Act, Char
Dulcinea	Br	Slow	Old, Mood, Romant

SHOW AND SONG	VOCAL	TEMPO	TYPE/EMPHASIS
I Like Him	T	Med	Char, Com, Chm
It's All the Same	A	Med	Bitt, Semi Dr
MAN WITH A LOAD OF MISCHIEF			
Little Rag Doll	M	Slow	Chm, Act
Make Way for My Lady	T	Med	V, Aud, Pre
Man with a Load of Mischief	S	Med	Lyr, Chm, Story
Once You've Had a Little . . .	M	Up	Char, Erg, Movmt
ME NOBODY KNOWS, THE			
If I Had a Million Dollars	Any	Med	Aud, Lyr
The Tree	Br	Slow	Story, Lyr
MERRILY WE ROLL ALONG			
Not a Day Goes By	T	Slow	V, Mood, Romant
MUSIC MAN, THE			
My White Knight	S	Slow	Romant, Act
MY FAIR LADY			
Just You Wait	M	Med	Anger, Story, Lyr
I've Grown Accustomed . . .	Br	Slow	Act, Story, Chm
On the Street Where You Live	T	Med	Movmt, Aud, Romant
NO, NO, NANETTE			
I Want to Be Happy	T	Up	Old, Movmt, Pre
NO STRINGS			
Loads of Love	M	Up	Movmt, Club
Nobody Told Me	Br	Slow	Aud, V, Romant
An Orthodox Fool	S	Med	Semi Dr, Aud, V
OF THEE I SING			
Who Cares?	Any	Up	Club, Movmt
OKLAHOMA!			
I Caint't Say No	A	Up	Char, Story, Prob
Kansas City	Br	Up	Movmt, Pre, Story
Lonely Room	Br	Med	Dr, Char, Strong
OLIVER!			
As Long As He Needs Me	A	Slow	Act, Semi Dr
Reviewing the Situation	Br	Med	Com, Char, Mid
ON A CLEAR DAY YOU CAN SEE FOREVER			
Come Back to Me	Br	Up	Romant, V, Strong
Hurry! It's Lovely up Here	M	Up	Chm, Movmt
She Wasn't You	T	Slow	Aud, V, Strong
What Did I Have . . . ?	M	Slow	Club, Semi Dr, Act
ONCE UPON A MATTRESS			
Happily Ever After	A	Med	Story, Com, Prob

SHOW AND SONG	VOCAL	TEMPO	TYPE/EMPHASIS
Sensitivity	A	Up	Char, Lyr, Rel
Very Soft Shoes	Br	Med	Chm, Dance, Styl
110 IN THE SHADE			
Love, Don't Turn Away	M	Slow	V, Act, Dr
Melisande	Br	Med	Act, Story, Char
Old Maid	M	Med	Act, V, Dr, Aud
Raunchy	M	Up	Com, V, Movmt
ONE TOUCH OF VENUS			
Speak Low	M	Slow	Club, Romant
That's Him	M	Slow	Com, Chm, Aud
ON THE TOWN			
I Can Cook Too	A	Up	Movmt, Char, Com
ON THE TWENTIETH CENTURY			
Never	S	Med	Anger, Com, V
Repent	M	Med	Char, Lt Com, Old
OVER HERE!			
Don't Shoot the Hooey . . .	Br	Med	Movmt, Styl, Bitt
Where Did the Good Times Go?	A	Slow	Club, Semi Dr
PACIFIC OVERTURES			
A Bowler Hat	Br	Slow	Char, Styl, Act
PAINT YOUR WAGON			
I Talk to the Trees	T	Slow	Romant, V, Aud
I Still See Elisa	Br	Slow	Chm, Romant, Mid
What's Goin on Here?	A	Up	Com, Prob, Story
PAL JOEY			
Bewitched, Bothered and . . .	M	Med	Club, Mid, Char
That Terrific Rainbow	A	Up	Club, Pre, Movmt
PIPE DREAM			
All at Once	Br	Slow	Romant, Mood
Everybody's Got a Home . . .	A	Slow	Char, Aud, Act
The Man I Used to Be	B	Up	Chm, Dance, Aud
PIPPIN			
Corner of the Sky	T	Med	Movmt, Char, Pre
I Guess I'll Miss the Man	M	Slow	Lyr, Act, Aud
No Time at All	A	Med	Old, Lyr, Char
PLAIN AND FANCY			
I'll Show Him!	S	Up	Char, Com, Anger
It's a Helluva Way . . .	A	Med	Char, Prob, Lyr

SHOW AND SONG	VOCAL	TEMPO	TYPE/EMPHASIS
It Wonders Me	S	Slow	Aud, V, Movmt
This Is All Very New . . .	S	Med	Aud, V, Movmt

PORGY AND BESS

I Got Plenty of Nothin'	Br	Up	V, Mood, Club
It Ain't Necessarily So	T	Med	Char, Movmt, Aud
Summertime	S	Slow	V, Aud, Mood
There's a Boat That's . . .	T	Med	Char, Movmt, Act

PROMISES, PROMISES

Knowing When to Leave	M	Med	Semi Dr, Strong
Promises, Promises	Br	Up	Semi Dr, Strong
She Likes Basketball	Br	Up	Movmt, Pre, Aud

PURLIE

I Got Love	M	Up	V, Aud, Mood
Purlie	M	Up	V, Aud, Mood

REDHEAD

Erbie Fitch's Twitch	M	Med	Pre, Styl, Story
I'm Back in Circulation	Br	Up	Strong, V, Aud
Merely Marvelous	M	Up	Movmt, Romant, Pre
The Right Finger of . . .	M	Slow	Chm, Mood, Act

ROAR OF THE GREASEPAINT, THE—THE SMELL OF THE CROWD

Feeling Good	T	Med	V, Aud, Act
The Joker	T	Med	V, Club, Semi Dr
Who Can I Turn To?	Br	Med	Semi Dr, Club, V

SECRET LIFE OF WALTER MITTY, THE

Aggie	Br	Slow	Mid, Chm, Semi Dr
Marriage Is for Old Folks	A	Med	Char, Movmt, Pre

SEESAW

He's Good for Me	A	Slow	Club, Semi Dr
I'm Way Ahead	M	Up	Act, V, Strong
It's Not Where You Start	Br	Up	Aud, V, Movmt
Nobody Does It Like Me	A	Med	Prob, Char

1776

Is Anybody There?	T	Slow	Semi Dr, Char
Molasses to Rum	Br	Med	Dr, Strong, Act
Piddle, Twiddle . . .	T	Med	Char, Anger, Lyr

SHE LOVES ME

Ice Cream	S	Up	V, Aud, Mood
I Resolve	A	Med	Char, Com, Strong

SHOW AND SONG	VOCAL	TEMPO	TYPE/EMPHASIS
I Resolve	A	Med	Char, Com, Strong
She Loves Me	Br	Up	Char, Movmt, Aud
A Trip to the Library	A	Med	Com, Story, Char

SHENANDOAH

I've Heard It All Before	Br	Med	Act, Strong, Char
Meditations, I and II	Br	Slow	Story, Dr, Act
The Pickers Are Coming	Br	Slow	Chm, Mood, Act

SHOW BOAT

Bill	M	Slow	Club, Chm, Lyr
Can't Help Lovin' That Man	M	Slow	Club, Semi Dr
Ol' Man River	Bs	Slow	V, Act, Char

SOMETHING'S AFOOT

I Owe It All	M	Med	Lyr, Char

SOUND OF MUSIC, THE (FILM)

I Have Confidence	M	Up	Aud, Movmt, Strong

SOUTH PACIFIC

A Cockeyed Optimist	M	Up	Movmt, Char, Pre
I'm in Love with a . . .	M	Up	Movmt, Char, Pre

STOP THE WORLD—I WANT TO GET OFF

Once in a Lifetime	Br	Med	Dr, Club, V, Act
Typically English	M	Med	Char, Com, Act
What Kind of Fool Am I?	Br	Slow	Mid, Semi Dr, V

STREET SCENE

A Boy Like You	S	Slow	Lyr, Mood, V
Lonely House	T	Slow	Mood, Semi Dr, Act
What Good Would the Moon Be	S	Med	Char, Semi Dr
When a Woman Has a Baby	T	Med	Prob, Chm, Char
Wouldn't You Like to . . .	Br	Up	Movmt, Pre, Rel

STREETS OF NEW YORK, THE

He'll Come to Me . . .	M	Med	Char, Lyr, Pre

SUGAR

It's Always Love	T	Slow	Chm, Mood

SUGAR BABIES

I'm Just a Song and Dance Man	Br	Med	Movmt, Pre, Styl

SHOW AND SONG	*VOCAL*	*TEMPO*	*TYPE/EMPHASIS*
SWEENEY TODD			
Epiphany	Br	Med	Dr, Act, Char
SWEET CHARITY			
If My Friends Could See . . .	M	Up	Styl, Movmt
Charity's Soliloquy	A	Med	Semi Dr, Char
THEY'RE PLAYING OUR SONG			
I Still Believe in Love	M	Slow	Romant, Club
They're Playing Our Song	Br, M	Up	Erg, Pre, Movmt
THREEPENNY OPERA, THE			
Barbara Song	S	Med	Story, Lyr
Pirate Jenny	A	Med	Bitt, Dr, Story
TWO BY TWO			
The Covenant	Br	Med	Semi Dr, Strong
An Old Man	S	Slow	Semi Dr, Chm, Act
Something, Somewhere	T	Med	Aud, Semi Dr
UNSINKABLE MOLLY BROWN, THE			
Leadville Johnny . . .	T	Med	Dr, Act, V
VERY GOOD EDDIE			
Thirteen Collar	Br	Med	Com, Prob, Chm
WEST SIDE STORY			
Something's Coming	T	Up	Aud, V, Strong
WHERE'S CHARLEY?			
Once in Love with Amy	Br	Up	Dance, Chm
WHOOPEE			
Love Me, or Leave Me	A	Slow	Club, Prob
Makin' Whoopee	Br	Up	Char, Story
Yes, Sir, That's My Baby	Br	Up	Pre, Styl
WIZ, THE			
Don't Nobody Bring Me No Bad News	A	Med	Com, Char
WONDERFUL TOWN			
One Hundred Easy Ways	A	Med	Char, Com, Prob
WORKING			
Cleanin' Women	A	Med	Mid, Pre, Strong
It's an Art	M	Up	Char, Movmt, Pre
Joe	Br	Slow	Chm, Char, Old
Just a Housewife	M	Slow	Char, Act, Semi Dr

SHOW AND SONG	VOCAL	TEMPO	TYPE/EMPHASIS
Millwork	M	Med	Story, Act, Dr
Nobody Tells Me How	M	Med	Char, Act, Lyr
YOUR OWN THING			
I'm on My Way to the Top	T	Up	V, Aud, Mood
YOU'RE A GOOD MAN, CHARLIE BROWN			
Little Known Facts	A	Med	Char, Strong
Suppertime	T	Up	Styl, Pre, Dance
ZORBA			
Life Is	A	Med	Club, V
I Am Free	Br	Med	Strong, Movmt
No Boom Boom	M	Med	Mid, Chm, Story

DUETS

SHOW AND SONG	VOCAL	TEMPO	TYPE/EMPHASIS
ALL IN LOVE			
A More Than Ordinary . . .	A,Bs	Med	Com, Char, Lyr
ALLEGRO			
A Fellow Needs a Girl	S,Br	Slow	Romant, Chm, Mid
AMOROUS FLEA, THE			
Lessons on Life	Br,S	Med	Com, Styl, Movmt
ANNIE			
I Don't Need Anything . . .	Br,M	Up	Chm, Rel, Dance
ANNIE GET YOUR GUN			
They Say It's Wonderful	A,Br	Slow	Romant, Chm
ANYONE CAN WHISTLE			
Come Play Wiz Me	M,Br	Med	Movmt, Mood
With So Little to Be . . .	M,Br	Slow	Semi Dr, Chm
ANYTHING GOES			
It's Delovely	S,Br	Med	Movmt, Romant
You're the Top	A,Br	Med	Rel, Styl, Lyr
BABES IN ARMS			
I Wish I Were in Love . . .	A,T	Med	Movmt, Rel
BABY			
What Could Be Better?	T,M	Med	Char, Rel
BELLS ARE RINGING			
Just in Time	Br,A	Med	Styl, Dance, Chm

SHOW AND SONG	VOCAL	TEMPO	TYPE/EMPHASIS
Mu Cha Cha	A,Br	Up	Dance, Pre
BOY FRIEND, THE			
Never Too Late	Br,M	Med	Styl, Char, Com
A Room in Bloomsbury	T,S	Med	Movmt, Chm
Won't You Charleston . . .	M,Br	Up	Pre, Rel, Dance
BOYS FROM SYRACUSE, THE			
This Can't Be Love	S,Br	Med	Romant, Mood
BRIGADOON			
Almost Like Being in Love	Br,S	Slow	Romant, Rel
Heather on the Hill	Br,S	Med	Romant, Movmt
BYE BYE BIRDIE			
Kids	T,M	Up	Com, Lyr
CABARET			
It Couldn't Please Me More	A,T	Med	Mid, Chm, Char
CALL ME MADAM			
It's a Lovely Day Today	T,S	Up	Chm, Movmt
CAMELOT			
What Do the Simple Folk Do?	Br,S	Med	Semi Dr, Rel
CANDIDE			
You Were Dead You Know	T,S	Med	Styl, Com, V
CARMEN JONES			
Finale	S,T	Med	Dr, V, Act
CARNIVAL			
Humming	A,Br	Med	Com, Char, Mid
CAROUSEL			
If I Loved You	S,T	Slow	Char, Rel, Act
When the Children Are . . .	M,T	Slow	Chm, Mood, Romant
You'll Never Walk Alone	2S	Slow	Dr, V, Strong
You're a Queer One/Snow	S,M	Med	Char, Story
CHARLIE AND ALGERNON			
I Really Loved You	T,S	Slow	Romant, Semi Dr
Whatever Time There Is	T,S	Slow	Chm, Semi Dr
CHICAGO			
Class	2A	Slow	Com, Lyr
DAMES AT SEA			
Choo Choo Honeymoon	M,Br	Up	Styl, Pre, Dance
It's You	T,M	Med	Movmt, Pre, Styl
DO RE MI			
Adventure	A,Br	Up	Rel, Mid, Story

SHOW AND SONG	VOCAL	TEMPO	TYPE/EMPHASIS
Ambition	S,Br	Up	Erg, Rel, 1 Mid
Take a Job	A,Br	Med	Char, Prob, Mid
EVITA			
I'd Be Surprisingly . . .	M,Br	Med	Rel, Act
A New Argentina	M,Br	Med	Rel, Act, Strong
Waltz for Che and Eva	T,M	Med	Semi Dr, Movmt
FADE OUT-FADE IN			
You Mustn't Be Discouraged	A,Br	Med	Styl, Pre, Dance
FANTASTICKS, THE			
Plant a Radish	2Br	Med	Styl, Mid, Movmt
Soon It's Gonna Rain	T,S	Slow	Romant, Story
FIDDLER ON THE ROOF			
Do You Love Me?	A,Br	Med	Com, Chm, Mid
Now I Have Everything	T,M	Med	Rel, Char, Act
FINIAN'S RAINBOW			
Old Devil Moon	T,S	Med	Chm, Romant
Something Sort of Grandish	Br,S	Up	Char, Movmt
FLOWER DRUM SONG			
The Other Generation	A,Br	Med	Mid, Rel, Char
FUNNY GIRL			
Who Taught Her Everything . . . ?	A,T	Med	Dance, Char, Styl
FUNNY THING HAPPENED ON THE WAY TO THE FORUM, A			
Free	Br,T	Med	Pre, Rel, Char
Impossible	Br,T	Med	Rel, Com, Pre
GEORGE M!			
You're a Grand Old Flag	A,T	Up	
GIRL CRAZY			
Treat Me Rough	A,Br	Up	Com, Char, Rel
GODSPELL			
All for the Best	2T	Up	Styl, Pre, Dance
GOLDEN APPLE, THE			
It's the Going Home . . .	S,Br	Med	Romant, Mood
Scylla and Charybdis	T,Bs	Up	Styl, Pre
GUYS AND DOLLS			
Guys and Dolls	T,Br	Up	Char, Pre, Com
I'll Know	S,T	Slow	Romant, Strong

SHOW AND SONG	VOCAL	TEMPO	TYPE/EMPHASIS
Marry the Man Today	A,S	Med	Com, Movmt, Char
Sue Me	A,Br	Med	Com, Char, Rel
GYPSY			
If Mama Was Married	A,M	Med	Rel, Movmt, Prob
HAPPY TIME, THE			
Seeing Things	S,T	Med	Semi Dr, V, Rel
HELLO, DOLLY!			
Put on Your Sunday Clothes	T,Br	Med	Char, Styl, Rel
HIGH BUTTON SHOES			
I Still Get Jealous	S,Br	Med	Mid, Chm, Romant
Papa Won't You Dance . . . ?	S,Br	Up	Mid, Chm, Dance
HOW TO SUCCEED IN BUSINESS WITHOUT REALLY TRYING			
The Company Way	2Br	Med	Char, Rel, 1 Old
Grand Old Ivy	2Br	Med	1 Old, Pre, Rel
I DO! I DO!			
Good Night	M,Br	Med	Char, Act
The Honeymoon Is Over	M,Br	Up	Anger, Semi Dr
Nobody's Perfect	M,Br	Up	Anger, Drama
I LOVE MY WIFE			
Everybody Today Is . . .	2Br	Med	Styl, Pre, Lyr
Lovers on Christmas Eve	A,Br	Med	Com, Romant, Movmt
KING AND I, THE			
Shall We Dance	S,Br	Med	Chm, Dance, Rel
KISS ME, KATE			
Brush up Your Shakespeare	2Br	Med	Styl, Pre, Lyr
LITTLE MARY SUNSHINE			
Colorado Love Call	Br,S	Slow	Styl, Romant, Com
Do You Ever Dream of . . . ?	S,Br	Slow	Styl, Mid, Chm
Once in a Blue Moon	A,T	Med	Styl, Chm, Romant
LITTLE ME			
Be a Performer	2Br	Up	Styl, Char, Movmt
LITTLE NIGHT MUSIC, A			
Every Day a Little . . .	A,S	Med	Semi Dr, Act
LITTLE SHOP OF HORRORS			
Mushnik and Son	T,Br	Up	Char, Rel
MAME			
Bosom Buddies	2A	Med	Mid, Char, Rel
MOST HAPPY FELLA, THE			
Don't Cry	S,T	Med	Dr, Rel, Act

SHOW AND SONG	VOCAL	TEMPO	TYPE/EMPHASIS
Big D	A,T	Up	Rel, Dance, Erg
I Don't Like This Dame	A,S	Med	Lyr, Pre, Rel
Recitative	A,S	Med	Char, Rel, Com
MUSIC MAN, THE			
Piano Lesson/If You . . .	S,A	Med	Lyr, Act, 1 Mid
MY FAIR LADY			
Without You	S,Br	Med	Anger, Semi Dr, Rel
NO, NO, NANETTE			
I've Confessed to the . . .	T,S	Med	Romant, Movmt
Tea for Two	T,S	Med	Dance, Rel, Romant
You Can Dance with . . .	Br,M	Up	Styl, Dance
NO STRINGS			
Love Makes the World . . .	2A	Med	Pre, Movmt
OF THEE I SING			
Who Cares?	Br,S	Med	Romant, Movmt
OKLAHOMA!			
All 'Er Nothin'	M,T	Up	Com, Char
Pore Jud is Daid	2Br	Med	Com, Rel, Story
People Will Say We're . . .	S,Br	Med	Romant, Rel
OLIVER!			
I Shall Scream	A,T	Med	Mid, Com, Char
ON A CLEAR DAY YOU CAN SEE FOREVER			
Wait Till We're Sixty-Five	M,Br	Med	Dance, Pre, Styl
ONCE UPON A MATTRESS			
Man-to-Man Talk	Br,NE	Med	Char, Movmt, 1 Mid
ON THE TOWN			
Carried Away	Br,M	Med	Com, Lyr, Char
110 IN THE SHADE			
You're Not Foolin' Me . . .	S,Br	Med	Dr, Anger, Rel
OVER HERE!			
Over Here!	M	Up	V, Movmt, Styl
PAJAMA GAME, THE			
I'll Never Be Jealous . . .	A,Br	Med	1 Mid, Char, Story
Small Talk	A,Br	Med	Romant, Pre

SHOW AND SONG	VOCAL	TEMPO	TYPE/EMPHASIS
PAL JOEY			
I Could Write a Book	S,Br	Slow	Romant, Mood, Chm
Take Him	2S	Med	Lyr, Char, Rel
PIPE DREAM			
The Next Time It Happens	Br,M	Med	Semi Dr, Act
PIPPIN			
On the Right Track	2T	Med	Dance, Pre
PORGY AND BESS			
Bess, You Is My Woman Now	Br,S	Med	V, Semi Dr
PROMISES, PROMISES			
You'll Think of Someone	Br,M	Med	Chm, Rel
PURLIE			
Down Home	A,Br	Slow	Char, Mood, Act
The Harder They Fall	S,Br	Up	Movmt, Erg
ROAR OF THE GREASEPAINT—THE SMELL OF THE CROWD, THE			
My First Love Song	T,M	Slow	Romant
RUNAWAYS			
Where Are Those People . . . ?	Br,A	Up	Lyr, Movmt
SEESAW			
Welcome to Holiday Inn	M,Br	Med	Rel
1776			
Till Then	Br,S	Med	Romant, Act
SHE LOVES ME			
I Don't Know His Name	S,A	Med	V, Char, Lyr
SHOW BOAT			
Goodbye, My Lady Love	A,T	Up	Pre, Styl
Only Make Believe	S,T	Med	Romant, Chm
SOUND OF MUSIC, THE			
An Ordinary Couple	M,Br	Med	1 Mid, Chm, Romant
How Can Love Survive?	A,Br	Med	Mid, Com, Lyr
You Are Sixteen[reprise]	S,M	Med	Rel, Semi Dr
SUGAR BABIES			
On the Sunny Side of the Street	M,Br	Up	Rel, Styl, Pre
SWEENEY TODD			
Kiss Me	S,T	Med	Com, V, Styl
A Little Priest	Br,A	Med	Com, Rel, Lyr

SHOW AND SONG	VOCAL	TEMPO	TYPE/EMPHASIS
SWEET CHARITY			
Baby, Dream Your Dream	A,A	Slow	Chm, Char, Mood
I'm the Bravest Individual	A,Br	Up	Com, Char, Rel
THREEPENNY OPERA, THE			
The Army Song	Br,T	Med	Strong, Rel
Jealousy Duet	S,A	Med	Anger, Com, Lyr
TWO BY TWO			
As Far As I'm Concerned	A,Br	Med	Char, Rel, Com
WEST SIDE STORY			
A Boy Like That/I Have a Love	A,S	Med	Dr, Rel, V, Act
One Hand, One Heart	S,T	Slow	Romant, Act
WHERE'S CHARLEY?			
Make a Miracle	Br,S	Med	Lyr, Styl, Pre
WONDERFUL TOWN			
Ohio	A,S	Slow	Com, V, Prob
YOU'RE A GOOD MAN, CHARLIE BROWN			
The Doctor Is In	A,Br	Slow	Rel, Char, Com
YOUR OWN THING			
Be Gentle	M,Br	Slow	Act, Char, Chm
ZORBA			
Goodbye, Canavaro	M,Br	Med	Char, Chm, Mid
Why Can't I Speak?	S,NE	Slow	Act, Movmt

TRIOS/QUARTETS

SHOW AND SONG	VOCAL	TEMPO	TYPE/EMPHASIS
ANNIE			
Easy Street	A,S,T	Up	Movmt, Char, Rel
ANNIE GET YOUR GUN			
There's No Business . . .	A,2Br,T	Up	Pre, Lyr, Erg
BABY			
I Want It All	3M	Up	Rel, Char, Pre
CHORUS LINE, A			
At The Ballet	S,M,A	Med	Char, Act, Movmt
COMPANY			
Getting Married Today	S,M,T	Up	Lyr, Erg, Pre
You Could Drive . . .	S,M,M	Up	Char, V, Styl

SHOW AND SONG	VOCAL	TEMPO	TYPE/EMPHASIS
DAMN YANKEES			
Heart	Br,Bs,2T	Med	V, Char, Pre
DO RE MI			
All You Need Is . . .	A,M,S	Up	Com, Movmt, Pre
FUNNY GIRL			
Find Yourself a Man	S,A,T	Med	Char, Com, Rel
FUNNY THING HAPPENED ON THE WAY TO THE FORUM, A			
Everybody Ought To . . .	3Br,T	Med	Com, Styl, Pre
GEORGE M!			
All Aboard for . . .	S,A,T,Br	Up	Pre, Styl, Movmt
GIRL CRAZY			
Bidin' My Time	T,Bs,2Br	Slow	V, Movmt, Pre
GUYS AND DOLLS			
Fugue for Tinhorns	Br,Bs,T	Med	V, Char, Pre
GYPSY			
You Gotta Get a Gimmick	A,M,S	Med	Char, Com, Styl
HALLELUJAH, BABY!			
Another Day	S,A,Br,T	Up	Movmt, Pre, Erg
HELLO, DOLLY!			
Elegance	S,M,Br,T	Med	Styl, Pre, Rel
HIGH SPIRITS			
What in the World . . . ?	S,A,Br	Med	Lyr, Anger, Rel
HOW TO SUCCEED IN BUSINESS WITHOUT REALLY TRYING			
Been A Long Day	S,A,Br	Med	Char, Pre, Rel
KISMET			
And This Is My . . .	S,T,2Br	Slow	Romant, V
KISS ME, KATE			
We Open in Venice	S,A,Br,T	Up	Movmt, Pre
Too Darn Hot	T,2Br	Med	Dance, Pre, Styl
MAME			
We Need a Little . . .	A,2S,T	Up	Pre, Erg, Rel
MOST HAPPY FELLA, THE			
Abbondanza	2T,Br	Up	Char, Com, V
Happy to Make Your . . .	S,A,T	Med	Chm, Rel
Standing on the . . .	T,2Br,Bs	Med	V, Movmt, Rel
MY FAIR LADY			
With a Little Bit . . .	T,2Br	Up	Pre, Movmt
Wouldn't It Be Loverly	S,T,2Br	Med	Chm, Mood, Movmt

SHOW AND SONG	VOCAL	TEMPO	TYPE/EMPHASIS
110 IN THE SHADE			
Poker Polka	4Br	Up	Com, Dance, Pre
ON THE TWENTIETH CENTURY			
I Rise Again	T,2Br	Slow	Pre, Styl
Never	S,2Br	Med	Com, Styl
OVER HERE!			
The Big Beat	A,S,M	Up	Styl, Pre, V
PAJAMA GAME, THE			
Steam Heat	A,2Br	Med	Dance, Styl
PLAIN AND FANCY			
Take Your Time . . .	A,S,Br	Med	Pre, Rel
REDHEAD			
Behave Yourself	2A,M	Med	2 Old, Char
Just for Once	M,T,Br	Med	Char, Rel
1776			
The Egg	2Br,T	Med	Char, Pre, Styl
SOMETHINGS'S AFOOT			
Carry On	A,S,2M	Up	Com, Char, Pre
SOUND OF MUSIC, THE			
Maria	2S,A,M	Med	Char, Rel
SWEET CHARITY			
There's Gotta Be . . .	2A, M	Up	Pre, Story, Erg
TWO BY TWO			
Put Him Away	M,2Br	Med	Char, Rel
You Have Got to . . .	2Br, 2T	Med	Char, Rel
WEST SIDE STORY			
I Feel Pretty	S,A,M	Up	Movmt, V
WONDERFUL TOWN			
What a Waste	2Br,A	Med	V, Story, Char

CHORUS

SHOW AND SONG	VOCAL	TEMPO	TYPE/EMPHASIS
ALLEGRO			
Money Isn't Everything	F	Up	Char, Lyr

SHOW AND SONG	VOCAL	TEMPO	TYPE/EMPHASIS
ANNIE			
We'd Like to Thank . . .	Mix	Med	Char, Lyr
ANNIE GET YOUR GUN			
Buffalo Bill	Mix	Up	Pre, Erg
APPLAUSE			
Applause	Mix	Up	Dance, Pre, Erg
BABY			
The Ladies Singing . . .	F	Med	Char, Pre, Act
BARNUM			
Come Follow the Band	Mix	Up	Pre, Erg
BEST LITTLE WHOREHOUSE IN TEXAS, THE			
Hard Candy Christmas	F	Low	Char, Semi Dr
BOY FRIEND, THE			
The Boy Friend	F	Up	Dance, Pre, Styl
Perfect Young Ladies	F	Up	Movmt, Char
CHICAGO			
Cell Block Tango	F	Med	Char, Act, Pre
DAMES AT SEA			
Good Times Are . . .	Mix	Up	Erg, Pre, Styl
Singapore Sue	Mix	Med	Story, Com, Styl
DAMN YANKEES			
The Game	M	Up	Com, Char, Pre
DAY IN HOLLYWOOD/A NIGHT IN THE UKRAINE, A			
Just Go to the Movies	Mix	Up	Styl, Pre, Erg
DO I HEAR A WALTZ?			
What Do We Do? We Fly	Mix	Up	Com, Lyr, Char
FIDDLER ON THE ROOF			
The Tailor Motel . . .	Mix	Med	Com, Char, Story
FIORELLO!			
Unfair	F,1Br	Up	Anger, Pre, Prob
FOLLIES			
Waiting for the Girls . . .	Mix	Med	V, Act, Dr
FUNNY THING HAPPENED ON THE WAY TO THE FORUM, A			
Comedy Tonight	Mix	Up	Styl, Pre, Lyr
GEORGE M!			
Yankee Doodle Dandy	Mix	Up	Movmt, Styl

SHOW AND SONG	VOCAL	TEMPO	TYPE/EMPHASIS
GIRL CRAZY			
Strike up the Band	Mix	Up	Pre, Erg
GOLDEN APPLE, THE			
By a Goona-Goona Lagoon	Mix	Med	Com, Styl, Pre
GREASE			
Summer Nights	Mix	Up	Pre, Styl
We Go Together	Mix	Up	V, Styl, Pre
HOW TO SUCCEED IN BUSINESS WITHOUT REALLY TRYING			
Brotherhood of Man	M, 1S	Up	Char, Movmt, Pre
Coffee Break	Mix	Med	Com, Char, Pre
KISS ME KATE			
Another Op'nin' . . .	Mix	Up	Movmt, Pre
L'IL ABNER			
Jubilation T Cornpone	Mix	Up	Movmt, Erg
Put 'Em Back	F	Up	Movmt, Prob, Pre
Rag Offen the Bush	Mix	Up	Movmt, Pre, Erg
LITTLE MARY SUNSHINE			
Mata Hari	F	Med	Styl, Movmt
LITTLE NIGHT MUSIC, A			
A Weekend in the Country	Mix	Med	V, Lyr, Styl
LITTLE SHOP OF HORRORS			
Skid Row	Mix	Med	Styl, V, Lyr
MAME			
Open a New Window	Mix	Up	Movmt, Pre, Erg
MUSIC MAN, THE			
Pick-a-Little . . . /Good . . .	Mix	Med	Char, Lyr, V
Wells Fargo Wagon	Mix	Up	Erg, Pre
MY FAIR LADY			
Get Me to the Church . . .	Mix	Up	Movmt, Pre
ONCE UPON A MATTRESS			
Song of Love	Mix	Up	Com, Pre
PACIFIC OVERTURES			
Chrysanthemum Tea	Mix	Med	Lyr, Styl
Please, Hello	M	Med	V, Movmt, Com
PAJAMA GAME, THE			
I'm Not at All in Love	F	Up	Pre

SHOW AND SONG	VOCAL	TEMPO	TYPE/EMPHASIS
PIPPIN			
Magic to Do	Mix	Up	Pre, Styl
PLAIN AND FANCY			
City Mouse, Country Mouse	F	Up	Pre, Lyr
1776			
But, Mr. Adams	M	Med	Char, Story, Styl
SHOW BOAT			
Life upon the Wicked Stage	F	Up	Pre, Styl, Movmt
SOUTH PACIFIC			
There Is Nothing . . .	M	Up	Char, Lyr, Pre
SWEET CHARITY			
Big Spender	F	Med	Char, Styl, Movmt
Rhythm of Life	Mix	Med	V, Char, Movmt
WEST SIDE STORY			
Gee, Officer Krupke	M	Up	Lyr, Char, Story
WIZ, THE			
Ease on down the Road	Mix	Up	Movmt, Erg
WONDERFUL TOWN			
Conversation Piece	Mix	Med	V, Lyr, Rel
YOU'RE A GOOD MAN, CHARLIE BROWN			
The Baseball Game	Mix	Med	Char, Story

Appendix B

Musical Theatre Annual _____

This calendar of shows is designed to help the reader determine what productions included in the text were playing opposite each other. The first Pulitzer Prize for Drama to be awarded a musical was in 1931. *Carousel* was the first musical recognized by the New York Drama Critics Circle. The Antoinette Perry Awards (Tonys) to honor "distinguished achievement in the theatre" were first given at the end of the 1947 season. As a result of this, the following chart lists the shows produced prior to 1947 by year of opening while those entries after 1947 are listed by season.

Pulitzer Prizes are marked PUL, Drama Critics DC and Tonys TY with the categories abbreviated as follows: Best Actor—a; Featured Actor—fa; Best Actress—as; Featured Actress—fas; Direction—d; Musical Direction—md; Choreography—ch; Music—m; Lyrics—l; Score—sc; Producer—p; Best Musical—mus; Book—b; Sets—s; Costumes—c; Lighting—lt.

1915
  Very Good Eddie
1919
  Irene
1925
  No, No, Nanette
1927
  Show Boat
1930
  Girl Crazy

1931
  Of Thee I Sing—PUL
1934
  Anything Goes
1935
  Porgy and Bess
1937
  Babes in Arms
1938
  The Boys from Syracuse
1940
  Pal Joey
1943
  Oklahoma!—Special PUL
  Carmen Jones
1944
  On the Town
1945
  Carousel—DC
1946
  Annie Get Your Gun
1946–47 Season
  Street Scene
  Finian's Rainbow—TY:ch
  Brigadoon—DC, TY:ch
1947–48 Season
  High Button Shoes—TY:ch
  Allegro
1948–49 Season
  Where's Charley?—TY:a
  Kiss Me Kate—TY:mus,p,b,m,c
1949–50 Season
  South Pacific—PUL, DC, TY: a,as,fa,fas,d,mus,p,b,m
1950–51 Season
  Call Me Madam—TY: as,fa
  Guys and Dolls—DC, TY: a,fas,d,mus,p,b,m,ch
1951–52 Season
  The King and I—TY: as,fa,mus,c,s,p,m
  Paint Your Wagon
  Pal Joey (Revival)—DC, TY: fas,ch,md
1952–53 Season
  Wonderful Town—DC, TY: as,mus,p,b,m,s,ch,md
1953–54 Season

Kismet—TY: a,mus,p,b,m,md
The Golden Apple—DC

1954–55 Season
  The Pajama Game—TY: fas,mus,p,b,m,ch
  Fanny—TY: a
  The Boy Friend (Off-Broadway)
  Plain and Fancy

1955–56 Season
  Damn Yankees—TY: a,as,fa,mus,b,p,m,md,ch
  The Threepenny Opera (Off-Broadway)—TY: fas
  Pipe Dream—TY: c

1956–57 Season
  My Fair Lady—DC, TY: a,mus,b,p,m,md,s,c
  The Most Happy Fella—DC
  L'il Abner—TY: fas,ch
  Bells Are Ringing—TY: as,fa
  Candide

1957–58 Season
  West Side Story—TY: s,ch
  The Music Man—DC, TY: a,fa,fas,mus,b,p,m,md

1958–59 Season
  Flower Drum Song—TY: md
  Redhead—TY: a,as,mus,b,p,m,c,ch
  Once Upon a Mattress

1959–60 Season*
  Gypsy
  The Sound of Music—TY: as,fas,mus,b,p,m,md,s
  Little Mary Sunshine (Off-Broadway)
  Fiorello!—PUL, DC, TY: fa,mus,b,p,d,m

1960–61 Season
  Bye Bye Birdie—TY: fa,mus,b,p,d,ch
  The Fantasticks (Off-Broadway)
  The Unsinkable Molly Brown—TY: fas
  Camelot—TY: a,md,s,c
  Do-Re-Mi

1961–62 Season
  No Strings—TY: as,m,ch
  Carnival—DC, TY: as,s
  How To Succeed in Business without Really Trying—DC, TY: a,fa,mus,b,p,d,md

1962–63 Season
  Oliver!—TY: m,l,md,s
  Stop the World—I Want to Get Off—TY: fas

*Separate category for direction of a musical initiated.

A Funny Thing Happened On The Way To The Forum—TY: a,fa,m,b,p,d
Little Me—TY: ch

1963–64 Season
  She Loves Me—TY: fa
  110 in the Shade
  Streets of New York, The (Off-Broadway)
  Funny Girl
  Anyone Can Whistle
  High Spirits
  Fade Out—Fade In
  Hello, Dolly!—TY: as,mus,b,p,d,m,l,md,c,ch

1964–65 Season*
  Fiddler On The Roof—DC, TY: a,fas,mus,b,p,d,m,l,c,ch
  Do I Hear a Waltz?
  The Roar of the Greasepaint—The Smell of the Crowd

1965–66 Season
  Man of La Mancha—DC, TY: a,m,d,mus,l,s
  On a Clear Day You Can See Forever
  Sweet Charity—TY: ch
  Mame—TY: as,fas,fa

1966–67 Season
  The Apple Tree—TY: as
  The Man with a Load of Mischief (Off-Broadway)
  Cabaret—DC, TY: fa,fas,mus,d,m,l,s,c,ch
  I Do! I Do—TY: a
  You're a Good Man, Charlie Brown (Off-Broadway)
  Annie Get Your Gun (revival)

1967–68 Season
  The Happy Time—TY: a,d,ch
  Hallelujah, Baby!—TY: as,fas,mus,p,m,l
  Your Own Thing—DC

1968–69 Season
  Zorba—TY: s
  George M!—TY: ch
  Promises, Promises—TY: a,fas
  1776—DC, TY: fa,mus,d,b,m,l
  Hair

1969–70 Season
  Purlie—TY: a,fas
  Applause—TY: as,mus,d,ch

1970–71 Season†
  Godspell (Off-Broadway)

*Musical direction as a Tony category deleted.

†Lighting design initiated.

The Me Nobody Knows (Off-Broadway)
Company—DC, TY: mus,p,d,b,sc,s
No, No, Nanette (revival)—TY: as,fas,c,ch
Two by Two

1971–72 Season
  Grease
  Follies—DC, TY: as,d,sc,s,c,ch,lt
  Two Gentlemen of Verona—DC, TY: mus,b
  Jesus Christ Superstar
  On the Town (revival)
  A Funny Thing Happened on the Way to the Forum (Revival)—TY: a,fa

1972–73 Season
  A Little Night Music—DC, TY: as,fas,mus,b,sc,c
  Sugar
  Pippin—TY: a,d,s,ch,lt
  Irene (revival)—TY: fa

1973–74 Season
  Candide (revised version)—DC, TY: d,b,s,c
  Raisin—TY: as,mus
  Seesaw—TY, fa,ch
  Over Here!—TY: fas

1974–75 Season
  Gypsy (revival)—TY: as
  Mack and Mabel
  The Wiz—TY: fa,fas,mus,d,sc,c,ch,s
  Shenandoah—TY: a,b

1975–76 Season
  A Chorus Line—PUL, DC, TY: as,fa,fas,mus,d,b,m,lt,ch
  Pacific Overtures—DC, TY: s,c
  Chicago
  Very Good Eddie (revival)
  Something's Afoot
  My Fair Lady (revival)—TY: a

1976–77 Season*
  Annie—DC, TY: as,mus,b,sc,s,c,ch
  I Love My Wife—TY: fa,d
  Godspell (moved to Broadway)
  Porgy and Bess (revival)—TY: most innovative production of a revival
  The Robber Bridegroom—TY: a
  Guys and Dolls (revival)
  Threepenny Opera (revival)

1977–78 Season
  On the Twentieth Century—TY: a,fa,b,sc,s
  Runaways

*Revival category added.

Timbuktu!
Working
Whoopee (revival)

1978–79 Season
The Best Little Whorehouse in Texas—TY: fa,fas
Ballroom—TY: ch
They're Playing Our Song
Sweeney Todd—DC, TY: a,as,md,b,sc,s,c
The Most Happy Fella (revival)
I'm Getting My Act Together and Taking It on the Road (Off-Broadway)

1979–80 Season
Evita—TY: lt,d,b,sc,fa,mus,as
Sugar Babies
Barnum—TY: c,s,a
Oklahoma! (revival)
A Day in Hollywood/A Night in the Ukraine—TY: ch,fas

1980–81 Season
42nd Street (rights unavailable). TY: mus,ch
Charlie and Algernon

1981–82 Season
Merrily We Roll Along
Dreamgirls (rights unavailable)—TY: b,as,a,fa,lt,ch
Joseph and the Amazing Technicolor Dreamcoat
Nine (rights unavailable)—TY: mus,sc,fas,d,c

1982–83 Season
Little Shop of Horrors (Off-Broadway)—DC
My One and Only—TY: fa,a (rights unavailable)
Cats (rights unavailable)—TY: mus,sc,d,fas,b,c

1983–84 Season
Baby
Le Cage aux Folles (rights unavailable)—TY: mus,d,b,sc,c,a
Oliver! (revival)
Sunday in the Park with George (rights unavailable)—PUL, DC, TY: lt,s
The Tap Dance Kid (rights unavailable)—TY: fa,ch
The Rink (rights unavailable)—TY: as
Zorba—(revival)—TY: fas

1984–85 Season*
Big River (rights unavailable)—TY: sc,fa,d,mus,b,s,lt
Grind (rights unavailable)—TY: fas,c
Quilters (rights unavailable)
The King and I (revival)
Leader of the Pack (rights unavailable)

*No best actor, actress or choreography award given.

Appendix C

Chronology of Included Long-Running Musicals

BROADWAY

A Chorus Line (still running)
Grease—3,388
Fiddler on the Roof—3,242
Hello, Dolly!—2,844
My Fair Lady—2,717
Annie—2,377
Man of La Mancha—2,329
Oklahoma!—2,212
Pippin—1,944
South Pacific—1,925
Hair—1,742
The Wiz—1,672
The Best Little Whorehouse in Texas—1,584
Evita—1,568
Mame—1,508
The Sound of Music—1,443
How to Succeed in Business Without Really Trying—1,415
The Music Man—1,375

Funny Girl—1,348

Promises, Promises—1,281

The King and I—1,246

1776—1,217

Sugar Babies—1,208

Guys and Dolls—1,200

Cabaret—1,166

Annie Get Your Gun—1,147

They're Playing Our Song—1,082

Kiss Me Kate—1,077

The Pajama Game—1,063

Shenandoah—1,050

Damn Yankees—1,019

A Funny Thing Happened on the Way to the Forum—964

Chicago—947

Bells Are Ringing—924

Applause—896

Carousel—890

Fanny—888

Camelot—873

No, No, Nanette (revival)—861; original—321

I Love My Wife—857

Barnum—854

Raisin—847

Fiorello!—795

Where's Charley?—792

Oliver!—774

Joseph and the Amazing Technicolor Dreamcoat—747

Candide (revival)—740

West Side Story—732

High Button Shoes—727

Finian's Rainbow—725

Jesus Christ Superstar—711

Carnival—719

Gypsy—702

L'il Abner—693

Company—690

Purlie—688

The Most Happy Fella—676

Irene—670; revival—605

Call Me Madam—644

Two Gentlemen of Verona—627

Sweet Charity—608

Bye Bye Birdie—607

A Little Night Music—601

Flower Drum Song—600

A Day in Hollywood/A Night in the Ukraine—588

The Me Nobody Knows—587

Kismet—583

Brigadoon—581

No Strings—580

Show Boat—572

One Touch of Venus—567

I Do! I Do!—560

Wonderful Town—559

Sweeney Todd—557

Stop the World—I Want to Get Off—556

Pal Joey (revival)—542; (original)—374

The Unsinkable Molly Brown—532

Godspell—527

Follies—522

Sugar—505

Carmen Jones—502

The Boy Friend—485

On the Town—463

The Apple Tree—463

Plain and Fancy—461

Once Upon a Mattress—460

On the Twentieth Century—460

Redhead—452

Of Thee I Sing—441

George M!—435

Do Re Mi—400

Very Good Eddie—341; revival—307

Whoopee—379; revival—204

OFF-BROADWAY

The Fantasticks (still running)
The Threepenny Opera—2,706
Godspell—2,118
Little Shop of Horrors (still running)
You're a Good Man, Charlie Brown—1,597
I'm Getting My Act Together and Taking It on the Road—1,165
Little Mary Sunshine—1,143
Your Own Thing—937
Curley McDimple—931

Bibliography

Altman, Richard, with Mervyn Kaufman. *The Making of a Musical. Fiddler on the Roof*. Crown, 1971.

Atkinson, Brooks. *Broadway*. Macmillan, 1970.

Balk, H. Wesley. *The Complete Singer-Actor*. University of Minnesota, 1977.

Bentley, Eric, (Ed). *The Modern Theatre* Volume 4- includes "Guys and Dolls." Doubleday, 1956.

Bloom, Ken. American Songs: the Complete Musical Theatre Companion: 1900–1984. Facts on File, 1985.

Blum, Daniel, (Ed). *Theatre World*, publisheed annually from 1944–1964. Greenberg, 1944–1957, Chilton, 1957–1964.

Bordman, Gerald. *American Musical Theatre*. Oxford University Press, 1978.

Chujoy, Anatole, *The Dance Encyclopedia*. Simon & Schuster, 1967.

Clurman, Harold. *On Directing*. Collier, 1974.

Craig, David. *On Singing Onstage*. Schirmer, 1978.

Dunn, Don. *The Making of No, No, Nanette*. Citadel Press, 1972.

Engel, Lehman. *The American Musical Theatre*. Collier, 1967.

————. *Getting Started in the Theatre*. Collier Books, 1973.

————. *The Making of a Musical*. Macmillan, 1977.

————. *Planning and Producing The Musical Show*. Crown, 1966.

————. *Words with Music*, Macmillan, 1972.

————. *Their Words Are Music*. Crown, 1975.

Ewen, David. *New Complete Book of the American Musical Theatre*. Holt, Rinehart and Winston, 1970.

————. *The Story of America's Musical Theatre*. Chilton Co., 1961.

Frankel, Aaron. *Writing the Broadway Musical*. Drama Book Specialists, 1977.

Gottfried, Martin. *Broadway Musicals*. Abrams, 1978.

Green, Stanley. *Encyclopaedia of the American Musical Theatre*. Dodd, Mead & Co.,
     1976, NY.
————. *The World of Musical Comedy*. Barnes, 1974.
Guernsey, Otis, Jr. (ed). *Playwrights, Lyricists, Composers on Theatre*. Dodd, Mead &
     Co., 1964.
Hagen, Uta. *Respect for Acting*, Macmillan, 1973.
Hammerstein, Oscar, II. *Lyrics*. Hal Leonard Books, 1985.
————. *Six Plays by Rodgers and Hammerstein*, includes: "Allegro, Carousel, The King
     and I, Me and Juliet, Oklahoma!, South Pacific,"Modern Library, 1953.
Herbert, Ian. *Who's Who In Theatre*. Pitman, 1977.
Hummel, David. *The Collector's Guide to the American Musical Theatre*. Scarecrow
     Press, 1984.
King, Larry. *The Whorehouse Papers*. Viking Press, 1982.
Kislan, Richard. *The Musical*. Spectrum Books, 1980.
Kosarian, Oscar. *The Singing Actor*. Prentice-Hall, 1983.
Kreiger, Miles. *Show Boat, The Story of a Classic American Musical*. Oxford, 1977.
Laufe, Abe. *Broadway's Greatest Musicals*. Funk & Wagnalls, 1973.
Laurie, Joe, Jr. *Vaudeville*. Holt, 1953.
Lerner, Alan Jay. *The Street Where I Live*. Norton & Co., 1978.
Lewine, Richard, and Simon, Alfred. *Songs of the American Theatre*. H. W. Wilson,
     1984.
Little, Stuart and Cantor, Arthur A. *The Playmakers*. Dutton, 1971.
Lynch, Richard Chigley. *Musicals!*. American Library Association, 1984.
Merman, Ethel. *Don't Call Me Madam*. W. H. Allen, 1955.
Moore, Sonia. *Training an Actor*. Penguin, 1979.
Paskman, Dailey. *Gentlemen, Be Seated!*. Potter, 1976.
Richards, Stanley (ed). *Great Musicals of the American Theatre*, volume two, includes:
     "Applause, Cabaret, Camelot, Fiorello!, Lady in the Dark, Leave It to Me, Lost
     in the Stars, A Little Night Music, Man of La Mancha, Wonderful Town,"
     Chilton, 1976.
————. *Great Rock Musicals*, includes "Grease, Hair, Jesus Christ Superstar, Prome-
     nade, Tommy, Two Gentlemen of Verona, Your Own Thing, The Wiz," Stein
     and Day, 1979.
————. *Ten Great Musicals of the American Theatre*, includes: "Brigadoon, Company,
     Fiddler on the Roof, Gypsy, Kiss Me Kate, Of Thee I Sing, One Touch of Venus,
     Porgy and Bess, 1776, West Side Story." Chilton, 1973.
Shurtleff, Michael. *Audition*. Walker, 1978.
Silver, Fred. *Auditioning for the Musical Theatre*. Newmarket, 1985.
Smith, Bill. *The Vaudevillians*. Macmillan, 1976.
Smith, Cecil. *Musical Comedy in America*. Theatre Arts, 1950.
Sobel, Bernard. *A Pictorial History of Burlesque*. Bonanza, 1956.
Tumbusch, Tom. *Guide to Broadway Musical Theatre*, Richards Rosen, 1984.
Stenson, Isabella. *The Tony Award*. Arno Press, 1975.
Vallance, Tom. *The American Musical*. Barnes, 1970.
Wilk, Max. *They're Playing Our Song*. Atheneum, 1973.
Willis, John (Ed). *Theatre World* Published Annually from 1957–1983. Crown.
Zadan, Craig. *Sondheim and Company*. Equinox Books, 1974.

Sources _____

Sources below include the addresses and phone numbers of the licensing agencies and the names, addresses and phone numbers for stores specializing in scripts, music and records. Many of the scripts, scores and records for the older shows are difficult to obtain from regional stores and help must be sought from New York specialty stores. Most "in print" music and records may be ordered from your local music store which is why their addresses and phone numbers are not included.

LICENSING AGENCIES

Dramatic Publishing Company (DPC), P.O. Box 41906, Chicago, Il 60641. (312) 545–2062. Scripts are available for purchase.

Dramatists Play Service, Inc. (DPS), 440 Park Avenue South, New York, NY 10016. (212) 683–8960. Scripts available for purchase.

Irving Berlin Music Corporation (Irving Berlin), 1290 Avenue of the Americas, New York, NY 10019. Although Hammerstein Library handles the rights to *Annie Get Your Gun*, the Irving Berlin Music Corporation handles the purchase of the script. (Send a check for $4.75 to cover script cost and mailing.)

Music Theatre International (MTI), 49 East 52nd Street, New York, NY 10019. (212) 975–6841. They will send up to three perusal copies of scripts and chorus books at a time. You can rent perusal scores for $25 for up to three weeks; when the score is returned $20 is refunded.

Rodgers & Hammerstein Library (R & H), 598 Madison Avenue, New York, NY 10022. (212) 486–0643. They will send up to two perusal copies of scripts at a time. The only fee you pay is for the postage and handling. Most of the scores may be ordered from your local music store.

Samuel French, Inc. (SF), 25 West 45th Street, New York, NY 10036. (212) 206–8990. Most scripts and published vocal selections may be purchased. Some scores are available for purchase and some manuscripts are *only* available for perusal. They will send perusal copies of the musical score if you send a $35 deposit plus $3 for postage and handling.

Tams Witmark Music Library (TW), 560 Lexington Avenue, New York, NY 10022. 1–800–221–7196, (212) 688–2525. They will send up to three perusal copies of scripts and scores at a time. They will bill you for the copies they send.

Theatre Maximus (MAX). Sole property is *Godspell*. 1650 Broadway, New York, NY 10019. (212) 765–5913.

BOOK, MUSIC AND RECORD STORES

Chappell & Co., 50 New Bond Street, London, W.1, England.

The Collectors Series, 51 West 52nd Street, Room 826, New York, NY 10019. (212) 975–4126.

Drama Book Shop, 723 Seventh Avenue, New York, NY 10019. (212) 944–0595. Specializing in theatre books.

DRG Records, 200 West 57th Street, New York, NY 10019. (212) 582–3040.

Footlight Records, 90 Third Avenue (between 12th and 13th streets), New York, NY 10003. (212) 533–1572. A store that specializes in out-of-print records with a sizeable collection of Broadway show albums. The proprietor, Gene Dingenary, is extremely helpful and knowledgeable.

Frank Music Co., 13 St. Geroge Street, London, W1A 2BR England.

Half Price Music, 160 West 56th Street, New York, NY 10036. (212) 582–2840. Specializing in out-of-print music.

Lincoln Square Music, Hotel Ansonia, 2109 Broadway, New York, NY 10023. (212) 724–7370. Specializing in out-of-print music.

Music Exchange, 151 West 46th Street, New York, NY 10036. (212) 354–5858. Specializing in out-of-print music.

Music Masters, 25 West 43rd Street, New York, NY 10036. (212) 840–1958.

Original Cast Records, P.O. Box 496, Georgetown, CT 06829. (203) 544–8288.

Records Ltd., 2818 West Pico Blvd., Los Angeles, CA 90006. (213) 737–2611. Specializing in out-of-print records.

Richard Stoddard, Out of Print Theatre Books, 90 East 10th Street, New York, NY 10013. (212) 982–9440.

Theatre Books, Inc., 1576 Broadway, Room 312, New York, NY 10036. (212) 757–2834.

ORGANIZATIONS

The rights to individual show tunes are usually controlled by ASCAP or BMI. Licenses are available on an annual or per song basis.

ASCAP, 1 Lincoln Plaza, New York, NY 10023. (212) 595–3050.

BMI, 320 West 57th Street, New York, NY 10019. (212) 586–2000.

Actors Equity, 165 West 46th Street, New York, NY 10036. (212) 869–8530. They will forward mail to members.

Dramatists Guild, 234 West 44th Street, New York, NY 10036. (212) 398–9366. They will forward mail to members.

National Music Publishers Ass., 110 East 59th Street, New York, NY 10022. (212) 751–1930.

Index of Shows and Years of Production

Index of Songs and Their Sources ___

Index of Professionals and Their Specialties _____

About the Author

CAROL LUCHA-BURNS is an Associate Professor of Theatre at the University of New Hampshire specializing in Youth Drama and American Musical Theatre. Since 1964 she has been director, performer or author of 105 musicals and plays. In 1965 she founded and acted as producing director of the Tokyo Junior Theatre, an international children's theatre company now celebrating its twentieth anniversary. Her earlier written texts include *Education through Dramatization* (with Susan Goldin), *Creative Dramatics,* and *Puppetry, A Practical Guide.*